Colonial Families of Delaware

Volume 1

F. Edward Wright

Colonial Roots
Lewes, Delaware
2010

Colonial Roots

17296 Coastal Highway

Lewes, Delaware 19958

1-800-576-8608

Printed in the United States of America

Reprinted 2010

CONTENTS

INTRODUCTION

The early limits of New Castle County are presumably defined in the order to the constables of New Castle and Christiana to list taxable persons, age 16 to 60, in 1677 on the "south side of Christeena Creeke, and so downwards to the south syde of St. George's Creek, including all the inhabitants between the two creeks ... " and persons "wch is all ye north syde of Cristeena Creeke up as far as ye Bogt Creek, above Oole fransen's house."[1] The hundreds[2] of New Castle County which existed in the colonial period were New Castle, Christiana, Brandywine, Mill Creek, White Clay Creek, Pencader, Red Lion, Appoquinimink, St. George's, and Drawyers Creek.

Few records of the Swedish Colony (1638-1655) have survived. From 1655 to 1664 and from 1673 to 1674, the Dutch West India Company and the City of Amsterdam were proprietors of the land which became Delaware (ignoring claims by the Calverts of Maryland). The surviving records are held by the Archives of New York at Albany. For an excellent treatment of the family histories of many of the Swedish families in Delaware, see Peter Stebbins Craig, *The 1693 Census of the Swedes on the Delaware.*[3]

The Duke of York was proprietor from 1664 to 1673 and from 1674 to 1682. These land records are also held at Albany. *Original Land Titles in Delaware, commonly known as The Duke of York Record, 1646-1679*, was printed by order of the General Assembly of the State of Delaware (1899).[4]

Kent County, originally a part of Whorekill District (created in 1664), became an independent territory under the name of St. Jones County in 1680. In circa 1682, simultaneous with the transfer of government from the Duke of York, the name was changed to Kent County. Kent County was comprised of the following hundreds: Duck Creek, Little Creek, Murtherkill or Murderkill (and many other variations), Mispillion (also Muspillion), Dover.

The following hundreds made up Sussex County during the period of this volume: Lewes and Rehoboth, Georgetown, Cedar Creek, Broadkiln, Indian River, Northwest Fork (originally a part of Maryland), Nanticoke. The southernmost portions of Sussex County were once part of Somerset and Worcester Counties,

---

[1] J. Thomas Scharf, History of Delaware, p,. 611.

[2] An old English term of uncertain origin referring to subsections of the county.

[3] Published in 1993 by SAG publications, Winter Park, Florida.

[4] Reprinted by Family Line Publications in 1989.

Maryland and an eastern portion was once part of Dorchester County. Lands as far north as the Nanticoke and Indian Rivers, plus most of Northwest Fork Hundred were claimed by both the Calverts and Penns for several generations.

The first settlement of Delaware was made at and near present-day Lewes, just north of Cape Henlopen, was called The Whorekill in the 17th century. On 8 May 1671 a census of Horekill was taken showing the following persons[5]:

Hilmonous Fredericks Wiltbank, his wife, two sons and a man servant
Alexander Moetsteen, his wife, two sons and a man servant
Otto Wolgart, his wife, one son and a man servant
William Klarson, with two daughters and a child
Jan Kipshaven, his wife and daughter
James Weedon, one daughter, one son, and four servants
John Rods (Roades), his wife, three sons and two daughters
Daniel Breen, his wife and partner, John Colloson
Jan Michael, Anthony Pieters, Abraham Peters, Peter Smith
Pieter Gronedick, Anthony Sandes
Herman Cornellsson, Herman Drooche, trader

Somerset County, Maryland, was created in 1666 with the Atlantic Ocean and Chesapeake Bay its eastern and western boundaries and its northern boundary which today lies well inside Sussex County ... the Nanticoke River. Dispute over the location of Delaware's southern boundary began in 1680 when William Penn received his charter. It continued until 1732 when both parties signed an agreement that the line would lie at 39 degrees, 43 minutes, 19 seconds and be surveyed to continue to the midpoint of the peninsula, then turn north to a point 15 miles south of Philadelphia. Unfortunately for Lord Baltimore, his decision to agree to this compromise was based on an inaccurate map which showed 39 degrees, 43 minutes, 19 seconds as lying at Cape Henlopen. In fact, Cape Henlopen lay 25 miles further north, and Lord Baltimore had inadvertently signed away present day Little Creek Hundred and parts of Broad Creek, Dagsborough and Baltimore Hundreds that had never been claimed by Penn. Realizing his mistake too late, Lord Baltimore fought the agreement in the courts for the next twenty years. When Worcester County was formed in 1742 from the eastern and southern sections of Somerset, he set the northern boundary of Worcester at Broad Creek Bridge, at the site of present-day Laurel, Delaware. From 1763 through 1768 Charles Mason and Jeremiah Dixon conducted the final survey of the so-called Mason-Dixon Line and finally, in January 1769, the new line was officially accepted.

Prior to 1769, therefore, all records of the residents of lands south of the Nanticoke and Indian Rivers should be sought in Maryland record books. For persons who

---

[5] *The History of Delaware*, by J. Thomas Scharf, p. 1201.

resided in the disputed territory near the two rivers, or in Northwest Fork Hundred, both Delaware and Maryland, should be consulted prior to 1769. A particularly good example is the Cannon family, covered in Volume 3. Land conveyances by members of this family appeared in the deed books of Dorchester County prior to appearing in the deed books of Sussex County.

Many of the early settlers of Delaware were Quakers. The first Quaker meeting of southern Delaware may have been in Lewes as early as 1692. However the earliest surviving records pertain to the monthly meeting of Duck Creek, formed in 1705. It was a part of the Chester Quarterly Meeting. This probably explains the connection of Chester families to Kent County families: note for example the families of Cowgill and Needham.

Subsequent to 1674 many Maryland settlers began to take up land in Kent County, Delaware. Note for example the Irons, Manlove, Paradee and Rawlings families, who first received patents for land from the Calverts of Maryland.

A large number of families of the Eastern Shore of Virginia, took up land in Sussex County. Notable are the families of Atkins, Bagwell, Bedwell, Burton, Carey, Draper, Hazzard, Lofland, Marriner, Manlove, Marsh, Nutter, Parker, Pettyjohn, Prettyman, Spencer, Staton, Stockley and Warrington.

F. Edward Wright
Lewes, Delaware
2010

SOURCES

ACCO: Accomack County Virginia Court Order Abstracts, compiled by JoAnn Riley McKey.

Adventurers of Purse and Person, Virginia M. Meyer and John Frederick Dorman, 1987. Published by Order of First Families of Virginia 1607-1624.5.

ARMD: *Archives of Maryland.* (71 vols.)

Bendler: *Colonial Delaware Records, 1681-1713.* By Bruce A. Bendler. Published by Family Line Publications, 1992.

BMM: Burlington Monthly Meeting, Burlington Co. NJ (Quakers)

British Roots: *British Roots of Maryland Families.* By Robert W. Barnes. Baltimore: Genealogical Publishing Co.

CANI: Records of the Nicholite Society whose members lived in Caroline and Dorchester counties of Maryland, and Kent County, Delaware. See *Joseph Nichols and The Nicholites*, Kenneth Carroll, 1962.

Chester Co. Wills: The Wills of Chester County, Pennsylvania as abstracted by Jacob Martin. Published by Family Line Publicatons.

CDA: *Colonial Delaware Assemblymen.* By Bruce A. Bendler. Published by Family Line Publications.

Chester Co. Deeds: *Abstracts of Chester County, Pennsylvania, Land Records* series, published by Family Line Publications

Chester Co., PA, Wills: *The Wills of Chester County, Pennsylvania* series, published by Family Line Publications

Citizens of the Eastern Shore: *Citizens of the Eastern Shore of Maryland.* By F. Edward Wright. Published by Family Line Publications, 1986.

Colonial Soldiers and Sailors: *Colonial Delaware Soldiers and Sailors 163801776*, compiled by Henry C. Peden, Jr. Published by Family Line Publications, 1995.

DCMM: Duck Creek Monthly Meeting Registers and Minutes (Society of Friends, or Quakers)

DE Recall: *Delaware Recall*, published by Delaware Genealogical Society

Delaware Bible Recds: *Delaware Bible Records* (6 vols.), compiled by Donald O. Virdin and Lu Verne V. Hall. Published by Heritage Books, Inc., 1991-1998.

ESVR: *Maryland Eastern Shore Vital Records* 5 vols.), compiled by F. Edward Wright. Published by Family Line Publications, 1982-1986.

GSP: *The Pennsylvania Genealogical Magazine*

Hinshaw/PA&NJ: Encyclopedia of American Quaker Genealogy Volume II: Pennsylvania and New Jersey. William Wade Hinshaw, Author and Publisher; Thomas Worth Marshall, Compiler.

Hinshaw/VA: Encyclopedia of American Quaker Genealogy Volume VI: Virginia. William Wade Hinshaw, Author and Publisher; Thomas Worth Marshall, Editor; Douglas Summers Brown, Collaborator and historian for Virginia.

Hinshaw/NC: Encyclopedia of American Quaker Genealogy Volume I: North Caroline

Immanuel Church: Records of Emanuel Protestant Episcopal Church of New Castle (established in 1704).

Irish Quakers: *Immigration of the Irish Quakers into Pennsylvania, 1682-1750*, by Albert Cook Myers, M.L. Originally published Swarthmore, 1902. Reprinted Genealogical Publishing Co., Inc., 1969, 1985, 1994.

KEDELR: Kent County, Delaware, Land Records

Kent Co. Court Records

Kent Co. Orphans court

KEORCF: Kent County Orphans Court Case Files

LCPC: Lewes and Coolspring Presbyterian Church records

Maryland Eastern Shore Vital Records (5 vols), F. Edward Wright. Published by Family Line Publications, 1982-1986.

Marshall: Abstracts of the Wills and Administrations of Northampton County, Virginia 1632-1802. Compiled by James Handley Marshall.

MGS Bulletin: *Maryland Genealogical Society Bulletin*

MMM: Middletown Monthly Meeting, Bucks County, Pennsylvania (Quakers)

MPL: Maryland Patent Land Records

MWB: Maryland Calendar of Wills (16 vols.)

NCDELR New Castle County, Delaware, Land Records

NCOC: *Orphans' Court Proceedings of New Castle County, Delaware. 1742-1761*. Abstracted by F. Edward Wright, Delmarva Roots (2001).

New Castle Co. Wills: *A Calendar of Delaware Wills New Castle County 1682-1800*. Compiled by The Historical Research Committee of The Colonial Dames of Delaware

Nottingham: *Wills and Administrations of Accomack County, Virginia 1663-1800. Compiled and edited by Stratton Nottingham.*

Nottingham Monthly Meeting Records (Quakers)

Old Swedes: Records of Old Swedes Church of Wilmington, DE, published as *Early Church Records of New Castle County, Delaware*, Volume 2. Family Line Publications (1994), reprint of *The Records of Holy Trinity (Old Swedes) Church, Wilmington, Del., 1713-1799*. Transcribed by Horace Burr.

PA Genealogies: *Genealogies of Pennsylvania Families*, a collection of articles taken from The *Pennsylvania Magazine of History and Biography*. Published by Genealogical Publishing Co., Inc., 1983.

Penna. Hist. Soc. Papers, vol. AM. 2013

PMM: Philadelphia Monthly Meeting (Quakers)

RPD: *Revolutionary Patriots of Delaware*, compiled by Henry C. Peden, Jr.

RPWS: *Revolutionary Patriots of Worcester and Somerset Counties, Maryland 1775-1783*, compiled by Henry C. Peden, Jr.

Runk: *Biographical And Genealogical History of the State of Delaware containing Biographical and Genealogical Sketches of Prominent and Representative Citizens, and many of the Early Settlers,* published in 1899 by

J. M. Runk & Co., Chambersburg, PA.
QALR: *Queen Anne's County, MD, Land Records*, R. Bernice Leonard.
SCGA: Sussex County Guardian Accounts
Scharf: *History of Delaware, 1609-1888*, by J. Thomas Scharf, A.M., LL.D.
SCOC: Abstracts of the Proceedings of Sussex County Orphans' Court, Delaware, Libers 1, 2, 3, 4, A (1708-1709 and 1728-1777). Compiled by Vernon L. Skinner, Jr., published by Willow Bend Books, Westminster, MD. (2000).
SCS: Sussex County Surveys
SCChR: Sussex County Chancery Court Records
SCCR: Sussex County Court Records
SCOR: Sussex County Obituary Records
SCW: Sussex County Wills
St. George's Episcopal Register, Indian River
SOSP: Stepney Parish Register, Somerset Co., Maryland
SUDELR: Sussex County, Delaware, Land Records
SUORCF: Sussex County Orphans Court Case Files
Sussex Court Records: *Records of the Courts of Sussex County, Delaware 1677-1710*, Craig W. Horle. University of Pennsylvania Press, 1991.
TALR: *Talbot County, Maryland, Land Records*, R. Bernice Leonard
The Duke of York Records: *Original Land Titles in Delaware Commonly Known as The Duke of York Record*, printed by General Assembly of the State of Delaware, 1903.
THMM: Third Haven Monthly Meeting, Talbot County, Maryland (Quakers)
Torrence: *Old Somerset on the Eastern Shore of Maryland*, Clayton Torrence, 1935.
Turner: *Some Records of Sussex County, Delaware*, compiled by H.B. Turner.
Welcome *Claimants: The Welcome Claimants Proved, Disproved And Doubtful With An Account Of Some Of Their Descendants*. By George E. McCracken. Published by The Welcome Society of Pennsylvania, 1985.
Whitelaw: *Virginia's Eastern Shore*, Ralph T. Whitelaw, first published by Virginia Historical Society, 1951.
WMM: Wilmington Monthly Meeting (Quakers) Register and minutes.
WOLR: *Land Records of Worcester County, Maryland*. By Ruth Dryden. Published by Family Line Publications

Wills and administration data were taken from the following: *Calendar of Kent County, Delaware, Probate Records, 1680-1800*, compiled by Leon de Valinger, Jr., published by Public Archives Commission (1944); *A Calendar of Delaware Wills, New Castle County 1682-1800*, published by National Society of Colonial Dames; *Calendar of Sussex County, Delaware, Probate Records, 1680-1800*, compiled by Leon de Valinger, Jr., published by Public Archives Commission (1964) All these publications, i.e., *Calendar of Wills* ..., are abstracts and as such are not complete. One might expect that all heirs would be included; however the names of heirs (including children) were sometimes inadvertently omitted. One should check the original records whenever possible. Mr. de Valinger in his work, includes both the reference to the original probate records in the Hall of Records, giving the Archives volume and page on which the original document is mounted; and the Register of Wills liber and folio as found at the court house.

ABBREVIATIONS

a.	acres
adj.	adjoining
admin.	administrator or administered
admx.	administratrix
afsd	aforesaid
b.	born
bapt.	baptized
bur.	buried
c	circa
d.	died
dec'd.	deceased
dau(s).	daughter(s)
DSA	Delaware State Archives, Dover (Hall of Records)
DO Co.	Dorchester County (Maryland)
e.	east
exec.	executor
extx.	executrix
FHL	Family History Library (The Morman Library, Salt Lake City, UT.
m.	married
MM	Monthly Meeting
n.	north
N	Names unknown
nunc.	nuncupative
QA Co.	Queen Anne's County (Maryland)
s.	south or shilling
sd.	said
s.p.	died without issue
TA Co.	Talbot County (Maryland)
v.p.	during father's lifetime
w.	west
wit(s).	witness(es)

THE ALLEE FAMILY

First Generation

1. JOHN ALLEY (Alee, Allei) d. leaving a will dated 19 Feb 1718, proved 16 March 1718. Heirs: sons Peter, Abraham, Johanus [Johanns]; daus. Hannah, Mary, Elizabeth, Rachell, Jane Vanwinkle (wife of Simon Vanwinkle), Susannah (wife of John Vangasco); son Jacob; sons-in-law Simeon Vanwinkle and John Vangasco. Execs.: sons Peter, Abraham and Johanns. Witnessed by John Hillyard, Isabell Smith, John Bradshaw, Sr. {Arch. Al:98. Reg. of Wills, D:7-8}

On 29 Oct 1725 Peter Allei, Abraham Allei and John Allei, all sons and heirs of John Allei, yeoman, late of Duck Creek Hundred, KE Co., dec'd., for £50 sold to Simon Vanwinkle of the same place, 384 a. John Allei (Allee), the father, was at the time of his decease possessed of sundry tracts of land and particularly three tracts within Duck Creek Hundred in a small neck between Dawsons Branch and Hirons His Branch, one tract called *Woodstock Bower* 600 a. and one tract of 360 a. called *Hillington* and also one other tract which was formerly granted to Frances Richardson by patent dated at Philadelphia, 4 Aug 1685, 1500 a. John Allee by his will dated 19 Feb 1718 bequeathed to his son Peter Allee 250 a. of land including about 1/2 his dwelling plantation within the small neck, provided the said Peter come thereon within 3 years after the decease of John Allee, otherwise the said Peter by virtue of the said will was to have 300 a. of land at the Beaver Dam and become possessed of 1/3 part of all the lands. Then he willed and distributed amongst his children [the remainder of the lands] and also impowered his sons Peter, Abraham and John his executors to convey unto Simon Vanwinkle afsd. 150 a. of land being the same the testator had sold unto him. {KEDELR I:26}

On 10 Dec 1727 Peter Allee, Gartrude Allee, widdow of John Allee, dec'd., Simon Vanwinkle and Jane his wife, Edward Long in right of his wife Susannah, John Hawkins and Ann [also Hannah] his wife, William Cahoon and Mary his wife, Elizabeth Allee and Rachell Allee, all sons and daus. or sons and daus. in law to John Allee, senr., late of KE Co., dec'd., for £100 sold to Jacob Allee of Duck Creek KE Co. a tract of land and plantation near Duck Creek which of late was the dwelling plantation of John Allee ye younger, to him by his father in his will by the name of Johannas Allee given, having been formerly part of two tracts of land one called *Woodfork Bower* and the other called *Islington*, and of late in pursuance of his fathers will, laid out from ye said tracts beginning at Dawsons Branch being also a corner of Abraham Allee's land. {KEDELR I:131}

On 14 Nov 1728 Deed and Articles of Agreement were made between Abraham and Jacob Allee (Allei) and Simon Vanwinkle all of Duck Creek Hundred, KE Co., yeoman. Whereas John Allee (Allei), father of the said Abraham and Jacob, being late of same place, dec'd., was at the time of his death the real owner of two tracts of land whereon he then did dwell both between Dawsons Branch and Hirons Branch and by his will dated 19 Feb 1718 did bequeath the upland part of the tracts amongst his children, Peter, Abraham, John, Jacob, Hannah and Mary Allee also ordering his executors to convey to Simon Vanwinkle and John Vangasco 150 a. each and reserving 30 a (reduced to 6 a. by agreement) in the *Pasture Point* to be a privilige place for all his children to have recourse to the marshes and secure hay for their stocks. Peter, Abraham and John Allee conveyed to Simon Vanwinkle 150 a. and Hanna and

Mary together with their husbands sold their part unto Abraham Allee. John Allee the son afsd. deceasing since the division the legatees have sold all his part unto Jacob Allee so now the whole of the upland is in the possession of Abraham and Jacob Allee and Simon Vanwinkle, exempting 150 a. yet to be conveyed to the heirs of John Vangasco. Final division to wit: Jacob's part, land which includes the dwelling house of John Allee the father w. of land called *Islington* and 100 a.; Simon Vanwinkle, 146 a.; Abraham to the Salt Water Point, 430 a. (signed) Abraham Allee, Jacob Allee, Simon Vanwinkle, Jane Vanwinkle, John Hawkins, Hannah Hawkins, William Cahoon, Mary Cahoon. Ackn 14 May 1730. {KEDELR K:25; see also KEDELR I:90; N:pg 43}

In a conveyance dated 5 Dec 1738 it was stated that John Alle the elder late of Duck Creek Hundred, Kent Co., by his will bearing date 19 Feb 1718 did appoint and impower his executor Abraham Alle (surviving and the principle acting executor) of same place to make over by a good suficient deed of sale 150 a. of land unto John Vangaseo which John Alle had sold unto him and whereas the said John Vangaseo, died before the land was conveyed and without a will leaving three children. By this indenture Abraham Alle for £50, paid to the estate of his dec'd. father John Alle by John Vangaseo in his life time, confirms unto John Vangaseo, Henry Vangaseo and Susannah Vangaseo, children of John Vangaseo. late of Duck Creek Hundred KE Co., yeoman, dec'd., 150 a. of land. {KEDELR M:69}

On 20 Aug 1744 Abraham Allei and Jacob Allei, sons and legatees of John Allei, late of Duck Creek Hundred, KE Co., dec'd., and William Cahoon and Mary his wife, dau. and legatee of the same John Allei (Allie), dec'd., all now of same place enter into agreement. Whereas John Allei by his will dated 19 Feb 1718 did give his lands to sundry of his children and some to be in common amongst them and it was generally understood amongst those children that his true intent was that each should have upland to the full quantity and each should have a right in the marshes adj. the upland, including his two daus. who were wives of Simon Vanwinkle and John Vangaseo at the time of his decease, and whereas John Hawkins and Hannah his wife, one of the daus. of John Allei, dec'd., by their deed of sale did convey her part of the marsh unto Abraham Allei, and Peter Allei eldest son of the same John Allei, dec'd., by his deed (Book I, fol. 26) did transfer all his right of said marsh unto Simon Vanwinkle, and John Vangaseo, son and heir to Susanna Vangaseo, wife of John Vangaseo the elder, by a deed of sale did convey all his rights of the marsh with other lands unto the Simon Vanwinkle, John Allei the younger being dec'd., his part is now in the possession of Jacob Allei, so that the whole right of the marsh is now lawfully vested in Abraham Allei, Jacob Allei, William Cahoon and Mary his wife and Simon Vanwinkle and Jane his wife, and they have agreed to certain divisions amonst themselves. Abraham Allei and Jacob Allei, William Cahoon and Mary his wife in consideration of the agreements and premisses above recited and also for 15 shillings give to Simon Vanwinkle all that piece of marsh land in Duck Creek Hundred being part of a tract granted to Francis Richardson by patent dated at Philadelphia 4 Aug 1685, beginning at a tract of land called *Woodstock Bower* formerly in possession of the said John Allei the elder and running down the Dawsons branch (alias Shearnest) to Irons branch ... 100 a. of marsh and all the rights they have in that 6 a. of upland now remaining in common amongst the parties afsd. lying in *Pasture Point*. {KEDELR N:42}

John was father of the following children: PETER (eldest son); ABRAHAM; JOHN; JACOB; JANE, m. Simon Vanwinkle; SUSANNAH, m. 1st John Vangasgo, m. 2nd Edward Long; ANN [or Hannah], m. John Hawkins; MARY, m. William Cahoon; ELIZABETH; RACHELL.

Second Generation

2. JOHN ALEE, son of John (1) Alee, m. Gartrude (N).

On 23 March 1719 it was agreed that Robert Draiton, aged 12 years, July next, son of Robert Draiton, would serve Johannes Alle. {DE Recall Kent WD1}

On 23 March 1719 it was agreed that William Sherar, aged 17 years, son of William Sherar, would serve Johannes Alle. {DE Recall Kent W-D14}

John d. leaving a will dated 20 Nov 1726, proved 22 March 1726. Heirs: wife Gartrude; bros. Peter, Jacob; sisters Jane VanWinkle, Susannah Long, Ann Hawkins, Mary Allee, Elizabeth Allee, Rachell Allee; cousin John Allee. Execs., wife and Jacob Allee, Simon VanWinkle. Wits., James Morris, Rebecka More, John Tilton. {Arch. Al:59. Reg. of Wills, F:21}

3. JANE ALLEI, dau. of John (1) Allei, m. Simon Vanwinkle of Duck Creek.

On 21 Aug 1744 Simon Vanwinkle of Duck Creek Hundred KE Co., yeoman, and Jane his wife, dau. and legatee of John Alei the elder late of same place, dec'd., for divers, good causes and considerations them thereunto moving which are now particularly sett forth and expressed in a certain indenture made between Abram Alei, Jacob Alei and William Cahoon and Mary his wife of the one part and the said Simon Vanwinkle of the other part dated 20 Aug 1744 and for 10 shillings give unto Abraham Alei and Jacob Alei, both of same place, yeomen, a piece of upland lying in *The Pasture Point,* being the same which was in common between the said Abraham and Jacob Allei, William Cahoon and Mary his wife, and the said Simon Vanwinkle and Jane his wife and conveyed to Simon by the afsd. deed and one piece marsh land adj. Irons branch and one other piece of marsh land adj. Shearnest alias Dawsons Branch, 6 a. Abraham Alei and Jacob Alei have free liberty of a roadway 50 yards in breadth to pass and repass for driving creatures or other occasions from one piece of the said marsh to the other and Simon Vanwinkle and Jane his wife reserve for themselves to make and keep such ditches or drains across the said roadway as they shall have occation of. {KEDELR N:42}

Simon Vanwinkle d. leaving a will dated 17 Dec 1748, proved 23 Jan 1752. Heirs: wife Jane; sons Jacob, John, Simon; dau. Susannah Talbort; grandson Simon Draughton. Extx. wife Jane. Wits., Wm. Cahoon, Mary Cahoon, John Cahoon. {Arch. A52:24-26. Reg. of Wills, K:50-51}

4. ABRAHAM ALLEE, probable son of John (1) Allee, m. 1st Isabelle (N).

On 23 March 1719 it was agreed that Elizabeth Draiton, aged 5 years, dau. of Robert Draiton, would serve Abraham Alee and Isabelle his wife. {DE Recall Kent W-D15}

On 23 March 1719 it was agreed that John Draiton, aged 9 years, would serve Abraham Alee and his wife Isabelle. {DE Recall Kent W-D15}

Abraham Allee m. 2nd Mary (N). On 12 Aug 1747 Abraham Allee of Duck Creek Hundred KE Co. and Mary his wife for £103 sold to John Draughton of same place, a tract of land (whereas Robert Draughton of same co.

did sell unto the afsd. John Draughton part of a tract of land called *Northampton*, patent was recorded for Robert Draughton in Phildelphia, 1702 Book A, fol. 3, pg 314, and John Draughton for £103 did sell the afsd. tract unto Abraham Allee, Book N, fol. 108) ... 100 a. of land 6 a. marsh. {KEDELR N:162}

Abraham Allee, Sr., Gentleman of Duck Creek, d. leaving a will dated 8 May 1770, proved 20 Aug 1770. Heirs: wife Mary; sons John and Jonathan; daus. Mary Carpenter, Sabrah Tilton; son-in-law Thomas Tilton; grandsons Abraham Allee (son of Jonathan), Abraham Allee (son. of John); grandchildren of dau. Mary Carpenter by her first husband, Henry Rothwell; grandchildren Isaac, Abraham, Jacob and Mary, children of son Abraham Allee, dec'd., Execs., sons John and Jonathan and son-in-law Thomas Tilton. Wits., James Tilton, John VanGaskin, Jr., John Hawkins, Jr. {Arch. Al:50-53. Reg. of Wills, L:83}

Abraham was father of the following children: ABRAHAM, had children Isaac, Abraham, Jacob and Mary; JOHN, had a son Abraham; JONATHAN, had a son Abraham; MARY, m. 1st Henry Rothwell, m. 2nd (N) Carpenter; SABRAH, m. Thomas Tilton.

5. SUSANNAH ALLEE, dau. of John (1) Allee, m. 1st John Vangasgo and m. 2nd Edward Long.

John Vangasco d. by 22 March 1726 when Edward Long was appointed admin. of his estate. {Reg. of Wills, F:23}

John Vangasgo was father of the following children: JOHN; HENRY; SUSANNAH.

Third Generation

6. ABRAHAM ALLEE, Jr., son of Abraham (4) Allee, m. Sarah (N).

Abraham Alee, Jr., d. by 21 May 1766 when his estate was administered by Sarah Allee, widow. {Reg. of Wills, L:21} On 27 May 1768 his estate was administered by Christopher Denney, next of kin. {Arch. Al:48-49. Reg. of Wills, L:45} Arch. Al:49 shows children, Isaac, Abraham, Jacob and Mary Allee.

Abraham was father of the following children: ISAAC; ABRAHAM; JACOB; MARY.

7. JOHN ALEE of Duck Creek Hundred, son of Abraham (4) Allee, d. leaving a will dated 8 Aug 1771, proved 14 Aug 1771. Mentioned were sons Abraham, Peter, John, Presley; dau. Mary. Execs., sons Abraham, Peter, John. Wits., Immanuel Stout, William Cook, Thomas Parry. {Arch. Al:60. Reg. of Wills, L:98}

John was father of the following children: ABRAHAM; PETER; JOHN; PRESLEY; MARY, m. (N) Vanwinckle.

Fourth Generation

8. PETER ALLEE, yeoman of Duck Creek Hundred, son of John (7), d. leaving a will dated 17 May 1773, proved 24 May 1773. Heirs: bros. Presley, Abraham and John Allee; sister Mary Allee; Frances Cooper. Execs., Abraham and John Allee. Wits., John Dawson, George Harris, Lucey Cooper. {Arch. Al:69-72. Reg. of Wills, L:133-136} Arch. Al:72 mentions a sister Mary Vanwinckle.

Unplaced

JACOB ALLE, Jr., yeoman, d. by 16 March 1762 when his estate was administered by John Alle, gentleman. {Reg. of Wills, K:278}

JOHN ALLEE, yeoman, d. leaving a will dated 16 Sep 1766, proved 13 Oct 1766. Heirs: wife unnamed; son John, Jr.; dau. Rebecca Killen, wife of William Killen; granddaus. Elizabeth and Mary, daus. of William and Rebecca Killen. Exec. son John, Jr. Wits., Abraham Allee, Jonathan Allee, Thomas Wild. {Arch.
Al:57-58. Reg. of Wills, L:19-20}

John was father of the following children: REBECCA, m. William Killen and were the parents of Elizabeth and Mary.

JOHN ALLEE, JR., d. by 6 March 1769 when his estate was administered by William Killen, Esq., next of kin. {Reg. of Wills, L:54}

THE ALSTON FAMILY

First Generation

1. ARTHUR ALSTON m. 1st Hannah (N) and m. 2nd Sarah (N).

In the 1693 tax assessment of Kent Co., DE, Little Creek Hundred, was shown Arthur Allstone, 100 a. {Bendler:21}

At the court of 16 Aug 1705 came Arthur Alston and acknowledged a deed of gift for 50 a. to Jasper Harwood and Hanna his wife and a deed of gift for 50 a. to David Duncan and Elizabeth his now wife. {Kent Ct:334}

On 6 Nov 1718 Thomas Allston of Little Creek Hundred, Kent Co. yeoman, eldest son of Arthur Allston, dec'd., and Sarah his wife for £40 sold to John Stott of same place, yeoman, a tract of land (being part of patent dated at Philadelphia 26 March 1684 granted to Arthur Alston called *Chester*, on s. side of Western (or s.w.) branch of Duck Creek, 800 a. Arthur Alston by deeds and his will sold and gave some parcells of land out of said tract, did also by his will give to his eldest son Thomas Allston all the remaining part of said tract, 100 a. {KEDELR F:45}[1]

On 13 May 1740 Henry Hayse of Kent Co., blacksmith, for £27 sold to Thomas Allstone of same co., yeoman, a tract of land called *Chester*, granted to Arthur Allstone who by deed of gift granted 50 a. to David Duncan and Elizabeth his wife, dau. to the said Arthur, which David and Elizabeth dyed intestate and the land descended to Arthur Duncan, their son and heir, who conveyed the same to Henry Hayse beginning near Allstones branch, 50 a.
{KEDELR M:136}

On 25 May 1748 Arthur Dunkan and James Keath (Keeth) both of Kent Co. for £30 sold to Israel Allston of same co. a tract of land. Whereas Arthur Allston late of Kent Co., dec'd., grandfather of the said Arthur Duncan

---

1 In the record of quit rents of Kent Co., DE, for the period, circa 1701-1713 is shown Arthr. Alston to whom a patent of 800 a. was granted which he alienated to Thos. Bostock. {Bendler: Colonial Delaware Records, 1681-1713}

did by his deed of gift bearing date 1 Oct 1705 give unto David Duncan father of the afsd. Arthur Duncan a tract of land in Little Creek Hundred bounded by 50 a. of land given by the afsd. Arthur Allston to Jesper Harred and Hannah his wife near Allstons Branch, 100 a. {KEDELR N:221}

Arthur and Hannah were parents of the following children: ELIZABETH, b. 8 July 1685, m. David Duncan and had a son Arthur; HANNAH, b. 1 Sep 1687, m. Jesper Harred (or Harwood). {KEDELR}

Arthur was also father of RACHEL who m. Hugh Rowland as revealed in the following deed. On 10 May 1744 Hugh Rowland and Rachel his wife of Kent Co. for 30 shillings sold to James Keith part of a tract of land (patent dated at Philadelphia, 26 March 1684, granted for 800 a. to Arthur Alston) part of the tract called *Chester*, on s. side of Duck Creek beginning at Allstons Branch. Arthur Alston is since dead and the remaining part of the said tract unsold having been divided among his surviving children of which Thomas Alston being his eldest son had for his share 100 a. (2 shares) and whereas there is left after such division about 50 a. which doth belong to Rachel ye wife of Hugh Rowland, one of the daus. and heirs of said Arthur Alston, lying to the s. of land that Thomas Alston sold to John Scott being his share now in the possession of William Blackson adj. the tract ye said Arthur Alston sold to a certain Thomas Bolstock.
{KEDELR N:29}

Arthur and Sarah had a son THOMAS (eldest son), b. 25 Aug 1688. {KEDELR}; ARTHUR (see below).

Second Generation

2. THOMAS ALLSTON, eldest son of Arthur (1) Alston, m. Sarah (N).

On 8 April 1738 a Deed of Mortgage was made. Thomas Allstone of Kent Co. and Sarah his wife for £30 sold to Isaac Pound of same place, a tract of land in the forrest of Little Creek Hundred being part of 200 a. of land taken up by virtue of a warrant 9 Nov 1734 beginning on s. side of Allstons Branch adj. a tract of land called *Chester*, 100a. Isaac Pound to clear the whole 200 a. from all demands of the trustees of the Loan. {KEDELR M:51}

Thomas d. leaving a will dated 13 Dec 1746, proved 19 Jan 1746. Heirs: sons Isreal, Randell, Arture; wife Seara; daus. Ester Reese, Seara Keth. Execs.: wife Seara and son Isreal. Wits., William Reese, Alexander McFarland.
{Arch. Al:120. Reg. of Wills, 1:129-130}

Sarah Alston was grandmother of Sarah Rees, dau. of William Rees as mentioned in the will of William Rees, written 9 Nov 1749 and proved 16 Nov 1749. Heirs: wife Elizabeth; sons David, William, Jonathan; daus. Sarah, Margaret; bros. John and Thomas. Execs., wife Elizabeth, John Rees, and Phillip Lewis. Wits., Randel Blackshare, James Edwards, Edward Norman. Codicil Hannah Rees; mentions Sarah Alston, grandmother of dau. Sarah Rees. {Arch.
A43:40-43. Reg. of Wills, K:12-13}

In the Kent Co. Orphans Court case file is recorded the petition of Charles Allen who m. the widow and extx. of her late husband Thomas Allston, dec. The accompt is given by Charles Allen and Israel Allston of all singular of goods and chattels. Charles Allen had m. Sarah, widow and extx. of Thomas Allston, and Israel Alstone another of the execs. {KEORCF Allston, Thomas - 1752}

Thomas was father of the following children: ISREAL; RANDELL;

ARTURE; ESTER, m. William Reese; SEARA, m. (N) Keth.[2]

3. ARTHUR ALSTON, son of Arthur (1) Alston, m. 1st Mary, dau. of John Clayton and m. 2nd Frances (N).

On 10 May 1721 Arthur Alston of Kent Co., yeoman, son of Arthur Alston of same place, dec'd., for £25 sold a parcel of land to Jasper Harwood of same place. Whereas Arthur Alston, dec'd., by his will did bequeath unto his son Arthur Alston 100 a. to be laid off at the upper end of a parcel he was then possessed in Little Creek Hundred and was part of a greater tract granted by patent to Arthur Alston ye father. {KEDELR G:28}

On 10 Oct 1727 Arthur Alstone (Allstone) and Mary his wife of KE Co. sold to Samuel Whitehart a tract of land being one-half of 100 a. of land and plantation of John Walker late, dec'd., of same county, being part of a greater tract called *Denby Town* conveyed by Elisha Snow to Arthur Alstone, 53 a. {KEDELR I:170}

On 11 Feb 1730 Mary Allstone, wife of Arthur Allstone in Little Creek Hundred, Kent Co., with the special advice and consent of her husband, and Hanna Levick, wife of John Levick, in the same place, yeoman, with the special advice and consent of her husband, and Arthur Allstone and John Levick for themselves and taking burthen in and upon for their said wives, Mary Allstone and Arthur her husband for £5 and Hannah Levick and John her husband for £8 sold to John Clayton Junr. of same place, their brother (as lawful daus. of the, dec'd., John Clayton from same place yeoman) a tract of land in Little Creek Hundred possessed by John Clayton their brother being part of the lands called formerly *London* now *Middlewith*. {KEDELR I:243}

On 9 March 1761 Abraham Vannoy (Vanhoy) of Kent Co., yeoman, and Susannah his wife, admins. of Jonathan Clayton late of Kent Co., yeoman, dec'd., for £150 sold to Henry Stevens of same county, yeoman, at publick vendue, half part of a 80 a. tract of land, whereas John Clayton the elder late of Kent Co., yeoman, dec'd., was in his life time seized in sundrie parcels of land in Little Creek Hundred and being so seized, died intestate, leaving 6 children, to wit, John Clayton the younger, the afsd. Jonathan Clayton, Mary wife of Arthur Alstone, Hannah wife of John Levick, the afsd. Susannah Vannoy and Elizabeth Clayton and after the death of the afsd. John Clayton on 11 April 1730 William Rodeney, late high sheriff of Kent Co. by virtue of a writ did cause the land to be divided into 7 parts, and 2 parts did allot to the said Jonathan Clayton and Elizabeth Clayton, beginning at the share of Abraham Vannoy and Susannah his wife, 30 a. and 50 a. next adj. which the said John Clayton, dec'd., in his lifetime purchased of Richard Richardson, in the whole 80 a. Jonathan Clayton became vested in half part of the 80 a. and d. intestate and without issue being indebted in divers sums of money and admininistration was granted to the afsd. Abraham Vannoy and Susanna his wife and they at an Orphans Court 24 Aug 1748 were granted an order of court to sell the lands of their intestate to discharge his debts. {KEDELR Q:36}

---

[2] This is probably James Keeth of Little Creek Hundred who d. leaving a will dated 22 Sep 1757, proved 24 Dec 1757. Heirs: wife Sarah; sons Thomas, James, John, Francis; daus. Miriam, Sarah, Jane, Hannah. {arch. A28:92-93. Reg. of Wills, K:173}

Arthur Alston, son of Arthur (1) Alston, d. by 11 Jan 1736 when his estate was administered by Frances Alstone. {Reg. of Wills, H:133}

In the Kent Co. Orphans Court File case of Arthur Allston in 1736 was referenced the estate late of Arthur Allston and Frances Allston, relict and admx. of sd. Arthur Allston. {KEORCF Allston, Arthur - 1736}

4. ELIZABETH ALSTON, dau. of Arthur (1) Alston, b. 8 July 1685, m. David Duncan and had an only son ARTHUR.

On 16 March 1738 Arthur Duncan of Kent Co. for £20 sold to Henry Hayes of same co. blacksmith, a tract of land which Arthur Allstone late of Kent Co., dec'd., grandfather of the said Arthur Duncan did, by his deed of gift bearing date 1 Oct 1705, give unto David Duncan father of the afsd. Arthur Duncan 50 a. of land in Little Creek Hundred bounded by 50 a. given by afsd. Arthur Allstone to Jasper Harrid and Hannah his wife near Allstons Branch. David Duncan so seized thereof dyed and the land descended to Arthur Duncan as only son and heir at law to his father. {KEDELR M:37}

Third Generation

5. ARTHUR ALSTON, possible son of Thomas (2) Alston, m. Sarah Raymond, sister of Jonathan Raymond and dau. of Sarah Gooding.

Sarah Gooding, Gentlewoman of Duck Creek Hundred, d. leaving a will dated 23 July 1763, proved 10 Aug 1763. Heirs: sons John and Jonathan Raymond; daus. Rachel Raymond, Sarah Alston. Execs., sons John and Jonathan, John Jones. Wits., Abraham Allee, Mary Steel, Thomas Tilton. {Arch. A19:132-133. Reg. of Wills, K:313-314}

(N) Alston m. Sarah Raymond, sister of Jonathan Raymond, before 10 May 1771. {Kent Wills L:96}

Jonathan Raymond, Gentleman of Duck Creek Hundred, d. leaving a will dated 10 May 1771, proved 16 May 1771. Heirs: sisters Sarah Alston, wife of Arthur and Rachel Tybout; niece Sarah Raymond, dau. of bro. John; cousin James Raymond; Edward McElroy. Execs., Thomas Collins, Esq., and Thomas Tilton. Wits., Matthew Crozier, Thomas Keith, Rachel Crozier. {Arch. A42:152 155. Reg. of Wills, L:96-97}

Arthur Allston, yeoman, d. leaving a will in Appoquinimick Hundred, New Castle Co., DE, dated 19 July 1775, proved 5 Sep 1775. Mentioned were wife Sarah; sons, Jonathon Allston and Thomas Allston; dau., Rachel; and two more younger children. Extx. Wife Sarah. {New Castle Co. Wills K:255}

Arthur was father of the following children: JONATHAN; THOMAS; RACHEL; Two children.

6. ISRAEL ALLSTON, son of Thomas (2), m. Sarah (N) who later m. Benjamin Eubanks.

On 14 Aug 1754, Israel Allston of Kent Co. planter and Sarah his wife for £16.6.3 sold to James Keeth of same co. part of a tract of land called *Chester* on n. side of Ellingsworths Branch in Little Creek Hundred extending with the said Keeth's land to land of Israel Allston's. ... 21 3/4 a. Wit: Randall Allston, John MacNeMamara. (o:pg 243) {KEDELR O: 243}

Israel Allston of Little Creek d. leaving a will dated 5 Nov 1760, proved 22 Nov 1760. Heirs: wife Sarah; sons Thomas, Abner, Joab (Job), Joshua, Israel, John; daus. Elizabeth, Sarah. Extx., wife. Wits., Randall Allston,

John Roach, Edward Norman. Codicil, bros. Randall and Arthur Allston. {Arch. Al:106-108. Reg. of Wills, K:247} Arch. Al:107 shows Sarah, the widow, later married Benjamin Hughbanks [Eubanks].

Israel was father of the following children: THOMAS; ABNER; JOAB (JOB, ZOAB); JOSHUA; ISRAEL; JOHN; ELIZABETH; SARAH.

7. RANDAL ALSTON, son of Thomas (2) Alston, m. Martha (N) who later m. John Bennett.

Randal d. leaving a will dated 5 Nov 1771, proved 19 Feb 1772. Heirs: daus. Hannah, Elizabeth; sons Stephen, Andrew, Thomas; wife Martha. Extx., wife Martha. Guardian, bro. Arthur Alston of New Castle Co. Wits., Joseph Smith, Mary Smith, Silas Snow. {Arch. Al:116-117. Reg. of Wills, L:108} Note: Arch. Al:117 shows John Bennett and wife Martha as execs.

Randal was father of the following children: HANNAH; ELIZABETH; STEPHEN; ANDREW; THOMAS.

Fourth Generation

8. ABNER ALSTON, son of Israel (6) and Sarah Alston, late of KE Co., DE, dec'd., and Hannah [Anna] Jenkins, dau. of Jabez and Hannah Jenkins, late of the same place, also, dec'd., m. 29th da., 5th mo., 1782 at Duck Creek. {DCMM}

On 28th da., 10th mo., 1780 Abner Allston requested to be joined in membership with Friends. {DCMM}

On 7th da., 3rd mo., 1795 Hannah Allston, wife of Abner Allston, produced a certificate of removal from Cecil Monthly Meeting.

Abner Alston of St. George's Hundred, d. leaving a will dated 14th da., 3rd mo., 1795, proved 30 March 1795. Mentioned were wife Hannah; dau. Hannah; nephew, Abner Alston, son of Brother Zoab; brothers, John, Zoab and Israel; sister, Elizabeth. Execs. John Hirons and John Alston. {New Castle Co. Wills O:63}

On 9th da., 5th mo., 1795, Appoquinimink Preparative Meeting requested a certificate for Hannah Allston, widow of Abner Allston, to be again joined to Cecil Monthly Meeting. {DCMM}

Abner and Hannah were parents of the following children {DCMM}: MARY, b. 9th da., 3rd mo., 1783, d. 25th da., 11th mo., 1783; HANNAH, b. 5th da., 11th mo., 1784; SARAH, b. 4th da., 1st mo., 1787. Hannah, mother of the above children d. 1st da., 2nd mo., 1787[3] about 2 a.m. and interred at Friends Meeting House at Appoqunimink.

9. ISRAEL ALLSTON, probable son of Israel (6) and Sarah Alston, m. on 31st da., 3rd mo., 1772, Mary Ozburn, dau. of Jonathan and Eunice Osburn, at the house of Jonathan Ozburn in Little Creek Hundred. {Duck Creek Monthly Meeting; Orphans Court E:100}

Jonathan Ozbun, yeoman of Little Creek Hundred, d. leaving a will dated 24 Aug 1773, proved 11 Nov 1773. Heirs: wife Eunice; son Jonathan; daus. Eunice and Tabitha Ozbun, Elizabeth Cowgill, Mary Alstone; son-in-law Israel Alstone. Extx., wife Eunice. Guardian, Robert Holliday. Wits., Robert Regester, Elizabeth Stevens, Thomas Parry. {Arch. A38:166-167. Reg. of Wills, L:143}

---

[3] Obvious discrepancy in this date.

Note: Will mentions grandfather Joshua Clayton, dec'd.

On 23rd da., 11th mo., 1771, Israel Allston with the concurrence of Little Creek Preparative Meeting requested to be joined in membership. {DCMM}

Israel and Mary were parents of the following children {DCMM}: JONATHAN, b. 8th da., 7th mo., 1773; ELISABETH, b. 24th da., 2nd mo., 1775; SARAH, b. 22nd da., 3rd mo., 1777; ---, b. 1779; MARY, b. 2nd da., 7(?)th mo., 1781, m. 22nd da., 5th mo., 1800, Preston Sharples of Appoquinimick Hundred, son of Thomas Sharples and his wife Martha; ISRAEL, b. 2nd da., 3rd mo., 1783; EUNICE, b. 24th da., 11th mo., 1784; SUSANNA, b. 10th da., 1st mo., 1787; ANNA, b. 27th da., 5th mo., 1793.

10. JOAB ALLSTON, son of Israel (6), m. Hannah Lamb.

On 23rd da., 2nd mo., 1788 Joab Allston requested a certificate to Cecil Monthly Meeting in order to accomplish his marriage with Hannah Lamb, a member of that meeting. {DCMM}

On 28th da., 6th mo., 1788, Hannah, wife of Joab Allston, produced a certificate from Friends of Cecil Monthly Meeting. {DCMM}

On 26th da., 12th mo., 1789, Appoquinimick Preparative Meeting informed that Joab Allston requested a certificate for himself, his wife and son Joshua, to be joined to Cecil Monthly Meeting. {DCMM}

Unplaced

Ruth, Henry and Mary Hyland, minor children of John Hyland. Petition of Matthias Morton and Elizabeth his wife at court appointed Matthias Morton, Ralph Winteron and ISRAEL ALSTON, uncles of Ruth, Henry and Mary, their guardIans. 15 Jan 1744/5. {Kent Co. Orphans court C:49}

REBEKAH ALLSTON m. John Greenwood.

On 10 Feb 1745 John Greenwood and Rebekah his wife of Kent Co. in consideration of a certain bond passed from Thomas and Israel Alstone wherein the said Thomas and Israel hath obligated themselves to find and allow the said Rebekah wife of John Greenwood a good and sufficient maintenance during natural life as by condition of the said bond, release unto Israel Alstone of same co, a plantation and tract of land in Little Creek Hundred formerly given unto Isaac Ellett, dec'd., by Alstone the older, dec'd., in marriage with his dau. Rebeka, partie to these presents, who since intermarried with the said John Greenwood ... adj. David Dunking's land, to Jasper Harwood's land, to land of the said Alstone, dec'd., 50 a. {KEDELR N:88}

THOMAS ALSTON m. Jane McDavett, dau. Of Daniel McDavett.

Daniel McDavett, yeoman of Duck Creek, d. leaving a will dated 27 Feb 1759, proved 29 Aug 1759. Heirs: dau. Jane; Margaret Moran; Christopher Wan. Execs., Jacob Allee, Sr., and James McMullan, merchant. Trustee, motherin-law Jane Keith. Wits., Peter McGlew, John Mason, Patrick Moran. {Arch. A32:158-160, 162. Reg. of Wills, K:212} Note: Arch. A32:159-160 show Jane (Jean] later married Thomas Alston; Margaret Moran later married Thomas Murphy.

Thomas Allston d. by 7 Sep 1772 when his estate was administered by Jane Allston, widow. {Arch. Al:121. Reg. of Wills, L:120}

THE BADGER FAMILY

1. EDMUND BADGER, cordwainer of Dover, m. 1st Elizabeth (N) and m. 2nd Letitia Blackshare, dau. of Thomas Blackshare.

On 6 Sep 1744 Edmund Badger of the Town of Dover, cordwainer, and Elizabeth his wife for £500 sold to Thomas Nixon of same place, taylor, all their lotts of land in Dover Town on w. side of Court House Square, formerly conveyed to Edmund Badger by James Gorrell and Thomas Skidmore, two of the persons apointed by Act of Assembly to convey the lots of Dover Town (one recorded Book M, pg 127). {KEDELR N:46}

On 12 May 1756 Edmund Badger of the Town of Dover, Kent Co. cordwainer, signed a release for the settling and assuring the several tracts of land and for divers other good causes and considerations release in trust unto John Miller of same county, clerk, a brick messuage or tenement with the lot of ground whereon Edmund Badger now dwells and formerly conveyed to him by Thomas Nixon and Anne his wife and also one lot of ground conveyed by Mark Manlove late of said county to Edmund Badger, also one other messuage and lot of ground called *Jayl* conveyed by Benjamin Chew and Robert Willcocks commissioners, all lots in the Town of Dover and the plantation and tract of land on s. side of Walkers Branch formerly conveyed by a certain Jonathan Sturges to the said Edmund Badger, 147 a., part of a larger tract called *Shoemakers Hall*, granted for the uses, trusts, intents and purposes herein after limited expressed that is to the use of Edmund Badger and his assigns for and during the term of his natural life and after his decease then to the only use of Eleazar Badger his eldest son and the messuage and lot of ground called *Jayl* after the decease of said Edmund Badger to the only proper use of his youngest son Edmund Badger.
{KEDELR O:337}

On 12 Aug 1757 Thomas Blackshare and Ursla (Ursley) his wife, both of Kent Co., for naturall love and affection and £5 gave to their son in law Edmund Badger of same place, cordwainer, a tract of land in Duck Creek Hundred granted to Thomas Blackshare by a warrant bearing date 19 May 1752 beginning at John Mclean's land to Edward Tilghman's land to head of Muddy branch ... 188 a. Witnessed by Eleazar Badger, Edmund Badger. {KEDELR P:33}

On 27th da., 12th mo., 1760, Edmund Badger requested to be taken into the membership of Friends. {DCMM}

2. EDMUND BADGER, son of Edmund (1) Badger, m. Margaret (N).

On 14 March 1763 Edmund Badger of the Town of Dover Kent Co. cordwainer, and Letitia his wife for £150 sold to Thomas Floyd of Murtherkill Hundred same county, weaver, a tract of land and plantation in Murtherkill Hundred on e. side of lower Kings Road.{KEDELR Q:141}

Edmund d. leaving a will dated 14 Dec 1763, proved 15 Dec 1763. Heirs: wife Letitia; sons Eleazor, Edmund; Society of Quakers (Little Creek). Exec., Samuel McCall, practitioner. Wits., Richard Wells, Thomas Skillington, James Maning. {Arch. A2:46-47. Reg. of Wills, K:327-328}

Apparently Letitia later m. (N) Moore, since Thomas Blackshear mentions dau. Letitia Moore in his will writen 15 Feb 1768. {Arch. A4:111. Reg. of Wills, L:41}

On 17 Dec 1764 Edmund Badger of the Town of Dover, Kent Co.,

cordwainer, and Margaret his wife for £36 sold to Vincent Loockerman of same town merchant, a small tract of land in Murtherkill Hundred on n. side of Spring Branch which Thomas Floyed, conveyed to Edmund Badger late of said town, dec'd., who was the father of the afsd. Edmund Badger, and whereas Edmund Badger the father by his will left to his son Edmund Badger, Junr., the afsd. land.
{KEDELR Q:264}

On 4 Jan 1765 Edmund Badger of Kent Co. yeoman and Margaret his wife for £210 sold to John Banning of same county, sadler, two lots of ground, whereas Edmund Badger the elder late of Kent Co., shoemaker, dec'd., father of Edmund Badger party hereto, became seized in a tract of land purchased on 6 Sep 1744 of Thomas Nixon and Ann his wife, whereon the afsd. Edmund Badger now dwells and a lot of ground adj. w. side of the Court House Square in the Town of Dover. The said Edmund Badger, the elder, in his life time became seized in all that other lot of ground adj. the afsd. lot beginning at High Street to North Street, 1 a., 39 perches, 45 ft. and Edmund Badger the elder being so seized made his will dated 14 Dec 1763 and did devise the same to the afsd. Edmund Badger his son excepting 1/2 a. conveyed by the afsd. Mark Manlove to Edmund Badger the elder adj. North Street. {KEDELR R:15}

On 4 Feb 1765 John Banning of Kent Co., sadler, for £215 sold to Casar Rodney of same county, esqr, a messuage and lot of ground now in the occupation of Edmund Badger, yeoman, on w. side of the Court House Square in the town of Dover adj. messuage late belonging to one Edmund Kearny on High Street and a lot adj. to afsd. lot beginning at High Street and North Street, 1 a. 39 perches excepting 1/2 a. laid out next adj. North Street which said premisses were lately belonging to Edmund Badger late of Kent Co., dec'd., who by his will bearing date 14 Dec 1763 did devise the said premisses to Edmund Badger his son who on 4 Jan last past did convey the same, except as herein excepted, to the said John Banning ... subject to a lease for some part of said premisses made between one James Moor and the afsd. Edmund Badger the son. {KEDELR R:21}

Edmund was father of the following children: ELEAZOR; EDMUND.

3. ELEAZAR BADGER, eldest son of Edmund (1) Badger.

On 26 Feb 1763 Eleazar Badger of the Town of Dover KE Co., taylor, for £20 sold to Edmund Badger, Senr., of same place cordwainer, two lotts of ground and brick messuage which is mentioned in a deed of gift to the Reverend John Miller in trust for the use of the said Eleazar Badger as the eldest son of the said Edmund Badger bearing date 12 May 1756 (Book O, fol. 337) ... in the Town of Dover w. side of Court House Square on n. side of Court House Lane. {KEDELR Q:138}

On 5 May 1764 Eleazor (Eliazor) Badger of the town of Dover Kent Co., taylor, being the eldest son of Edmund Badger late of same place, cordwainer, dec'd., for £150 sold to his brother Edmund Badger of same town, cordwainer, a lot of ground, called *Goal Lot*, which he purchased at publick vendue and conveyed by deed poll bearing date 19 Nov 1755 (Book O, fol. 310), and whereas the said Edmund Badger d. and by his will bearing date 15 Dec 1763 did bequeath the *Goal Lot* to the afsd. Eleazor Badger, on Kings Street and Court House Square, 32 1/4 perches. {KEDELR Q:229}

Unplaced

JOHN BADGER of Sussex Co., d. leaving a verbal will, proved 6 March 1687/8. Heir: Antony Inloyce. Wits., Robert Tomlinson, James Hughs. {Penna. Hist. Soc. Papers, vol. AM. 2013:88}

THE BAILEY FAMILY

First Generation

1. ELIAS BAILY m. Sarah (N). Elias, his wife Sarah and their son Seattown Baily, were mentioned in the will of James Seattown or Sealtown of Sussex Co., written 21 Jan 1717 and proved 4 Feb 1717. {Arch. A67:130. Reg. of Wills, A:120-121}

Elias Baily of Kent Co., yeoman, d. before 7 Nov 1727 when his estate was administered by Sarah Baily. {Reg. of Wills, F:33}

Elias Baily was father of the following children: SEATTOWN; ELIAS (eldest son); JONATHAN; JAMES; NATHANIEL; SARAH; MARY; HANNAH, m. Griffith Griffiths; ABIGAL, m. Isaac Jones.

Second Generation

2. ELIAS BAILY, eldest son of Elias (1) Baily, late of Murderkill Hundred, on 10 Nov 1733 sold land to Thomas Langley. Whereas Elias Baily, his father, became seized of a tract of land in the forrest of Murderkill Hundred of 200 a., being part of a tract of land called *Dundee* whereon the said Elias at the time of his death dwelled and whereas Elias the father dyed intestate the land descended into the possession of his children Elias afsd. and Jonathan, James, Nathaniel, Sarah, Mary, Hannah and Abigal ... Elias Baily the son for £11 sold to Thomas Langley now of same place planter the afsd. tract of land. {KEDELR K:173}

3. JONATHAN BAILY of Sussex Co., probable son of Elias (1) Baily, was paying quit rent, in 1693 on land in Sussex Co. and in 1702-1713, on part of 112 a. in Sussex Co. {Bendler:27, 49}

Jonathan d. leaving a will dated 1 Aug 1737, proved 13 Sep 1737. Heirs: sons James and Jonathan; daus. Sarah Baily, Mary Naws and Hannah and Abigail Jacobs; seven grandchildren unnamed (children of son Elias, dec'd.) Execs., sons James and Jonathan and daus. Sarah Baily; Mary Naws, Hannah and Abigail Jacobs. Wits., Nehemiah Field, Luke Shield, Phil. Russel. {Arch. A58:76. Reg. of Wills, A:293-295}

On 31 July 1758 Sanders Darby of Sussex Co., sawyer, for £35 sold to Samuel David of same co., pilot, a lott of land in the town of Lewes binding on Mulberry Street 60 ft. breadth, 200 ft length, granted by the Court of Sussex to a certain Joseph Russell who sold the same to Jonathan Baily the elder, who by his will bequeathed all his lands to his sons James Baily and Jonathan Baily. They according to the will divided the lands and the afsd. lott was allotted to the said Jonathan Baily. {SUDELR I:177}

Jonathan was father of the following children: ELIAS; JAMES; JONATHAN; SARAH; MARY, m. (N) Naws; HANNAH; ABIGAIL.

4. NATHANIEL BAILY, son of Elias (1) Baily, m. 1st Hannah, widow of

William Cale and m. 2nd Jennet Simonton, dau. of John Simonton who later m. William Dodd.

On 10 Aug 1747 Nathaniel Baily of Sussex Co., yeoman, one of the sons of Elias Baily late of Kent Co., dec'd., and Griffith Griffeths of Sussex Co., house carpenter, and Hannah his wife and Abigail Baily of same co., spinster, daus. of the afsd. Elias Baily, dec'd., for £22 released unto Richard Jackson of Kent Co. yeoman ... a plantation about 6 miles from the Town of Dover being part of a greater tract called *Dundee* being the same land and plantation whereof the afsd. Elias Baily lived on when he dyed, who dyed intestate and is actually now in the possession of the afsd. Richard Jackson. {KEDELR N:166}

On 1 Feb 1757 Nathaniel Baily and Hannah his wife formerly the widow and relict of a certain William Cale, late of same co., dec'd., and John Cale, son of the afsd. William Cale, all of Sussex. Co., for £80 quit claimed a plantation which was 1/2 of a tract of land called the *New Forrest* in Rehoboth Neck ... 138 1/2, a. also 22 a., part of a 80 a. tract of land called *South Hampton* on Gordons Branch and also one other parcel part of *South Hampton*, 35 a.
{SUDELR I:141}

On 29 Sep 1757 Nathaniel Baily the son of Elias Baily, late of Sussex Co., dec'd., and Isaac Jones of same co., yeoman, and Abigail his wife dau. of the afsd. Elias Baily, for £50 paid to Elias Baily in his lifetime by John Little in his lifetime sold to John Little of same co. the only surviving heir of the said John Little, late of same co., dec'd., 1/2 part of a tract of land, whereas the afsd. Elias Baily in his life time did sell and give his bond unto the afsd. John Little in his life time for the conveying a tract of land on n. side of Long Loved Branch alias Bundicks Bridge adj. to a tract formerly taken up by Samuel Gray being first called *Okeys Fortune* and now the *Childrens Portion* and since the deaths of the afsd. Elias Baily and John Little, Martha Little, widow of the afsd. John Little, who intermarried with one Matthew Rankin, they got a warrant from Benjamin Easburn bearing date at Philadelphia 18 Aug 1737 and William Shankland deputy surveyor for Sussex Co. resurveyed for the children of the afsd. John Little, dec'd., the tract of land on 11 Nov 1743 adj. Samuel Gray ... 262 a. {KEDELR I:154}

On 2 March 1763 John Clark and Mary his wife, execs. of the estate of Margery Miers, spinster, dec'd., of Sussex Co. by order of the court to discharge a bond and for £30 paid by John Simonton, Senr., dec'd. sold to the heirs of John Simonton, dec'd., to wit Jenet Baily, wife of Nathaniel Baily, Sarah Shankland, wife of John Shankland and Mary Davison wife of James Davison, spinsters, all of Sussex co. ... a parcel of land in Lewes Hundred binding on John Simonton, son of John Simonton, dec'd. ... 11 3/8 a. and whereas the said Margery Milers on 4 Aug 1749 by articles of agreement entered into with John Simonton, Senr., dec'd., that the said Margery Miers shall convey to said John Simonton the land afsd, and Margery Miers is since dec'd. without conveying said land, and John Simonton in his will bearing date 29 May 1751 bequeathed the land unto his 3 daus to wit Jenet, Sarah and Mary Simonton whom lately married as above.
{SUDELR I:439}

Nathaniel Bailey, yeoman, Lewes and Rehoboth Hundred, d. leaving a will dated 28 May 1782 [no date of probate]. Heirs: wife Jennet; sons William, Jonathan and Nathaniel Bailey; daus. Peggy and Comfort Bailey and Sarah Coulter (wife of William). Extx., wife Jennet Bailey. Wits., Jno. Russel, Jean Russel, Elizabeth Russel. {Arch. A58:85-86. Reg. of Wills, C:310} Arch. A58:86 shows that Jennet Bailey later m. William Dodd.

Nathaniel was father of the following children: WILLIAM; JONATHAN; NATHANIEL; PEGGY; COMFORT; SARAH, m. William Coulter.

5. JAMES BALEY, son of Elias (1) Baley late of Murtherkill Hundred, Kent Co., dec'd., on 13 Feb 1744 for £33 sold to Archabald Carsey of same place all his rights in a tract of land ... (whereas Elias Baley the father, in his lifetime became seized in a tract of land in the forrest of Murtherkill Hundred 200 a. being the w. part of a tract of land called *Dundee* whereon ye said Elias at the time of his decease did dwell, and Elias the father dyed intestate and it became in the possession of his children Elias, Jonathan and James afsd, Nathaniel, Sarah, Mary, Hannah and Abigall) ... whereon the said Archabald now dwells. {KEDELR N:58}

James Bailey, pilot of Sussex Co., DE, d. leaving a will dated 29 April 1745, proved 6 March 1744. Heirs: sons James and Steward; daus. Hannah and Ann. Execs. Jonathan Bailey and Jacob Phillips. Wits., Richard Metcalfe, Albertus Jacobs, Francis Richardson. {Arch. A58:69. Reg. of Wills, A:392-393}

On 8 April 1767 Ann Baily of Sussex Co., spinstres, for £27.0.2 sold to Jacob Kollock, of same county, several parcels of land in Pilot Town which descended to the afsd. Ann Baily by the death of her father James Baily, viz one lot 138 ft front 200 ft back between the grave yard and a 18 ft front and 200 ft back lot laid off for Samuel Arnall who purchased of Stuart Baily, one of the heirs of afsd. James Baily, also 1/2 of land that was divided between Samuel Arnold and said Ann Baily, likewise all her part of the marsh between Jacob Art's marsh and Lewes Creek by a deed of release from Samuel Arnall to the said Ann Baily. If Ann Baily shall pay unto the afsd. Jacob Kollock £27.0.2 before 1 March next with lawfull interest, then this present indenture shall cease. {KEDELR K:257}

James was father of the following children: JAMES; STEWARD; HANNAH; ANN.

Third Generation

6. JONATHAN BAILY, of Lewes, Sussex Co., probable son of Jonathan (3) Baily, d. leaving a will dated 9 March 1746, proved 8 Sep 1748. Heirs: wife Bethiah; sons John and Joseph; daus. Mary and Esther. Execs., wife Bethiah and friend Joseph Turner. Wits., John Maull, Shephard Kollock, William Rowland.
{Arch. A58:75. Reg. of Wills, A:394-395}

On 30 July 1763 John Adams, late of Pilot Town, Sussex Co., pilot, at present residing in Philadelphia and Cornelia his wife for £200, released unto Joseph Baily of Pilot Town, pilot, all the estate right in the messuages and lotts in Pilot Town, 50 a. in the whole, the estate of John Baily, dec'd., who was the brother of said Joseph Baily. {KEDELR K:20}

Jonathan was father of the following children: JOHN; JOSEPH; MARY; ESTHER.

7. ANN BAILY, dau. of James (5) Bailey.
On 14 Dec 1756 Ann Baily of Sussex Co., spinster, sold 2 tracts in Rehoboth Hundred, 3 miles from Lewes, devised to the said Ann by her father James Baily, late of Sussex Co. by his will. {KEDELR I:135}

8. STUARD BAILEY, son of James (5) Bailey.

On 2 March 1761 Joseph Shankland, high sheriff of Sussex Co., conveyed 2 tracts of land being divided amongst the heirs of James Bailey, dec'd., and whereas Jacob Kollock, Junr. and Daniel Nunez in Nov Term -- did each recover a judgment against Stuard Bailey of same co., pilot, by virtue of a writ the sheriff seized in execution 2 tracts of land formerly belonging to James Bailey in Rehoboth Hundred. {SUDELR I:295}

9. HANNAH BAILEY, dau. of James (5) Bailey, m. Jacob Art.

On 21 April 1761 Steward Baily of Sussex Co., pilot, for £75 sold to Samuel Arnal of same co., pilot, a tract of land at Lewes and Rehoboth Hundred at Pilot Town, part of a larger tract which James Baily of same co., dec'd., devised by his will to his 4 children, James, Hannah, Ann and Steward Baily, and the said [blank][4] intermarried with a certain Jacob Art, who became investedwith 1/4 part and Jacob Art also purchased the said James Baily the younger's part who then possessed 1/2 of the land and 2 shares of an island of marsh called *Balys Island* in Lewes Creek, and Ann Baily and Steward Baily are invested with a property in the land being undivided and also to the said island of marsh in an equal degree with the said Jacob according to the will of their father James Baily, dec'd. ... being the 1/4 part of the land whereon the afsd. Jacob Art now dwells and 1/8 part of *Bailys Island.* {SUDELR I:329}

Fourth Generation

8. JOHN BAILY, son of Jonathan (6) Baily.

In the land records of Sussex Co., is mentioned Jonathan Bailey, dec'd. father of John Baily who mortgaged a parcel of land in Rehoboth on 8 Jun 1754 which had been bequeathed to him by his father. {KEDELR I:17}

9. JOSEPH BAILY of Sussex Co., pilot, son of Jonathan (6) Baily.

On 22 Jul 1757 Joseph Baily of Sussex Co., pilot, for £20 quit claim unto John Adams of same place, pilot, several tracts of land one on the bank of Pilot Town and the other in Rehoboth being all the lands that were bequeathed to his brother John Baily by the will of his dec'd. father Jonathan Baily, mortgaged to the afsd. John Adams by the afsd. John Baily. {SUDELR I:153}

Unplaced

EDMUND BAYLEE m. Alice (N).

On 15 Aug 1753 Edmund Baylee (Bailey, Bayley) of Muspillion Hundred Kent Co., yeoman, and Alice his wife, for £80 sold to Benjamin Rasin, taylor, of same place, a tract of land, which John Crippen by his deed dated 11 Aug 1740 did convey unto Edmund Bayle.... 150 a. {KEDELR O:193}

EDMOND BAILY m. Ann, widow of Stephen Hairgrove.

Stephen Hairgrove, Murderkill Hundred, d. by 15 Feb 1768 when his

4

[4] By the process of elimination this has to be Hannah.

estate was administered by Ann Hairgrove, widow. {Arch. A21:69-70. Reg. of Wills, L:40} Arch. A21:69 mentions heirs, Mary, George, Anne, Katherine and Thomas Hairgrove; page 70 shows that Ann Hairgrove, widow, later married Edmond Baily.

JOHN BALY of Long Island.

30 Oct 1689 John Baly of Long Island, NY, sold unto William Lawrence of Kent Co. PA one light gray horse marked on left buttock with letters TP. {KEDELR}

THOMAS BAILY of Little Creek Hundred, d. by 4 June 1773 when his estate was administered by Mary Baily, widow. {Arch. A2:76. Reg. of Wills, L:137}

THE BARTLET FAMILY

1. NICHOLAS BARTLET m. Sarra (N).

On 21 Dec 1680 Nicholas Bartlet of St. Jones Countie in the province of NY "appoints my deare and loveing wife Sarra Bartlet to be my trusty and well beloved attorney."

On 22 Dec 1680 Nickoles Bartlet was granted a license to keep a house of entertainment for the county of St. Jones, for victualls, drinke and lodging for horses and men. {Kent Ct.:10}

At court of 15 March 1680/1 Nickoles Bartlet claimed that Peter Bawcombe had slandered his wife by calling her a whore; she was accused of throwing a block at Bawcombe. {Kent Ct.:15}

In the Kent County Rent Roll, 1681-1688, Nich. Bartlet is paying rent on 1000 a. called *Longacre*. Also listed were Jane Bartlet paying rent on *Poplar Ridge*, 380 a. and Rich. Bartlet paying rent on 1150 a. called *Bartlets Lot*. {Bendler:1}

On 16 Aug 1681 Nicholas Bartlett and his wife Sarah, conv. to William Eaterson of TA Co., mariner, 150 a. in Tredhaven Creek adj. *The Exchange* called *Petty France*. {TALR 4:56}

In a court case dated 20 Dec 1681 Sarah Bartlet complained that her husband Nickoles Bartlet abused her. The jury agreed and ordered that Nickoles alllow his wife 2000 lbs. of tobacco per year. {Kent Ct.:48}

In a court case of 12-13 Sep 1682, William Bourne against Nichls. and Sarah Bartlet, it was set forth that Bourne disbursed £16 for Sarah Bartlett in consideration thereof the said Sarah Bartlet engaged to serve the peticioner 2 years as a housekeeper and he craves her service or the £16. Nichols Bartlett, her husband, being present in Court consented to the same and that she the said Sarah Bartlett, should keepe and injoy hur sun untill he shall be of full age and in the meantime to dispose of him as she shall think fitt. {Sussex Court Records}

On 21 June 1682 Nickoles Bartlet with the consent of Jane his daughter, agreed to her indenture to John Betts for 4 years. {Kent Ct.:80}

In 27-29 April 1683 Court Joseph Low gave his testamony in open court that he did see William Beaverly a bed together [with Sarah Bartlet] with their clorth of [with their clothes off], acting in an unseemly manner. William Beaverly being excamined confessed that he have lay upon the bead with the said Sarah Bartlett, and William Borne confessed in open court that he have been tempted by the said Sarah Bartlett to committ the act of uncleannes and that he did committ the said act with her. It was ordered that Sarah Bartlett shall have 21 lashes laid upon her naked back, well laid on, and to returne to hur husband or otherwise to depart out of this province and territories within tenn days. William Borne and William Beaverly were ordered to sitt two hours in the stocks and pay £5 a piece as a fine. {Sussex Court Records}

On 25 March 1689 Nicholas Bartlett of Kent Co., admin. of estate of Joseph Groves of same place, dec'd., discharged William Berry of same co. from all bills bonds debts owing unto estate of Joseph Groves, dec'd., {KEDELR}

Nicklos Bartlet of Kent Co., Delaware, d. by 12 Feb 1689 when his estate was administered by Sarah Bartlet, widow. {Penna. Hist. Soc. Papers, AM. 2013:112}

On 4 April 1690 William Berry of Kent Co. acquitted, discharged and released Sarah Bartlett, admin. of estate of Nicholas Bartlett, dec'd., from all manner of debts, bills and bonds. {KEDELR}

On 10 March 1690/1 Sarah Bartlett, admin. of estate of Nicholas Bartlett of Kent Co. for a valuable consideration in hand by her said, dec'd., husband Nicholas Bartlett sold unto John Richardson, Senr. of same co. a tract of land called *Bartletts Lott* on s. side of Jones Creek, 300 a. {KEDELR}

Nicholas Bartlet was father of JANE; JOHN.

2. JOHN BARTLET, b. c1679, son of Nicholas (1) and Sarah Bartlet of KE Co., DE, m. Elizabeth (N).

On 15 Aug 1729 John Bartlet of Talbot Co., MD, ship carpenter, and Elizabeth his wife, he the son and heir of Nicholas Bartlet, late of Kent Co., dec'd., for £24 sold to William Marchant of KE Co., 100 a. being part of a tract of land called *Bartlets Lott.* {KEDELR I:202}

On 10 Feb 1729/30, before Thomas Berry and Jno. Housman, justices, came John Bartlet, aged 50 years or thereabout, on his solemn oath deposeth and saith that he well remembers he heard his mother Sarah Bartlet say that John Price, commonly called The Fidler, had taken up land on Murder Creek and the said Price had the chief of his abode at her husbands house in Kent Co. and that the said Bartlett doth further say that he was well acquainted with the said Price ever since he can well remember, and have heard him the owner of the land say that the tract of land was called *Oxford* and contained 1200 a. and further Bartlet saith that he knew John Price, Junr., the son of the said John Price who being heir to the said Price sold ye tract of land to Andrew Caldwell and he was an evidence to the above deed and sale. {KEDELR K:1}

On 20 April 1730 John Bartlett of TA Co. MD, son and heir of Nicholas Bartlett, late of Kent Co., dec'd., for £60 sold to John Newell the younger of Kent Co. yeoman, a tract of land in Murderkill Hundred beginning at the corner of Peter Groundick's ... (973 a. granted by warrant unto Nicholas Bartlett, dec'd., and surveyed in his life time 18 Jan 1680 which he conveyed unto John Newell, dec'd., father of the afsd. John Newell 100 a. and to John Richardson, dec'd., 300 a. John Bartlett the son since the decease of Nicholas Bartlett hath sold two other parcells, to wit, 100 a. to William Marchant and 100 a. more to Thomas Skidmore) ... remaining part of the afsd. tract called *Bartletts Lott* ... 373 a. (excepting such land of Edward Williams lately sold him by the said John Bartlett as part of another tract.). {KEDELR K:31}

On 30 Sep 1729 John Bartlet of [TA] Co. MD. son and heir at law to

Nicholas Bartlet, late of Kent Co., dec'd., for £40 and also the great love, good will and affection he hath for Edward Williams, son of Edward Williams, and Rebecca his wife released unto Edward Williams and Rebecca his wife of Kent Co. ... a parcell of land on s. side of Mill branch of Dover River ... bounded by William Marchant's land ... to line of John Housman's land ... 100 a. being part of two greater tracts of land formerly laid out for the afsd. Nicholas Bartlet and John Bartlet ... to the only proper use of Edward Williams the father and Rebecca his wife during their natural lives and after both their decease then to Edward Williams the son and to the lawful issue of his body. {KEDELR I:213}

THE BEDWELL FAMILY

Ref. A: *Bedwell Beaux and Belles. A Brief History of the Bedwell Family*. By Carolyn Reeves Ericson. 1614 Redbud St., Nacogdoches, TX 75961. 1972. Printed by King Printing Nacogdoches, Texas. A copy is held by the Delaware State Archives.

The following was taken from above Ref A:

"The first records we find in America is of a Robert Bedwell in Old Rappahannock County, Virginia where he received a grant of land in 1661. (*Cavaliers and Pioneers*: 335). He also received land for paying the passage for two persons other than his family. In the earlier deed records he is joined by wife Ann. (Rappahannock County, Virginia Deeds, 1668-1672:94) Her death took place between 1669 and 1680 when Robert is joined by wife Susanna (widow Fisher) in signing deeds. (Rappahannock County, Virginia Deeds, 1672-1682, pg. 105-6)

"Apparently Robert Bedwell and his son-in-law Isaac Webb journeyed to Kent Co., DE in the summer of 1679. There they obtained a grant of land, spent the fall and winter making improvements on it, then returned to Virginia where final preparations for the move were completed. In April 1680 Robert and Susanna sold their final holdings in the state of Virginia. (Rappahannock County, Virginia Deeds, 1672-1682, pg. 1056)

"In March 1682-3, Robert Bedwell traveled to Philadelphia to take part in the first scheduled Pennsylvania Assembly, as one of six delegates from Kent County on Delaware. (Hist of Delaware by Scharf:86). ...."

First Generation

1. ROBERT BEDWELL m. Susannah (N).

Robert was granted a patent to land on the s.e. side of St. Jones Creek called *Folly Neck*, 800 a., dated in New Yorke, 20 Aug 1679. {The Duke of York Records:155} On 20 Dec 1680 a tract called *Playners* on the west side of Jones Creek was laid out adjoining the first tract. On 22 Feb 1681/2 1200 a. as laid out for his sons. {KEDELR} During the period, 1681-1688 Robert was paying rent on the tract called *The Folly Neck*, 1050 acres (surveyed on 21/6/1685 and granted on 20/6/1679). Robert d. by 14 June 1686 when Susannah Bedwell, widow, was appointed as admin. {Penna. Hist. Soc. Papers, vol. AM. 2013:66}

On 8 Dec 1691 Adam Fisher of Kent Co. PA sold to Jacob Salter of same place, 137 a. of land being part of a tract of land of 1100 a. on s. side of Dover River called *Longreach,* formerly laid out for Thomas Bedwell, Henry Bedwell, Robert Bedwell and the said Adam Fisher as by patent 20 Jul 1684 beginning at a corner of Ezekiell Needham's and Gabrill Jones' land.

Robert was father of the following children; MARY (oldest dau.), m. 1st in Richmond Co., VA {DE Recall 1:3} Isack Webb by whom she had a son Robert, m. 2nd James Clayton, m. 3rd Michael O'Donahoe[5] ; THOMAS (oldestson); ELIZABETH, m. 1st Annanias Turner and m. 2nd Richard Swan; ROBERT; HENRY.

Second Generation

2. THOMAS BEDWELL, son of Robert (1) Bedwell, m. Millicent (N), dau. of Thomas Hewthate and sister of Ralph Hewthat, Prisala Edmonds (wife of Robert Edmonds), Anne Needum (wife of Edmond Needum), and Elenor Robertson (wife of John Robertson). Thomas Bedwell, m. 2nd Honor, widow of William Clark.

At the initiative of Thomas Bedwell *Folly Neck* was resurveyed by warrant on 10th da., 11th mo., 1685 and confirmed by patent for 1050 a. to Robt. Bedwell on 6 March 1690/1. {KEDELR}

On 9 Aug 1688 Thomas Bedwell acknowledged receiving of Susana Bedwell, admin of the estate of Robert Bedwell, his full share the estate of his father, Robert Bedwell.

On 4 Sep 1688 Thomas Bedwell of Kent Co. gave one light gray maire filly about one year and a half olde unto his nephew Robert Webb, his sister Marie's son, with her increase to him the said Robert Webb, except first horse coult of said maire shall be James Clayton's his said sisters present husband and in case Robert Webb shall hapen to die before he comes of age then one half of ye increase to go to my said sister his mother and James Clayton her husband, other half of increase to return to me. {KEDELR}

On 8 Feb 1691 Thomas Bedwell son and heir of Robert Bedwell, dec'd., of Kent Co. PA and admin. to his estate, for brotherly love and deare affection Thomas Bedwell gives to Elizabeth Turner, dau. to said Robert Bedwell, dec'd., and new wife to Annamias Turner and sister to said Thomas Bedwell of same co., a tract of land called *Elizabeth Chance*, s. side of Dover River beginning at Mary Clayton and Henry Bedwell's land, 150 a., part of a tract of land said Robert Bedwell dyed possessed of. {KEDELR}

On 9 Jan 1692 Thomas Bedwell acknowledged and delivered one deed to Henry Bedwell for 175 a. of land. {KEDELR}

In 1693 Thomas Bedwell was assessed for 100 a. Thomas Bedwell was the 1693 tax collector at Murderkill. {Bendler:26}

On 8 Feb 1695 Thomas Bedwell, son and heir and admin. of estate of Robert Bedwell of Kent Co. PA for love and affection gave to his sister Mary Clayton, late widdow of Isack Webb, oldest dau. to the said Robert Bedwell, dec'd., and now wife to James Clayton, a tract of land called *Claytons Lott* on s.w. side of Dover River, parallel with land of Henry Bedwell, 175 a.

5

[5] According to Reference A.; no documentation is given.

On 8 Aug 1696 the births of the children of Thomas Bedwell and Malecent his wife of KE Co. were recorded: dau. Anna Bedwell was borne on Fryday 10 Dec 1691 about 11 oclock at night, son Robert Bedwell was borne on Sunday 18 Nov 1694 about 2 oclock in the afternoon. {KEDELR}

8 March 1696/7. Birth. Melleccent Bedwell dau. of Thomas Bedwell and Melleccent his wife was borne on Munday about 4 oclock in the morninge. {KEDELR}

In the will of Simon Hirons, Sr. written 12 Oct 1706 was mentioned Anna Bedwell, dau. of Thomas and Milicent Bedwell. {Arch. vol. A24, page 97. Reg. of Wills, Liber B, folio 56}

On 6 Aug 1709 Thomas Bedwell of Murderkill Hundred Kent Co. sold to John Hall of same place in consideration of said John Hall's intermarriage with Hannah, his dau. and for 10 shillings, a tract of land s. side of Dover River, 175 a. Acknowledged 12 Aug 1715. {KEDELR D:99}

Mellesent, wife of Thomas Bedwell, was the dau. of Thomas Hewthat. In his will, written 29 Nov 1695, Thomas Hewthat mentioned his daus. Priscilla Edmunds [Edmonds], Ann Needham, Elliner Robisson, Mellesent Bedwell;and son Ralph Hewthat. {Prob. 24 Dec 1695. Arch. A23:196. Reg. of Wills, A:20}

On 20 May 1713 Elenor Robertson, wife of John Robertson of Kent Co., dau. and coheir of Thomas Hewthate of same co., yeoman, dec'd., whereas said Thomas Hewthate in his lifetime was seized of a tract of land part of a greater tract on Mutherkill Creek called *Ousby* and by his will did give and bequeath his land to his son Ralph Hewthat and failing him said Ralph heirs the said land to be equally divided among his four daus, Prisala Edmonds wife of Robert Edmonds, Anne Needum wife of Edmond Needum and the said Elenor Robertson wife of John Robertson and Mellecent Bedwell wife of Thomas Bedwell and whereas said Ralph Hewthat is since, dec'd., without heirs of his body begotten, the said lands were by the will vested in the said Prisalla, Anne, Elenor and Mellecent and whereas the said John Robertson and Elenor his wife by deed bearing date 11 Jun 1700 did sell unto Samuel Brooks of same co. all that tract of land said Hewthate died possessed of called *Hopewell* on Murtherkill Cr. Acknowledged 12 May 1716. {KEDELR E:89}

Thomas was paying quit rent during the period c1701-1713 on 375 a. of 1050 a. called *Folly Neck*, originally layed out to Robt. Bedwell, granted by patent in 1697. Thomas purchased of his bro. Robert, 50 a. of the same tract.
{Bendler:32}

On 14 Nov 1710 Thomas Bedwell and Honor his wife, executrix of the will of William Clark, late of Lewistown in Sussex Co., esqr., dec'd., for £40 sold to James Brooks the elder of Murtherkill Hundred, Kent Co., a tract of land called *Brimleys*. on s. side of Dover River formerly granted and laid out for William Dorrington who sold the same to Richard Mitchell who dyed intestate and by indenture bearing date 13 Jun 1700 William Dixon one of the admin. sold to William Clark ... near the land called *Amsterdam* formerly surveyed and laid out for Henry Johnson ... 549 a. {KEDELR G:111}

On 15 Aug 1711 Thomas Bedwell of Kent Co. and Honour his wife, executrix of the will of Wm. Clarke, late of Lewistown Sussex Co., conveyed unto David Row a tract of land s. side of Mother Creek called *Fairfield*, 2000 a., patent bearing date 29 May 1689 granted to William Clarke, dec'd., {KEDELR E:138}

On 2 Feb 1713 Thomas Bedwell, of Murtherkill Hundred Kent Co.

gentlemen and Honour his wife for £185 sold to John Coe of same place, a tract of land on s. side of Dover River in Murtherkill Hundred, 550 a. part of a 1050 a. tract of land called *Folly Neck*, by patent 6 March 1690 granted unto Robert Bedwell father of Thomas Bedwell, former patent granted by Govr Edmond Andross unto Robert Bedwell 20 Aug 1679 and resurveyed 10 Jan 1685. Thomas Bedwell being eldest son and heir of their father Robert Bedwell, dec'd., did grant unto his brother Robert Bedwell, 175 a., who sold but did not convey back to Thomas Bedwell and Robert Bedwell since, dec'd., and by his will 4 Oct 1713 did appoint his well beloved wife Elizabeth Bedwell to make over in open court a good title for 175 a. unto Thomas Bedwell (1 Feb 1713 Elizabeth Bedwell did assign over unto Thomas Bedwell 175 a.) ... 175 a. and 375 a. remainder of said 550 a. {KEDELR D:133}

On 10 April 1713 Thomas Bedwell, Robert Bedwell and Adam Fisher all of Kent Co. gentlemen for £15 sold to Mark Barden of same co., carpenter, a tract of land (patented to Thomas Bedwell and Henry Bedwell [his] brother and unto Robert Bedwell and Adam Fisher 1100 a.) called *Long Reach* in Murtherkill Hundred on a branch of Dover River ... to line formerly belonging to Ezekiel Needham ... to corner of land formerly belonging to Edmond Needham ... 100 a. ... Henry Bedwell is since, dec'd., without heirs. Acknowledged 10 Nov 1715 by Thomas Bedwell and Elizabeth Bedwell relict of and executrix of Robert Bedwell, dec'd., and Adam Fisher. {KEDELR E:12}

On 8 Aug 1715 Thomas Bedwell of Kent Co., gentlemen, and Honor his wife, executrix of will of William Clark, late of Lewis Town, Sussex Co., dec'd., for £35 sold to Thomas Nock of Kent Co., a tract of land on w. side of St. Jones Creek alias Dover River by Tidbury Branch, 445 a., patent dated 2 Aug 1690, granted unto Ezekiel Needham and by his deed 10 Sep 1690 conveyed unto William Clark, dec'd., {KEDELR D:122}

Thomas Bedwell of Sussex Co. d. leaving a will dated 18 Nov 1716, proved 6 Nov 1717. Heirs: daus. Mary Anne and Elenor Bedwell, Anna Hall and Mellicent Hill; grandson John Hill (son of Mellicent Hill). Execs., daus. Mary Anne and Elenor, and son-in-law John Hall. Wits. James Clayton, Michal Donohoe, Mary Donohoe. {Arch. A59:26. Reg. of Wills, A:95-96}

On 3 May 1720 Honor Bedwell, widow and extx. of William Clark, dec'd., conveyed to Alexander Draper part of a tract of 300 a. {SUDELR F6:28}

Thomas was father of the following children: HANNAH (Anna), b. 10 Dec 1691, m. John Hall; ROBERT, b. 18 Nov 1694; MELLECCENT, b. 8 March 1696/7, m. (N) Hill and had a son John; MARY ANNE; ELENOR.

3. ROBERT BEDWELL, son of Robert (1) Bedwell, m. Elizabeth (N). Robert d. prior to 1 Feb 1713.

On 12 May 1708 Thomas Bedwell and Robert Bedwell surviving sons and heirs of Robert Bedwell, late of Kent Co., gentlemen, for £5 sold to Mary Shaw of same co., widdow of Thomas Shaw, late of same co., dec'd., a tract of land being part of a greater tract of land on n. side of Dover River called *Longreach* formerly belonging to Gabriell Jones, 137 a. {KEDELR D:pg 83}

Robert Bedwell was paying quit rent, ca. 1701-1713, on 125 a. of *Holly Neck*, granted to his father, Robert Bedwell. {Bendler:33}

On 10 April 1713 Thomas Bedwell, Robert Bedwell and Adam Fisher all of Kent Co., gentlemen, for £15 sold to Mark Barden of same co., carpenter, a tract of land (patented to Thomas Bedwell and Henry Bedwell [his] brother and unto Robert Bedwell and Adam Fisher, 1100 a.) called *Long Reach* in Murtherkill Hundred on a branch of Dover River ... to line formerly belonging to Ezekiel Needham ... to corner of land formerly belonging to Edmond Needham ... 100 a. ... Henry Bedwell is since, dec'd., without heirs. Wit: Francis Allen, Wm. Annand. Ackn 10 Nov 1715 by Thomas Bedwell and Elizabeth Bedwell relict of and executrix of Robert Bedwell, dec'd., and Adam Fisher. {KEDELR E:12}

On 1 Feb 1713 Elizabeth Bedwell of Murderkill Hundred, Kent Co., widdow and relict of Robert Bedwell late of same place, yeoman, dec'd., one of the sons of Robert Bedwell late of same co., gentlemen, dec'd., whereas Robert Bedwell the younger in his lifetime 1 March 1708 for £50 did sell but not convey unto Thomas Bedwell of same co., gentlemen, a tract of land on s. side of Dover River, 175 a., and is part of 500 a. whereof said Robert Bedwell the elder dyed possessed of being part of a 1050 a. tract of land called *Follyneck* whereof the said Robert Bedwell, John Goodson and Samuell Carpenter, commissioners, on 6 March 1690 granted to Robert Bedwell in his lifetime patent on 20 Aug 1679, resurveyed 10 Jan 1685 unto Robert Bedwell being one of the sons of Robert Bedwell, dec'd., and whereas Robert Bedwell the younger late, dec'd., by will 4 Oct 1713 did appoint his well beloved wife Elizabeth Bedwell a party to these presents to makeover in open court a good title to said 175 a. unto Thomas Bedwell. {KEDELR D:115}

On 9 May 1717 William Rodeney, son and heir of William Rodeney, late of Kent Co., dec'd., for a certain sume of money in hand payed sold to Robert and James Bedwell, sons and coheirs of Robert Bedwell, late of Kent Co., dec'd., a tract of land called *Wedmore* wherewith the said William Rodeney, dec'd., did in his life time sell unto [page torn] by deed dated 14 Feb 1717 but not fully executed. Therefore William Rodeney's son conveys unto Robert and James Bedwell the afsd. tract of land ... by Isaac's Branch, 254 a. {KEDELR E:289}

Whereas there was a certain sum of money in hand paid by Robert Bedwell in his life time to William Rodeney, dec'd., for a tract of land, William Rodeney, son and heir of William Rodeney. late of Kent Co., released to Robert and James Bedwell, sons and coheirs of Robert Bedwell late of same co., dec'd., all his rights to tract of land called *Wedmore*, 354 a. Acknowledged 15 May 1717. {KEDELR F:39}

On 11 Aug 1748 John Webb of Murtherkil Hundred Kent Co. yeoman for £40 sold to Robert Bedwell, son of Robert Bedwell of same place, dec'd., part of a parcel of his dividend (whereas Robert Bedwell, dec'd., was at the time of his death possessed of a tract of land called *Wedmore* and by his will did give the same to be divided between his two sons James and Robert afsd, and whereas Robert Bedwell did sell all his right of the said land unto John Webb, Book M, fol. 109, and whereas James Bedwell and John Webb have since divided the afsd. tract on w. side of Bedwells Branch ... binding on Isaacs Branch between the present dwelling plantations of the said Jno. Webb and Robert Bedwell ... 110 a. {KEDELR :226}

James Bedwell, one of the heirs of Robert Bedwell submitted a petition stating that the dec'd. purchased a tract of old Captain William Rodney but the said Rodney and petitioner's father both died without making any ... for the land and and William Rodney, son and heir of sd. William Rodney the elder did by his deed of seasen ... sd. land to petitioner and his brother Robertt Bedwell according to the intention of petitioners's father who it is said made a will but no such will can be found. Requests a division of the land be made. The tract was called *Wedmore*. (Plat shown). {KEORCF Bedwell, Robert - 1754}

Robert was father of the following children: JAMES; ROBERT.

4.MARY BEDWELL, dau. of Robert (1) Bedwell, m. 1st 16 April 1678 in Old Rappahannock Co., VA, Isaack Webb {A} and m. 2nd James Clayton.

5.HENRY BEDWELL, son of Robert (1) Bedwell, m. Sarah Needham[6] who later m. Joshua Clayton. {Ericson cites Court Records of Kent Co., DE, 1680-1705. DeValinger, p. 287}

He d. leaving a will dated 3 May 1698, proved 14 June 1698. Heirs: wife Sarah; dau. Sarah; John Robisson; child unnamed. Exec.: wife Sarah. Wits., Robert Bedwell, Adam Fisher, Anthony Jones. {Arch. A3:141. Reg. of Wills, B:28}

During the period c1701-1713 Henry Bedwell's heirs, now Joshua Clayton, were paying quit rent on 175 a., part of *Holly [Folly?] Neck*, granted to Henry's father. {KE Co. Quit Rents, circa 1701-1713}

6. ELIZABETH BEDWELL, dau. of Robert (1) Bedwell, was paying quit rent (later her husband, Richd. Swan) during the period c1701-1713 on 100 a. of *Holly Neck (Folly Neck?)* sold by Tho: Bedwell, 8 Feb 1691, then 150 a. of which 50 a. are sold to Jno. Barnes, about 13 years earlier. {Colonial DE Records:34}

Elizabeth m. 1st Annanias Turner, m. 2nd Richard Swan and m. 3rd Michael O'Donahoe (the latter according to {A}).

Third Generation

7. JAMES BEDWELL, son of Robert (3) Bedwell, d. by 15 Feb 1771 when his estate was administered Robert Bedwell, next of kin. {Arch. A3:142. Reg. of Wills, L:91}

The following is based on ref {A}:

Kent Co. Orphans Court Records show eight heirs sold his land. They were: ROBERT, m. Anne Wilson; THOMAS, m. Jemima Johnson (?); SUSANNAH, b. ca. 1737, m. (N) Harper, had a son John; JAMES, b. ca. 1740; JOHN, b. ca. 1743; ELIJAH, m. Mary Seenea; CALEB, d. ca. 1823 in Lincoln Co., TN, m. Rebecca (N); ELIZABETH, b. ca. 1752.

8. ROBERT BEDWELL, probable son of Robert (3) Bedwell, m. Margaret (N).
On 6 Feb 1765 a Letter of Administration was granted to Margaret Bedwell of Kent Co. widow and proper admx., whereas Robert Bedwell of Kent Co. lately died intestate. {KEDELR R:268}

9. ADAM FISHER, step-son of Robert (3) Bedwell, was frequently listed as the son of Robert Bedwell. Adam m. Mary Molleston, dau. of Henry and Ann Molleston. Adam d. leaving a will proved 18 May 1725 in Kent Co., DE in

---

[6] Probably Sarah, b. 27 May 1674, dau. of Ezekiel Needham. See Needham Family in this volume

which the following children were named: Adam, Jr. m. Lydia Poynter; John, m. Hannah (N); Joseph, whose will was proved 19 March 1731; Isaac; Molleston; Mary; Susannah; Sarah. {A}

Fourth Generation

10. ROBERT BEDWELL, son of James (7) Bedwell, m. Anne Willson.

Robert Willson d. leaving a will dated 10 Sep 1757, proved 4 Oct 1757. Heirs: wife Sarah; son Robert; dau. Anne; son-in-law Robert Bedwell. Execs., son Robert and son-in-law Robert Bedwell. Wits., William Manlove, Jr., Nathan Williams, Sarah Forcum. {Arch. A56:2. Reg. of Wills, K:167}

The following is based on reference {A}:

Robert and his brothers moved to North Carolina after the death of their father. After about twelve years in North Carolina, Robert moved to Grayson Co., VA. Robert left a will in Grayson Co., VA. {Will Book 1, 1796-1839}

Robert was father of the following children {A}: JAMES, m. Jane Wells; ELISHA, m. Mary; ROBERT T., m. Elender Black; JOHN, m. 22 May 1799 Sarah Ogle; REUBEN; THOMAS; MICHA, b. ca. 1790, m. 30 Aug 1807; MARY.

11. ELIJAH BEDWELL, son of James (7) Bedwell, m. Mary Seena.

Owen Seenea d. leaving a will dated 16 Oct 1771, proved 22 Nov 1771. Heirs: wife Martha; sons John, William, Owen, Bryan; daus. Elizabeth, Ann, Elenor, Martha Powell (wife of William Powell), Mary Bedwell (wife of Elijah Bedwell). Execs., wife Martha and son Bryan. Wits., Thomas Bedwell, Jemima Beadwell, Maleston Maxwell. {Arch. A45:120-121. Reg. of Wills, L:108}

12. THOMAS BEDWELL, son of James (7) Bedwell. The following is based on reference {A}:

Thomas Bedwell m. Jemima (Johnson?). After a brief stay in North Carolina, Thomas and Jemima returned to Kent Co., DE in 1775 with all their children except son Caleb. Thomas left a will dated 23 Feb 1794 which named the following children: THOMAS, b. ca. 1769, m. Mary Lovitt 28 Jan 1790; GEORGE, b. ca. 1770; JAMES JOHNSON, b. ca. 1772; PRESTON, b. ca. 1774; SARAH, b. ca. 1775, m. William Jones 5 March 1793; ELIZABETH, b. ca. 1776, m. Thomas Stant 8 March 1792, had a dau. named Easter; CALEB, b. ca. 1777.

13. JAMES BEDWELL, son of James (7) Bedwell. The following is based on reference {A}:

James, b. ca. 1740 in Kent Co., DE, was found in Pasquotank Co., NC, at the time of the 1790 census. The 1800 census revealed James lived in Union Co., SC. According to tradition some of James' children moved to Tennessee. Two of the children are known: JAMES, b. ca. 1795, SC, m. Mary Nicholson; WILLIAM, b. ca. 1807, m. Nancy Smith.

THE BETTS FAMILY

1. JOHN BETTS, bro. of Edward Betts, was listed on the rent roll of KE Co., DE, paying quit rent on a tract called *Middletowne*, 1000 a., surveyed

25/2/1685, granted 21/12/1681. His name is crossed out of a land patent dated 11 March 1676/7. {Duke of York Record:51}

John Betts is shown on the Kent Co. rent roll, 1681-1688, as owing on the tract *Middletowne*, 1000 a. In the quit rents of ca. 1701-1713 John Betts' widow owes on 530 a., part of 1000 a. granted to John Betts by warrant in 1680. Geo. Robinson holds 300 a. and Jno. Hall holds 170 a. {Bendler:1, 31, 40}

John Betts m. Mary Stacie, widow of (N) Stacie, sister of Elizabeth Brinkloe (wife of John Brinkloe). On 15 Feb 1686 John Betts of Kent Co. PA, planter and Mary Betts his wife for a valuable consideration sold to Richard Hogbane of same co., ship carpenter, a tract of land called *The Fast Landing* on
e. side of Murther Creek ... 100 a. {KEDELR}

On 12 Sep 1687 John Betts of Kent Co. PA and Mary his wife for £30 sold to George Robinson of same co., 200 a. being part of a tract of land called *Bettses Purchase* on s. side of Murder Creek ... corner of land formerly laid out for Richard Hogbane. {KEDELR}

On 10 Jun 1689 John Betts of Kent Co. PA and Mary his wife for a valuable consideration sold to John Foster of same co. ... a tract of land called *Fosters Purches* on n. side of Bacombrigg Creek beginning at the corner of land belonging to George Roboson ... 170 a., surveyed 8 Feb 1689.

John Betts d. 1697. In the land records is shown: 20 Nov 1697. Death. John Betts, sherriff of Kent Co., departed this life on a Saturday and was buryed on the Thursday following.{KEDELR} He left a will dated 16 Nov 1697, proved 3 Jan 1697/8. Heirs: children of William Freeman; Elizabeth, wife of William Freeman; heirs of Richard and Sarah Williams; heirs of Edward and Mary Killingsworth; George Robisson; heirs of John Robisson; wife's dau. Susanna Stacie; wife's dau. Jane Stacie; wife's granddau. Mary Burbary. dau. of Samuel Burbary; bro. Edward Betts; wife Mary; William Rodeney, Jr. Execs., Mary Betts and William Rodeney, Jr. Wits., Mathew Bryan, Elizabeth Miller, Susanna Miller. {Arch. A4;35. Reg. of Wills, A:22}

Benjamin White mentioned his mother-in-law in his will dated 7 Oct 1709, proved 11 Oct 1709. Heirs: mother-in-law, Mary Betts; son not named. Exec. Thomas Skidmore. Wits., William Steel, Walter Hamilton, Francis Steel, Robert Miller. {Arch. A54:101. Reg. of Wills, C:81}

On 11 Aug 1731, whereas John Betts late of Kent Co., dec'd., in his life time was possessed of 300 a. of marsh in Muspelion Hundred which was granted to him by patent bearing date 14 July 1694 and in his will bequeathed the marsh to his wife Mary Betts, in her will she bequeathed 100 a. between Thomas Winsmore and Robert Winsmore and 100 a. unto Benjamin White, the other 100
a. she did not dispose of, therefore as to that part of her estate she dyed intestate and Thomas Winsmore dyed intestate and without issue, his share descended into the possession of Robert his brother and likewise Robert and Benjamin as heirs of Mary Betts, became possessed of the 100 a. of marsh not disposed of ... this indenture Robert Winsmore of Kent Co. yeoman for £30 sold to Henry Molleston of same place yeoman his part of the 300 a. being 150 a. {KEDELR K:96}

Mary Betts, Murther Creek, d. leaving a will 5 Dec 1709, proved 30 Jan 1709/10. Heirs: grandsons Benjamin White, Thomas, Robert and William Winsmore; Elizabeth Crawford; sister Elizabeth Brinckloe; Samuel Burberry; John Brinckloe; Anne, dau. of George Robisson. Execs., John Brinckloe, Arthur Meston, Stephen Nowell. Wits., Samuel Burberry, Walter Hamilton, James

Miller. {Arch. A4:36 and 37. Reg. of Wills, C:85-86}

On 6 Sep 1728 Henry Molleston of Mispillion Hundred Kent Co. yeoman, and Jemimah his wife, widdow, and relict of Benjamin White, dec'd., and Robert Winsmore of same place yeoman. Whereas Mary Betts widdow and relict of John Betts late of same place, dec'd., by her will did bequeath unto her grandson Benjamin White her dwelling plantation and also 300 a. adj, did also bequeath unto her two grandsons Robert and Thomas Winsmore 200 a., that is 100 a. each, part of the same tr. Thomas deceasing before the age of 21 years and without issue, the 200 a. came into the possession of Robert Winsmore, and Benjamin White by his will did bequeath the 300 a. of land and plantation in such a manner that since the decease of Benjamin's child it came into the possession of Henry Molleston and Jemimah his wife ... having the land surveyed and divided, it is agreed that Robert Winsmore shall have the land of Mary Betts, dec'd., on the s. side of the division line and Henry Molleston and Jemimah his wife shall have the land of Mary Betts, dec'd., on the n. side of the division line. {KEDELR I:265}

On 5 Sep 1751 Thomas Brannock and Ann his wife for £30 sold to Daniel Robisson, a tract of land and marsh adj. (whereas Mary Betts by her will did give unto Ann Robisson a parcel of land lying between the land of George Robisson and the land of Abraham Skidmore in Mispillion Hundred and whereas Ann Robisson hath since entermarried with the afsd. Thomas Brannock).
{KEDELR O:122}

On 14 April 1763 John Hall of the Borough of Bristol, Bucks Co., PA for £20 sold to Joseph Hall of Philadelphia, soap boyler and tallow chanlor, a tract of land, whereas John Betts being seized in a tract of land called *Betts Purchase*, also a piece of marsh did by his will devise the same to his wife Mary Betts, she being so seized devised the same with plantation she then lived on to her grandson Benjamin White, he being so seized by his will[7] (I give to my wife Jemima the plantation I now dwell on called *Betts Purchase* with all the land and marsh thereunto belonging to her and her heirs in case she proves not with child, but if she is with child and it lives, to it and its lawfull issue forever) and whereas a child was born alive and died living, Peter White the only brother of the devisor became legally seized to the afsd. tract of land, so as afsd. devised he being then heir at law to his brother Benjamin White, dec'd., and whereas the said Peter White by will devises the said estate to Joseph White and John Hall, and the said Joseph White being since, dec'd., the said estate became only and solly the property of the afsd. John Hall.
{KEDELR R:41}

Mary Betts was mother of the following children: JEMIMA, m. 1st Benjamin White by whom she had a son Benjamin and m. 2nd Henry Molleston; by (N) Stacie: SUSANNA; JANE, m. 26 Nov 1697 William Winsmore by whom she had Thomas, Robert, and William. {KEDELR}

2. ROBERT BETTS, b. c1672, of unknown relationship to John (1) Betts.

Robert Betts and John King paid quit rent on 1200 a., surveyed 13/10/1683 and granted 17/10/1682. {Bendler:39}

---

[7] I believe reference is being made to the will of Mary Betts'son-in-law Benjamin White not her grandson Benjamin White, Jr. -Ed.

Robert Betts m. Elizabeth Manlove, dau. of Mark Manove before 11 Nov 1703. {Deeds E:154}

On 22 Nov 1727 Robert Betts, aged 55 years, on his solemn oath declareth that he did see Vincant Emerson per virtue of a power of atty from Wm. Molleston acknowledge in open Court of Common Pleas, a deed from William Molleston. {KEDELR I:144}

Robert Betts, planter, Mispillion Hundred, d. leaving a will dated 27 March 1726, proved 15 Feb 1727. Heirs: sons John and William; dau. Elizabeth; Mark, Jr. and Matthew, Jr., children of Mark and Matthew Manlove. Exec., bro.in-law Matthew Manlove. Guardians, William Molleston, Tobitha Williams. Wits., John Ashley, Robert Cuming, William Barnabey. {Arch. A4:38, 39. Reg. of Wills G:5-6}

On 15 May 1740 Pemberton Brown of Mispillion Hundred, yeoman, and Elisabeth his wife for £60 sold to William Molliston of same place, yeoman, a tract of land (whereas Robert Betts of same place in his life was seized in a tract of land in Mispillion Creek Hundred beginning at a fork of Fishing Creek to corner of Ryneir Williams, 153 a., being part of a larger tract called *Goosebery*. Robert Betts made his will bearing date 27 March 1726 and bequeathed the afsd. tract of land to wit: I give and bequeath to my son William Betts my plantation with 153 a. of land which adjoins the land that William Molliston bought of Henry Molliston, and if my son John should die without issue my will is that my son William shall have the land and plantation given and bequeathed to him, and my dau. Elizabeth (party hereto) shall have the land and plantation herein given to my son William, afsd. William, son and legatee of Robert Betts, dec'd., pursuance of his fathers intentions, after the death of his brother John, by his indenture of release bearing date 7 Dec 1739 released unto Pemberton Brown and Elizabeth his wife, sister to the afsd. William, the 153 a. of land. {KEDELR M:74}

Robert was father of the following children: JOHN; WILLIAM; ELIZABETH, m. Pemberton Brown.

Second Generation

3. WILLIAM BETTS, son of Robert (2) Betts, m. Elizabeth Newell, dau. of John Newell.

William Betts, referring to a deed recorded in 1738, declared most humbly that your petitioner's father purchased of one Mark Manlove a tract of land in Muspellion Hundred [1714] contiguous thereto for which the said Mark gave your petitioners father whose name was Robert Betts a deed and the same put in the Rolls Office in order to have same recorded but by the neglect of the then officer appointed for such purposes the same was not done nor is yet, therefore your petitioner prays your worships that you allow him to procure such evidences as will make it appear that the same deed from the said Mark was signed, sealed and delivered to your petitioners father according to law in order to confirm to your petitioners father a title to the same land and marsh that he have the same recorded as the law directs. {KEDELR L:233, 234}

William Betts, laborer, son of Robert Betts, d. by 29 Dec 1740 when his estate was administered by Elizabeth Betts. {Reg. of Wills, I:33} Note: Arch. A4:40-41. shows a later admin. by John Caton, Jr., and Elizabeth Caton, his wife, mentioning son William and dau. Ruth Betts.

John Newell d. leaving a will dated 16 Jan 1639/40 proved 4 Feb 1739. Heirs: sons William, John, Thomas; dau. Elizabeth; grandson James Clayton; granddau. Ruth Betts; wife Mary., {Arch. A37: 190. Reg. Of Wills I:14}

Elizbeth later m. 2nd John Caton and m. 3rd William Carpenter.

John Newell d. leaving a will dated 16 Jan 1739/40, proved 4 Feb 1739. Heirs: sons William, John, Thomas; dau. Elizabeth; grandson James Clayton; granddau. Ruth Betts; wife Mary. {Arch. A37:190. Reg. Of Wills I:14}

John Caton d. leaving a will dated 28 May 1765, 19 Aug 1769. Heirs: wife Elizabeth; bro. Benjamin; sisters Esther Pearce and Jenat Chaplin; stepson William Betts; nephews James Caton (son of bro. Benjamin), John and Sampson Williamson. Extx. wife Elizabeth. Wits., William Thomas, Periscilla Walker. Codicil - Wit., Charles Ridgely. {Arch. A8:74 and 84. Reg. of Wills, L:63-64} Note: Arch. A8:84 shows Elizabeth as wife of William Carpenter.

Ruth Betts (alias McSparren) d. by 17 Aug 1759 when her estate was administered by John McSparran, merchant. {Reg. of Wills, K:211}

On 10 Oct 1749 John Catten and Elizabeth his wife of Kent Co. for £12 sold to Mathew Lowber of same place, the rights we have in a tract of land and marsh surveyed by Thomas Noxon ye then surveyor unto William Molliston, Luke Manlove, William Bettes and Thomas Jestor in company in Mispellion Hundred adj. land of Nathaniel Bowman, dec'd., 564 a., called *Companeys Adventure* and John Catten did intermary with Elizabeth Bettes widow of the afsd. Wm. Bettes, dec'd., having a rite to here third or dowry of said land. {KEDELR O:30}

Petition of William Betts, that petitioner's father William Betts d. intestate and at the time of his death was seazed in fee simple of 200 a. and 40 a. of marsh, being part of tract *Mount Pleasant* in Mispillion Hundred and 1/2 part of 176 1/4 a. of marsh and 100 a. of marsh called *Struckill* on Delaware Bay in same hundred. Petitioner's father left a widow, now the wife of John Caton, Esqr. and two children, viz: Ruth Betts and your petitioner and his afsd. dau. Ruth Betts m. John McSparran and is since dead but left issue, viz: a son called William McSparran. Requests division of the land. {KEORCF Betts, William, dec. -1765-66}

William was father of the following children: WILLIAM; RUTH, m. John McSparren.

Third Generation

4. RUTH BETTS, dau. of William (3) Betts, m. John McSparran.

Ruth Betts was mentioned in the will of John Newell, written 16 Jan 1739/40, proved 4 Feb 1739. Heirs: sons William, John, Thomas; dau. Elizabeth; grandson James Clayton; granddau. Ruth Betts; wife Mary. Exec. wife Mary. Wits., James Clayton, John Hall, Rebecca Welsh. {Arch. A37:190. Reg. of Wills, 1:14}

John Newell d. by 30 Aug 1764 when his estate was administered by Andrew Caldwell. {Arch. A38:54} Note: Shows that John Newell was guardian to Ruth Betts, wife of John McSparran, and Rachel Newell, wife of Henry Sapp; also mentions Henry and William Newell.

Ruth was mother of a son WILLIAM McSparran.

5. WILLIAM BETTS, son of William (3), m. Elizabeth (N).

William Betts d. By 13 Feb 1784 when his estate Elizabeth Betts was appointed admx. of his estate. {Arch. A4:42-44. Reg. Of Wills, M:20} Note: Arch. A4:44 mentions heirs, Isaac, Elizabeth, Ann, Ruth and Susannah Betts. Page 42 shows that Elizabeth Betts m. Job Meredith.

THE JOSEPH BOOTH FAMILY

1. JOSEPH BOOTH m. 1st Francis Spencer, dau. of Benjamin Cowdry and widow of Major William Spencer. Francis Spencer had sons Henry and Samuel Spencer. Joseph m. 2nd Elinor Robinson.

Joseph Booth after marrying Frances Spencer, sold 100 a. to Benj. Cowdry, father of Frances. {KEDELR F6:195}

Joseph Booth owned land in Sussex Co. as early as 5 Dec 1694 for on that date Joseph Booth did make over 200 a. in Sussex Co. unto a certain Peter Goyte [or Goyle] of Sussex Co., merchant. {SUDELR I:56}

On 31 Oct 1710 Joshua Cowdry of Northamton Co., VA, appointed his uncle Joseph Booth of Kent Co. as his attorney to convey land in Sussex Co. {F6:199}

The orderly marriage of Joseph Booth, Senr., and Elinor Robinson was reported on 20th da., 6th mo., 1716. {DCMM} She was the widow of John Robinson and mother of Mary who m. Her step-son Joseph Booth, Jr.

On 30 Nov 1718 Joseph Booth of Murderkill Hundred Kent Co., yeoman, and Elinor his wife, for 11 shillings sold to Richard Underwood of Mispillion Hundred same co., a tract of land patent bearing date 26 Feb 1716/7 granted unto Joseph Booth 200 a., surveyed 10 April 1718, on n. side of Pemberton's branch on s.e. side of the present dwelling of Richard Underwood.
{KEDELR F:100}

On 12 Aug 1729 Benjamin Shurmer and Richard Richardson, gent., by act of authority given to them, for £2 sold to Waitman Sipple and Joseph Booth, Junr., and Joseph Booth, Senr., gent and Eliner his wife all of Kent Co., two lotts of land being part of the Town of Dover beginning at a corner of John Lunt's lott on the s. side of Water Street ... 2 a. called *Elinors Dowry*. {KEDELR I:204}

Benjamin Shurmer and Richard Richardson of Kent Co. by their deed bearing date 12 Aug 1729 did sell unto Joseph Booth, Junr., and Waitman Sipple and their heirs in trust for the use of Joseph Booth, Senr., and Elinor his wife during the natural life of Joseph Booth, Senr., and after his decease to the only proper use of Elinor Booth two lotts of land but there happening a mistake in the deed in consideration of which and for the consideration of £2, Joseph Booth, Senr., and Elinor his wife, Joseph Booth, Junr., and Waitman Sipple all of same co., gent., quitt claim unto Benjamin Shurmer and Richard Richardson in trust, the afsd. tract of land. {KEDELR K:37}

Joseph Booth d. leaving a will dated 10 Dec 1732, codicil 11 Dec 1732, proved 12 Nov 1744. Heirs: son Joseph; grandson Thomas Booth. Exec., son Joseph. Wits., Mark Manlove. Abraham Wynkoop, John Morice, William Servant. Wits., Mark Manlove, Isaac Mason. {Arch. A4:231. Reg. of Wills, H:65}

The estate of Joseph Booth was administered on 28 Nov 1732 by John Reynolds. {Reg. of Wills, H:109}

On 11 March 1755 Nathan Spencer of Sussex Co., for £90 sold to John Clark of same place, a tract of land on s. side of Mispillion Creek, part of 1000

a. tract formerly surveyed for Richard Hill called *Hills Content* which land was conveyed by the said Hill unto Benjamin Cowdry who by deed of gift confirmed the same unto Francis Spencer (dau.), Henry Spencer and Samuel Spencer, sons of the afsd. Francis, to be divided amongst them, that is 500 a. to Francis and the other 500 a. to be divided between the afsd. sons Henry and Samuel. The said Francis Spencer intermarried with a certain Joseph Booth who having only 1 son named Joseph Booth he became heir to the afsd. Francis and whereas the said Joseph Booth Junr. did convey the 500 a. unto the said Samuel Spencer, and he by his will bequeathed 100 a. unto his son the afsd. Nathan Spencer on Panters Branch, 100 a. {SUDELR I:91}

Joseph was father of JOSEPH.

Second Generation

2. JOSEPH BOOTH, Junr., son of Joseph (1) Booth, m. 1st Margaret Fisher, dau. of Thomas Fisher.

Thomas Fisher made his will 17 Nov 1713 with these words "I give and bequeath to my dau. Margaret Fisher the now wife of Joseph Booth, Junr., of Kent Co. yeoman 500 a. which I purchased of David Rowe" and soon after dyed ... whereas David Rowe since made his will bearing date 20 Aug 1717 and therein did appoint Susannah Rowe his sole executrix with these words "I do hereby authorize and impower my said executrix to make over ... all lands that I have sold" and soon after dyed ... for £50 paid by Thomas Fisher in his life time unto David Rowe before his decease and for 10 shillings paid by Joseph Booth and Margaret his wife unto Susannah ... Susannah conveys afsd. land. Acknowledged 13 Aug 1718. {KEDELR F:28}

Joseph Booth, only son of Joseph Booth, m. 2nd Mary Robinson (b. 21st da., 3rd mo., 1705), dau. of John Robinson before 4 May 1720. {Deeds N:224} On 21st da., 11th mo., 1722 he produced a paper in behalf of himself and wife in relation to their being married out of the approved way. {DCMM} Mary later m. George Morgan.

Richard Richardson of Little Creek and Philadelphia d. leaving a will dated 10 Dec 1730, proved 12 May 1731. Heirs: daus. Mary Watters, Miriam and Ann Richardson; sons Richard and John; wife Ann; children of sister-in-law Mary Booth; bro.-in-law Joseph Booth. Execs., wife Ann and Joseph Booth. Wits., Thomas Empson, John Holliday, Lewis Howell, James Steel. {Arch. A43:166-167. Reg. of Wills, H:15-17}

Anna Richardson, Little Creek, and sister of Mary Booth, d. leaving a will dated 22 Oct 1732, proved 28 Dec 1732. Heirs: four youngest children unnamed; dau. Mary Waters. Exec., Joseph Booth, bro.-in-law. Wits., Timothy Hanson, Susanah Hanson. {Arch. A43:160-161. Reg. of Wills, H:64 and 103} Note: These names are mentioned with no relationship shown: Mariam, Richard, John and Anna Richardson.

Joseph Booth of Murderkill Hundred d. leaving a (nunc.) will dated 4 Jan 1736, proved 8 Jan 1736. Heirs: wife Mary; sons Thomas, John, Joseph; daus. Eleanor, Anna, Frances. Execs., wife Mary and Mark Manlove. Wits., Miriam Richardson, William Fisher. Prob. Jan. 8, 1736. {Arch. A4:232. Reg. of Wills, H:119-120} Note: Arch. A4:236 shows that Mary Booth later married George Morgan.

On 21 Oct 1742 Daniel Robisson of Kent Co., yeoman, for £300 paid by Joseph Booth in his life time and also in pursuance of a certain deed lately made by the justices of the Court of Equity to wit 23 Sep last upon the complaint of the said Daniel Robisson against George Morgan and Mary his wife have sold to George Morgan and Mary his wife who was admx. by the name of Mary Booth of Joseph Booth late of same co., dec'd., in trust for the heirs of the afsd. Joseph Booth, a tract of land and marsh in Murderkill Hundred called *Whitewells Delight*, 694 a., now in actual possession and occupation of the said George Morgan and Mary (175 a. parcell of the said tract by Daniel Robisson unto John Bowers lately sold) ... 320 1/2 a. {KEDELR M:204}

On 12 Aug 1743 George Morgan of Kent Co. yeoman and Mary his wife for the settling and assuring the lands and for divers, other good causes and considerations sold to John Clayton, Junr., of same co. yeoman, two tracts of land (now in his actual possession by virtue of a bargain and sale made for 1 whole year) part of a large tract called *Ousby* which Thomas Heathers and Ann his wife 12 Sep 1787 [sic] conveyed to John Robinson father of the said Mary (Book B, Vol 2, fol. 39) which John Robinson by his will bearing date 28 Sep 1708 devised to his dau. the afsd. Mary in Murtherkill Hundred, 200 a. and all that other parsel of land also part of the afsd. tract called *Ousby* which Thomas Heather and Ann his wife on 10 Sep 1687 conveyed to Robert Edmonds together with 200 a. more, and he by deed bearing date 4 May 1720 (Book F, fol. 29) conveyed to the said Mary by the name of Mary Robisson on n. side of Murther Creek in Motherkill Hundred to the e. side of Cranberry Branch ... 100 a. ... to and for the several uses, trust, intents and purposes herein after declared to wit to the use of George Morgan during the term of his natural life and after the decease of George to the use of Mary the wife of George for and during the term of her natural life, then to the use of their son George Morgan and his heirs, and for default of such issue to the use of Mary Morgan, dau. of the afsd. George Morgan and Mary his wife, and her heirs, and for default of such issue to the use of Grace Morgan second dau. of George and Mary and her heirs, and for default of such issue to the use of John Booth son of the afsd. Mary wife of of George Morgan by her former husband Joseph Booth, dec'd., and to his heirs, and for default of such issue to the use of Anna Booth dau. of said Mary by Joseph Booth, and her heirs, and for default of such issue to the use of Francina Booth another dau. of Mary by Joseph Booth and her heirs, and for default of such issue to the use of the heir at law of the said Mary wife of George. {KEDELR N:224}

The estate of Joseph Booth was administered by 14 May 1747 by John Booth. {Reg. of Wills, I:176}

On 28 May 1755 Thomas Stratten of Murtherkill Hundred, yeoman, and Hannah his wife for £50 sold to William Walker of the Town of Dover, cordwainer, a tract of land, whereas Benjamin Shurmer and Richard Richardson late commissioners appointed for granting of lotts within the Town of Dover on 13 May 1730 did sell unto Joseph Booth, Junr., of Kent Co. two lots of ground in Dover bounded by High Street, Water Street and Church Lane, 2 a., and Joseph Booth died intestate leaving issue, to wit Anna Booth, John Booth and Frances Booth and on the petition of the said John Booth to the justices of an Orphans Court they did appoint 5 sufficient freeholders to make division of all such lands ... on 26 Aug 1749 allotted unto John Booth eldest surviving son that part of said lotts n. side of the Courthouse branch 1 a., to Anna Booth by name of Anna Morgan 1/2 a. and Anna together with her husband conveyed it to her brother John Booth ... John Booth entered into a bond with the said Thomas

Stratten conditioned for the conveying the said 1 1/2 a. but died before the said bond was complyd with and Andrew Caldwell and Mary his wife admx. of John Booth sold the land to Thomas Stratten in discharge of the afsd. bond ... 1 1/2 a. {KEDELR O:297}

In a petition of John Booth eldest surviving son of Joseph Booth, dec. it was stated that petitioner's father Joseph Booth d. intestate about 12 years ago leaving 6 children, to wit: Thomas, Elinor, John your petr., Anna, Frances and Joseph and at the time of his decease was seized in his demesne of 500 a. in Muspillion Hundred being part of a larger tract called *Fairfeild* and of 2 lotts in Dover. Thomas, Elinor and Joseph died soon after their sd. father in their minority and without issue; Anna has m. George Morgan and is still living. Frances your petitioner's other sister is also living. That a division be made of the afsd. lands. 11 March 1748. (PLat after division shown) {KEORCF Booth, Joseph, Jr., 1736-49}

Joynt petitions of George Morgan, Junr. and Anna his wife lately called Anna Booth and Waitman Sipple, Junr., the guardian of John Booth and Frances Booth showed that Joseph Booth late of the county, dec., by his will gave to Thomas Booth his grandson, one Negro boy named Simon and Negro girl named Fenny, 15 cows and calves and feather bed and furniture belonging to the testator, and horse and mare that were called Thomas Booth's. His son Joseph Booth to be his exec. That Joseph Booth the exec. took into his possession all the estate of his father and is since dead and left his wife Mary his extx. together of Mark Manlove and Mary took the admin of the estate and she m. George Morgan of this county. That the sd. Thos. Booth the legatee died intestate and that the legacies became the sole right of the afsd. George Morgan. Petitioner and Anna his wife the sister and the afsd. John Booth and Frances Booth also the brother and sister of sd. Thos. Booth and altho the sd. Joseph Booth the elder besides the legacies afsd. did leave a considerable estate over and above what would pay all his debts and altho the sd. George and Mary his wife (which sd. Mary is since dead). {KEORCF Booth, Joseph, Sr., dec. - 1744-45}

Joseph was father of the following children: THOMAS; JOHN; JOSEPH; ELEANOR; ANNA (HANNA), m. George Morgan and moved out of the Province; FRANCES, m. Theodore Parke and d. without issue.

Third Generation

3. THOMAS BOOTH, son of Joseph (2) Booth, d. by 25 Feb 1756 when his estate was administered by Andrew Caldwell. {Reg. of Wills, K:129-130}

On 14 May 1747 John Booth of Kent Co., yeoman, for £50 sold to William Manlove, Junr., of same co., yeoman, a tract of land (whereas Joseph Booth, Senr., by his will did bequeath unto his grandson Thomas Booth a tract of land 115 a. and whereas Thomas Booth did decease before the age of 21 years that the said John Booth being then his nearest are at law became seazed of the afsd. tract of land) ... in Mispillion Creek adj. where John Brown now dwells and to the e. of the plantation whereon the afsd. Joseph Booth formerly did dwell being part of a larger tract called *Saw Mill Range*, to Cullens Branch n.w. side of the Mill Road ... 115 a. {KEDELR N:128}

4. JOHN BOOTH, eldest son of Joseph (2) Booth, m. Mary Sipple, dau. of Waitman Sipple. He had an only son WAITMAN. Mary later m. Andrew Caldwell.

On 24 Aug 1749 John Booth of Kent Co., yeoman, for £105 sold to William Shirley of same place, a tract of land (whereas Joseph Booth father to ye afsd. John Booth died seized of a tract of land in Muspellion Hundred on *Pemberton's Savanah* and dying intestate the land was divided amonst his heirs whereby the said John Booth became seized into 1/2 part) ... beginning at Kings Road to Mill Branch ... 341 1/2 a. {KEDELR O:30}

Whereas a tract of land granted by pattent to a certain William Framton on s. side of Jones Creek allies Dover River beginning at land of John Fullerton late of this co., dec'd., to dividing line between John Booth and his sister Francis Booth ... 482 a. called *Whightwells (Whitewells) Delight* or *Dover Peer* which land was survaid and allotted by men appointed by an Orphans Court 15 March 1748, unto John Booth late of this co., dec'd., as his share of the land of which his father Joseph Booth who died intestate was saized in at the time of his death, and John Booth was seized of the land att the time of his death and Benjaman Chew of Kent Co. did obtain a judgment for £228.18.6 whereupon a writ of execution was dirycted to Thomas Parke the high shirife who seized in execution the afsd. land and sold att publick vandue. {KEDELR O:262}

John d. leaving a will dated 8 March 1750, proved 30 March 1751. Heirs: wife Mary; son Waightman. Exec. wife. Wits., Waitman Sipple, Daniel Robison, Mary Jones. {Arch. A4:215. Reg. of Wills, K:34}

Also recorded was a second will which shows the following: John d. leaving a will dated 9 Dec 1752, proved 3 Jan 1753, proved 3 Jan 1753. Heir: wife Mary. Extx. wife Mary. Wits., Richard Morris, Mary Bartlet. {Arch. A4:216 217. Reg. of Wills, K:83} Note: Arch. A4:217 shows Mary, the widow, later m. Andrew Caldwell.

On 29 May 1754 Andrew Caldwell and Mary his wife admins. of John Booth, dec'd., of Kent Co. for £7.10 paid to the dec'd. in his lifetime released unto Thomas Stratten a lot of land. The said John Booth on 22 Jan 1747 had executed and delivered unto the said Thomas Straten a bond with a penalty of £50 conditioned that the said John Booth would execute a deed of sale of all his right and title of a lot of land in the Town of Dover 1 1/2 a. which land being the lot that was divided between the said Booth and his two sisters by an order of court and the said Booth being the surviving eldest brother was intitled to 2 shares and 1 other share he purchased of his sister Hannah Morgon so that he became vested with 3 shares and the said John Booth before executing any such deed died and administration was granted to Mary Booth, who had now m. afsd. Andrew Caldwell, and Thomas Straton at May Term 1753 proved said bond and Andrew Caldwell and Mary his wife at May Term 1754 were impowered to make over the said lot unto Thomas Straton. {KEDELR O:260}

On 13 May 1768 Waitman Booth of Kent Co., yeoman, grandson to Joseph Booth, and only son of John Booth who was the only son of afsd. Joseph Booth, and the only heir of Joseph Booth in this government confirmed he was willing to fulfill that which is just and right and for 5 shillings convey unto Charles Townsend of same place, a tract of land, whereas Joseph Booth of said co. did by his bond bearing date 26 March 1736 bind himself in the sum of £100 to make over unto Charles Townsend a 200 a. tract of land called *Hope* and the consideration money appears to have been paid and Joseph Booth did never in his life time convey the afsd. land but afterwards d. leaving issue to wit John Booth, Hannah Booth and Frances Booth, and whereas Frances Booth died without issue and John Booth died leaving issue only one son Waitman Booth, party afsd, and Hannah Booth intermarried with a certain George Morgan and having removed out of this government, and whereas the said John Booth and Frances Booth 2 of the heirs of the afsd. Joseph Booth did never in their lifetime convey the afsd. land unto Charles Townsend as heirs ought to have done ... on Murther Creek adj. land of Robert New. {KEDELR R:264}

5. FRANCES BOOTH, dau. of Joseph (2) Booth, m. Theodore Parke.

In a petition of Frances Booth a minor of about 16 years of age, desirous of choosing a guardian, she requests appointment of Waitman Sipple. Recorded 29 Nov 1744. {KEORCF Booth, Francis - 1744}

On 6 May 1751 Theodore Parke of Kent Co., taylor, and Frances his wife for £350 sold to Thomas Parke of same place, gent., a parcel of land alloted and divided to the afsd. Frances, one of the children of Joseph Booth, late of same place, dec'd., in full of her share of her fathers estate, 225 a. of 787 a. on St. Jones Creek adj. John Bower's ditch ... and 1/2 a. of 2 a. in the Town of Dover beginning at John Lunt's lott in Water Street to Anna Booth's lott being one of the children of Joseph Booth now the wife of George Morgan, Junr., to lott of John Booth being the eldest son and heir of Joseph Booth. {KEDELR O:90}

On 10 Aug 1752 Theodorah (Theodore) Parke of Kent Co., tayllor, for £40 sold to John Bowars of same place, yeoman, a tract of marsh (whereas George Robisson by a deed of sale from Francis Richardson of Philadelphia became seazd of a parcel of land and marsh, being part of a larger tract called *Whitewells Delight*, and George Robisson by a deed of gift did confirm the said parcel unto his son Daniel Robisson and he conveyd the same unto Joseph Booth who died intestate whereby the land devolved amongst his children, to wit John Booth, Annah Booth and Frances Booth, Frances hath since intermarried with the said Theodorah Parke and she did convay her part unto her husband) beginning at Griffen's ditch ... 60 a. of marsh. {KDERL O:148}

On 16 April 1761 Thomas Parke of Kent Co. esqr. and Hugh Parke of same co., hatter, for £165 sold to Daniel Robisson of same co. gent, a tract of land, whereas Joseph Booth, late of same co., gent, dec'd., was in his life time seizd in 707 a. on s. side of St. Jones Creek or Dover River part of a larger tract called *Whitwells Delight* and being so seized died intestate leaving issue, to wit, John Booth, his eldest son and 2 daus. Anna Booth and Frances Booth. John Booth by his petition to the justices of the Orphans Court, 5 sufficient freeholders were appointed to make a division of the afsd. land on 15 March 1748 and did allot unto Frances Booth, 225 a., by the return of said division 25 Aug 1749, and whereas Frances Booth afterwards m. Theodore Parke who together did on 6 May 1751 convey the afsd. 225 a. unto the afsd. Thomas Parke, and Thomas Parke together with Anne, his wife, on 30 May 1751 did reconvey to the said Theodore Parke, gent., the afsd. land, and Theodore Parke sold to John Bowers, 60 a. of the said tract but before disposition of the residue died intestate leaving issue only Theodore Parke his son which said Theodore Parke the younger died intestate and without issue by means whereof the residue now is vested in the said Thomas Parke and Hugh Parke as uncles of the said Theodore Parke the younger and brothers of the said Theodore Parke the elder ... beginning at John Bower's ditch on Jones Creek adj. John Fisher's land. {KEDELR Q:49}

6. ANNA (HANNA) BOOTH, dau. of Joseph (2) Booth m. George Morgan,

Junr.

On 25 May 1749 George Morgan, Junr., of Dover Hundred Kent Co. yeoman and Anna, his wife, dau. of Joseph Booth, Junr., late of this co., dec'd., for £50 sold to Elisabeth Manlove dau. and co. legatee of William Manlove, Junr., late of this co., dec'd., a tract of land (whereas Joseph Booth died seized in a 500 a. tract of land) in Mispillion Hundred on s. side of Western Branch of Murther Creek being part of a larger tract called *Farefield* which was granted by patent to William Clark bearing date 29 May 1694 (Book H, fol. 5) and the afsd. Joseph died intestate by which means the afsd. Anna became heir to 1/4 of the afsd. 500 a. ... 120 a. {KEDELR N:279}

THE JOHN BOOTH FAMILY

1. JOHN BOOTH, Wicomico, Somerset Co., MD, d. leaving a will dated 16 May 1698, proved 25 June 1698. Mentioned were Bridget Spence, dau. Of James Spence and the following children: JOHN; DANIEL; PETER; ISAAC; ELLINOR; EASTER; ELIZABETH. {MWB 6:143}

2. PETER BOOTH, farmer of Duck Creek, and possible son of John (1) m. Sarah (N) who later m. Phillip Hillyard.

Peter d. leaving a will dated 29 Jan 1770, proved 13 Feb 1770. Heirs: wife Sarah; son Isaac; dau. Tamer; children of wife's sister, Sarah and Mary Stuart. Exec. wife Sarah. Wits., Cuthbart Green, Thomas Wilson, Thomas Brown. {Arch. A4:246-248. Reg. of Wills, L:71} Note: Arch. A4: 248 shows that Sarah Booth married ... Hillyard; also shows Tamer Booth as wife of John Steward.

Peter was father of the following children: ISAAC; TAMER, m. John Steward.

Phillip Hilliard of Duck Creek Hundred d. leaving a will proved 29 Dec 1781. Heirs: wife [Sarah from admin. acct.]; bros. Christopher, Thomas and John; nephew Thomas Hilliard, son of Christopher. Execs. wife and bro. Christopher. Wits., Samuel Wilson, Evan Denny, Isaac Booth. {Arch. A24:43. Reg. of Wills, L:250}

3. ISAAC BOOTH, probable son of Peter (2) Booth, m. Elizabeth, widow of William Willson.

William Dyer d. leaving a will dated 19 Oct 1728, proved 19 Nov 1728. Heirs: bro. Thomas Clifford; cousins John Clayton, Hannah Levick and children of Elizabeth Booth; Isaac Booth; John Pound. Execs., bro. Thomas Clifford and Isaac Booth. Wits., Philip Denny, Isaac Snow. {Arch. A15:230-231. Reg. of Wills, G:16-17}

On 14 Aug 1740 Isaac Booth and Elizabeth his wife, late widdow of William Willson of Kent Co., dec'd., for £10 quit claim unto William Willson, son of the said, dec'd., Willson, her thirds of the land called *Cambridge*. {KEDELR M:76}

<u>Unplaced</u>

ELINER BOOTH was dau. of Sarah Fisher.

Mary Little d. leaving a will dated 6 Jan. 1748, proved 14 Jan 1748.

Heirs: daus. Susannah Edmonds, Sarah Morgan, Mary Walker; grandson Addam Fisher; granddaus. Mary Fisher, Eliner Booth, dau. of Sarah Fisher; children of John and Mary Walker; Molliston Fisher; Robert and Susannah Edmonds. Execs., friends John Walker and John Fisher. Wits., William Newell, John Waller, William Silliven. {Arch. A30:196-197. Reg. of Wills, I:261}

THE JOHN BRINCKLOE FAMILY

1. JOHN BRINCKLOE m. Elizabeth (N).

A land patent to *Lisburne*, 600 a., was granted by Whorekill Court in 1679-80 to John Brinkle. {KEDELR}

John Brinklow was listed on the Kent Co. Rent Roll, 1681-1688, owing on tracts *Lisbon*, 750 a.; *Brinklow's Gift*, 575 a.; and another 1000 a. Capt. John Brinkloe was listed in the 1693 Tax Assessment List of Kent Co., owing on 500 a. in Dover Hundred. The list of quit rents for Kent Co., ca. 1701-1713, show that Jn. Brinckloe owned a tract named *Freeland.*

Whoso names are here under written are witnesses to the said mariage this day and year. John Brinckloe and Eliz Brinkloe, Nicholas Bartlett, Susanah Freeland, William Leo, Mary Morgan, Susanah Stasey, William Freeland, Eliz. Jackson, Jonathan Riall, Geo. Morgan, Eliz Haile, Arthur Meston, Hollen Ago. [Recorded ca. 14 Feb 1686] {KEDELR B1, part 2}

Jepeth Griffin before his death 24 Feb 1682 did give and bequeath to John Brinckloe and Elizabeth his wife all his land in the province of MD and also all his land in Kent Co. and all his personal and reall estate his will being proved by Daniell Jones and Samuell Burbery. {KEDELR}

John Brinkloe of Kent Co. and Elizabeth his wife, became seized in a tract of land and by their indenture dated 16 March 1685 sold same to Daniel Toes of Stockton in the Bishoprick of Durham in Great Brittain, marriner. {KEDELR N:75}

On 16 March 1685 John Brinckloe of Kent Co. PA and Elizabeth his wife in consideration of £80 sold to Daniell Jones of Markston Co., Bishopricke of Durham in England, mariner, a tract of land called *Addition* on w. side of Jones Creek, neare unto Robert Betts house, containing 1200 a. {KEDELR}

On 20 Feb 1688 John Brinckloe and Elizabeth his wife of Kent Co. PA for 7000 pounds of tobacco sold to Thomas Rogers of same co. ... a tract of land called *Rogers Foly*, part of a tract of land called *Lisburn*, on n. side of Dover River ... corner of a tract of land called *The Good Speed*, 100 a. {KEDELR}

On 5 Nov 1689 John Brinckloe and Elizabeth his wife of Kent Co. PA for five cows and calves in hand paid sold to John Foster a tract of land called *Lisborn,* on n. side of Dover River, 100 a. {KEDELR}

On 18 Sep 1686 John Brinckloe and Elizabeth his wife of Kent Co., PA, for £40 sold to John King of Philadelphia, mariner, a plantation and parcell of land called *Troy* on n.e. side of Dover River alias St. Jones Creek, 300 a. {KEDELR}

On 20 Feb 1688 John Brinckloe and Elizabeth his wife of Kent Co. PA for 6000 pounds of tobacco sold to Evan Davice of same co., a tract of land called *Lisburn*, on n. side of Dover River, beginning at the corner of a tract of land called *Wickes Fortune*, 100 a. {KEDELR}

On 10 June 1695 John Brinckloe of Kent Co. PA in consideration of naturall affection and love gives to my well beloved kinsman William Brinckloe, Junr., of same place a tract of land called *Lisbon* on n. side of Dover River alias Jones Creek beginning at the corner of Thomas Rogers land, 77 a. {KEDELR}

On 10 Dec 1695 John Foster of Kent Co., PA, felt maker for £12, sold to Robert French of same co., merchant, a tract of land called *Fosters Chance*, being part of a tract of land called *Lisborne* on n. side of Dover River, 100 a. Acknowldeged unto John Foster in Kent Co. Court 5 Nov 1689 by John Brinckloe and Elizabeth his wife. Witnessed by John Brinckloe, Thomas Bedwell. {KEDELR}

Mary Betts of Murther Creek d. leaving a will dated 5 Dec 1709, proved 30 Jan 1709/10. Heirs: grandsons Benjamin White, Thomas, Robert and William Winsmore; Elizabeth Crawford; sister Elizabeth Brinckloe; Samuel Burberry; John Brinckloe; Anne, dau. of George Robisson. Execs., John Brinckloe, Arthur Meston, Stephen Nowell. Wits., Samuel Burberry, Walter Hamilton, James Miller. {Arch. A4:36 and 37. Reg. of Wills, C:85-86}

On 1 Aug 1710, an agreement was made by John Brinckloe of Dover Hundred Kent Co. and Elizabeth his wife for love and goodwill and £100 to be paid unto their dau. Elizabeth so soon as she shall arrive of full age or be maryed which first shall happen sold to Thomas Crawford of same place, clerk, and Elizabeth his wife, granddau. of said John and Elizabeth, a tract of land two miles above St. Jones Creek, s.e. side of a swamp which divideth this from a piece of land called *Poplar Neck*, 60 a., by patent bearing date 14 Aug 1678 by Sir Edmond Andrews granted to John Briggs who by assignment 23 April 1681 granted to Henry Stevenson who by indenture 19 Aug 1684 granted same to above named John Brinckloe and whereas there is alsoe a tract of land called *Brinckloe His Choice*, on n. side of Dover River beginning at the corner of the land of John Brinckloe called *Poplar Ridge*, to land of Richard Bassnett ... 250 a. by patent bearing date 17 Jun 1693 granted to above named John Brinckloe ... formerly granted to Arthur Meston as butted and bounded in the deed ... Thomas Crawford and Elizabeth shall not during the natural life of said John Brinckloe and Elizabeth his wife sell or dispose of the land without their consent. {KEDELR D:79}

Captain John Brinckloe of Dover Hundred d. leaving a will dated 10 May 1720, proved 8 Dec 1721. Heirs: friend Thomas Crawford; Evis, Mary, Letetia, Elizabeth, daus. of Thomas Crawford; cousin Peter Brinckloe; wife Elizabeth Brinckloe. Execs., wife and Thomas Crawford. Wits., Charles Hillyard, John Plessenton. {Arch. A5:221. Reg. of Wills, D:47-49}

Elizabeth Brincklow, widow, Dover Hundred, d. leaving a will dated 9 Dec 1721, proved 28 Sep 1723. Heirs: great-grandchildren, Elizabeth, Mary, Evis, Letitia Crawford, children of Thomas and Elizabeth Crawford; grandsonin-law Thomas Crawford. Exec., grandson-in-law Thomas Crawford. Wits., Else Mahan, Charles Hyliard, Ann Gream. {Arch. A5:179. Reg. of Wills, D:62-63}

On 9 Aug 1722 John Turner of Kent Co., yeoman, for £52.13.6 sold to Elizabeth Brinkle, widow, and John Curtis of same place, a tract of land on n.w. side of Swan Creek and n.w. side of Mispillion Creek, 300 a. {KEDELR G:99}

John was father of ELIZABETH, b. after 1692 and grandfather of Elizabeth Crawford, wife of Thomas Crawford who had children, Evis, Mary, Letitia, and Elizabeth.

THE PETER BRINCKLE FAMILY

First Generation

1. PETER BRINCKLE, m. Elizabeth (N). Peter d. by 15 April 1728 when his estate was administered by
Elizabeth and Curtis Brinckle. {Reg. of Wills, G:10}

Peter Brinckle was father of Richard. {See KEDELR N:188}

Elizabeth Brinckle, wife of Peter Brinckle, d. leaving a will dated 9 April 1741, proved 9 Nov 1743. Heirs: sons Curtis, Peter, Richard, Daniel, William; dau. Elizabeth. Exec., son Richard. Wits., John Brinckle, Ruth Brinkle, Susanna Brinkle. {Arch. A5:165-166. Reg. of Wills, I:129} Admin. acct. Arch. A5:166 shows dau. Elizabeth married Herman Vanburkeeloe; mentions her father Peter Brinckle.

Peter and Elizabeth were parents of the following children: CURTIS; PETER; RICHARD; DANIEL; WILLIAM; ELIZABETH, m. Herman Vanburkeeloe.

Second Generation

2. CURTIS BRINCKLE, son of Peter (1) and Elizabeth Brinckle, m. Mary Manlove, dau. of Matthew Manlove.

Matthew Manlove, 29 Jan 1679, d. leaving a will dated 17 May 1735, proved 18 July 1735. Heirs: wife Susannah; daus. Jemima Moleston. Mary Brinckle (wife of Curtis Brinckle), Susannah, Miriam, Tabitha, Elizabeth Manlove; sons Matthew, Jonathan; grandsons Abner and Obediah Manlove. Exec., son Matthew. Wits., Nathaniel Bowman, John Clark, Anthony Woodward. {Arch. A32:42-43. Reg. of Wills, H:115-117}

3. PETER BRINCKLE, Little Creek Hundred, probable son of Peter (1) and Elizabeth Brinckle, m. Mary (N) who later m. Aaron Hart.

Peter d. leaving a will dated 10 Jan 1764, proved 30 March 1765. Mentioned were wife Mary to whom he left a third of all his lands during her natural life and the best bed and furniture thereunto belonging, and the third of all personally estate. To son William Brinckle, the plantation whereon I now dwell and a sorrell horse called Rock and a saddle and bridle. To son Jesse Brinckle the plantation in Murtherkill forrest on n. side of Cow Marsh binding on a tract of land called *Cabben Ridge*. To son Peter Brinckle plantation bought of Thomas Irons on Muddy Branch Bridge adj. to Thomas Parker's land and to the plantation whereon I now dwell. To dau. Mary Brinckle a negroe girl named Kate and her increase to be delivered to her when she comes to the age of 16 years. Execs., wife Mary and son William Brinckle. {KEDELR R:272?; Arch. A5:193200} Reg. of Wills, L:4-5. Arch. A5:194 shows Mary, the widow, later m. Aaron Hart.

Jessy Brincle, minor under 14 years, Mary, minor under 14 years, and Peter, minor under 14 years, children of Peter Brincle. Guardian Mary Hart late wife of Peter Brincle. 14 Jan 1768. {KE Co. Orphans Court B:32}

Mary Hart, late wife of Peter Brinckley, dec'd., petitioned the court on 14 Jan 1768. Peter left three children: Jessee now going in his 14th year; Mary now of the age of 10 years; Peter, aged 7 years. James Mortin (Morton) requested to be guardian of Jessee and Stokely Sturgis as guardian of Mary and

Peter. {KEORCF Brinckley - 1768}

In a petition of James Tilton of Dover, Practitioner of Physick. Dec 1769 he stated he became bound with William Brinckle and as his surety in a guardian bond to Jessey Brinckle for the said William Brinckle's execution of the trust reposed in him as guardian. Petr. apprehends that he is in danger of suffering by his becoming surety for said William Brinckle as afsd. {KEORCF
Brinkle, Jesse - 1770}

Peter was father of the following children: WILLIAM; JESSE, b. c1755; PETER, b. c1761; MARY, b. c1758.

4. RICHARD BRINCKLE, son of Peter (1) and Elizabeth Brinckle. Richard m. Tabitha (N)[8] who later m. Andrew Gray.

Richard d. by 5 Sep 1759 when his estate was admin. by Tabitha Brinckle and Andrew Gray. {Arch. A5:203} The administration shows that Tabitha, the widow, later married Andrew Gray.

Richard's estate was again administered on 27 Aug 1761 by Andrew Gray, D. B. N. {Arch. A5:204}

Petition of Ezekiel Brinckle, being of the age of 21 years. Whereas Richard Brinckle was seized of a tract in Mispillion Hundred and died intestate leaving issue: Ezekiel Brinckle and Elizabeth. Ezekiel requests division of land 29 May 1767. {KEORCF Brinkle, Ezekiel - 1768}

Richard was father of the following children: EZEKIEL; ELIZABETH.

5. DANIEL BRINCKLE of Little Creek Hundred, son of Peter (1) and Elizabeth Brinckle, m. Kesiah (N) who later m. Isaac Carty.

Daniel d. leaving a will dated 28 Sep 1754, proved 4 Nov 1754. Heirs: wife Kesiah; bros. Curtis, Peter, Richard; Ezekiel, Peter and Susanna, children of bro. Richard; sister Elizabeth Davis; cousins, Phebe Bessex [Beswick], William Brinckle, Peter Brinckle, Margaret Vanburkeloe and Mary Bessex (Beswick]. Extx., wife Kesiah. Wits., Robert Hall, Mark Hirons, John Brinckle. {Arch. A5:163-164. Reg. of Wills, K:97} Arch. A5:164 shows Kesiah, the widow, later married Isaac Carty; also shows John Hirons as a child of Charles Hirons. Will mentions mother Elizabeth Brinckle, dec'd.

On 25 Feb 1767 Isaac Carty of Little Creek Neck and Hundred for £300 sold to Charles Hillyard of Murtherkill Hundred same co., a tract of land and marsh in Little Creek Neck and Hundred on n. side of Herring Branch or Gut which said tract was surveyed for the said Isaac Carty 20 Oct 1763 by order of William Killen esqr then surveyor of said co. by virtue of a warrant granted to the said Isaac Carty and Kesiah his wife bearing date 3 April 1760 which Kesiah is since, dec'd., but return not being made, it was made for the said Isaac Carty the surviving partner and returned in to the surveyor generals office at Philadelphia 17 Feb present by Saml Mccall now deputy surveyor of said co.

---

[8] This is probably Tabitha Williams, dau. of Reynear Williams, noting that Reynear Williams mentions a dau. Tabitha Brinckle in his will dated 5 Dec 1743, proved 9 Oct 1745. Also mentioned was dau. Susannah Brinckle. {Arch. A55:138. Reg. of Wills, 1:12}

bounded by land claimed by John Brinckle (Brinckley) ... 111 1/2 a. Isaac Carty will defend against the heirs of his late wife Kesiah and against the heirs of Daniel Brinkle the former husband of the said Kesiah. {KEDELR R:176}

The estate of Daniel Brinckle was administered on 14 Jan 1771 by Isaac Carty. {Reg. of Wills, L:89}

6. WILLIAM BRINCKLE, son of Peter (1) and Elizabeth Brinckle, m. Elizabeth (N).[9]

On 14 Sep 1698 William Rodeney and Sarah his wife for love and naturall affection and 5 shillings sold to William Brinckloe and Elizabeth his wife a tract of land being part of a tract of land called *Denbigh*, w. side of Dover River, 394 a. {KEDELR}

William d. leaving a will dated 1 April 1722, proved 8 May 1722. Heirs: sons William, Winnlock (Winlock], and John Brinckle and John Curtis; daus. Elizabeth, Mariam [Miriam], and Sarah Brinckle and Mary Curtis; wife Elizabeth. Execs.: wife Elizabeth, son-in-law Jehu Curtis. Wits., Andrew Freasure, William Mulroney, Hannah Freasure. {Arch. A5:217. Reg. of Wills, D:52-54}

John Curtis on 18 March 1718 did grant a tract called *Pasture Point* to William Brinckle, esqr, of Kent Co, and he in his will did devise unto his son John Brinckle all that tract of land and plantation called *Ivy Hill* together with a small tract called *Pasture Point* adj. 250 a., whereas Richard Brinckle of Kent Co. being lawfully seized in one half of the afsd. 400 a. tract of land called *Hill* which is divided by a line projected by the said William Brinckle and Peter Brinckle father to the afsd. Richard Brinckle in their life times. {KEDELR N:188}

William's estate was administered on 1 Oct 1748 by bros. Peter, Richard, Daniel Brinkle and sister Elizabeth VanBurkelo. {Arch. A5:218. Reg. of Wills, 1:238-239}

William was father of the following children: WILLIAM; WINLOCK; JOHN; MARY, m. Jehu Curtis, son of Winlock Curtis; CURTIS; ELIZABETH, m. 1st John Clark, Jr. and m. 2nd Peter Lowber; MARIAM, m. (N) Hyland; SARAH, m. Spencer Cole. William probably had a dau. Mary, noting that the will of Samuel Low mentioned Mary Brinckloe, dau. of William Brinckloe as a creditor. {Arch. A31:92. Reg. of Willas B:58, written 19 Aug 1707 and proved 23 Sep 1707}

7. ELIZABETH, dau. of Peter (1) and Elizabeth Brinckle, m. (N) Davis. Third Generation

8. CURTIS BRINCKLE, farmer, probable son of William (6) Brinckle, m. Sarah (N) who later m. George Ogle.

Curtis d. leaving a will dated 21 March 1767, proved 8 April 1767. Heirs: wife Sarah; dau. Phebe Bessix, wife of John; cousins William Brinckle (son of Peter), Ezekiel Brinckle, Brinckle Davis, George Manlove (son of Matthew); Robert Hamilton, tenant. Extx., wife Sarah. Wits., John Haslet, John Molleston, Joshua Jester. {Arch. A5:159-162. Reg. of Wills, L:28} Note: Arch. vol. A5, page 160 shows that Sarah Brinckle later married George Ogle.

---

9 Probably dau. of John Curtis.

9. ELIZABETH BRINCKLE, dau. of William (6) Brinckle, m. Peter Lowber.

On 5 Feb 1766 Peter Lowber and Elizabeth his wife, one of the sisters of John Brinckle, dec'd., for natural love, good will and affection give unto Anne Clark of Kent Co., mantuamaker, and also for the better maintenance lively hood and perserment of her ... a parcel of land allotted as the share of the afsd. Peter Lowber and Elizabeth his wife being their shear of the lands of the afsd. John Brinckle esqr, dec'd., which he was seized of in his life time, beginning at the share laid off to Mariam Hyland one of the sisters of the afsd. John Brinckle to Browns Creek to Sandy Gravely Vally to Chappell branch to field left to the heirs of Winlock Clark ... 200 a. part of the lands that belonged to John Brinckle by the will of his father William Brinckle and also the right which they have to all that 1/2 part of the lands of the afsd. John Brinckle, dec'd., laid off to Jemimah Haslet who was the widow and relique of the afsd. John Brinckle ... reserving to my self and my wife for and during our natural life the use and occupation of the said lands and premisses. {KEDELR R:163}

10. JOHN BRINCKLE, son of William (6) Brinckle, m. Jemima Molleston, dau. of Henry Molleston. Jemima later m. John Haslet.

Jemima Molleston, wife of Henry Molleston, d. leaving a will dated 20 Aug 1760, proved 11 Nov 1760. Heirs: sons John, Jonathan, Henry and William; dau. Jemima Brinckle, wife of John Brinckle. Execs., sons John and Henry. Wits., Elizabeth Faries, G. Russell, Mark Manlove. {Arch. A35:211-212. Reg. of Wills, K:245-246}

Henry Molleston d. leaving a will dated 21 Dec 1761, proved 23 Feb 1762. Heirs: sons Henry, Jonathan, William; dau. Jemimah Brinckle; granddau. Mary Molleston, dau. of son Henry; grandson Henry Molleston, son of son Henry; Eleanor Hall. Exec., son Henry. Wits., Daniel Robisson, William Manlove, Elizabeth Miller. {Arch. A35:204-205. Reg. of Wills, K:280}

John Brinckle, Esq., d. by 9 Oct 1764 when his estate was admin. by Jemima Brinckle, widow. {Reg. of Wills, K:348-349} Note: Arch. A5:177-181 show Jemima, the widow, later married John Haslet.

On 20 May 1766 a petition was submitted by Peter Lowber who was one of the heirs of John Brinkley, Esq. Brinkley died intestate leaving a widow but no children. He had four sisters, Mary, Elizabeth, Mariam, and Sarah who are the only surviving ones. An undated petition of Peter Lowber states John Haslet m. Jemima, widow of John Brinckle. An undated petition of John Revel, yeoman, and Amelia his wife states John Brinckle died intestate sometime in 1764 without issue leaving a widow Jemima. Mentioned were sisters of John Brinckle: Mary Vanbebber, wife of Jacob; Elizabeth Lowber, wife of Peter; Mariam Highland, widow of Kent Co.; and Sarah Cole, late wife of Spencer Cole of Kent Co., dec'd. Also mentioned were daus. of Sarah Cole: Penelope, wife of Reynear Williams; Sarah, wife of John Peterkin; Mary, wife of Joshua Clark; Amelia, wife of petitioner John Revel. {KEORCF Brinckle, John, Esq. 1767-95}

11. SARAH BRINCKLE, dau. of William (6) Brinckle, m. Spencer Cole. They were parents of the following children: PENELOPE, m. Reynear Williams; SARAH, m. John Peterkin; MARY, m. Joshua Clark; AMELIA, m. 1st Southey Brinckle and m. 2nd John Revel. {KEORCF Brinckle, John, Esq. 1767-95; Brinckle, Southey 1769-74}

THE JOHN BRINCKLE FAMILY

1. JOHN BRINCKLE m. Hester Tilton, dau. of Thomas Tilton. She was mother of the following children: ELIZABETH, m. (N) Durborow; HANNAH, m. (N) Fisher; JOHN; THOMAS, m. Mary (N) who later m. (N) Pleasanton; DANIEL; BENJAMIN. John later m. Ruth (N).

Hester Brinckle, gentlewoman, d. leaving a will dated 19 Jan 1739/40, proved 3 May 1740. Heirs: daus. Elizabeth Durborow, Hannah Fisher; sons John, Thomas, Daniel and Benjamin. Exec., son John. Wits., Daniel Brinckle, Susannah Brinckle, Isaac King. Prob. May 3, 1740. Arch. A5:170. Reg. of Wills, I:19}

At Orphans Court of Sussex Co. 4 Sep 1744 John Brinkle, Junr., exec. of the testament and one of the devisees of Hesther Brinkle, dec'd., who was one of the dau. of Thomas Tilton of Sussex Co., dec'd., petitioned the court setting forth that the said Thomas Tilton died possessed of 3 tracts consisting of 800 a. and prays to have the land divided. {Sussex Co. Orphans Court}

John d. leaving a will dated 31 Jan 1748/9, proved 4 March 1748. Heirs: wife Ruth; daus. Hannah Fisher, Elis Durborow; sons John, Daniel and Benjamin; grandson Joseph Brinckle; granddau. Hester Brinckle. Execs., sons John and Benjamin. Wits., Jno. Brinckle, Curtis Brinckle, Sarah Brinckle. {Arch.
A5:171-172. Reg. of Wills, 1:263}

On 11 Jan 1754 Mary Pleasanton of Kent co. widow for £15 sold to John Brinckle of same place yeoman, 3 tracts of land, whereas a certain Thomas Tilton of Sussex Co. being possessed of 3 tracts of land in Slaughter Neck whereon the said Thomas Tilton formerly dwelt and he dying intestate the tracts descended to his 3 children, to wit John Tilton, Hester Brinckle and Sarah Sharp, afterwards Hester Brinckle makes her will and bequeathed her part of the lands to her 4 sons, John, Thomas, Daniel and Benjamin Brinckle, lastly Thomas Brinckle makes his will and dies and leaves his part of the land to be sold and leaves his wife Mary sole executrix, party to these presents ... 800 a. {KEDELR I:139}

On 1 Aug 1754 Daniel Brinckle of Murtherkill Hundred Kent Co. yeoman quit claim unto John Brinckle of Little Creek Hundred same co. yeoman ... a tract of land, whereas John Brinckle, Senr., of Mispillion Hundred same co., dec'd., possessed of a tract of land 440 a. in Murtherkill Hundred being the same which the said John Brinckle, Senr., purchased of Jehu Curtis and by his will did bequeath unto his two sons John and Daniel and grandson Joseph Brinckle, that is to say 220 a. to his son John Brinckle and grandson Joseph Brinckle to include *Loftis's Point*, the dwelling house and plantation on w. side of County Road where Thomas Brinckle, dec'd., formerly dwelt to road which leads to Jonne Cake Bridge. {KEDELR P:210}

On 10 Dec 1756 John Brinckle, Daniel Brinckle and Benjamin Brinckle of Kent co. gent for £220 sold to John Smith of Slaughter Neck, Sussex Co., yeoman, a tract of land, whereas at a Court of Orphans held at Lewes on 4 Feb 1755 Thomas Tilton of Kent co. son of John Tilton late of Kent Co., dec'd., petitioned setting forth that his grandfather Thomas Tilton, dec'd., d. intestate leaving a son and 2 daus. and at the time of his death was possessed of 800 a. in Cedar Creek Hundred, the court did appoint Thomas Till and Nehemiah Draper esqrs, Avery Draper, William Fowler and John Haverlee, with the assistance of a skillfull surveyor, to divide the land among the heirs of the said Thomas Tilton, dec'd., on 11 Jun 1755 the gent divided the land and alloted the heirs of Esther Tilton who intermarried with John Brinckle of Kent co. who by her will devised her right in the lands to her 4 sons, John, Thomas, Daniel and Benja. Brinckle, 3 of whom viz John, Daniel and Benjamin are parties to these presents (Thomas long being dead and whose right was vested in John), on Slaughter Creek ... 483 a. {KEDELR I:145}

Second Generation

2. JOHN BRINCKLE, son of John (1) Brinckle, m. Charity Robbison, dau. of George Robbisson. John had sons Joseph and John Brinckle.

George Robbison d. leaving a will dated 15 Aug 1730, proved 16 March 1733. Heirs: Children of son William, dec'd; sons George, Daniel, John, Samuel; wife Mary; son-in-law John Bland; daus. Ann Bland and Charity Brinkly; son-in-law John Brinkly; grandsons Lawrence, son of George, and William, son of John. Exec., son Samuel. Wits., George Nowell, Robert Cumming, Daniel Rodney, Robert Hodgson, John Maysom, Train Hodgson. {Arch. A44:40. Reg. of Wills, H:67-68}

On 11 May 1759 Joseph Brickle and John Brinckle his father both of Kent Co. in consideration of a bond, released unto Andrew Caldwell all their right in a tract of land, whereas George Robisson did in his life time make a deed of gift to his three children Laurence Robisson, Daniel Robisson and Charity Robisson for a tract of land called *Whitewells Delight*, on s. side of Jones Creek being the place whereon the said George Robisson did dwell and Charity afterwards intermaried with the afsd. John Brinckle and the said John Brinckle sold the land by consent of his wife to Daniel Robisson and give his bond of £100 5 July 1738 for the conveying all their right in the tract of land and marsh but Charity dyed before the said conveyance was made. {KEDELR P:121}

On 2 March 1761 a Memorandum of Agreement was made between Joseph Brinckle of Kent Co. and Caleb Sipple of same co., Joseph Brinckle hath sold all that plantation and the land thereunto belonging which was left to him and his father John Brinckle, by his grandfather John Brinckle, dec'd., in Murtherkill Hundred near the draw bridge unto the said Caleb Sipple for £450 to be paid on or before 10 May 1762, and Joseph Brinckle doth promise and agree to take Benjamin Warren Junr's bond for any sum therein mentioned in discharge of the afsd. £450 and Joseph Brinckle doth covenant for himself togeather with his father John Brinckle to convey by a good and sufficient deed in open court all the afsd. plantation and lands. {KEDELR Q:76}

On 27 Feb 1765 Joseph Brinckle and John Brinckle (Brinckley) of Kent Co. yeoman for 5 shillings released unto John Sipple, Caleb Sipple, Garret Sipple and Thomas Sipple of same co. yeomen, Nancy Sipple, Mary Sipple and Elizabeth Sipple of same co. spinsters, the children and heirs of Caleb Sipple late of same co. yeoman, dec'd., a tract of land, whereas the said Joseph Brinckle and John Brinckle the elder, dec'd., late father of the said Joseph and John Brinckle, in the lifetime of the said John Brinckle the elder, became seized in a 440 a. tract of land granted to one James Steel by patent bearing date 25 March 1727 on n. side of the Murther Creek beginning below Kings Road from Dover to the draw bridge ... to Johnneycake Bridge ... and Joseph Brinckle and John Brinckle the elder being seized of 220 a. Joseph Brinckle entered into a writing of agreement bearing date 2 March 1761 whereby the said Joseph Brinckle had sold the 220 a. to the said Caleb Sipple for £450 paid by the said Caleb Sipple, that the said Joseph Brinckle his father would convey the tract unto the said Caleb Sipple the father and whereby Caleb Sipple was in his lifetime peacably possessed of the land. Whereas the said Joseph Brinckle and John Brinckle the elder in his lifetime after the death of Caleb Sipple the father in consideration of the agreement entered into a bond bearing date 17 Jul 1762 bound unto Sarah Sipple widow of Caleb Sipple then, dec'd., for £900 with condition to convey unto John Sipple, Caleb Sipple party hereto Garret Sipple, Thomas Sipple, Nancy Sipple, Mary Sipple and Elizabeth Sipple as heirs to the said Caleb Sipple their father the 220 a. John Brinckle the elder died leaving issue, the said Joseph Brinckle and John Brinckle party hereto only, before the condition of the bond was complyed with. {KEDELR R:20}

3. THOMAS BRINCKLE, planter of Murderkill, son of John (1) Brinckle, m. Mary Marim, dau. of Charles Marim {see *Colonial Families of Delaware*, v. 2}. She later m. John Pleasanton. Thomas and Mary were parents of Easter [or Hester].

Thomas d. leaving a will dated 23 July 1741, proved 6 Aug 1741. Heirs: wife Mary; dau. Hester; bros. John, Daniel, Benjamin; Alexander Bryer. Extx., wife. Wits., John Brinckle, Jr., Ann Brinckle, John Newton. {Arch. A5:216. Reg. of Wills, L:38} Grandfather Tilton is mentioned in the will.

John Pleasanton, yeoman of Dover Hundred, d. leaving a will dated 8 Dec 1753, proved 15 Dec 1753. Heirs: wife Mary; sons John, Charles, George and David; granddau. Elizabeth Field; grandson Jonathan Pleasanton. Exec., son David. Wits., Ebenezer Manlove, William Shurmer, Abraham Barber. {Arch. A40:108-110. Reg. of Wills, K:88} Will mentions wife's dau. Easter; Arch. A40:109 shows Mary Maxwell and Thos. Brinckle as parents of Hester Brinckle, dec'd.

On 11 Jan 1754 Mary Pleasanton of Kent Co., widow, for £15 sold to John Brinckle of same place yeoman ... 3 tracts of land, whereas a certain Thomas Tilton of Sussex Co. being possessed of 3 tracts of land in Slaughter Neck whereon the said Thomas Tilton formerly dwelt and he dying intestate the tracts descended to his 3 children, to wit, John Tilton, Hester Brinckle and Sarah Sharp, afterwards Hester Brinckle makes her will and bequeathed her part of the lands to her 4 sons, John, Thomas, Daniel and Benjamin Brinckle, lastly Thomas Brinckle makes his will and dies and leaves his part of the land to be sold and leaves his wife Mary sole extx., party to these presents ... 800 a. Proved and Ackn 2 Feb 1757. (I:pg 139)

4. BENJAMIN BRINCKLE, son of John (1) Brinckle, m. Bettey (N) who later m. George Monro.

Benjamin d. by 8 June 1764 when his estate was administered by Bettey Brinckley, widow. {Arch. A5:154-156. Reg. of Wills, K:344-345} Arch. A5:154 shows that Betty Brinckle later married George Monro; also mentions heirs, Mary, William, Benjamin and Joseph Brincklee and Leah Brinckley, wife of Joshua Cottman.

Petition of Southy Brinkle [eldest son]. That petitioners's father, Benjamin Brinckle, d. intestate seized of a tract and marsh in Mispillion Hundred and left a widow, now the wife of George Manloe [?], Esq., and seven children, viz: Southy Brinkle, John Brinkle, William Brinkle, Leah Brinkle, Mary Brinkle, Joseph Brinkle and Eliza. Brinkle. Southy Brinkle requests a division of the land. 20 June 1766. The commission decided the land could not be divided without spoiling the value. {KEORCF Brinckle, Benjamin, dec. 1766-67}

Joseph Brinckle, minor under 14 years, Sarah and John, minors, children of Benjamin Brinckle. Guardian was their brother Southy Brinckle. May 1767. {KE Co. Orphans Court B:15}

Benjamin was father of the following children: SOUTHY (eldest son); JOHN; WILLIAM; LEAH, m. Joshua Cottman; MARY; JOSEPH; ELIZABETH; SARAH.

Third Generation

5. JOSEPH BRINCKLE, son of John (2) Brinckle, m. Ruhamah, dau. of John Marim; they had a son John who d. intestate and without issue and without siblings, survived by his father.

On 20 May 1766 Joseph Brinckle of Kent Co. yeoman for £3 for each a. of upland sold to James Stevens of same place yeoman ... a tract of land in Jones Neck part of a larger tract lately belonging to John Marim and upon his decease conveyed to his dau. Ruhama late wife of Joseph Brinckle and upon her decease descended to John Brinckle son of said Joseph and Ruhama by the decease of which said child the estate is now vested in the said Joseph Brinckle bounded by land of Charles Marim and John Nickerson, 100 a. {KEDELR R:89}

On 3 Dec 1766 James Stevens of Kent Co. yeoman for £222.10 sold to William Rodney of said co. gent ... 1/3 part of a tract of land, whereas John Marim late of Kent Co. yeoman, dec'd., was in his life time seized in a tract of land 210 a. on w. side of Pipe Elm Branch and on s. side of Little Creek in Dover Hundred, part of 2 larger tracts called *Little Pipe Elm* and *Edington* and being so seized the said John Marim by his will bearing date 19 May 1755 did devise the said tract to his 3 daus, viz Ruhamah, Mary and Elizabeth (Registers Office Book K, fol. 113), the land became vested in said Ruhamah, Mary and Elizabeth Marim devisees as tenants in common, and whereas afterwards the said Ruhamah Marim m. Joseph Brinckle of Kent Co., yeoman, by whom they had issue only John Brinckle, and died whereby 1/3 part of said premisses descended to the said John Brinckle her son, and after the death of Ruhamah the said John Brinckle also died intestate without issue, brothers or sisters, whereby the 1/3 part came to the said Joseph Brinckle who survived the said John Brinckle his son, and Joseph Brinckle being seized of the premises on 20 May now last past did sell unto the said James Stevens his share (Book R, fol. 89). {KEDELR R:141}

6. HESTER (Esther) BRINCKLE, dau. of Thomas (3) Brinckle and dau. of Mary Pleasenton, d. leaving a will dated 13 Sep 1754 but unwitnessed. Heirs: sister Mary Campbell; mother Mary Pleasenton. Extx., mother Mary Pleasenton. Wits., Stephen Paradee, Nimrod Maxwell, Anna Maxwell. {Arch. A5:167-169. Reg. of Wills, K:136} The Will mentions father Thomas Brinckle, dec'd; Arch. A5:169 shows Mary Maxwell, nee Pleasanton, as extx.

The second will of Esther [Hester] Brinckle, dau. of Thomas, dec'd., was written 17 Sep 1754 and proved 10 Oct 1754. Heirs: sister Mary Campbell; mother Mary Plesonton. Extx., mother. Wits., Stephen Paradee, Nimrod Maxwell, Annah Maxwell. {Arch. A5:167-168. Reg. of Wills, G, appendix 5} Note: The first unwitnessed will is recorded in Arch. A5:168 and Reg. of Wills, K:136}

The estate of Esther Brinckle was administered by Nimrod Maxwell,

d. b. n., 24 Nov 1763. {Arch. A5:169}

7. SOUTHBY (SOUTHY) BRINCKLE, son of Benjamin (4) Brinckle, m. Emily or Amelia Cole, dau. of Spencer Cole. Amelia later m. John Revell.

Southby d. by 9 Dec 1769 when his estate was administered by Emily Brinckle, widow, and Reynear Williams. {Arch. A5:212-215. Reg. of Wills, L:68} Arch. A5:212 shows heirs, bros. William and Joseph Brinckle; Elizabeth Brinckle, dau. of Benjamin Brinckle; page 213 shows that Amelia Brinckle married John Revell; page 215 mentions a son Southey Brinckle.

Southby was father of SOUTHBY.

Unplaced

ELIZABETH BRINKLEE d. by 31 May 1733 when her estate was administered by Caesar Rodney. {Reg. of Wills, H:107-108}

JOHN BRINCKLE, Little Creek Hundred, m. Ann (N).[10]

John d. leaving a will dated 30 July 1762, proved 7 June 1763. Heirs: wife Ann; sons John and Joseph. Exec., son John. Wits., Peter Brinckle, Robert Hall, William Brinckle. {Arch. A5:173. Reg. of Wills, K:312-313}

JOHN BRINCKLE d. by 19 Dec 1769 when his estate was admin. by John Brinckle, next of kin. {Arch. A5:183-186. Reg. of Wills, L:68}

JOHN BRINCKLE d. leaving a will (unsigned), made 25 Sep 1764 (no probate). Heirs: wife unnamed; nephew Spencer Cole; nieces Sarah, Mary and Emilia Cole; Penelope Williams; Brinckle Adams; John Molleston; Reynear Williams; Joseph Nicholls. Execs., wife and Reynear Williams. Wits., John Haslet, Curtis Brinckle, Sarah Brinckle. {Arch. A5:174-176. Reg. of Wills, K:1-2}

JOHN BRINCKLE m. Susanna (N) [11].

On 5 Aug 1743 John Brinckle of Kent Co. esqr and Susanna his wife for £150 sold to William Shirley of same place yeoman ... a tract of land called *Pasture Point* on s. side of Murder Creek beginning at the corner of John Cabellis, 50 a. and one other tract on s. side of Murder Creek, 200 a. William Brinckle, esqr., of Kent Co, in his will bequeathed unto son John Brinckle all that tract of land called *Ivey Hill* together with a small tract called *Pasture Point* adj.thereunto... both tracts 250 a. {KEDELR M:229}

---

10 This may be Ann Brinckle mentioned as dau. Ann Draper of Ann Draper, widow of Alexander of Sussex Co., in the will of Ann Draper, written 5 Sep 1743 and proved 20 March 1753. {Arch. A69:187. Reg. of Wills, A:354-356}

11 This is probably Susanna Williams, dau. of Reynear Williams, noting that Reynear Williams mentions a dau. Susanna Brinckle in his will dated 5 Dec 1743, proved 9 Oct 1745. Also mentioned was dau. Tabitha Brinckle. {Arch. A55:138. Reg. of Wills, 1:12}

MARGARETT BRINCKLE, widow, d. by 14 Dec 1725 when her estate was administered by Peter Brinkle. {Reg. of Wills, F:8}

PETER BRINKLE m. Elizabeth, dau. of William Manlove.

On -- -- 1747 Peter Brinkle of Kent Co. yeoman and Elizabeth his wife, dau. and heiress of William Manlove late of Little Creek Hundred Kent Co., yeoman, dec'd., for £60 sold to Daniel Brinkle of same co. yeoman a tract of land (whereas William Manlove dyed seized in a tract of land in Little Creek Hundred 300 a. called *Wheel of Fortune* purchased 10 Jul 1716 and William Manlove dyed intestate leaving issue a son named William and the said Elizabeth Brinkle, and William her brother is since dead whereby the said tract of land descended to her - s. side of s.w. branch of Duck Creek beginning at Muddy branch, 300 a. {KEDELR N:171}

RICHARD BRINCKLE m. Phebe Calloway, widow of James Calloway who d. by 29 Dec 1769 when Phebee Calloway, widow, and Joseph Marrett were appointed admins. of the estate of James Calloway. {Arch. A7:145-147. Reg. of Wills, L:69} Note: Arch. A7:146 shows that Phebe Calloway married Richard Brinckle.

SARAH BRINCKLE was dau.-in-law of John Hammitt.

John Hammitt, farmer, d. leaving a will dated 18 Dec 1740, proved 31 Dec 1740. Heirs: dau.in-law Sarah Brinckle; housekeeper Catherine Owen. Execs., Sarah Brinkle and Catherine Owen. Wits., William Shurley, Harman Burkeloe, Spencer Cole. {Arch. A21:190. Reg. of Wills, 1:25}

WILLIAM BRINCKLE m. Mary Hamilton, dau. of Mary Hamilton.

Mary Hamilton d. leaving a will dated 19 March 1773, proved 2 Oct 1773. Heirs: dau. Mary Brinckle, wife of William; grandchildren Peter Moore and Mary Moore, children of John Moore; grandsons Curtis and Joseph Brinckle, sons of William Brinckle; Robert Hamilton. Exec., Robert Hamilton. Wits., Ann Harris, John Ham. {Arch. A21:165. Reg. of Wills, L:141-142}

THE BURTONS

Ref A: Notes on The Ancestry of Robert Burton (1730-1785) ... *The Penn. Gen. Magazine*, XVIII, pp. 143-152, by John Goodwin Herndon.[12] In this article is stated that there lived in Accomack County, Virginia, during the second half of the seventeenth century Robert Burton and William Burton and their families. Each of these men acquired interests in Sussex county, Delaware, at an early date. One of William's sons married one of Robert's daughters, and another son of William's married one of Robert's step-daughters. We have discovered no

---

12 This source discusses the mystery of Robert's identity and describes in more detail the early records of the Burtons of Accomack County, Virginia.

proof of the relationship of Robert and William Burton, but notes collected by the late Miss M. Atherton Leach indicate that they were first cousins. See this article for more discussion on the Ancestry of Robert and William Burton.

Ref B: Information generously furnished by Carole A. Sherr of Lancaster, Pennsylvania.

Ref C: "William Burton (ca. 1640 - 1695/6), Landowner In Accomac, Somerset, and Sussex," by Mary Burton Derrickson McCurdy, Ph.D. This was later published in the *Pennsylvania Genealogical Magazine*.

In *Biographical And Genealogical History of the State of Delaware*, published by J. M. Runk, 1899 the following is given: Robert Burton, b. England; came to America c1677 and settled in Virginia. He m. 11 Feb 1676, Catherine Cotton. His three sons took up land in Indian River Hundred, Sussex Co. One of the sons, William, was b. in Virginia 11 Nov 1677, and died in Delaware, leaving a son Woolsey.

THE WILLIAM BURTON FAMILY

1. WILLIAM BURTON of Accomack Co., Virginia m. Ann Stratton, dau. of Thomas and Agnes Stratton of Northampon Co. Virginia. {C}

William was elected to the vestry of Hungar's parish in 1672. On 16 June 1673 he purchased 1000 a. adj. 400 he owned at that time. {C}

William was assigned a patent in Sussex Co., DE, in 1694 which he later devised to his son Jacob.

William Burton of Accomack Co., VA, was granted a land patent (from New York land office) to a tract called *Long Neck* between the Indian River and Rehoboth Bay. {SUDELR}

On 8 May 1772 William Burton of *Long Neck*, Indian River Hundred, conveyed to his son William Burton, Junr., a tract in *Long Neck* whose patent of 600 a. was assigned to William Burton of Accomack, 5 Sep 1694 and by him in his last will dated 5 Jan 1695 devised to his son Jacob Burton who devised same to his nephew the above named party in his last will dated 14 Nov 1716 - 223 a.
{SUDELR}[13]

William Burton of Accomack Co., VA, Gent., by his last Will devised to his son Joseph Burton of Sussex Co. a tract called *Cheet*, 715 a. which descended to William Burton, yeoman, being the eldest son of afsd. Joseph Burton. William Burton on 3 Dec 1734 conveyed same to William Prettyman. {Sussex Co. Land Records}

William Burton d. leaving a will dated 5 Jan 1695. To eldest son William, land on the seaboard side, situate in Forked Neck near where I now live. To 3rd son Thomas Burton the South side of the said Forked Neck. To 6th son Stratton Burton land purchased of Col. John West and adj. the land given

---

13 The Duke of York Record, p. 177, shows a grant to William Burton of 1000 a. called *Loving Neck*, no date given, probably ca 1675

Thomas. To 2nd son John Burton 500 a., being 1/2 of 1000 a. in Sussex Co. in the Territories of Pennsylvania granted me by patent called *Long Neck.* To 4th son Benjamin 600 a. near Assateag on the seaboard side in Somerset Co., MD. The other 1/2 of the of the 1000 a. in Sussex Co. was conveyed by me to Thomas Bagwell, of Accomack, dec'd., To 5th son Joseph Burton 387 1/2 a. on the north side of Indian River in Sussex Co., PA. being 1/2 a. of 775 a. purchased of John Parker. To 7th son Woolsey Burton 387 a. being the other 1/2 of said tract. To sons William, Thomas and Stratton my interest in *Cedar Island* in Accomack Co. To 8th son Jacob Burton 450 a. near Lewis Towne in PA on Indian River, being part of 600 a. purchased of Thomas Jones and adj. the land given my son John - The other 150 a. was due William Bagwell of Accomack. To 9th son Samuel Burton 500 a. on the south side of Indian River. Wife Ann Burton. To dau. Agnes Revell - To grandchildren. Wife Ann and son William, execs. Capt. William Custis, William Nock and son in law John Revell overseers in Accomack and John Hill of Lewis Town, PA. Wit: John Revell, Robert Scott, James Smith, Robert Edge. {Accomack Co. Wills:100}

Following the death of William Burton, Ann m. James Alexander. James Alexander d. leaving a will dated 14 Jan 1708, proved 1 Feb 1708. To son in law William Burton after the decease of his mother, my wife. To John, Thomas, Benjamin, Joseph, Stratton, Woolsey, Jacob and Samuel Burton, 100 a. at Jengoteague. To wife Ann 1/2 of my new sloop now in Pungoteague and the other 1/2 of my kinsman Benjamin Clungston, but if he come not within 12 months to claim this gift I give the same to Stratton Burton. Wife Ann residuary legatee and exec. Wit: William Custis, Francis Wharton, Delight Sheald. {Accomack Co. Wills 463}

Ann Alexander d. leaving a will dated 6 Sep 1711, proved 4 March 1711/12. Mentioned: son William Burton; son William's son William; son Thomas Baurotn; son Thomas Baurton's wife and his two children, Thomas and Patience; Ann Burton, dau. of son Thomas; son Benjamin Burton and his son William, dau. Ann and son John; son Joseph and his son; son Stratton's dau. Leeze; son Benjamin's wife Elizabeth; son Woolsey Burton; sons Jacob and Samuel Burotn; grandau. Agnes Burton; graudaus. Elizabeth and Ann Revell; son in law John Revell; grandaus. Rachell and Sarah Revell; grandson Edward Revell. Son William, exec. Wit: William Custis, Christopher Brooks, John Daggen. {Accomack Co. Wills:560}

William was father of the following children: WILLIAM, b. 19 Nov 1677; JOHN; THOMAS; BENJAMIN; JOSEPH; STRATTON; WOOLSEY; JACOB; SAMUEL; AGNESS, m. John Revell and had children {B}: Frances, Elizabeth, Edward Revell, Rachel, Ann and Sarah.

Second Generation

2. WILLIAM BURTON, son of William (1) Burton, b. 19 Nov 1677, m. Mary (West) Snead, widow of Robert Snead. Mary was the dau. of Col. John West{Whitelaw: 957, 959}.

William Burton d. leaving a will dated 18 Nov 1730, proved 2 Feb 1730/31. Mentioned: wife Mary; daus. in law Ann Snead and Catherine Snead; dau. Agnes and for want of heirs to her children. To son William, 250 a. bought of William Clark on Pothook Creek near Lewis Town. To nephew Thomas Burton. To nephews Joshua, Samuel and Joseph. To nephews Caleb and Abner Burton. To grandson John West. To the children of dau. Agnes already born or to be born. Wife and 2 children residuary legatees. Wife extx. Wit: Stratton Burton, William Arbuckle. {Accomack Co. Wills:122}

Mary Burton d. leaving a will dated 14 April 1765, proved 27 Jan 1767. Grandau. Anne Arbuckle, now Anne Teackle, wife of Levin Teackle. To great-grandau. Anne Purnall, dau. to my granddau. Euphime Purnell. To grandau. Mary Stewart. To great-grandau. Anne Snead Stewart. To grandau. Catherine Arbuckle. To grandson Archibald Campbell. To each of grandchildren in NC, viz: Leah and Eupheme Snead. To great-grandson John Eustace. To grandau. Anne Snead, dau. of son John Snead in NC. To Anne Snead, dau. of John Snead in Accomack Co. To my 4 grandchildren in NC, viz: Jane, Catherine, Leah and Eupheme Snead. Jane and William Wilson Snead, children of son John in NC. Greatgrandau. Catherine Arbuckle, dau. of James Arbuckle. Great-grandau. Catharine Murray in Worcester Co. MD. Grandchildren Eupheme Purnall, Mary Stewart and Catharine Arbuckle, residuary legatees. Friends Col. Thomas Parramore, John Snead and grandson James Arbuckle, execs. Wit: Levin Stewart, George Millechops, William Arbuckle. {Accomack Co. Wills:707}

William and Mary were parents of the following children {B}: AGNESS; WILLIAM, m. Margaret Robins and had a children Caleb {Whitelaw:862} and Margaret,[14] d. 6 Dec 1772, and who m. Littleton Savage {Whitelaw:144}.

3. JOHN BURTON, son of William (1) Burton, d. leaving a will dated 10 Feb 17[0]8, proved 1708. Mentioned: Samuel, Benjamin, Thomas, Joseph, Stratton, Jacob, Woolsey and William Burton, Sr.; Ann Bagwell; Frances Kaning; and Aminadal Hangar. Exec., bro. William. Wits., William Bagwell, Thomas Gear, Mary Oakey. {Sussex Co. Probate - Arch. A61:183. Reg. of Wills, A:443-444}

4. THOMAS BURTON, son of William (1) Burton, m. Amey Wallace.

Thomas Burton d. leaving a will dated 4 May 1735, proved 1 July 1735. Mentioned: son Joshua to whom land was devised wherein I now live, 500 a.; sons Samuel, Joseph, Joshua; dau. Patience Armistrader. Balance of estate to all my children except for dau. Patience. Son Joshua, exec. Wit: Samuel Beech, John Wharton, Robert Coleburn. {Accomack Co. Wills:459}

Amey Burton d. leaving a will dated 24 Nov 1745, proved 30 July 1746. Mentioned: sons Joseph Burton; dau. Patience Armitrader; dau. Agnes Garrison; daus. Susannah, Amey and Anne Burton residuary legatees; son Joseph and dau. Susannah Burton, execs. {Accomack Wills:296}

Thomas and Amey were parents of the following children {B}: JOSHUA, m. Elizabeth Garrison; SAMUEL; JOSEPH; PATIENCE, m. (N) Armistrader; AGNES, m. (N) Garrison; SUSANNAH; AMEY; ANNE; THOMAS.

5. BENJAMIN BURTON, son of William (1) Burton, m. Elizabeth (N). Benjamin was living in Bogerternorton Hundred, Somerset Co., MD, in

---

[14] Her tombstone inscription is given in Whitelaw:223. She d. 6 Dec 1772 in the 35th year of her age. Savage later m. Leah Teackle.

1723 and 1725, as revealed in the tax lists. {*Maryland Genealogical Society Bulletin* 31:1 and *Citizens of the Eastern Shore of Maryland* by Wright}

He d. leaving will dated 17 March 1728, proved 21 Aug 1728. Mentioned were son John to whom was devised 600 a., *Divell*, and 86 a., *Burtton's Chance*, adj. reserving to wife Elizabeth, 1/3 of same. Each of daus. (unnamed), personalty at age. Wife Elizabeth, extx., residue of estate. Wit: Henry Turner, Edward Franklyn, John Donelson. {MWB 19:475}

On 18 July 1730 a cattle mark was recorded for John Burton, son of Benjamin Burton. {KEDELR F6:270}

Elizabeth Burton of Somerset Co., widow of Benjamin Burton, d. leaving a will dated 1 April 1728, proved 7 Nov 1755. Mentioned were son John Burton, dau. Ann Burton, eldest dau. Agnis Burton, 3rd dau. Comfort Burton, 4th dau. Sarah Burton, youngest dau. Ester Burton. Bro.-in-law Woollsey Burton, as trustee over the children. {MWB 29:535}[15]

Benjamin and Elizabeth were parents of the following children: JOHN, d. intestate and without heirs; ANN; AGNIS; COMFORT; SARAH; ESTER.

6. JOSEPH BURTON, son of William (1) Burton, m. Elizabeth Burton, dau. of Robert Burton. {See The Robert Burton Family following this section.}

John Barker of Sussex Co. on 8 Feb 1686 conveyed a tract unto William Burton of Accomack Co. VA, gent., and he by his will did bequeath the tract unto his son Joseph Burton of Sussex Co. and the tract descended by heirship unto William Burton of Sussex Co., yeoman, he being the eldest son of the afsd. Joseph Burton, and he on 3 Dec 1734 conveyed the tract unto William Prettyman of Sussex Co., 140 a. {SUDELR I:141}

Joseph d. leaving a will dated 19 Nov 1719, proved 25 Feb 1719/20, proved 19 Feb 1719/20. Heirs: wife Elizabeth; sons William, Cornelius and youngest son Jacob; and dau. Ann Catherine. Execs., wife Elizabeth and bro. Woolsey. Wits., Phil. Askie, Paul Waples, Frances Bagnell. {Arch. A61:202. Reg. of Wills, A:124-126}

On 5 Nov 1766 Isaac Prettyman of Sussex Co., yeoman, for £30 sold to Joshua Richard of same place, cooper, a tract of land, whereas there is a tract of land called *Cheet* on n. side of Indian River in Indian River Hundred between *Stevens Creek* and Southerns Creek granted by order of Sussex Court and laid out 23 April 1684 for 775 a. and confirmed by patent under Thomas Loyd, James Claypool and Robert Turner, commissioners of property for PA bearing date 3 Nov 1684 unto Thomas Welborne of Accomack co. VA, and Thomas Welborne did by his letter of atty to his loveing friend William Clark bareing date 25 Jan 1685 as per deed bearing date 8 Feb 1686 the said Welborne did convey the tract unto John Barker of Sussex Co., and he on 8 Feb 1686 did convey the tract unto William Burton of Accomack Co., VA, gent., and he by his will did bequeath the tract unto his son Joseph Burton of Sussex Co. and the tract descended unto William Burton of Sussex Co., yeoman, being the eldest son of Joseph Burton, and he on 3 Dec 1734 did convey the tract unto William

---

[15] John is listed as a taxable living with John Nock in Bogerternorton Hundred in 1730, 1731, 1733 and 1734. Noting that the estate of Benjamin Burton was administered by John Nock and his wife Elizabeth suggests that Benjamin's widow had married John Nock. {Maryland Admin. Accts (SO Co.) 10:58, 10 Oct 1729}

Prettyman, and he obtained a warrant of resurvey bearing date 28 Jan 1735, and found it to contain 1750 a. then called *Honesty*, and William Prettyman by his will bearing date 20 Feb 1743 bequeathed unto his son the afsd. Isaac Prettyman part of the tract ... 30 a. {KEDELR K:230}

Reference is made to Willm. Prettimon who m. Elizabeth Burton, widow and extx. of Joseph Burton, dec'd. {Sussex Co. Orphans Court, 3 March 1733, pp. 58}

Joseph was father of the following children: WILLIAM; CORNELIUS; JACOB; ANN CATHERINE.

7. STRATTON BURTON, son of William (1) Burton, m. Rebecca (N).

On 10 Sep 1725 Straton Burton with wife Rebecca Burton sold 170 a. to Charles Rackliffe, purchased of William Fassitt, called *Goshen*. {Dryden Worcester Land:268}

Stratton was father of the following children {B}: LEEZE; CALEB; ABNER.

8. WOOLSEY BURTON, son of William (1) Burton, m. Ann Burton, step-dau. of Robert Burton.

On 7 Nov 1758 Jacob Burton of *Long Neck*, Sussex Co., house carpenter, for £15.10 sold to Patience Burton of same co., a tract of land between the Indian River and Rehoboth Bay in *Long Neck* adj. the afsd. Jacob Burton and Joseph Burton, dec'd., 1 1/4 a. part of the pattent called *Long Neck* granted to William Burton of Accomack Co., VA, which was bequeathed to Woolsey Burton and thence to John Burton of same co., and he did sell unto the afsd. Jacob Burton and Joseph Burton the tract of land. {SUDELR I:187}

Woolsey d. leaving a will dated 9 April 1728, proved 18 July 1730. Heirs: wife Anne; sons John, Woolsey and Benjamin; and daus. Anne, Agnes, Comfort and Patience. Extx., wife Anne. Wits., --- Cummings, Esq., Thomas Gear, Phil. Russel. {Sussex Co. Probate - Arch. A62:46-47. Reg. of wills, A:231-234} Arch. A62:46 mentions dec'd. father-in-law Robert Burton.

At Orphans Court of Sussex Co., on 4 March 1745, William Burton, son of Woolsey Burton, petitioned to choose his brother, Woolsey as his guardian. {Sussex Co. Orphans Court}

Ann's tombstone indicates she d. 23 Dec 1762, aged 69 years, 1 mo, 23 days. Woolsey's tombstone reads that he d. 21 May 1730, aged 42 years, 3 mos, 1 day. {C}

Woolsey and Ann were parents of the following children: JOHN, b. 22 Nov 1711; WOOLSEY, b. 9 March 1713/4; ANN, b. 16 April 1716; BENJAMIN, b. 28 Jan 1718; AGNES, b. 6 Oct 1721, m. (N) Hathaway {B}; COMFORT, b. 28 April 1724, ; PATIENCE, b. 24 July 1727, m. Joseph Burton {B}; WILLIAM, b. 7 Dec 1729, m. Elizabeth Cord {B}. {St. George's Episcopal Register, Indian River}

9. JACOB BURTON, son of William (1) Burton.

Stratton of Jacob Burton bapt. at St. George's Chapel, 8 Feb 1745. {St. George's Episcopal Register, Indian River}

Sarah, dau. of Jacob Burton, bapt. ca. 1746. {St. George's Episcopal Register, Indian River}

Jacob, son of Jacob and Ann Burton, b. 2 Sep 1753, bapt. 18 Nov 1753. {St. George's Episcopal Register, Indian River}

Jacob d. leaving a will dated 14 Nov 1716, proved 20 Jan 1716/7. Heirs: bros. Joseph, Stratton, Woolsey and Benjamin; niece Ann (dau. of Benjamin); and nephews William (son of Joseph) and John (son of Woolsey). Exec. bro. Woolsey. Wits., Samuel Davis, Jr., Thomas Stockley, W. White. {Sussex Co. Probate - Arch. A61:156. Reg. of Wills, A:94-95}

10. SAMUEL BURTON, son of William (1) Burton, m. Procilla Eyre, dau. of John Eyre {Whitelaw:66}.

Samuel Burton d. leaving a will dated 29 March 1728, proved 3 Dec 1728. Mentioned: wife Procilla; son John to whom was left the plantastion at Magette Bay in Northampton called *Golden Quarter*, 534 a. To son Samuel the plantation where I now live, 216 a. To son Eligals Burton, 100 a. in the woods near Gingoteague. Daus. Ann and Mary Burton. Wife and 4 of my children, Samuel, Eligals, Ann and Mary, residuary legatees. Bro. Stratton Burton to have the care of my son John and his estate until he is 21. Wife extx. Wit: Bennet Scarburgh, John Tankerd, Elizabeth Abbott, Temperance Scarburgh. {Accomack Co. Wills:272}

Samuel and Procilla were parents of the following children {B}: JOHN, m. Esther (N); SAMUEL, m. Tabitha Bailey; ELIGALS; ANN; MARY.

Third Generation

11. WILLIAM BURTON, probable son of John (3) Burton.

Hog Ridge was patented on 24 Dec 1715 by William Burton for 100 a. on the s. side of the Baltimore River. On 20 Aug 1773 William Burton sold same to his bro. Jacob Burton. {Dryden Worcester Land:308}

12. ABNER, son of Stratton (7) Burton, m. Susannah (N). They were parents of the following children: CALEB; BENJAMIN; JOHN; SARAH; COMFORT. {B}

13. JOHN BURTON, b. 22 Nov 1711, son of Woolsey (8) Burton, had a son Woolsey who m. Patience, dau. of William Bagwell.

On 6 Feb 1759 John Burton, son of Woolsey Burton, dec'd., of Sussex Co., yeoman, for £1.10 sold to his brother William Burton Junr. a tract of land part of a larger tract in *Long Neck* pattented 29 Sep 1677 adj. William Burton, Senr., 1 1/2 a. {SUDELR I:192}

On 7 Feb 1759 Woolsey Burton son of John Burton and grandson of Woolsey Burton, dec'd., yeoman, and his wife Patience, dau. of William Bagwell, dec'd., for £20 sold to William Burton, Junr., son of the afsd. Woolsey Burton, dec'd., yeoman, all of *Long Neck* in Indian River Hundred, part of tract of land in *Long Neck* as per pattent dated 29 Sep 1677 bounded by 1 1/2 a. William Burton, Junr., afsd. purchased of his brother John Burton, lands of William Burton Senr, William Bagwell, dec'd., Jacob Burton and John Burton Senr., 20 a. {SUDELR I:195}

14. WOOLSEY BURTON, son of Woolsey (8) Burton, b. 9 March 1713/4, m. Elizabeth Burton, dau. of William Burton. They were parents of the following children {B}: JOHN STRATTON; WILLIAM; WOOLSEY; ELIZABETH; ANN.

15. BENJAMIN BURTON, son of Woolsey (8) Burton, b. 28 Jan 1718, d. 5

Nov 1783, m. Hester (N), sister of Hezekiah Cord.

Hester is mentioned in the will of her bro. Hezekiah Cord in his will dated 16 April 1767, proved 4 June 1767. {Sussex Co. Wills - Arch. A66:179-180. Reg. of Wills, B:321-323} Arch. A66:179 mentions dec'd. father, Thomas Bagwell as husband of Ann and Benjamin Burton as husband Joseph Cord and dec'd. bro. John; page 180 shows William Burton as husband of Elizabeth of Hester.

Daniel, son of Benjamin and Hester Burton, b. 9 Sep 1768, bapt. 10 Oct. {St. George's Episcopal Register, Indian River}

Benjamin and Hester were parents of the following children {St. George's Episcopal Register, Indian River}: WOOLSEY, b. 4 April 1751, m. Molly Walton {B}; BENJAMIN, b. 10 Aug 1753; JOSEPH, b. 12 Sep 1755, d. 3 Oc t 1785; LYDIA, b. 2 June 1757; LEAH, b. 4 Feb 1759; BENJAMIN, b. 29 Sep 1760; JOHN, b. 19 April 1762; ELIZABETH, b. 17 Feb 1764; WILLIAM, b. 28 Jan 1766, m. Cornelia Steveson {B}; DANIEL, b. 9 Sep 1768, d. 1809, m. Arcadia Milby {B}; HESTER, b. 1770, m. (N) Hopkins {B}.

16. JOHN BURTON, son of Samuel (10) Burton, m. Esther Harmonson, dau. of Thomas Harmonson III. They had a son John. Esther m. 2nd John Respess. {Whitelaw: 66, 209}

16. SAMUEL BURTON, son of Samuel (10) Burton, m. Tabitha Bayley.

Samuel Burton d. leaving a will dated 7 Jan 1750/51, proved 29 Jan 1750/51. Mentioned: son John, wife and 3 children Ann, John and Priscilla residuary legatees. Friend Edmund Bayley, exec. Wit: William Gray, George Abbott, John Sturgis. Tabitha Burton, widow of the testator. {Accomack Co. Wills:157}

Tabitha Burton, wife of Samuel Burton, was mentioned as dau. in the will of Edmund Bayley, written 13 Jan1750/51, proved 26 March 1751. {Accomack Co. Wills:186}

Samuel and Tabitha were parents of the following children {B}: ANN; JOHN, m. Annabella White; PRISCILLA.

17. JOHN STRATTON BURTON, son of Woolsey (14) and Elizabeth Burton, m. Sarah Parker. They were parents of the following children: JOHN; ISAIAH; WOOLSEY; ELI; LYDIA; LEAH. {B}

18. JOSEPH BURTON, son of Benjamin (15) Burton, m. Elizabeth Bagwell {B}.

Mary, dau. of Joseph and Elizabeth Burton, b. 10 March 1768, bapt. 5 June. {St. George's Episcopal Register, Indian River}

Elizabeth, dau. of Joseph and Elizabeth Burton, b. 27 Feb 1774. {St. George's Episcopal Register, Indian River}

19. JOHN BURTON, son of John Stratton (17) Burton, m. Rachel Burton, dau. of William and Rachel (Russell) Burton. They were parents of the following children: CORNELIUS, b. 1773, d. 1813; WILLIAM, b. 1784; ROBERT, d, 1854; JOSEPH, b. 1789, d. 1842; GEORGE LEWIS, b. 1790; MOLLY; JEHU, b. 1795, d. 1878. {B}

20. ISAIAH BURTON, son of John Stratton (17) Burton, d. 15 March 1840, m. 20 Feb 1791, Cornelia (b. 17 Nov 1770, d. 5 Jan 1830), dau. of William Burton

and granddau. of Woolsey Burton. {A} They were parents of the following children: MARIA, b. 15 Feb 1792, bapt. d. Oct 1853. {St. George's Episcopal Register, Indian River}; GIDEON, b. 16 Dec 1793, a sailor who d. on board his vesssel, 6 March 1833; DEBORAH, b. 15 March 1795, m. John Burton; ADAN C., b. 3 Sep 1797; LYDIA, b. 11 Oct 1798, d. age 70; BENJAMIN, b. 18 June 1800; CORNELIA, b. 25 June 1802, d. 10 Nov 1835, m. Azel Dodd; ELHANAN, b. 17 Sep 1804, buried at sea, 1841; PATIENCE, b. 6 Nov 1806, d. 9 Sep 1807; JOHN, b. 24 Feb 1809, d. March 1809; JAMES F., b. 27 June 1810; ADELAIDE JANE, b. 7 Aug 1814. {A; St. George's Episcopal Register, Indian River}

THE ROBERT BURTON FAMILY

1. ROBERT BURTON, formerly called Robert Spencer,[16] yeoman, arrived in Virginia prior to 18 Dec 1665.

Reference {A} notes that on 18 Dec 1665 a certificate was issued to John Davis for the transportation to Accomack County, Virginia, of 14 persons, one of whom was Robert Spencer. The name Robert Burton appears first appears on the Accomack County records on 16 Dec 1676 when he was appointed guardian of John Truit. {Accomack County Records, vol. i:107}

Robert Burton first purchased land in Sussex County, DE, in 1693. {SUDELR A:142, 158, 159} He served as one of Sussex County's members of the Provincial Council in 1700. {A}

Robert m. 1st on 11 Feb 1676/7 Catherine Cotton. {A} He m. 2nd Mrs. Comfort (Bagwell) Leatherbury, widow of Peter Leatherbury, and dau. of Thomas and Ann Bagwell.{A}[17]

Perry Leatherbury d. by 3 Sep 1717 when Robert Burton, his father in law of Sussex Co. upon Delaware, as greatest creditor, was appointed admin. of his estate with consent of Edmund Leatherbury, brother of said Perry. William Burton and Samuel Welburne, securites. {Accomack Co. Court orders:1}

Robert Burton d. in Sussex Co., leaving a will dated 16 Sep 1724,

---

16 [16] In the Accomack County Records, vol. vi:84 was recorded on 29 Jan 1677/8 the following: "These are to certifie ... that whereas I the subscriber have formerly gone under the name of Robert Spencer from my infancy and now being better Informed out of England by letters from my Relations my true and right name is Robert Burton ... "

[17] Reference {A} establishes the identity of Robert's wife Comfort from three sources: (1) On 3 Sep 1717 Robert Burton of Sussex Co. petitioned the Court fo administration of the estate of his son-in-law [meaning step-son] Perry Leatherbury; (2) The Will of Perry Leatherbury dated 1708/9, proved 5 April 1709 in Accomack Co., mentioned several sons including son Perry and also mentioned wife Comfort; (3) The Will Thomas Bagwell, dated 15 Apr 1690, proved 16 Sep 1690 in Accomack Co., mentioned dau. Comfort Leatherbury (also mentioned William Burton's Branch and appoined Capt. Wm. Burton and Wm. Parker as overseers of his children).

proved 16 Oct 1725. Heirs: wife Comfort; son William; daus. Sarah, Anne and Patience Burton, Elizabeth Prettyman (wife of William Prettyman), and Comfort Walker; grandchildren Robert, Joseph, Samuel, Catherine, Elizabeth, Comfort and Sarah children of Robert Burton, dec'd.), Joseph and William (sons of Joseph Burton), Thomas Bagwell (son of Francis), Robert Prettyman (son of Robert Prettyman), Catherine, Cornelius, Jacob and Joseph (children of dau. Elizabeth Prettyman by her former husband Joseph Burton), nine children [unnamed] of dau. Mary Waples, dec'd. (wife of William Waples), two children [unnamed] of dau. Comfort Walker by her first husband Thomas Prettyman; Elenor Letherberry. Execs., wife Comfort and daus. Anne Burton, Sarah Prettyman and Patience Burton. Wits., Thomas Leatherbury, Job Barker, Oliver Stockley. Overseers: John Rhods and Richard Henman. {Arch. A61:241-242. Reg. of Wills, A:187-190}

On 1 Aug 1763 Paull Waples and his son William Waples, Comfort Burton, widow and relict of Joshua Burton, now dec'd., Baker Wharton and his wife Betty all of Worcester Co., MD, and now deemed southern Sussex Co. PA for £155 sold to Burton Waples of Sussex Co., blacksmith, 408 1/2 a. part of 3 tracts of land on Ivy Branch of Middle Creek of Rehoboth Bay, conveyed to Robert Burton, Senr., in 1715, and he did by his will bearing date 16 Sep 1724 bequeath the tract unto his wife Comfort and 3 daus. Sarah, Ann and Patience, and whereas Comfort Prettyman and her 2 children Thomas Prettyman and Elizabeth Prettyman became invested in the right by the will of Robert Burton, dec'd., who was father to afsd. Comfort Prettyman and grandfather to her 2 children, and whereas Paul Waples having purchased all the right of a certain Thomas Walker and his wife Comfort, dau. of afsd. Robert Burton, dec'd., and afsd. Thomas and Elizabeth Prettyman and afsd. 2 sisters Sarah and Ann together with Paull Waples by joint consent did divide the 1100 a. unto 3 divisions, and 408 1/2 a. fell to Paull Waples and his wife Patience. {KEDELR K:22}

On 7 Aug 1765 William Burton of Sussex Co., yeoman and Elizabeth, his wife for £400 sold to Absalom Littell of same co., a parcel of land in Broadkill Hundred on n. side of Broadkill Creek or Great Creek called *Swan Point*, part of a larger tract. Robert Burton, being seized of the 150 a. dec'd., leaving the same to his several heirs, viz, William Burton of Summerset Co. who purchased all the property of the other several heirs (Woolsey Burton and Ann his wife, Sarah Pretyman, widow, William Waples, William Preteman and Elizabeth his wife, Thomas Walker and Comfort his wife, Paul Waples and Patience his wife) for £25 as in quit claim bearing date 8 Sep 1729, and the said William Burton of Summerset co. at his decease by his will demised the lands to his grandson Ebenezar Burton, son of Richard Burton who dec'd. without issue leaveing said lands to his several brothers and sisters, which after being examined was judged not to bear division and tract was sold to highest bidder of said heirs and conveyed to Purnal Johnson who was then husband to Sarah, the dau. of Richard Burton afsd, Purnal Johnson did convey the same unto William Burton of Sussex Co., son of said Richard Burton and party to these presents which 2 pieces of land containeth 200 a. bounded as by a survey made by Purnal Johnson adj. Isaac Jones fence, Broadkill Creek, Bryant Rowls and Helmanas Wheelbanck ... resurvey containeth 360 a. {KEDELR K:183}

Robert was father of the following children: WILLIAM; JOSEPH, had sons Joseph and William; SARAH; ANNE (step-dau.?),[18] m. Woolsey Burton; PATIENCE (step-dau.?), m. Paul Waples; ELIZABETH, m. 1st Joseph Burton (by whom she had Catherine, Cornelius, Jacob and Joseph) and m. 2nd William Prettyman; COMFORT (step-dau.), m. 1st Thomas Prettyman (by whom she had two children), m. 2nd (N) Walker and m. 3rd Reese Woolf; ROBERT (father of Robert, Joseph, Samuel, Catherine, Elizabeth, Comfort and Sarah); MARY, m. William Waples and had 9 children; CATHERINE, m. Francis Bagwell; FRANCIS {B}.

Second Generation

2. WILLIAM BURTON, b. 19 Nov 1677 in Accomack Co., VA, son of Robert (1) Burton, m. Frances Bagwell.

William was living in Baltimore Hundred, Somerset Co., 1730-1740. {Somerset Co. Tax Lists, 1730-40}

William Burton d. leaving a will proved 1 Feb 1744/5. Mentioned were six children: Richard, John, Joshua, Catharine and Elizabeth Burton, and Sarah Ingram to whom were left the profits and ground rents of land called *Worwick*, which was laid out for a town. Wife Francis received use of the dwelling plantation and the island, and use of all the slaves. Grandson Robert, son of William, 1/2 of *Hopewell* on north side of Indian River; if he dies to his brother John Russell Burton. Grandson John Russell Burton to have 50 a. of *Conclusion* and part of tract *Folly*. Grandau. Elizabeth Burton, dau. of William Burton, other half part of a slave. Son Richard as devised use of plantation where he dwelled of 405 a. and use of 200 a. on the north side of the head of Broad Kill Creek. Grandson William Burton, son of Richard Burton, was devised the plantation whereon his father then dwelled, 405 a. after the death of his father and mother. To grandson Ebenezer Burton, son of Richard Burton, 200 a., in Sussex Co., and on north side of head of Broadkill Creek. To son John Burton, plantation where testator lived, 400 a. called *Brooked Project*, a mill on Swan Creek and 150 a. thereunto. Dau. Catharine Morris to have use of the land where she and her husband dwelled, 340 a. called *Chance*; also slaves. Grandsons, sons of dau. Catharine: William, John and Joshua Morris, to have plantation where their father and mother dwelled, at the death of their mother. Dau. Elizabeth Burton was devised land purchased of Abraham Ingram, 400 a. To grandson Woollsey Burton, son of dau. Elizabeth, land bought of Abraham Ingram, 400 a. To dau. Sarah Ingram, land on n. side of Sheep Pen Branch called *Rich Island* and 150 a. whereon they dwelled, being the n. part of tract *Conclusion*. {MWB 24:37}

Francess Burton, Worcester Co., widow, d. leaving a will dated 25 Feb 1750, proved 23 March 1750. Mentioned were children Richard, Catharine Morris, Elizabeth Burton, and Sarah Ingram. To grandchildren: Elizabeth Burton, Robert Burton, Wm. Burton, John Russell Burton, children of eldest son William, dec.; Elizabeth Hall, Sarah Burton, Francess Burton, Ann Burton, John

---

[18] Reference {A} offers the convincing argument that Comfort Walker, Patience Waples and Ann Burton were daughters of Comfort by her husband Perry Leatherbury, noting that he (Perry Leatherbury) mentioned the names of daughters Comfort, Patience and Ann in his will. Thus it appears that they were the step-daus. of Robert Burton

Burton, Tabitha Burton, children of son Richard Burton; Ann Robertson, Elizabeth Morris, Joseph Morris, children of dau. Cathrine Morris; John Stratton Burton, Elizabeth Burton, Wm. Burton and Ann Burton, children of dau. Elizabeth Burton; Joshua Burton, John Burton, Sarah Burton and Wm. Burton, children of son John Burton; Ann Burton, Wm. Burton, children of son Joshua Burton; Ann Ingram, Wm. Ingram, Joshua Ingram. {MWB 28:139}

According to a Sussex County deed William Burton of Worcester Co., MD, by his last will desired be paid to his 6 children on lots laid out in town he called *Warwick*. His children were Richard; Elizabeth Prettyman; Catharine Morris; and three others. Richard Burton, son of William d. before he was able to convey a lot to Henry Draper. The conveyance was done by his execs. Elizabeth Burton and Job Ingram. {SUDELR}

On 5 Sep 1756 Elizabeth Burton and Job Ingram execs. of the will of Richard Burton late of Sussex Co., dec'd., for £20 paid before the decease of the said Richard Burton sold to Henry Draper of same co., shipwright, part of the tract of land on n. side of Indian River called *Warwick* which did formerly belong to a certain William Burton late of Worcester co. MD and part of which tract the same William caused to be laid out in lotts of a town which he named *Warwick* under the yearly rent of 6 shillings 8 pence each lott to be paid by the possessors on 1 Jan yearly as quitrent, and William Burton by his will gave the ground rents of the afsd. lotts to be equally divided amongst his 6 children, Richard Burton, John Burton, Joshua Burton, Catharine wife of John Morris, Sarah wife of Job Ingram and Elizabeth wife of Woolsey Burton, and Richard Burton in his life time bound himself unto the afsd. Henry Draper to convey 10 a. of *Warwick* but died without complying. {KEDELR I:119}

William and Frances were parents of the following children {St. George's Episcopal Register, Indian River}: CATHERINE, b. 12 Nov 1705, bapt. 6 April 1708, m. John Morris; WILLIAM, b. 24 Feb 1702/3,[19] bapt. 6 April 1708; RICHARD, b. 31 Jan 1708, bapt. 12 May 1709; JOHN, b. 21 July 1713, bapt. 30 July 1714; JOSHUA, b. 31 May 1716, bapt. 16 Oct 1719; ELIZABETH, b. 29 Nov 1717, bapt. 16 Oct 1719, m. (N) Prettyman and m. 2nd Woolsey Burton; SARAH m. Job Ingram; ANN, b. 11 Feb 1721, bapt. 18 March 1721, probably d. young.

3. SARAH BURTON, dau. of Robert (1) Burton, m. 1st Anderson Parker, m. 2nd (N) Lacey; m. 3rd Perry Leatherbury; m. 4th Robert Prettyman. Sarah and Robert Prettyman were parents of the following children: SARAH; WILLIAM; ANN; CATHERINE.

4. ROBERT BURTON, Jr., yeoman, son of Robert (1) Burton, m. Catharine (N).

He d. leaving a will dated 25 April 1725, proved 28 May 1724. Heirs: wife Catharine; sons William, Samuel, Robert and Joseph; daus. Catharine, Elizabeth, Comfort and Sarah. Execs., wife Catharine and son William. Wits., Samuel David, William Burton, Danet Penoyre. {Arch. A61:243. Reg. of Wills, A:184-

---

19 Reference {A} noting that the register omitted the year of the birth date and that the parents were m. at the end of Dec 1700 and since both parents' Wills listed William ahead of Catherine this birth date was suggested.

186} Robert owned land in Angola Neck on the Indian River and 100 a. tract called *Privilege* in Somerset Co., MD, for which a certificate was issued to him in 1718. {A}

Robert was father of the following children: WILLIAM; ROBERT; JOSEPH; SAMUEL; CATHERINE; ELIZABETH; COMFORT; SARAH.

5. COMFORT BURTON, probable step-dau. of Robert (1) Burton, m. 1st Thomas Prettyman, m. 2nd (N) Walker and m. 3rd Reese Wolf.

On 3 Aug 1762 Reese Woolf of Sussex Co., yeoman, and Comfort his wife, a dau. of Robert Burton, late of same co. dec'd., for love and affection and 5 shillings give unto Thomas Prettyman of same co., son of ye afsd. Comfort, all their right unto any lands within Indian River Hundred. {SUDELR I:389}

On 1 March 1765 Thomas Prettyman of Worcester Co., MD, for £10 sold to Burton Waples of Sussex Co., a tract of land, whereas a certain Robert Burton of Sussex Co. dec'd. by his will bearing date 16 Sep 1724 did direct a 1100 a. tract of land in Indian River Hundred to be divided in 7 equal parts and one of those parts he devised 1/2 to his dau. Comfort Walker and the other 1/2 he gave to his said daughter's 2 children which she had by a former husband, and Comfort intermarried with a certain Reese Woolf and the said Reese Woolf and Comfort his wife on 3 Aug 1762 did give to Thomas Prettyman afsd. who is one of said Comfort's children all their right unto the afsd. land whereof the same Thomas Prettyman became intitualed to 3/4 of the 1/7 part of the whole tract. Wit: William Burton, Stockley Waples. {KEDELR K:141}

Comfort by her first husband Thomas Prettyman had two children: THOMAS; ELIZABETH.

6. ELIZABETH BURTON, dau. of Robert (1) Burton, m. 1st Joseph Burton, son of William and Ann (Stratton) Burton (by whom she had children, CATHERINE, CORNELIUS, JACOB and JOSEPH and m. 2nd William Prettyman by whom she had ELIZABETH who m. Samuel Coulter.

On 8 Aug 1765 Elizabeth Coulter, widow, late of Sussex Co., granddau. to Robert Burton, ye elder dec'd. for £3.6.8 sold to Burton Wapels of same co., blacksmith, part of 1100 a. tract of land in Indian River Hundred which the afsd. Robert Burton did by his will bearing date 16 Sep 1724 devise to be divided among his several heirs, the afsd. Elizabeth Coulter then Elizabeth Preteman by virtue of the will hath good right to part of the 1100 a. Wit: John Clowes Junr, James Coulter. {KEDELR K:176}

7. ANN BURTON, step-dau. of Robert (1) Burton, m. 1st Woolsey Burton, son of William and Ann (Stratton) Burton and m. 2nd (N) Plasket. {A}

On 8 Aug 1734 Ann Burton, widow and relict of Woolsey Burton, late of Sussex co. dec'd. was firmly bound unto Paul Waples of Summerset Co., MD, yeoman, in the sum of £24, the condition of this obligation was such that if the said Ann Burton, dau. of Robert Burton, late of same co. dec'd. doth no manner of way lay any right unto a certain 408 1/2 a. parcel of land part of a 1117 a. belonging unto said Robert Burton, and on ye contrary suffer said Paul Waples to have quiet and peaceable possession of said land, then this obligation to be void. {KEDELR K:24}

On 8 Aug 1734 Anne Burton, widow and relict of Woolsey Burton, late of Sussex Co. dec'd. was firmly bound unto Anderson Parker of Sussex Co., yeoman, in the sum of £24, the condition was such that if Ann Burton, widow and dau. of Robert Burton, late of same co. dec'd., suffered Anderson Parker to have quiet and peaceable possession of a 300 a. tract of land, then this obligation to be void. {KEDELR K:50}

Ann and Woolsey were parents of the following children: WOOLSEY; JOHN; ANN; BENJAMIN; AGNES; COMFORT; PATIENCE; WILLIAM.

8. PATIENCE BURTON, step-dau. of Robert (1) Burton, m. Paul Waples. Paul and Patience(?) were parents of WILLIAM.

On 8 Aug 1734 Paul Waples of Summerset Co., MD, yeoman, was firmly bound unto Anderson Parker of Sussex Co., yeoman, in the sum of £24; the condition of this obligation is such that if Paul Waples, whose former wife was dau. of Robert Burton, late of Sussex Co., dec'd., suffered the said Anderson Parker to have quiet and peaceable possession unto a 300 a. parcel of land part of 117 a. tract belonging unto afsd. Robert Burton on s. side of Ivy Branch, then this obligation to be void. {KEDELR K:49}

9. CATHERINE BURTON, dau. of Robert (1) Burton, m. Frances Bagwell, son of Francis and Catherine Bagwell. {A}

10. SARAH BURTON, dau. of Robert (1) Burton, m. 1st (N) Lacey, m. 2nd Robert Prettyman, m. 3rd Perry Leatherbury, m. 4th Anderson Parker. {A, B}

Robert Prettyman d. leaving a will dated 13 July 1721, proved 1 Aug 1721. He named his wife Sarah, extx. and his son-in-law and dau.-in-law Robert and Elizabeth Lacey, son William and daus. Sarah, Catherine and Ann, under age. {A}

On 16 Dec 1731 Anderson Parker and his wife, Sarah, late wife of Robert Prittyman, cordwainer, dec'd., of Sussex Co., DE, gave to Sarah's son, Robert Prittyman, 300 a. on Ivey Branch of Middle Creek in Indian River Hundred, part of 1117 a., belonging to Robert Burton, dec'd., father of Sarah. {KEDELR F6:420}

Robert and Sarah were parents of the following children {B}: SARAH; WILLIAM; ANN; CATHERINE; ROBERT.

11. MARY BURTON, dau. of Robert (1) Burton, m. William Waples, son of Peter Waples. The will of Robert (1) Burton refers to the nine children of dau. Mary. Among those children were Peter Waples, Paul Waples who m. Temperance Derrickson, Thomas Waples, Burton Waples, Elizabeth (Waples) Carey, and Mary (Waples) Derrickson. {A}

Third Generation

12. CATHERINE BURTON, dau. of William (2) Burton, b. 12 Nov 1705, bapt. 6 April 1708, m. John Morris. They were parents of the following children: WILLIAM; JOHN; JOSHUA; ANN, m. (N) Robertson; ELIZABETH; JOSEPH. {See will of William (2).}

13. WILLIAM BURTON, son of William (2) Burton, b. 24 Feb 1702/3, m. Rachel Russell who later m. John Marriner, son of Thomas Marriner, as revealed in the following record of the Orphans Court at Lewis Town, 6 March 1738/9. It was recorded that John Marriner who m. Rachel Burton, widow and

relict of Willm. Burton, charged themselves with the amount of the dec'd. William Burton's inventory (appraised at £73.11.0). After the widow's third it was "dividable among the dec'd..'s heirs, in number Four, the eldest son to have two shares."

At a Orphans Court on 12 March 1749 John Burton, late of Worcester Co., MD, was by the court appointed guardian to the children of William Burton, dec., viz., Robert, William, John and Elizabeth.

William was father of the following children: ROBERT, b. 25 April 1730; WILLIAM; JOHN RUSSELL, d. by 12 March 1749; ELIZABETH. {All named in the will of their Burton grandparents}

14. ROBERT BURTON, probable son of William (2) Burton, m. Ann Dobson, dau. of Richard Dobson.

On 2 March 1756 Robert Burton of Indian River, Sussex Co. and Ann his wife for £30 sold to Robert West of same co., cordwainer, a 60 a. tract of land in Broadkill Hundred, part of a larger tract which a certain Richard Dobson, dec'd., was possessed of who died intestate whereupon the land was divided amonst his children, the 60 a. was laid off to the said Ann being one of the daus. of the said Richard Dobson, on the n.w. part of a tract which Robert Burton and Ann his wife conveyed to Alexr. McCullah, dec'd., adj. other lands of the said Mccullah and William Robinson. {SUDELR I:131}

From Bible presented to St. Peter's Parish, Lewes, DE, by Hon. H. R. Burton, M.D. Date of Bible 1761.
Family of Robert Burton b. 25 April 1730.
Robert Burton m. Ann his wife by Anderson Parker, 19 Dec 1751.
They were parents of the following children: SARAH, b. 5 Nov 1752, d. 23 June 1755; ROBERT, b. 24 June 1756; JOHN, b. 12 Oct 1759; ANN, b. 15 April 1762; JOSHUA, b. 4 Nov 1764; WILLIAM, b. 8 April 1767; MARY, b. 26 Oct 1771, d. 4 July 1864. Robert, Senr. d. 30 March 1785. Ann his wife d. 15 March 1790.

Sarah, dau. of Robert and Anne Burton, b. 1 Nov 1752, bapt. 18 Nov 1753. {St. George's Episcopal Register, Indian River} Mary, dau. of Robert Burton and Ann his wife, b. 26 Oct 1771, bapt. 29 March following. {St. George's Episcopal Register, Indian River}

15. RICHARD BURTON, son of William (2) Burton, b. 31 Jan 1708, bapt. 12 May 1709, m. Elizabeth Ingram.

Richard d. leaving a will proved 3 Feb 1753. Mentioned were wife Elizabeth and brother in law, Job Ingram of Worcester Co., MD, execs.; sons: William (eldest), son Ebenezer; youngest sons John and Robert, dau. Sarah; youngest daus., Frances, Ann and Tabitha; dau. Elizabeth, wife of Thomas Hall of KE Co. {Sussex Co. Probate A61:240. Reg. of Wills, B:48}

On 4 Sep 1759 William Burton, son of Richard Burton, dec'd.. and Thomas Hall and Elizabeth his wife all of Sussex Co. for £25 quit claim unto Purnel Johnson of same place yeoman ... all their right in a tract of land in Broadkill Hundred originally pattented to a certain Bryan Rolls and called *Swan Point*. {I:SUDELR 224}

On 7 Feb 1764 William Burton, Junr. of Sussex Co., yeoman, for £900 sold to Purnal Johnson of same co., yeoman, 405 a. of land and marsh adj. Coolspring Creek in Broadkill Hundred being the same whereon the said Purnal

Johnson dwelled. Synopsis of Title: William Piles, dec'd., who was the patentee by his will devised the 405 a. to his 3 sons, viz., William, Isaac and Joseph, the 2 first dying intestate and without issue, the same descended to Joseph who conveyed the same to a certain William Burton who by his will devised the same to his grandson William Burton, son of Richard Burton which said William Burton is the granter afsd. {KEDELR K:51}

William (2) Burton in his will devised to his grandson William Burton, son of Richard Burton, part of a tract which William, Jr., conveyed on 7 Feb 1764 to Purnal Johnson. Reference is made to Ann, widow of William Burton. {Sussex Co. Land Records}

Richard was father of the following children {mentioned in the wills of the grandparents, William and Frances Burton and the will of their father}: WILLIAM (eldest son); EBENEZER; ELIZABETH, m. Thomas Hall; SARAH, m. Purnal Johnson; FRANCESS; ANN; JOHN; TABITHA; ROBERT.

16. JOHN BURTON, son of William (2) Burton, b. 21 July 1713, bapt. 30 July 1714, probably m. Elizabeth (N).

The tax lists of Somerset Co., MD, show that John was living with his father, 1730-1738, in Baltimore Hundred. jIn 1739 and 1740 he was head of household nearby. {See *Tax Lists of Somerset County*, 1730-1740 by Jean Russo.}

On 1 May 1749 John Burton with wife Elizabeth Burton, Joshua Burton with wife Comfort Burton sold *Green Swamp* to Uriah Brookfield. {Dryden Worcester Land:275}

John Burton d. leaving a will dated 18 Jan 1750, proved 27 Feb 1750. Heirs: sons Joshua, John and William; dau. Sarah. Exec. bro. Joshua. Wits., Job Ingram, William Burton, John Russel Burton. Guardian, bro. Joshua. {Arch. A61:177-178. Reg. of Wills, A:428-429}

On 8 Feb 1758 Temperance Waples of Sussex Co., widow, for £26.10 sold to Joshua Burton, John Burton, William Burton and Sarah Burton, heirs of John Burton, late of same co., dec'd., a tract of land in Indian River Hundred 129 a. part of a larger tract called *Silent Grove*. If Temperance Waples shall pay unto the said Joshua Burton, John Burton, William Burton and Sarah Burton for £26.10 on or before 1 Feb next ensuing with lawfull interest, then this present indenture shall cease. {SUDELR I:162}

John was father of the following children {mentioned in the wills of the grandparents, William and Frances Burton}: JOSHUA; JOHN; SARAH; WILLIAM.

17. JOSHUA BURTON, son of William (2), b. 31 May 1716, bapt. 16 Oct 1719, m. Comfort (N).

Reference was made to Comfort Burton, widow, in a deed of 3 May 1726. {F6:286}

On 3 Aug 1727 Comfort Burton gave to her son Thomas Leatherbury, yeoman, of Sussex Co., 315 a. {F6:268}

Patience of Joshua Burton bapt. ca. 12 April 1747. {St. George's Episcopal Register, Indian River}

Jacob, son of Joshua Burton and Comfort, b. 21 July 1751. {St. George's Episcopal Register, Indian River}

Joshua Burton d. intestate possessed of 217 a. in Indian River Hundred, Sussex Co., the original grant made to William Kanning 11 April 1682; the land was sold to William Burton on 17 Aug 1705. William devised the land in his

Will to his son Joshua Burton.

On 3- April 1768 John Wingate and Ann, his wife, of Worcester Co., MD for £40 quit claim unto Thomas Robinson and Peter Robinson, both of Sussex Co., merchants, all their right to a tract of land that Joshua Burton, died intestate of in Indian River Hundred supposed to contain 217 a.; Luke Watson, High Sheriff, sold the same to the said William Burton, 217 a., and the said William Burton by his will devised the residuary part of his real estate unto the afsd. Joshua Burton, and the said Joshua Burton haveing died intestate and left issue, viz., Burton [sic], Jacob Burton, Ann, wife of the afsd. John Wingate and Sarah Burton. {KEDELR K:323}

In 1744 William Burton conveyed the tract *Ackequesanne* to son Joshua Burton. On 15 April 1761 Joshua Burton with wife Comfort Burton sold 100 a. of said tract to William Holland. {Dryden Worcester Land}

Joshua Burton d. intestate leaving the following issue: William, Jacob; Ann, m. John Wingate; Sarah. The land was released by William Burton of Worcester Co., MD, on 5 Sep 1770. {Sussex Co. Land Records}

Joshua was father of the following children {Wills of the grandparents William and Frances Burton}: ANN, m. John Wingate; WILLIAM; JACOB; SARAH; PATIENCE, probably d. prior to 5 Sep 1770.

18. ELIZABETH BURTON, dau. of William (2) Burton, b. 29 Nov 1717, bapt. 16 Oct 1719, m. (N) Prettyman and m. 2nd Woolsey Burton.

Elizabeth had the following children by Woolsey Burton {Wills of William and Frances Burton, grandparents to the following children}: WOOLSEY, d. intestate; JOHN STRATTON; ELIZABETH; WILLIAM; ANN.

William Burton, Broadkill Hundred, acquired from Elizabeth Prettyman, John Stratton Burton, William Burton, joyner, William Bagwell and Ann his wife, all of Sussex Co., for £109.4, a parcel of marsh of 91 a. that William Burton of Worcester Co., MD, d. possessed of and by his last will devised to his grandson Woolsey Burton who d. intestate, situated acknowledged 25 April 1772. {SUDELR}

19. SARAH BURTON, dau. of William (2) Burton, m. Job Ingram, and was mother of the following children {Wills of William and Frances Burton, grandparents to the following children}: ANN; WILLIAM; JOSHUA.

20. COMFORT BURTON, dau. of Robert (3) Burton, m. Thomas Prettyman. They were parents of a dau. MARGARET who m. Oliver Stockley.{B}

21. ROBERT BURTON, probable son of William (12) Burton, m. Sarah Evans, dau. of Elisha Evans. On 11 May 1776 Robert Burton with wife Sarah (dau. of Elisha Evans, dec.) sold to John Covington, 1/3 of her rights to tract *Buckingham*. {Dryden Worcester Co. Land}

On 28 May 1764 Robert Burton of Sussex Co., DE, sold to Job Ingram of Worcester Co., land left by grandfather William Burton to John Russell Burton who d. and it fell to Robert as heir, 250 a. of *Conclusion* and *Folly*.

Robert Burton, Sussex Co., bought a tract in Angola Hundred, 3 Aug 1769.

On 7 April 1779 Robert Burton, Senr., of Angola and Indian River

Hundred, yeoman, sold to his son Luke Burton, Sussex Co., a parcel in Angola Neck whereon Robert Burton dwelled, which had been devised to Robert by his father and afterwards confirmed to him by the will of his grandfather. {Sussex Co. Land Records}

The will (1781) of Robert Burton of Worcester Co., (written in Sussex Co., DE), devised to son William Burton, lands in Worcester Co.

Robert was father of the following children: LUKE; WILLIAM.

22. LUKE BURTON, probable son of above Robert (13) Burton, m. Patience (N).

Watson, son of Luke and Patience Burton, b. 11 Sep 1767, bapt. 3 April 1764. {St. George's Episcopal Register, Indian River}

Patience Hathaway, b. 23 Aug 1784, dau. of Luke Burton and Patience his wife, bapt. 10 April 1786. Angola. {St. George's Episcopal Register, Indian River}

On 28 May 1764 Robert Burton of Sussex Co. DE, sold to Job Ingram of Worcester Co., left by grandfather William Burton to John Russell Burton who died and it fell to Robert as heir, 250 a. of *Conclusion* and *Folly*. {Dryden Worcester Land:229}

23. MARGARET PRETTYMAN, dau. of Thomas and Comfort (20) Prettyman, m. Oliver Stockley and by him had the following children: ALEXANDER, JOHN, OLIVER, PRETTYMAN, ELIZABETH, JANE, SARAH. {B}

24. PRETTYMAN STOCKLEY, son of Oliver and Margaret (23) Stockley m. Ann (N). They were parents of the following children: NANCY; BETSY; JACOB; PRETTYMAN; DAVID; COMFORT; NEHEMIAH. {B}

Unplaced

On 1st da., 6th mo., 1755 AARON BURTON produced a certificate from Burlington Monthly Meeting for himself and wife. {DCMM}

Bayly Johnson d. leaving a will dated 26 March 1761, proved 26 Nov 1761. To kinsman ABNER BURTON. To Caleb Burton, son of Abner. To sister Rebecca Burton. {Accomack Co. Wills:451

AMEY BURTON d. leaving a will dated 13 Nov 1759, proved 29 Jan 1760. To Joshua Burton, enough to pay him for burying me. Son John residuary legatee. Joshua Burton, exec. Wit: John Spiers, Robert Peel, Thomas Burton. {Accomack Co. Wills:166}

BENJAMIN BURTON, m. Ann Bagwell, widow of William Bagwell. They were parents of the following children: ANN, b. 18 Sep 1744; COMFORT, b. 1 Feb 1746.{St. George's Episcopal Register, Indian River}

At Orphans Court of 21 Sep 1751 it was noted that Benjamin Burton had m. Ann Bagwell, widow of William Bagwell; they came into court and presented an account. {Sussex County Orphans Court}

BRIDGET BURTON was mentioned as grandau. in the will of Joanna Finney, written 7 Jan 1768. {Accomack Co. Wills:97}

CALEB BURTON d. by 24 Nov 1761 when Michael Burton was appointed admin. of his estate. {Accomack Co. Court:430}

CORNELIUS BURTON, son of Jno. Burton, b. 12 April 1747. {St. George's Episcopal Register, Indian River}

JACOB BURTON, Indian River, had a son Joseph, bapt. 13 June 1774. {St. George's Episcopal Register, Indian River}

JAMES BURTON m. Mary (N); resided at Indian River. Their dau. Ruth, bapt. 14 Aug 1768. {LCPC}

JOHN BURTON m. Isabell (N).

On 13 Sep 1684 Joseph [John?] Burton of Dover in Kent Co. planter and Issabella his wife sold to Henry Stevenson of Dover planter a tract of land formerly Japhet Griffins on n.e. side of Dover River formerly called St. Jones Creek buting to the land of Gabriell Jones and Christopher Jackson ... containing 100 a. ... in consideration of 3500 pounds of tobacco. {KEDELR}

On 10 Feb 1684 John Burton of Kent Co. PA and Isabell his wife for 1000 pounds of tobacco sold to Richard Michell of same co. ... [the rest is missing]. {KEDELR}

On 10 March 1684/5 John Burton of Dover River, planter, and Issabella his wife sold to John Smith of Long Island, husbandman, a tract of land named *Short Island*, n.e. side of Dover River butting to the land of Henry Stephenson, containing 100 a. adj. to said John Burton's land for the consideration £23.

On 23 Dec 1692 John Burton of Dover River, planter, and Isabelle his wife in consideration of £23 sold to John Smith of Long Island NY, husbandman, a tract of land called *Short Island* lying on the n.e. side of Dover River butting on the land of Henry Stephenson, between John Smith and James Clayton, containing 100 a. {KEDELR}

John Burton d. by 18 March 1706 when his estate was administered by Isabella Burton and John Burton. {Reg.of Wills, B:54}

JOHN BURTON was mentioned as son in law in the will of Andrew Gilchrist dated 21 Aug 1760.{Accomack Co. Wills:251}

JOHN BURTON m. Mary (N). They were parents of the following children {St. George's Episcopal Register, Indian River}: ROBERT, b. 15 Oct 1772, bapt. 17 Jan 1773; BETSEY, b. 29 Jan 17--, bapt. 23 July -- ca. 1774; ELIZABETH, b. 29 July 1775.

JOHN BURTON m. Elizabeth (N).

On 24 Nov 1679 John Burton received a warrant for 600 a., *Burton's Delight.* {KEDELR}

On 22 Jul 1701 Robert French of Kent Co. PA, merchant, for £138 sold to John Burton of same co. carpenter and Elizabeth his wife a tract of land being remainder of a greater tract of land called *Burtons Delight* adj. with land formerly sold by said John Burton to Daniell Jones, dec'd., 180 a. John Burton to pay unto Robert French the afsd. sum at one whole and entire payment at or upon 20 Dec 1705. {KEDELR D:8}

On 22 July 1701 John Burton of Kent Co. PA, carpenter, and Elizabeth his wife for £138 sold to Robert French of same co., merchant, a tract of land being the remainder part of a tract called *Burton's Delight* adj. land of Captain John Brinckloe and on the n.e. with the land formerly sold by said John Burton to Daniell Jones, dec'd., {KEDELR F:25}

John Burton d. by 2 Feb 1708 when his estate was administered by Elizabeth Glover, wife of Richard. {Reg. of Wills, B:73} Richard Glover d. leaving a will dated 25 Dec 1719, proved 13 Jan 1719; wife Elizabeth was not mentioned. {Arch. A-19:70. Reg. of Wills, D:11-12 and 17}

JOHN BURTON m. Ann Catherine (N). They were parents of PHEBE, b. 24 Feb 1753, bapt. 18 Nov 1753. {St. George's Episcopal Register, Indian River}

JOHN BURTON m. Mary (N), residing at Indian River. They were parents of the following children {LCPC}: ELIZABETH, bapt. 7 Oct 1770; JOHN, bapt. 26 May 1776.

Jesse, son of JOHN BURTON, Indian River, bapt. 6 Oct 1774. {LCPC}

JOSEPH BURTON m. Patience (N).

Joseph d. leaving a will dated 9 Dec 1756, proved 20 Dec 1757. Heir: wife Patience. Wits., Henry Draper, Benjamin Burton, James Hathaway. {Arch. A95:27. Reg. of wills, B:138-140}

MARGARET BURTON was mentioned as grandau. of Tabitha Reese in her will written 16 Aug 1773. {Accomack Co. Wills:131} Richard Savage mentioned his dau. MICHAL BURTON, written 2 May 1739. {Accomack Wills:140}

Cornelia, dau. of PATIENCE BURTON presented to baptism by William and Comfort Burton, b. Sep 177-, bapt. 13 Nov 1772. {St. George's Episcopal Register, Indian River}

REBECCA BURTON d. by 29 March 1768 when Abner Burton was appointed admin. of her estate. {Accomack Court orders:460}

ROBERT BURTON had a son Samuel. A parcel in Indian River Hundred called *Rock Hole* was surveyed to Robert Burton 30 Dec 1723, and devised by his will, dated 25 Aug 1724 to his son Samuel Burton who conveyed same on 5 Aug 1752 to Thomas Coullour and Asher Mott. {SUDELR}

William, son of ROBERT and Sarah BURTON, b. 18 Aug 1753, bapt. 18 Nov. {St. George's Episcopal Register, Indian River}

David, son of ROBERT and Elizabeth BURTON, Junr., b. 25 Nov 1773. {St. George's Episcopal Register, Indian River}

SAMUEL BURTON

Vallance, dau. of Samuel Burton, b. 18 March 1749/50, bapt. 16 April 1750. {St. George's Episcopal Register, Indian River}

William, son of Samuel and Edy Burton, b. 25 Oct 1752, bapt. 9 Dec 1753. {St. George's Episcopal Register, Indian River}

STRATTON BURTON d. by 2 Feb 1736/7 when Caleb Burton was appointed admin. of his estate. {Accomack Co. Court orders:203}

STRATTON BURTON m. Mary West 2 Aug 1773. {LCPC} Mary Burton, wife of Stratton Burton, formerly West, buried at Indian River 20 April 1778. {LCPC} Richard Armitrader d. leaving a will dated 13 March 1762. Mentioned was his dau. SUSANNA BURTON. {Accomac Co. Wills:148}

WILLIAM BURTON m. Elizabeth (N). They were parents of Ann Cord, b. 15 Jan 1769. {St. George's Episcopal Register, Indian River}

WILLIAM BURTON m. Rachel (N). They were parents of the following children {St. George's Episcopal Register, Indian River}: SARAH, b. 31 Aug 1772, bapt. 7 Feb 1773; WILLIAM, b. 17 April 1776.

WILLIAM BURTON had a son WILLIAM, William, bapt. ca. 13 July 1746. {St. George's Episcopal Register, Indian River}

WILLIAM BURTON m. Bethsheba (N). They were parents of POLLY, b. 2(?) Dec 1768, bapt. 24 March. {St. George's Episcopal Register, Indian River}

WILLIAM BURTON had a dau. ANN CATHERINE, bapt. ca. 1749. {St. George's Episcopal Register, Indian River}

WILLIAM BURTON of KE Co., MD, d. leaving a will dated 30 April 1698 and proved 10 Dec 1699. To son William, dwelling plantation. To dau. Margarett, land taken up jointly with Thomas Carman. To daus. Mary and Hannah, personalty. Execs.: John Hamar and Thomas Head. {MWB 12:160}

WILLIAM BURTON m. Comfort (N). They were parents of WOOLSEY, b. 6 Sep 1753, bapt. 18 Nov 1753. {St. George's Episcopal Register, Indian River}

WILLIAM BURTON (called Long Burton) of Sussex Co., m. Elizabeth, had a son Joseph. Joseph d. intestate leaving children: SARAH; MARY; THOMAS; ELISABETH; WILLIAM BAGWELL; PATIENCE.

On 8 Aug 1787 Woolsey Burton [son of Benjamin] of Dagsberry Hundred, yeoman, bought from Sarah Burton of Angola and Indian River Hundred, spinster a parcel of land cont. 90 a., being part of a tract called *Bottle and Cake*, whereof William Burton, commonly called Long Burton, last of Sussex Co. by his will devised same to his son Joseph, father of afsd. Sarah, subject to the thirds or dower of Elizabeth, the widow of said William which being alloted to her by virtue of an order of the Orphans Court and whereas Joseph d. intestate, seized of the remaining 2/3 leaving a widow and 6 children, afsd. Sarah, and Mary, Thomas, Elisabeth, William Bagwell and Patience to whom the lands descended. Tract adjoining land devised by Benjamin Burton to his son the afsd. Woolsey Burton and runs along Herring Creek. {Sussex Co. Land Records}

WILLIAM BURTON, son of John, Sr.

Jesper Jesop d. leaving a will dated 25 July 1694, proved 13 Dec 1694, in which he mentioned William, son of John Burton, Sr. Exec. was John Burton, Sr. Wits., John Brinckloe, John Lane, Arthur Meston. {Arch. A27:5. Reg. of Wills, A:9}

WOOLSEY BURTON had a dau. ANN, bapt. ca. 1749. {St. George's Episcopal Register, Indian River}

WOOLSEY BURTON m. Elizabeth (N).

Woolsey d. leaving a will written [1751], proved 8 May 1751. Heirs: wife Elizabeth; sons Woolsey and William; dau. Elizabeth; and child unnamed. Extx., wife Elizabeth. Wits., Peter Waples, Burton Waples, Jacob Burton, Henry Blackwood. {Arch. A62:48. Reg. of Wills, B:1-4}

Woolsey was father of the following children: WOOLSEY; WILLIAM; ELIZABETH; UNNAMED.

WOOLSEY BURTON.

On 3 Dec 1773 Isaac Smith, Mary Smith, Woolsey Burton, Arcada Burton, Margaret Hazzard, Ann Hazzard of Sussex Co., DE, appointed William Hazzard to convey to William Holland 150 a. *Hills Folly* and *Woodsman Folly*.
{Dryden Worcester Land:298}

THE CLAYTON FAMILY

1. JAMES CLAYTON, b. c1632, probably in or near Middlewich, Cheshire, where he practiced the trade of blacksmith and m. 1st Jane (N), aged 48 in 1682. With his wife and the children listed below he came to America in 1682 on the ship *Submission* of Penn's 1682 fleet. {Welcome Claimants}

In *The Welcome Claimants Proved, Disproved And Doubtful*, hereafter cited as Welcome Claimants, the following account is given of the Clayton family of Delaware: James was father of the following children: JAMES, b. England c1666, aged 16 in 1682; SARAH, b. England c1668, aged 14 in 1682; JOHN, b. England c1671, aged 11 in 1682; MARY, b. England c1674, aged 8 in 1682; JOSHUA, b. England 1677, aged 5 in 1682, possibly twin of Lydia, d. c1761; LYDIA, b. England c1677, aged 5 in 1682.

Second Generation

2. JAMES CLAYTON, son of James (1) Clayton, b. c1666, m. 2nd Mary Bedwell.[20]

[20] Carolyn Reeves Ericson in *Bedwell Beaux and Belles A Brief History Of the Bedwell Family*, states Joshua Clayton who m. Sarah Bedwell and James Clayton who m. Mary Bedwell were brothers, and sons of James and Jane Clayton who came from England to Pennsylvania in 1682 with their children.

On 30 May 1696 James Clayton of Kent Co. PA, blacksmith, and Mary his wife for £10 sold to Daniell Ruttey a tract of land on s. side of St. Jones Creek alias Dover River being part of land of Thomas Bedwell called *Holy Neck*, 50 a. {KEDELR}

James Clayton d. by 13 March 1696/7 when Mary Clayton and Thomas Bedwell administered his estate. {Reg. of Wills, A:19} In a court case of 12, 13, 14 March 1699, Mary Clayton who had since m. to Michael Dennahoe, and Thomas Bedwell, admins. of the estate of James Clayton were complainants against Robert Hudson. {Kent Ct.:165}

In a petition of Thomas Bedwell and Michael Odonahoe and Mary his wife, admins. of the estate of James Clayton, blacksmith, it was noted that James Clayton had been obliged in certain indentures to John Clayton, his brother, for making over 100 a. on Ivy Branch of Murther Creek. John Clayton had been bound to James as apprentice, to learn the trade of blacksmith. {Kent Ct.:325}

On 14 Aug 1766 Joshua Clayton of Kent Co. MD, physician, eldest son of James Clayton, late of Kent Co., dec'd., for £500 sold to Isaiah Wharton of Kent Co. a tract of land, whereas the afsd. Joshua Clayton by his petition to the Orphans Court held at Dover on 15 Nov 1764 praying the Court to grant an order of 5 freeholders to go upon and view and divide the lands of James Clayton afsd. who died intestate who after viewing the land did return 28 Nov 1762 that the said land would not bear division without spoiling the whole. The commissioners on 14 May 1765 valued the land, 558 a., to the sum of £1100 over and above the widows right of dower, the Court ordered the lands to the afsd. Joshua Clayton in Murderkill Hundred beginning on Isaacs Branch to lands called *Claytons Chance* and *Burtons Chance* and *Mill Square*, 100 a. which includes the land called *Mill Square* and also all the mills n. side of Isaacs Branch adj. said tract. {KEDELR R:113}

3. JOHN CLAYTON, son of James (1), b. England c1671, aged 11 in 1682, d. by 5 Jan 1718 when his estate was administered by Mary Clayton. {Reg. of Wills, D:6} He probably m. Mary Smith.[21]

On 23 Jan 1718 Joshua Clayton, Jr., orphan son of John Clayton, aged 19 years, asked that his Uncle Joshua Clayton, Senr. be his guardian. {Wills D:10} On 17 March 1720 John Clayton, an orphan son of John, dec'd., asked that his Uncle Joshua Clayton, Senr., be his guardian. {Wills D:8}

John was father of the following sons: JOSHUA, b. c1699; JOHN.

4. JOSHUA CLAYTON, sometime of Middlewich, Cheshire, b. c1677, son of James (1), m. before 12th da., 4th mo., 1699, Sarah (Needham) Bedwell. On 12 June 1699

Joshua Clayton and Sarah his wife, executor of Henry

---

[21] Mary Clayton was mentioned as dau. in the will of Maurice Smith, dated 9 March 1695/6, proved 25 June 1698. Heirs: wife Bethia; sons John, Solomon, & Maurice, Jr.; daus. Mary Clayton, Martha, Alce, Elizabeth Smith. Extx. wife Bethia. Wits., Jacob Smith, John Clayton, John Evans, William Rodeney, James Clayton. {Arch. A47:123. Reg. of Wills, B:30}

Bedwell, dec'd., of Kent Co. PA for £14 sold to John Robbisson of same co., 100 a. taken out of a tract of land called *Longreach*, on s. side of St. Jones. {KEDELR}

On 10 Feb 1717/8 Joshua Clayton of Little Creek Hundred, Kent Co., yeoman, and Sarah his wife, for £20 sold to David Morgan of same place planter, a tract of land David Morgan now dwells upon, 50 a. {KEDELR E:336}

On 11 May 1750 Joshua Clayton of Kent Co., yeoman, for love, goodwill and affection give to my loving dau. Sarah Cowgill, widow of Thomas Cowgill, late of same co., part of a tract of land called *Willinbrook* in Little Creek Hundred, 88 a. Wit: John Clayton, Nico. Loockerman. {KEDELR O:46}

On 20th da., 2nd mo., 1758 Joshua Clayton requested a certificate in behalf of his grandson Henry Cowgill to recommend him to Nottingham Monthly Meeting. {DCMM}

Joshua Clayton of Little Creek Hundred d. leaving a will dated 2 Sep 1760, proved 1761. Heirs: wife Sarah; grandsons John, Henry, Thomas, Ezekiel and Clayton Cowgill; granddaus. Eunice Ozbun [Osborne], Sarah Hand, Elenor Cowgill, Rachel Grewell, Sarah Register, Elizabeth Neal, Jean Smith and Lydia Durborow. Execs., friend Timothy Hanson and grandson-in-law Jonathan Ozbun. Wits., Mary Manlove, Elizabeth Manlove, Sarah Needham. {Arch. A9:121-122. Reg. of Wills, K:254-255} Note: Will mentions dau. Sarah Cowgill, dec.

On 10 May 1763 a Deed of Partition was prepared between Jonathan Ozbun of Kent Co. yeoman and Eunice his wife and Ezekiel Cowgill of same co. yeoman, which said Eunice and Ezekiel Cowgill are 2 of the devisees named in the will of Joshua Clayton late of Kent Co., yeoman, dec'd., ... in division of several tracts of land, whereas the said Joshua Clayton in his life time was seized in a tract of land called *Highams Ferry* in Little Creek Hundred, 136 a., also in one other parcel of land part of a larger tract called *Willingbrook* and being so seized he on 2 Nov 1760 did make his will and did devise, to wit I give unto my grandson Ezekiel Cowgill 12 a. to be laid off at the w. end of that land which I gave by deed to my, dec'd., dau. Sarah Cowgill and to incommode as little as may be the tract whereon I now dwell, I give unto my grandau. Unice Ozbun my now dwelling plantation part of a tract called *Highams Ferry*, and part of a tract called *Willingbrook* bounded on the s. with land given to my afsd. dau. Sarah Cowgill on the n.w. with land of Ralph Needham, on the e. with the land left herein to my grandson John Cowgill. {KEDELR Q:159}

On 10 Nov 1763 John Cowgill of Kent Co. yeoman and Jonathan Ozburn (Ozbun) of same co., yeoman, and Unice (Eunice) his wife release each to the other several tracts of land, whereas Joshua Clayton late of Kent Co., yeoman, dec'd., grandfather of the said John Cowgill and Unice Ozburn was in his lifetime seized in 100 a. which heretofore belonged to one Robert Porter then late of said co., dec'd., also in another parcel part of a larger tract called *Highams Ferry*, also in one other parcel part of 2 larger tracts called *Wellingbrook* and *Highams Ferry* including the late dwelling plantation of the said Joshua Clayton, and being so seized made a will bearing date 2 Nov 1760 and devised to the said John Cowgill his grandson all the land and plantation which formerly belonged to Robert Porter late of said co. beginning at Herring branch e. side of road from Muddy branch to Little Creek Landing, to land of Ralph Needham, dec'd., to land by me sold to David Morgan, the will did further devise to the said Unice Ozburn his granddau. all my now dwelling plantation bounded by land given to my dau. Sarah Cowgill. {KEDELR Q:200}

Jonathan Ozbun, yeoman of Little Creek Hundred, d. leaving a will dated 24 Aug 1773, proved 11 Nov 1773. Heirs: wife Eunice; son Jonathan; daus. Eunice and Tabitha Ozbun, Elizabeth Cowgill, Mary Alstone; son-in-law Israel Alstone. Extx., wife Eunice. Guardian, Robert Holliday. Wits., Robert Regester, Elizabeth Stevens, Thomas Parry. {Arch. A38:166-167. Reg. of Wills, L:143} Note: Will mentions grandfather Joshua Clayton, dec'd.

Joshua was father of the following children {Welcome Claimants}: LYDIA, m. 16th da., 12th mo, 1720, John Cowgill who was b. 8th da., 5th mo., 1698, son of John and Bridget (Croasdale) Cowgill {Middletown Monthly Meeting}[22]; SARAH, m. at Duck Creek Monthly Meeting, 11th mo. 1727, Thomas Cowgill, also son of John and Bridget (Croasdale) Cowgill, b. Bucks Co., PA, 21st da., 4th mo., 1696, removed to New Castle Co., DE, 1713, d. Kent Co., DE, before 7 Dec 1749 when his widow, Sarah Cowgill, administered his account; ELIZABETH, m. 3 Sep 1730 Mark Manlove, Jr.

Third Generation

5. JOSHUA CLAYTON, son of John (3) Clayton, b. c1699, probably m. Sarah Cummings. [*Although not definite, the following items probably pertain to Joshua of John and not his uncle Joshua of James.*]

On 18th da., 3rd mo., 1747, it was reported that Joshua Clayton and Sarah Cummings, widow, had announced their intentions to marry. {DCMM}

Joshua Clayton, yeoman, of KE Co., DE, m. Sarah Cummins of Sussex Co. on 21st da., 5th mo., 1747, at the Little Creek Meeting House. {DCMM}

6. JOHN CLAYTON the elder, probable son of John (3), d. 11 April 1730 when his land was divided for his children.

Whereas John Clayton d. intestate leaving an estate in land in Little Creek Hundred to be divided between his children, John Clayton, Jonathan Clayton, Mary Allstone, Hannah Levick, Susannah Vannoy and Elizbeth Clayton. On 13 Feb 1730 a request is made to divide the land. {KEORCF Clayton, John - 1730}

On 9 March 1761 Abraham Vannoy (Vanhoy) of Kent Co., yeoman, and Susannah his wife, admins. of Jonathan Clayton, late of Kent Co., yeoman, dec'd., for £150 sold to Henry Stevens of same co., yeoman, at publick vendue he being the highest bidder, half part of a 80 a. tract of land, whereas John Clayton the elder late of Kent Co., yeoman, dec'd., was in his life time seized in sundrie parcels of land in Little Creek Hundred and being so seized, died intestate leaving 6 children, to wit, John Clayton the younger, the afsd. Jonathan Clayton, Mary wife of Arthur Alstone, Hannah wife of John Levick, the afsd. Susannah Vannoy and Elizabeth Clayton and after the death of the afsd. John Clayton on 11 April 1730 William Rodeney, late high sheriff of Kent Co. by virtue of a writ did cause the land to be divided into 7 parts, and 2 parts did allot to the said Jonathan Clayton and Elizabeth Clayton, beginning at the share of Abraham Vannoy and Susannah his wife, 30 a. and 50 a. next adj. which the said John Clayton, dec'd., in his lifetime purchased of Richard Richardson, in the

---

22 John Cowgill m. 2nd Hannah (N) and d. intestate, with administration to widow Hannah, 29 July 1752. Hannah m. 2nd Robert Hall.

whole 80 a. Jonathan Clayton became vested in half part of the 80 a. and d. intestate and without issue being indebted in divers sums of money and adminr was granted to the afsd. Abraham Vannoy and Susanna his wife and they at an Orphans Court 24 Aug 1748 were granted an order of court to sell the lands of their intestate to discharge his debts. {KEDELR Q:36}

John Clayton m. Mary Wilson, dau. of William Wilson the elder; following the death of John Clayton she m. Joseph Buckmaster and had a son Wilson Buckmaster.

On 1 Feb 1753 Robert Wilson, the only surviving son of William Wilson formerly of Kent Co., dec'd., John Wilson son of William Wilson, late of Kent Co., dec'd., which said William Wilson last mentioned was the eldest son of the first afsd. William Wilson the elder, John Clayton, son of Mary, one of the daus. of William Wilson the elder by her husband John Clayton, Abraham Vannoy and Susanah his wife one of the daus. of Mary by her husband John Clayton, Wilson Buckmaster another of the sons of Mary by her husband Joseph Buckmaster with whom she intermarried after the death of her former husband John Clayton - all of Kent Co. for £6 sold to Nicholas Ridgely of same co., a tract of land (warrant dated at Philadelphia 15 Jun 1703 surveyd and laid out 20 July 1703 unto afsd. William Wilson the elder by Jonas Greenwood deputy surveyor) adj. the land of William Rodney and Edward Starkey above the Kings Road beginning at a peice of land formerly surveyed for Daniel Jones, Senr., to land formerly laid out for Richard and John Walker, 118 a. William Wilson the elder d. intestate and his wife died soon after him. Robert Wilson, John Wilson, John Clayton, Abraham Vannoy, Susanah Vannoy and Wilson Buckmaster do impower John Vining and Richard Wells of Kent Co. or either of them our attys to ackn this deed in open court. {KEDELR O:174}

On 1 March 1758 a petition was submitted by William Gray, showing that John Clayton d. intestate seized of a tract of land in fee simple in Little Creek Hundred and at his death left issue, three sons and 4 daus.: John, Jonathan, Daniel, Susannah, Hanah, Mary, and Elisabeth. Jonathan and Daniel died intestate and without issue. Hannah died and left issue now living. Mary died and left issue but whether was alive was unknown to petitioner. Elisabeth m. with your said petitioner and died and left issue now living and John and Susannah are still alive. Petitioner requested land be divided. {KEORCF Clayton, John - 1758}

John was father of the following children: JONATHAN (eldest son), d. intestate; JOHN; DANIEL; MARY, m. Arthur Alstone; HANNAH, m. John Levick; SUSANNAH, m. Abraham Vannoy; ELIZABETH, m. William Gray.

7. LYDIA CLAYTON, dau. of Joshua (4) Clayton, m. 16th da., 12th mo., 1720, John Cowgill (b. 8th da., 5th mo., 1698, son of John and Bridget (Croasdale) Cowgill. On 13th da., 1st mo., 1721, the orderly marriage of Lydia Clayton and John Cowgill, Jr. was reported. {DCMM}

Lydia and John Cowgill were parents of the following children {Welcome Claimants}: JOHN, m. Mary Worrell; CLAYTON; SARAH, m. John Register; ELIZABETH, m. Francis Neal; HENRY, m. Elizabeth Osborne; LYDIA, m. (N) Durborow.

8. SARAH CLAYTON, dau. of Joshua (4) Clayton, m. 11th mo., 1727, Thomas Cowgill. On 19th da., 12th mo., 1727, the orderly marriage of Thomas Cowgill

and Sarah Clayton was reported. {DCMM}

Sarah and Thomas were parents of the following children: EZEKIEL; THOMAS; SARAH, m. 22nd da., 12th mo., 1756, Samuel Hand; ELLEN (Eleanor); RACHEL, m. Jonathan Grewell; JANE (Jean), m. Daniel Smyth.

9. ELIZABETH CLAYTON, dau. of Joshua (4) Clayton, m. Mark Manlove, Jr.

On 19th da., 8th mo., 1730 it was reported that Elizabeth Clayton and Mark Manlove, Jr. had married. {DCMM}

Elizabeth and Mark Manlove were parents of dau. EUNICE who m. 1750 Jonathan Osborne.

Fourth Generation

10. JONATHAN CLAYTON, son of John (6) Clayton, d. by 23 Aug 1748 when his estate was administered by Abraham Vanhoy and wife Susanna Vanhoy. {Arch. A9:120. Reg. of Wills, 1:234}

On 25 Aug 1748 a petition was submitted by Abraham Vannoy and Susanna his wife showing that Jonathan Clayton, bro. to afsd. Susanna, one of your petitioners about the month of Sep last d. intestate and was seized in fee of a tract in Little Creek Hundred, 40 a., but left no personal estate. Letters of admin granted to your petitioner and dec'd. was indebted for £60.8.6 for which there is not personal estate to pay. Hence requests to sell the land. Granted. In the account was bill from Abraham Vannoy and Susannah his wife admins., for boarding and maintaining of him being a poor infirm creature subject to fits for 10 years. {KEORCF Clayton, Jonathan - 1748}

On 9 March 1761 Henry Stevens of Kent Co. yeoman for £150 sold to Abraham Vannoy, Junr., of same co., yeoman, half part of a tract of land, whereas Jonathan Clayton, late of same co., yeoman, dec'd., was in his lifetime seized in half part of a parcel of land in Little Creek Neck and Hundred beginning at the land of Abraham Vannoy the elder, 30 a. and also a half part of one other parcel 50 a. adj. the 30 a. conveyed by a certain John Richardson to John Clayton the elder since, dec'd., who was the father of the said Jonathan Clayton which two tracts were allotted to the said Jonathan Clayton and Elizabeth Clayton, one other of the children of the said John Clayton the elder, in a partition made of his lands among all his children by virtue of a writ. The 80 a. became vested in Jonathan Clayton and he d. intestate and indebted in divers sums of money, by virtue of an order of the justices of an Orphans Court held 24 Aug 1748 for the sale of so much of the lands to discharge such debts, the afsd. Abraham Vannoy (Vanhoy) the elder and Susannah his wife of Kent Co. yeoman admins. of Jonathan Clayton late of Kent Co. yeoman, dec'd., on 9 March 1761 did sell unto Henry Stevens half part of the 80 a. which did belong to Jonathan Clayton at the time of his death. {KEDELR Q:35}

11. JOHN CLAYTON, eldest son of John (6).

John Clayton of Little Creek Hundred Kent Co., blacksmith, mortgaged a plantation with 90 a. of land to Mark Manlove and Richard Richardson, trustees of the Generall Loan Office. John Clayton, for paying and discharging the mortgage deed and also £63.2.6, sold to Joshua Clayton of same place, farmer, the tract of land called *Middle Wicke*, formerly purchased by John Clayton father to the said John Clayton of William Rodeney by deed of sale bearing date 1 May 1700 beginning at the corner of London near the mouth of Timothy Hanson's land, 90 a. Acknowledged 9 May 1732. {KEDELR K:131}

On 10 Nov 1736 Joshua Clayton of Kent Co., yeoman, for £90.14 sold to Henry Stephens of the same place farmer, a tract of land and plantation, being part of a tract of land called *Midlewick,* formerly purchased by John Clayton of William Rodeney 1 May 1700, and John Clayton the eldest son of the afsd. John Clayton, dec'd., did sell the same being his part of the tract unto Joshua Clayton 8 May 1732 ... John Clayton the younger did mortgage the land unto the trustees of the General Loan Office ... Henry Stephens to discharge the several payments in the mortgage ... beginning at the land called *London* to Timothy Hanson's land ... 90 a. {KEDELR L:177}

On 17 Feb 1738 John Clayton of Mutherkill Hundred Kent Co. yeoman for love, good will and affection gave to his son John Clayton, Junr., my grist mill on n. side of Isaacs Branch and also 100 a. of land including the mill beginning at the corner of a tract of land called *Mill Square* adj. land called *Claytons Chance* and one other tract called *Bartons Chance* to Isaacs Branch, 100 a. laid out to me by virtue of a warrant dated at Philadelphia 14 March 1734 and the s. part of my tract called *Claytons Chance* conveyed to me by John Hall about 1722 and also the s. part of my tract called *Bartons Chance.* {KEDELR M:14}

On 13 Feb 1739 John Clayton of Little Creek Hundred Kent Co. for £4 released his undivided rights to William Willson of same co. in two tracts of land one called *Cambridge* in Duck Creek Hundred on n. side of s.w. branch of Duck Creek bounded on the e. side by a tract of land formerly belonging to one Simkins now to the widow Mary Heath and on the w. by the other tract of land formerly taken up by William Rodeney called *Brunford,* both tracts were taken up by William Willson the elder, dec'd., who died seized intestate, part of the said land descended unto John Clayton being son to the dau. of the said Willson. {KEDELR M:70}

On 11 Feb 1761 John Clayton of Kent Co., Esqr., for £600 sold to James Clayton of same co., miller, one grist mill on n. side of Isaacs branch and also 100 a. including the said mill beginning at land called *Mill Square* to tract called *Claytons Chance,* to land called *Burtons Chance*, 100 a., which includes the land called *Mill Square* laid out to John Clayton Senr., dec'd., by virtue of a warrant dated at Philadelphia on 14 March 1734 and the s. part of the land called *Claytons Chance*, conveyed to the said John Clayton, Senr., dec'd., by John Hall in 1722 and also the s. part of the tract called *Burtons Chance*, conveyed from William Lawrance to the said John Clayton, Senr., dec'd., on 10 Nov 1713 which the afsd. lands were conveyed to the afsd. John Clayton, Esqr by his father John Clayton, Senr., dec'd., by a deed of gift dated 17 Feb 1738 (Book M, fol. 14) and afterwards the said John Clayton Esqr obtained a patent for the part called *Mill Square* bearing date at Philadelphia of 6 Nov 1749 (Book A vol 15 pg 351). {KEDELR Q:25}

Unplaced

JAMES CLAYTON, Gent., d. by 20 May 1761 when his estate was administered by John Clayton, Esq. {Arch. A9:110-111. Reg. of Wills, K:262}

JOHN CLAYTON, yeoman, d. by 27 Jan 1724 when his estate was administered by Moses Freeman. {Reg. of Wills, D:69}

JOHN CLAYTON, Sr., yeoman, m. Grace (N).

John d. leaving a will dated 24 Dec 1754, proved 9 May 1759. Heirs: wife Grace; sons James and John; dau. Sarah Caldwell; granddau. Sarah Caldwell; grandson John Caldwell. Exec. son James. Wits., Elizabeth Armitage, James Egnew, Robert Teat. {Arch. A9:112. Reg. of Wills, K:203}

John was father of the following children: JAMES; JOHN; SARAH, m. (N) Caldwell and had a son John.

On 31 Jan 1761 James Clayton of Kent Co. yeoman and Grace his wife for £500 sold to Thomas Hanson of same co. yeoman and Joshua Gregg of same co., millwright, three parcels of land in Murtherkill Hundred, the one tract on s. side of Isaacs branch adj. land of John Vining on Kings Upper Road leading from Three Runs to the Town of Dover to land late claimed by Allan Delap, 29 a., 148 sq perches, part of a larger tract called *Brecknock*, also a parcel adj., 45 a., part of the larger tract called *Brecknock*, also a parcel of land on n. side of Isaacs Branch, part of a tract called *Smyrna*, 2 a. heretofore laid out to a certain John Hill for the use of building a grist mill. {KEDELR Q:33}

Joshua Gregg of Kent Co. mill-right, together with Thomas Hanson of same co. purchased on 31 March 1761 (Liber Q pg 33) of James Clayton and Grace his wife 3 tracts of land with a grist mill and other improvements on Isaacs Branch in Murtherkill Hundred 96 a., 148 perches. {KEDELR Q:257}

In a petition of Joshua Clayton, eldest son of JAMES CLAYTON, dec'd., and now of the age of 21 years, sheweth that your petiioner's father James Clayton, d. intestate possessed of land. Requests land be divided. On 6 Jan 1762 a commission was appointed to lay out the land of James Clayton dec'd, for his widow now wife of Isaiah Wharton. In 1762 Grace, widow and relict of James Clayton was alloted all the plantation where James Clayton dwelt (except the mill standing thereon, of which she was alloted 1/3 part only). 100 a and 20 a. of unimproved land. {KEORCF Clayton, James - 1761-70}

JOSHUA CLAYTON d. by 17 May 1720 when his estate was administered by Abraham Brooks. {Reg. of Wills, D:18}

JOHN CLAYTON m. Mary, dau. of George Manlove.

George Manlove, farmer of Little Creek Hundred, d. leaving a will dated 10 May 1766, proved 20 May 1766. Heirs: sons Matthew, John and Tredwell; grandson George Manlove, son of Matthew; daus. Mary Manlove, Sarah Emerson (wife of Govey Emerson). Execs., sons Matthew and John. Trustee, James Sykes, Esq. Wits., Clayton Levick, Mary Hunter, John Molleston. {Arch. A33:92-94. Reg. of Wills, L:11-12} Note: Arch. A33:92 shows that dau. Mary Manlove married John Clayton.

JAMES CLAYTON had a son John.

On 12 Feb 1745 Robert Fitsgerell (Fitzgerrald) of Kent Co., yeoman, and Elizabeth his wife for £60 sold to Samuel Dickinson of same place, gent., part of a tract of land called *Burtons Delight*, on n.e. side of Dover River adj. John Hart's land, 50 a. Said land was given to the afsd. Robert Fitsgerell by the will of James Fitsgerell, his father, who purchased it from George Hart, who purchased the same with another 50 a. adj. of John Clayton, eldest son and heir of James Clayton, which James Clayton purchased the 100 a. of John Burton the pattentee. {KEDELR N:87}

JOHN CLAYTON, son of James.

John Edingfield of St. Jones's Hundred d. leaving a Will dated 22 Oct 1771. [No date of probate] Heirs: dau. Elizabeth Parke; grandsons Thomas Parke (son of Hugh and Elizabeth Parke) and John Clayton (son of James Clayton). Extx. dau. Elizabeth Parke. Wits., Richard Butler, Anake Lucas, John Irons, John Irons, Jr. [No. prob.]. {Arch. A16:16. Reg. of Wills, L:100-103}

JAMES CLAYTON, grandson of John Newell.

John Newel d. leaving a will dated 16 Jan 1739/40, proved 4 Feb 1739. Heirs: sons William, John, Thomas; dau. Elizabeth; grandson James Clayton; granddau. Ruth Betts; wife Mary. Extx., wife Mary. Wits., James Clayton, John Hall, Rebecca Welsh. {Arch. A37:190. Reg. of Wills, 1:14}

On 24 Feb 1758 James Clayton of Kent Co., blacksmith, for £100 sold to Daniel Robisson of same co., a tract of land, whereas John Newell, late of this co., dec'd., was seased of a tract of land in Murderkill Hundred between the land cald *The Downs* and the land cald *Clappom* and did in his will give unto his Grandson James Clayton party to these presents 150 a., beginning at land called *Bartlets Lot* on e. side of Hethers Road. {KEDELR P:55}

On 24 Aug 1756 James Clayton, Junr., of Kent Co., blacksmith, for £10 sold to John Newell of same place blacksmith, a tract of land which formerly did belong to Thos. Newell, dec'd., he dying intestate the land falling to his brethren their legal representatives of which James Clayton is one and also a percil of land adj. to afsd. land, 10 a. {KEDELR O:344}

James Clayton and (N) Newell, dau. of John Newell, m. before 16 June 1737. She had a son James Clayton this date. {Arch. A37:100}

JOHN CLAYTON was mentioned as brother of George Morgan.

George Morgan d. leaving a will dated dated 12 Aug 1755, proved 27 Aug 1755.Heirs: wife Martha; sons Jacob, Robert, George; daus. Elizabeth, Hannah, Mary, Grace; son-in-law John Boyd, son of John Boyd, dec'd., Execs., wife Martha and bro. John Clayton, Esq. Wits., Mark Smith, James Clayton, Robert Buchanan. {Arch. A36:145-148. Reg. of Wills, K:117}

JOHN CLAYTON was a cousin of William Dyer.

William Dyer d. leaving a will dated 19 Oct 1728, proved 19 Nov 1728. Heirs: bro. Thomas Clifford; cousins John Clayton, Hannah Levick and children of Elizabeth Booth; Isaac Booth; John Pound. Execs., bro. Thomas Clifford and Isaac Booth. Wits., Philip Denny, Isaac Snow. {Arch. A15:230-231. Reg. of Wills, G:16-17}

SARAH CLAYTON d. by 19 Nov 1766 when her estate was administered by Jonathan Ozburn, next of kin. {Arch. A9:124. Reg. of Wills, L:18}

THE CLIFFORD FAMILY

1. THOMAS CLIFFORD, Little Creek, m. Elizabeth (N) who later m. Dennis Dyer.

On 13 Dec 1690 Thomas Cleford and Elizabeth his wife of Dover River alias Jones Creek PA planter, conveyed a tract of land called *Aberdeene* n.e. side of Dover River, for £14 in corn and tobacco, sold to Alexander Chance of same place. {KEDELR}

On 20 July 1696 Thomas Clifford, Senr., of Kent Co. ordered his children's ages be recorded: Thomas Clifford, Junr., aged 11 years the 4 Sep next, John Clifford aged 9 years the 20 Aug next, Elizabeth Clifford aged 5 years the 20 Nov next, Mary Clifford aged 1 yeare the 25 April last. {KEDELR}

Thomas d. leaving a will (unwritten) made 26 March 1698. Heirs: sons Thomas and John; wife Elizabeth; daus. Elizabeth and Mary; bro. George. Extx. wife Elizabeth. (No probate.) {Reg. of Wills, A:25}

Thomas Clifford, aged 16 years, middle of Septenber next chose Wm. Winsmore as guardian. John Clifford, aged 14 years, the later end of Aug next is ordered to remain with his mother who has lately m. Dennish Dyer. Whereas Timothy Kairons by will (30 Oct 1700) to Thomas and John Clifford, sons of widow Clifford, Elizabeth, now wife of Dennish Dyer, mother of the afsd. Thomas and John, 13 March 1700. {Kent Co. Court Records}

In his will Timothy Kairone [Hirons?] dated 28 Oct 1700 and proved 28 Oct 1700, mentioned Thomas and John Clifford, children of the widow Clifford. Execs., John and Thomas Clifford. Guardians, William Winsmore, Dennish Dyer. Wits., Robert Porter, Dennish Dyer, John French. {Arch. A28:80. Reg. of Wills, B:37 and 41}

Thomas was father of the following children: THOMAS, b. 4 Sep 1685; JOHN, b. 20 Aug 1687; ELIZABETH, b. 20 Nov 1691; MARY, b. 25 April 1695. {KEDELR C:174}

William Dyer d. leaving a will dated 19 Oct 1728, proved 19 Nov 1728. Heirs: bro. Thomas Clifford; cousins John Clayton, Hannah Levick and children of Elizabeth Booth; Isaac Booth; John Pound. Execs., bro. Thomas Clifford and Isaac Booth. Wits., Philip Denny, Isaac Snow. {Arch. A15:230-231. Reg. of Wills, G:16-17}

Second Generation

2. THOMAS CLIFFORD, son of Thomas (1) Clifford, d. leaving a will dated 2 July 1703, proved 12 July 1703. Heirs: Elizabeth, Mary and Parnell Clifford; bro. John Clifford. Execs., John Clayton, John Evans. Wits., William Morton, William Winsmore. {Arch. A9:139. Reg. of Wills, B:49}

3. JOHN CLIFFORD, son of Thomas (1) Clifford, m. Ann (N).

On 10 Feb 1718 John Clifford of Kent Co. yeoman (son and heir of Thomas Clifford late of same co. dec'd.) and Ann his wife for £26 sold to Benjamin Barret of Little Creek, taylor, a tract of land called *Simsons Choice* on n. side of Little Creek (404 a. patent bearing date 25 March 1676 granted unto William Simson), part of which tract of land of 50 a. was conveyed late in the tenure of Thomas Clifford unto John Clifford, bounded by the land of Andrew Hamilton to the w. and the land where Benjamin Barret dwelleth to the e., 50 a. {KEDELR F:66}

John Clifford, Little Creek Hundred, d. leaving a will dated 9 Dec 1726, proved 20 March 1726. Heirs: son-in-law William Dyer; wife Ann; son Thomas. Extx., wife. Trustee, Daniel Needham. Wits., Richard Richardson. Thomas Slater, Agnes Slater. {Arch. A9:138. Reg. of Wills, F:22}

John was father of THOMAS.

4. ELIZABETH CLIFFORD, dau. of Thomas (1) Clifford, m. (N) Hillyard.

On 17 Nov 1727 Elizabeth Hillyard of Kent Co. one of the daus. of Thomas Clifford, late of same co., dec'd., for £3 quitt claim unto Benjamin Shurmer of Kent Co. gent., all her right, title and interest in a tract of land called *Sciptop*, 400 a. in Murderkill Hundred, originally granted to the afsd. Thomas Clifford between the lands of Daniell Jones called *London* to the n.e. and the lands formerly of [blank] Bedwell called *Long Reach* to the w. and the Phuchion Run formerly called Walkers Branch to the s. {KEDELR I:108}

Third Generation

5. THOMAS CLIFFORD, probable son of John (3) Clifford, yeoman, m. Esther (Hester) Coudratt, dau. of Peter Coudrat. She later m. Wilson Buckmaster.

On 13 Feb 1739 Thomas Clifford of Kent Co. for £7 released all his undivided rights unto Jonathan Willson in a tract of land called *Cambridge* in Duck Creek Hundred. {KEDELR M:70}

On 14 Aug 1742 Thomas Clifford of Kent Co., yeoman, for £45, sold to John Mifflin of same place, carpenter, a tract of land in Murther Creek Hundred being part of a larger tract called *Skipton* which said larger tract was formerly sold by John Clifford father of the said Thomas Clifford (and who Thomas is heir at law) to Benjamin Shurmer, dec'd., some part thereof was released unto the said John Clifford, bounded by John Clayton's land on the Puncheon Run, 100 a. {KEDELR M:178}

Thomas d. leaving a will dated 7 April 1747, proved 9 May 1747. Heirs: wife Esther; sons John, Peter; daus. Anne, Mary, Martha, Elizabeth, Esther. Extx., wife. Trustees, father Peter Coudrat and friend Thomas Irons. Wits., John Coudrat, Hannah Irons, Samuel McCally. {Arch. A9:140-142. Reg. of Wills, 1:149-150} Note: Arch. A9:141 shows Esther later married Wilson Buckmaster.

Peter Coudrat d. leaving a will dated 28 Feb 1747, proved 14 March 1747. Heirs: wife Frances; sons John, Peter; children of daus. Hestor Clefford and Mary Harper; children of son Daniel Coudrat, dec'd., Execs., wife Frances and son John. Wits., David White, William Jackson, John Clayton, Jr. {Arch. A-11:47. Reg. of Wills, I:189}

In 1755 John Coudratt of Kent Co. for £80 sold to John Vining of same place a tract of land. Sarah widow of John Register sold 125 a. to Peter Coudrat (Coudratt) on 20 Nov 1734 (Book L, fol. 51) and he made his will 28 Feb 1747 (Book I, fol. 189) and bequeathed unto to my beloved wife Frances Coudrat my dwelling plantation and house during her natural life and after her decease that then it to be sold and the money equally divided between my beloved son John Coudrat, my son Peter Coudrat and my dau. Hester Clifford's children, only the dau. now born, and my dau. Mary Harper, and also the children of my son Daniel Coudrat, dec'd., to have one share equally divided amongst them and if any of my sons and daus. will come and live on my plantation that then they shall gett two sufficient freeholders to appraise the value of the said land and premisses and they shall pay unto my children the sum of money the said freeholders say the land to be worth then it to belong to them, after the death of Frances Coudrat, tenant for life, John Coudrat the eldest son of Peter removed with his family and settled and possessed and lived upon the said land, appraised by James Caldwell and James Train good and lawfull freeholders of this co, to the sum of £80 ... adj. w. side of lands late in the possession of Alexander Pinder, dec'd., to Bettys Branch. Acknowldeged 9 Sep 1755. {KEDELR O:307}

THE CLOWES FAMILY

Much of the following information was taken from *Genealogies of Pennsylvania Families*, published in 1983 by Genealogical Publishing Co., which was taken from articles of *The Pennsylvania Magazine of History and Biography* up to 1935. It is hereafter cited as PA Genealogies.

1. SAMUEL CLOWES, b. 1684[23], d. 1760, bur. at Jamaica. He m. Catherine Donne (d. 27 Aug 1760). They were parents of the following sons: PETER, "left no children who settled in Lewestown, Delaware"; JOHN; CALEB; JOSEPH; SAMUEL; GERARDUS, had sons, Samuel, Timothy and John, "who all lived on Long Island, at Hampstead and New York City." {PA Genealogies:846}

Second Generation

2. PETER CLOWES, son of Samuel (1) Clowes. Peter Clowes was high sheriff of Sussex Co. in 1754 and 1765. {SUDELR}

On 1 Jul 1768 Peter Clowes of Orange Co., NY, yeoman, for £20 sold to Jacob White of Sussex Co., yeoman ... a small island of marsh in Lewes Town Creek which was surveyed 1715 by Robert Shankland then surveyor by virtue of a warrant from Jacob Taylor surveyor general dated at Philadelphia 24 Oct 1715 which required him to survey 2 small islands for Alexander Molleston fronting his own land which island is the lowermost island s side of an island belonging to said Shankland ... 4 a. Peter Clowes appointed Rhoads Shankland, esqr., high sheriff of Sussex Co. and John Clowes, Junr, of same place to ackn this deed in open court. Wit: John Clowes, Johanna Clowes. Ackn 6 Sep 1768. {SUDELR K:332}

3. JOHN CLOWES, son of Samuel (1) Clowes, settled in DE, 25 Aug 1727, at 5 o'clock, d. 24 April 1769 of pleurisy, aged 66 years and 9 days. John m. Mary (N) by Rev. William Beckett at Lewes Town. {PA Genealogies:846}

Mary, widow of John, d. 5 Feb 1770 of pleurisy, aged about 63 years. {PA Genealogies: 847}

John Clowes by his will dated 8 April 1761 did devise unto his 4 sons and 3 daus, William, John, David, Gerhardus, Catharine, Mary and Lydia all the lands, and the said William dyed intestate, leaving issue 4 children Catharine, party to this deed, Mary, Lydia and John to whom his part of the said lands descended, and the survivors of the afsd. 7 children did on 17 Dec 1772 divide all the testators lands, when Lot No 5 became the property of the afsd. William's

---

23 PA Genealogies quotes Thompson's History of Long Island as saying that Samuel was born at Derbyshire, England, March 16, 1674. For more detail on Samuel see PA Genealogies: 845-850

4 children (Lib L, fol. 270), and Catharine, dau. of the afsd. William, m. Peter Dickerson who petitioned the Orphans Court for a division of Lot No 5 amongst the heirs of the said William, being granted 3 freeholders were ordered to set a true valuation thereon which order being complyed with the said Peter Dickerson accepted the same in right of his wife Catharine ... 17 1/2 a. adj. Hazard's old field. Proved and Ackn 3 Sep 1788. {SUDELR B:363}

John Clowes of Sussex Co., dec'd., by his will dated 8 April 1761 devised to his four sons and three daus., William, John, David, Gurhardus, Catharine, Mary Junr., and Lydia Clowes, all his land in said county to be equally divided. John Clowes, John Young and Catharine his wife, John Sheldon Dormon and Mary his wife, Jeremiah Conwell and Lydia his wife being at full age, heirs and legal representatives of this afsd. John Clowes, dec'd., caused a draught to be made of the land [described]. {SUDELR - signed 17 Dec 1772} The will mentioned dec'd. father Samuel. {Arch. A65:54-55. Reg. of Wills, B:368-374}

As of 29 July 1773 Gerhardus Clowes had d. without issue and his right became the property of his surviving brothers and sisters. Lydia Conwell was now a widow. {SUDELR - recorded 4 Aug 1773}

John and Mary were parents of the following children {PA Genealogies:846-847}: WILLIAM, b. 28 June 1728, 4 a.m. at Broadkill, Sussex Co., d. 26 Oct 1766; JOHN, b. 5 Nov 1730, 11 a.m.; ALETTA, b. 28 Aug 1732, at Lewes, d. 6th inst., bur. in churchyard at Lewes; DAVID, b. 16 Sep 1733 at 5 a.m. in Lewistown; CATHERINE, b. 9 July 1736 at 9 a.m. at Lewistown; SAMUEL, b. 31 Dec 1737 at 6 a.m. at Lewestown, d. 19 March 1758 bur. at Broadkill in the burying ground of his mother's relations; MARY, b. 7 Feb 1739 at 5 a.m. at Lewes, d. 6 Aug 1813; LYDIA, b. 19 May 1742, at 7 a.m. at Lewestown; GERARDUS, b. 12 March 1747 at 10 a.m. at Parkton on the Broadkill, Sussex Co., d. by 29 July 1773. {PA Genealogies: 847-849}

Third Generation

4. WILLIAM CLOWES, son of John (3) Clowes, b. 28 June 1728, 4 a.m. at Broadkill, Sussex Co., d. 26 Oct 1766 of pleurisy and interred at Eliza Staton's at Broadkill, where his former wife wsa buried. He was father of the following children: CATHERINE; MARY; LYDIA, b. 15 Nov 1762; JOHN, b. 18 March 1765; GERARDUS, d. in a violent storm of snow on Accoqunamen Beach, being driven in a vessel there and bur. there in an old Burying Ground. {PA Genealogies:847}

On 20 June 1777 John Sheldon Dormon, Sussex Co., yeoman, bought from Peter Dickerson and wife Catharine. Whereas John Clowes, Esqr., (grandfather to afsd. Catharine Dickerson), dec'd., by his last will devised all his land to his seven children, William, John, David, Catharine, Mary, Lydia and Gerhardus, share alike by lots to be drawn. William Clowes, father to the afsd. Catharine Dickerson, predeceased his father, and his share became the right of his four children, Catharine, Mary, Lydia and John. Whereas John, Catharine, Mary, Lydia, four of the seven children of John Clowes, along with John Young, husband of afsd. Catharine (dau. of John Clowes), John Sheldon Dormaon, husband of afsd. Mary (dau. of John Clowes), and Jeremiah Conwell, husband of afsd. Lydia (dau. of John Clowes) on 17 Dec 1772 entered into an agreement to divide the land. Ackn 6 May 1778.

5. JOHN CLOWES, son of John (3) Clowes, b. 5 Nov 1730, 11 a.m., d. 24 Feb 1790 at 5 a.m. of a violent pleurisy and inflamation of the lungs.

John m. 7 Sep 1758 Mary Draper, by Rev. Mathias Harris at John Spencer's, her step-father. Mary, b. 10 Nov 1739, dau. of Isaac and Sarah (Hines) Draper (who later m. John Spencer).

On 2 Nov 1764 John Clowes of Sussex Co., esqr., was appointed as one of the justices of the state supreme court. {SUDELR A:323} On 10 June 1788 John Clowes of Sussex Co. was appointed Third Justice of the Court of Common Pleas and Orphans Court of Sussex Co. {SUDELR B:313}

John Clowes d. leaving a will dated 20 Aug 1784, proved 15 March 1790. Heirs: wife Mary Clowes; sons Isaac and Peter Clowes; daus. Alletta and Sarah Clowes. Execs., wife Mary Clowes and son Isaac Clowes. Wits., John Wilson Dean, John Tam, Benedict Pennington. {Arch. A65:56-58. Reg. of Wills, D:288289} note: Arch. A65:56 mentions bro. David Clowes, dec'd.

On 10 May 1792 Mary Clowes and Isaac Clowes, execs. of John Clowes, late of Sussex Co. esqr., dec'd., submitted a petition showing that the said John Clowes in his lifetime became bound unto George Conwell ... that John Clowes, since dec'd. and no deed of conveyance hath yet been made altho part of the consideration money was paid to the said John Clowes in his lifetime and the residue since his death to your petitioner, your petitioner prays your honors to give an order impowering them to convey the tract of land to the said George Conwell. Granted 10 May 1792. {SUDELR B:481}

John and Mary were parents of the following children: SARAH, b. 17 Aug 1759, d. 1 Jan 1767 of a choking fit; SAMUEL, b. 22 March 1762 between 1 and 2 p.m., lost in the Delaware Bay in a violent storm on 21 Nov 1780; JOHN, b. 7 Oct 1764 at 2 p.m., d. 21 Sep 1766 with a flux of 4 days; ALETTA, b. 7 April 1767 at 9:30 a.m.; SARAH, b. 12 June 1769 at 8:30 a.m.; JOHN, b. 16 July 1771, bur. 7 inst.; ISAAC, b. b. 20 Aug 1772, at 3:30 p.m.; PETER, b. 2 Feb 1775, Doctor of Medicine, d. aged 31 years and 7 months of a billious fever, leaving a son Ezekiel William; JOHN, b. 12 Sep 1777, d. 27 Jan 1784 of a malignant quinsey or the putrid sore throat; MARY, b. 17 May 1780 at 11 a.m., taken with diarrhea and d. 3 Sep 1781. {PA Genealogies: 846-849}

6. DAVID CLOWES, son of John (3) Clowes, b. 16 Sep 1733 at 5 a.m. in Lewistown, d. 25 May 1770 after a disorder of nearly 4 years. He m. Sophia (N).

Ann Crow with Isaac Jones by their writing obligatory dated 7 March 1763 obliged themselves to convey 44 3/4 a. to David Clowes and the land was conveyed by John Bound Jump and his wife Jemima, admins. of Ann Crow, and Isaac Jones, to David Clowes. And David Clowes by his last will devised same to his wife Sophia who later m. David Stewart. Ackn 27 Nov 1773. {SUDELR}

David Clowes, shipcarpenter, d. leaving a will dated 13 April 1770, proved 29 May 1770. Heirs: wife Sophia; dau. Hannah; bro. John; sisters Catherine and Mary. Exec., bro. John Clowes. Wits., Jeremiah Conwell, William Hazzard, Solomon Wright. Guardian, bro. John Clowes. {Arch. A65:52-53. Reg. of Wills, B:389-391} David was father of a dau. HANNAH, b. at Nanticoke on 22 April 1767, d. 9 Dec 1783 of quinsey at midnight. {PA Genealogies: 849}

7. CATHERINE CLOWES, dau. of John (3) Clowes, b. 9 July 1736 at 9 a.m. at

Lewistown, m. John Young. They were parents of JOHN, b. 28 Feb 1772. {PA Genealogies: 849}

8. MARY CLOWES, dau. of John (3) Clowes, b. 7 Feb 1739 at 5 a.m. at Lewes, d. 18 Jan 1791, 3 a.m., m. John Sheldren (Sheldon) Dorman. The were parents of the following children: GERARDUS, b. 23 Aug 1772; NEHEMIAH, b. 31 July 1774; ELIZABETH, b. 29 July 1776; JOHN, b. 22 May 1779. {PA Genealogies: 849}

9. LYDIA CLOWES, dau. of John (3) Clowes, b. 19 May 1742, at 7 a.m. at Lewestown, d. 25 Nov 1781 of nervous fever.

Lydia m. 1st Jeremiah Conwell by whom she had the following children: SHEPHARD, b. 23 July 1765; GERARDUS, b. 12 Nov 1767; JOHN, b. 29 Jan 1770. {PA Genealogies: 847-848}

Lydia m. 2nd (N) Lott Clark by whom she had the following children: MILICENT, b. 29 Sep 1776; ANNA, b. 27 April 1778; CHARLOTTE, b. 12 Feb 1780. {PA Genealogies: 849}

Fourth Generation

10. CATHERINE CLOWES, dau. of William (4) Clowes, m. 2nd 30 Jan 1774, Peter Dickison. {Rev. C. H. B. Turner}

11. SARAH CLOWES, dau. of John (5) Clowes, b. 12 June 1769 at 8:30 a.m., d. 9 Dec 1789, m. John Clarke. They were parents of a dau. JOANNA, b. 4 Oct 1787, m. 1809 Martin Duwaeli; JOHN, b. 6 Dec 1789, d. Jan 1812. {PA Genealogies: 849}

12. ALETTA CLOWES, dau. of John (5) Clowes, b. 7 April 1767 at 9:30 a.m., m. Miers Clark (b. 2 May 1761, d. 17 Dec 1810) 1785. They were the parents of the following children: MARY, b. 28 Aug 1786; SARAH, b. 9 May 1792; HANNAH, b. 10 Sep 1794; ELIZABETH, b. 24 Oct 1798; LIDIA, b. 18 July 1800; ESTER, b. 1 Feb 1803; ANNA, b. 6 Feb 1805; ALETTA, b. 30 April 1807. {PA Genealogies: 850}

THE COWGILL FAMILY

Ref.: A. See also *The Descendants of Ellin Cowgill 1682-1800*, by H. G. Stuebing and Carole J. Cowgill-Stuebing. Gateway Press, Inc., Baltimore, 1994. The authors state that John Cowgill [1 below], assumed son of Ellin Cowgil and assumed brother of Jane, Jennitt, Ralph, and Edmund, was probably born in England. John arrived in Bucks Co., PA in the fall of 1682 on the *Friend's Adventure* or *The Lamb* as an indentured servant to Cuthbert Hayhurst and remained until 1712 when he moved to New Castle County. For more details on the early generations of this family see this reference.

1. JOHN COWGILL, m. 1st 19th da., 8th mo., 1693, Bridget, dau. of Thomas and Agnes (Hathornthwaite) Croasdale, of Neshamina and m. 2nd 1703, Rachel Bunting, widow of Jobe Bunting, of Bristow, Berks Co., PA and dau. of Henry

Baker[24] of Newtown Twp. Bucks Co. {PA Genealogies:62} Bridgett Cowgill, wife of John Cowgill, d. 26th da., 2nd mo., 1701. {Middletown Monthly Meeting}

John and Bridget were parents of the following children {Middletown Monthly Meeting}: ELIZABETH, b. 24th da., 6th mo., 1694, m. 1st da., 10th mo., 1715, William Brown; THOMAS, b. 21st da., 4th mo., 1696; JOHN, b. 8th da., 5th mo., 1698; ELLIN, b. 14th da., 10th mo., 1700.

John Cowgill and Rachel Bunting announced their intentions of marriage by 10th da., 2nd mo. 1703. {Middletown Monthly Meeting}

On 1 May 1708 John Cowgill of Trevose in the county of Burks, yeoman, and Rachell his wife, widow and sole extx. of the will of Jobe Bunting, late of Bristow, Bucks Co., miller, and William Smith, late of Concord but now of the province of Maryland, conveyed to Nathan Baker of Concord, 300 a., originally granted to Jobe Bunting. {Chester Co. Deeds B2:224}

On 6th da., 9th mo., 1712, a certificate was requested for John Cowgill and his family to New Castle Co. {Middletown Monthly Meeting}

William Brown, son of William Brown of Nottingham in Chester Co. and Elizabeth Cowgil, dau. of John Cowgil of Duck Creek in Newcastle Co., m. 1st da., 10th mo., 1715 at Duck Creek. {DCMM}

On 4 Feb 1722/3 John Cowgill of Duck Creek in Newcastle Co., yeoman, and Rachel his wife, for £6 sold to James Hogg of same place, cordwinder, a lott of ground in the town of Salsbury ... about 66 foot from the Mill Dam. {KEDELR H:42}

John Cowgill and Rachael his wife, widow of John [Job] Bunting, were parents of the following children {Middletown Monthly Meeting, Bucks Co.}: HENRY, c1704 {A}; RACHAEL, b. 3rd da., 3rd mo., 1706, m. Thomas Sharp; MARY, b. 23rd da., 11th mo., 1707, m. Alexander Adams, Jr.; EBENESER, b. 19th da., 10th mo., 1709; ELEASOR, b. 21st da., 1st Mo., 1710.

Rachel had previously m. Job Bunting and by him had the following children {Middletown Monthly Meeting, Bucks Co.}: Rebecah, b. 5th da., 1st mo., 1691; Sarah, b. 27th da., 3rd mo., 1694.

John Cowgill d. by 2 Sep 1731 when Rachel Cowgill was appointed admx. of his estate. {Reg. of Wills, H:20}

In a petition on 26th of 6th month 1746 Henry Cowgill and Eleazor Cowgill stated that they doth understand that the admin. of our bro. Ebnazar Cowgill, dec'd., hath not long since passed. On 26 Aug 1746 the court ordered that William Maxwell and Elizabeth his wife who was admx. by the name of Elisabeth Cowgill, give a full acount. {KEORCF Cowgill, Ebenezer - 1746}

Second Generation

2. ELIZABETH COWGILL, dau. of John (1) and Bridget Cowgill, b. 24th da., 6th mo., 1694, m. 1st da., 10th mo., 1715, William Brown.

William Brown, son of William Brown of Nottingham in Chester Co. and Elizabeth Cowgil, dau. of John Cowgil of Duck Creek in Newcastle Co., m. 1st da., 10th mo., 1715 at Duck Creek. {DCMM}

---

24 Rachel was dau. of Henry and his 1st wife Margaret Hardman. Rachel was b. in Lancashire, 23rd da., 2nd mo., 1669 and m. Job Bunting of West Jersey. {PA Genealogies:71}

3. THOMAS COWGILL, son of John (1) and Bridget Cowgill, b. 21st da., 4th mo. 1696, m. in 1727, Sarah Clayton, dau. of Joshua Clayton and Sarah Clayton. {Welcome Claimants}

On 19th da., 12th mo., 1727, the orderly marriage of Thomas Cowgill and Sarah Clayton was reported.

Thomas Cowgle d. by 7 Dec 1749 when his widow, Sarah Cowgle, widow, was appointed admx. of his estate. {Arch. A-11:119. Reg. of Wills, K:4} Note: Arch. A-11:119 shows Ezekiel Cowgill, admin., d.b.n.

On 11 May 1750 Joshua Clayton of Kent Co., yeoman, for love, goodwill and affection give to my loving dau. Sarah Cowgill, widow of Thomas Cowgill, late of same co, part of a tract of land called *Willinbrook* in Little Creek Hundred ... 88 a. Wit: John Clayton, Nico Loockerman. {KEDELR O:46}

Sarah Cowgill, widow, d. leaving a will dated 15 July 1750, proved 16 Aug 1750. Heirs: sons Ezekiel and Thomas; daus. Sarah, Ellen, Rachel and Jane Smyth. Execs., son Ezekiel and son-in-law Daniel Smith. Wits., Clayton Levick, William Snow, Samuel McCall. {Arch. A-11:116. Reg. of Wills, K:22}

Joshua Clayton of Little Creek Hundred, d. leaving a will dated 2 Sep 1760, proved 26 Jan 1761. Heirs: wife Sarah; grandsons John, Henry, Thomas, Ezekiel and Clayton Cowgill; granddaus. Eunice Ozbun, Sarah Hand, Elenor Cowgill, Rachel Grewell, Sarah Register, Elizabeth Neal, Jean Smith and Lydia Durborow. Execs., friend Timothy Hanson and grandson-in-law Jonathan Ozbun. Wits., Mary Manlove, Elizabeth Manlove, Sarah Needham. {Arch. A9:121
122. Reg. of Wills, K:254-255} Note: Will mentions dau. Sarah Cowgill, dec'd.

Thomas and Sarah were parents of the following children: EZEKIEL; THOMAS; SARAH, m. 22nd da., 12th mo., 1756, Samuel Hand; ELLEN (Eleanor), probably m. Timothy Jenkins[25]; RACHEL, m. Jonathan Grewell; JANE (Jean), m. 21 st da., 5th mo., 1747, Daniel Smyth.

4. JOHN COWGILL, Jr., son of John (1) and Bridget Cowgill, b. 8th da., 5th mo., 1698, m. 1st, Lydia Clayton, dau. of Joshua Clayton, and m. 2nd Hannah Tomblin.

On 13th da., 1st mo., 1721, the orderly marriage of John Cowgill, Jr., and Lydia Clayton, was reported. {DCMM}

John and Lydia were parents of the following children {Third Haven Monthly Meeting, A}: JOHN; HENRY; CLAYTON, m. 27th da., 5th mo., 1763, Martha Neal; SARAH, b. 23rd da., 9th mo., 1722, m. John Register, b. 5th mo., 1709; ELIZABETH, m. 18th da., 3rd mo., 1743, Francis Neal; LYDIA, m. 1st da., 8th mo., 1753, Williamm Webb and m. 2nd (N) Durborow.

John Cowgill m. Hannah Tobmlin, widow of John Tomblin.

John Tomblin d. by 3 Nov 1747 when Hannah Tomblin, widow, was appointed admx. of his estate. {Reg. of Wills, 1:166-167} Note: Arch. A50:172-173 show Hannah, the widow, m. John Cowgill and later married Robert Hall; also

---

[25] Timothy Jenkins and ELLEN COWGILL, both of Kent Co., DE, m. 31st da., 3rd mo., 1773. {DCMM}

shows sons Joseph and John Tomblin; dau. Susannah, who married James Piper.

On 21st da., 9th mo., 1748 was reported the marriage of John Cowgil and Hannah Tomblin. {DCMM}

John Cowgill [Cowgle], Little Creek Hundred, d. by 29 July 1752 when Hannah Cowgill, widow, was appointed admx. of his estate. {Reg. of Wills, K:60-61} Note: Arch. All:96 shows Hannah, the widow, later m. Robert Hall; also mentions dau. Lydia Cowgill.

On 22nd da., 1st mo., 1753, a certificate was prepared for Lydia Cowgil to Third Haven Meeting, Maryland. {DCMM}

On 9 Feb 1767 Robert Hall of Little Creek Hundred, Kent Co., yeoman, for £52 sold to Isaac Carty of same place, yeoman, a parcel of land in Little Creek Neck and Hundred, part of a larger tract called *Willingbrook*, part of the real estate of John Hall, late of said co., dec'd., beginning at land of John Cowgill, as by deed from Andrew Caldwell and Hugh Durborow to John Cowgill, father to the present John Cowgill, bearing date 13 Aug 1723 (Book H, fol. 33), to land of John Frazier and Henry Cowgill, to land late purchased by Jonathan Caldwell from John Bell and Letitia his wife, to land of the said Isaac Carty ... 13 a. {KEDELR R:177}

5. ELLEN (Eleanor) COWGILL, dau. of John (1) and Bridget Cowgill, b. 14th da., 10th mo., 1700. m. Thomas Brown.

On 15th da., 12th mo., 1718, Thomas Brown from New Garden Monthly Meeting and Ellen Cowgill signified their intentions of marriage. {DCMM}

Thomas Brown, son of --- Brown, Senr. of Nottingham in Chester Co., PA, and Ellin Cowgil, dau. of John Cowgil, Senr., of Duck Creek of New Castle Co. on Delaware, yeoman, m. with consent of parents and relations. [no date] {DCMM}

Thomas Brown d. 19th da., 12th mo., 1746/7 between 10 and 11 a.m. in his 53rd year. {Nottingham Monthly Meeting}

Thomas d. leaving a will dated 3rd da., 2nd mo., 1745, proved 12 May 1747. He left his wife Ellen the plantation except for 25 a. for son John when he came of age. To son Nathan, 100 a., already conveyed to him and another 25 a.; To sons Thomas and Eleazer remainder of plantation. To sons Thomas and Eleazer, 231 a. in Little Britain in Lancaster Co. Also mentioned were daus. Rebecca Long; and Rachel, Anne and Elizabeth Brown. Execs. were wife Ellen and son Nathan. {Chester Co., PA, Wills B:220}

Thomas and Eleanor were parents of the following children {Nottingham Monthly Meeting}: NATHAN, b. 24th da., 3rd mo., 1720; THOMAS, b. 12th da., 1st mo., 1722/3; REBEKAH, b. 3rd da., 2nd mo., 1725; RACHEL, b. 23rd da., 12th mo., 1727/8; JOHN, b. 23rd da., 2nd mo., 1730; ANNE, b. 27th da., 9th mo., 1733; ELEAZER, b. 24th da., 8th mo., 1736; LYDIA, b. 7th da., 11th mo., 1739; ELIZABETH, b. 10th da., 12th mo., 1742.

6. HENRY COWGILL, son of John (1) Cowgill of Duck Creek, New Cassel Co., PA, m. 4th da., 4th mo., 1724, Mary Boulton, dau. of Edward and Sarah (Pancoast) Boulton, late of Mansfield Twp, Burlington, Co., NJ. {BMM}

Ca. 11th mo., 1723 Henry Cowgill requested a certificate to Burlington Monthly Meeting in order for marriage with a Friend belonging thereto. {DCMM}

Sarah Cowgill, dau. of Henry Cowgill and his wife Mary, b. 28th da., 2nd mo., 1725. {DCMM}

7. RACHAEL COWGILL, dau. of John (1) and Rachael Cowgill, b. 3rd da., 3rd mo., 1706, m. Thomas Sharp.

Rachal Sharp, wife of Thomas Sharp, d. 10th da., 12th mo., being dau. of John and Rachel Cowgil, in her 23rd year in 1728/9. {DCMM}

8. MARY COWGILL, dau. of John (1) and Rachael Cowgill, b. 23rd da., 11th mo., 1707, m. Alexander Adams, Jr.

On 19th da., 8th mo., 1724, Alexander Adams Jr. and Mary Cowgill announced intentions of marriage. {DCMM}

9. EBENEZER COWGLE, son of John (1) and Rachael Cowgill, b. 19th da., 10th mo., 1709.

On 21st da., 12th mo., 1742 Ebenezer Cowgill acknowledged his outgoing in marriage. {DCMM}

Ebenezer d. by 7 May 1743 when Elizabeth Cowgle was appointed admx. of his estate. {Reg. of Wills, I:65}

On 18th da., 2nd mo., 1754 a certificate was prepared for Rachel Cowgil, dau. of Ebenezer Cowgil to Nottingham Monthly Meeting. {DCMM}

Ebenezer was father of RACHEL.

10. ELEAZER COWGIL, son of John (1) and Rachael Cowgill, b. 24th da., 8th mo., 1736; m. 29th da., 6th mo., 1739, Martha Pain, dau. of Josiah Pain of Chester Co., PA.

On 19th da., 4th mo, 1732 Eleazer Cowgill informed the meeting that he intended to move to Nottingham and requested a certificate. {DCMM}

Eleazer Cowgill, son of John, dec'd., of West Nottingham, Chester Co., PA, m. Martha Pain, dau. of Josiah of the same place, on 29th da., 6th mo., 1739 at the public meeting of Friends at West Nottingham. {Nottingham Monthly Meeting}

On 17th da., 5th mo., 1756 there was a complaint from Nottingham Monthly Meeting against Eleazer Cowgil for leaving his affairs unsettled. {DCMM}

Eleazer and Martha were parents of the following children {Nottingham Monthly Meeting}: RACHEL, b. 6th da., 10th mo., 1744; ELISHA, b. 1st da., 1st mo., 1742; ELEANOR, b. 23rd da., 8th mo., 1745; ELIZABETH, b. 26th da., 2nd mo., 1747; JOHN, b. 29th da., 12th mo., 1748; MARTHA, b. 11th da., 1st mo., 1751; ELEAZER, b. 21st da., 11th mo., 1752.

Third Generation

11. JANE (Jean) COWGILL, dau. of Thomas (3) and Sarah Cowgill, m. 21st da., 5th mo., 1747, Daniel Smith (b. 11th da., 11th mo., 1722) of Kent Co. on Delaware and Jane Cowgill, having consent of parents and relations concerned, at Little Creek Meeting house.

Daniel Smith d. 27th da., 2nd mo., 1769. {DCMM} On 20 March 1769 Jane Smith, widow, was appointed admx. of his estate. {Arch. A47:13. Reg. of Wills, L:55}

Daniel and Jane were parents of the following children: EZEKIEL, b. 26th da., 5th mo., 1748; JOSEPH and BENJAMIN, b. 1st da., 8th mo., 1750

(Benjamin d. 4th da., 11th mo., 1784); SARAH, b. 11th da., 5th mo., 1752, d. 17th da., 10th mo., 1790, m. Joseph Nock (b. 15th da., 6th mo., 1750, d. intestate 1793), son of Daniel and Barthia (Hales) Nock {Welcome Claimants}; WILLIAM, b. 11th da., 7th mo., 1754; DANIEL, b. 30th da., 3rd mo., 1756; JANE, b. 5th da., 3rd mo., 1758; MARY, b. 24th da., 2nd mo., 1760, d. 16th da., 4th mo., 1799; LYDIA, b. 30th da., 11th mo., 1761; ELIZABETH, b. 29th da., 6th mo., 1764; SAMUEL, b. 8th da., 11th mo., 1766. {DCMM}

12. EZEKIEL COWGILL, son of Thomas (3) and Sarah Cowgill, m. Mary Sipple, widow of Christopher Sipple [26].

On 20th da., 11th mo., 1751 Ezekiel Cowgil and Susannah Tomblin announced their intentions of marriage. {DCMM}

On 17th da., 2nd mo., 1752 the intention of marriage between Ezekiel Cowgil and Susannah Tomblin was closed, she being married to another man by a priest, he being of another society. {DCMM}

On 20th da., 8th mo., 1753 Ezekiel Cowgil brought a paper condemning his disorderly marriage by a Priest to one not in membership with the Society. {DCMM}

Christopher Sipple d. leaving a will dated 7 Dec 1751, proved 24 Feb 1752. Heirs: wife unnamed; sons Christopher, Raymond, Silva; daus. Mary, Elizabeth, Alice and Priscilla Sipple and Sarah Goforth and Mary Ann Jenkins; granddau. Mary Jenkins. Execs., wife, bro. John Sipple and friend Mark Manlove. Wits., John Emerson, William Gray, Unity Emerson. {Arch. A46:110-115. Reg. of Wills, K:52} Note: Arch. A46:115 shows Mary, the widow, later married Ezekiel Cowgill.

On 10 May 1763 Jonathan Ozbun of Kent Co, yeoman, and Eunice his wife and Ezekiel Cowgill of same co., yeoman, which said Eunice and Ezekiel Cowgill are 2 of the devisees named in the will of Joshua Clayton late of Kent co. yeoman dec'd. ... in division of several tracts of land, whereas the said Joshua Clayton in his life time was seized in a tract of land called *Highams Ferry* in Little Creek Hundred, 136 a., also in one other parcel of land part of a larger tract called *Willingbrook* and being so seized he on 2 Nov 1760 did make his will and did devise, to wit, I give unto my grandson Ezekiel Cowgill 12 a. to be laid off at the w. end of that land which I gave by deed to my dec'd. dau. Sarah Cowgill and to incommode as little as may be the tract whereon I now dwell, I give unto my grandau. Unice Ozbun my now dwelling plantation part of a tract called *Highams Ferry* and part of a tract called *Willingbrook* bounded on the s. with land given to my afsd. dau. Sarah Cowgill on the n.w. with land of Ralph Needham, on the e. with the land left herein to my grandson John Cowgill. {KEDELR Q:159}

On 15 Aug 1753 Mary Cowgill and Mark Manlove of Kent Co., surviving execs. of Christopher Sipple, dec'd., for £100 released unto Thomas Christophers of same place, a tract of land (whereas Christopher Sipple, dec'd., did in his life time bargain with said Christopher to let him have a tract of land called *Sipples Choice* in Murderkill Hundred and whereas by Sipple's will bearing date 7 Dec 1751 he impowered his executors, to wit the afsd. Mark

[26] Ref. A. states that Mary was the dau. of Christopher Sipple.

Manlove, Mary Cowgill then Mary Sipple and John Sipple since dec'd. to comply with his part of the said covenants upon said Christopher complying with his). {KEDELR O:199}

Ezekiel Cowgil and Mary were parents of the following children: DANIEL, b. 13th da., 5th mo., 1754; ELIZABETH, b. 10th da., 8th mo., 1760, d. 31st da., 12th mo., 1789, bur. at Little Creek meeting house. Mary, mother of the above d. 22nd da., 8th mo., 1788, bur. Little Creek Meeting house on 23rd. Ezekiel Cowgil, father of the above d. 8th da., 9th mo., 1792, bur. Little Creek Meeting House on 10th da., 9th mo., 1792. {DCMM}

13. THOMAS COWGILL, son of Thomas (3) and Sarah Cowgill, m. Susanna Dawson.

On 26th da., 3rd mo., 1765, was reported the marriage of Thomas Cowgill and Susanna Dawson. {DCMM}

Thomas Cowgill d. by 14 May 1767 when Benjamin Dawson was appointed admin. {Arch. A11:120. Reg. of Wills, L:26}

On 26th da., 11th mo., 1768, a certificate was being drawn for Susanna Cowgill who was removing to within the compass of Uwchland Monthly Meeting, Chester Co. {DCMM}

On 26th da., 5th mo., 1770, Susanna Cowgill produced a certificate from Uchland Monthly Meeting in behalf of herself and dau. Sarah Cowgill. {DCMM}

On 25th da., 9th mo., 1773, Susanna Cowgill, now wife of John Smedley of Chester Co. offered a paper condemning her outgoing in marriage. {DCMM}

Thomas was father of SARAH, b. 24th da., 2nd mo., 1766, m. Richard Cox. {A}

14. ELIZABETH COWGILL, dau. of John (4) Cowgill, m. 18th da., 3rd mo., 1743, Francis Neall, Jun., of TA Co., MD, at Little Creek Meeting house. {DCMM}

Francis and Elizabeth were parents of the following children: LYDIA, b. 17 April 1744; MARY, b. 30 June 1746, m. Aaron Parrott. {For more on this Neall family see *Colonial Families of the Eastern Shore of Maryland*, Vol. 4.}

15. SARAH COWGILL, b. 23rd da., 9th mo., 1722, dau. of John (4) Cowgill, m. John Regester, b. 5th mo., 1709, son of Robert Regester of TA Co., MD, dec'd., at the public meeting house at Little Creek [date missing]. {DCMM}

On 29th da., 10th mo., 1742 John Regester requested a certificate to be directed to the monthly meeting in KE Co. on Delaware, signifying his clearness in marriage.

On 15 April 1752 - 12 May 1752 John Regester and his wife Sarah conv. to William Troth 8 1/4 a., part of *Darlington.* {TALR 18:59}

John Register, d. 17 Feb 1758, 49 years.{TATH}

John Register, TA Co., d. leaving a will dated 17 Feb 1758, proved 25 April 1758. Mentioned were wife Sarah and children: Samuel, John, Robert, Lydia, Joshua, David and Sarah Register. The will was witnessed by Wm. Taylor, Francis Neale, Jonathan Neale, Jr., Wm. Troth. {MWB 30:477}

On 16 da., 11 mo., 1768 Sarah Regester manumitted Negroes Jacob and Jane. {TALR 19:543} On 25th da., 4th mo., 1771, Sarah Register manumitted

Jacob and Jane.

Sarah Register, widow of John Register, of TA Co. d. 5 Feb 1771 and proved 5 May 1772. She mentioned her children: Joshua, David, Sarah, John, Robert and Lydia. William and Henry Troth were execs. The will was witnessed by Henry and Elizabeth Troth. {MWB 38:875}

John was father of SAMUEL; and John and Sarah were parents of the following children: JOHN; ROBERT; LYDIA; JOSHUA; DAVID, b. 17 Jan 1752 {TATH}; SARAH, b. 27 Jan 1754 {TATH}.

16. JOHN COWGILL, probable son of John (4) Cowgill, m. 19th da., 8th mo., 1756, Mary Worrel, both of KE Co. DE, at the dwelling house of Joshua Clayton of KE Co. {DCMM}

On 17th da., 1st mo., 1757 there was a report of orderly marriage of John Cowgill and Mary Worrall, having consent of parents and relations. {DCMM}

Children of John Cowgil and Mary his wife: Lydia, b. 20th da., 7th mo., 1759, d. 3rd da., 12th mo., 1759; Mary, b. 13th da., 5th mo., 1764; Elizbeth, b. 11th da., 10th mo., 1763; d. 19th da., 10th mo., 1763; Clayton, b. 6th da., 11th mo., ---; John, b. 13th da., 2nd mo., ---, d. 1767; John, b. 25th da., 6th mo., 1768; Sarah, b. 21st da., 1st mo., 1771; Joseph, b. 8th da., 11th mo., 1773; Worrell, b. 1777. {DCMM}

On 26 Aug 1761 a petition was submitted by John Cowgill to sheweth that his father John Cowgill, dec'd., d. intestate and his lands, 50 a. on Little Creek Hundred being part of the same plantation whereon he d. and whereas he has left 5 heirs besides your petitioner. He requests division of the land. {KEORCF Cowgill, John - 1761}

On 10 Nov 1763 John Cowgill of Kent Co., yeoman, and Jonathan Ozburn (Ozbun) of same co., yeoman, and Unice (Eunice) his wife released each to the other ... several tracts of land, whereas Joshua Clayton, late of Kent Co., yeoman, dec'd., grandfather of the said John Cowgill and Unice Ozburn was in his lifetime seized in 100 a. which heretofore belonged to one Robert Porter then late of said co. dec'd., also in another parcel part of a larger tract called *Highams Ferry*, also in one other parcel part of 2 larger tracts called *Wellingbrook* and *Highams Ferry* including the late dwelling plantation of the said Joshua Clayton, and being so seized made a will bearing date 2 Nov 1760 and devised to the said John Cowgill his grandson all the land and plantation which formerly belonged to Robert Porter late of said co. beginning at Herring Branch on e. side of road from Muddy Branch to Little Creek Landing, to land of Ralph Needham, dec'd., to land by me sold to David Morgan, the will did further devise to the said Unice Ozburn his granddau. all my now dwelling plantation bounded by land given to my dau. Sarah Cowgill. {KEDELR Q:200}

On 14 Aug 1766 John Cowgill of Kent Co., yeoman, and Mary his wife for £200 sold to John Spruance of same place, yeoman, a tract of land part of a tract called *Banefield* ... 100 a. {KEDELR R:112}

17. CLAYTON COWGILL, probable son of John (4) and Lydia Cowgill, m. 27th da., 5th mo., 1763, Martha Neal. {TATH}

On 24th da., 10th mo., 1761 Clayton Cowgill and Thomas Cowgill both produced certificates from Philadelphia Monthly Meeting dated 31st da., 7th mo., 1761. {DCMM}

Clayton Cowgill of Kent Co. on Delaware and Martha Neal in TA Co., m. 27th da., 5th mo., 1763 at the dwelling house of Francis Neal in TA Co. {THMM}

Clayton Cowgill d. by 2 Aug 1764 when Martha Cowgill was appointed admx. of his estate. {Reg. of Wills, K:346} On 4 Dec 1764 Henry Cowgill was appointed admin. of his estate. {Arch. All:83. Reg. of Wills, K:353}

18. HENRY COWGILL of Kent Co., PA [DE], son of John (4) and Lydia Cowgill, m. 4th da., 1st mo., 1741/42, Alice Pain, dau. of Josiah Pain, of Nottingham in Chester Co. {Nottingham Monthly Meeting}

On 17th da., 12th mo., 1745 Henry Cowgil requested a certificate for himself and wife in order to join them to Nottingham Monthly Meeting. {DCMM} On 27th da., 6th mo, 1761 a certificate was produced for Henry Cowgill from East Nottingham. {DCMM}

Fourth Generation

19. JOHN COWGILL, son of Henry (18) Cowgill, dec'd., and Alice of Fawn Twp., York Co., PA, m. 12th da., 11th mo., 1772, Catherine Sheppard, dau. of William and Hannah of East Nottingham Twp., Chester Co., PA. {Nottingham Monthly Meeting}

Unplaced

(N) COWGILL m. Elizabeth Ozbun, dau. of Jonathan Ozbun.

Jonathan Ozbun, yeoman of Little Creek Hundred, d. leaving a will dated 24 Aug 1773, proved 11 Nov 1773. Heirs: wife Eunice; son Jonathan; daus. Eunice and Tabitha Ozbun, Elizabeth Cowgill, Mary Alstone; son-in-law Israel Alstone. Extx., wife Eunice. Guardian, Robert Holliday. Wits., Robert Regester, Elizabeth Stevens, Thomas Parry. {Arch. A38:166-167. Reg. of Wills, L:143} Note: Will mentions grandfather Joshua Clayton, dec'd.

On 27th da., 10th mo., 1764, ELIZABETH COWGILL produced a certificate from East Nottingham Monthly Meeting dated 30th da., 6th mo., 1764. {DCMM}

On 24th da., 8th mo., 1765, a certificate was drawn for ELIZABETH and ELLEN COWGILL who are removed to Nottingham. {DCMM}

On 18th da., 12th mo., 1744 there was a complaint against ELIZABETH COWGILL for marrying out of the Unity of Friends. {DCMM}

On 25th da., 2nd mo., 1764, ELLEN COWGILL appeared and produced a paper condemning the misconduct for which she was formerly disowned in 1759. {DCMM}

On 20th da., 8th mo., 1764, ELINOR COWGILL produced a certificate from East Nottingham Monthly Meeting dated 26th da., 5th mo., 1764. {DCMM}

On 21st da., 2nd mo., 1735, HENRY COWGILL by his brother John requested a certificate to Chesterfield Monthly Meeting, Crosswicks, where he intends to move. On 21st day., 5th mo., William Farson reported that Henry Cowgill had changed his mind. {DCMM}

On 23rd da., 4th mo., 1768, there was a complaint against HENRY COWGILL for accomplishing his marriage by assistance of a priest (minister of another denomimation) with his first cousin's dau., being a Friend. {DCMM}

On 18th da., 9th mo., 1758 a certificate was being drawn for MARTHA COWGILL. {DCMM}

On 26th da., 5th mo., 1764, MARTHA COWGILL produced a certificate from Third Haven Monthly Meeting dated 26th da., 1st mo., 1764. {DCMM}

MARTHA COWGILL d. by 4 Dec 1764 when Henry Cowgill was appointed admin. of her estate. {Arch. All:111. Reg. of Wills, K:352}

On 22nd da., 11th mo., 1766, testimony was being drawn against MARY COWGILL, now the wife of David Thornton, for marrying with a man not of the Society, after being precautioned. {DCMM}

THE CURTIS FAMILY

Ref: A. For more information on the Curtis Family see *Genealogies of Pennsylvania Familes*. From the *Pennsylvania Genealogical Magazine*. Vol. 1, 1982. Some of the following information is included below.

1. RICHARD CURTIS of Philadelphia m. Ann, dau. of John (2) and Elizabeth Curtice. Richard arrived on the ship *Lion* of Leverpool, 14th da., 8th mo., 1683, as servant to Robert Turner. {Welcome Claimants}

On 3 Feb 1687/8 Richard Curtice of Philadelphia appointed his friend William Berry of Kent Co. as atty to appear in court to receive a deed of gift from John Curtice for 100 a. and one deed of sale from Joseph Hillyard for 100 a. {KEDELR}

On 1 March 1687/8, whereas there was intentions of mariage between Richard Curtice of Philadelphia batchelor and Ann Curtice dau. of John Curtice yeoman and Elizabeth his wife ... published and certified same under hands of Samuell Carpenter, Thomas Fitzwater, Thomas Duesott, Joshua Carpenter, Robert Turner, Edward Low, John Fuller, Phillip England and Anthony Morris all of Philadelpia ... Wit: Wm. Berry, clerk.

On 1 March 1687/8 Richard and Ann [above] at house of John Curtice took each other for man and wife. Wit: Ana Heathord, Naomy Berry, Prosila Bowers, Mary Betts, Miloson Hotherd, Ellinor Roboson, An Manloe, Sarah Jones, John Walker and John Betts Justices, Richard Hogbain, Geo Bowers, Wm. Freeman, Tho Skidmore, John Fostor, Robert Edmons, Wm. Berry, Daniell James, John Curtice, Tho Heatherd, John Roboson, Winlock Curtice, Daniell Jones, Geo Manloe, Ezekiell Jones, Johanes Groundyck.

Richard Curtis of Mispillion Creek Hundred d. leaving a will dated 20 May 1695, proved 14 Dec 1695. Heirs: Jehu Curtis; Winlock, son of Jehu

Curtis; sister-in-law Elizabeth Jones; Nathaniel Hun; Samuel Low; son, Samuel Curtis; dau. Elizabeth Curtis; James Howell; John Arriskin; father-in-law John Curtis. Execs., John Curtis and James Howell. Wits., Robert French, Samuel Atkins, Priscilla Curtis. {Arch. A12:163. Reg. of Wills, A:17}

On 2 Jan 1698/9 John Curtis, James Howel and William Brinkloe were appointed admins. of the estate of Richard Curtis. {Reg. of Wills, B:32}

Richard was father of the following children: SAMUEL; ELIZABETH.

2. JOHN CURTIS, b. c1642 at Appledore, County Kent, England; m. 1st Elizabeth Cabley, dau. of John Cabley, and m. 2nd Priscilla (Kitchen) Bowers. Priscilla was b. c1647 in Salem Massachusetts, dau. of John and Elizabeth (Grafton) Kitchen. Priscilla m. 1st Nathaniel Hunn, m. 2nd George Bowers, m. 3rd John Curtis and m. John Gilbert. {A}

John Cabley of Mother Creek d. leaving a Will dated 9 Nov 1683 [no probate]. Heirs: Caleb Curtis, Ann Curtis, Winlock Curtis, Elizabeth Curtis, John Curtis. [No extx.]. Wits., Ann Carter, Cornelis Collton. (No probate.] {Penna. Hist. Soc. Papers, AM 2013:16}

On 4 Oct 1687/8 John Curtis of Kent Co. in consideration of the love goodwill and affection which I have for my loving friend Richard Curtis of Philadelphia, I give to Richard Curtis a plantation tract of land 100 a. part of tract of land belonging to said John Curtis called *Stratham* and to be that part adj. tract which John Curtis sold unto George Manloe called *Point Looke Out*. {KEDELR}

On 7 Nov 1687 John Curtis of Kent Co. and Elizabeth his wife for £50 sold to William Monloe of same co., a tract of land called *Stratham*, 300 a. On the same day John Curtis of Kent Co. and Elizabeth his wife for £37 sold to Georg Manloe of same place, a tract of land called *Point Look Out*, 300 a. {KEDELR}

On 23 Dec 1689 Frances Spencer quitt and discharged and released "from all ingagements as concerning mariage between me and my friend John Curtice." Witnessed by Hugh Luft, Thomas Huflam.

On 29 Dec 1689, whereas John Curtice of Kent Co., PA, widdower and Prisilla Bowers of same place widdow hath intentions of mariage ... Frances Spencer, widdow, certified [see below] ... it is certified that John and Prisilla take each other for husband and wife at the house of Thomas Heatherd ... Wit: James Cooper, Hugh Luft, Thomas Bedwell, Thomas Heatherd, Samuell King, John Parker, John Newell, Cornelias Collin, Thomas Skidmore, William Berry, Anna Heatherd, Rose Skidmore, Naomy Berry, Anna Price, Mary Killingworth, Elizabeth Curtice, Malesent Heatherd.

John Curtis, Gentleman of St. Jones Hundred, d. leaving a will dated 22 April 1698, proved 3 May 1698. Heirs were wife unnamed; son Caleb; daus. Elizabeth and Ruth; grandson Jehu Curtis; Samuel Low. Execs., Caleb Curtis and Priscilla Curtis (from Admin. Acct.). Wits., Richard Jackson, Michael Donoho, Jno. Foster. {Arch. A12:159. Reg. of Wills, B:26 and 32}

John was father of the following children: (by 1st wife Elizabeth Cabley): WINLOCK, b. 1668, lost at sea c1693/4; ANN m. Richard (1) Curtis; CALEB; ELIZABETH, m. 1st William Brinckle and m. 2nd John Hammitt; RUTH.

On 10 March 1768 by virtue of a warrant dated 26 Feb 1681 there was surveyed and laid out for John Curtis a 50 a. tract of land called *Pasture Point* on s. side of Murther Creek adj. afsd. tract, and John Curtis by his will dated 22 April 1698 did devise all of *Pasture Point* and 1/2 of *Ivy Hill*, 270 a. in both pieces, to his grandson Jehu Curtis, and Jehu Curtis by his deed poll bearing date 18 March 1718. {KEDELR R:254}

On 13 Nov 1747 William Shirley (Sherley) of Kent Co. yeoman for £150 sold to John Emerson of same place, two tracts of land (whereas there is a tract of land called *Pasture Point* on s. side of Murther Creek, 50 a. laid out unto John Curtis by a warrant dated 26 Feb 1681, also one other tract s. side of Murder Creek 400 a. by virtue of a warrant bearing date 20 April 1681 unto John Cabelie, and he did convey the same unto John Curtis of same co, and John Curtis by his will to wit, 22 April 1698 did devise unto his grandchild Jehu Curtis, 270 a. on s. side of Murtherkill Creek adj. to the land of Richard Curtis and on the other side which is called *Cedar Landing Neck.* {KEDELR N:pg 188}

Second Generation

3. WINLOCK CURTIS, son of John (2) and Elizabeth Curtis, b. c1668, lost at sea c1693/4, m. Ann Bowers (b. 1668, d. 1723/4, dau. of Benanuel and Elizabeth (Dunster) Bowers of Charlestown, MA, and sister of George Bowers.) They were parents of the following children: ANN, b. 1690, d. 1747, m. 1st Robert Clay and m. 2nd Robert Bolton, both Philadelphia merchants; JEHU, b. 1692, d. 1753, Speaker of the Assembly, m. Mary Brinkloe, his first cousin and had issue. {A}

4. ELIZABETH CURTIS, dau. of John (2) and Elizabeth Curtis, b. c1671, probably m. William Brinckle.

5. CALEB CURTIS, son of John (2) and Elizabeth Curtis, probably m. Cornelia (N).

On 7 April 1722 John Curtis of Kent Co., yeoman, (son and heir of Caleb Curtis late, dec'd., of same co. gentleman) and Sarah his wife appoint our trusty friend Andrew Caldwell of same co. gentleman to be our atty to deliver and convey [above] deed of sale in open court. {KEDELR G:73}

Caleb Curtis d. by 20 March 1702 when his estate was administered by Cornelia Curtis. {Reg. of Wills, B:46}

On 7 April 1722 John Curtis, son and heir of Caleb Curtis, to whom John Curtis, Senr., late of Kent Co., gentleman, dec'd., father of said Caleb Curtis, devised the hereafter mentioned land by his will bearing date 22 April 1698 ... and John Curtis, Junr., now of same co., yeoman, son and heir of said Caleb, and Sarah his wife for £60 sold to James Maxwell of same co., yeoman ... 400 a. which John Curtis, Senr., was lawfully possessed (pattent granted from York 29 Sep 1678) unto John Briggs who sold same by an assignment on the pattent bearing date 5 May 1679. {KEDELR G:97}

On 12 Feb 1722 James Maxwell of Kent Co. for £74 sold to John Clark, Junr., of same co. yeoman, a tract of land in Mispillion Hundred called *Aberdeen* (400 a. patent from York bearing date 5 May 1679 unto John Briggs late of Kent Co., dec'd., from whom it came into the tenure of John Curtis who in his life time and at the time of his death was seized thereof and by his will bearing date 22 April 1698 bequeath the same unto his son Caleb Curtis and his grandson John Curtis, Junr., son of said Caleb which said John Curtis, Junr., sold half part of 400 a. unto afsd. James Maxwell) ... 200 a. {KEDELR H:57}

On 10 Aug 1725 Elizabeth Curtis, dau. and one of the heirs of Caleb Curtis, late of Kent Co., dec'd., for £10 sold to John Clark of same place, a tract of land in Mispilion Hundred called *Aberdeen*, 400 a., and was originally granted by pattent from NY bearing date 5 May 1679 unto John Briggs late of the same co., dec'd., and came into the possession of John Curtis who in his life time and at the time of his death was seized thereof and did by his will bearing date 22 April 1698 bequeathed same to his son the afsd. Caleb Curtis, father to Elizabeth Curtis and the said Caleb Curtis afterwards dyed intestate ... Caleb Curtis leaving behind only one son John Curtis and one dau. the afsd. Elizabeth Curtis, she is lawfully seized of 1/3 part of of the 400 a. conveying same unto John Clark. {KEDELR H:148}

Caleb was father of JOHN who m. Sarah (N) and ELIZABETH.

6. RUTH CURTIS, b. c1690, dau. of John (2) and Priscilla Curtis, m. William Rodney. See The Rodney Family.

On 10 May 1725 William Rodeney and Ruth his wife of Kent Co. for £8 sold to Jehu Curtis of same place esqr., a tract of land which is not mentioned in the will of John Curtis late of same co., dec'd., father to the said Ruth, in Mispilion Hundred called *Swamp Baron*, 160 a., also two other parcells of land in Dorchester Co. MD one called *Indian Quarter* and the other *Rochester* 100 a. each. {KEDELR H:199}

Third Generation

7. JEHU CURTIS, son of Winlock (3) Curtis, b. 1692, d. 1753, m. Mary Brinckloe, dau. of William and Elizabeth Brinckle. Mary was his first cousin.[27] Jehue was Speaker of the Assembly. {A}

On 1 Jul 1725 Jehu Curtis of Newcastle Co., gent., and Mary his wife for £220 sold to John Brinklo of Kent Co., a tract of land on n. side of Murther Creek, by the land of John Edmonds ... 440 a. {KEDELR I:9}

Elizabeth Hammitt,[28] wife of John Hammitt, d. leaving a will dated 31 Oct 1725, proved 8 Dec 1725. Heirs: sons Winlock and John Brinkle; daus. Mary Curtis, wife of Jehu Curtis, Elizabeth Clark, wife of John, Jr., Miriam and Sarah Brinkle. Execs., sons John and Winlock Brinkle. Trustees, bros.-in-law John and Peter Brinkle. Wits., Elizabeth Brinkle, Hannah Masten, Curtis Brinkle. {Arch. A21:189. Reg. of Wills, F: 6}

8. JOHN CURTIS, son of Caleb (5), m. Sarah (N).

On 19 March 1718/19 John Curtis of Philadelphia, mariner, for £30 sold to William Brinkloe of Kent Co. esqr ... a tract of land called *Pasture Point* on s. side of Murder Creek ... 50 a. (granted unto John Curtis by virtue of a warrant for 1200 a. dated 21 Feb 1681/2 surveyed 18 Oct 1687) and one other tract on s. side of Murther Creek ... 200 a. lower half part (400 a. granted by virtue of a warrant bearing date 20 April 1681 surveyed 28 Jan 1681 unto John

---

[27] It is likely that they were cousins, through having John Curtis as their grandfather.

[28] Elizabeth was the widow of William Brinckle and mother of Jehu's wife.

Cabley and John Cabley sold to John Curtis) ... John Curtis in his life time 22 April 1698 did make his will ... I give to my grandchild John Curtis 270 a. of land s. side of Murther Creek adj. land of Richard Curtis and on the other side of that which is called *Ceder Landing Neck.* {KEDELR F:63}

On 7 April 1722 John Curtis, Junr., son and heir of Caleb Curtis, to whom John Curtis, Senr., late of Kent Co., gent., dec'd., father of the said Caleb Curtis devised the hereafter mentioned land by his will dated 22 April 1698... whereas the afsd. John Curtis son, dec'd., was possessed of 400 a. of land (pattent bearing date 29 Sep 1678 granted unto John Briggs who on 5 May 1679 sold the same) John Curtis, Junr., (son and heir of said Caleb) now of Kent Co. yeoman together with Sarah his wife for £100 sold to Nathaniel Luff of same co. yeoman the one halfe of afsd. tract of land called *Abardeen.* {KEDELR H:90

On 12 May 1722 John Curtis late of Kent Co., gentleman, and Sarah his wife for a valuable consideration in hand paid sold to John Mathon of same place yeoman ... a tract of land called *The Reserve*, on s.w. side of Dover River 400 a. {KEDELR G:72}

On 12 Feb 1723 John Curtis of Kent Co., yeoman, for £60 sold to Mathew Manlove of same place, a tract of land formerly surveyed and laid out 11 Oct 1687 for John Curtis of same co., dec'd., grandfather to said John Curtis, confirmed by patent bearing date 5 April 1690, called *Hickbery* but by patent called *Swamp Barow* in Mispelion Hundred, at the corner of land of James Shakerly and John Curtis land called *Aberdeen* ... 160 a. {KEDELR H:68}

On 5 Aug 1743 John Curtis in his life time 22 April 1698 did make his will and devised to his grandchild John Curtis 270 a. next adj. the land of Richard Curtis called *Ceder Landing Neck* which includes the afsd. tract of 50 a. and the lower half part of the 400 a., and John Curtis 18 March 1738 for £30 conveyed the same to William Brinckle of Kent Co. {KEDELR M:229}

On 16 Mary 1740 Sarah Curtis was appointed admx. of the estate of John Curtis, laborer. {Reg. of Wills, I:32}

9. ELIZABETH CURTIS, dau. of Caleb (5) Curtis, moved to Queen Anne's Co.

On 15 Jan 1724 Elizabeth Curtis of Queen Anns Co., MD, spinster, dau. of Caleb Curtis of Baukcombs Creek in Mismillion Hundred, Kent Co., dec'd., appoint my loveing brother John Curtis of place afsd. to recover and receive all such debts as are due and oweing to me and also to deliver [above] deed in open court. {KEDELR H:150}

Unplaced

JOHN CURTIS and MARY CURTIS and son in law JEHU CURTIS.

William Brinckle d. leaving a will dated 1 April 1722, proved 8 May 1722. Heirs: sons William, Winnlock (Winlock], and John Brinckle and John Curtis; daus. Elizabeth, Mariam [Miriam], and Sarah Brinckle and Mary Curtis; wife Elizabeth. Execs., wife Elizabeth, son-in-law Jehu Curtis. Wits., Andrew Freasure, William Mulroney, Hannah Freasure. {Arch. A5:217. Reg. of Wills, D:52-54}

WILLIAM CURTIS m. Mary (N) and had a son JOHN.

William d. by 23 April 1748 when his estate was administered by Mary Curtis, widow. {Reg. of Wills, I:207} Note: Arch. A12:167 mentions son John

Curtis; also Mary Oleger as admx.

THE FARSON FAMILY

1. WILLIAM FARSON of the Kingdom of Ireland but later of Duck Creek in Kent Co. upon Delaware, m. 1st Rachel Veal of Georges Creek, New Castle Co. upon Delaware, dau. in law of John Kinsey of Woodbridge and dau. of Grace Kinsey, his wife, of East Jersey, on 25th da, 4th mo, 1719, at Georges Creek.

William m. 2nd Sarah Hales of Georges Creek in New Castle Co., 23rd da, 8th mo, 1724 at the meeting house at Georges Creek. She was the widow of John Hales and had children by her earlier marriage to Hales. {DCMM}

On 21st da, 5th mo, 1735 William Farson reported that Henry Cowgill has altered his mind about going to Crosswicks. {DCMM}

On 11 May 1763 Edmund Liston of Appoquinomink Hundred, Newcastle Co., yeoman, and Rachel his wife in consideration of Henry Farson and Mary his wife making and executing a deed of release by an agreement and 5 shillings quit claim unto Henry Farson of Duck Creek Hundred yeoman ... part of the real estate of William Farson Esqr., dec'd., whereas William Farson Esqr. late of Duck Creek Hundred Kent Co. dec'd. by virtue of sundry mesne conveyances and by a proprietary grant to him confirmed became in his life time and was at the time of his death seized in part of a tract of land called *Branford* and of another called *Lurgan* and also of a tract part of the *Manner of Freith*, and died intestate leaving issue, to wit afsd Henry Farson the only male, and one dau. Rachel being the afsd wife of Edmund Listen, and Henry Farson and Edmund Liston have mutually agreed upon a division of the several trs of land, lying contiguous to each other, and release to each other ... containing the brick dwelling house where William Farson dec'd. lately did dwell beginning on road to Duck Creek Town to Permains branch ... 249 3/4 a. in Duck Creek Hundred and also 1 small piece of land on Greens branch ... 13 a. (Q:pg 195)

William Farson d. 2nd da, 5th mo, 1762. {DCMM}

On 13 May 1762 Jane Farson and Henry Farson were appointed admins. of his estate. {Reg. of Wills, K:283}

William and Rachel Farson were parents of the following children {DCMM}: HENRY, b. 20th da, 6th mo, 1720; MARTHA, b. 10th da, 3rd mo, 1722, d. 23rd da, 8th mo, 1722.

Rachel, wife of William, d. 23rd da., 8th mo, 1722. {DCMM}

William and Sarah Farson were parents of the following children {DCMM}: RACHEL, b. 5th mo, 1726, m. Edmund Liston.

Sarah, wife of William Farson, d. 27th da, 1st mo, 1748.

2. HENRY FARSON, son of William (1) m. Mary Hales, late of New Castle Co., dec'd., 14th da, 2nd mo, 1743 at Duck Creek Meeting House. {DCMM}

The orderly marriage of Henry Farson and Mary Hales was reported on 18th da, 2nd mo, 1743. {DCMM}

On 19th da, 6th mo, 1758 Henry Farson produced a paper condemning his past misbehaviour in drinking strong liquor to excess. On 26th da, 6th mo, 1762 there was a complaint against Henry Farson for using spiritous liquors to excess. {DCMM}

Malachi Roan of Duck Creek d. leaving a will dated 25 July 1759, proved 16 Aug 1759. Heirs: Jane McDevet, dau. of Daniel McDevet; William Farson, son of Henry Farson; Roger Magee (in Ireland); bros. & sisters unnamed. Exec'r, friend Daniel McDevet. Wits., Mary Farson, Martha Turner, Henry Farson. {Arch. A44:19-20. Reg. of Wills, K: 210}

On 25 Aug 1762 Henry Farson and Mary his wife of Duck Creek Hundred, Kent Co., for £20 sold to Molleston Currey of same place a tract of swamp or meadow ground in the hundred afsd beginning at Greens Branch alias Spring Branch being the last corner stone of Henry Farson's lower meadow ... 4 a. part of a large tract called *Branford.* {KEDELR Q:114}

On 26th da, 3rd mo, 1763 a certificate for Jane Farson to Wilmington Monthly was to be prepared. {DCMM}

On 11 May 1763 Henry Farson of Duck Creek Hundred Kent Co. yeoman and Mary his wife in consideration of Edmund Liston and Rachel his wife making and executing a deed of release by an agreement and 5 shillings quit claim unto Edmund Liston of Appoquinimink Hundred New Castle Co. yeoman and Rachel his wife, part of the real estate of William Farson Esqr dec'd. containing a messuage & tract of land and plantation in Duck Creek Hundred on e. side of the plantation whereon William Farson Esqr lately did dwell part of a tract called *Branford* and also part of another tract called *Lurgan* ... adj. Andrew Jamison's land 229 a. 137 perches. {KEDELR Q:198}

On 28th da, 9th mo, 1771 a certificate was being prepared for Ann Farson, dau. of Henry Farson to Wilmington Monthly Meeting. {DCMM}

On 23rd da, 1st mo, 1768, Jane Farson informed the meeting that she intended to embark for Old England and requested a certificate. {DCMM}

On 24th da, 6th mo, 1769 preparation was being made to deal with Mary Farson (that was) now wife of Samuel Starr. {DCMM} On 23rd da, 1st mo, 1773 a certificate was produced from Wilmington Monthly Meeting for Ann Farson, dau. of Henry Farson. {DCMM}

Henry and Mary Farson were parents of the following children {DCMM}: WILLIAM, b. 19th da, 12th mo, 1744, d. 20th da, 1st mo, 1745; WILLIAM, b. 31st da, 5th mo, 1746, d. 25th da, 9th mo, 1753; MARY and RACHEL, b. 3rd da, 1st mo, 1748/9 (Rachel d. 26th da, 10th mo, 1767); HENRY, b. 28th da, 1st mo, 1751; JOHN, b. 15th da, 8th mo, 1753; JANE, b. 14th da, 10th mo, 1755; ANN, b. 1st da, 11th mo, 1757; SARAH, b. 9th da, 1st mo, 1760; HENRY, b. 3rd da, 3rd mo, 1762; JOSEPH, b. 22(?), 3rd mo, 1764, d. 7th da, 4th mo following; DAVID, b. 29th da, 3rd mo, 1766.

Mary Farson, wife of Henry and mother of the above children, d. 21st da, 4th mo, 1769 at about 11 o'clock at night, having been in poor health for about 7 years. {DCMM}

3. RACHEL FARSON, dau. of William (1) and Sarah Farson, b. 5th mo, 1726, m. Edmund Liston.

They were parents of the following children: SARAH, b. 22nd da, 2nd mo, 1748; WILLIAM, b. 16th da, 1st mo, 1752.

Mary, wife of Edmund, d. 12th da, 4th mo, 1755.

4. WILLIAM LISTON, son of Rachel (3) and Edmund, b. 16th da, 1st mo, 1752, m. Mary (N). {DCMM} They were parents of the following children {DCMM}: ANN, b. 11th da,

5th mo, 1776; SARAH, b. 4th da, 2nd mo, 1778; WILLIAM, b. 4th da, 7th mo, 1781.

THE GLOVER FAMILY

1. JOHN GLOVER m. Alse/Alec/Aloe (N)..

John Glover was due to pay rent roll on the tract *Teyneds Court*, 93 a., in the Kent County Rent Roll, 1681-1688. In the same rent roll is shown the names of John and Rich. Glover, oweing rent roll on 1200 a. {Bendler:3}

John Glover d. by 17 Dec 1684 when his wife Alse Glover was appointed admx. of his estate. {Penna. Hist. Soc. Papers, AM 2013:36}

On 6 Jan 1684 it was ordered to be recorded by Alec Chant, widow, formerly of Robert Nogust ... by aprobation of present husband John Chant her choyce of cattle when she divides ye stock with John Glover her former husband John Glover's son one cow called Cherry and cow called Prittoy one cow Fortin one cow Bob one yearling heifer called White Back one yearling bull called Roben. {KEDELR}

On 6 Jan 1684 in the Last Will and Testament of Aloe Gloveare appointed William Darvall exec. to take care of the estate "as if it were his owne until my two sons John Glover and Richard Glover shall come to age and I appoint William Darvall and Robert Bedwell to take the tuition of my two sons John and Richard Glover into their care and prudence ... when John and Richard Glover come into age the estate shall be divided equally. {KEDELR}

On 10 Dec 1687 John Glover of Talbot Co., MD, son of John Glover late of same place give to Richard Glover his brother of Kent Co, MD, in consideration of ye dear love and good will and natural effection which I ever had and still have for my said brother Richard Glover ... a tract of land called *Timehead Court* on s. side of Little Creek, 570 a. as by patent with plantation 21 Sep 1680 and surveyed 24 Nov 1680 ... another tract of land called *Stenning Court* on s. side of Little Creek ... 93 a. ... if said Richard Glover shall die without issue lawfully begotten of his body that 400 a. of above land with ye plantation shall return to John Glover ... John Glover appoints my friend John Brinckloe to ackn and deliver these presence. {KEDELR}

On 20 Nov 1693 John Glover of Talbot Co., MD, son and heire of John Glover, late of Kent Co., PA, dec'd., by his deed of 10 Dec 1687 gave to his brother Richard Glover of Kent Co., two parcells of land, one called *Time Head Court*, 570 a., the other called *Steninge Court*, 93 a. John Glover for £20 revokes the provision in deed that if Richard Glover shall dye without issue land shall return to John Glover ... Richard Glover can dispose of land at his pleasure.

John was father of the following sons: JOHN; RICHARD

2. RICHARD GLOVER, son of John (1) m. 29 Dec 1690, Mary Winsemore, dau. of William Winsmore.

On 24 Dec 1690 Richard Glover and Mary Winsemore, both of Kent Co., PA, published their intentions and stood up publickly ... Wit: John Brinckloe.

On 29 Dec 1690 Richard Glover and Mary Winsemore take each other for husband and wife ... Wit: John Brinckloe, William Wilson, John Wilson, Elizabeth Wilson, Ezekiell Needham, Edmund Needham, John Everett, Thomas Everett, James Fitzgerrell, Thomas Wilson Senr, Mathew Wilson, Thomas Wilson Junr.

On 10 Dec 1694 Richard Glover of Kent Co., planter, and Mary his wife for £8 sold to Allexander Chance of same co., a tract of land being in the fork of Little Creek, lower part of that tract of land formerly belonging to William Winsmore of same co., dec'd., called *Pipe Ealme*. {KEDELR}

On 20 July 1696 Richard Glover of Kent Co. ordered his children's ages be recorded: Elizabeth Glover, aged 3 years on 8 March next, William Glover, aged 1 yeare the 24 Jan next.

In the c1701-1713 list of quit rents of Kent Co., DE, is listed Elizabeth Glover owing on 263 a., the title not made out but belonged to Wm. Winsmore and he gave it to his dau. Mary, mother to the child Elizabeth Glover. {Bendler:36}

On 22 Jun 1702 personally appeared Richard Glover who desired his son's age to be recorded, John Glover, son to Richard Glover and Elizabeth, his wife, born in Kent Co., PA, and was three years old 27 Jan last. {KEDELR D:12}

Richard Glover d. leaving a will dated 25 Dec 1719, proved 13 Jan 1719. Heirs: daus. Mary and Elizabeth; son John. Execs., sons John Glover and John Stevens. {Arch. A-19:70. Reg. of Wills, D:11-12 and 17}

Richard was father of the following children: MARY; ELIZABETH, b. 8 March 1694; WILLIAM, b. 24 Jan 1696; JOHN, b. 27 Jan 1699.

3. JOHN GLOVER, son of John (1) Glover.

On 10 Dec 1687 John Glover of TA Co., MD, ye son and heir of John Glover, late of Kent Co., PA, dec'd., gave to Richard Glover his brother of Kent Co., 2 tracts of land called *Tinehead Court* on s. side of Little Creek, 570 a. granted by Kent Co. Court 21 Sep 1680 surveyed 24 Nov following ... the other called *Stonning Court* on s. side of Little Creek ... 93 a. {KEDELR}

John Glover was witness to the Will of John Hall of TA Co. dated 25 Jan 1669. {MWB 1:381}

John, son of John and Mary Glover, b. 27 Oct 1695.{TAPE}

Elizabeth, dau. of John and Mary Glover, b. 19 Dec 1694, christened by Joseph Leech 14 Dec 1695.{TAPE}

John Glover, d. 3 Sep 1705.{TAPE}

Mary Glover, d. 12 Nov 1708.{TAPE}

At November Court 1708, John Glover, son and orphan of John Glover, dec'd., chose John Henricks as his guardian. {TAJU CR 6399-1:597}

In the administration of the estate of John Glover of TA Co., payments were made to Daniel Walker and Mr. Finley. Distribution was made to Mary Glover, widow, dead, 1/3. The estate was unadministered by Mary Glover and admin. d.b.n. by Richard Holmes on 23 Oct 1716. {INAC 37C:150}

In the administration of the estate of Richard Holmes on 9 May 1724 payments were made to John Glover and to Sarah Glover for her filial portion of the estate of John Glover.

John Glover was probably father of the following children: SARAH; JOHN, b. 27 Oct 1695; ELIZABETH, b. 19 Dec 1694.

4. ELIZABETH GLOVER, b. 19 Dec 1694, dau. of John (3) Glover, m. Henry

Harden 6 Jan 1713.{TAPE}

5. JOHN GLOVER of TA Co., probable son of John (3) Glover, b. 27 Oct 1695, m. Eliz: Henricks 29 July 1717.{TAPE}

On 18 Feb 1717 John Glover and his wife Elizabeth conv. to Isaac Kitson of London, mariner, 50 a., part of *Dover.* {TALR 12:316}

Mary Glover(?) dau. of John Glover and Elizabeth his wife b. 28 Dec 171-. {TAPE}

John Glover was listed as a taxable in TA Co. in 1733. {Citizens of the Eastern Shore:25}

John died leaving a will dated 7 March 1750/1 and proved 3 April 1751. The heirs named were son Richard Glover, lands and tenements called *Mount Hope*; but if he die without issue, the land to dau. Elizabeth Glover. To grand-son Thomas Pickering, £10 money. To grand-dau. Elizabeth Pickering, £10 money. To grand-dau. Rachel Glover, dau. of John Glover, late of this county, dec'd., £5 money. To dau. Mary Pickering, wife of Francis Pickering, 1s. money. The exec. was son Richard. The will was witnessed by James Dickinson, John Barwick and Wm. Troth (Quaker). {MWB 28:1}

John was father of the following children: RICHARD; ELIZABETH; JOHN; MARY, m. Francis Pickering and had children, Thomas and Elizabeth.

6. JOHN GLOVER Junr, son of John (5) Glover, m. Elizabeth Elston 25 Oct 1740. {TAPE}

Rachel, dau. of John Junr. and Elizabeth Glover, b. 11 Aug 1741.{TAPE}

John Glover, Junr., d. 21 Feb 1742.{TAPE}

John Glover, the Younger, d. by Nov 1744, leaving a dau. Rachel. {TAGU A}.

7. RICHARD GLOVER, probable son of John (5) Glover.

On 4 June 1759 Richard Glover and his wife Elizabeth of DO Co. conv. to Philip McManus 46 a., part of *Upper Range,* 114 3/4 a.; 114 3/4 a., part of *Upper Dover;* 54 a., part of *Mt. Hope.* {TALR 18:537}

On 12 Nov 1761 Phillip McManus of TA Co. sold to Richard Glover and his wife Elizabeth of DO Co. a tract named *Busby*, 500 a., selling part of it to Elizabeth Caile, widow, on 26 July 1762. {DOLR 18 Old 24, 18 Old 170}

<u>Unplaced</u>

DANIEL GLOVER was granted a tract called *Hope* in TA Co., 200 a., on 6 Nov 1684. {MPL 25:190}

Daniel Glover of TA Co., d. leaving a will dated 15 April 1699 and proved 27 April 1699. The heirs named were son-in-law John Hadley, 50 a., part of *Gray's Inn*, a tract of 200 a. formerly laid out for Thos. Hinson. To Sarah, Rachel, and John Moore, child. of Francis and Ann Moore, residue of estate, real and personal, at death of their mother. The extx. was Ann Moore, life interest in estate afsd. The will was witnessed by Robt. Sealey and Rich'd. Macklyn. {MWB 6:266}

JOHN GLOVER and wife Elizabeth of TA Co., MD, received a grant for service in 1667. {MPL 11:176}

MARY GLOVER, probable dau. of John (5) Glover, m. Thomas Stewart 31 Dec 1737.{TAPE}

THE HANSON FAMILY

1. (N) HANSON m. Barbary (N).

Barbary Hanson, mother to Timothy and Samuel Hanson Jenkins and Mary Barrat, d. 6th da, 11th mo, 1718; bur. by Little Creek meeting house. {DCMM}

2. TIMOTHY HANSON, Jr., son of (N) (1) Hanson, m. 9th da, 9th mo, 1704, Susannah Freeland, dau. of William Freeland.

Timothy Hanson, Jun. of Frankfort in the county of Philadelphia, carpenter, and Susannah Freeland, dau. of William Freeland, late of Philadelphia, dec'd., m. 9th da, 9th mo, 1704 with her mother in law, Esther James, consenting. He produced a certificate from Dublin Monthly Meeting.
{Phila Monthly Meeting}

On 14 Feb 1709 Timothy Hanson & Susanna his wife one of the daus. of William Freeland late of Philadelphia, dec'd., for £150 sold to Robert Porter of Dover Hundred, Kent Co., yeoman, a tract of land on n. side of Little Creek beginning at the corner of John Stevens' land called *London* ... 158 a. by patent 5 July 1684 granted to John Richardson which 1 Aug 1685 he did give & grant to said William Freeland & Susannah his wife which William Freeland by his will bearing date 23 Feb 1697 did bequeath to above named Susanna his dau.
{KEDELR D:77}

On 3 May 1714 Timothy Hanson of Kent Co., yeoman, and Susannah his wife for £200 sold to John Bowers of same co., a tract of land in Mispillion Hundred by Bawcomb Brigg Creek ... 303 a. {KEDELR E:110}

On 3 May 1714 Timothy Hanson of Kent Co. and Susanah his wife for £10 sold to Luke Manlove of same co., a tract of land in Mispillion Hundred beginning at the Bawcomb Brigg Creek ... by the land and plantation whereon the said Luke Manlove now dwells ... binding with the land of John Bowers ... 140 a. {KEDELR E:126}

On 16 March 1726 Timothy Hanson of Little Creek Hundred, Kent Co., gent., and Susannah his wife for £10 sold to John Clarke Junr. of Mispillion Hundred same co., part of the ancient tract called *Baucom Brigg* and was included therein by virtue of a resurvey lately granted in behalf of the afsd Timothy Hanson ... beginning at the corner of land which the afsd Timothy Hanson sold unto John Bowers ... 100 a. {KEDELR I:71}

Susanna, wife of Timothy Hanson, d. 30th da, 11th mo, 1740. {DCMM}

On 1 Aug 1746 Timothy Hanson of Kent Co., yeoman for love, good will and affection give to my son Samuel Hanson a tract of land being part of a tract called *Northampton* and part of a tract called *The White Oak Survey* in Dover Hundred beginning at Little Creek Bridge to the bridge that passes between the plantation belonging to my son Timothy Hanson and *Northampton*, to *The Exchange* ... 300 a. Wit: John Francis, William Lynch, Timothy Hanson, Junr. {KEDELR N:118}

Timothy Hanson, yeoman of Little Creek Hundred, d. 18th da, 9th mo,

1754. {DCMM} He left a will dated 31 July 1754, proved 14 Oct 1754. Heirs: sons Timothy, Samuel, Thomas; daus. Mary & Elizabeth Hanson & Rebecca Train, wife of James Train; children of dau. Susanna Course; children of dau. Barbara. Exec., son Thomas. Wits., Eliz. Jenkins, Ann Chicken, Hugh Shannon. {Arch. A21:218. Reg. of Wills, K:95-96}

Timothy and Susanna were parents of the following children {DCMM}: SUSANNA, b. 9th da, 7th mo, 1705, m. John Course; BARBARA, b. 16th da, 1st mo, 1707/8; MARY, b. 7th da, 7th mo, 1710; TIMOTHY, b. 27th da, 5th mo, 1712; WILLIAM, d. about 5 weeks old in 1714; WILLIAM (2nd of that name), d. 1st da, 12th mo, 1715; FREELAND, b. 13th da, 9th mo, 1717; SAMUEL, b. 22nd da, 19th mo, 1719; THOMAS; ELIZABETH; REBECCA, m. James Train.

3. TIMOTHY HANSON, son of Timothy (2) Hanson, m. Elizabeth Skillington of TA Co. on 20th da, 2nd mo, 1743 at Tuckahoe meeting house. {THMM}

On 7 March 1758 Timothy Hanson of Kent Co. for love, good will and affection give to my loving cousen Joseph Barrett son of Benjamin Barrett of same co. a lott of land with the dwelling house of George Hogg, late of the town of New Castle, being in the town of New Castle ... if the said Joseph Barrett should die before he come to lawfull age and without issue then the afsd granted premisses shall be to the proper use of the afsd Benjamin Barrett during his natural life and at his decease to the next heir at law, the afsd George Hogg. {KEDELR R:205}

Timothy Hanson d. by 9 May 1762 when Elizabeth Hanson, widow, was appointed admx. of the estate of Timothy Hanson. {Reg. of Wills, K:281}

On 28th da, 9th mo, 1771 a certificate was prepared for Elizabeth Hanson and her children, to wit, Lydia, Susanna and Ann Hanson, to Wilmington Monthly Meeting. In the minutes of Wilmington Monthy Meeting is shown that Lydia was a young girl and the other daus. shown as young. {DCMM, WMMM}

Timothy and Elizabeth were parents of the following children {DCMM}: JOHN, b. 3rd da, 6th mo, 1744, d. 20th da, 11th mo, 1746; WILLIAM, b. 9th da, 11th mo, 1745, d. 25th da, 8th mo, 1747; TINDLEY, b. 22nd da, 2nd mo, 1747, d. 9th following; SUSANNA, b. 23rd da, 11th mo, 1748, d. 30th same mo; ELIZABETH, b. 23rd da, 12th mo, 1749; LYDIA, b. 3rd da, 5th mo, 1752/3; ANN, b. 15th da, 3rd mo, 1755, d. 21st da, 9th mo, 1758; SUSANNA, b. 14th da, 11th mo, 1756; ANN, b. 31st da, 12th mo, 1759.

4. SAMUEL HANSON, son of Timothy (2) Hanson, b. 22nd da, 19th mo, 1719, m. Sarah Levis.

On 16 May 1735 Robert Howard of Kent Co. for 5 shillings assigned unto Samuel Hanson, son of Timothy Hanson, his mark which I usually make to my creatures being one crop in the left ear as appears now on records of said co. to his own proper use, excepting those that are at the date hereof already marked with said mark. Attest: Jno. Housman, recorder. {KEDELR N:15}

On 5th da, 8th mo, 1755 Samuel requested by a friend a certificate in order for marriage with a young woman belonging to Newark Monthly Meeting. {DCMM}

Samuel Hanson, son of Timothy Hanson, late of Little Creek, Kent Co., DE, dec'd., m. 19th da, 11th mo, 1755, Sarah Levis, dau. of William Levis, late of Kennett, Chester Co., dec'd. at Kennett meeting house. {WMMM}

Samuel m. 2nd, 22nd da, 12th mo, 1741, Priscilla Sipple, dau. of Weightman Sipple, at the meeting house at Little Creek. {DCMM}

Samuel and Priscilla were parents of the following children: SUSANNA, b. 14th da, 6th mo, 1744; TIMOTHY, b. 11th da, 19th mo, 1749.

5. THOMAS HANSON of Little Creek Hundred, son of Timothy (2) Hanson, m. 22nd da, 9th mo, 1756, Mary Levis of Kennett, Chester Co., PA, dau. of William Levis. {New Castle Co. Quaker marriages}

On 12 Jun 1766 Thomas Hanson of Kent Co., yeoman, and Mary his wife for £300 sold to Joshua Gregg of same co., a tract of land called *Friendship* at the head of the main branch of Dover River near Horsehead in the forrest of Murtherkill Hundred ... 481 1/4 a. which was purchased by the afsd Thomas Hanson from a certain John Smithers and Nathaniel Smithers (Book Q, fol. 200). {KEDELR R:100}

Thomas d. 18th da, 4th mo, 1783 about 3 o'clock in the morning, bur. Little Creek meeting house on 19th.

On 22nd da, 4th mo, 1786, a certificate was prepared for Mary Hanson, relict of Thomas Hanson, to Wilmington Monthly Meeting. {DCMM}

Thomas and Mary were parents of the following children {DCMM}: ELIZABETH, d. 30th da, 6th mo, 1759, d. 17th da, 8th mo, 1760; SUSANNA, b. 17th da, 7th mo, 1761.

6. SUSANNA HANSON, b. 9th da, 7th mo, 1705, dau. of Timothy (2) and Susanna Hanson, m. John Course.

On 17th da, 11th mo, 1725 John Course of Cecil Monthly Meeting in Maryland and Susannah, dau. of Timothy Hanson, announced their intentions of marriage, he producing a certificate from Chester Meeting in Maryland. {DCMM}

On 10th da, 2nd mo, 1762 a certificate was prepared for Susannah Hanson to Duck Creek Monthly Meeting, signifying her clearness of marriage engagements. {WMMM}

7. MARY HANSON, dau. of Timothy and Susanna Hanson, b. 7th da, 7th mo, 1710, m. 1730 Thomas Empson. On 22nd da, 12th mo, 1730 the orderly marriage of Thomas Empson was reported. {DCMM}

8. TIMOTHY HANSON, son of Samuel (4) Hanson of Little Creek, m. 1st Mary Way (d. 24th da, 2nd mo, 1790) dau. of Caleb Way.

On 11th da, 4th mo, 1770 a certificate was prepared by Wilmington Monthly Meeting to Duck Creek Monthly Meeting for Timothy Hanson, having served out his apprenticeship. {WMMM}

Timothy Hanson (of the borough of Wilmington) m. 2nd, 17th da, 5th mo, 1792, Mary Robinson, dau. of James Robinson of the borough of Wilmington and his wife Elinor, both dec'd. {WMMM}

Timothy d. 20th da, 10th mo, 1798. {WMMM} He (Timothy Hanson, cabinet-maker) left a will dated 6 Sep 1798, proved 16 Nov 1798. Mentioned were wife Mary; daus. Susanna and Elizabeth; sons Samuel and Thomas; Eli Mendinhall, Thomas Little, Bridget Woodward, Thomas Davis, William Wilson, John Simpson, Thomas Wilson, Joseph Warner, James Brobson, John

White. Exec. son in law, William Robinson and Peter Brynberg. {New Castle Co. Wills O:393}

Timothy was father of the following children by his marraige with Mary Way {WMMM}: SUSANNA, b. 6th da, 10th mo, 1775, d. 26th da, 4th mo, 1800; ELIZABETH, b. 13th da, 7th mo, 1778. In addition he was father of the following children: SAMUEL; THOMAS.

9. SUSANNA HANSON, dau. of Samuel (4) and Priscilla Hanson, b. 14th da, 6th mo, 1744.

Susanna Hanson of Jones Hundred, dau. of Samuel Hanson, and Isaac Cox of Little Creek Hundred, son of Isaac Cox, late of TA Co., Md, dec'd., m. 7th da, 4th mo, 1763 at Little Creek meeting house. {DCMM}

10. SUSANNAH HANSON, b. 6th da, 10th mo, 1775, d. 26th da, 4th mo, 1800, dau. of Timothy (7) and Mary Hanson, m. 18th da, 9th mo, 1794, Jesse Shenton Zane, son of Joel Zane and his wife Esther of Wilmington.

Susannah and Jesse Zane were parents of the following children {WMMM}: MARY HANSON, b. 19th da, 12th mo, 1795; NATHAN SHENTON, b. 18th da, 3rd mo, 1797; HESTER, b. 18th da, 7th mo, 1798; TIMOTHY HANSON, b. 19th da, 4th mo, 1800.

Susannah d. 26th da, 4th mo, 1800. {WMMM}

11. ELIZABETH HANSON, dau. of Timothy (8) and Mary Hanson (dec'd.), m. 24th da, 5th mo, 1798, William Robinson of Wilmington, son of Nicholas Robinson and his wife Mary (dec'd.). {WMMM}

Unplaced

MARY HANSON, dau. of Samuel Hanson, b. 11th da, 11th mo, 1730 {DCMM}.

SAMUEL HANSON and Mary Guest announced their intentions of marriage on 20th da, 4th mo, 1720. {DCMM}

Mary Hanson, wife of Samuel Hanson, d. 22nd da, 6th mo, 1723. {DCMM}

On 17th da, 8th mo, 1726, the orderly marriage of SAMUEL HANSON and Patience Bentley was reported. {DCMM}

On 5th da, 8th mo, 1755, SAMUEL HANSON, Jr., requested a certificate in order for marriage with a young woman of Third Haven Monthly Meeting. {DCMM}

Samuel Hanson, Jr., of Kent Co. on Dillaware and Lydia Berry of TA Co., m. 28th da, 10th mo, 1768 at the dwelling house of Sarah Berry in TA Co. {THMM} Lydia d. 21st da, 3rd mo, 1794.

Samuel and Lydia were parents of the following children {DCMM}: TIMOTHY, b. 19th da, 8th mo, 1769, d. 5th da, 5th mo, 1814; SARAH, b. 26th da, 8th mo, 1770, d. 26th da, 1st mo, 1771; PRISCILLA, b. 26th da, 8th mo, 1770, d. 7th da, 11th mo, 1770; SARAH, b. 28th da, 10th mo, 1771, d. 27th da, 11th mo, 1772; THOMAS, b. 28th da, 10th mo, 1771, d. 29th da, 11th mo, 1788.

SUSANNA, wife of Samuel Hanson, d. 7th da, 1st mo, 1791. {DCMM}

THE SYMON IRONS FAMILY

1. SYMON IRONS immigrated to the province of Maryland by 1679. With him were wife Dorothy, and Elizabeth, Francis and Susannah Irons. {MPL WC2:68} A William Irons (possibly William, son of Symon, mentioned below) was transported into the province of Maryland by 1678. {MPL 15:530}

On 27 Oct 1684 Simon Irons of Kent Co. and Doreathy his wife in consideration of 6000 pounds of tobacco sold to Timothy Pade of the same co. a tract of land being part of a 600 a. tract called *Hillyards Adventure* on s. side of Duck Creek, containing 200 a. {KEDELR}

On 2 Feb 1692/3 Simon Hirons, Senr. (on behalf of Simon Hirons the younger) and his son Francis Hirons both of Kent Co., PA, for the consideration of £20 sold to Walter Thompson and Walter Price both of Philadelphia a tract of land on the n. side of the main branch of Dover River containing 570 a. with the plantation, part of a patent for 670 a., granted to Francis Simon and Elizabeth Hirons for 1500 a. granted named *Concord.* {KEDELR}

A tract of land (patent granted in 1684 unto Simon Hirons then of Kent Co., yeoman, 600 a. on Duck Creek Neck) and Simon Hirons conveyed the 600 a. unto his two elder sons, to wit Francis Hirons and Simon Hirons, Junr., (division made on 6 Feb 1705 by Jonas Greenwood then surveyor of Kent Co). {KEDELR O:223}

On 2 Feb 1692/3 Simon Hirons, Senr., and Francis Hirons of Kent Co. PA, were held and firmly bound unto Walter Thompson and Walter Price, both of Philadelphia, in the sum of £500 to be paid upon demand. Condition of obligation was such that Simon Hirons, Senr., and Francis Hirons sold 570 a. of land, part of a tract containing 670 a. (being part of a tract of 1500 a. granted to Francis Simon and Elizabeth Hirons) the said Elizabeth being dec'd., and the said Simon the natural son of Simon Hirons, Senr., not being of age, will be required to sign over the 570 a. of land when he becomes of age.

Simon Hirons, Sr., d. leaving a will dated 12 Oct 1706, proved 16 Dec 1706. Heirs: sons Francis, Simon, Robert, William, and John; wife Percess; dau. Margaret; Sarah Rodney, dau. of Capt. Wm. and Sarah Rodney; Anna Bedwell, dau. of Thomas and Milicent Bedwell; Samuel Berry, son-in-law; John Portess, son of John and Deborah Portess; Silvanus Portess, son of John and Deborah Portess. Extx., wife Percess. Wits., James Moore, Timothy Hanson, Joshua Clayton, Stephen Paradee. {Arch. A24:97. Reg. of Wills, B:56}

On 7 Feb 1716 Perces and William Hirons, widow and son of Simon Hirons, late of Kent Co., dec'd., for £40 sold to James Potter of same co., yeoman, a tract of land called *Brookshear*, formerly taken up by Francis Whitwell, patent dated at Yorke Jan 167- and 10 Dec 1685 conveyed to Simon Hirons, dec'd., by William Berry and William Southebe, admin. of the estate of Francis Whitwell and Simon Hirons in his lifetime did make his will and did give 50 a. out of the 400 a. called *Brookshear* on s. side of Richard Wilson's plantation to be by his executrix sold for the payment of his debts and the other 50 a. of the same tract out of the part of William Hirons near *Chippennorton* line, 100 a. Witnessed by Simon Hirons, Robert Hirons, David Morgan, Nathaniel Roach. Ackn 15 Feb 1716. {KEDELR E:256}

On 7 Feb 1716 Perses, William and John Hirons all of Kent Co. for £160 sold to Simon Hirons of same place, two tracts of land commonly the dwelling plantation of Simon Hirons who did make his will and did bequeath plantation and tract of land to be divided between his two sons William and John. William to have the north part and John the south part. Witnessed by James Potter, Robert Hirons. {KEDELR E:266}

On 16 Aug 1716 Francis Vannoy and Kathrine his wife of Kent Co., for a valuable consideration sold to George Green, conveyed 80 a. of a tract of land called *Bets Endeavour* which was formerly conveyed by Cristopher Standly to Simon Hirons and from Perses Hirons executrix to Simon Hirons, dec'd., to George Green and from him to Francis Vannoy. {KEDELR E:177}

Perciss Hirons, widow of Simon Hirons, d. intestate by 6 Nov 1718. On that date William Hirons and John Hirons both of Little Creek Hundred Kent Co. yeomen sons of Simon Hirons late of same place, dec'd., for £40 sold to James Potter of same place yeoman ... (whereas Simon Hirons in his lifetime was seized of a tract of land called *Brulshaw* and by his will bequeathed to his sons William and John Hirons all said tract of lands only excepting 50 a. he gave to his wife Perciss who dying intestate the said 50 a. descended into the possession of the eldest son William Hirons). {KEDELR F:pg 49}

On 10 May 1720 Francis Hirons, Simon Hirons and Robert Hirons of Little Creek Hundred Kent Co., yeomen, for £22 sold to Joshua Clayton of same place, gentleman, a tract of land patent dated at Philadelphia 25 Feb 1691/2 unto Francis Hirons, Simon Hirons and Robert Hirons (and Elizabeth Hirons was without issue, dec'd.) called *Mount Pleasant* in Little Creek Hundred between land called *Highams and Chippanorton*, on w. side of Ralph Needham's land ... 130 a. {KEDELR F:129}

On 2 Jun 1743 Samuel Berry of Kent Co., for 5 shillings gave to his son in law Andrew Craige, yeoman, a tract of land (whereas Simon Hirons the elder of same co. d. possessed of a tract of land called *Oxford* upon Choptank Road near the Black Swamp adj. to a tract of land formerly taken up by William Morton called *Camebridge*, 500 a., Simon Hirons by his will bearing date 12 Oct 1706 bequeathed to Samuel Berry, his son in law, 100 a. of land part of *Oxford* and next adj. 100 a. of the same tract which he the testator devised to his son Simon Hirons), 100 a. {KEDELR M:232}

On 23 Feb 1749 George Gillespie of White Clay Creek, New Castle Co., clergy man, for £150 sold to William Killen of Kent Co., surveyor, a tract of land (patent dated 30 Jul 1688 granted unto Simon Hirons 1000 a. called *The Range* on n. side of Dover River and whereas Francis Hirons his son as heir at law by deed bearing date 9 Oct 1722 did convey unto Benjamin Shurmer of Kent Co. 600 a. and Shurmer released it to the said Hirons again on 10 Oct 1722.
{KEDELR O:47}

Simon was father of the following children: FRANCIS (eldest son); SIMON (a minor in 1692/3); ROBERT; WILLIAM; JOHN; MARGARET.

Second Generation

2. FRANCIS HIRONS, eldest son of Simon (1) Hirons, m. Frances (N) and had a son Charles.

On 17 Oct 1721 Francis Hirons of Kent Co., yeoman, son and heir of Simon Hirons, late of same place, dec'd., by virtue of a warrant bearing date 20 Jun 1682 there was surveyed the 12 Nov 1686 unto Simon Hirons a tract of land called *The Range*, 1000 a. on n. side of Dover River and by patent granted bearing date 30 March 1688. Simon Hirons in his life time did sell afsd. tract of land unto William Berry and Joseph Phips joyntly and by indenture bearing date 1 Feb 1689 they did sell the same unto John Richardson, Senr., late of same co., and by his will dyed possessed of the 1000 a. to be divided between Mary Richardson his executrix, John Richardson, his grandson John Levick and the children of George and Judith Row. 300 a. of afsd. tract do now belong unto John Hall and Benjamin Shurmer of Kent Co. gentlemen and because the first mentioned conveyance from Simon Hirons has been misplaced. Francis Hirons for 10 shillings released unto John Hall and Benjamin Shurmer 300 a., part of the 1000 a., to be laid out by virtue of the will afsd. {KEDELR G:44}

On 5 Oct 1722 Frances Hirons of Kent Co. yeoman son and heir of Simon Hirons late of same place, dec'd., did by deed bearing date 17 Oct 1721 release and convey to Benjamin Shurmer of same place gentleman and John Hall a tract of land called *The Range*, 1000 a., on n. side of Dover River. John Hall by articles of agreement bearing date 19 Dec 1720 hath released and quit claim to said Benjamin all his right and title to 300 a. Benjamin Shurmer for 10 shillings quit claims 300 a. unto Simon Hirons excepting all the land belonging to the 1000 a. called *The Range*. {KEDELR G:109}

On 9 Oct 1722 Francis Hirons of Kent Co., yeoman, son and heir of Simon Hirons, late of same place, dec'd., in consideration of a deed dated 17 Oct 1721 released unto Benjamin Shurmer of same place, gentleman, and John Hall, all his rights to 300 a. of land being part of a tract on n. side of Dover River called *The Range* (Book A, folio 44). In this indenture Francis Hirons for £10 sold to Benjamin Shurmer afsd. 300 a. {KEDELR G:108}

On 1 June 1723 Articles of Agreement were made between Francis Hirons of Kent Co. yeoman and Andrew Caldwell of same co., yeoman, to wit: Francis Hirons and Frances his wife shall release all his right and claim unto 700 a. of that tract of land called *The Range* on the main branch of Dover River adj. *Berrys Range* whereon Thomas Parke now dwelleth unto the said Andrew Caldwell for the use of Nicholas Lokerman and Sarah his wife, in consideration whereof the said Andrew Caldwell on behalf of the said Nicholas Lokerman shall pay unto Francis £10 and to Frances his wife one pistole or the value thereof and 200 a. of land in *Bootte Neck* or *Dukes Manner*, wheresoever in the neck or manner said Frances shall have the same out of 500 a. or 600 a. which now belongs to the said Andrew and Hugh Durborow in partnership. {KEDELR I:8}

Francis Hirons d. by 17 Feb 1740 when his estate was administered by William Hirons. {Arch. A24:92. Reg. of Wills, I:30}

According to a recorded deed, there was surveyed and laid out unto Simon Hirons gent being the elder and first of the name who was an inhabitant of Kent Co. a tract of land being in *Dukes Mannor* called *Oxford* in the forrest of Murtherkill Hundred near ye side of Black Swamp adj. w. side of land called *Cambridge* which was surveyed and laid out to William Morton then of same place and later called *The Cave Land* and whereas Simon Hirons the elder by his will did bequeath unto his son Frances Hirons 100 a. of land part of the afsd. tract called *Oxford* (will proved 16 Dec 1706 Book:17 fol. 66) and whereas Francis Hirons did sell unto his son Charles Hirons the afsd. 100 a. 17 May 1740 and Charles Hirons (since dec'd.) conveyed it to Thomas Green 11 May 1749 (Book N, fol. 274). {KEDELR O:26}

3. SIMON HIRONS, son of Simon (1) Hirons, m. Mary (N).

On 27 Aug -- [acknowledged 27 Aug 1747] Joseph Dowding, gent., and William Hirons, yeoman, both of Kent Co., executors of the will of Simon Hirons, Senr., of Little Creek Hundred same co., for £500 sold to John Brinckle, Junr, now of same hundred and co., the land and plantation whereon the said Simon Hirons did dwell (whereas Simon Hirons father to the afsd. Simon did formerly purchase and settle a tract of land called *Brubshaw* in Little Creek Hundred in a neck of land and marsh between Simons Creek and Herring branch in Herring Gutt Marsh and did obtain a grant for a tract of up land and marsh called *Hirons Addition* adj. the e. part of the said tract, the said Simon Hirons the father the first settler afsd. being so possessed did by his will give the same lands and marsh to his sons William Hirons and John Hirons, and whereas William Hirons and John Hirons sold to the said Simon Hirons the testater first afsd. all their rights to the afsd. lands except two parcels which they had sold out of the tract called *Brubshaw* at the w. end, to wit 100 a. sold by William to James Potter and 50 a. sold by John to John Hall, so that Simon Hirons the testator becamed possessed of all the tract called *Hirons Addition* and all the residue of *Brubshaw*, and whereas Simon Hirons the son and testator did purchase from Andrew Caldwell and Hugh Durborow a part of a tract called *Willingbrook* on n. side of Herring Branch adj. to some of the afsd. land, and being so possessd of the several tracts excepting one parcel to Robart Blackshaw, one parcel to James Smith, one parcel to his son Simon and one persel to his son William who is partie to these presents, on 11 Feb 1741 Simon became bound to the afsd. John Brinckle for £1000 conditioned that on the receipt of £250 he should execute a good and vallid deed of conveyance to the said John Brinckle). {KEDELR N:175}

On 10 Feb 1724/5 Simon Hirons of Little Creek Hundred Kent Co., yeoman, and Mary his wife for £45 sold to Robert Blackshaw of same place, yeoman, a part of a tract of land called *Brubshaw* whereon Simon now dwelleth and also one other tract call *Hirons Addition* adj. to the n. side of *Brubshaw*, in Little Creek Hundred including a part of *Brubshaw* and also a part of *The Addition* land beginning at Whetstone Island Branch being the corner of a piece of land which John Hall purchased of John Hirons, by Dear Island to Simons Creek, 150 a. {KEDELR H:171}

On 8 Aug 1726 Simon Hirons of Little Creek Hundred, Kent Co., yeoman, and Mary his wife for £40 sold to Lancelot Lewis of same place, planter, a tract of land warrant dated at Philadelphia 8 Dec 1718 granted unto Simon Hirons afsd, 200 a. in the forrest called *Simons Choice* in Little Creek Hundred beginning at the s. corner of land called *Ye Exchange*, surveyed 10 April 1719. {KEDELR I:44}

On 12 Nov 1739 Simon Hirons of Kent Co., yeoman, for good will, love and natural affection and £20 gave to his son Simon Hirons, Junr., a tract of land being part of a tract called *Willingsbrook* beginning at Herring branch, 100 a. {KEDELR M:61}

On 13 Feb 1739 Simon Hirons of Kent Co., yeoman, for 5 shillings and for love and affection gave to his son William Hirons of same co., a parcel of land in Little Creek Hundred being part of the land and plantation whereon the said Simon dwells on the s. side thereof, 128 a. {KEDELR M:63}

On 13 Aug 1740 Simon Hirons of Little Creek Hundred, yeoman, for natural love and affection gave to his granddau. Mary Hemer (Hamer), dau. of John Hemer and Hannah his wife, a tract of land being part of a greater tract called *Oxford*, beginning at the corner of Charles Hirons his land, 100 a. Witnesses were Thomas Green and William Hirons. {KEDELR M:88}

On 13 Aug 1742 by a deed bearing date 13 Feb 1739 Simon Hirons the elder of Kent Co., yeoman, intended to give to William Hirons of same place son of the said Simon, 128 a. of land and marsh in Little Creek Hundred. The said deed doth not contain the said quantity intended to be conveyed and this conveyance is for remedying thereof and the better conveying the said quantity of land and marsh. For natural love and affection and 5 shillings Simon Hirons gives to his son William Hirons all that parcell of land in Little Creek Hundred being part of the land whereon the said Simon Hirons lately dwelt, 128 a. {KEDELR M:189}

Simon d. leaving a will dated 21 Dec 1742, proved 6 Jan 1742. Heirs: sons Mark, Luke, Matthew, William, Simon; daus. Rebecca Hirons, Hannah Hamer, Abigall Fropp; wife Mary. Execs., wife Mary, son William, Joseph Dowding. Wits., Grace Leatherberry, Jonathan Griffin, Jonathan Leatherberry. {Arch. A24:98-99, 103, 105. Reg. of Wills, 1:49-50}

On 12 April 1749 Luke Hirons and Elizabeth his wife of Little Creek Hundred, Kent Co., for £26 sold to Samuel Barnett of same place, one half of a tract of land (whereas Simon Hirons, father of the said Luke Hirons, d. seized of 200 a. of land in Little Hundred beginning on w. side of Hillyards Branch, to land lately laid out for John Newton, to s.w. branch of Duck Creek, to land called *The Mill Range*, to land of John Hillyard called *The Exchange,* as by deed of sale from Stephen Heargrove dated 13 Aug 1716, and Simon Hirons by his will after bequeathing of divers legacies unto his beloved wife Mary Hirons and also unto divers of his elder children, did bequeath the remaining part of his estate unto his two youngest sons Mark Hirons and Luke Hirons to be equally divided between them part of which the afsd. tract is). {KEDELR N:282}

Mark Hirons being under the age of 21 and his father being dec'd, leaving him some estate and he being not capable of taking care of it himself, begs leave to chuse a guardian. 27 Feb 1744. {KEORCF Hirons, Mark - 1744}

Simon was father of the following children: MARK; LUKE; MATTHEW; WILLIAM; SIMON; REBECCA; HANNAH, m. John Hamer; ABIGALL, m. (N) Fropp. Mark and Luke were the youngest sons of Simon Hirons.

4. ROBERT HIRONS, son of Simon (1) Hirons, had a son SIMON the only surviving issue of said Robert. Robert d. by 5 Feb 1724 when his estate was administered by Mary Hirons. {Reg. of Wills, D:69}

On 24 Aug 1748 Simon Hirons of Kent Co., planter, son of Robert Hirons late of same co. yeoman, grandson to Simon Hirons, gent., formerly of same place, for £40 sold to Thomas Green of Dover a tract of land surveyed and laid out unto the afsd. Simon Hirons, being the elder and first of that name who was an inhabitant of the co. afsd, called *Oxford* in the forrest of Murtherkill Hundred near the e. side of Black Swamp adj. w. side of a tract of land called *Cambridge* which was surveyed and laid out to William Morton then of same place and is now called the *Cave Land*, whereas Simon Hirons the elder by his will duly executed and proved 16 Dec 1706 recorded in Book 17, fol. 66, did give unto his son Robert Hirons afsd. 100 a. being part of a parcel called *Oxford*, the said Robert Hirons dyed intestate in possession of his part, the tract descended into the possession of the said Simon Hirons party to these presents and the only surviving issue of the said Robert Hirons, dec'd., 100 a. {KEDELR N:229}

There was surveyed and laid out unto Simon Hirons, gent., being the elder and first of that name who was an inhabitent of Kent Co. a tract of land in *Dukes Mannor* called *Oxford* in the forrest of Murtherkill Hundred near ye e. side of Black Swamp adj. w. side of land called *Cambridge* which was surveyed and laid out to William Morton then of the same place and is now called *The Cave Land* and whereas Simon Hirons the elder by his will (proved 16 Dec 1706 Book N:17 fol. 66) did bequeath unto his son Robert Hirons 100 a. part of ye tract called *Oxford*, and whereas Robert Hirons died intestate and in possession of his part of the said land it descended into the possession of Simon Hirons his only surviving son and issue, which 100 a. was conveyed by Simon son of Robert, dec'd., 24 Aug 1748 who is now [20 Dec 1749], dec'd., (Book N, fol. 229). {KEDELR O:25}

5. WILLIAM HIRONS, son of Simon (1) Hirons, m. Leah (N).

On 9 May 1716 Francis Whitwell late of Kent Co., dec'd., did take up a tract of land on side of s.w. branch of Duck Creek called *Brookhoss*, 400 a., patent granted Jan 1675 and since conveyed to William Berry and from him to Simon Hirons, dec'd., Now William Hirons and Peirses Hirons, widow and son of Simon Hirons, late, dec'd., of Kent Co., joyntly for a valuable consideration in hand paid sold to James Potter of same co., 100 a. {KEDELR E:82}

On 12 Nov 1718 William Hirons of Kent Co. appointed his friend and brother John Hirons of same place to be his attorney to acknowledge a deed of sale in open court for 200 a. and one for 500 a. to Simon Hirons. {KEDELR F:50}

On 12 Feb 1746 William Hirons of Kent Co. and Leah his wife for £63 sold to Daniel Brinckle of same co., bricklayer, a tract of land (whereas Simon Hirons of the same co. late, dec'd., did buy from his brother William Hirons a tract of land and the said Simon Hirons by his deed of sale, Book M, fol. 189, granted unto the said William Hirons, his son, a part of the afsd. land and plantation whereon the said Simon dwelt) binding on Herring Gut, 128 a.
{KEDELR N:118}

William Irons of Duck Creek d. leaving a will dated 13 Aug 1757, proved 12 Sep 1757. Heirs: son John; dau. Grace. Execs., John Draughton and James Morris. Wits., Arnold Hawkins, Margaret Doney, Samuel McCall. {Arch. A24:106-108. Reg. of Wills, K:166}

On 27 Feb 1760 William Leatherbury was appointed admin. of William's estate. {Reg. of Wills, K:223-224}

William was father of the following children: JOHN; GRACE.

6. JOHN HIRONS, son of Simon (1) on 10 Nov 1718 in consideration of a tract of land, sold to Simon Hirons a tract of land being one half of the plantation of Simon Hirons his father, dec'd., and his part of land thereunto given him by his fathers will with his part of the addition bounded according to pattent and according to ye division line run between him and his brother William except 50 a. sold to John Hall. {KEDELR F:pg 41}

Third Generation

7. CHARLES HIRONS, son of Francis (2) Hirons, m. Mary (N).

According to a deed recorded in 1754, Simon Hirons, dec'd., by his will did give unto his son Francis Hirons 100 a. of land called *Oxford* to be laid off continguous to a tract of land called Cambridge) and Francis Hirons died intestate by which means the land did decend to his son and heir Charles Hirons who on 4 Aug 1748 (Book N, fol. 269) sold the same to Thomas Green. (KEDELR O:224)

On 11 May 1749 Charles Hirons of Little Creek Hundred Kent Co., yeoman for £40 sold to Thomas Green of the Town of Dover same co., yeoman, a tract of land being part of a larger tract called *Oxford* in *Ducks Mannor* granted by warrant to Simon Hirons 7 Dec 1692 which parcel of land Francis Hirons son of the afsd. Simon Hirons did convey to Charles Hirons 17 May 1740 (Book M fol. 78), 100 a. in the forest of Murtherkill Hundred near ye Black Swamp. {KEDELR N:274}

Charles d. leaving a will dated 5 April 1752, proved 11 April 1752. Heirs: sons Charles, John; wife Mary. Execs., wife Mary and Stokely Sturgis. Wits., Daniel Shanen, John Swaney, James Small. {Arch. A24:89-91. Reg. of Wills, K:58} Note: Arch. A24:91 shows Daniel Brinkley, exec. of Mary Ann Hirons, dec'd.

Mary Ann Hirons d. leaving a will dated 29 June 1752, proved 28 July 1752. Heirs: eldest son John; other children unnamed. Execs., Daniel Brinckle of Little Creek Hd., Stokley Sturgis. Guardian, Daniel Brinckle, of other children unnamed. Wits., Mary Jones, Catherine Rannels, James Small. {Arch. A24:96. Reg. of Wills, K:81} Note:Will mentions husband, Charles Hirons, dec'd.

Charles was father of the following children: CHARLES; JOHN.

8. MARK HIRONS, son of Simon (3) Hirons and brother of Luke Hirons, m. Sarah (N).

On 12 May 1749 Mark Hirons (Irons) of Kent Co. yeoman for £30 sold to Thomas Green of the Town of Dover same co., yeoman, one half of a tract of land (whereas Simon Hirons, father of the said Mark Hirons, died seized in 200 a. of land in the forest of Little Creek Hundred on w. side of Hillyards Branch to land lately laid out for John Newton, to land called the *Mill Rainge*, to land of John Hillyard's called *The Exchange*, by deed of sale from Stephen Heargrove dated 13 Aug 1716 and whereas the said Simon Hirons by his will did bequeath the afsd. land between Mark Hirons and Luke Hirons). {KEDELR N:269}

Mark d. by 3 April 1769 when his estate was administered by Sarah Hirons, widow. {Reg. of Wills, L:57}

9. LUKE HIRONS, son of Simon (3) Hirons, m. Elizabeth, dau. of John Lewis. She d. c1761 and Luke then m. Mary Vannoy.

On 27 Feb 1750 Luke Hirons of Little Creek Hundred Kent Co. yeoman and Elizabeth his wife for £35 sold to Stokely Sturgis of same place yeoman, half part of a tract of land called *Content* in Little Creek Hundred on n.w. side of Muddy Branch whereon the said Stokely Sturgis now dwells, 100 a. which did formerly belong to a certain John Lewis late of this co., dec'd., father of the afsd. Elizabeth Hirons and by his will did devise and give unto the said Elizabeth and Keziah Lewis his two daus. the 100 a. to be equally divided between them which said division hath not been yet made, 50 a. {KEDELR O:84}

Luke Hirons of Kent Co., DE., in a petition stated it had been about 18 years since married with Elizabeth Lewis who died about 1761 leaving the petitioner 3 children, to wit, Sarah, Pheebe and Keziah, all very young and yet living. That on the death of your petitioner said late wife his poverty was so great as to render him altogether incapable to keep house and his children being at that time and for many years after too young to bind but to honest housekeeper, he was obliged to board them out at a very great expense and has incurred a great debt, £44. Abut 2 years since he agains m. Mary Vannoy his second wife who is still living by whom he has two children both very young. By the death of John Wells the younger intestate and without issue who was maternal uncle to your petioner's children by his said first wife, his said children became intitled to a distribution share of all the real and personal estate of their said dec. uncle which distribution share is of the value of £194. Have thought fit to commit the custody or guardianship of said Sarah, Phoebe and Keziah your petitioner's children by first wife and their estate to Samuel Hanson. Seek payment for boarding. {KEORCF Hirons, Elizabeth - 1773}

Luke Hirons d. by 2 Jan 1769 when his estate was administered by Elizabeth Hirons, widow. {Arch. A24:94-95. Reg. of Wills, L:50} Note:-Arch. A24:94 shows heirs, Phebe and Keziah Hirons}

Petition of Keziah Hirons, only surviving child of Elizabeth Hirons dec. late wife of Luke Hirons (and which by her maiden name was Elizabeth Lewis) and one of the heirs of the estate John Wells dec'd., for to have Abraham Vannoy appointed her guardian - 24 Feb 1773. Whereas Samuel Hanson was formerly appointed guardian for the heirs and representatives of said John Wells and your petitioner being one of the said heirs in right of her mother and being of the age of 14 in last August and being now willing to change her guardian and being desirous of having Abraham Vanhoy Jr. appointed for that purpose. {KEORCF Hirons, Elizabeth - 1773}

Luke was father of the following children by Elizabeth: SARAH; PHOEBE; KEZIAH. Luke had two children by wife Mary.

10. SIMON HIRONS, probable son of Simon (3) Hirons, m. Perces Berry, dau. of Samuel Berry. Perces later m. John Edenfield.

Samuel Berry of Little Creek Hundred d. leaving a will dated 15 Sep 1742, proved 27 Aug 1743. Heirs: wife Sarah; son-in-law Josiah Gascoine; son Daniel; daus. Percis Heirons, Sarah Wade, Margarett Craige; granddau. Elizabeth Heirons. Execs., wife Sarah and son Daniel. Wits., Thomas Cockron, Alex. McKenny, John David. {Arch. A4:12-13. Reg. of Wills, I:67}

On 16 Feb 1744 Simon Hirons of Little Creek Hundred Kent Co. yeoman and Perses his wife for £116 sold to Daniel Brinkle, late of Mispillion Hundred same co., bricklayer, a tract of land. Andrew Caldwell and Hugh Durborow did convey a certain part of their share of *Willingbrook* unto Simon Hirons, father to the afsd. Simon Hirons (Book H, fol. 28), the said Simon the father by his deed of gift (Book M, fol. 61) did convey the same piece of land to his son Simon partie to these presents together with 15 a. of other adj. lands which together with the forrest piece contains 100 a.) beginning at Herring Branch, 100 a. {KEDELR N:64}

Simon d. by 20 Feb 1746 when his estate was administered by Pearcee Hirons. widow. {Arch. A24:104. Reg. of Wills, I:144}

John Edenfield d. by 29 May 1759 when his widow, Persis Edenfield, was appointed admx. of his estate. {Arch. A16:15. Reg. of Wills, K:206}

Petition of Benjamin Winne of Kent Co., blacksmith, and Elizabeth his wife, one of the daus. of Simon Hirons late of said co. yeoman, dec. That Simon Hirons d. owner of about 120 a. , part of a larger tract called *London* in Little Creek Hundred, died intestate leaving a widow and four children: Simon, eldest son, Elizabeth Winne your petitioner, Robert Hirons and Mary Hirons. Recorded 30 Aug 1764. Plat of land divided. {KEORCF Simons - 1764-1773}

Pearsis (Persis) Edengfield d. by 17 April 1772 when her son Robert Hirons, was appointed admin. of her estate. {Reg. of Wills, L:111}

In a petition of John Bell, Junr., on 24 Feb 1773 it was stated that some years since there was a division of the real estate of Simon Hirons, late of Little Creek Hundred amongst his heirs and legal representatives to wit Perses Edenfield formerly the wife of the said Simon and Simon, Robert, Elizabeth and Mary his children and as the said Perses is lately dead it now becomes necessary that the part alloted to her as her dower should be divided amongst the children. And your petitioner having purchased of Robert, one of the children of said Simon the elder, as well the part alloted to him by the division afsd. as his share of the allotment made to his mother which should fall to him afer her decease. {KEORCF Simons - 1764-1773}

Simon was father of the following children: SIMON; ELIZABETH, m. Benjamin Winne; ROBERT; MARY.

Fourth Generation

11. JOHN HIRONS, probable son of Charles (7) Irons, is mentioned in the will of Daniel Brinckle, written 28 Sep 1754, proved 4 Nov 1754. {Arch. A5:163-164. Reg. of Wills, K:97}

12. SIMON HIRONS, son of Simon (10) Hirons, m. Leticia (N).

On 27 Jul 1764 a Bond of Conveyance was made. Simon Hirons of Kent Co. was firmly bound unto Timothy Jenkins of same co in the sum of £250. If Simon Hirons shall well and sufficiently convey to Timothy Jenkins 6 a. of land on n.e. side of the present mansion plantation and a tract of land of Timothy Jenkins, being part of a larger tract late belonging to Simon Hirons, dec'd., father of the afsd. Simon Hirons in Little Creek Neck and Hundred which 6 a. is to be laid out next adj. the land of the said Timothy Jenkins along the line of Simon Hirons, dec'd., to include the dwelling house of one Benjamin Wynn, then this obligation to be void and of none effect. {KEDELR R:95}

On 17 May 1765 Simon Hirons of Little Creek Neck and Hundred, Kent Co., yeoman, and Leticia his wife for £118.3 sold to Benjamin Winn (Wynn) of same place, blacksmith, a lot of ground in the hundred afsd, part of the real estate of Simon Hirons late of Kent Co., dec'd., the father of the afsd. Simon Hirons as laid off for the share of the said Simon Hirons by the men appointed by the Orphans Court to make division among the heirs of the said Simon Hirons, dec'd., dated 7 Nov 1764 beginning at widows thirds in the line of *York* to land of Timothy Jenkins to part of said estate laid off by said division for the said Benjamin Winn, 33 a. and 138 square perches. {KEDELR R:30}

Simon d. by 12 Oct 1765 when his estate was administered by Letitia Hirons, widow. {Arch. A24:100. Reg. of Wills, L:8}

On 4 March 1773 John Bell, was appointed administrator, D. B. N. {Reg. of Wills, L:128} Note: Arch. vol. A24, page 101 mentions a dau. Perce Irons.

Petition of John Bell the younger, admin, d.b.n. of Simon Irons, dec. unadministered by Letitia Irons. That Letitia Irons during the course of her administration overpaid the estate of said Simon the sum of £13.16.6 by an accompt she passed 27 Nov 1766 now filed. Sundry debts still are due and also a charge against a child of Simon Irons along with the maintenance of the child. {KEORCF Simons - 1764-1773}

Simon was father of PERCE.

THE TIMOTHY IRONS FAMILY

1. TIMOTHY IRONS m. Catherine (N) and had a son Timothy.

On 7 March 1760 Catherine Irons of Kent Co., widow and devisee under the will of Timothy Irons her late husband, dec'd., and Timothy Irons of same co., yeoman, son and devisee also under the will of Timothy Irons, dec'd., for £200 sold to Thomas Irons of same co., two tracts of land, whereas the said Timothy Irons, dec'd., by virtue of a deed bearing date 9 May 1709 (Lib E, fol. 16:17) was in his life time seized in 50 a. of land, part of a larger tract called *Burtons Tract* in Dover Hundred beginning near the line of John Hall and James Fitzgerald, and by a deed bearing date 3 May 1721 (Lib G, fol. 161) the said Timothy Irons, dec'd., was in his life time seized in a tract of land called *Edinton Tract* in the same place, 26 a., and Timothy Irons being so seized by his will bearing date 10 March 1739 devised the same to the afsd. Catherine Irons his wife during her natural life and after her decease to the afsd. Timothy Irons his son, and Catherine Irons in Nov Term 1759 did levy a common recovery of the afsd. 2 tracts of land and vouched to warranty to the said Timothy Irons who vouched over the common vouchee. Witnessed by Henry Irons, Benjamin Brown, Mark Hirons, Ann Gray. {KEDELR P:226}

Timothy d. leaving a will dated 10 March 1739/40, proved 9 April 1740. Heirs: sons John, Thomas, Timothy, Henry, Owen; daus. Catherine, Mary, Sarah, Meriam; wife Catherine. Extx., wife. Wits., Isaac Freeland, George Gordon, James Gordon. {Arch. A25:228. Reg. of Wills, 1:18}

Timothy was father of the following children: JOHN; THOMAS; TIMOTHY; HENRY; OWEN; CATHERINE; MARY; SARAH; MERIAM.

Second Generation

2. THOMAS IRONS, probable son of Timothy (1) Irons, m. Hannah, widow of Henry Stevens.

Henry Stevens of Little Creek Hundred d. leaving a will dated 13 Dec 1744, proved 2 Jan 1744. Heirs: wife Hannah; sons-in-law Clayton Levick, John Levick; daus. Mary, Elizabeth; sons Henry, Daniel. Execs., wife Hannah and cousin Thomas Irons. Wits., Samuel McCall, Darby Carty, Benjamin Barret, Jr. {Arch. A48:217-218. Reg. of Wills, I:100} Note: Later administered by Thomas Irons and widow Hannah, who later intermarried with Thomas Irons.

On 19th da., 3rd mo., 1746 Hannah Irons produced a paper condemning her outgoing in marriage with a man not of the Society. {DCMM}

This may be the same Thomas Irons who m. Jennett, widow of Robert Bellach, admx. of her husband's estate on 21 June 1748. {Arch. A3:206-207. Reg. of Wills, 1:229-230} A3:206 mentions children, John, James and Ann Bellach, son-inlaw Robert Graham; and shows Thomas Irons and wife Jennett as admins.}

3. TIMOTHY IRONS, son of Timothy (1) Irons, m. Elizabeth Rees, widow of William Rees.

William Rees, planter, d. leaving a will dated 9 Nov 1749, proved 16 Nov 1749. Heirs: wife Elizabeth; sons David, William, Jonathan; daus. Sarah, Margaret; bros. John and Thomas. Execs., wife Elizabeth, John Rees and Phillip Lewis. Wits., Randel Blackshare, James Edwards, Edward Norman. Codicil: Hannah Rees; mentions Sarah Alston, grandmother of dau. Sarah Rees. {Arch. A43:40-43. Reg. of Wills, K:12-13} Note: Arch. A43:42 shows Elizabeth m. Timothy Hirons.

On 14 May 1760 Timothy Irons of Kent Co., yeoman, and Elizabeth his wife for £25 sold to Thomas Irons of same co., a tract of land, 46 a. {KEDELR P:227}

Timothy Irons d. by 6 April 1761 when his estate was admin. by his widow, Elizabeth. {Arch. A25:229. Reg. of Wills, K:261}

In the land records is recorded the will of Elizabeth Irons of Little Creek Hundred written 4 March 1765 and proved 6 March 1765, "being verry sick and weak in body but of perfect mind and memory thanks be given unto God do make and ordain this my last will and testament ... I give and bequeath to Jonathan Rees my eldest son 2 horses, one of about 8 years old and one of 1 year old and one chest of drawer, I give and bequeath unto my 2 sons Thimathy and William Irons the whole residue of my estate to bequally devided, I do constitute Thomas Irons esqr my sole executor." Wit: Thomas Blackshear, Mary Jolly. Proved 6 March 1765. {KEDELR R:272?; also recorded with the wills of Kent Co. in Arch. A25:215-216. Reg. of Wills, L:4}

On 6 March 1765 a Letter of Administration was granted to Thomas Irons, esqr., to administer the will of Elizabeth Irons of Kent Co., dec'd., {KEDELR R:272?}

Petition of Jos: David, Junr, atty in fact for Jonan. Rees for the acceptation of Timothy Irons's lands. 25 Feb 1774 [1779?] Whereas a commission was appointed to view and divide real estate of Timothy Irons which they would not divide. On 15 April 1767 came James Ballach guardian to Timothy Irons, minor above age of 14, and prays the court would appoint three freeholders to view land of Timothy Irons, dec'd. Petition of Jonathan Rees now of Bedford Co., PA but late of Kent Co., husbandman, by Joseph David Junr. of Kent Co., yeoman, his atty. That Timothy Irons, yeoman, dec'd., became seized of about 180 a. being in the forrest of Little Creek Hundred and he died intestate leaving issue only two sons, Timothy Irons his eldest son and William Irons. That the son Timothy the younger since the death of his said father, to wit on or about 1 Aug 1772 also died intestate and without issue leaving the afsd. William Irons his only brother of the whole blood and your petitioner his brother of the half blood. {KEORCF Irons, Timothy - 1767-73}

Elizabeth Irons was mother of the following sons: JONATHAN REES and TIMOTHY and WILLIAM IRONS.

4. TIMOTHY IRONS, probable son of Timothy (1) Irons, d. by 13 Jan 1773 when his estate was administered by James Bellach, next of kin. {Reg. of Wills, L:124}

5. OWEN IRONS, probable son of Timothy (1) Irons, m. Penelope Freeman.

On 27 Aug 1765 Thomas Collins, high sheriff of Kent Co., for £20.5

conveyed unto Thomas Irons of Little Creek Hundred esqr a tract of land and plantation in the forrest of Murtherkill Hundred, the property of Owen Irons, appraised by James Wells and David Caldwell, originally surveyed for the said Owen Irons and Moses Freeman in partnership, the 1/2 part hath since been conveyed by the said Moses Freeman to the said Owen Irons, beginning at land now belonging to John Freeman a minor and land sold by Thomas Morris, to land of the heirs of Richard Jackson, dec'd., to land belonging to Doctor Samuel Mccall and also land survyed for Penelope Freeman the now wife of the said Owen Irons, 200 a. {KEDELR R:61}

On 26 May 1767 Thomas Irons, esqr., of Little Creek Hundred, Kent Co., for fraternal love and good will and 5 shillings released unto Owen Irons of the forrest of Murtherkill Hundred same co., yeoman, the remainder of a tract of land, whereas the said Thomas Irons lately purchased at a sherriff's vendue, a 200 a. tract of land in the forrest of Murtherkill Hundred, as the property of the said Owen Irons taken in execution at the suit of sundry persons to whom the said Owen Irons was indebted, and afterwards the said Thomas Irons sold 150 a. of said premisses to a certain James Voshall and thereby reimbursed to himself the money he had paid for the said Owen Irons and being now willing to reconvey the remainder to the said Owen Irons ... bounded by Benjamin Start and land now belonging to said Owen Irons formerly surveyed to Penelope Freeman now wife of the said Owen Irons, Horse Pen Swamp and land of Thomas Morris, 62 a. {KEDELR R:244}

Unplaced

(N) IRONS m. Elizabeth Stanton.

Elizabeth Stanton of Little Creek d. leaving a will dated 1 March 1769, proved 21 March 1769. Heirs: daus. Sara Miller, Ann Smith, Elizabeth Irons; sons Mathais and Jonathan; granddau. Sara Stanton; Mary Cahoon (alias Stanton). Exec., son-in-law Conrad Miller. Wits., James Jones, John Russel. {Arch. A48:147-148. Reg. of Wills, L:55-56}

CHARLES HIRONS d. by 7 April 1772 when his estate was administered by William Hirons. {Reg. of Wills, L:111}

TITUS IRONS d. by 14 April 1774 when his estate was administered by George McCall. {Reg. of Wills, L:153}

WILLIAM IRONS m. Jane, dau. of Jacob Kollock, merchant of Lewes. Jane was mentioned in the will of her father written 30 Dec 1720 and proved 14 March 1720/1. {Arch. A83:3. Reg. of Wills, A:130-134}

On 14 May 1755 John Johnson, sold to Jane Hirons 100 a. of tract called *London Derby* and she on 10 Feb 1761 sold same to Thomas Robinson and wife Jane. {Dryden Worcester Land:372}

On 16 May 1755 Johnson sold to Jane Hirons 150 a. of *Friendship*. On 10 Nov 1755 John Dixon of Sussex Co., DE, sold to Aaron Hirons of Worcester Co., 250 a. of *Friendship*. {Dryden Worcester Land:247}

THE HUNN FAMILY

1. (N) HUNN m. Prisilla (N) who later m. 2nd George Bowers and m. 3rd John Curtice and m. 4th (N) Gilbert.

On 23 Nov 1689 Prisilla Bowers, widdow and admx. of George Bowers of Kent Co., dec'd.,gave to her loveing son Nathaniell Hunn ... three yeareling calves being two heifers and one bull. {KEDELR}

Prissila Gilbert, widow, d. leaving a will 22 Jan 1719/20, proved 10 May 1721. Heirs: daus. Sarah Bowman, Prissila Walton and Ruth Rodney; son John Bowers; grandsons Nathaniel Hunn and Nathaniel Luff; granddau. Penelop Rodney, dau. of William and Ruth Rodney; Thomas Bowman, son of Nathaniel Bowman. Execs., son John Bowers and son-in-law Nathaniel Bowman. Wits., Jonathan Manlove, Hannah Manlove. {Arch. A19:28. Reg. of Wills, D:44}

(N) Hunn was father of the following children: NATHANIEL; SARAH.

Second Generation

2. SARAH HUNN, dau. of (N) (1) Hunn, m. Hugh Luff.

On 25 Aug 1688 Hugh Luff of Kent Co., PA, batcheler, and Sarah Hunn of same place, spinster, having intentions of marriage, publish same. Wit: Wm. Berry, Clerk. On 25 Aug 1688 Hugh Luff did take Sarah Hunn to be his wife at house of Thomas Hethard at Murder Creek in Kent Co., PA. Wit: Robert Edmonds, ? Hunn, Anna Price, Ellinor Robeson, M(?) Hethard, Tho Skidmore, Sam King, Winlock Curtis, John Robbinson, ? Hethard, Georg Bower, John Curtis, Mark ?, Wm. Me(?), Wm ? [page torn]. {KEDELR}

Hugh Luff d. leaving a will dated 7 Jan 1709, proved 16 April 1709. Heirs: wife Sarah; daus. Sarah, Hannah; son Nathaniel; one other child. Execs., Nathaniel Hunn, John Bowers. Wits., Charles Austin, Zacaria Goforth, Anne Burgess. {Arch. A31:223}. Reg. of Wills, B:79}

Sarah m. 2nd Nathaniel Bowman of Mispillion Hundred who d. leaving a will dated 16 Nov 1740, proved 31 Dec 1740. Heirs: wife Sarah; son Thomas; grandson Henry Bowman. Exec., son Thomas. Wits., Matthew Manlove, Isaac King, Nathaniel Luff. {Arch. A5:79. Reg.of Wills, I:24}

Sarah Bowman of Mispillion Hundred d. leaving a will dated 14 Sep 1741, proved 25 Feb 1741. Heirs: sons Nathaniel Luff, Thomas Bowman; daus. Hannah Robisson, Sarah Clark; grandau. Ann Clark; grandson Henry Bowman. Exec., son Nathaniel Luff. Wits., John Brickle, Sarah Jester, Precillar Tharp. {Arch. A5:86. Reg. of Wills, I:42}

Sarah was mother of the following children: NATHANIEL Luff; THOMAS Bowman; HANNAH, m. (N) Robisson; SARAH, m. Clark.

3. NATHANIEL HUNN, son of (N) (1) Hunn, m. Elenor (N) who later m. James Maxwell. Nathaniel d. by 25 Aug 1718 when Ellinor Hunn was appointed admx. {Reg. of Wills, D:5}

On 5 Sep 1741 John Hunn of Kent Co., son of Nathaniel Hunn late of same co., dec'd. and Elenor his wife sold to John Clark of same place, yeoman, a tract of land (Nathaniel Hunn was in his life time possessed and d., seized in a tract of land in Mispillion Hundred, 348 a. called *Peter's Neck* and dying intestate and leaving children Caleb Hunn, Nathaniel Hunn, Mary Hunn,

Elizabeth Hunn and the afsd. John Hunn. John Hunn pursuant to his petition, the tract of land with the assistance of Benjamin Johnson, surveyor, was laid off by Peter Galloway, Jonathan Raymond, John Brinkle, Daniel Rodeney and Robert Willcosks appointed by the court their legal representatives) ... in Muspellion Hundred, lately laid off by persons afsd. for the said John Hunn, part of a bigger tract called *Peters' Neck* reserving to the said John Hunn 36 sq. perches of ground to go to and from the said grave yard with corps and a company of people to bury his dead and to build, repair and make up the said yard as occasion may require ... beginning at the land called *Aberdean* ... 80 a. for £120 John Hunn and Tabitha his wife [sic] convey the afsd. tract. {KEDELR N:54}

On 28 Nov 1749 James Maxwell and Elenor his wife of Kent Co., for £8.5 quit claim unto John Hunn of ye same co. yeoman ... all their estate right of 1/3 part of two tracts of land (whereas Nathaniel Hunn, late of Kent Co., yeoman, married with ye said Elenor and afterwards died intestate and among other lands left one tract of land in St. Jones Hundred, 170 a. called *Town Point* and also one other parcel of land of 64 a. adj. the afsd. tract which he purchased from a certain George Nowell and Elenor afterwards intermarried with James Maxwell whereof James in right of his wife became possessed of 1/3 part of the afsd. two tracts to hold to him during the natural life of his said wife Elenor). Wit: Daniel Robisson, Mary Sipple. {KEDELR O:29}

On 10 March 1728 Caleb Hunn and Nathaniel Hunn of Kent Co., yeomen, sons of Nathaniel Hunn, late of same place dec'd., Waitman Sipple, Junr, of same place, yeoman, and Mary his wife, dau. of the afsd. Nathaniel, dec'd., sold to John Killinsworth of Mispelion Hundred, a tract of land in Mispillion Neck.... 100 a. called *Northhampton* heretofore belonging to John Curtis, late of same co., dec'd., and by him sold unto the afsd. Nathaniel Hunn, the father and is part of the *Mills His Choice*, and Nathaniel Hunn in his lifetime did sell but not actually convey the 100 a. unto John Bowers of same co., cooper, bearing date 21 May 1716 and did bind himself to convey the same but hapened to dye intestate before he could perform the conveyance, and whereas the said John Bowers did assign his right and interest in the afsd. bond unto a certain John Wilson. {KEDELR I:181}

On 26 May 1762 Mary Sipple, widow, relict and late wife of Waitman Sipple, Junr, late of Kent Co., yeoman, dec'd., and dau. and one of the heirs of Nathaniel Hunn, late of said co., yeoman, dec'd., for £20 sold to Nathaniel Hunn of same co., yeoman, a tract of land, whereas the said Nathaniel Hunn, dec'd., was in his lifetime seized of a 303 a. tract of land called *Peters Neck* on s. side of Bawcombriggs Creek in Mispillion Neck and being so seizd d. intestate leaving issue living at the time of his death, to wit Caleb Hunn since dec'd., the said Nathaniel Hunn and Mary Sipple parties hereto, and John Hunn also since dec'd., and whereas after the death of Nathaniel Hunn the father on 28 Jul 1744 the justices of the Orphans Court did on the humble petition of the afsd. John Hunn make an order thereby appointing 5 discreet freeholders of said co. to go on the lands whereof the said Nathaniel Hunn, dec'd., d. seizd and make a division thereof among his children, and in pursuance of the order of the said court the 5 freeholders with the assistance of a skilfull surveyor did make a division of the said tract and thereby did lay off and allott unto the said Mary Sipple ... 49 a., 40 sq. perches. Wit: Sarah Sipple, Will Killen. {KEDELR Q:88}

Nathaniel was father of the following children: CALEB; NATHANIEL; MARY, m. Waitman Sipple; JOHN; ELIZABETH.

Third Generation

4. CALEB HUNN, son of Nathaniel (3) Hunn, m. Ruth Manlove.

On 19th da., 8th mo., 1730 the marriage of Caleb Hunn and Ruth Manlove was reported. {DCMM} {DCMM}

Caleb d. by 13 Dec 1737 when Ruth Hunn was appointed admx. of his estate. {Arch. A25:131. Reg. of Wills, H:138-139}

Anna Whitaker (Whitacre] d. leaving a will dated 30 Aug 1741, proved 1 Oct 1741. Heirs: grandson Caleb Hunn's four children Mary, Hannah, Ruth, Pricilla Hunn; grandsons Nathaniel Hunn, Waitman Sipple, Jr.; great-grandson Caleb Sipple. Exec. grandson Waitman Sipple, Jr. {Arch. A54:75. Reg. of Wills, 1:54-55}

Mark Manlove d. leaving a will dated 16 March 1747, proved 8 Jan 1749. Heirs: sons Absolam, Ezenezer, William, Mark, and Gideon; grandsons Nathan (son of Mark Manlove), Matthew (son of Absolam Manlove), Mark, son of Ebenezer Manlove, William, son of William; granddaus. Eunice (dau. of Mark Manlove), Kesiah Wheler, Margaret Manlove, Mary, Hannah, Ruth, and Priscilla Hunn, daus. of Ruth Hunn. dec'd. Execs., sons Absolam, Ebenezer and Mark. Wits., Samuel Bussee, Samuel Bussee, Jr., George Brown, Mary Bussee. {Arch. A32:38. Reg. of Wills, K:18-19}

Caleb was father of the following children: MARY; HANNAH, m. John Levick; RUTH, m. 2 Nov 1752, John Rodney, son of William[29]; PRICILLA, m. David Pleasontine; NATHANIEL.

5. NATHANIEL HUNN, son of Nathaniel (3) Hunn, probably m. Mary, dau. of Renear Williams. Nathaniel was father of REYNEAR and JONATHAN; dau. SARAH.

Reynear Williams of Mispillion Hundred, d. leaving a will dated 5 Dec 1743, proved 9 Oct 1745. Heirs: daus. Mary Hunn, Tabitha Brinckle, Susannah Brinckle, Elizabeth Williams; sons Aaron, Reynear. Exec., son Aaron. Wits., Thomas Davis, Lewes Davis, Ralph Basnet. {Arch. A55:138. Reg. of Wills, 1:125}

6. MARY HUNN, dau. of Nathaniel (3) Hunn, m. Waitman Sipple.

On 11 Aug 1749 Waitman Sipple, Junr, and Mary his wife for £30 sold unto John Hunn of same co. all rights in two tracts of land which Nathaniel Hunn of Kent Co., late dec'd., purchased from Isaac Hill on n. side of St. Jones Creek, 170 a. called *Town Point* and also one other parcel 65 a. adj.afsd. tract and purchased from George Newell, and Nathaniel Hunn d. intestate and his dau. Mary Hunn has since m. Waitman Sipple, Junr, of same co. {KEDELR O:10}

7. JOHN HUNN, probable son of Nathaniel (3) Hunn, m. Tabitha (N).

John Hunn d. leaving a will dated 26 May 1750, proved 21 June 1750. Heirs: wife Tabitha; mother Elinor Maxwell; sons David, John, Caleb; dau. Susanna. Extx., wife Tabitha. Wits., Benjamin Chew, Richard Johns, Isaiah Wharton. {Arch. A25:142-143. Reg. of Wills, K:23} Note: Arch. A25:143 shows Tabitha, the widow, later m. Silas Crispin.

On 28 Feb 1767 John Hunn of Little Creek Hundred, Kent Co., blacksmith, for £155 sold to David Hunn of same place, mason, ... his part of 2

---

29 See the Rodney section.

tracts of land he being seized in by the will of his father John Hunn, late of this co., Esqr., dec'd., 1/2 part of a tract of land called *Town Point* and 1/2 part of another tract adj. the afsd. land being that part of 2 tracts which was divided and laid off to John Hunn late of said co., dec'd., he being one of the heirs of Nathaniel Hunn of same co. dec'd., in St. Jones Hundred and now in the tenure of John Williams of St. Jones and co. afsd. and adj. the said Williams's land on n. side of St. Jones Creek adj. the Baymarsh ... 106 a. Wit: Elizabeth David, Ruth Manlove. {KEDELR R:212}

John was father of the following children: DAVID; JOHN; CALEB; SUSANNA.

8. ELIZABETH HUNN, dau. of Nathaniel (3) Hunn, m. Waitman Trippett.

On 12 Nov 1740 Waitman Treppett (Trippett) and Elizabeth his wife, dau. and one of the heirs at law to Nathaniel Hunn, late of Kent Co., dec'd., for £40 released unto John Bowers of same co., a tract of land (whereas Nathaniel Hunn did in his life time sell unto the said John Bowers and received full satisfaction for a parcel of land now in occupation of the said John Bowers called *Mulbery Point*, 300 a. of land and 170 a. of marsh) being part of an antient tract of land called *Whitewells Delight*, but Nathaniel Hunn did die before the said land and marsh was conveyed. {KEDELR M:97}

Fourth Generation

9. HANNA HUNN, dau. of Caleb (4) Hunn, m. John Levick.

On 27 May 1762 John Levick of Kent Co., yeoman, and Hannah his wife, one of the daus. and heirs of Caleb Hunn, late of said co., yeoman, dec'd., for £30 sold to Nathaniel Hunn of Kent Co., yeoman, one share of a tract of land, whereas Nathaniel Hunn, late of said co., yeoman, dec'd. father of the said Nathaniel Hunn was in his lifetime seized in a tract of land called *Peters Neck* on s. side of Bawcombriggs Creek in Mispillion Neck, 303 a., and being so seized d. intestate leaving issue the afsd. Caleb Hunn his eldest son, Nathaniel Hunn party hereto, John Hunn of said co. since dec'd. and Mary Sipple late wife of Waitman Sipple, Junr, late of said co., yeoman, dec'd., and after the death of Nathaniel Hunn the father on 28 July 1744 the justices of an Orphans Court on the petition of the afsd. John Hunn make an order appointing 5 discreet freeholders of said co. to go on the lands whereof the said Nathaniel Hunn, dec'd., d., seizd and make a division thereof among his children ... did allot and lay off to the afsd. Caleb Hunn part of the tract ... 98 a., 80 sq perches ... Caleb Hunn d. intestate seized of the said tract and leaving issue 3 daus, to wit Mary, the afsd. Hannah Levick, Ruth and Priscilla who afterwards m. David Pleasontine of Kent Co., yeoman, and is since dec'd. without issue living at the time of her death, by means of which said deaths of the said Caleb Hunn and Priscilla Pleasontine intestate the 98 a. 80 sq perches descended to the afsd. Mary, Hannah Levick, Ruth now wife of a certain John Rodeney, children and heirs of the said Caleb Hunn. {KEDELR Q:104}

10. JONATHAN HUNN, son of Nathaniel (5) Hunn, m. Ann Willson (d. 28th da., 7th mo., 1780), dau. of George and Patience Wilson of TA Co.

On 16th da., 7th mo., 1753 the marriage of Jonathan Hunn and Ann Willson was reported. {DCMM}

Jonathan and Ann were parents of the following children {DCMM}: MARY, b. 25th da., 8th mo., 1754, m. Caleb Bickham of Philadelphia; REYNEAR, b. 22nd da., 2nd mo., 1756, d. about 2 1/2 years old; GEORGE, b. 10th da., 10th mo., 1757, d. about 15th da., 2nd mo., 1782; NATHANIEL, b. 28th da., 9th mo., 1759; DWIDIN (Durdin?), b. 10th da., 4th mo., 1762, d. 13th da., 2nd mo., 1782; JONATHAN, b. 22nd da., 1st mo., 1764, m. Patience Mifflin; PATIENCE, b. 9th da., 1st mo., 1766, m. Jabez Jenkins of Jabez and Hannah; SARAH, b. 24th da., 3rd mo., 1768, d. 16th da., 9th mo. 1768, m. John Brown; CALEB, b. 10th da., 2nd mo., 1770, d. an infant; ANN, b. 1st da., 3rd mo., 1772, d. an infant; EZEKIEL, b. 1st da., 3rd mo., 1774, m. Tabitha Newell (b. 27th da., 11th mo., 1777, dau. of Henry and Margaret Newell).

George Wilson d. leaving a will dated 31 Aug 1756, proved 23 Oct 1756. Heirs: wife unnamed; sons Derdin, William, George; daus. Ann Hunn, Mary Hunn, Margaret Wilson. Extx., wife. Appraisers, Govey and Jonathan Emmerson. Wits., Ezekiel Nock, Jabez Jenkins. Codicil written 1 Sep 1756, names sons-in-law Jonathan and Renear Hunn as alternate execs. Wits., Thomas Nock. {Arch. A55:203-204. Reg. of Wills, K:148} Note: Arch. vol. A55, page 204 shows Patience married Daniel Robisson.

11. RENEAR HUNN, probable son of Nathaniel (5) Hunn, m. Mary Wilson, dau. of George Wilson. {See will of George Wilson}

Rynear Hunn m. Mary Wilson, both of the county of Kent on Delaware, 28th da., 11th mo., 1754, at the dwelling house of George Wilson in Kent Co. {DCMM} On 16th da., 12th mo., 1754 the marriage of Rynere Hunn and Mary Willson was reported. {DCMM}

Reynear Hunn, farmer, d. leaving a will dated 29 July 1762, proved 11 Aug 1762. Heirs: father Nathaniel Hunn; bro. Jonathan; nephew Nathaniel son of bro. Jonathan; niece Mary, dau. of bro. Jonathan; sister Sarah Hunn; Skidmore Wilson, son of William Wilson. Execs., father Nathaniel and bro. Jonathan. Wits., Nathan Adams, John Plesenton, Joice Lynch. {Arch. A25:170. Reg. of Wills, K:288}

12. DAVID HUNN, son of John (8) Hunn.

On 26 Aug 1767 David Hunn of Kent Co., bricklayer, for £117 sold to Ebenezer Manlove of same place, yeoman, the estate right of Caleb Hunn in 2 tracts of land, whereas Nathaniel Hunn, late of Kent Co., dec'd., in his lifetime by sundry good conveyances became seized in 2 tracts of land in Jones Hundred, one called *Town Point* and the other thereunto adj. called *The Addition* and being so seized d. intestate leaving issue, Caleb Hunn and John Hunn to whom the afsd. did descend, and the said John Hunn being so seized to a share of the 2 trs died leaving behind his will wherein he did bequeath the lotts of land and marsh which were lately laid off and allotted unto me by virtue of an order of the Orphans Court part of 2 tracts of land which my father in his life time purchased of George Nowell and Isaac Hill in Jones Neck unto my 2 sons John and Caleb, and whereas David Hunn by his bond bearing date 8 May 1767 became bound unto the said Ebenezar Manlove in the sum of 500 pounds conditioned for his conveying by a good and sufficient deed all the estate right in the afsd. 2 trs of land. (signed) David Hunn, Tabitha Crispen. {KEDELR R:218}

On 21st da., 2nd mo., 1757 Silas Crispen on behalf of his wife requested certificates for her two sons John Hunn and Caleb Hunn to be taken under the care of Friends. {DCMM}

Fifth Generation

14. PATIENCE HUNN, dau. of Jonathan (10) and Ann Hunn, b. 9th da., 1st mo., 1766, m. Jabez Jenkins.

Jabez, son of Jabez Jenkins, late of Kent Co., on Delaware, and Hannah his wife, both dec'd., m. Patience Hunn, dau. of Jonathan Hunn of the same place and Ann his wife, dec'd., 3rd da., 4th mo., 1782, at a publick meeting at Murtherkill. {DCMM}

15. NATHANIEL HUNN of Kent Co. on Delaware, son of Jonathan (10) Hunn, the same place, and Ann his wife, dec'd., m. Mary Mifflin, dau. of Daniel Mifflin and his wife of Accomack, VA, 1st da., 8th mo., 1781, at a publick meeting at Murtherkill. {DCMM}

Unplaced

On 28th da., 1st, mo., 1775, Murtherkill Preparative Meeting brought a complaint against JONATHAN HUNN for having purchased a negro about three years ago. {DCMM}

TABITHA HUNN, m. William Willson

On 20th da., 2nd mo., 1758, the marriage of Wm. Willson and Tabitha Hunn, having consent of parents and relations, was reported orderly accomplished. {DCMM}

THE KELLY FAMILY

1. JOHN KELLY, m. Sarah Word, dau. of Patrick Word. Sarah later m. Samuel Glue.

Patrick Word by his will dated 16 Jan 1697 did give to the afsd. John Kelly then his son in law, 45 a., being part of a tract called *Kingsale* adj. to the n.e. side of the tract called *Galloway* divided by Willsons Branch, afterwards the land called *Kingsale* being confirmed by patent to James Jackson and Margarett his wife, granddau. to the said Patrick Word, they released the 45 a. unto William Kelly, son of the afsd. John Kelly 15 Feb 1715/6, John Kelly, dec'd., one surviving son named William and several daus. who are all dec'd. without issue except one named Margarett who became married to James Jackson late of Kent Co. and is now also, dec'd., leaving issue, only one son named James Jackson one of the parties to these presents, and William Kelly who died in possession of the afsd. tract of land called *Galloway*, except the part thereof which his father's executors conveyed to William Freeman (Book H, pg 15-17), and also in possession of the 45 a. part of *Kingsale*, being dec'd., intestate and without issue his two half sisters, daus. of his mother, to wit Rebecca now wife of Nicholas Powel and Rachel now wife of William Hazard all parties to these presents now claim a right in the said lands and James Jackson the son afsd. likewise partie to these presents also claims in right of his mother who was whole sister to the said William Kelly, dec'd., all the 441 a. called *Galloway* excepting 200 a. conveyed to Lowber.

Patrick Word of Duck Creek d. leaving a will dated 16 Jan 1697, proved 12 April 1698. Heirs: granddaus. Honor Kelly, Margaret Kelly, Judity Dwyer (dau. of Mary); sons-in-law John Kelly and Thomas Dwyer; dau. Sarah Kelly, wife of John Kelly; dau. Mary Dwyer. Exec. John Kelly. Wits., James Fitzjarrell. Simon Hirons, Jr., William Annand {Arch. A56:135-136. Reg. of Wills, A:24-25} Note: Order from the Commissioners to John Kelley respecting Tobias Tunissen and wife, Mary (dau. of Patrick Word). 13 Dec 1698. Reg. of Wills, Liber B, folio 32.

John Kelly d. by 10 March 1700 when his estate was administered by Sarah Kelly. {Reg. of Wills, B:40-41}

On 12 Aug 1767 Lewis Jones and Evan Jones both of Little Creek Hundred Kent Co., yeomen, for £236 sold to John Ham of same place, yeoman, a tract of land, whereas 400 a. called *Galloway* formerly surveyed for a certain John Kelly by virtue of a warrant from court of Kent Co. dated 16 Nov 1681 but the return of survey not being found in the surveyor generals office a resurvey was made for the said Kelly and found to contain 441 a. in Little Creek Hundred on s. side of Thomas Willson's Branch of Little Duck Creek and whereas the said John Kelly soon after dyed and Sarah his widow having intermarried with a certain Samuel Glue. Whereas the said John Kelly at the time of his death left issue viz, a son named William and sundry daus. all of whom dyed without issue except one dau. named Margaret who intermarried with a certain James Jackson, they by the decease of the other children of John Kelly became vested with a title by inheritance to the whole estate which was of said Kelly. Said James Jackson and wife left issue, viz one son who was also named James Jackson who together with Rebecca his wife conveyed the said 200 a. to a certain James Tybout. {KEDELR R:219}

John was father of the following children: HONOR; MARGARET, m. James Jackson; WILLIAM.

Second Generation

2. MARGARET KELLY, dau. of John (1) Kelly, m. James Jackson. They had a son JAMES who m. Rebecca (N).

3. WILLIAM KELLY, son of John (1) Kelly.

On 12 Feb 1715 James Jackson of Little Creek Hundred, Kent Co., yeoman, and Margit his wife for love and affection and 5 shillings sold to their brother William Kelly, a tract of land on s. side of Duck Creek, running to corner of tract of land formerly layd out to John Kelly. {KEDELR E:45}

William Kelly d. by 2 Sep 1720 when his estate was administered by James Jackson. {Reg. of Wills, D:24}

Unplaced

JAMES KELLY m. Ann Mercer 4 Dec 1766. {LCPC}

JOHN KELLY, farmer of Murderkill Hundred, d. leaving a will dated 14 March 1764, proved 24 April 1764. Heirs: son Enock; son-in-law Samuel Goodwin; dau.in-law Elizabeth Goodwin. Exec. friend William Wallace, Sr. Trustee, Charles Ridgly. Wits., Mark Harper, Daniel Coudret, Joshua Wallace. {Arch.

A28:99, 106-108. Reg. of Wills, K:342} Note: Arch. A28:106 shows William Wallace, dec'd, and Catherine, his wife, admins.

SAMUEL KELLY, son of Anipil who is sister to Samuel Man.

Samuel Man d. by 17 July 1752, proved 12 Aug 1752. Heirs: sisters Agness, Isable Hudson, Rachel Wilson, Annalana Man, Abigail Man; niece Marget Hudson, dau. of sister Isable; nephew Samuel Kelly, son of sister Anipil. Execs., sister, Rachel Wilson and Hugh Craige. Wits., Ephraim Shaw, Elizabeth Craige, Leah Craige. {Arch. A33:74-76. Reg. of Wills, K:78-79} Arch. A33:75 shows Rachel Wilson later married Francis Murrey.

WILLIAM KELLY, laborer, d. by 17 Nov 1762 when Vincent Loockerman, merchant, was appointed admin. to his estate. {Arch. A28:110. Reg. of Wills, K:297}

THE LANCELOTT LEWIS FAMILY

1. LANCELOTT LEWIS, Duck Creek, d. leaving a will dated 24 July 1720, proved 25 July 1720. Heirs: sons Lancellot and John; daus. Martha, Elizabeth and Mary, wife of Alexander Humphries. Wits., John Foster, James Tire, William Fortescue. {Arch. A30:107. Reg. of Wills, D:21}

Lancelott was father of the following children: LANCELLOT; JOHN; MARTHA; ELIZABETH; MARY, m. Alexander Humphries.

Second Generation

2. LANCELOTT LEWIS, son of Lancelott (1) Lewis, m. 1st Mary Portice, sister of John and Silvanus Portice of Cecil Co., MD, and m. 2nd Bridgett (N).

On 6 Aug 1726 Simon Hirons and Lancelott Lewis and Mary his wife of Kent Co. for £17 sold to Robert Buchar of same place a tract of land in Little Creek Hundred near the head of Dover River being part of a greater tract called *Simons Choyce* formerly taken up by Simon Hirons beginning at the s. corner of land called *Ye Exchange* ... 71 a. {KEDELR I:38}

On 27 Aug 1741 Mariam Lewis, dau. of Lancelot Lewis and Mary his former wife who was sister of John and Silvanus Portice, for £5 sold to John Hamer of Kent Co. a tract of land (whereas Simon Hirons, late of same co., dec'd., stood possessed of a 500 a. tract of land called *Oxford*, 100 a. of which he left in his will to afsd. John and Silvanus Portices, uncles to Mariam, which died without issue) ... beginning near a path that goes from John Bosticks's to Daniel Griffin's ... 100 a. {KEDELR M:120}

On 16 Feb 1743 Lancelot Lewis and Bridgett his wife of Kent Co. for £22 sold to Alexander Umphris of same co. a tract of land ... 100 a., part of the 200 a. beginning at the n. corner of John Lewis his land which is also a part of the said 200 a. {KEDELR N:23}

On 28 Aug 1753 Clemment Carter and Mary his wife (formerly Mary Lewis who is now one of the surviving heirs of John and Silvanus Portes late of Kent Co., dec'd.) of Cecil Co., MD, for £10 sold to William Hirons of Kent Co. a parcel of land on Choptank Road near the Black Swamp adj. a tract of William Morton's called *Cambridge* and it being a part residue of that tract of land called *Oxford* which was left to John and Silvanus Portes afsd. (Hiron's will recorded Book B, No. 17 in Kent Co.) 50 a. {KEDELR O:198}

Lancelott and Mary were parents of the following children: MARIAM; probably MARY.

3. JOHN LEWIS, son of Lancelot (1) Lewis, had a dau. Elizabeth who m. Luke Hirons and dau. Kesiah Lewis.

On 10 May 1721 John Hall of Little Creek Hundred, Kent Co., gentleman for £25 sold to John Lewis of same co., son of Lancelot Lewis, blacksmith, dec'd., a tract of land in Little Creek Hundred on n. side of Muddy Branch called *Content* ... 100 a. being the upper part of 200 a. called *Content* ... to the corner of land now in the possession of Lancelot Lewis, son of Lancelot Lewis, dec'd. {KEDELR G:27}

On 27 Feb 1750 Luke Hirons of Little Creek Hundred, Kent Co., yeoman, and Elizabeth his wife, for £35 sold to Stokely Sturgis of same place half part of a tract of land called *Content* in Little Creek Hundred on n.w. side of Muddy Branch whereon the said Stokely Sturgis now dwells ... 100 a. which did formerly belong to a certain John Lewis late of this co., dec'd. father of the afsd. Elizabeth Hirons and by his will did devise and give unto the said Elizabeth and Keziah Lewis his two daus. the 100 a. to be equally divided between them which said division hath not been yet made ... 50 a. {KEDELR O:84}

On 10 Nov 1756 Stokley Sturgis of Little Creek Hundred, Kent Co., yeoman, for £50 sold to Thomas Parker of same place ... 1/2 undivided part of a 100 a. tract of land called *Content* in Little Creek Hundred on n. side of Muddy Branch being the same tract Sturgis purchased of a certain Luke Hirons and his wife Elizabeth which did formerly belong to a certain John Lewis late of this co., dec'd. father of the afsd. Elizabeth Hirons and by his will did devise the tract of land unto said Elizabeth and Kesiah Lewis his two daus. to be equally divided between them ... 50 a. {KEDELR O:348}

John was father of two daus.: ELIZABETH, m. Luke Hirons; KESIAH.

THE REES LEWIS FAMILY

1. REES LEWIS of Duck Creek m. Mary (N).

Rees d. leaving a will dated 15 Oct 1744, proved 14 Nov 1744. Heirs: wife Mary; sons John, David, James, Rees, Daniel, Mark; grandson Joell Lewis, son of James. Execs., wife Mary and sons Rees, Daniel. Wits., Lewis Williams, Jenkin David, John David. {Arch. A30:121. Reg. of Wills, I:88-89}

Rees was father of the following children: JOHN; DAVID; JAMES; REES; DANIEL; MARK.

Second Generation

2. JOHN LEWIS, probable son of Rees (1) Lewis, d. leaving a will dated 26 Nov 1769, proved 4 Dec 1769. Heirs: sons Rees, Mark and Amram. Exec., friend John Russel. Trustee, friend John Russel. Wits., James Lewis, Timothy Russel, Hugh Russel. {Arch. A30:95. Reg. of Wills, L:68}

John was father of the following children: REES; MARK; AMRAM.

3. DAVID LEWIS, probable son of Rees (1) Lewis, m. Susannah Lowber, dau. of Michael Lowber and widow of Benjamin Furbey.

David Lewis, yeoman, d. leaving a will dated 19 Dec 1744, proved 12

Jan 1744. Heirs: wife Susannah; heirs of Thomas Noxon; children unnamed. Extx., wife. Wits., Abraham Morris, Matthew Lowber, John Dowling. {Arch. A30:66, 67, 149. Reg. of Wills, I:101-102}

Michel Lowber d. leaving a will dated 2 Jan 1744, proved 7 April 1746. Heirs: daus. Unity (wife of John Emerson), Susannah Lewis; sons Michael, Peter, Matthew, Isaac; daus. Garty Muncy, Margarett Manlove, Agnes Walker; wife Rachel; grandchildren of dau. Grace Brown; grandsons Michael (son of Peter Lowber), John and Michael Reynalds, Michael Emerson (son of Unity and John Emerson), granddau. Susannah Reynalds. Exec'rs, wife Rachel and son Peter. Wits., Isabella Brooks, Arthur Brooks, Mary Brooks, now Mary Jackson. {Arch. A31:172-174. Reg. of Wills, I:122-123}

Susannah Lewis d. leaving a will dated 20 March 1763, proved 18 May 1763. Heirs: sons Bowers, Michael, Caleb and Benjamin Furbey, Daniel, David, Joseph and Stephen Lewis; dau. Elizabeth Boyer. Exec., son Michael Furbey. Trustees, friends John Caton, Daniel Robisson. Wits., Daniel Robisson, Hanahretta Anderton, Febey Pecue. {Arch. A30:147-148. Reg. of Wills, K:312} Note: Arch. A30:148 shows James Boyer and Mary Furbee, adm'rs, D. B. N.

Michael Forbee [son of Susannah Lewis] d. leaving a will dated 9 April 1765, proved 15 May 1765. Heirs: wife Mary; son Benjamin; daus. Mary and Nancy; a child unnamed. Execs., wife Mary and friend James Boyer. Wits., Caleb Furbee, Stephen Lewis, Alexander Craige. {Arch. A18:166-169. Reg. of Wills, L:6} Note: Will mentions Susannah Lewis as mother of Michael; Arch. A18:169 shows Mary, the widow, later married Arthur Wheatley and mentions Michael Furbee as a son.

David was father of the following children: DANIEL; DAVID; JOSEPH; STEPHEN.

4. JAMES LEWIS, probable son of Rees (1) Lewis, m. Rachel (N).

On 14 Nov 1753 James Lewis of Kent Co. and Rachel his wife for £50 sold to Stephen Durborow of same co. a plantation and tract of land in the forest of Joneses Hundred in a fork of Joneses being the now dwelling plantation of James Lewis and allso part of two tracts of land that William Sidden of same co. purchased of Robert Wilson of same co. and William Sidden sold it to James Lewis 12 Feb 1750. {KEDELR O:202}

James was father of JOELL.

Third Generation

5. DANIEL LEWIS, son of David (3) Lewis, m. Margaret (Peggy) Paradee, dau. of Stephen Paradee and she later m. Jonathan Caldwell.

On 24 Nov 1759 Stephen Paradee, esqr., and Lydia his wife of Kent Co. for £100 sold to Daniel Lewis, farmer, and Margaret his wife of same co. a tract of land and plantation in Dover Hundred in actual possession of Daniel Lewis and Margaret, his wife, beginning at Pipe Elm Branch and land late of George Robinson now belonging to Aron Hart, the whole formerly belonging to William Winsmore called *Great Pipe Elm,* adj. Casar Rodney's land and John Paradee's land ... 176 a. also a small piece of meadow ground part of the tract of land called *Shoulder of Mutton* near Bucks Bridge to land called *Paradees Venture* ... 5 a. {KEDELR P:164}

Stephen Paradee d. leaving a will dated 29 Nov 1759, proved 18 Dec 1759. Heirs: wife Lydia; dau. Mary; son Stephen; grandsons Daniel and Stephen

Lewis; granddaus. Ruhamy, Hannah and Mary Lewis. Execs, wife Lydia and son-in-law Daniel Lewis. Appraisers, James Clayton and Charles Marim. Wits., Charles Inglis, Richard Wells, James Sykes. {Arch. A38:243-244 and A39:1-2. Reg. of Wills, K:217-218} Note: Arch. A39:2 shows Jonathan Caldwell and wife Peggy, late Peggy Lewis, admins., d.b.n.

Daniel Lewis of Dover Hundred d. leaving a will dated 22 June 1761, proved 22 July 1761. Heirs: wife Peggy; sons Daniel and Stephen; dau. Elizabeth. Execs., wife Peggy and son Stephen. Wits., Caesar Rodney, Charles Marim, Wilson Buck [master]. {Arch. A30:59-62. Reg. of Wills, K:265} Note: Arch. A30:61 shows Daniel Lewis a relative of Stephen Paradee; also mentions Geo. Gordon and wife Mary, dau. of John Parradee; page 59 shows Margaret, the widow, later married Jonathan Caldwell. {KEORCF Lewis, Daniel - 1768-73}

Expenses for Elizabeth Lewis, dau. of Danl. Lewis, dec'd., submitted by Jonathan Caldwell her guardian: To cash paid John Boyd for your schooling, do. to John Cotton. To boarding you from July 1761 at which time you were about 1 yr. and 3 mo. old to the present time 11 yrs and about 8 mos. At the bottom of account is written, "Elizabeth born April 29th 1760." {KEORCF Lewis, Daniel – 1768-73}

The account of Jonathan Pleasanton includes bill for a velvet side saddle for Hannah Lewis ... To boarding cloathing and schooling Ruhama Lewis from 22d July 1761 (at which time she was about 11 years and 8 mos. old) to the 29th of July 1767 at which time she intermarried with said Jona. Pleasonton ... {KEORCF Lewis, Daniel - 1768-73}

Whereas Stephen Paradee in his last will gave to the children of his dau. Peggy in the event of the death of his dau. Mary without issue (which was the case) she was to have three Negroes. Petitioners, Stephen Lewis, Jonathan Pleasonton and John Gordon request a division be made of said Negroes. {KEORCF Lewis, Daniel - 1768-73}

In an account of the expenses for Daniel Lewis, son of Danl. Lewis, dec'd. is shown, "Daniel born Decr. 12th 1756." {KEORCF Lewis, Daniel - 1768-73}

A commission was chosen by Stephen Lewis, Jonathan Pleasanton who m. Ruhamah Lewis and also guardian to Hannah Lewis and Jonathan Caldwell, guardian to Mary Lewis, Daniel Lewis and Elizabeth Lewis, heirs and representative of Daniel Lewis, to view and value the Negroes Jo., Daniel and Phebe which were left to the children of said Daniel Lewis by his last will. {KEORCF Lewis, Daniel - 1768-73}

In a petition of Stephen Lewis he stated that Daniel Lewis, a minor, age 15 years or thereabouts and Elizabeth Lewis, an infant under the age of 14 years, to wit, of the age of 13 years, children of Daniel Lewis, late of said county, yeoman, dec'd., are owners of and intituled to a considerable personal as well as real estate and having neither any testamentary or other guardian to take a proper care of their persons or estates. Petitioner is brother to the said infants. {KEORCF Lewis, Daniel - 1768-73}

Daniel was father of the following children: STEPHEN; RUHAMAH, b. ca. 22 Nov 1749, m. 29 July 1767, Jonathan Pleasonton; HANNAH; DANIEL, b. 12 Dec 1756; ELIZABETH, b. 29 April 1760; MARY.

6. DAVID LEWIS, son of Daniel (3) Lewis, m. Sarah Sipple, widow of Caleb Sipple.

Caleb Sipple, yeoman, d. by 10 Feb 1762 when Sarah Sipple, widow, was appointed admx. {Reg. of Wills, K:275} Note: Arch. A46:87-89 shows Sarah, the widow, later married David Lewis; also mentions children Nancy, John, Caleb, Mary, Thomas, Elizabeth and Garret.

On 24 Aug 1763 David Lewis of Kent Co., yeoman, and Sarah his wife, late the wife of Caleb Sipple, late of said co., yeoman, dec'd., and admin. of Caleb Sipple, dec'd., sold to Benjamin Warren of same co., a tract of land part of a larger tract called *Ousby* on n. side of Murtherkill Creek in Murtherkill Hundred beginning at land late of Benjamin Warren, Senr, to land late of Waitman Sipple, Junr ... 142 1/2 a., also that other parcel on s. side of Service Branch in the hundred afsd. beginning at land late of John Brown ... 84 a. {KEDELR Q:170}

On 24 Aug 1763 the humble petition of David Lewis of Kent Co., yeoman, and Sarah his wife, admx. of Caleb Sipple late of said co., yeoman, dec'd., sheweth that the said Caleb Sipple in his lifetime was seized of 2 parcels of land, in the whole 226 1/2 a., and being so seized by his agreement in writing made 2 March 1761 did agree with one Benjamin Warren, Junr, that he would convey the tract of land by a good and sufficient deed containing a general warranty for the consideration of 20 shillings per a. but died before a deed was made. The consideration money of £226.10 has since the death of said Caleb Sipple been paid by Benjamin Warren to the afsd. Sarah. The Court ordered that the parties within mentioned execute and acknowledge a deed. {KEDELR Q:170}

7. JOSEPH LEWIS, probable son of Daniel (3) Lewis, m. Ruth (N).

Joseph Lewis d. by 3 April 1773 when Ruth Lewis, widow, was appointed admx. of his estate. {Arch. A30:103-104. Reg. of Wills, L:130}

<u>Unplaced</u>

ADAM LEWIS m. Mary Watson, dau. of Luke Watson.

On 8 April 1718 Adam Lewis of Philadelphia and Mary his wife, dau. of Luke Watson, late of Lewis Town, Sussex Co., dec'd. ... whereas Luke Watson by his will bearing date 6 Sep 1705 did devise to his then wife Sarah and his dau. Mary Watson all the rest and residue of his estate and he died seized of a tract of land on n. side of Main Branch of Mispillion beginning at the corner of land of W -illiam Clark ... 1500 a. of which said land by virtue of the devise afsd. does of right belong to the said Mary Lewis. By this indenture Adam Lewis and Mary his wife for £20 sold to Berkly Cood and Mary his wife halfe part of the afsd. tract of land. {KEDELR H:174}

On 9 April 1718 Adam Lewis and Mary my wife of Philadelphia constitute our trusty friend Preserved Coggeshall of Sussex Co. our atty to make over a tract of land according to a deed bearing date 8 April 1718 by me in Philadelphia in open court. {KEDELR H:112}

DAVID LEWIS, probable son of David Lewis, yeoman, d. by 10 Jan 1757 when Rachel Lewis and John Lewis were appointed admins. {Reg. of Wills, K:155}

JONATHAN LEWIS of Chester Co., PA., son of Alexander Lewis and Hannah his wife.

On 22 March 1763 Jonathan Lewis of Chester Co., PA, for £55 sold to Thomas Murphy of Kent Co., blacksmith, 1/4 part of a tract of undivided land in

Little Creek Hundred now in possession of Joseph David by virtue of a power of atty received from his father and mother Alexander Lewis and Hannah his wife. {KEDELR Q:157}

MARY LEWIS d. by 4 Sep 1769 when Ebenezar Clampitt was appointed admin. of her estate. {Reg. of Wills, L:65} Note: Arch. A30:117 shows that Jane Clampitt married Benjamin Sparks. On 22 Nov 1769 Jean Clampit, next of kin, was appointed admx. d.b.n. Reg. of Wills, L:67}

PHILIP LEWIS m. Mary (N).

On 13 Nov 1740 Phillip Lewis and Mary his wife of Kent Co. for £110 sold to Thomas Dawson of same place a tract of land (warrant from the Whorekill Court dated 21 Jan 1679/80 a tract of land was laid out unto Isaac Webb of Kent Co., dec'd., called *Shoemakers Hall* on s. side of St. Jones Creek, 400 a. {KEDLER M:87}

On 14 May 1752 Phillip Lewis of Kent Co., yeoman, and Mary his wife, for £400 sold to Wm. Corse of Dover Hundred but late of Little Creek Hundred, same co., a tract of land on n.w. side of Dover River and on s. side of Kings Road from Dover to Salisbury Town ... 330 1/4 a. part of a larger tract called *Concord* and also of another larger tract surveyed to the said Philip Lewis in pursuance of a warrant bearing date 9 Oct 1751. {KEDELR O:143}

Philip Lewis of Little Creek Hundred d. leaving a will dated 17 Oct 1769, proved 1 Nov 1769. Heirs: wife Mary; son Philip. Extx., wife Mary. Wits., Richard Smith, John Evans, Thomas Murphey, Jr. {Arch. A30:118-120. Reg. of Wills, L:65-66}

Philip was father of PHILIP.

STEPHEN LEWIS m. Mary Furchas, widow of Tobias Furchas.

Tobias Furchas, farmer of Mispillion Hundred, d. leaving a will dated 6 March 1747, proved 4 April 1748. Heirs: wife Mary; children unnamed. Execs., wife and John Caten. Wits., Nathaniel Hunn, Thomas Bowman, Jr., Spencer Cole. {Arch. A18:188-189. Reg. of Wills, I:194-195} Note: Arch. A18:189 shows Stephen Lewes and his wife Mary as execs.

On 12 May 1760 Stephen Lewis and Mary his wife of Kent Co. for £50.7.8 sold to John Furchase of same place a tract of land in Mispillion Hundred beginning near Bacombrig Creek adj. land of James Martin now in the posesion of William Smith ... as by a deed of conveyance from John Bowers of same co. to the said Mary Lewis ... 150 a. {KEDELR P:220}

STEPHEN LEWIS m. Sarah Dickenson, widow of William Dickinson.

William Dickinson [Dickerson) d. by 8 Jan 1768 when Sarah Dickinson, widow, was appointed admx. of his estate. {Arch. A14:65-67. Reg. of Wills, L:39} Note: Arch. A14:67 shows Sarah Dickinson married Stephen Lewis; page 65 mentions children, John, William, Elizabeth and Anne.

Walter Dickenson d. by 18 Feb 1769 when Sarah Dickenson, next of kin, was appointed admx. of his estate. {Reg. of Wills, L:54} Note: Arch. A14:64 shows that Sarah Dickenson married Stephen Lewis.

STEPHEN LEWIS m. Deborah, dau. of Nathaniel Luff and widow of David Pleasanton.

Nathaniel Luff, Sr., Gentleman, d. leaving a will dated 3 Feb 1760, proved 27 Feb 1760. Heirs: wife Deborah; sons Caleb, Nathaniel, John; daus. Hannah Paradee, Deborth Pleasanton. Execs., sons Caleb and Nathaniel. Wits., Samuel Merydith, Sarah Maston, Thomas Clark. {Arch. A31:229-238. Reg. of Wills, K:225} Note: Arch. A31:235 shows John Paradee as husband of Hannah; David Pleasanton as husband of Deborah; Deborah later married Stephen Lewis. Page 236 shows Deborah, the widow, later married Jonathan Manlove. Page 238 shows Philip Reason [Rasin] only son of Sarah had heirs, Jemiah Ford, Robert Meeks and Joseph Rasin.

David Pleasanton of Dover Hundred d. leaving a will dated 28 March 1774, proved 5 April 1774. Heirs: wife Deborah; dau. Sarah; sons Nathaniel, John, David, Caleb. Exec'rs, wife Deborah and William Rodney. Commissioners, Caleb Luff, John Williams, James Sykes, Esq., William Rodney, Samuel Hanson. Wits., James Stevens, Jonathan Pleasanton, Benjamin Nixon. {Arch. A40:94-99. Reg. of Wills, L:152} Note: Arch. A40:96 shows that Deborah Pleasanton married Stephen Lewis.

THOMAS LEWIS m. Mary (N).

Thomas Lewis of Duck Creek Hundred d. leaving a will dated 13 May 1769, proved 23 May 1769. Heirs: wife Mary; cousin Hannah Morris, wife of Thomas Morris; Thomas Jones and Elizabeth Jones, children of David Jones; Dr. John Lewes. Execs., wife Mary and friend Robert Blacksheare. Wits., James Moore, Richard Meradith. {Arch. vol. A30, pages 150-152. Reg. of Wills, Liber L, folio 60}

(N) LEWIS m. Phebe Whitman and she later m. Jonathan Griffin.

Samuel Whitman d. leaving a will dated 26 April 1733, proved 7 Feb 1733. Heirs: sisters Elizabeth Whitman and Phebe Lewis; wife Elizabeth; bro. Jonathan; son-in-law Joseph Freeman; son Samuel. Extx., wife. Wits., James Justice, Hugh Rowland, Isaac Snow. {Arch. A54:209-211. Reg. of Wills, H:73} Note: Arch. A54:211 shows that Elizabeth Whitman, widow of Samuel, married John Craig and later married Richard James; that Elizabeth, the sister, married Thomas Green; and Phebe Lewis married Jonathan Griffin.

THE LOWBER FAMILY

1. PETER LOWBER (Loper) emigrated from Holland to New York ca. 1677. He m. Gartre (N). In 1684 he purchased land near Dover in Kent Co., DE.

Peter d. leaving a will dated 2 April 1698, proved 2 May 1698. Heirs: wife Gartre; son Michael; daus. Mary Nichols (widow of William), Margaret Paradee, Gartre Loper, Agnes Smith. Extx., wife Gartre. Wits., Thomas Bedwell, William Nichols, Daniel Hudson. {Arch. A31:136. Reg. of Wills, B:27}

Peter was father of the following children: MICHAEL; MARY, m. William Nichols; MARGARET, m. Stephen Paradee; GARTRE; ANGES, m. John Smith.

Second Generation

2. MICHAEL LOWBER, son of Peter Lowber, b. c1677, m. 1st Unity Paradee and m. 2nd Rachel Brooks, dau. of Arthur Brooks.

On 20 Feb 1721 Micheal Lowbar (Lowber) of Kent Co., yeoman, for love and fatherly respect gives to his dau. Susanah and her husband Benjamin Furby, 100 a. where Benjamin Furby now dwelleth it being part of a 400 a. tract of land I bought of Daniel Rutty called *Southhemton* which 100 a. is now called *Furbys Lott*. {KEDELR G:60}

In Oct 1722 Michael Lowber, aged 45 years or thereabouts, made oath regarding a deed of Thomas Bedwell and Honor his wife to James Brooks, Senr., made about 12 years earlier. {KEDELR G:112}

On 13 Sep 1735 Michael Lowbar of Kent Co. for natural love and affection gave to his well beloved son Michael Lowbar, Junr., a tract of land in DO Co., n. side of Cow Marsh that lyes at the head of Great Choptank River, 200 a. Wit: Mathew Lowber, Elizabeth Brinkloe, Peter Brinkloe, Agnas Logan. {KEDELR L:60}

On 16 Sep 1735 was recorded a true copy of the original deed exhibited to the office by Unity Lowber, wife of Michael Lowber, Senr., the granter grandfather and by her order recorded the reason by her given for it being not first acknowledged in the court of this co. is that the said premises and appurtances is situate in Dorsett Co. MD. {KEDELR L:62}

On 8 Feb 1741 Michael Lowber of Murther Creek Hundred, yeoman, and Rachel his wife, for £10 sold to Peter Lowber of same place, yeoman, a tract of land called *Cabin Ridge* in the forrest of Murther Creek Hundred near the s. side of Bear Swamp, 200 a. {KEDELR M:190}

Michael Lowber d. leaving a will dated 2 Jan 1744, proved 7 April 1746. Heirs: daus. Unity (wife of John Emerson), Susannah Lewis; sons Michael, Peter, Matthew, Isaac; daus. Garty Muncy, Margarett Manlove, Agnes Walker; wife Rachel; grandchildren of dau. Grace Brown; grandsons Michael (son of Peter Lowber), John and Michael Reynalds, Michael Emerson (son of Unity and John Emerson), granddau. Susannah Reynalds. Execs., wife Rachel and son Peter. Wits., Isabella Brooks, Arthur Brooks, Mary Brooks, now Mary Jackson. {Arch. A31: 172-174. Reg. of Wills, I:122-123}

On 25 Feb 1761 John Gooding and Susannah his wife of Kent Co. for £70.10 sold to John Growell of same co. a parcel of land in the forrest of Murderkill Hundred in Cow Neck (whereas John Gooding and Susannah his wife being seized in 270 a. formerly surveyed unto one William Welch and afterwards became vested to Daniel Reynolds who dying and left three children under age and Michal Lowber grandfather of the said children obtained a warrant in trust for the said children dated 30 April 174- by which the 270 a. was returned into the Secretarys Office 18 Aug 1760 and by a division amoungst the heirs of said Daniel Reynolds there was laid out for Susanah wife of John Gooding 75 a. of land and after her mothers death there was laid out for Susannah, share of her mothers thirds 28 a. 106 perches), 113 2/3 a. {KEDELR Q:32}

Rachel, widow of Michael Lowber, m. John Bowers, yeoman, 24th da., 1st mo., 1746, at the Little Creek Meeting House. {DCMM} John Bowers of Murderkill Hundred d. leaving a will dated 13 Aug 1765, proved 25 June 1766. Heirs: wife Rachel; son John; daus. Elizabeth Corse, Mary Lowber, Ruth Bowers. Execs., wife Rachel and friends Samuel Hanson and Thomas Hanson. Wits., John Gray, Prudence Gray, Agness McElhenny. {Arch. A5:27-28. Reg. of Wills, L:12-13}

On 26 Aug 1747 Peter Lowber, exec. of Michael Lowber, came to court with an account of the estate. The widow refused to abide by the Will and requested her thirds which was done. Legatees: Unity Emerson, a large church Bible appraised at £2.5.0 and pays the widow 1/3 the value thereof; Michael Lowber, Negro Prince; Susannah Lewes, Negro woman Betty; Margret Manlove, Negro Woman Doll; Grace Brown, Negro man Jacob; Matthew and Peter Lowber working and plantation tools; Agnes Walker, a Negro boy Tom; Isaac Lowber, three young Negroes and other things. Residue of the estate to the testator's six daus.: Unity Emerson, Susannah Lewes, Gartrey Munsey, Margaret Manlove, Agnes Walker, Grace Brown. {KEORCF Lowber, Michael - 1747}

On 31 March 1768 Rachel Bowers the widow of John Bowers late of Murtherkill Hundred Kent Co., dec'd., and Arthur (Arther) Brooks of same place, brother to the said Rachel Bowers, they being children of Arther Brooks, Senr., late of same place, dec'd., for love and good will and 5 shillings give unto Isaac Lowber, son of said Rachel Bowers, of same place, a parcel of land part of land called *New Line* whereof the said Arther Brooks, Senr., was in his lifetime possessed in Murtherkill Hundred near n. side of Double Run branch adj. land of William Brown and near other land of said Isaac Lowber called *Amsterdam*, to land of said Arthur Brooks, 25 a. {KEDELR R:261}

Michael was father of the following children: UNITY, m. John Emerson and had children Unity and John; SUSANNAH, m. 1st by 20 Feb 1721 Benjamin Furby and m. 2nd David Lewis; MICHAEL; MATTHEW; ISAAC; GARTY, m. (N) Muncy (Munsey); MARGARETT, m. 1st Absolem Manlove and m. 2nd Alexander Craige; AGNES, m. (N) Walker; GRACE, m. 1st Daniel Reynalds and m. 2nd (N) Brown; PETER, had a son Michael.

3. MARGARET LOWBER, dau. of Peter (1) Lowber, m. 4 Nov 1697, Stephen Paradee.

On 29 Oct 1697 it was recorded that Stephen Paradee and Margarett Loober, both of Kent Co., PA, have published their intention of marriage - William Rodeney, Clerk. {KEDELR}

On 4 Nov 1697 The marriage of Stephen Paradee and Margaret Loeber, both of Kent Co. PA, was duly solomnized by Thomas Bedwell, justice of the peace. {KEDELR}

4. AGNIES LOWBER, dau. of Peter (1) Lowber, m. John Smith.

On 15 Jun 1693 John Smith of Kent Co., PA, did take Agnies Loper to be his lawfull wife. Witnessed by Peter Louber, Jane Cowe, Guarte Wood, Michall Loper, John Brinckloe, John Waskenton, Timothy Thorold, Jacob Smith, Daniell Rutey, James Clayton, Thomas Hodgkines, Isacc Freeland, George Clifford, Abell Willson, John Chant, Grace Thorold. {KEDELR}

Third Generation

5. MATTHEW LOWBER, son of Michael (2) Lowber, m. Hannah, widow of Samuel Robinson (Robison).

Samuel Robinson (Robison], yeoman, d. leaving a will dated 21 June 1747, proved 20 Jan 1747. Heirs: wife Hannah; sons Daniel, Samuel, Asa; daus. Miriam, Hannah; nephew Samuel, son of bro. Daniel; bro. Daniel. Extx. wife Hannah. Wits., Thomas Clark, James Gorrell, Peter Lowber. {Arch. A44:84-85. Reg. of Wills, I:177-178} The Will mentions George Robinson as the father; settlement of estate completed by Mathew Lowber and Hannah, his wife.

Matthew d. leaving a will dated 8 June 1772, proved 29 July 1772.

Heirs: wife Hannah; sons Matthew, Jr., Peter and Jonathan; daus. Susanna, Elizabeth and Meriam; son-in-law William Virdin; granddau. Elizabeth Virdin, dau. of William; grandson Hugh Durborrow. Exec., son Peter. Wits., Richard Bassett, Jacob Duhadway, Sr., Daniel Duhadway. {Arch. A31:128-126. Reg. of Wills, L:117} Note: Arch. A31:125 mentions a dau. Susanah Durbrow.

Matthew was father of the following children: MATTHEW; PETER; JONATHAN; SUSANNA, m. (N) Dubrow; ELIZABETH; MERIAM.

6. ISAAC LOWBER, probable son of Michael (2) Lowber, m. Mary (N). They were parents of the following children {DCMM}: PRISCILLA, b. 27th da., 3rd mo., 1765; RACHEL, b. 12th da., 9th mo., 1767; RUTH, b. 24th da., 3rd mo, 1769; ELIZABETH, 24th da., 3rd mo., 1771; LYDIA, b. 24th da., 5th mo., 1773, d. 5th da., 9th mo., 1854; ISAAC and MARY, b. 8th da., 5th mo., 1776; MARGARET, b. 8th da., 2nd mo., 1778, m. Aaron Williams near Milford; MICHAEL, b. 14th da., 9th mo., 1780; JOHN, b. 8th da., 12th mo. 1781; BOWERS, b. 11th da., 1st mo., 1783, d. 3rd da., 10th mo., 1870; MICHAEL, b. 23rd da., 2nd mo., 1785, m. Ann Jenkins of Jabez.

7. MICHAEL LOWBER, eldest son of Michael (2) Lowber.

On 1 April 1747 Michall Lowber of Kent Co. for the sum of £4.10 sold to Mathew Lowber, all rights to a tract of land called *The Plains* (whereas Peter Lowber grandfather to the afsd. Michall Lowber and Mathew Lowber did in his lifetime purchase two parsells of land one called *Amsterdam*, the other *The Plains* from Henry Johnson and Daniell Ruttey and Peter by his will gave the afsd. lands to his son Michell Lowber father to Michall and Mathew, and Michall did by his will dispose of all his estate excepting that parsell of land called *The Plains* adj. *Amsterdam* and part of the plantation where the said Michael Lowber did dwell, and he did note dispose of that persell of land in his will it becomes so much of the estate intestate, Michall Lowbar being the eldest son is intitled to 2 shares). {KEDELR N:153}

8. PETER LOWBER, probable son of Michael (2) Lowber, had a son MATHEW.

On 17 Jun 1762 Mathew Lowber, Junr., son of Peter Lowber of Murtherkill Hundred Kent Co. for £147 sold to Mathew Lowber, Senr., of same place ... a parcel of land, 209 1/4 a., part of a tract which said Mathew Lowber, Junr., son of Peter Lowber sold 30 a. unto Michael Reynolds and also 1 a. unto Margaret Grier of the tract in the forrest of Murtherkill Hundred on s. side of Cowmarsh adj. John Gray's land and William Wheeler's land on Choptank Road. {KEDELR Q:102}

On 11 Feb 1767 Michael Raynolds of Murtherkill Hundred, Kent Co., for £9.26 sold to Mathew Lowber of same place, part of a 30 a. tract of land purchased of Mathew Lowber, Junr., son of Peter Lowber in the forrest of Murtherkill Hundred near Cow Marsh or Beaver Dam Branch on Forrest Road adj. Margret Green's land and Mathew Lowber's land, 9 a., 23 perches. {KEDELR R:164}

9. SUSANNAH LOWBER, dau. of Michael (2) Lowber, m. 1st by 20 Feb 1721 Benjamin Furby and m. 2nd (N) Lewis.

Benjamin Furby d. by 9 May 1733 when Susannah Furby was

appointed admx. of his estate. {Arch. A18:147. Reg. of Wills, H:105-106}

10. GRACE LOWBER, dau. of Michael (2) Lowber, m. 1st Daniel Reynolds, m. 2nd Thomas Brown and m. 3rd Anthony Pindegras.

Daniel Reynals, yeoman, d. leaving a will dated 4 May 1736, proved 14 June 1736. Heirs: sons John, Miyckel and dau. Susannah; wife Grace. Extx., wife. Wits., Hugh Marydith, John Thomas, William Thompson, Margaret Males. {Arch. A43:91, Reg. of Wills, H:147}

Thomas Brown d. by 21 Nov 1746 when Grace Brown was appointed admx. of his estate. {Reg. of Wills, I:142} Note: Arch. A6:92 shows Grace m. Anthony Pandergrass; also mentions daus. Agnis and Rachel Brown.

In the petition of Anthony Pindegras and Grace his wife, one of the daus. of Michael Lowber, dec'd., it was shown that Grace one of your petitioners formerly intermarried with Daniel Reynolds who was seized and possessed by sundry goods and etc. and a certain tract of land in Murderkill Hundred by whom this Grace, one of your ... had three children, to witt, John, Michael and Susanna and after the death of the sd. Daniel it was found that that no grant or warrt. had ever been made from the land offices for the same and Michael Lowber discovering the truth afsd. applied to the land office afsd. and obtained a warrant for the same in trust for his three grandchildren afsd. and Grace your petitioner. {KEORCF Lowber, Michael - 1755}

Daniel and Grace were parents of the following children: JOHN; MICHAEL; SUSANNAH, m. John Gooding.

Unplaced

PETER LOWBER had a dau. Catrine who m. Daniel Duhadway.

On 11 Feb 1767 Peter Lowber, Senr., of Kent Co. for love, good will and affection give to my son in law Daniel Duhadway and my dau. Catrine his wife of Kent Co., a parcel of land in the forest of Murderkill Hundred, part of 2 tracts of land the one surveyd unto a certain Joseph Harrison in pursuance of a warrant bearing date 4 May 1737 and the right whereof was afterwards vested in said Peter Lowber and returned in the secretary's office at Philadelphia 10 Oct 1747, the other tract of land was surveyed unto the afsd. Peter Lowber in pursuance of an order bearing date 22 Jun 1748 called *The Addition to Caben Ridge*, 97 a., 152 perches, part of the afsd. 2 tracts of land, beginning at land of Joseph Harrison to Francis Cain's land. {KEDELR R:164}

PETER LOWBER m. Elizabeth Brinckle, sister of John Brinckle.

On 5 Feb 1766 Peter Lowber and Elizabeth his wife, one of the sisters of John Brinckle, dec'd., for natural love, good will and affection gave unto Anne Clark of Kent Co., mantuamaker, and also for the better maintenance lively hood and perserment of her, a parcel of land allotted as the share of the afsd. Peter Lowber and Elizabeth his wife being their shear of the lands of the afsd. John Brinckle Esqr, dec'd., which he was seized of in his life time, beginning at the share laid off to Mariam Hyland one of the sisters of the afsd. John Brinckle to Browns Creek to Sandy Gravely Vally to Chappell Branch to field left to the heirs of Winlock Clark, 200 a., part of the lands that belonged to John Brinckle by the will of his father William Brinckle and also the right which they have to all that 1/2 part of the lands of the afsd. John Brinckle, dec'd., laid off to Jemimah Haslet who was the widow and relique of the afsd. John Brinckle, reserving to my self and my wife for and during our natural life the use and occupation of the said lands and premisses. Witnessed by David Caldwell, Matthew Lowber, Miriam Caton. {KEDELR R:163}

PETER LOWBER m. Elizabeth, widow of John Clark.

John Clark, farmer, d. by 25 Jan 1755 when his estate was administered by Elizabeth Clark, widow. {Reg. of Wills, K:104-105} Note: Arch. A9:4-5 shows Elizabeth, the widow, later married Peter Lowber.

On 1 Nov 1762 John Clark of Mispillion Hundred, the son of John Clark late of same place gent, dec'd., and also Peter Lowber of Murtherkill Hundred, tavernkeen, and Elizabeth his wife, all of Kent Co, the said Elizabeth Lowber having been the relict and widow of the afsd. John Clark, dec'd., for £259.4 sold to Nathaniel Luff of Mispillion Hundred Kent Co. gent ... a parcell of marsh in Mispillion Neck, 288 a {KEDELR Q:123}

THE MANLOVE FAMILY

{A} Refers to material generously contributed by Bruce Bendler, Bear, DE, published by him in 1987, along with information more recently discovered by him.

First Generation

1. MARK MANLOVE, immigrated into the Province of Maryland by 1665 with his wife Elizabeth and other members of the family: John, Ann, Marke, Jr, William, George, Christopher, Hannah, Perce and Thomas Manlove and Ann Williams and Thomas, Mary and John Gille. {MPL SR 8203; Transcript 9:204-9 [SR7351]} He settled in Somerset Co. The records also show Elizabeth Manloe had been transported by 1672 by her husband John of Somerset Co. {MPL 17:386; SR 7358} This is probably the same Elizabeth Manlow, wife of John, transported by 1673 with her husband. {MPL LL:139; SR 7548}

Mark Manlove patented on 20 Jan 1665 100 a. in Brinkleys, southeast, the tract *Pimore.*

Mark Manlove of Pocomoke, Somerset Co., d. leaving a will[30] dated 14 Sep 1666, proved 3 Jan 1666/7. To his wife Elizabeth and the children begotten of her, he devised 500 a. on n. side of Pocomoke River, "beginning at a little branch on the south side of my new dwelling house ..." Mentioned were wife and sons Mark, William, Christopher, George and Luke. To sons John and Thomas 100 lbs. of tobacco each. Legacies to daus. Hannah, Abijah and Persy Manlove, and grandchildren Hannah Gilley and Richard Hackworth. Execs. wife Eliza: and son-in-law Richard Hackworth. Overseers: William Stephens Horsey and Wm. James Meeden. Witnesses by Wm. Greene and Wm. Stephens. {See the orginal will held by MSA. See also MWB 1:268 which does not mention sons John and Thomas.}

Mark was father of the following children: GEORGE; LUKE; MARY,

---

30 The will as transcribed by Jane Baldwin in the Maryland Calendar of Wills does not mention sons John and Thomas.

m. 23 Nov 1661{A} Thomas Gilley; HANNAH, m. 25 June 1667, John Marrett; ABIJAH; PERSY; MARK, b. c1651; WILLIAM; CHRISTOPHER; JOHN; THOMAS, m. 30 July 1667 Jane Delamas{A}.

Second Generation

2. JOHN MANLOVE, son of Mark (1) Manlove, m. Ann (N). They were parents of Elizabeth, b. 27 Feb 1666/7. Ann, wife of John Manlove, d. Feb 1670/1. John m. 2nd 9 Aug 1672, Elizabeth Loe. They were parents of John, b. 1 May 1673.

Bruce Bendler states that John may have also had a son RICHARD {A}.

John Manloe, Richard Manloe, and John, Junr. Manloe, recorded their cattle marks at court, 4-6 Oct 1687. {Sussex County Court Records}

Reference is made in the Kent Co. deeds to a John Manlove (dec.), who conveyed land and then d. leaving a will in which he bequeathed the land to his wife Sarah, now wife of Wm. Milnor of Sussex Co. William and Sarah Milnor now release same to James Miers for £5 on 30 Aug 1735. {KEDELR F6:45}

John was probable father of ELIZABETH; JOHN; RICHARD.

3. THOMAS MANLOVE, son of Mark (1) Manlove, m. 30 July 1667, Jane Delamas. They were parents of the following children: COMFORT, b. 13 July 1671{A}; SARAH, b. 6 Feb 1680{A}; THOMAS, b. 4 Feb 1679{A}; DELAMAS (son), b. 1 Aug 1686{A}; JANE, b. 2 April 1684{A}; MARK; JOHN; JANE.

Thomas patented *Elliotts Improvement* on 9 May 1673 by Thomas Manlove who made it over to Matthew Dorman for 200 a. in West Prince Anne District. On 1 Oct 1679 Thomas Manlove and wife Jane, sold to Matthew Dorman 200 of same. {Dryden Somerset Land:147}

Thomas Manlove patented on 20 Nov 1678 *Hockley* for 50 a. in East Princess Anne Dist. He and wife Jane later sold the land. {Dryden Somerset Land:214} Thomas on 20 Nov 1679 patented 100 a. called *Wansborough* in East Princess Anne Dist. {Dryden Somerset Land:405} On 23 March 1687 Thomas Manlove patented *Bear Ridge*, 200 a., in East Princess Anne Dist. {Dryden Somerset Land:30}

4. GEORGE MANLOVE, son of Mark (1) Manlove, b. 1660 in VA, m. Ann (N).

On 6 April 1680 William Stevens patented a tract called *Georges Marsh* and assigned it to George Manlove for 50 a., in Pocomoke Hundred. {Dryden Worcester Land:254}

On 12 Sep 1693 Georg Manlow (Manlove) of Kent Co. PA and Anna Manlow (Manlove) his wife for a valuable consideration already paid sold to John Moroney of afsd. co. planter, 300 a. part of a tract of land fomerly surveyed for Georg Manlow (Manlove) called *Manlows Plott* at head of Stroutkill. {KEDELR}

On 8 Aug 1695 is recorded the second article in the Last Will and Testament of George Manlove, dec.; secondly it is my will that my well beloved wife Ann Manlove and my children that is Jonathan Manlove, Ann Manlove, Tabitha Manlove and Elizabeth Manlove shall have my full and whole stock of cattle male and female equally divided. Ann Manlove widdow and relict of

George Manlove, dec'd., has fullfilled the contents thereof. Wit: William Thompson, James Lawrence, Hugh Luffe, Michael Donnahoe. {KEDELR}

George d. leaving a will dated 7 Nov 1694, proved 12 Feb 1694/5. Heirs: wife Ann; son Jonathan; daus. Ann, Tabitha, Elizabeth; bros. Mark, Luke; John Walton. Wits., John Mulrony, John Walker. {Arch. A33:91. Reg. of Wills, A:14}

George was father of the following children: JONATHAN, d. 1721; ANN; TABITHA, m. (N) Williams {A}; ELIZABETH.

5. LUKE MANLOVE, son of Mark (1) Manlove, b. 26 Aug 1666.{A} He m. 1st Anna Brown[31]; m. 2nd Katherine (N).

Luke d. leaving a will dated 29 Dec 1708, proved 5 Jan 1709/10. Heirs: sons Luke, William, George, John, Joseph; daus. Anne and Mary. Execs., sons Luke and William. Trustees, Joseph Booth and Mark Manlove. Wits., William Simson, Rachel Manlove, Mark Manlove. {Arch. A32:31. Reg. of Wills, C:84-85}

2 April 1689. Birth. Luke Manloe son of Luke Manloe and Katherine his wife was born. {KEDELR}

Luke was father of the following children: LUKE, b. 2 April 1689; WILLIAM; GEORGE; JOHN; JOSEPH; ANNE; MARY; THOMAS {mentioned in the probate of his father's estate}.

6. ABIJAH MANLOVE, dau. of Mark (1) Manlove.

On 12 Oct 1669 Thomas Miller sold to Abijah Manlove, dau. of Mark Manlove, 250 a. of *Greens Chance*. {Dryden Worcester Land:275}

7. MARK MANLOVE of Mispillion Creek, son of Mark (1) Manlove, m. 4 April 1671, Elizabeth Green, dau. of William and Elizabeth Greene of Somerset Co., MD{A}. Following Mark's death Elizabeth m. (N) Clark.{A}

On 18 Sep 1678 Mark Manlove sold to David Linzey 133 1/3 a. of tract *Sonnes Choice*.

On 4 May 1686 Mark Manlove with wife Elizabeth, sold 100 a. of *Cowley* to William Bradshaw called *Bradshaws Purchase* and sold balance to William Brittingham. {Dryden Worcester Land:147}

Mark d. leaving a will dated 24 Nov 1694, proved 20 Feb 1694/5. Heirs: wife Elizabeth; sons. Mathew, Mark; daus., Rachel, Elizabeth, Rebecca, Sarah, Hannah Hillyard; son-in-law John Hillyard; bro. John Manlove; Henry Spencer. Execs., wife Elizabeth and son Mathew. Wits., Alce Manlove, Mark Manlove, Jr., Richard Curtis, James Howell. {Arch. A32:36. Reg. of Wills, A:13}

On 1 Jan 1716 Mark Manlove of Mispillion Hundred, Kent Co., yeoman, for £60 sold to Henry Hall of same place, a tract of land called *Mount Pleasent* on n. side of Mispillian Creek by Beaver Dam Branch ... by Fishing Branch ... 212 a. ... (412 a. of land and 88 a. of marsh adj. to said land was granted by order of St. Jones Court 20 Sep 1680 and surveyed 13 Jan following to William Clark and confirmed by patent 26 March 1684 ... William Clark sold to Griffith Jones late of Philadelphia, dec'd., merchant ... Griffith Jones 10 Sep 1694 sold unto Mark Manlove late of Kent Co., dec'd., father of afsd. Mark

---

[31] On 20 June 1698 he was charged in a Kent Co. court with marrying contrary to law. He pled ignorance, claiming to have been married by virtue of a license from the King's attorney in Maryland; he was fined £10.

Manlove ... Mark Manlove on 24 Nov 1694 did make his will and bequeathed afsd. tract of land, now being leased to John Clark, to son Mark ... Mark Manlove the younger sold unto Robert Betts of Kent Co. 200 a. of said land). {KEDELR E:284}

On 10 Jun 1695 Mark Manlove, Senr., and Elizabeth his wife of Kent Co. PA for £30 sold to Samuell Manlove, son of William Manlove of same co., a tract of land called *Samuells Lott* being part of a tract of land called *Mount Plesant*, on n. side of Mispillion Creek, 200 a. {KEDELR}

On 27 Aug 1697 Hannah Hillyard wife of John Hillyard do release, acquit and discharge my mother Elizabeth Clark alias Manlove and my brother Mathew Manlove both executors to the estate of my father Mark Manlove lately, dec'd., of a legacy of cattell left me by his will ... Wit: Rachel Manlove, Mark Manlove. {KEDELR}

On 10 Nov 1703 Samuel Webster and Rachel his wife of Sussex Co., PA and Robert Beets and Elizabeth his wife of Kent Co. for £10 sold to John Clark of Kent Co., 300 a., being part of a tract called *Mount Pleasant*, on n. side of Mispilion Creek by Fishing Branch being a parcel of land given to Rachel and Elizabeth by their father Mark Manlove. {KEDELR E:154}

On 23 Jan 1713/14 Mark Manlove, Junr., batchelor of Kent Co. was bound unto Robert Betts of same co. farmer for £100 to be paid unto the said Robert Betts, Mark Manlove to make over unto Robert Betts a tract of land of 200 a. beginning at the lower line of Mark Manlove's *Long Point* adj. with the Beaver Dam, adj. the marsh next unto Muspillion Creek, then this obligation to be void. {KEDELR L:232}

On 9 Aug 1714 Mark Manlove, batchelor son of Mark Manlove, dec'd., of Kent Co. for £22 sold to Robert Betts of same co. farmer, 200 a. of land and 40 a. of marsh in Muspillion Hundred by Bever Dam Branch n. side of Muspillion Cr. {KEDELR L:233}

On 1 Aug 1718 Mathew Manlove son and heir of Mark Manlove late of Kent Co. yeoman, dec'd., for £30 sold to William Mulroney of same place, yeoman, a tract of land on n. side of Mispillian Creek, 100 a., part of a 300 a. tract sold by John Curtis late of Kent Co., dec'd., unto Mark Manlove, dec'd., bearing date 5 Jan 1693 on the eastern line of Thomas Jester's land ... binding with a tract of land called *Maidens Plott*. {KEDELR F:21}

On 11 May 1722 Henry Hall of Mispelion Hundred Kent Co., yeoman, for £30 sold to Mathew Manlove of same place, yeoman, a tract of land called *Mount Pleasant*, on n. side of Mispillion Creek by Beaver Dam Branch, 412 a. of land and 88 a. of marsh adj., granted by order of St. Jones court 21 Sep 1680 surveyed 13 Jan following to William Clark and confirmed by patent 26 March 1684 and conveyed unto Griffith Jones late of Philadelphia merchant, dec'd., On 10 Sep 1694 Griffith Jones by deed sold to Mark Manlove late of same co., dec'd., father of Mark Manlove which Mark Manlove in his lifetime 24 Nov 1694 did make his will and bequeathed unto his son Mark the afsd. plantation. Mark Manlove the younger by deed sold unto Robert Betts of Kent Co. 200 a. and 1 Jan 1716 sold unto Henry Hall of same co. yeoman the residue of afsd. tract of land. {KEDELR G:83}

Mark Manlove of same co. from whom the whole or part thereof a tract called *Mount Pleasant*, n. side of Mispillion Creek, descended unto his son Mathew Manlove and he on 10 Jun 1701 conveyed 200 a. part of the tr, Book D, fol. [1?], unto John Hall, 200 a. and the remaining part of 300 a. which the said

John Clark bought of Robert Betts, Samuel Webster and their wives and afterwards sold with the afsd. 200 a. on 1 Oct 1718 unto the afsd. John Hall, 200 a. in all 400 a. {KEDELR O:248}

Mark was father of the following children: MARY, b. c1674{A}; MATHEW, b. 25 Jan 1679{A}; MARK; RACHEL, m. Samuel Webster[32]; ELIZABETH, b. 1 May 1673, m. Robert Betts; REBECCA; SARAH; HANNAH, b. 22 March 1676{A}, m. John Hillyard.

8. WILLIAM MANLOVE, son of Mark (1) Manlove, m. 1 Nov 1676{A} Alce Robbins, dau. of Samuel and Mary Robins {A}.[33] Following the death of William Manlove his widow Alce m. 10 July 1698 John Foster at the house of William Clark in the town of Lewis. {Some Records of Sussex County, Delaware:134}

On 25 Nov 1678 William Manlove patented *Manloves Lott* and assigned same to Cornelius Morris. {Dryden Somerset Land:277}

On 27 Feb 1679 William Manlove and his wife Alice sold to Mark Manlove 133 1/3 a. now called *Brothers Love*. {KEDELR}

On 1 Feb 1686 William Manlove and wife Alice sold to Thomas Lister 250 a. of tract *Morris's Hope* and 250 a. of the tract *Persimon*. {Dryden Somerset Land:301}

On 27 Feb 1734 Mark Manlove, son of William Manlove, sold to Robert Boyer, 250 a. {Dryden Somerset Land:301}

William Manlove d. leaving a will dated 16 Sep 1694, proved 10 Oct 1694. Heirs: wife, Alce; sons Mark, William, Samuel; daus. Hannah, Mary, Elizabeth; bros. John, Mark and George. Execs., wife Alice and son Mark. Trustees, bros. Mark and George. Wits., George Robisson, Richard Curtis {Arch. A33:131. Reg. of Wills, A:8}

Ephraim Emmerson and his wife Mary, sold land on 10 July 1716 to William Manlove of Little Creek same co, and after his death it descended to his only surviving children William Manlove and Elizabeth Manlove who afterwards marryed with the said Peter Brinckle, and by their deed 13 Aug last sold same to the said Daniel Brinckle. {KEDELR N:182}

William was father of the following children: MARK; WILLIAM[34], b. 25 Dec 1691, d. 1761; SAMUEL, d. 1731; HANNAH; MARY, b. 9 March 1681; ELIZABETH, m. Peter Brinckle.

9. CHRISTOPHER MANLOVE, son of Mark (1) Manlove.

On 20 Nov 1685 Christopher Manlove, son of Mark Manlove, sold 130 a. to John Walton. {Dryden Somerset Land:332}

---

[32] Rachel Manlove, dau. of Mark Manlove m. Samuel Webster before 11 Nov 1703.{KEDE Deeds E:154}

[33] Bruce Bendler states that Samuel d. before his 1662 will but mentions an expected child. The widow subsequently m. Richard Allen who brought Mary and Alice Robins from Virginia to Somerset Co. {A}

[34] William Manlove was mentioned in the Will of John Foster, dated 30 March 1722 as his son in law. {Arch. A18:43. Reg. of Wills, D:60}

Third Generation

10. JOHN MANLOVE, son of John (2) Manlove, was father of the following children {A}: MANUEL; JOHN; PATIENCE, d. 1776 at age 65, m. 8 July 1736, Charles Polk; MARY.

11. RICHARD MANLOVE, possible son of John (2) Manlove, d. leaving one son and two daus. Richard was father of the following children: SON, d. in his minority without issue; ELIZABETH, m. Evan Morgan; TABITHA, m. Daniel Clifton. This is shown in the conveyance in which William Manlove of KE Co., DE, and Daniel Clifton and his wife Tabitha, of Dorchester Co., MD, sold land to Abraham Wynkoop of Sussex Co. The land was part of a larger tract called *Cedar Town* which was sold to Richard Manlove by James Brown. {Sussex Co. Land Records: D:382; F6:381}

On 11 Dec 1727 Evan Morgan and his wife Elizabeth, dau. of Richard Manlove, conveyed land to Wm. Manlove, carpenter of Kent Co., DE. {F6:241}

According to Bruce Bendler {A} Richard d. leaving the following children: TABITHA, m. Daniel Clifton; ELIZABETH, m. Evan Morgan; WILLIAM.

12. THOMAS MANLOVE, son of Thomas (3) Manlove, d. leaving a will dated 26 Jan 1709, proved 24 Sep 1710. Heirs: wife Mary Manlove; dau. Sarah Manlove; a child unnamed. Extx. wife Mary Manlove. Wits., Richard Manlove, John Clandene, Philip Grende. {Sussex Co. Probate - Arch. A86:44. Reg. of Wills, A:75-76}

13. JONATHAN MANLOVE, farmer, probable son of George (4) Manlove, m. Hannah Spencer who later m. George Robbisson.

Jonathan d. leaving a will dated 3 March 1721, proved 3 April 1721. Heirs: daus. Mary, Ann; sister Sarah Molleston; wife Hannah; cousins Tabitha and Mary Williams; bros. Henry Molestone, Joseph Spencer; sister Tabitha's children. Execs., wife Hannah, father-in-law Samuel Spencer. Wits., Mathew Manlove, Henry Hall, Luke Manlove. {Arch. A33:111. Reg. of Wills, D:41}

On 24 Aug 1737 was a complaint of Thomas Nixon and Anne his wife, one of the daus. of Johnathan Manlove, late of the co., dec'd., against George Robbisson and Hannah his wife. That Johnathan Manlove made his last Will and bequeathed to his two daus., to wit, Mary and Anne Manlove, two mares of 4 years old ... Execs. wife Hannah and Samuel Spencer. And the said Hannah did afterward intermarry with ... ... afsd. Samuel Spencer is since removed out of the county. Now the said Anne, dau. of afsd. Jonathan being past the age of 15 years and since married with afsd. Thomas Nixon who in behalf of himself and the said Anne his wife did often require the said George and Hannah his wife to account with them for the one moiety of the said mares and their increase which the said Thomas and Ann his wife saith did amount to five head of horsekind but said George and Hannah his wife execs. afsd. have refused, sometimes pretending that they know now what became of them. {KEORCF Manlove, Jonathan - 1721}

On 15 Feb 1739/40 Thomas Tarrant, innholder, and Mary his wife, Thomas Nixon, taylor, and Ann his wife all of Kent Co. ... whereas Jonathan Manlove father of the said Mary and Ann late of same co., dec'd., in his life time caused to be surveyed a parcel of land in the forrest of Mispillion near Marshy Hope ... 210 a. and by his will devised his lands to his daus. Mary and Ann who haveing since intermarried with Thomas Tarrant and Thomas Nixon, they on 19 Jul 1737 obtained a warrant ... Thomas Tarrant and Mary his wife, Thomas Nixon and Ann his wife in consideration of the sum of £5 paid by George Robbisson, Junr., late of this co., dec'd., discharge the said George Robbisson and have released unto Richard Underwood of same co. yeoman (for whose use the afsd. £5 was paid by George Robbisson) all our rights unto the afsd. land by virtue of the bequest of the said Jonathan Manlove. {KEDELR M:77}

On 6 Oct 1739 Hannah Robbisson of Kent Co., widdow of George Robbisson, lately of same co., dec'd., for £30 quitt claim unto Thomas Nixon of same co., a plantation, devised to her by the will of Jonathan Manlove, her former husband, bearing date 3 March 1722. {KEDELR M:67}

On 17 Jul 1740 Thomas Tarrant of the Town of Dover Kent Co. innholder and Mary his wife one of the daus. of Jonathan Manlove of same co., dec'd., for £5 quit claim unto Thomas Nixon of same place taylor and Ann his wife also one of the daus. of Jonathan Manlove ... one half part of a tract of land in Mispillion Hundred (bequeathed by Jonathan Manlove, dec'd., to his two daus. by his will) part of a tract called *Point Look Out* ... to John Brinkloe Junr's land to the widow Brinckle's land ... adj. land called *Hickery Point* ... 266 a. including the old plantation and 1/2 of 150 a. of marsh granted by patent 15 May 1740 to Thomas Tarrant and Thomas Nixon and Ann his wife. {KEDELR M:92}

On 17 Jul 1740 Thomas Nixon of the Town of Dover Kent Co. taylor and Ann his wife, one of the daus. of Jonathan Manlove of same co., dec'd., for £5 release unto Thomas Tarrant of the same place innholder and Mary his wife, also one of the daus. of the afsd. Jonathan Manlove, dec'd., ... a tract of land in Mispillion Hundred adj. the marshes of the bay and is 1/2 bequeathed by Jonathan Manlove, dec'd., to his two daus. by his will ... adj. land of John Brinckle, Junr., to Great Turkey Glade ... to land called *Point Look Out* and *Hickery Point* ... 288 a. and also 1/2 of 150 a. of marsh granted by patent bearing date 16 May 1740 to Thomas Tarrant and Thomas Nixon and Ann his wife. {KEDELR M:83}

On 16 Nov 1759 Manlove Tarrant of Kent Co. yeoman for £390 sold to John Brinckle of same co. esqr and Curtis Brinckle, yeoman, 1/2 of two tracts of land, whereas Jonathan Manlove by sundry good and mesne conveyances became seized in two tracts of land in Mispillion Hundred called *Point Look-out* and *Hickory Point*, 554 a., and being so seized he made his will bearing date 3 March 1721 (Book D, fol. 41) and divided the said tracts unto his two daus. Mary Manlove and Ann Manlove, and soon after died, Mary Manlove soon after m. Thomas Tarrant and Ann Manlove also m. Thomas Nixon of the Town of Dover Kent Co. ... adj. land of John Brinckle, Junr., ... 288 a. by virtue of the patent bearing date 16 May 1740 there was surveyed and laid out for Thomas Tarrant and Mary his wife 1/2 of the tract of land in Mispillion Hundred adj. the afsd. tract called *Point Look Out* (patent Book A, Vol 9:195 at Phila) on Strunt Hill Creek ... 75 a. Thomas Nixon and Ann his wife on 17 Jul 1740 did release the same unto Thomas Tarrant and Mary his wife (Book M, fol. 83) and Thomas Tarrant and Mary his wife died leaving issue, the afsd. Manlove Tarrant. {KEDELR P:169}

Jonathan was father of the following daus.: MARY, m. Thomas

Tarrant, innholder; ANN, m. Thomas Nixon, taylor.

14. LUKE MANLOVE, farmer, b. 2 April 1689, son of Luke (5) Manlove, m. 1st Mary Walker, dau. of John Walker before 12 May 1743 {KEDELR B2:115} and m. 2nd Alce [Ellse] Trippett, widow of John Trippet.

John Walker by his will bearing date 2 Nov 1707 recorded in Registers Office at Dover (Book 17 fol. 70) did devise unto his dau. Mary Walker 100 a. and she afterward m. Luke Manlove by whom she had three daus. to wit Elizabeth who m. Daniel Brown, Grace who m. Charles Dickinson and Mary who m. George Pratt and whereas Daniel Brown and Elizabeth his wife on 12 May 1743 did convey unto Charles Dickinson all their rights in the afsd. land, and Charles Dickinson and Grace his wife and George Pratt and Mary his wife on 14 Aug 1745 did convey the 100 a. unto the afsd. George Manlove on e. side of Beaver Dam Branch, near John Walker's land. {KEDELR N:277}

John Trippet d. leaving a will dated 17 Feb 1738, proved 7 March 1738. Heirs: sons John, Waitman and Gove; dau. Prinelopey; cousin Sarah Trippet; wife Ellse. Execs., wife and bro. John Sipple. Wits., Mark Smith, Christopher Sipple. {Arch. A51:79. Reg. of Wills, H:149}

On 12 May 1743 Daniel Brown and Elizabeth his wife and Mary Manlove being daus. and coheirs of Luke Manlove and Mary his wife for £30 sold to Charles Dickinson yeoman of same co., a tract of land, part of a 100 a. tract called *Woodfort* in Mispillion Hundred which tract of land John Walker, dec'd., by his will did bequeath to his dau. Mary Walker who m. Luke Manlove beginning at the line of John Killingsworth, dec'd., on s.e. side of Beaverdam Branch, 67 2/3 a. which is our part of the said tract. {KEDELR N:181}

Luke Manlove, a Quaker of KE Co., DE, aged 61 years, qualified on estate in Virginia of Wm. Tyndle, late of KE Co., who d. at his father-in-law Luke Manlove's house, 31 Aug 1750. Proved in Accomack Co., VA 25 Sep 1750, p. 111. Proved in DE by Luke Manlove, aged 61 years and Paree Trippett, aged 19 years.

William Tyndle, d. leaving a will dated 28 Aug 1750, proved 31 Aug 1750. Heir: father-in-law Luke Manlove. Exec., Luke Manlove. Wits., Gove Trippett, Luke Manlove. {Arch. A51, 190. Reg. of Wills, K:25} In the Wills of Accomack Co., VA, is recorded that William Tyndle, late of Kent Co, DE, d. at his father in law Luke Manlove's house 31 Aug 1750, about the rising of the sun. Proved 31 Aug 1750. Proved in Accomack 25 Sep 1750. Wholte estate to Luke Manlove. Proved in Kent Co. by Paree Trippett, age 19 or thereabouts and Luke Manlove, Quaker, age 61 or thereabouts. {Accomack Co. Wills 1749-1752:113}

Luke d. leaving a will dated 10 April 1755, proved 15 Aug 1755. Heirs: wife Alce; son Emanuel; daus. Elizabeth Frashar, Mary Pratt, Grace Dickenson; granddau. Sarah Moleston. Extx., wife Alce. Wits., Jonathan Manlove, Wateman Treppett, Mary Davis. {Arch. A32:34-35. Reg. of Wills, K:118}

Thomas Groves sold a 400 a. tract of land on s. side of Murtherkill Creek to John Walker (Book B, Vol. 2, fol. 72), and John Walker by his will bearing date 2 Nov 1707 recorded in Registers Office at Dover (Book 17, fol. 70) did devise unto his dau. Mary Walker 100 a. adj. Zachariah Goforth, and she afterward m. Luke Manllove by whom she had three daus. to wit, Elizabeth who m. Daniel Brown, Grace who m. Charles Dickinson and Mary who m. George Pratt and whereas Daniel Brown and Elizabeth his wife on 12 May 1743 did convey unto Charles Dickinson all their rights in the afsd. land, and Charles

Dickinson and Grace his wife and George Pratt and Mary his wife on 14 Aug 1745 did convey the 100 a. unto the afsd. George Manlove on e. side of Beaver Dam Branch, to John Walker's land. Ackn 25 May 1749. {KEDELR N:277}

Luke was father of the following children: LUKE {A}; EMANUEL; By his wife Mary, Luke was father of: ELIZABETH, m. 1st Daniel Brown and m. 2nd William Frashar; MARY, m. George Pratt; GRACE, m. Charles Dickenson.

15. WILLIAM MANLOVE, son of Luke (5) Manlove, m. Susannah Clark, dau. of John and Catharine Clark. Following William's death Susannah m. Robert Winsmore.

On 9 Aug 1720 William Manlove by virtue of certain goods conveyance to him made and executed in open Court of Common Pleas 15 Aug 1716 by Ephraim Emerson of Kent Co. and Mary his wife became lawfully seized in a tract of land in Little Creek Hundred adj. to the n. side of Muddy Branch 300 a. ... corner of land late in the possession of John Hall called *Content* ... said William Manlove of Little Creek Hundred, same co., yeoman, and Susannah his wife, for £29 sold 100 a. of land to Alexander Humphrys of same place yeoman. {KEDELR F:118}

On 15 May 1723 Josiah Bradley of Kent Co. planter for a valuable sum of money paid sold to William Manlove, son of Luke Manlove, dec'd., of same place, yeoman, a tract of land (warrant dated at Philadelphia 14 June 1718 granted unto Josiah Bradley 200 a.) in the forest and surveyed 15 July 1718 there was laid out an island within the glades of Marshehope being the land where Mark Marrett now dwells, 40 a. called *Marks Island.* {KEDELR H:20}

On 14 Aug 1723 William Manlove, son of Luke Manlove, late of Kent Co., dec'd., for £70 sold to John Killingsworth, a parcell of land called *Fishing Point*, on n. side of Mispelion Creek formerly surveyed and laid out for Mark Manlove of same co. and bequeathed unto his son Mathew by his will, since sold by Mathew Manlove unto Luke Manlove, dec'd., and by his will gave unto William Manlove, 100 a. {KEDELR H:59}

William Manlove d. leaving a will dated 13 April 1724, proved 15 Dec 1725. Heirs: son Hezekiah; bro. Luke; wife Susannah. Execs., wife Susannah and bro. Luke. Wits., William Manlove (carpenter), Joseph Manlove, Isaac Marratt. {Arch. A33:132. Reg. of Wills, F:8}

John Clark d. leaving a will dated 29 Nov 1727, proved 11 Feb 1729. Heirs: sons William and John; daus. Sarah, Elizabeth and Susannah Winsmore; wife Katherine; Mary and Elias Williams. Execs., wife Katherine and son John. Wits., John Hamnitt, Luke Manlove, James Taylor. {Arch. A9:2-3. Reg. of Wills, G:35
36 and H:74-75}

On 15 Jun 1730 Katherine Clark of Kent Co. for the good will and affection I have towards William Manlove, dec'd., and Susanna his wife of same co. have given unto William Manlove son of the afsd. Wm. Manlove, dec'd., and Susanna his wife, one 2 year old heifer and her increase conditionaly, that is one half of the increase of the said heifer to William Manlove and the other half of the increase to the said Wm. Manlove his father in law until the said William Manlove arrive to the age of 16 years and after ye age he the said William Manlove is to have the full power and priviledge of and belonging to the heifer and her increase forever, but if this William Manlove happen to die under age then the heifer and her increase is to remain unto Elizabeth Manlove sister of the afsd. William and in case Elizabeth Manlove happen to die under age then the heifer and her increase is to remain with Susanna Winsmore mother of the above said William and Elizabeth Manlove of same co. {KEDELR K:180}

Note: that Elizabeth Manlove, dau. of Elizabeth Manlove, dec., m. (N) Winsmore, son of Robert Winsmore.

On 18 March 1729/30 Robert Winsmore of Kent Co. yeoman for good will give to my dau. in law [step-dau.] Elizabeth Manlove dau. to Elizabeth Manlove, dec'd., of same co., one negro girl named Martha being about 5 years old and also one cow the said negro girl and her increase to desend after this manner to wit if the said Elizabeth should hapen to die without issue that then the negro and her increase to William Manlove brother to the said Elizabeth, but if William should hapen to dye without issue that then the said negro and her increase to remain to my wife Susanah and the heirs of her body lawfully begotten. {KEDELR I:268}

William was father of the following children: HEZEKIAH.

16. GEORGE MANLOVE, son of Luke (5) Manlove, m. Susannah. {Bible Records published by GSP}

On 8 Aug 1727 George Manlove son and legatee of Luke Manlove late of Mispelion Hundred Kent Co., dec'd., for £28 sold a parcel of land to Luke Manlove Junr, son of Luke Manlove, dec'd., yeoman, now living in same place. Luke Manlove, dec'd., was seized of a parcell of land in Mispelion Hundred adj. to the s.w. side of land whereon he did dwell, 200 a. on s. side of Bawkin Brigg Creek to land called *Williams His Choice* to corner of James Martin's land to the lands of Owen Williams and by his will dated 9 Dec 1708 did bequeath the 200 a. unto his son George Manlove. {KEDELR K:11}

On 25 Aug 1747 George Manlove of Kent Co. yeoman and Susannah his wife for £300 sold to Philip Fields of same place, 150 a. Whereas John Edmonds late of same co., dec'd., did by his will give unto his son Robert Edmonds the plantation whereon he then dwelt together with 150 a. and he on 18 of this present Aug sold it unto George Manlove in Murtherkill Hundred. {KEDELR N:168}

George Manlove, farmer, Little Creek Hundred, d. leaving a will dated 10 May 1766, proved 20 May 1766. Heirs: sons Matthew, John and Tredwell; grandson George Manlove, son of Matthew; daus. Mary Manlove, Sarah Emerson (wife of Govey Emerson). Execs., sons Matthew and John. Trustee, James Sykes, Esq. Wits., Clayton Levick, Mary Hunter, John Molleston. {Arch. A33:92-94. Reg. of Wills, L:11-12}
Note:-Arch. vol. A33, page 92 shows that dau. Mary Manlove married John Clayton.

On 28 Aug 1766 Matthew Manlove and John Manlove, both of Little Creek Neck and Hundred, Kent Co., yeomen, executors of the will of George Manlove late of same place, dec'd., for £49.3.9 sold to Caleb Luff of St. Jones Neck and Hundred same co. yeoman, a tract of marsh, whereas George Manlove on 10 May 1766 did make his will wherein after he had disposed of his estate both real and personal in Little Creek Neck and Hundred on which he lived at the time of his sickness, near the close of said will stands the paragraph, to wit I give and bequeath unto my sons Matthew and John all my residue of my estate, and shortly after making said will died, whereas the said George Manlove in his lifetime, to wit 22 April 1735, obtained a warrant for a piece of vacant marsh on n. side of Mispillion Cr, survey was made 15 Oct 1765 by Samuel Mccall deputy surveyor of Kent Co, and also George Manlove in his lifetime had sold the said marsh unto the afsd. Caleb Luff for 12 shillings 6 pence per a. but not conveyed, and the sons Matthew and George Manlove are vested with authority to convey the land, in Mispillion Neck and Hundred beginning by the Beachand land being the s. part of marsh surveyed for William Molleston, Luke Manlove, William Betts and Thos Jester called *Company Adventure* to *Great Fishing Gutt*, 78 7/10 a. {KEDELR R:112}

On 10 Nov 1766 Matthew and John Manlove, executors of the will of George Manlove, late of Little Creek Hundred Kent Co. yeoman, dec'd., we being sons of the said George Manlove and of the same place for money already paid confirm unto Samuel Griffen a parcel of land whereon he now dwells by virtue of two warrants granted to our father dated at Philadelphia 21 April 1735 there was surveyed by Hugh Durborow then surveyor of Kent Co. on 29 and 30 May following a tract of land in the forrest of Mispillion Hundred on the head of Marshyhope including a piece called *Pond Neck*, and the survey being so made was returned into the Surveyor Generals Office at Philadelphia by Hugh Durborow, but for some reason the return was not received but together with many others filed in a bundle now known by the name of *Durborows Rejected Bundle*, and whereas our father soon after sold the said tract agreeable to the said survey in sundry parcels seperately to sundry persons, and whereas discovery hath lately been made by Saml. McCall now deputy surveyor of said co. that the return made by Hugh Durborow was rejected, and that on discovery thereof our father promised to convey again to the several purchasers now in possession so that nothing should be lacking on his side, copies of warrants are lately sent to said Saml. McCall to survey the tract and make return, in pursuance to which the survey was made 11 Jun 1766, and whereas our father hath not lived to fullfill his promise and we being desirous to fullfill every just contract made by our father and we being enabled by his will and we finding that a certain Samuel Griffen and Thomas Wyatt had purchased a quantity of said tract in partnership and they afterwards made partition thereof and passed releases between them, and Samuel Griffen is still in possession of his 1/2 part of said purchase, beginning at land now in the possession of Elijah Morris to s. side of *Miery Arm*, to land formerly belonging to Thomas Wyatt but now belonging to John Crumpton, to land called *New Bern*, 253 3/4 a. {KEDELR R:130}

George and Susannah were parents of the following children {Bible records published by GSP}: MATTHEW, b. 17 Dec 1736, d. 20 Dec 1777; JOHN; TREDWELL; MARY, m. John Clayton; SARAH, m. Govey Emerson.

17. JOHN MANLOVE, probable son of Luke (5) Manlove, m. (N)[35] Huling, dau. of Walton Huling.

Arbitors awarded on 9 Feb 1722 to George Walton[36] a tract, 250 a., *The Point* and 2 lots in Lewes and to John Manlove, 400 a., in the division of land of

[35] Probably Elizabeth, the only sister of Esther Huling mentioned in the will of their father, Walton Huling. {Sussex Wills Arch. A79:93. Reg. of Wills, A:54-55}

[36] George Walton, bachelor, m. Hester Huling, dau. of Walton Huling, dec'd, on 31 Oct by Jonathan Baily, Justice of Sussex Co.. {SUDELR F6:174}

Walton Huling, dec'd., of Sussex Co., in the right of their wives. {F6:30}

On 6 May 1756 Charles Polk and Patience his wife of Worcester Co., MD, Ephraim Polk and Mary his wife of Sussex Co. for £16 quit claim unto Jonathan Manlove of Sussex Co., yeoman, 80 a. of a 200 a. tract of land in Cedar Creek Hundred which a certain John Manlove died seized of who died intestate leaving 2 sons and 2 daus, to wit Patience and Mary, by reason they had a right to 1/5 part of the said land. {SUDELR I:128}

John was the father of two sons and PATIENCE, m. Charles Polk; MARY, m. Ephraim Polk; possibly JONATHAN.

18. JOSEPH MANLOVE, son of Luke (5) Manlove, d. leaving a will dated 10 April 1727, proved 29 Nov 1727. Heirs: cousin Mary Nicholds, dau. of Wm. and Ann Nicholds; bros. Luke Manlove, Thomas. Skidmore. Exec.., bro. George Manlove. Wits., Stephen Simons, Adam Fisher. {Arch. A32:30. Reg. of Wills, F:32, 33 and 26}

19. MARK MANLOVE, son of William (8) Manlove, m. 1st Margaret, dau. of Robert Hart and m. 2nd Ruth, widow of William Rodeney.

On 12 May 1731 Mark Manlove of Kent Co. yeoman for good will, love and natural affection give to my son Mark Manlove, Junr., a parcell of land being part of a tract of land called *Farmselswood* in Murderkill Hundred ... bounded by John Tomlin's land ... s. side of Spring Branch ... 300 a. {KEDELR K:80}

Robert Hart devised to his dau. Margret part of a tract which Mark and Margaret conveyed 100 a. to Samuel Webster who d. intestate having one dau. Mary who m. Robert Smith. {Sussex Co. Land Records F6:417, acknowledged 3 Nov 1731}

On 7 Nov 1735 Mark Manlove, Senr. of Kent Co. yeoman did by his deed of gift, give unto his son Mark Manlove, Junr., a tract of land about 300 a. being part of a tract of land called *Farms Elsworth* on the n. side of the main branch of Murtherkill Creek. Mark Manlove, Junr., in consideration that my father Mark Manlove hath passed a bond bearing date 16 Nov 1735 to me, to confirm unto me 250 a. of land being the lower part of a tract of land called *Heathers Adventure* and including part of the plantation whereon my father now dwells. Mark Manlove, Junr., quit claims the above recited land unto my father Mark Manlove. {KEDELR L:143}

On 7 Feb 1754 Ruth Manlove, widow and relict of Mark Manlove, late of Kent Co., dec'd., but formerly ye widow and adminr of William Rodeney of same co., dec'd., Whereas her said husband William Rodeney, dec'd., with Solomon Cale who is also, dec'd., were executors of John Cale, dec'd., at a Orphans Court held at the Town of Dover 27 Dec 1730 before Charles Hilliard, John Hall, John Housman and William Manlove esqrs, there was not personal estate enough to pay the debts of said, dec'd., by order of the court the land of John Cale, dec'd., were to be sold, 50 a. part of a larger tract called *Holly Neck* in Murtherkill Hundred with a messuage thereon adj. land then of Richard Jackson, John Jackson and Carron Manner sold at publick vandue unto John Housman of ye Town of Dover, esqr., he being the highest bidder for £15. William Rodeney and Solomon Cale dyed soon after and no deed to him made Ruth Manlove now conveys the afsd. tract of land unto John Housman and do appoint my friends William Killen and Edmund Badger of ye Town of Dover or either of them to ackn this deed in open court. {KEDELR O:213}

On 12 Aug 1747 Mark Manlove, Senr., of Kent Co. yeoman for good will and affection and 5 shillings give to my son Ebenezer Manlove a tract of land in Murtherkill Hundred beginning on s. side of Spring Branch near the line of John Hunter, to William Berry's land, to line of Mark Smith, 371 a. the one being part of a greater tract called *Farms Elsworth* was surveyed and taken up by Daniel Brown, who conveyed the same unto James Wells, who dyed seized of the said lands whereby the same descended unto his son Thomas Wells, who conveyed the same unto me and other land hereby given by me was by virtue of a warrant taken up and called *Manloves Berry*. {KEDELR N:159}

On 11 May 1749 Mark Manlove of Kent Co. yeoman for the good will and natural affection and 5 shillings give to my son Absalom Manlove, a parcell of land being part of two tracts the one called *Farms Elsworth* formerly laid out for Daniel Brown the other called *The Exchange* formerly laid out for Peter Grouendike and now of which I am seized on n. side of Murtherkill Creek to Spring Branch to Ebinezer Manlove's land, 270 perches. {KEDELR N:273}

Mark Manlove d. leaving a will dated 16 March 1747, proved 8 Jan 1749. Heirs: sons Absolam, Ebenezer, William, Mark, and Gideon; grandsons Nathan (son of Mark Manlove), Matthew (son of Absolam Manlove), Mark, son of Ebenezer Manlove, William, son of William; granddaus. Eunice (dau. of Mark Manlove), Kesiah Wheler, Margaret Manlove, Mary, Hannah, Ruth, and Priscilla Hunn, daus. of Ruth Hunn., dec'd. Execs., sons Absolam, Ebenezer and Mark. Wits., Samuel Bussee, Samuel Bussee, Jr., George Brown, Mary Bussee. {Arch. A32:38. Reg. of Wills, K:18-19}

On 15 Aug 1750 Mark Manlove and Ebenezer Manlove of Kent Co., gent., execs. of the will as well as residuary legatees of the estate of their late father Mark Manlove, dec'd., for 5 shillings quit claim unto George Willson of same place, a tract of land, whereas Mark Manlove, dec'd., by his deed bearing date 23 Oct 1749 did sell unto the afsd. George Willson 100 a. of land being part of a tract called *Ready Plains* in Murderkill Hundred and whereas some mistake hath been committed in the said deed in the description. {KEDELR O:57}

On 13 Feb 1760 Mark Manlove, Junr., and Ebenezer Manlove of Kent Co. yeomen executors and heirs of Mark Manlove, Senr., dec'd., for £20 sold to William Wells of the Town of Dover same co. innholder, two lotts of land, whereas Mark Manlove, Senr., in his life time became seized in two lotts of ground in the Town of Dover w. side of Queen Street and n. side of Water Street, 3 a. and 98 1/2 perches and being so seized made his will and soon after died. {KEDELR P:184}

Mark Manlove acquired 178 a. (Book M, fol. 199) and in his will did direct the afsd. land should be disposed of excepting 50 a. which he left unto his grandson Matthew Manlove son of Absalom Manlove. Whereas Mark Manlove and Ebenezer Manlove of Kent Co. yeoman are the surviving executors of the said Mark Manlove, dec'd., and according to the direction of the said will and for £90 they doth sell the afsd. land excepting the 50 a. unto Zachariah Goforth of same place, yeoman, beginning at Indian Branch ... 137 a. {KEDELR O:167}

On 11 Aug 1762 Mark Manlove, Junr., of Kent Co., son of Mark Manlove the elder, for 5 shillings released unto Mark Manlove, Rachel Williams, Absolem Manlove and Mathew Manlove of same co. representatives of Absolem Manlove who was son to the afsd. Mark Manlove the elder, a tract of land, whereas the said Mark Manlove the elder by his will bearing date 16 March 1747 did devise unto the afsd. Mark Manlove, Junr., and Absolem

Manlove a tract of marsh and ground in Dover Hundred adj. n. side of Dover River alias Jones Creek to be equally divided, and the said Mark Manlove's share is to lie to the e. next adj. the Bay, and the said Absolem Manlove's proportionable part to the w., and the said Absolem Manlove died before there was any division made ... beginning at Isaacs Island, to Jonathan and Vincent Emerson's marsh, to land called *Town Point*, 65 a. {KEDELR Q:114}

Mark was father of the following children: ABSOLAM (had son Matthew); EBENEZER (had son Mark); WILLIAM (had son William); MARK (had children Nathan and Eunice); GIDEON; RUTH (had children, Kesiah Wheler, Margaret Manlove, Mary, Hannah, Ruth, and Priscilla Hunn).

20. MATTHEW MANLOVE, son of Mark (7) Manlove, b. 29 Jan 1679, m. Susanna Williams, sister of William Williams and dau. of Reynear Williams and Susannah (Arents) Williams.

William Williams, merchant of Mispillion Hundred, d. leaving a will dated 19 Jan 1720/21. Heirs: dau. Susannah Pecker; sisters Susanna Manlove (wife of Mathew Manlove) and Gartrude Dingeesly. Exec., Mathew Manlove. Wits., Henry Hall, Robert Betts, Thomas May, Jr. [No probate.] Arch. A55:172. Reg. of Wills, D:35}

Reynear Williams d. leaving a will dated 12 Dec 1709, proved 20 Dec 1709. Heirs: sons Reynear, William Aaron; wife Susanna; daus. Gerthy Nangisell, Susannah Manlove, Cathrine, Mary. Exec., son Reynear. Wits., Mark Manlove, Archibald Douglas, Lewis Aways. {Arch. A55:137. Reg. of Wills, C:82}

On 15 May 1723 Matthew Manlove of Mispillion Hundred Kent Co. gent and Susannah his wife for £48 sold to John Brinkle of same place gent., a parcel of land in Mispillion Hundred adj. to the n. side of the land where the said John Brinkle now dwelleth and to the w. side of a piece of land whereon William Brinkle, dec'd., did dwell, part of a 300 a. tract of land formerly laid out to John Curtis called *Strathame*, 150 a. {KEDELR H:113}

Matthew d. leaving a will dated 17 May 1735, proved 18 July 1735. Heirs: wife Susannah; daus. Jemima Moleston. Mary Brinckle (wife of Curtis Brinckle), Susannah, Miriam, Tabitha, Elizabeth Manlove; sons Matthew, Jonathan; grandsons Abner and Obediah Manlove. Exec. son Matthew. Wits., Nathaniel Bowman, John Clark, Anthony Woodward. {Arch. A32:42-43. Reg. of Wills, H:115-117}

Susannah Manlove, d. leaving a will 15 Jan. 15, 1740, proved 21 Feb 1740. Heirs: daus. Jemima Moleston, Mary Brinckle, Miriam Bowman, Elizabeth Loper, Tabitha Manlove, Susannah Needham; sons Matthew, Jonathan. Exec. son Matthew. Wits., Reynear Williams, Nathaniel Hunn, Mary Hunn. {Arch. A33:124. Reg. of Wills, I:84}

Matthew was father of the following children: JEMIMA, m. 1st Henry Moleston {A}; MARY, m. Curtis Brinckle, son of Peter and Elizabeth (Curtis) Brinckle; SUSANNAH, m. 21 Aug 1740 Daniel Needham {A}; MIRIAM, m. (N) Bowman; TABITHA; ELIZABETH, m. Michael Lowber, son of Michael and Unity Lowber {A}; MATTHEW; JONATHAN; EPHRAIM, d. leaving sons Abner and Obediah.

21. MARK MANLOVE, bro. of Mathew, farmer, son of Mark (7) Manlove, m. Mary (N). Mark d. leaving a will dated 7 May 1720, proved 18 June 1720. Heirs:

wife Mary; dau. Sarah Manlove. Execs., wife Mary, bro. Mathew. Wits., Charles Maring, William Mucklegeare. {Arch. A32:37. Reg. of Wills, D:20}

Mark was father of SARAH.

22. WILLIAM MANLOVE, son of William (8) Manlove, b. 25 Dec 1691, d. 1761, m. 1st 6 Dec 1716 Mary Bibe and m. 2nd Alce (N).

On 15 Feb 1715 William Manlove of Little Creek Hundred Kent Co., yeoman, son of William Manlove late of Mispillion Hundred in same co., dec'd., sold for £50 a tract to John Clark. William Manlove did by his will bequeath unto his son William Manlove all of afsd. tract of land. William Manlove the son for £50 sold afsd. tract of land to John Clark of Mispillion Hundred, same co., yeoman. {KEDELR E:104}

On 6 Dec 1716 was the marriage of William Manlove and Mary Bibe both of Kent Co. being published were joyned together in the Holy Estate of Matrimony. Wit: Isaac Uptgrave, Waitman Sipple, Thomas Jestor, Edward Burrows, Thomas Hammons, Nathan Luff?, John Cripin, John Murphey, Darethy? Burrows, Wm. Brinkloe, Nathan Hunn, Mary Brinkloe, Hannah Manlove. {KEDELR K:88}

On 25 May 1749 George Morgan, Junr., of Dover Hundred Kent Co. yeoman and Anna (Annah) his wife dau. of Joseph Booth, Junr., late of this co., dec'd., for £50 (paid by William Manlove, Junr., before the time of his decease but land was not conveyed which said Manlove did by his will give the land to his dau. Elisabeth) ... sold to Elisabeth Manlove, dau. and co-legatee of William Manlove, Junr., late of this co., dec'd., which said Elisabeth is now a minor ... a tract of land (whereas Joseph Booth died seized in a 500 a. tract of land) in Mispillion Hundred on s. side of Western branch of Murther Creek being part of a larger tract called *Farefield* which was granted by patent to William Clark bearing date 29 May 1694 (Book H, fol. 5) and the afsd. Joseph died intestate by which means the afsd. Anna became heir to 1/4 of the afsd. 500 a. ... 120 a. {KEDELR N:279}

Mary, wife of William Manlove, d. 1 Dec 1757 around 5 p.m. {Some Records of Sussex County, Delaware:333}

William d. leaving a will dated 16 Aug 1760, proved 24 March 1761. Heirs: wife Alse; daus. Mary Mason and Sarah Masten; son-in-law Joseph Mason; granddaus. Sarah Mason (dau. of Joseph and Mary Mason), Mary and Elizabeth Manlove; grandson William Masten, Jr. Exec., Joseph Mason. Wits., Elias Mason, Isaac Codery, Samuel Burrows. {Arch. A33:137-139. Reg. of Wills, K:260}

On 24 May 1765 Joseph Mason of Mispillion Hundred Kent Co. for £6 sold to Thomas Way merchant of same place, a lott of land on Swan Branch near the wharf on Mispillion Creek, part of a tract called *The Improvement* and was purchased of William Manlove by the afsd. Thomas Way but before the making over of said lott said Manlove died which then fell into the hands of the afsd. Joseph Mason sole heir and executor of the said William Manlove, dec'd., 1/4 a. {KEDELR R:46}

William was father of the following children {A - Bible records of Genealogical Soc. of PA}: NATHANIEL, b. 6 Jan 1718, d. 27 April 1729; WILLIAM, b. 29 June 1721, d. 27 April 1748; MARY, b. 27 Oct 1723, d. 7 Nov 1779, m. Joseph Mason; RUTH, b. 10 Dec 1726, d. 5 April 1746; SARAH, b. 28 Sep 1730, d. 27 Feb 1776, m. William Masten.

23. SAMUEL MANLOVE, son of William (8) Manlove, m. Elizabeth, dau. of Samuel Glue.

On 10 May 1720 James Steel of Philadelphia gentleman for £105 sold to Samuel Hanson of Kent Co. carpenter 325 a. [same as above] ... a tract of land patent bearing date 4 May 1715 granted unto James Jackson of Kent Co., yeoman, and Margaret his wife on s. side of s.w. branch of Duck Creek 750 a. ... by indenture bearing date 5 Feb 1717 James Jackson and Margaret his wife sold unto James Steel afsd. 750 a. ... some parcels thereof granted to other persons ... by a deed of Samuel Manlove and Elizabeth his wife [date blank] did grant unto James Steel 140 a. part of the afsd. 750 a. being one of the parcells sold. {KEDELR F:108}

Samuel Glew [Glue] d. leaving a will dated 10 Feb 1725, proved 30 April 1731. Heirs: wife, former wife of Edward Berry; daus. Rachel, Elizabeth. and Rebecca; sons-in-law Samuel Manlove, Nicholas Powell. Execs., dau. Rachel and Samuel Manlove. Wits., Lancelot Lewis, Edward Nickolls, Nickolas Greenaway. {Arch. A19:67 and 71. Reg. of Wills, R:14} Note: Arch. A19:71 shows William Hazzard and wife Rachel as execs.

Samuel Manlove, yeoman, Dover Hundred, d. leaving a will dated 13 Sep 1731, proved 24 May 1734. Heir: wife Elizabeth. Execs., wife and bro. Mark Manlove. Mentioned was made to his residence "in the forest of Dover Hundred." Also mentioned was his father-in-law Samuel Glover (Glovis). Wits., Katherine Roberts, Rachel Glue, Hugh Durborough, Jr. {Arch. A33:119. Reg. of Wills, H:53; Kent Co. Wills H:79}}

24. ELIZABETH MANLOVE, dau. of William (8) Manlove, m. Peter Brinkle.

On 13 Aug 1747 Peter Brinkle (Brinckle) of Kent Co. yeoman and Elizabeth his wife, dau. and heiress of William Manlove, late of Little Creek Hundred, yeoman, dec'd., for £60 sold to Daniel Brinkle of same co. yeoman, a tract of land whereas William Manlove dyed seized in a tract of land in Little Creek Hundred 300 a. called *Wheel of Fortune* purchased of Ephraim Emerson and Mary his wife, Book E:184-6, on 10 July 1716 and William Manlove dyed intestate leaving issue a son named William and the said Elizabeth Brinkle, and William her brother is since dead whereby the said tract of land descended to her ... s. side of s.w. branch of Duck Creek beginning at Muddy branch adj. land formerly laid out for William Jacocks ... 300 a. {KEDELR N:171}

Fourth Generation

25. MANUEL MANLOVE, cordwinder, son of John (10) Manlove, m. Magdalene.

Manuel d. leaving a will dated 19 Oct 1743, proved 25 Nov 1743. Heirs: wife unnamed; sons Jonathan, Manuel and Boaz Manlove. Extx. unnamed wife. Wits., William Burroughs, Edward Burroughs, Geo. Grier. {Arch. A86:39. Reg. of Wills, A:345-347}

At the Orphans Court of 4 March 1745 Magdelen Manlove petitioned the court for the allowance of an account against Jemimah Goldsmith, a minor, for cloathing and the court ordered James Averlo who m. Frances Parsley admx. of Abraham Parsley who was exec. of Thos. Goldsmith to pay the sad Magdaln. Manlove £5.

Magdalene Manlove d. leaving a will dated 21 March 1770, proved 22 Nov 1770. Heirs: sons Jonathan, Boas and Manuel Manlove; daus. Elizabeth

Manlove, Ann Burroughs; grandson James Owens; granddaus. Eunice Waller, Sarah and Betty Manlove (daus. of George). Wits., Charles Polk, Sr., Charles Polk, Jr., George Polk. {Arch. A86:38. Reg. of Wills, B:406-407}

Manuel was father of the following children: JONATHAN; BOAZ; MANUEL; ELIZABETH; ANN, m. (N) Burroughs; GEORGE.

26. PATIENCE MANLOVE, dau. of John (10) Manlove, d. 1776 at age 65, m. 8 July 1736 Charles Polk.

On 8 Jul 1736 was recorded the marriage of Charles Polk (Polke) and Patience Manlove both single persons having published their intentions of marriage ... did solemnize their mariage at the house of Mark Manlove. Wit: Mark Manlove, Manuel Manlove, Edward Burroughs, John Pollock, Ephraim Polk, John Burrough, Ebenezer Manlove, Owen Caine, Mark Manlove Junr, Mary Manlove, Sarah Bradly, Esther Bibble, Ann Manlove. {KEDELR L:209}

Patience was mother of CHARLES who m. Mary Manlove, his mother's cousin.{A}

27. LUKE MANLOVE, son of Luke (14), m. Tabitha (N).

Luke d. leaving a will dated 27 May 1740, proved 30 June 1740. Heirs: son William; dau. Sarah; one child unnamed; wife [in guardian acct. named Tabitha]; Nathaniel Hunn. Execs., wife and Nathaniel Hunn. Wits., John Hammitt, Henry Molliston. {Arch. A32:32-33. Reg. of Wills, I:19}

Luke was father of the following children: WILLIAM; SARAH; UNNAMED CHILD.

28. EMANUEL (Amanuell) MANLOVE, son of Luke (14) and Alce Manlove, d. leaving a will dated 11 June 1760, proved 19 Aug 1760. Heirs: bros. Waitman and Govey Trippet; sisters Mary Pratt and Penelope Caton; niece Sary Molleston, wife of Henry Molleston, Jr.; mother Alce Manlove; Sary and William Trippet, children of bro. John Trippet; friend William Smith. Execs., bro. Waitman Trippet and friend Robert Caton. Wits., Samuel Merydith, Ailse Annet, James Corkeran. {Arch. A33:86-87. Reg. of Wills, K:236}

29. ELIZABETH MANLOVE, dau. of Luke (14) and Mary Manlove, m. 1st Daniel Brown and m. 2nd after 12 May 1743, William Frashar.

Daniel Brown of Mispillion Hundred d. leaving a will dated 6 March 1748/9, proved 18 March 1748. Heirs: wife Elizabeth; son Steven; daus. Susannah and Elizabeth; Charles Dickinson; cousin Daniel Brown. Extx., wife Elizabeth. Wits., Charles Dickinson, Luke Manlove, Grace Dickinson. {Arch. A6:36. Reg. of Wills, I:266} Note Arch. A6:34 shows the widow later m. William Freasure.

30. MARY MANLOVE, dau. of Luke (14) and Mary Manlove, m. George Pratt.

George Pratt, farmer, d. leaving a will dated 30 March 1767, proved 15 April 1767. Heirs: wife Mary; sons Nathan, Luke, George, Frederick; daus. Esther Taylor, Ann, Dinah, Mary and Ruth Pratt. Extx., wife Mary. Wits., George Sexton, Leven Gibson, Esther Jarrard. {Arch. A41:82-85. Reg. of Wills, L:26-27}

Mary Pratt, widow of Murderkill Hundred, d. leaving a will dated 20 May 1774, proved 11 Feb 1775. Heirs: sons Nathan, Luke, Frederick, George;

daus. Ann Reed, Dinah Clampitt, Mary Pratt; granddau. Mary Taylor. Exec. son Nathan. Wits., Patrick Crain, John Pegg, Sarah Pratt. {Arch. A41:120-123. Reg. of Wills, L:161 and 230}

31. MATTHEW MANLOVE, son of George (16) and Susannah Manlove, b. 17 Dec 1736, d. 20 Dec 1777, m. Sarah, dau. of Richbell Mott (b. 13 July 1739, d. 10 Dec 1787). {Bible Records of HSP} They were parents of the following children {Bible Records of HSP}: GEORGE, b. 27 June 1760, d. 6 Jan 1822; MOTT, b. 22 Feb 1763, d. 8 Oct 1790; JOHN, b. 8 April 1766, d. 30 Aug 1733; SARAH, b. 21 Dec 1776, d. 6 Aug 1778.

32. JOHN MANLOVE of Little Creek, son of George (16) Manlove, m. Margaret who later m. Ezekiel Hales.

John d. leaving a will dated 23 Feb 1770, proved 11 April 1770. Heirs: wife Margett; dau. Susannah; a child unnamed; nephew John Manlove, son of bro. Matthew. Execs., wife Margett and bro. Matthew Manlove. Wits., Mary Manlove, Joseph Galloway, Govey Emmerson. {Arch. A33:101-102. Reg. of Wills, L:76} Note: Arch. A33:102 shows that Margett Manlove married Ezekiel Hales.

John was father of the following children: SUSANNAH; UNNAMED CHILD.

33. RUTH MANLOVE, dau. of Mark (19) Manlove, d. by 16 March 1747, m. Caleb Hunn in 1730.

On 19th da., 8th mo., 1730 the orderly marriage of Caleb Hunn and Ruth Manlove was reported. {DCMM} She was mother of the following children {see her father's will}: KESIAH m. (N) Wheeler, MARGARET m. (N) Manlove, MARY, HANNAH, RUTH and PRISCILLA.

34. EBENEZER MANLOVE[37], probable son of Mark (19) Manlove, m. Sarah Cook, dau. of Capt. Thomas Cook and Sarah Newell (dau. of Stephen). {A}

On 14 Feb 1754 Ebenezer Manlove of Kent Co., yeoman, and Sarah his wife for £335 sold to Samuel Griffith of same place, a tract of land in Murderkill Hundred on s. side of Spring Branch near the line of John Hunter, dec'd., to William Berry's land to Mark Smith's land, 371 a. {KEDELR O:216}

Ebenezer d. by 2 Nov 1772 when his estate was administered by Sarah Manlove and Asa Manlove. {Arch. A33:83-85 Reg. of Wills, L:120} Note:-Arch. vol. A33, page 83 mentions heirs, Mary Hall (wife of David), Ellis Fisher (wife of James), Thos. Manlove, Sara Coleman, Asa Manlove and Sarah, the widow.

On 26th da., 11th mo., 1768, Alice Manlove, dau. of Ebenezer Manlove, with concurrence of Little Creek Preparative Meeting, requested to come under the care of Friends. {DCMM}

Ebenezer was father of the following children: GEORGE {Logan Papers} predeceased his parents and had a dau. Mary, b. by 1750 and m. David Hall; ELLIS (Alice) m. James Fisher; THOMAS, d. without issue c1789; SARA, d. without issue, m. James Coleman {A}; ASA (oldest surviving son), b. c1750, d.

---

[37] A great amount of the following information on Ebenezer was found by Bruce Bendler in Volume 26 of the Logan Papers at the Historical Society of Pennsylvania which deals with the settlement of the estate of Ebenezer Manlove and will be hereafter cited as Logan Papers.

1797, m. Deborah (N) and had sons David and Robinson {A}; EBENEZER {A}; ELIZABETH, m. Caleb Luff; MARK, b. c1760, d. before 1794 without issue.

35. MARK MANLOVE, son of Mark (19) Manlove, m. 1st 23 Sep 1730 Elizabeth Clayton, dau. of Joshua Clayton; he m. 2nd Anne Smith and m. 3rd Anne Hall, dau. of John Hall and Anna Bedwell. {A}

On 19th da., 8th mo., 1730 the orderly marriage of Mark Manlove, Jr. and Elizabeth Clayton was reported. {DCMM}

John Smith d. leaving a will dated 23 April 1745. Heirs: son John Smith; daus. Mary, Sarah, and Ester Smith; sister, Ann Manlove. Exec., Mark Manlove, bro.-in-law. Wits., Joshua Wheelor, Sarah Smith and Elizabeth Wheelor. [No prob.] {Arch. A47:71}

On 19th da., 1st mo., 1750 the marriage of Jonathan Ozburn and Eunice Manlove, dau. of Mark Manlove, Junr. was reported. {DCMM}

Mark Manlove, age 60 years, deposed that on 23 Sep 1730 he m. the dau. of Joshua Clayton. {Deposition Hist. Soc. Dela.}

John Hall d. leaving a will dated 28 Jan 1758, proved 2 Oct 1760. Heirs: sons William, Thomas, Isaac; daus. Mary Goforth, Isable Clark and Anne Manlove, wife of Mark Manlove; grandsons John Smith, son of dau. Sarah, dec'd, and Benjamin Spencer, son of dau. Elizabeth; Sarah Richards and Esther Steel, sisters of grandson John Smith. Exec., son Isaac. Wits., John Brinckle, Daniel Jestor, Arthur Steel. {Arch. A21:93. Reg. of Wills, K:239}

On 8 Aug 1758 Mark Manlove and Nathan Manlove both of Kent Co. doth agree that they together with their wives shall clear of all incumbrances and convey unto William Carpenter of New Castle Co. part of two tracts of land, one called *Hathers Adventure* and the other called *Edmunds Choice* which deed shall be with general warrantee, William Carpenter doth agree that if Mark Manlove and Nathan Manlove shall before or at the next May Court clear the land afsd. from the supposed incumbrances and make over the deed, then William Carpenter doth promise to pay £100 at the May Court, £100 on 1 May 1760 and £100 more 1 Oct 1760 which several sums of money together with £100 in hand paid by William Carpenter to Mark Manlove is in full consideration for the afsd. tracts of land which are the same whereon Mark Manlove and Nathan now lives 450 a. ... penal sum of £1000. {KEDELR P:80}

On 23 Feb 1765 Mark Manlove of Kent Co. yeoman and Ann his wife and Nathan Manlove of same co. yeoman and Jean (Jane) his wife for £400 sold to William Carpenter of Kent Co. gent, two tracts of land, whereas Mark Manlove the elder late of Kent Co. yeoman, dec'd., father of the said Mark Manlove was in his life time seized of a 300 a. tract of land called *Heathards Adventure* on n. side of Murther Creek in Murtherkill Hundred said to have been originally granted by patent to one Thomas Heathard also 150 a. said to be 1/2 part of a tract called *Edmunds Chance* otherwise *Choice* adj. *Heathards Adventure* and whereas the said Mark Manlove the elder being seized afsd. did on 14 May 1747 convey to the said Mark Manlove party hereto 207 a. part of the said tract called *Heathards Adventure* (Book M fol. 173) and also 38 a. another part of *Heatherds Adventure* (Book O fol. 23) and Mark Manlove the elder by his will bearing date 1747 did devise to said Nathan Manlove his grandson all the remaining part of the land and plantation whereon he then dwelt part of the afsd. two tracts of land, 300 a. and 150 a. {KEDELR R:19}

Mark was father of the following children by his first marriage {See will of Mark (12).}: NATHAN, m. Jean; EUNICE, m. Jonathan Osborne. Mark was father of the following children by his marriage to Anne Hall {A}: VINCENT; SUSANNA, b. 26 May 1752, d. 9 Feb 1802, m. William Levick Jr., son of William Levick and Sarah Crippen. {A}

36. ABSOLOM MANLOVE, son of Mark (19) Manlove, m. Margaret Lowber, dau. of Michael Lowber and Unity Pardee. {A} Margaret later m. Alexander Craige.

Michael Lowber d. leaving a will dated 2 Jan 1744, proved 7 April 1746. Heirs: daus. Unity (wife of John Emerson), Susannah Lewis; sons Michael, Peter, Matthew, Isaac; daus. Garty Muncy, Margarett Manlove, Agnes Walker; wife Rachel; grandchildren of dau. Grace Brown; grandsons Michael (son of Peter Lowber), John and Michael Reynalds, Michael Emerson (son of Unity and John Emerson), granddau. Susannah Reynalds. Execs., wife Rachel and son Peter. Wits., Isabella Brooks, Arthur Brooks, Mary Brooks, now Mary Jackson. {Arch. A31:172-174. Reg. of Wills, I:122-123}

Absolom d. by 18 July 1749 when his estate was administered by Margaret Manlove, widow. {Reg. of Wills, I:257} Note: Arch. Vol. A33, page 80 shows children, Mark, Absolom, Matthew and Rachel Manlove; also the widow Margaret later married Alexander Craige ante 30 May 1751.

On 26 Aug 1763 Mark Manlove, Junr., of Kent Co. yeoman one of the sons and heirs of Absolem Manlove of same co., dec'd., and John Williams of same co. yeoman and Rachel his wife formerly Rachel Manlove dau. to the afsd. Absolem Manlove by virtue of an order of Court and £268.12.6 sold to Isaac King of Mispillion Hundred same co., a tract of land, whereas the afsd. Absolem Manlove in his life time by sundry good and mesne conveyances became seized in a parcel of land part of 2 tracts the one called *Farms Elsworth* formerly laid out for Daniel Brown, the other called *The Exchange* formerly laid out for Peter Groundick in Murtherkill Hundred which land was conveyed by deed of gift to the afsd. Absolem Manlove by a certain Mark Manlove, father to the said Absolem Manlove (Book N, fol. 273) on n. side of the main branch of Murther Creek and s. side of Spring Branch adj. Owen Griffin's land, 307 a. and being so seized Absolem Manlove died intestate and administration was committed unto Margaret Manlove, and whereas the afsd. John Williams in 176- by his petition to the Orphans Court praying to appoint 5 substantial freeholders to divide the premisses, which was granted and who made a return that the premises would not bear a division, on 16 Dec 1763 Court appointed Thomas Clark esqr, William Rhodes and Zachariah Goforth, who valued the same at 17 shillings, 6 pence per a., Mark Manlove being the eldest brother accepted the several lotts and shares. {KEDELR Q:167}

Absolom was father of the following children: MARK; ABSOLOM; MATTHEW; RACHEL, m. John Williams {KEDELR I:113}.

37. WILLIAM MANLOVE, son of Mark (19).

On 9 Aug 1727 Mark Manlove of Kent Co. for naturall love, goodwill and affection give to my son William Manlove of the same place, the tract of land whereon the said William Manlove now dwells being part of a tract of land formerly made over in open court by Peter Groundeck admin. to the estate of Cornelius Verhoof unto John Hillyard for satisfaction of an execution against the said estate and afterwards sold by John Hillyard unto Mathew Manlove who sold the same to Mark Manlove, called *The Exchange* on the main branch of Murtherkill, 300 a. {KEDELR I:94}

Mark Manlove late of Kent Co. gent, dec'd., was in his lifetime seized in 300 a., part of the afsd. tract, and on 9 Aug 1727 did convey unto his son William Manlove 300 a. called *The Exchange* (Book I, fol. 93), and William Manlove being so seizd died intestate leaving issue William Manlove his only son and 2 daus., to wit Kesiah Manlove and Margaret Manlove, and William Manlove the younger being seized of 3/4 part of the 300 a. did on 15 Nov 1754 release unto the said Thomas Whittington 224 a., and whereas a certain John Wheeler of Kent Co, who m. the afsd. Kesiah Manlove, with Kesiah on 13 May 1760 did convey to the said Daniel Robisson her part of the tract near the head of Spring Branch, 80 a. {KEDELR Q:48}

William d. by 5 June 1730 when his estate was administered by Elizabeth Manlove. {Arch. A33:133. Reg. of Wills, H:6}

On 12 Aug 1751 Margaret Manlove, tayloress, of Kent Co., for £53 sold unto William Manlove of same place, yeoman, a tract of land, whereas a certain William Manlove, father to Margaret and William Manlove, died possessd of a tract of land on n. side of Murther Creek called *The Exchange* and leaving no will the said lands became to be divided between his three children, to wit Kesiah, Margaret and William Manlove, which said division was made by Thomas Clark, Esqr., John Emerson and Waitman Sipple, Junr. indiferently chosen by the parties for that purpose did lay off to the said Margaret Manlove as her part beginning at John Wheeler's and Kesiah his wife her land, 80 a. {KEDELR O:105}

On 12 Aug 1751 John Wheeler of Kent Co., taylor, and Kesiah his wife quit claim unto William Manlove, Junr., and Margaret Manlove both of same place, part of a tract of land (whereas a certain William Manlove father of the said Kesiah Wheeler, William and Margaret Manlove dyed possessed of a tract of land) Kesiah and John Wheeler her husband having their part of the said tract laid off to them by Thomas Clark, John Emerson and Waitman Sipple, Junr., men indifferently appointed by the parties for that purpose on the n. side of Murther Creek called *The Exchange* adj. land of John Wheeler and Kesiah his wife, 224 a. {KEDELR O:104}

On 12 Aug 1751 William Manlow and Margaret Manlow both of Kent Co. quit claim unto John Wheeler of same place, taylor, and Kesiah his wife, a tract of land (whereas a certain William Manlove, father of the said William Manlove, and Margaret Manlove and Kesiah Wheeler died possessed of a tract of land) William and Margaret Manlove having their part of the tract laid off to them by Thomas Clark, John Emerson and Waitman Sipple, Junr., men indifferently appointed by the parties for that purpose, on n. side of Murther Creek called *The Exchange* near the head of Spring Branch adj. land of John Wheeler and Kesiah his wife, 80 a. {KEDELR O:105}

On 13 May 1760 John Whealor (Wheelor) and Kesiah his wife of Kent Co. for £77 quit claim unto Daniel Robisson of same place a tract of land, whereas John Whealor became seased of a parcel of land being part of a larger tract called *The Exchange* in Murderkill Hundred on n. side of the main branch of Murder Creek in right of his said wife by a deed from William Manlove and Margret Manlove bearing date 12 Aug 1751 (Book O, fol. 104), on the head of Spring branch adj. land of William Manlove and his sister Margret Chipmon, 80 a. Witnessed by William Rhoades, William Manlove Junr. {KEDELR Q:14}

William Manlove, son of Mark Manlove, was father of the following children: WILLIAM, MARGARET who m. (N) Chipman and KESIAH who m. John Wheeler.

38. JONATHAN MANLOVE, son of Matthew (20) Manlove, m. Deborah, widow of Nathaniel Luff.

Nathaniel Luff, Sr. Gentleman, d. leaving a will dated 3 Feb 1760, proved 27 Feb 1760. Heirs: wife Deborah; sons Caleb, Nathaniel, John; daus. Hannah Paradee, Deborth Pleasanton. Execs., sons Caleb and Nathaniel. Wits., Samuel Merydith, Sarah Maston, Thomas Clark. {Arch. A31:229-238. Reg. of Wills, K:225} Note:-Arch. vol. A31, page 235 shows John Paradee as husband of Hannah; David Pleasanton as husband of Deborah; Deborah later married Stephen Lewis. Page 236 shows Deborah, the widow, later married Jonathan Manlove. Page 238 shows Philip Reason [Rasin] only son of Sarah had heirs, Jemiah Ford, Robert Meeks and Joseph Rasin.

Jonathan was father of the following children {A}: MATTHEW; SUSANNAH; MARY, m. Charles Polk; ELIZABETH; SARAH; JEMIMA.

39. MATTHEW MANLOVE, son of Matthew (20) Manlove, m. Mary (N).

Matthew d. leaving a will dated 16 April 1743, proved 6 May 1743. Heirs: wife Mary; son George; daus. Mary, Elizabeth, Susanna, Sarah; bro. Jonathan. Extx., wife. Wits., John Brinckle, John Clark, Isaac King. {Arch. A32:44
46. Reg. of Wills, I:53} Note: page 44 mentions Daniel Needham and wife Mary Manlove; page 45 mentions father Matthew Manlove, dec'd; page 46 shows that Mary Manlove was wife of Phillip Reasin; mentions Benjamin Reasin, son of Phillip.

Matthew was father of the following children: GEORGE[38]; MARY; ELIZABETH; SUSANNA; SARAH.

40. EPHRAIM MANLOVE, son of Matthew (20) Manlove, m. Sarah (N).

He d. leaving a will dated 29 Nov 1732, proved 23 Dec 1732. Heirs: wife Sarah; sons Abner, Obediah; bro. Matthew Manlove. Exec., Matthew Manlove. Trustee, Matthew Manlove. Wits., Matthew Huse, Elizabeth Manlove. {Arch. A33:90. Reg. of Wills, H:57-58}

Ephriam was father of the following children: ABNER; OBEDIAH.

Fifth Generation

41. WILLIAM MANLOVE, son of William (22) Manlove, b. 29 June 1721, d. 27 April 1748, m. Elizabeth (N). They were parents of the following daus.: MARY, b. 19 Feb 1746; ELIZABETH, m. 15 April 1748. {A}

42. MANUEL MANLOVE, son of Manuel (25) Manlove, m. Betty (N) who later m. Levin Crapper.

Manuel of Dorchester Co., merchant, d. leaving a will dated 30 Jan 1773, proved 11 March 1773. Wife Betty Manlove, extx., was devised the plantation at the head of Sussex Co., *The Golden Field*, 300 a., also 100 a. lying

---

38 George Manlove, son of Matthew, was mentioned in the will of Curtis Brinckle, dated 21 March 1767 as his cousin. {Arch. A5:159-162. Reg. of Wills, L:28}

in the *Duke of Yorks Manner*. At her death to bro. Boaz Manlove's 2 daus., Mary and Elizabeth Manlove. If either dies without issue the survivor to get the whole tract. Wife Betty Manlove to also to receive the tract *Mount Pleasant*, 350 a.; at her death to be divided between bro. Jonathan Manlove's eldest son George Manlove and sister Sarah Manlove's youngerst son Jonathan Manlove. To grandmother Dorrithy Burris, £3 yearly during her lifetime. {MWB 39:536}

43. BOAZ MANLOVE, son of Manuel (25) Manlove, had daus. MARY and ELIZABETH.

Boaz served as Justice of the Peace in Sussex Co. from 20 March 1767 to 10 April 1773, and later as sheriff. During the Revolutionary War he shifted to the side of Loyalists and eventually his land was confiscated. {A}

44. JONATHAN MANLOVE, son of Manuel (25) Manlove, had a son GEORGE.

45. ALICE MANLOVE of KE Co. DE, dau. of Ebenezer (34) Manlove, d. c1787, m. 28th da. (or 29th), 2nd mo., 1769, James Fisher of Sussex Co., DE. They were the parents of the following children {DCMM}:JOHN, 12th da., 2nd mo., 1770, lived near or at Broadkiln in Sussex Co. without issue; SARAH, b. 13th da., 1st mo., 1772; ELISABETH, b. 26th da., 3rd mo., 1774; EBENEZER, b. 16th da., 10th mo., 1776, d. c1794; RACHEL, b. 17th da., 9th mo., 1779; RUTH, b. 28th da., 8th mo., 1780. Alice and James d. c1786. In 1794 infants Ruth and LYDIA were living with Philadelphia Lay, widow of Baptist Lay and Stephen Wood c1795. {Logan Papers}

46. ELIZABETH MANLOVE, dau. of Ebenezer (34) Manlove, m. Caleb Luff. They were parents of the following children: CALEB, d. an infant after the death of his father and mother (d. before 1794) leaving half bros. Dr. Nathaniel Luffe and John Luffe.

47. GEORGE MANLOVE, probable eldest son of Ebenezer (34) Manlove, had a dau. MARY who m. David Hall and d. without issue c1788.

On 18 July 1765 a Letter of Administration was granted to Ebenezar Manlove of Kent Co., next of kin, for the estate of George Manlove of Kent Co., taylor, who d. intestate. {KEDELR R:274?; Reg. of Wills, L:6}.

48. ASA MANLOVE, son of Ebenezer (34) Manlove, b. c1750, d. 1797, m. 1st (N), dau. of Parker Robinson and m. 2nd Deborah, widow of Carmon Mason (d. 1790). Issue: DAVID; DANIEL; ROBINSON; SARAH.

49. NATHAN MANLOVE, probable son of Mark (35) Manlove, m. Jane (N).

On 24 Oct 1765 Nathan Manlove of Kent Co. yeoman and Jane his wife for £30 sold to James Purdin of same place ... a parcell of land part of a larger tract called *Trinairia* beginning at a tract of land called *Seaton* near where the Old Kings Road formerly did run ... 30 a. {KEDELR R:71}

50. VINCENT MANLOVE, son of Mark (35) Manlove, m. Elizabeth, widow of Alexander Humphries.

Alexander Humphries d. by 28 April 1773 when his estate was

administered by Elizabeth Humphries, widow. {Reg. of Wills, L:131} Note: Arch. A25:129 shows that Elizabeth Humphries m. Vincent Manlove.

51. MARK MANLOVE, son of Absalom (36) Manlove, m. Violet, dau. of Robert Cummins, Junr. and granddau. of Robert Cummins.

On 21 May 1766 Mark Manlove, Junr., of Kent Co. and Vilet (Vilott) his wife for £60 sold to Thomas Woodly of same place ... a parcell of land, whereas the afsd. Vilet Manlove became the proper heir of a certain Robert Cummins the younger who was the son of Robert Cummins of same place physitian, part of a larger tract called *Clappeam* being the same peice of land which was conveyed by Thomas Skidmore unto Robert Cummins bounded by *Johanness Hall* and *Caroon Manner*, 102 a. {KEDELR R:91}

On 21 May 1766 Mark Manlove and Violet his wife, she being the dau. and heirest of Robert Cummins, Junr., late, dec'd., of Murtherkill Hundred Kent Co. for £37.10 sold to William Baker of same place yeoman ... a tract of land in hundred afsd. on e. side of Double Run branch of Murtherkill Creek and is part of the real estate of Robert Cummings of same place late, dec'd., and also being part of a larger tract called *Johanness Hall*, beginning at the New Bridge by the e. end of the causway, 50 a. {KEDELR R:87}

On 21 May 1766 Mark Manlove of Kent Co. yeoman and Violet his wife for £160 sold to Thomas Skidmore of same place yeoman ... a tract of land late in the possession of Robert Cummins and upon his decease the estate became vested in the said Violet, wife of Mark Manlove, who was heir of the said Robert Cummins, dec'd., on s. side of Double Run branch in Murderkill Hundred adj. land called *Arundall* ... 60 a. with 1 grist mill thereon, and also one other tract of land adj. afsd. land on n. of Double Run branch, 40 a., and is land the said Robert Cummins purchased of John Housman in his life time. {KEDELR R:89}

On 14 Nov 1766 Mark Manlove, Junr., of Murderkill Hundred, Kent Co., and Violet his wife, for £100 sold to John Cadwalader and Lambert Cadwalader of Philadelphia, merchants, 100 a. next adj. to the land formerly sold by the said Mark and his wife to Bowers Furbee part of a tract devised to Robert Cumming father of the said Violet by her grandfather Robert Cumming. {KEDELR R:121}

Mark was father of the following children {A}: MATTHEW, d. intestate ca. 1773-1791 {A}; ANN, m. John Chambers and they and their children moved to Allegany Co., MD in 1790 and eventually to Muskingum Co., OH; possibly MARK, progenitor of Cecil Co. MD Manloves {A}.

52. ABSALOM MANLOVE, shallopman, son of Absolom (36) Manlove, m. (N) Williams.

Absalom d. leaving a will 26 Nov 1769, proved 1 Dec 1769. Heirs: bro.-in-law John Williams, son of John Williams; Thomas Cockrum. Exec., bro.-in-law John Williams. Wits., Mary Hunn, Richard Furbush, Rachel Bullen. {Arch. A33:81. Reg. of Wills, L:67-68}

53. MATTHEW MANLOVE, son of Absolom (36) Manlove, m. Sarah, dau. of Richbell Mott.

On 21 April 1768 Seaman (Seman) Mott of Kent Co. and Nancy his wife for £240 sold to Govey Emmerson of same co. yeoman, part of a tract of land, whereas Richbell Mott in his life time was seized in 300 a., part of 2 larger tracts one called *York* and one called *Willingsbrook* in Little Creek Hundred and being so seized d. intestate leaving 4 children, to wit Sarah now wife of Matthew Manlove, Richard Mott, afsd. Seaman Mott and Elizabeth wife of Solomon Seamans of MD, beginning at land of the said Govey Emmerson to Thomas Irons's land which he purchased of Richard Mott eldest son afsd, to Matthew and Sarah Manlove's land, 44 a. {KEDELR R:251}

Matthew Manlove, farmer, d. leaving a will dated 13 Dec 1773, proved 28 Dec 1773. Heirs: sister Margret Craige; bro. Mark Manlove; nephew Matthew Manlove, son of bro. Mark. Exec., bro. Mark Manlove. Wits., Jonathan Sipple, James Reed, Silvanus Swallow. {Arch. A32:47. Reg. of Wills, L:147-148}

Unplaced

On 10th da., 9th mo., 1747 a complaint was made against ELIZABETH MANLOVE in marrying out of the Unity of Friends. {DCMM}

JONATHAN MANLOVE m. Elizabeth Miers, dau. of James and Margery Miers, before 13 Sep 1749. {KEDE Deeds H:238}

LUKE MANLOVE m. Ann (N).

In 1707 Luke Manlove and his wife Ann of Kent Co., PA [DE}, farmer, conveyed to John Rider of Dorchester Co., Gent., *Pennipe Point* on s. side of Ireland Creek, 100 a. {DOLR 6 Old 104}

MARK MANLOVE, yeoman, Cedar Creek Hundred, d. leaving a will dated 5 March 1717/18 [no date of probate]. Heirs: wife Anne Manlove; son Thomas Manlove; dau. Mary Manlove; servants George and Hugh Perkins. Extx. wife Anne Manlove. Wits., Art Vankirke, Sr., George Walton, Thomas May, Jr. {Sussex Co. Probate - Arch. A86:41}

On 22nd da., 12th mo., 1755 Murtherkill Friends brought a complaint against MARK MANLOVE for drinking to excess and absenting himself from meetings. {DCMM}

MARK MANLOVE of Kent Co. on Delaware purchased 50a. called *Hudsons Lott* from William Trippe and Margaret his wife in Dorchester Co. on 9 June 1731. {DOLR 8 Old 417}

On 17th da., 5th mo., 1738, it was reported that MARK MANLOVE had acknowledged his outgoing in marriage. {DCMM}

MARK MANLOVE m. Rachel (N).

On 13 May 1726 Mark Manlove of Kent Co. yeoman and Rachell Manlove for £36 sold to James Armitage of New Castle Co., smith, a tract of land called *Chance*, being part of an antient tract of land formerly granted to Benony Bishop of Kent Co., dec'd., called *Bishops Choice* the said part of land being the upper part ... 200 a. {KEDELR H:227}

MARK AND MATTHEW MANLOVE
Betts, Robert. Planter. Will (copy). Made March 27, 1726. Mispillion Hd. Heirs: sons John and William; dau. Elizabeth; Mark, Jr. and Matthew, Jr., children of Mark and Matthew Manlove. Exec., bro.-in-law Matthew Manlove. Guardians, William Molleston, Tobitha Williams. Wits., John Ashley, Robert Cuming, William Barnabey. Prob. Feb. 15, 1727. Arch. Vol. A4, pages 38 and 39. Reg. of Wills, Liber G, folios 5-6.

SUSANNAH MANLOVE d. 27th da., 3rd mo. 1795, age 49 years; buried in the Family burial ground, KE Co., DE. {DCMM}

WILLIAM MANLOVE m. (N) Robisson and had daus.: Hannah, Elizabeth and Sarah and son George.

Daniel Robisson d. leaving a will dated 10 Jan 1764, proved 28 Jan 1764. Heirs: wife Patience (former wife of George Willson, dec'd.); sons Joseph, Samuel; dau. Elizabeth Hudson, wife of William Hudson; granddaus. Hannah, Elizabeth and Sarah Manlove, daus. of William Manlove; grandson George Manlove; son-in-law William Manlove. Exec., son Samuel. Wits., Samuel Skidmore, James Edmunds, John Hinds. Codicil, wife's son George Willson. {Arch. A44:36-39. Reg. of Wills, K:335-336}

WILLIAM MANLOVE had a dau. Elizabeth.

George Morgan, Jr. of Dover and Anne his wife, dau. of Joseph Booth, Jr., sold land to Elizabeth Manlove, dau. of William Manlove - Elizabeth Manlove, a minor. {KEDELR Deeds N:279, 25 May 1749}.

WILLIAM MANLOVE, Jr., m. Elizabeth (N).

William d. leaving a will dated 1 May 1748, proved 3 June 1748. Heirs: wife Elizabeth; daus. Mary, Elizabeth. Execs., wife Elizabeth, friends Joseph Mason, William Walton. Wits., George Walton, John Brown, James Freeland. {Arch. A33:134-136. Reg. of Wills, I:226} Note: Arch. A33:135 shows Elizabeth, the widow, later married Jacob Warrington.

William was father of the following children: MARY; ELIZABETH.

WILLIAM MANLOVE m. Hannah (N).

On 27 May 1760 William Manlove, Junr., and Hannah his wife of Kent Co. for £150 sold to Stephen Lewis of same place, a tract of land whereon the afsd. William Manlove of late did dwell part of a larger tract called *Wedmore* in the forrest of Murtherkill Hundred beginning at corner of John Webb and the afsd. William Manlove, s. side of Isaacs Branch to James Bedwell's land, 112 1/2 a. {KEDELR P:203}

THE GEORGE MARTIN FAMILY

1. GEORGE MARTIN m. 1st Constant (N) and m. 2nd Ursula Colliner.

On 8 Oct 1685 George Martin and Constant his wife of Kent Co., PA, sold to David Straughan [also written Daniell] of same co. for 1000 pounds of tobacco, a tract of land called *Coventry*, being part of a tract which George Martin now dwelleth on n. side of Duck Creek. {KEDELR}

On the Kent Co. Rent Roll, 1681-1688 is shown George Martin owning *Woodstock Corner*, 1500 a.; *Bradshaws Choice*, 270 a.; *Price's Choice*, 100 a.; *James' Choice*, 100 a.; and another 200 a. {Bendler:4}

The 1693 Tax Assessment List of Kent County shows Capt. George Martin of Duck Creek Hundred having a value of £300. {Bendler:20}

George Martin d. by 12 March 1694/5 when Ursilla Martin, widow, was appointed admx. {Reg. of Wills, A:11; Reg. of Wills, Liber B, folio 31}

On 9 June 1698 at Philadelphia Wm. Hoakey and Ursula Martin, widower, and widow, both of Kent Co., have made known there intentions of marriage ... Wm. Markham grants a license. {KEDELR}

On 21 Jul 1698 Ursula Martin, widdow and relict of Georg Martin of Kent Co., PA, late dec'd., for love good will and affection give to my deare and well beloved children Georg Martin, Josiah Martin and Elizabeth Martin (alsoe children of the said Georg Martin, dec'd.) ... I give to my son Georg Martin one gun called Black Bess and one law book entitled Shepards Epitome it being a large thick book ... I give to Josiah Martin two cows ... I give unto my dau. Elizabeth Martin one feather bed and bolster weighing about 60 pounds, two blankets and one rugg, six pewter dishes and six pewter plates weighinge about 55 pounds, one small brazeale cabbinet, one leather trunck marked with the letters UC, one small bible, one box iron and heater, one black framed lookinge glass, one small iron pott with pott hook and hangers, and two cows ... the said Georg, Josiah and Elizabeth Martin being now in their minority and of tender years not of ability to take care for themselves ... Ursula Martin put Simon Hirons and William Rodeney both of same co. in peaceable and quiet possession of all the afsd. ... Wit: William Hawkey, John Mohon.

On 25 Jul 1698 the marriage of William Hawkey and Ursilla Martin was solomnized by John Brinckloe justice of the peace ... Wit: Griffith Jones, Arthur Meston, William Rodeney.{KEDELR}

On 25 Jul 1698 Ursula Martin, late wife of Georg Martin of Kent Co., PA, dec'd., in consideration of the performance of former agreement between Ursula Martin and said Georg Martin her late husband before their intermarriage and more especially for the naturall love good will and affection for my children George, Josiah and Elizabeth Martin hath quit claimed unto said children ... all right and title of dower on lands of said Georg Martin's ... especially a tract of land called *Gloster* 400 a. on n. side of Duck Creek being same whereon she now dwells ... Georg, Josiah and Elizabeth Martin now in their minority and of tender years Ursula Martin appoint my friends Simon Hirons and William Rodeney both of afsd. co. to be guardians of my said children untill they arrive and be at lawfull years of discretion ... Wit: William Hawkey, John Mohon. Memorandum. afsd. tract of land ... was delivered by Ursula Martin unto William Rodeney ... Wit: William Hawkey, John Mohon.

On 10 Feb 1701 William Hawker of Kent Co., PA, planter, and Ursula his wife, relict and admx. of George Martin, late of same co., dec'd. whereas the said George Martin at the time of his decease left behind him several young children to the nature and education of Ursula ... William Hawker and Ursula his wife petitioned court and at a court held 20 Dec 1699 court ordered lands of George Martin, dec'd., to be sold for bringing up the said children being young and chargable ... William Hawker and Ursula his wife for £20 sold to Robert French of Newcastle, PA, merchant, a tract of land called *Elkes Horn* lying near Duck Creek bounded with a tract called *Gloucester* heretofore belonging to

George Martin, dec'd., and the land called *Coventry* belonging to Robert French on the one side and on the n.e. with the land of Alburt Muntford ... 85 a. {KEDELR F:32}

Ursilla Hawkey, wife of Wm. Hawkey, formerly wife of George Martin, nee Collinner, d. leaving a will dated 17 March 1702, proved 12 May 1703. Heirs: sons Samuel Hawkey, Josiah Martin and George Martin; daus. Ruth Hawkey and Elizabeth Martin; Evan Jones; Elizabeth Jones, wife of Evan Jones. Execs., Evan Jones, Elizabeth Jones. Wits., John Bradshaw, Jonas Greenwood, Elizabeth Morris. {Arch. A23:9. Reg. of Wills, B:47}

On 12 Aug 1712 whereas George Martin in his lifetime ... did sell unto John Bradshaw of same co. ... a tract of land on n. side of s.w. branch of Duck Creek, 300 a. called *Bradshaws Chance* in consideration of a tract of land that said John Bradshaw did grant to George Martin in his lifetime for payment of said 300 a. ... witness to bond was David Strawhin and Walter Jones both dec'd. ... Feb 1684 George Martin did deliver possession of 300 a. and Richard Mitchell and Evan Jones signed as witnesses ... Know ye that George Martin, William Annand and Elizabeth Annand his wife all of Kent co. son and dau. of George Martin late of same place dec'd. ... quitt claim unto John Bradshaw afsd. tract of land ... Wit: A Hamelton, Hoyidiah Ofley?, Wm Hawkey. Ackn 12 Aug 1712. {KEDELR E:30}

On 17 May 1716 Elisabeth Annand of Murtherkill Hundred, Kent Co., widow, dau. of George Martain of Duck Creek, late, dec'd., for good will, love and affection and for £30 sell to my well beloved brother George Martain of same place, a tract of land that said George Martain now lives upon in Duck Creek Hundred called *Gloster*. {KEDELR E:175}

George was father of the following children: ELISABETH, m. William Annand; GEORGE; JOSIAH.

Second Generation

2. GEORGE MARTIN of Duck Creek, son of George (1) Martin, m. 25th da., 10th mo., 1717, Rachel Cook, dau. of John and Mary Cook of Duck Creek. {DCMM} Rachel later m. (N) Tybout.

Mary Cook, widow of Duck Creek, d. leaving a will dated 10 July 1726, proved 20 Oct 1726. Heirs: sons Robert and Michall; dau. Rachel Martin; dau.-in-law Hannah Cook. Execs., sons Robert and Michall. Wits., John McKebb. Richard Empson, and Dorethy Empson. {Arch. A10:123. Reg. of Wills, F:16}

George d. leaving a will dated 21 July 1729, proved 1 Sep 1729. Heirs: son George; wife Rachel; bro. Josiah Martin; David French; one child unnamed. Execs., wife Rachel and William Collins. Trustees, Charles Hillyard, John Hall, and George Newell. Wits., Philip Denny, Alexander McKenzie, John Tilton. {Arch. A33:205-206. Reg. of Wills, G:27-28} Note: Arch. A33:206 shows that Rachel Martin later married ... Tybout.

George was father of the following children: GEORGE; UNNAMED.

Third Generation

3. GEORGE MARTIN, probably the unnamed child of George (2) Martin, d. leaving by 12 Jan 1756 when Elizabeth Martin, widow, and Thomas Collins, were appointed admins. of his estate. {Arch. A33:207-208. Reg. of Wills, K:123-124} Note: Arch. A24:25 shows this acct. later administered by Mary Raymond,

admx. of Charles Hillyard, who with his wife Elizabeth and Thomas Collins was admins. of the estate of George Martin.

Elizabeth Martin later m. Charles Hillyard.

PATRICK MARTIN

PATRICK MARTIN m. Mary Ridgely, dau. of Nicholas Ridgely by whom a child was born. Mary d. by 31 March 1755.

On 15 Nov 1753 Patrick Martin of Kent Co., merchant, and Mary his wife, for £80 sold to John Rash of same place, yeoman, a tract of land in Murtherkill Hundred called *Barnses Chance* or *Choise* alias *Gidishaw* beginning at Rash's fence to original tract *Barneses Chance* formerly belonging to a certain Robert French ... 100 a. being the land formerly belonging to a certain Thomas Nichols which land was mortgaged by him to Robert French. Wit: Nicholas Ridgely, John Clayton Junr. {KEDELR O:201}

On 1 April 1754 James Byrne of Kent Co., for barring and docking and cutting off all estate tail and remainders in tail of ye lands and for settling and assuring of same sold to Nicholas Ridgely of same co. gent and Patrick Martin of same co., gent, and Mary his wife, dau. of afsd. Nicholas Ridgely ... all those tracts of plantable land, a tract called *Newberry* on s. side of Duck Creek, 500 a., one other tract in Duck Creek Hundred, beginning at Hillyards Branch to land sold by Samuel Harraway to one Andrew Trebow, 150 a., part of a larger tract formerly belonging to William Harraway, also one other tract on n. side of Parimains Branch beginning at land of William Sherrer by Gravelly Run to Rainold's land, 100 a., also one other tract called *Golden Grove* and also part of a tract which was formerly conveyed by a certain John Brinckle to a certain Robert French, 300 a., part of a larger tract called *Hillyards Adventure* ... James Wells did enter into ye warranty of said lands ... all agree in a good and perfect common recovery. {KEDELR O:255}

On 20 Aug 1754 Patrick Martin of Kent Co., yeoman, and Mary his wife, for £533.0.6 sold to John Bell of Philadelphia, merchant, a tract of land in Duck Creek Hundred, beginning at Hillyards Branch ... 150 a., also one other tract of land in same hundred called *Golden Grove*, 209 a., also one other tract of land in the same hundred called *Newberry* on s. side of Duck Creek ... 400 a., also one other tract of land in same hundred on n. side of Pairmains Branch ... 100 a. ... on condition that if the said Patrick Martin shall well and truly pay unto the said John Bell the sum of £533.0.6 at the end of 2 years together with lawfull interest then this indenture shall cease and become void. Wit: Benjamin Chew, George Martin. Ackn 15 Feb 1755. Mary did declare that she freely and voluntarily became a party to this deed. Attest: Geo. Martin, justice. {KEDELR O:261}

On 31 March 1755 Patrick Martin of Kent Co., yeoman, for £400 sold to James Trotter of Philadelphia, merchant, a tract of land, whereas Robert French late of New Castle Co., dec'd., by his will bearing date about 23 Jan 1712 did devise to his son David French 500 a. called *Giddishaw* or *Barnes's Chance* or *Choice* and in case the son should die without issue then the said tract to his dau. Ann French provided she should have children and David French died without issue and Ann French m. Nicholas Ridgely and had by him one dau. named Mary and Ann also died and Mary Ridgely m. afsd. Patrick and had by him a child born alive and Mary is since dead ... in the forest of Jones in Murderkill Hundred s. side of Isaacs Branch adj. land formerly belonging to Thomas Nichols ... 500 a. Wit: Chas. Gordon, Wm. Rasin (Rason). {KEDELR O:293}

On 9 May 1758 Charles Ridgely, practitioner, was appointed admin. of the estate of Mary Martin, wife of Patrick Martin. {Reg. of Wills, K:182}

Patrick Martin, gentleman, d. by 14 March 1761 when John Clayton, Esq., was appointed admin. of his estate. {Arch. A33:210. Reg. of Wills, K:259}

Unplaced

CHARLES MARTEN m. Elizabeth (N).

Charles d. leaving a will dated 14 Sep 1724, proved 7 June 1725. Heirs: sons Nathaniel and John; daus. Jane and Mary; wife Elizabeth. Extx., wife Elizabeth. Wits., William Morriss, Philip Brady, John Clampet. {Arch. A33:204. Reg. of Wills, F:4}

Charles was father of the following children: NATHANIEL; JOHN; JANE; MARY.

JAMES MARTIN m. Elizabeth (N) who later m. (N) Frost.

On 20 Oct 1735 Elizabeth Frost, widow and relict of James Martin, late of Kent Co., dec'd., for £18 in hand paid, for and towards her support and maintenance, sold to Samuel Smith of same co. blacksmith ... a tract of land (whereas the said James Martin in his life time was possessed of a tract of land in Mispillion Hundred, 200 a., and is the same which Nathaniel Hunn, dec'd., sold James Martin and which John Bowers sold Nathaniel, called *George Bowers His Old Feild*, on s. side of Bawcombrig Branch, bounded on the n. side by Luke Manlove, on the e. side by Mathew Manlove, on the s. side by Big Bellyed Swamp and on the w. with land Owen Williams bought of the said Nathaniel, of which said land James dyed possessed and it descended to his children who all of them dyed before they came of lawfull age and without issue whereby the said Elizabeth became the lawful heir thereto) ... 200 a. {KEDELR L:149}

JAMES MARTAIN d. by 15 Oct 1739 when Samuel Smith was appointed admin. of his estate. {Reg. of Wills, H:157}

JOHN MARTAIN m. Mary Maffet.

John Maffet, planter of Jones' Hundred, d. leaving a will dated 1757, proved 25 Oct 1757. Heirs: wife Janet; sons John, William, James, Robert; daus. Susannah, Rachael and Mary, wife of John Martain. Execs., wife Janet and son John. Wits., John Hardin, William Maffet, Thomas Hardin. {Arch. A35:189. Reg. of Wills, K:169}

WILLIAM MARTIN, Duck Creek, d. by 2 Oct 1750 when Richard and Ann Wooderson were appointed admins. of his estate. {Reg. of Wills, K:43-44} Note: Arch. A33:211 shows Jean Martin as a dau.

William was father of JEAN.

THE MAXFIELD/MAXWELL FAMILY

1. JAMES MAXWELL m. 1st on 25 Feb 1686 Damsin Low and m. 2nd on 2 May 1688 Alce (Alice) Adams who later m. John Machan.

James Maxfield is listed on the Kent Co. Rent Rolls, 1681-1688 as owing on 50 a. {Bendler:4} James Maxwell of Dover Hundred is shown as owing on 150 a. in the 1693 Tax Assessment of Kent Co. {Bendler:22} In a list of Kent Co. Quit Rents owed in the period 1701-1713 are shown the names of the sons of James Maxwell, i.e., James and Robert Maxwell, for 75 a., part of the same tract of which Thos. Mahon held 175 a., laid out as *Berry's Range*. {Bendler:38}

On 25 Feb 1686 James Maxwell of Kent Co. and Damsin Low have published their intentions to marry ... William Berry, Clerk. {KEDELR}

This couple James Maxwell and Damsin Low hath taken each other as husband and wife in the presence of us Thomas Hoatherd, John Robsson, Anna Hoathord, Jacob Amorson, Mary Walker, John Newell, Prosila Edmuns, Stephen Simons, Ann Walker, George Robsson, Elliner Robsson, Robert Edmons, Mahason Hoathers. {KEDELR}

On 2 May 1688 James Maxwell of Kent Co. and Alice Adams, widow, haveing intentions of marriage have publish same ... Wit: William Berry, Clerk. {KEDELR}

On 2 May 1688 James Maxwell and Alice Adams take each other for man and wife at house of William Berry ... Wit: Samuell Burbery, John Richardson, Arthur Meston, Patrick Grady, Neomy Berry, Ann Heckleyer, Damarice Wally, John Newell, Wm. Morton, Tho. Bedwell, Wm. Darvall, John Brinkloe, Wm. Wilson, John ---, Wm. [page torn]. {KEDELR}

James Maxwell d. by 20 Dec 1695 when the administration of his estate was assigned to wife Alce and Robert French. {Reg. of Wills, B:37}

On 13 Feb 1710 John Berry, son and heir of William Berry, late of Kent Co., yeoman, dec'd., for £5 sold to William Maxwell, James Maxwell and Robert Maxwell, sons of James Maxwell, late of same co., dec'd. ... (whereas Naomy Berry, mother of the afsd. John Berry in her life time as admx. of the estate of William Berry, dec'd., by her deed bearing date 16 July 1695 sold unto afsd. James Maxwell, dec'd., in his life time a tract of land called *Cowhill*, 250 a., being part of a tract called *Berrys Range* on n. side of Dover River ... to corner of 100 a. late belonging to James Maxwell whereon he then lived and was formerly also part of *Berrys Range*) ... afsd. 250 a. {KEDELR H:13}

On 8 Aug 1721 William Maxwell, eldest son of James Maxwell late of Kent Co., dec'd., and Robert Maxwell, younger son of the said James Maxwell, dec'd., and Meliston his wife, all of Little Creek Hundred ... whereas James Maxwell in his lifetime became seized of a tract of land adj. e. side of Dover River called *Berrys Range* whereon he did then dwell ... dying intestate the land descended unto his sons William, James and Robert Maxwell ... James Maxwell by a deed of sale dated 10 May 1712 did sell to John Register a parcel of land of the lower end of the tract as his share ... William Maxwell by one other indenture did sell to John Mahan a parcel of afsd. tract including part of the plantation whereon Thomas Parbo now dwelleth (Book D, folio 15) ... this indenture William Maxwell and Robert Maxwell and Meliston his wife for £30 sold to Edward Jennings of Dover same co., one parcel of land between the two afsd. parcels ... 130 a. {KEDELR G:30}

On 20 May 1728 Alice Machan of Kent Co., relict of John Machan, dec'd., upon the trust and confidence I have in my son James Maxwell of same place, by letter of atty do make him my atty to make sale of the land, goods, chattles, rights and creditts that did of right belong unto me as 1/3 part of the estate of my dec'd. husband John Machan. {KEDELR I:131}

James was father of the following sons: WILLIAM; JAMES; ROBERT.

Second Generation

2. WILLIAM MAXFIELD, eldest son of James (1) Maxfield, m. Aldery (N).

On 31 Oct 1702 William Maxwell of Kent Co., PA, planter, eldest lawfull son of James Maxwell, late of same co., dec'd., for £35 sold to John Mahon of same co., planter ... tract of land whereupon James Maxwell in his life time did dwell called *Berrys Range* near and towards the head of Jones Creek ... bounded by a tract of land containing 100 a. purchased by James Maxwell of William Berry ... 95 a. {KEDELR D:22}

On 12 Feb 1704 William Maxfield (Maxwell), eldest son of James Maxfield of Kent Co., PA, and Alderey his wife for £11 sold to John Monghon (Mohon) of same co., 80 a. of land adj. the land and plantation where the said John Mohon now liveth at the side of St. Jones Branch ... side of Kings Road to Duck Creek ... to a parcell of land formerly sold by William Maxfield to John Mohon ... part of a 300 a. tract purchased by James Maxwell, father to William Maxfield, of William Berry, late of same co., dec'd., being part of a tract of land called *Berrys Range*. {KEDELR I:2}

3. JAMES MAXWELL, Jr., son of James (1) Maxwell, Joiner.

On 10 May 1712 James Maxwill of Kent Co., planter, younger son of James Maxwill, late of Dover, yeoman, dec'd., for £16 sold to John Rigester of same co., carpenter, ... whereas James Maxwill, dec'd., was in his lifetime and at the time of his death seized of a 350 a. tract of land in Dover Hundred near the head of Dover River, part of a greater tract called *Berrys Range* which said James Maxwill dyed intestate ... 81 a. {KEDELR E:47}

James d. leaving a will dated 2 Oct 1752, proved 11 Oct 1752. Heirs: daus. Elizabeth Maxwell, Anna Helford, Ann Darling (dau. of my wife); bro. Robert. Exec., bro. Robert. Trustee, Henry Upprithart. Wits., Samuel Robisson, John Taylor, Jr., Mathew Claghorn. {Arch. A34:80-84. Reg. of Wills, K:80}

On 5 March 1755 Robert Maxwell, exec. of [his bro.] James Maxwell, yeoman, dec'd., petitioned to sell some of the land. {KEORCF Maxwell, James 1755-61}

James was father of the following children: ELIZABETH; ANNA, m. (N) Helford.

4. ROBERT MAXWELL, son of James (1) Maxwell m. Meliston (N).

Robert d. leaving a will dated 12 June 1744, proved 20 Oct 1744. Heirs: sons William, Robert, Moses, Thomas, James, Adam, Mark; daus. Elce, Sarah; George and Ebenesor Russell, sons of George Russell, dec'd. Execs., sons Robert and Moses. Wits., John Talbutt, James Maxwell, Jr. {Arch. A34:92-95. Reg. of Wills, 1:88}

Robert Maxwell, exec. of the estate of Robert Maxwell [his dec'd. father], requested to sell enough of the lands to discharge demands. {KEORCF Maxwell, Robert 1745-46}

Robert was father of the following children: WILLIAM; ROBERT; MOSES; THOMAS; JAMES; ADAM; MARK; ELCE; SARAH.

Unplaced

ALEXANDER MAXWELL b. 23 Jan 1670. {TA Co. Court Proceedings}

ESTHER MAXFIELD d. 1751, age 2 years. {THMM}

JAMES MAXWELL, possible son of Robert (4) Maxwell, m. Eleanor Hunn, widow of Nathaniel Hunn.

On 17 Aug 1739 James Maxwell of Kent Co., yeoman, and Eleanor his wife for £140 already paid by Alexander Farquhar in his life time and for £37.10 with interest to be paid to the trustees of the Loan Office in discharge of the mortgage, sold to Mary Farquhar, extx., and James Gorrel, exec. of the will of Alexander Farquhar, late of same co., dec'd. ... a tract of land (James Maxwell did by his writing obligatory dated 2 Aug 1737 bind himself to convey unto Allexander Farquhar sufficient deed of sale of one grist mill and a tract of 400 a. ... John Hall, late sheriff by deed of sale 13 May 1731 reciting that James Maxwell, admin. of John McHan late of Kent Co. in Aug Term last past did recover against Thomas Parke of same co., yeoman, a debt of £61.17.3 and 128 shillings damages and by a writt bearing date 14 Aug sheriff had seized in execution the afsd. grist mill and land in Mutherkill Hundred and by one other writ 14 Nov land was exposed to sale by publick vendue to the highest bidder ... appraized by Thomas Wells and Thomas Tarrant to the value of £230 ... 400 a. purchased by James Maxwell afsd. he being the greatest bidder at £151) ... in Murtherkill Hundred by Dover River by Isaacs Branch ... 400 a. Mary quit claims her right of dower. {KEDELR M:44}

On 28 Nov 1749 James Maxwell and Elenor his wife of Kent Co. for £8.5 quit claim unto John Hunn of ye same co., yeoman, all their estate right of 1/3 part of two tracts of land (whereas Nathaniel Hunn, late of Kent Co., yeoman, married with ye said Elenor and afterwards died intestate and among other lands left one tract of land in St. Jones Hundred, 170 a. called *Town Point*, and also one other parcel of land of 64 a. adj. the afsd. tract which he purchased from a certain George Nowell and Elenor afterwards m. James Maxwell whereof James in right of his wife became possessed of 1/3 part of the afsd. two tracts to hold to him during the natural life of his said wife Elenor). {KEDELR O:29}

John Hunn d. leaving a will dated 26 May 1750, proved 21 June 1750. Heirs: wife Tabitha; mother Elinor Maxwell; sons David, John, Caleb; dau. Susanna. Extx., wife Tabitha. Wits., Benjamin Chew, Richard Johns, Isaiah Wharton. {Arch. A25:142-143. Reg. of Wills, K:23} Note: Arch. A25:143 shows Tabitha, the widow, later married Silas Crispin.

James Maxwell, yeoman, d. by 10 Sep 1755 when Elinor Maxwell, widow, was appointed admx. of his estate. {Arch. A34:83. Reg. of Wills, K:121}

Elinor Maxwell d. by 14 March 1758 when Nimrod Maxwell, planter, was appointed admin. of her estate. {Reg. of Wills, K:178}

JAMES MAXFEALD of Duck Creek, m. Hannah (N) who later m. Charles Tool and still later m. John Spruance.

James d. leaving a will dated 21 Jan 1748, proved 15 Feb 1748. Heirs: wife Hannah; son James; daus. Mary, Jean, Hannah; one child unnamed. Execs., wife Hannah and friend Daniel Nock. Wits., Mathew Steel, Samuel Griffeth, William Pope. {Arch. A34:74-76. Reg. of Wills, I:262}

On 5 Nov 1759 Joseph Galloway of Philadelphia, and Elizabeth Johns of Kent Co., widow, sold to Charles Tool of Kent Co., yeoman, and Hannah his wife, late the wife of James Maxwell, late of Kent Co., yeoman, dec'd., and James Maxwell and Robert Maxwell, children and devisees of the said James Maxwell, dec'd., ... 1/2 of a tract of land called *The Manor of Frieth.* {KEDELR P:170}

On 18 March 1771 when John Spruance and wife Hannah, late Hannah Maxwell, were appointed admins. of the estate of James Maxwell {Arch. A84:85} Note: Mentions heirs, Hannah and Joan Maxwell and Mary Craige, wife of Moses Craige.

Jean Maxwell, dau. of James Maxfeald, d. by 7 Oct 1769 when Sarah Hirons was appointed admx. of her estate. {Reg. of Wills, L:65}

James was father of the following children: JAMES; MARY, m. Moses Craige; JEAN, d. by 7 Oct 1769; HANNAH; ROBERT.

On 10th da., 9th mo., 1753 there was a complaint against JESTINIA Needham, now MAXFIELD, for marrying out and for having carnal knowledge of him before marriage. {DCMM}

JOHN MAXWELL m. Anne (N).

On 13 Jan 1764 John Maxwell of Kent Co., gent., and Anne his wife for 5 shillings leased unto James Wells of same co., 1/2 part of several tracts of plantable land, one called *Tynehead Court* on s. side of a branch of Little Creek and land now of John Nikerson but late of one George Morgan, dec'd. ... 410 a. including all those several parcels of *Tynheads Court* heretofore conveyed by sundry persons to a certain Robert French now dec'd., also 1/2 part of all that other tract called *Tyneds Court* ... 93 a., also 1/2 part of one other parcel on n. side of Jones Creek or Dover River in Dover Hundred. ... 170 a., for the term of 1 year. {KEDELR Q:211}

On 31 Jan 1764 John Maxwell of Kent Co., gent., and Ann his wife, and Richard Butler of same co., in a good and perfect common recovery, for docking and baring of all estates tail and for 5 shillings sold to James Wells of same co. several tracts of land. {KEDELR Q:215}

JOHN MAXFIELD of Kent Co., MD, m. Elizabeth (N). They were parents of JOHN, b. 9 April 1714. {KESP}

The name John Maxfields is shown on the 1693 Tax Assessment List of Sussex Co. {Bendler:29}

John d. leaving a will dated 31 Jan 1721, proved 2 June 1722. Mentioned were wife Eliza. and 4 children: Eliza., John, Gawin, and another dau. unnamed. Son John to the care of his uncle Thos. Ricand. {MWB 17:179}

JOHN MAXWELL m. Elizabeth (N). They were parents of WILLIAM, b. 27th da., 6th mo., 1754. {KESP}

JOSEPH MAXFIELD of Worcester Co., MD, m. Sarah Warner of Kent Co.,

MD, at Cecil Meeting House, on 14th da., 9th mo., 1744.

Joseph was living in the Mulberry Grove area of Worcester Co., MD, in 1744; he d. in 1750, leaving his widow Sarah, son Stephen, and daus. Susanna and Esther.

Sarah, widow of Joseph Maxfield, m. 27th da., 9th mo, 1753, Ezekiel Nock of Kent Co., DE, at the home of Daniel and Mary (Warner) Mifflin in Accomack Co., VA. {Quakerism on the Eastern Shore:97-98}

On 27th da., 4th mo., 1765, Sarah Nock by a Friend requested a certificate on behalf of her son Stephen Maxfield who is bound an apprentice in Philadelphia. {DCMM}

Susanna Maxfield of Kent Co., DE, m. James Berry of TA Co., MD, 29th da., 3rd mo., 1768, at a publick meeting at Murderkill. {DCMM}

Joseph and Sarah were parents of the following children: SUSANNA, b. 15th da., 8th mo., 1740, m. 29th da., 3rd mo., 1768, James Berry of TA Co[39]; STEPHEN, b. 21st da., 11th mo., 1748; ESTHER, b. 25th da., 10th mo., 1749. {THMM}

MARY MAXWELL m. Ebenezer Blackiston 14 April 1737. {KESP}

NIMROD MAXWELL m. 1st Mary (N) and m. 2nd Elizabeth Taylor {MD Genealogies:499}.

Mary Maxwell, wife of Nimrod Maxwell, d. by 27 May 1760 when Nimron (Nimrod) Maxwell was appointed admin. of her estate. {Reg. of Wills, K:229}

On 23rd da., 10th mo., 1762 Elizabeth Maxfield produced a certificate from Third Haven Monthly Meeting dated 29th da., 7th mo., 1762. {DCMM}

Nimrod and Elizabeth were parents of the following children {DCMM}: SARAH, b. 28 Sep 1761, m. 19 Feb 1777, Coe Gordon {MD Genealogies:499}; EDMONDSON, b. 16th da., 3rd mo., 1766; NIMROD.

Elizabeth Maxwell d. 28th da., 2nd mo., 1791, age 50 years, bur. Motherkiln Meeting, Kent Co., DE. {DCMM}

ROBERT MAXWELL m. Esther (N).

On 26 April 1741 Robert Maxwell of Kent Co., yeoman, and Esther his wife for £106 sold to Solomon Wallace ... a tract of land (1100 a.) granted unto Thomas Bedwill, Henry Bedwill and Robert Bedwill Junr and Adam Fisher called *Longrech* in Murtherkill Hundred. {KEDELR N:28}

ROBERT MAXWELL m. Joanna (N).

On 11 June 1754 Robert Maxwell of Kent Co., carpenter, and Joanna (Joannah) his wife for £70 sold to David Hall of same co. ... a tract of land called *Gravesend* which was sold by Samuel Robisson, sheriff of Kent Co., for the trustees of the General Loan Office to Samuel Morris putt in by James Steward for the whole tract and Samuel Morris for £24 have sold unto Robert Maxwell 100 a. of the original tract. {KEDELR O:231}

Robert Maxwell d. leaving a will dated 20 Sep 1769, proved 4 Nov

---

39 For more on the Berry Family, see *Colonial Families of the Eastern Shore of Maryland*, Vol. 3.

1769. Heirs: sons David, James, Bedwell; daus. Joannah and Mellesent. Execs., friends Edward Gibbs, William Meredith. Trustee, William Meredith. Wits., Daniel Virdin, Oliver Crawford, Elizabeth Virdin. Codicil, dau. Elizabeth. {Arch. A34:96-98. Reg. of Wills, L:66-67}

ROBERT MAXFIELD m. Ann Park 2 Oct 1702. {KESP} Ann was the dau. of Robert Park. Robert and Ann were parents of the following children {KESP}; MARY, bapt. 15 Aug 1703; ANN, bapt. 23 Sep 1706; WILLIAM, bapt. 13 July 1712.

Robert Park of KE Co., MD, d. leaving a will dated 10 June 1718, proved 2 June 1722. Mentioned was his dau. Ann, wife of Robert Maxfield to whom he left 50 a., part of tract *Hinchman*, joining land of Michael Miller and at her death to her second dau. Mary, she dying without issue to granddaul. Eliza. Maxfield. {MWB 17:171}

ROBERT MAXWELL d. by 10 June 1751 when Nicholas Ridgely was appointed admin. of his estate. {Reg. of Wills, K:38}

ROBERT MAXWELL m. Marah (N).

Jonathan Jester d. by 15 Feb 1764 when Mary Jester, widow, was appointed admx. of his estate. {Reg. of Wills, K:338-339} Note: Arch. A28:241 shows that Robert Maxwell and wife Marah later administered on the acct.

ROBERT MAXWELL

David Maxwell, guardian to Bedwell Maxwell, a minor, above the age of 14 years, son of Robert Maxwell, late of Murthurkill Hundred, yeoman, dec'd., showing that Robert Maxwell was seized in his demesne as of fee in certain lands and tenements in the hundred afsd., and d. making his last will and testament wherein he gave to Bedwell Maxwell a part of said lands. The land was valued on 29 May 1771. {KEORCF Maxwell, Robert - 1771-76}

THOMAS MAXWELL, taylor, m. Mary (N).

On 13 Feb 1765 Thomas Maxwell of Murderkill Hundred, Kent Co., taylor, and Mary his wife for £70 sold to William Morris, tanner, of same place, a tract of land in the forrest of Murderkill, part of a tract that belonged to Owen Cain, dec'd., and by virtue of a deed bareing date 25 Feb 1762 from Owen Cain and Manasse Cain the heirs of the said Owen Cain, dec'd., to the said Thomas Maxwell ... 50 a. including the plantation where Owen Cain, dec'd., dwelt. {KEDELR R:14}

WILLIAM MAXWELL m. Sarah Goodwin, widow of Samuel Goodwin and dau. of Mark Bardon.

Samuel Goodwin d. by 5 March 1747 when Sarah Goodwin, widow, was appointed admx. of his estate. {Reg. of Wills, I:186-187} Note: Arch. A19:144 shows the widow Sarah later m. William Maxwell; mentions dau. Elizabeth and son Samuel Goodwin.

Mark Bardon d. leaving a will dated 15 Dec 1750, proved 26 March 1750. Heirs: grandsons Daniel and Mark Coudrat, sons of Daniel Coudrat, dec'd; daus. Sarah Maxwell, Presemene Brian (wife of John Brian), Elizabeth Armitage (wife of Daniel Coudrat, dec'd). Execs., sons-in-law John Bryan and

Joseph Powell. Wits., Robert Wilson, David Pugh, Mary Ann Willson. {Arch. A2:156-157. Reg. of Wills, K: 82 and 115}

William d. leaving a will dated 8 Oct 1753, proved 16 Oct 1753. Heir: wife Sarah. Extx., wife Sarah. Wits., Elizabeth Armitage, Alice Maxwell, John Clayton, Jr. {Arch. A34:104. Reg. of Wills, K:87}

WILLIAM MAXFIELD m. Naomi (N).

On 26th da., 12th mo., 1767, Naomi, wife of William Maxfield, requested to come under the care of Friends. {DCMM}

On 1 March 1769 Thos. Parry in behalf of Lydia Maxwell, dau. of William Maxwell, dec'd., an orphan under age, prays the court to appoint a guardian for her. {KDORCF Maxwell, Lydia 1769}

WILLIAM MAXWELL d. by 27 Jan 1738 when Alexander Donaldson was appointed admin. of his estate. {Reg. of Wills, H:154}

WILLIAM MAXWELL d. by 26 April 1739 when Thomas Skidmore, Jr. was appointed admin. of his estate. {Arch. A34:103. Reg. of Wills, I:11-12}

WILLIAM MAXFIELD d. by 28 Feb 1778 when John Draughton, Sr. was appointed admin. of his estate. {Reg. of Wills, L:127-128}

WILLIAM MAXWELL m. Jane (Jean).

William Maxwell, yeoman of Little Creek Hundred, d. by 6 March 1762, proved 13 June 1761. Heirs: wife Jane [Jean]; sons William, James, Samuel; daus. Mary, Sarah, Lydia, Elizabeth. Extx., wife Jane [Jean]. Trustee, friend Henry Stevens. Wits., William Levick, Clayton Levick, Mark Hirons. {Arch. A34:105. Reg. of Wills, K:264}

William was father of the following children: WILLIAM; JAMES; SAMUEL; MARY; SARAH; LYDIA; ELIZABETH.

WILLIAM MAXWELL m. Chastina (N).

By virtue of an order of the Orphans court of Kent Co. to value the lands of Chastina Maxwell, dec'd., late wife of William Maxwell, now also dec'd., lands in Littlecreek Hundred. On 23 Nov 1774 came Samuel Maxwell, son and one of the representatives of Chastina Maxwell, dec'd., requesting a commission to divide the lands of Chastina, between petitioner and Lydia, dau. of Chastinia Maxwell and now the wife of John Cowgill, Junr., the children and only heirs of said Chastina Maxwell. {KEORCF Maxwell, Chastina - 1774}

THE MIFFLIN FAMILY

1. JOHN MIFFLIN m. Eleanor (N). John Mifflin, senr. of the three of the same name, d. 4th da, 7th mo, 1716. {PMM}

John Mifflin, Senr., of Blockley Twp., Philadelphia Co., yeoman, d. leaving a will dated 5th da, 10th mo, 1715, proved 22 Sep 1716. Wife Elinor. Extx., Elizabeth, dau. in law, wife of John Mifflin, Junr. Witnesses: Thomas Shute, Jacob Qubri and John Mifflin, Junr.

Second Generation

2. JOHN MIFFLIN the younger, and son of John (1) Mifflin, from Wiltshire, and Elizabeth Hardy from Derbyshire m. 6th da, 12th mo, 1683/4 at the house of Henry Lewis near Schuykill. {PMM}

On 27th da, 9th mo, 1696 it was reported that John Hood and John Mifflin had a difference between them. {PMM}

John Mifflin of the Northern Liberty of Philadelphia, yeoman, d. leaving a will dated 10 Sep 1713, proved 11 July 1714. Children: Edward, George, John, Patience, Elizabeth, Jane, Samuel, Jonathan. Philip Kearney and widow Fonderslayse mentioned. Extx., wife Elizabeth. witnesses: David Evans, Thomas Potts, John Cadwalader. {{Phila Wills D:4}

John Mifflin bur. 4th da, 4th mo, 1714. {PMM}

Elizabeth Mifflin, widow of John, bur. 21st da, 6th mo, 1736. {PMM}

John and Elizabeth Mifflin were parents of the following children {PMM}: EDWARD; GEORGE; JOHN; JONATHAN d. 15th da, 3rd mo, 1700; JONATHAN, b. 12th da, 4th mo, 1704; JANE, m. John Waln; PATIENCE d. 23rd da, 9th mo, 1717; SAMUEL, d. 1st da, 8th mo, 1724.

Third Generation

3. EDWARD MIFFLIN, son of John (2) and Elizabeth Mifflin, m. Mary Eyre, widow of Southy Littleton and sister of Daniel Eyre and probable dau. of Daniel Eyre I. {Whitelaw:67, 678}

On 26th da, 1st mo, 1714, John Mifflin requested a certificate on behalf his son, Edward, who intends to take a wife in Virginia. {PMM}

A certificate was issued to Edward Mifflin on 30th da, 2nd mo, 1714, to Virginia, on account of marriage. {PMM}

Mary Mifflin, wife of Edward Mifflin of Northampton Co., VA, is mentioned as a sister of Daniel Eyre in the will of Daniel Eyre, written 14 Sep 1720, proved 24 Oct 1720. {Sussex Co. Wills Arch. A71:54. Reg. of Wills, A:138-139}

Edward d. leaving a will dated 7 Sep 1740, proved 31 May 1743. To son Daniel the tract where I now live lying in the mouth of Swans Gut Creek, with my water mill and plantations in MD. To son Samuel plantation situate in the Northern Liberties of Philadelphia near Schoolcill whereon my father John Mifflin lived, 270 a. To son Southy my house and lot in High Street in Philadelphia near the great meeting house. "Whereas there is a dispute with my brothers and sisters children about part of my above given plantation near Philadelphia which if they recover their claim I desire that my son Samuel Mifflin may have £200 in lieu of what they recover." To granddau. Ann Eyre. Balance of estate to wife and 3 sons. Wife Mary to have her natural life in the plantation where I live, also my water mill and plantation in MD, the profits of my house in Philadelphia and all my plantation on Schoolkill until my sons Samuel and Southy come to the age of 21. Estate not to be divided until son Daniel is 21. Son Daniel, Joseph Maxfield and wife Mary, execs. Wit: Joseph Maxfield (Quakier), John Watson, Jacob Hill, William Gore. {Accomack Co. Wills p. 470}

Mary Mifflin d. leaving a will dated 18 June 1772, proved 28 March 1775. To my son Samuel Mifflin's two children Edward and Mary Mifflin whatever is due me from the estate of Samuel Mifflin, dec., and should both die to go to my grandsons Warner Mifflin and Daniel Mifflin and my great-grandson Daniel Nock, son of James Nock. To great-grandau. Mary Mifflin, dau. of Southy Mifflin, dec. "I give and bequeath unto the Monthly Meeting at Little Creek, Kent Co. on Dellaware Bay, PA, of the People called Quakers, £30, to be disposed of as the members of the meeting shall see fit Great-grandson Charles Mifflin, son of George Mifflin. To Ann Roberts. To Stephen Maxfield and Susannah Beary. Great-grandau. Mary Mifflin, dau. of Warner Mifflin. To Susannah Nelson. Son Daniel Mifflin, residuary legatee. Son Daniel and grandson Warner Mifflin, execs. Wit: George Stewart, Annabellah Willet. {Accomack Co. Wills p. 312}

Edward was father of the following children: DANIEL; SAMUEL; SOUTHY; GEORGE, m. Ann Eyre, dau. of Neech Eyre and she later m. 2nd Humphrey Roberts of Norfolk {Whitelaw:1267}.

4. GEORGE MIFFLIN, son of John (2) and Elizabeth Mifflin, m. 29th da, 11th mo, 1723, Esther (Hester) Cordery, dau. of Hugh Cordery[40]. {PMM}

On 31st da, 10th mo, 1736, George Mifflin applied on behalf of his son John Mifflin for a certificate to Boston Monthly Meeting in relation to marriage.

On 25th da, 2nd mo, 1740, Benjamin Mifflin complained against his uncle, George Mifflin, who refused to refer. {PMM}

On 28th da, 7th mo, 1744, George Mifflin applied on behalf of his son George, for a certificate to Friends in London. {PMM}

On 26th da, 5th mo, 1745, George Mifflin, complained against his brother, Jonathan Mifflin, there being a difference between them. {PMM}

On 29th da, 5th mo, 1745, George Mifflin was reported as returning from London. {PMM}

Hugh Cordery, City of Philadelphia, block maker, d. leaving a will dated 16 June 1741, proved 24 July 1751. Children: Esther Mifflin, Senior, Mary and Deborah. Grandchildren: John, George and Sarah Mifflin. Exec.: Deborah Cordery. Witnesses: Wm. Heaslton, Barth Penrose, Job Goodson. {Philadelphia Wills J:411}}

George Mifflin, City of Philadelphia, merchant, d. leaving a will dated 1 Jan 1755, proved 16 May 1758. Wife: Esther. Children: John and Sarah. Grandchildren: Charles Thomas and George Mifflin. Exec.: John and Sarah Mifflin. Witnesses: Jno. Bleakley, Jno. Ord, Paul Isaac Voto. {Philadelphia Wills L:119}

George and Hester were parents of the following children {PMM}: JOHN; SARAH; MARY, d. 17th da, 3rd mo, 1719; MARY, d. 8th da, 6th mo, 1723; GEORGE, d. 5th da, 7th mo, 1724; GEORGE {mentioned in his grandfather's will}.

5. JOHN MIFFLIN, yeoman, son of John (2) and Elizabeth Mifflin, late of Northern Liberties of Philadelphia, m. 23rd da, 2nd mo, 1717, Sarah Shurmer, dau. of Benjamin Shurmer of Duck Creek, having consent of parents and relations, at Duck Creek. {DCMM}

On 22nd da, 12th mo, 1716, John Mifflin applied for a certificate to Duck Creek with respect to marriage. {PMM}

---

40 Hugh Cordry presented a certificate from Ratclif Monthly Meeting in England on 27th da, 10th mo, 1700 at Philadelphia Monthly Meeting, along with his wife Deborah. {Philadelphia Monthly Meeting}

On 9 Feb 1719 John Mifflin of Kent Co., yeoman, and Sarah his wife for £16 sold to Benjamin Shurmer, prothonotary of same co. a lott of land ... 69 a. {KEDELR F:94}

On 12 Nov 1740 Benjamin Shurmer Miflin and John Miflin of Philadelphia, carpenters, for £60 sold to Robert Willcocks of Kent Co., merchant, 1/5 part of of a tract of land (whereas Benjamin Shurmer late of Kent Co. was in his life time seized in 5 lotts of land containing 5 1/4 a. in the Town of Dover ... Benjamin Shurmer Miflin and John Miflin, sons & coheirs of Sarah Miflin & John Miflin, dec'd., which said Sarah was dau. of the afsd Benjamin Shurmer, dec'd., became seized in 1/5 part of the afsd lots, that is to say each of them in 1/10 part). {KEDELR M:92}

On 30th da, 2nd mo, 1742, a certificate was prepared for John Mifflin, son of John Mifflin, to Duck Creek. {PMM} On 19th da, 5th mo, 1742, John Mifflin produced a certificate from Philadelphia Monthly Meeting. {DCMM} A certificate was received for John Mifflin from Duck Creek on 16th da, 12th mo, 1746. {PMM}

On 24 Dec 1747 William Shurmer of Kent Co., yeoman, only son of Benjamin Shurmer, late of same co., gent., dec'd., for £30 sold to Joseph Dowding of same co., atty at law, 2/5 part of a tract of land, whereas Benjamin Shurmer was in his life time seized in a tract of land in Murtherkil Hundred called *Canterbury* adj. to land of Hugh Durborow near *Vincents Marsh* (warrant for 500 a. unto Benjamin Shurmer) and died intestate the land descended to his children, to wit his son William Shurmer partie to these presents 2/5, & his grandsons Benjamin Mifflin & John Mifflin only children of Sarah Mifflin, dau. of Benjamin Shurmer 1/5 and 1/5 to Ester now the wife of Nicholas Lockerman, another dau. of Benjamin Shurmer, and 1/5 residue of said land to his other dau., Margaret now wife of Joseph Nixon. {KEDELR O:183}

Benjamin Shurmer died intestate leaving issue William Shurmer his only son, the afsd Benjamin Mifflin and John Mifflin the lawfull issue & only representatives of Sarah his eldest dau., Hesther the wife of Nicholas Loockerman and Margaret late the wife of Joseph Nixon to whom his estate did descend, and whereas Thomas Green Esqr late high sheriff of Kent Co. by his deed poll -- May 1745 (Lib N, fol. 71) did convey unto the afsd John Mifflin all the right and estate of the afsd William Shurmer in all the afsd five lots of land to contain in the whole 132 6/10 a. and whereas the afsd Joseph Nixon and Margaret his wife 17 Aug 1745 (Lib N, fol. 69) did convey all their right and estate in the afsd lots of land unto John Mifflin. John Mifflin and Hannah his wife, Benjamin Mifflin & Hannah his wife and Nicholas Loockerman & Hester his wife impower Benjamin Chew and James Gorrell of same co. gent or either of them to ackn this indenture in open court. Memorandum: That 50 ft sq including the present burying ground being part of one of the within mentioned town lots is hereby excepted and reserved for the use of the afsd John Mifflin, Benjamin Mifflin & Nicholas Loockerman for a burying place for ever. {KEDELR N:235}

On 13 May 1757 William Shurmer of Kent Co. yeoman, John Mifflin and Benjamin Mifflin of Phila merchants as the heirs and legal representatives of a certain Benjamin Shermur dec'd. for 50 pounds quit claim unto Vincent Loockerman of the Town of Dover Kent Co., merchant, a tract of land in Murtherkill Hundred called *Brinckles Rainge*. {KEDELR P:39}

John Mifflin [of Kent Co. DE] d. leaving a will dated 1720, proved 9

Dec 1720. Heirs: sons Benjamin, John; servant Samuel Greenwood; friend Timothy Hanson; bros. & sisters not named; Israel Pemberton; Clymon Plomstead. Execs., Israel Pemberton & Clymon Plomstead. Wits., Samuel Greenwood, Richard Smith, Rachell Hillyard. {Arch. A35:8. Reg. of Wills, D:27-28}

John and Sarah were parents of the following children: BENJAMIN and JOHN.

6. JONATHAN MIFFLIN, son of John (2) and Elizabeth Mifflin, b. 12th da, 4th mo, 1704, m. Sarah Robinson in Philadelphia on 30th da, 3rd mo, 1723. {PMM}

Sarah Mifflin, wife of Jonathan, d. 29th da, 5th mo, 1745. {PMM}

Jonathan was at liberty to marry Rebecca Evans on 28th da, 8th mo, 1752. {PMM}

Jonathan Mifflin bur. 15th da, 10th mo, 1781, age 78.

Jonathan and Sarah were parents of the following children {PMM}: SAMUEL, b. 13th da, 12th mo, 1724/5; ELIZABETH, b. 19th da, 3rd mo, 1727; SARAH, b. 16th da, 8th mo, 1729; LIDDYA, bur. 5th da, 1st mo, 1732; PATIENCE, b. 3rd da, 11th mo, 1735/6; JONATHAN, d. 1st da, 9th mo, 1738; JONATHAN, d. 16th da, 6th mo, 1745.

7. SAMUEL MIFFLIN, son of John (2) and Elizabeth Mifflin, d. 1st da, 8th mo, 1724.

On 24th da, 9th mo, 1721, application was made for a certificate for Samuel Mifflin, who intended a voyage to the West Indies. {PMM}

Fourth Generation

8. DANIEL MIFFLIN, son of Edward (3) Mifflin, m. 1st Mary Warner of Kent Co., MD on 15th da, 9th mo, 1744 at Cecil Meeting. {Cecil Monthly Meeting; Whitelaw:1373}. They resided in Accomac Co., VA.

They were parents of the following children {DCMM}: WARNER, b. 21st da, 8th mo, 1745; EDWARD, b. 15th da, 7th mo, 1747, died an infant; ANN, b. 2nd da, 10th mo, 1748, d. an infant; SARAH, b. 10th da, 2nd mo, 1751; DANIEL, b. 7th da, 4th mo, 1754, m. Debby Howell of Philadelphia.

Daniel Mifflin of Accomack Co., VA, farmer, and Ann Walker of the same place, having consent of parents and parties concerned, m. 17th da, 10th mo, 1757 at Little Creek Meeting House, Kent Co. {DCMM} Ann was dau. of John Walker of Accomack Co. {Whitelaw:1216}

Daniel m. 3rd Mary Pusey. {*Life and Ancestry of Warner Mifflin*:15, by Hilda Justice}

Daniel d. leaving a will dated 22 Dec 1795, proved 27 April 1796. Mentioned: sons Warner Mifflin, Daniel Mifflin; grandson Jonathan Walker Mifflin; daus. Patience Hunn, Elizabeth Howell Eyre Mifflin, Rebecca Mifflin, and grandau. Ann Hunn. Refers to his former wife Ann. {Accomack Co. Wills 365}

Daniel and Ann were parents of the following children {DCMM}: WALKER, b. 5th da, 8th mo, 1758, d. 1st da, 3rd mo, 1790, m. Sarah Blundel; MARY, b. 11th da, 6th mo, 1760, m. Nathaniel Hunn; ANN, b. 10th da, 10th mo, 1762; ELIZABETH, b. 18th da, 2nd mo, 1765; PATIENCE, b. 17th da, 12th mo, 1766, m. Jonathan Hunn; ELIZABETH, b. 5th da, 10th mo, 1769, m. Samuel F. Howell; SARAH, b. 21st da, 5th mo, 1773; EYRE, b. 26th da, 6th mo, 1774, m. Thomas Berry of Cecil Monthly Meeting; REBECCA, b. 21st da, 1st mo, 1777, m. Joseph Galloway Rowland, son of Isaiah and Ann Rowland.

9. SAMUEL MIFFLIN, son of Edward (3) Mifflin. A certificate was received from Accomack Co., VA, for Samuel Mifflin on 26th da, 9th mo, 1747. {PMM}
Samuel was father of the following children {mentioned in the will of Mary Mifflin, mother of Samuel}: EDWARD; MARY.

10. SOUTHY MIFFLIN of Swan Gutt, Accomack Co., VA, son of Edward (3) Mifflin, m. Johana Thomas of Kent Co., MD, 13th da, 6th mo, 1753, at the house of George Rasin in Kent Co. {Cecil Monthly Meeting}

11. JOHN MIFFLIN, son of George (4) Mifflin, m. Sarah (N).

John d. 10th da, 2nd mo, 1759. {PMM}

John Mifflin, City of Philadelphia, merchant, d. leaving a will dated 7 Feb 1759, proved 26 Feb 1759. wife: Sarah. Children: Thomas and George. Sister Sarah. Exec.: Sarah and Thomas Mifflin, Joseph Saunders. Witnesses: Hannah Moore, Rachel Hill, William Sturgeon. {Philadelphia Wills L:217}

John was father of the following children: MARY, d. 3rd da, 4th mo, 1742 {PMM}; ELIZABETH, d. 18th da., 5th mo, 1742 {PMM}; BENJAMIN, d. 14th da, 11th mo, 1747 {PMM}; SARAH, d. 19th da, 2nd mo, 1750 {PMM}; ELIZABETH, d. 2nd da, 10th mo, 1750 {PMM}; THOMAS {Will of his father}; GEORGE {Will of his father}.

12. SARAH MIFFLIN, dau. of George (4) Mifflin, m. 7th da, 6th mo, 1759, Jacob Lewis, son of Henry of Philadelphia, late of Haverford of Chester Co., dec'd., at Philadelphia Monthly Meeting. {PMM}

13. JOHN MIFFLIN of the city of Philadelphia, carpenter, son of John (5) Mifflin of Kent Co., on Delaware, dec'd., and Hannah Taylor of the city afsd, dau. of Joseph Taylor of said city, dec'd., m. 7th da, 3rd mo, 1747. {PMM}

On 26th da, 1st mo, 1742, John Mifflin, son of John Mifflin, dec'd., was provided a certificate to Friends at Little Creek. {PMM}

On 15 July 1748 John Mifflin of Philadelphia, carpenter, and Hannah his wife, Benjamin Mifflin of same place, carpenter, and Hannah his wife and Nicholas Loockerman of Dover Hundred, Kent Co., gent., and Hester his wife for £200 sold to Nicholas Ridgely of the Town of Dover Kent Co., five tracts of land. {KEDELR}

On 22 Nov 1759 John Mifflin Junr. of Philadelphia, merchant, and Hannah his wife and William Shurmer of Kent Co., yeoman, and Sarah his wife, for £45 sold to James Carbine of Kent Co., yeoman, a tract of land. {KEDELR P:191}

14. BENJAMIN MIFFLIN, son of John (5) Mifflin, m. 1st Hannah (N) and m. 2nd Sarah, widow of Lawrence Riley.

On 30th da, 2nd mo, 1742, Benjamin Mifflin brought in a paper condemning his breach of discipline respecting marriage. {PMM}

On 2 Dec 1746 Benjamin Mifflin and Hannah his wife of Philadelphia and Nicholas Loockerman and Hester his wife, William Shurmer and Mary his wife, Joseph Nixon and Margrett his wife and John Mifflin of Kent Co. for £16 sold to Roger Pugh of Chester Co. PA but now of Kent Co., cooper, a tract of land on the head of Duck Creek adj. the Town of Salisbury adj. the ground belonging to the Meeting House of the people called Quakers ... 8 a. and also another lott a little below the Town of Salisbury front of the New Mill House to Duck Creek ... 4 a. both of which said pieces of land were taken out of a tract of 500 a. called *Graves End.* {KEDELR N:146}

Hannah Mifflin, dau. of Benjamin, d. 10th da, 6th mo, 1746. {PMM}

Elizabeth Mifflin, dau. of Benjamin, d. 8th da, 6th mo, 1750. {PMM}

Benjamin Mifflin, son of Benjamin, d. 14th da, 11th mo, 1758. {PMM}

On 28th da, 12th mo, 1764 Hannah, wife of Benjamin Mifflin, requested to become a member of the Society of Friends. {PMM}

On 10th da, 10th mo, 1765, Hannah McCarty, late Mifflin, reported as married contrary to discipline. {PMM}

On 27 da, 8th mo, 1768, a certificate was produced from Philadelphia Monthly Meeting for Benjamin Mifflin and wife Hannah, and their children, Elizabeth, Esther, Susanna and Benjamin, dated 29th da, 3rd mo, 1765. {DCMM}

On 23rd da, 2nd mo, 1771 a certificate was received by Philadelphia Monthly Meeting for Benjamin Mifflin, wife and son, from Duck Creek Monthly Meeting. {PMM}

Benjamin Mifflin d. leaving a will dated 1784, proved 7 June 1787. Heirs: wife Sarah Mifflin; son Benjamin Mifflin; daus. Hannah McCaskey (wife of Alexander), Elizabeth Draper (wife of Isaac), Susannah Caldwell (wife of Train) and Esther Irwin (wife of Matthew of Philadelphia); son in law Capt. John Ashmead. Extx., wife Sarah Mifflin. Wits., John Clowes, Esq., John Wilson Dean. {Sussex Co. Wills Arch. A88:157. Reg. of Wills, D:145}

On 26th da, 6th mo, 1773, a committee had dealt with Elizabeth Draper (formerly Mifflin) for accomplishing her marriage by the assistance of a priest with one not of the same society. {DCMM}

On 18 Dec 1780 Mariah, a Negro woman, aged 45, was manumitted by Benjamin Mifflin and his wife Sarah. Mariah was formerly the property of John Spencer, afterwards of Lawrence Riley by marriage with his widow, and on decease of said Riley, purchased by his widow Sarah, now the wife of Benjamin Mifflin. {SUDELR B:437}

Benjamin was father of the following children: MARY, m. Capt. John Ashmead; BENJAMIN; HANNAH, m. Alexander McCaskey; ELIZABETH, m. Isaac Draper; SUSANNAH, m. Train Caldwell; ESTHER, m. Matthew Irwin of Philadelphia.

15. SAMUEL MIFFLIN, son of Jonathan (6) Mifflin, b. 13th da, 12th mo, 1724/5, m. Rebekah Edgett, dau. of Simon Edgett.

It was reported on 28th da, 10th mo, 1750, that Samuel Mifflin, son of Jonathan Mifflin, and Rebekah his wife, dau. of Simon Edgett, dec'd., have lately married contrary to disclipline. {PMM}

Jonathan, son of Samuel Mifflin, bur. 30th da, 3rd mo, 1777, age 23. {PMM}

16. SARAH MIFFLIN, dau. of Jonathan (6) Mifflin, b. 16th da, 8th mo, 1729, m. John Jones, son of John of Philadelphia.

John Jones of the city of Philadelphia, merchant, son of John Jones, late of the city afsd, dec'd., and Sarah Mifflin, dau. of Jonathan Mifflin of the city afsd, m. 28th da, 8th mo, 1745. {PMM}

17. ELIZABETH MIFFLIN, dau. of Jonathan (6) Mifflin m. Morris Morris.

On 31st da, 11th mo, 1743, a certificate was issued for Morris Morris to marry Elizabeth Mifflin, from Gwynedd Monthly Meeting. {PMM}

Morris Morris of Upper Dublin in the county of Philadelphia, son of Morris Morris of Richland, county of Bucks and Elizabeth Mifflin, dau. of Jonathan Mifflin of the city of Philadelphia, m. 22nd da, 1st mo, 1743/4. {PMM}

18. PATIENCE MIFFLIN, dau. of Jonathan (6) and Sarah Mifflin of the Northern Liberties, b. 3rd da, 11th mo, 1735/6, m. 7th da, 10th mo, 1767, Isaac Paschall, merchant, son of Joseph of Philadelphia, dec'd. {PMM}

Fifth Generation

19. WARNER MIFFLIN, son of Daniel (8) and Mary Mifflin, b. 21st da, 8th mo, 1745, m. 1st Elizabeth Johns, dau. of James and Elizabeth Johns. {DCMM}

On 26th da, 3rd mo, 1768, there was a complaint from Mutherkill Preparative Meeting against Warner Mifflin for accomplishing his marriage with another Quaker with the assistance of a priest (a minister other than Quaker). {DCMM}

On 27th da, 8th mo, 1768, Elizabeth, wife of Warner Mifflin, appeared (as did Warner Mifflin) and offered a paper condemning for outgoing in marriage. {DCMM}

Elizabeth, wife of Warner Mifflin, d. 3rd da, 6th mo, 1786. {DCMM}

Warner and Elizabeth were parents of the following children {DCMM}: MARY, b. 21st da, 4th mo, 1768, d. 23rd da, 2nd mo, 1783; ELIZABETH, b. 14th da, 2nd mo, 1770, d. same day; ELIZABETH, 26th da, 1st mo, 1771, d. 29th da, 2nd mo, 1785; SARAH, b. 4th mo, 1773, d. 7th mo, 1773; ANN, b. 20th da, 9th mo, 1774, m. Warner Rasin, MD; WARNER, b. 6th da, 4th mo, 1777, d. 1848; SUSANNA, b. 24th da, 8th mo, 1779; HANNAH, b. 30th da, 10th mo, 1781, d. 5th da, 11th mo, 1785; SARAH, b. 9th da, 12th mo, 1784, m. Daniel Neall.

Warner produced a certificate from Duck Creek Monthly Meeting to marry Ann Emlen, Jr., dated 23rd da, 8th mo, 1788. {DCMM}

Warner Mifflin of Kent County on Delaware, son of Daniel Mifflin of Accomack Co., VA, and Mary his late wife, dec'd., and Ann Emlen, dau. of George Emlen. late of the city of Philadelphia, dec'd., and Anne his wife, m. this 9th day of the 10th month, 1788. {PMM}

On 28th da, 11th mo, 1788, Anne Mifflin, removed with her husband Warner Mifflin - to the Monthly Meeting at Motherkiln in Kent County, DE.

Warner and Ann were parents of the following children {DCMM}: SAMUEL E., b. 6th da, 4th mo, 1790; LEMUEL, b. 23rd da, 3rd mo, 1792; MARY ANNA, b. 3rd mo, 1795, d. 8th mo, 1795.

Warner Mifflin, d. 10th mo, 1798, age 54 years, bur. Motherkiln Meeting, son of Dan. Mifflin.

20. DANIEL MIFFLIN, son of Daniel (8) Mifflin, b. 7th da, 4th mo, 1754 m. Debbe Howell.

On 22nd da, 8th mo, 1778 Daniel Mifflin, Jr., requested a certificate in order for marriage with a woman who was a member of the monthly meeting of the Northern District of Philadelphia. {DCMM}

Daniel Mifflin of Kent County, Delaware, merchant, son of Daniel

Mifflin of Accomac Co., VA, and Mary his wife, dec'd, m. 6/10/1778, Debbe Howell, dau. of Samuel and Ann Howell of Philadelphia.

On 23rd da, 1st mo, 1779, Debbe Mifflin produced on her own behalf [along with her husband] a certificate from the monthly meeting of the Northern District of Philadelphia dated 24th of the 11th mo mo. last to Duck Creek Monthly Meeting. {DCMM}

They were parents of the following children {DCMM}: DANIEL, b. 30th da, 9th mo, 1779, d. 28th da, 12th mo, 1852; ANN, b. 28th da, 7th mo, 1781, unmarried; SAMUEL, b. 16th da, 1st mo, 1784, m. Ann Hunn of Nathaniel; JOSHUA HOWELL, b. 28th da, 8th mo, 1786; EDWARD, b. 5th da, 6th mo, 1789, d. 24th da, 4th mo, 1791; MARY, b. 25th da, 8th mo, 1791, m. Thomas Wilson and J. W. Mifflin; DEBBY, b. 26th da, 1st mo, 1794, d. 9th da, 10th mo, 1795; THOMAS, b. 13th da, 7th mo, 1796, m. Sarah Turner of Joseph who d. and m. Susan M. Kemp of Robert Bartlet.

Daniel Mifflin, Sr., d. 31st da, 12th mo, 1795. {DCMM} Nathaniel Hunn of Kent Co. DE, son of Jonathan Hunn, the same place, and Ann his wife, dec'd., and Mary Mifflin, dau. of Daniel Mifflin and Ann his wife of Accomack Co., VA, m. on 1st da, 8th mo, 1781, at a publick meeting at Murtherkill. {DCMM}

21. WALKER MIFFLIN, son of Daniel (8) Mifflin of Accomack Co., VA, and his wife Ann, dec'd., m. 1st da, 1st mo, 1789, Sarah Blundell, dau. of James Blundell of Kent Co., DE, and his wife Susanna, both dec'd. - at Little Creek Meeting. {DCMM}
Jonathan Walker, son of Walker and Sarah Mifflin, b. 2nd da, 1st mo, 1790. {DCMM}

22. MARY MIFFLIN, dau. of Daniel (8) and Ann Mifflin of Accomack Co., VA, m. 1st da, 8th mo, 1781, Nathaniel Hunn of Kent Co., son of Jonathan Hunn, and his wife Ann, dec'd. {DCMM}

23. THOMAS MIFFLIN of the city of Philadelphia, merchant, son of John Mifflin (10), late of the same place, dec'd., and Sarah Morris of the Northern Liberties, daughter of Morris Morris, late of the city aforesaid, deceased, mar this 4th day of the 3rd month, 1767. {PMM}

24. GEORGE MIFFLIN, of the city of Philadelphia, merchant, son of John (10) Mifflin, late of the same place, dec'd., and Martha Morris, dau. of Joseph and Martha Morris of Philadelphia aforesaid, m. this 15th day of the 10th month, 1772. {PMM}

25. SUSANNAH MIFFLIN, dau. of Benjamin (13) Mifflin, m. Train Caldwell. On 25th da, 1st mo, 1777 a committee dealt with Susanna Caldwell, late Mifflin, for going out in marriage. {DCMM}

On 22nd da, 11th mo, 1777, a certificate was produced for Benjamin Mifflin and his wife from Philadelphia Monthly Meeting dated 23rd da, 4th mo, 1777. {DCMM}

On 22nd da, 12th mo, 1770, application was made for a certificiate for Benjamin Mifflin, his wife and children, who have removed back to Philadelphia. {DCMM}

26. MARY MIFFLIN, dau. of Benjamin (14) Mifflin, m. John Ashmead, son of John and Ann (Rush) Ashmead. {PA Genealogies:667, 668}

The Philadelphia Monthly Meeting minutes dated 28th da, 1st mo, 1763, show that Mary Mifflin was disowned for marrying (N) Ashmead. Capt. John Ashmead is mentioned as son in law in the will of Benjamin Mifflin.

They were parents of the following children {PA Genealogies:668: JOHN; BENJAMIN; ANN; JOSEPH; WILLIAM; MARY; ELIZA.

27. HANNAH MIFFLIN, dau. of Benjamin (14) Mifflin, m. Alexander McCaskey.

On 28th da, 6th mo, 1771, Hannah McCaskey, late Mifflin, condemned her breach of discipline in marriage. {PMM}

Unplaced

On 28th da, 8th mo, 1762, BENJAMIN MIFFLIN and Samuel Massey regret their being concerned in buying and selling a negro slave.

On 23rd da, 2nd mo, 1771, BENJAMIN MIFFLIN, his wife and son were received by certificate from Duck Creek. {PMM}

CHARLES MIFFLIN, son of George Mifflin, Jr., b. 13th da, 12th mo, 1753. {PMM}

A certificate was received from Boston for ELIZABETH MIFFLIN, lately married on 10th da, 9th mo, 1737. {PMM}

On 30th da, 11th mo, 1764, BENJAMIN MIFFLIN expresses his sorrow for taking up arms in the 2nd month past. {PMM}

CHARLES MIFFLIN of Philadelphia, merchant, son of George Mifflin, dec'd, and Ann his wife, m. 11/2/1777, Mary Waln, dau of Richard and Mary Waln, late of Germantown, dec'd.

On 24th da, 4th mo, 1777, Mary Mifflin had removed to live with her husband, Charles, within the limits of Philadelphia Monthly Meeting for the Southern District. {PMM} Children of Charles and Mary Mifflin: SARAH, b. 20th da, 12th mo, 1777 and d. 23rd da, 8th mo, 1793; ANN, b. 16th da, 5th mo, 1779 and d. at Germantown.

Charles Mifflin d. 16/4/1783, age 29 yrs.

Mary Mifflin, dau of Charles, dec'd, d. 26/10/1785, age 2 yrs.

Mary Mifflin, widow of same, d. 20/2/1786, age 31 yrs.

On 31st da, 10th mo, 1794, ELIZABETH MIFFLIN was recommended to the Monthly Meeting for the Southern District.

ESTHER MIFFLIN d. 21st da, 9th mo, 1776, age 85 yrs. {PMM}

On 27th da, 7th mo, 1753, GEORGE MIFFLIN, Jr, and Ann his wife, have sometime since been married contrary to the rules of discipline. {PMM}

On 31st da, 10th mo, 1755, JOHN MIFFLIN and Sarah Fishbourne declared their intentions to marry, his parents and her guardian being present. {PMM}

On 30th da, 4th mo, 1756, JOHN MIFFLIN and Joseph Fox were disowned for being concerned in promoting and advising to the late Declaration against the Indians and offering rewards for scalping them. {PMM}

JOHN MIFFLIN d. 29th da, 5th mo, 1798, age 78 yrs. {PMM}

JONATHAN MIFFLIN of the city of Philadelphia, merchant, and Sarah Powell of the said city, widow, m. 9th day of the 11th month, 1758.

Mary Mifflin, wife of JONATHAN, d. 24th da, 12th mo, 1778, age 21 yrs. {PMM}

JOSEPH MIFFLIN d. 24th da, 1st mo, 1791, age 40 yrs. {PMM}

On 26th da, 5th mo, 1773, Joseph Mifflin, son of John Mifflin, on account of marriage was given a certificate to Chester Monthly Meeting held at Providence. {PMM}

On 30th da, 5th mo, 1774, Joseph Mifflin- from Chester Monthly Meeting, held at Providence. {PMM}

On 28th da, 11th mo, 1781, Deborah Mifflin, wife of Joseph Mifflin, who came received from Chester Monthly Meeting with her three children, Mary, Hannah and Joseph - to Nottinham. {PMM}

Deborah Mifflin, wife of Joseph, d. 14th da, 11th mo, 1789, age 36 yrs. {PMM}

MARTHA MIFFLIN d. 9th da, 1st mo, 1793, age 42 yrs. {PMM}

On 28th da, 9th mo, 1753, SAMUEL MIFFLIN, of Maryland, disowned for misdemeanor. {PMM}

On 28th da, 5th mo, 1756, SAMUEL MIFFLIN was granted a certificate to the Monthly Meeting at Haddenfield. {PMM}

On 28th da, 7th mo, 1775, THOMAS MIFFLIN, merchant, having for a considerable time past been active in the promotion of military measures, is disowned. {PMM}

THE MURPHEY FAMILY

1. NICHOLAS MURPHY

On 14 May 1752 Wm. Shirvan and Johannah his wife of Duck Creek Hundred Kent Co. for £39 released unto David Murphy of same place ... a tract of land (600 a. patent called *Pearmains Choice* granted and confirmed to Henry Pearmain) and he sold 100 a. to a certain Nicholas Murphy, father of afsd. David Murphy and Johanna the wife Wm. Shirvan, part of tract called *Pearmains Choice*, beginning on the w. branch of Duck Creek, being the corner of land formerly sold by said Pearmain to Wm. Edwards, it appears that the said Nicholas Murphy did give to his son Samuel Murphy, brother to said David Murphy and Johannah wife of Wm. Shirvan all the afsd. land, and Samuel is since dead, and David and Johannah the only surviving heirs of said Samuel Murphy ... 100 a. {KEDELR O:141}

On 10 Nov 1762 David Murphey of Duck Creek Hundred, Kent Co., yeoman, and Susanah his wife, for £110 sold to John Joy of same place a tract of land, whereas a certain Henry Pearmain did obtain a patent for a tract of land in Duck Creek Hundred on s. side of the s.w. branch of Duck Creek called *Pearmains Choice* and did sell a tract unto a certain Ralph Prime beginning on Western Branch bounded by 200 a. formerly sold by the said Henry Pearmain to William Edwards ... 100 a., and Ralph Prime did sell the afsd. 100 a. to Nicholas Murphey father of the said David Murphey, and by his will Nicholas Murphey did give the land to his son Samuel Murphey who died intestate and without issue, and having 1 brother, to wit the said David Murphey, and 1 sister named Johanah who intermarried with a certain William Shirvan, and the said Shirvan and Johanah his wife did sell their right of the afsd. tract to the said David Murphey. {KEDELR Q:118}

NICHOLAS MURPHEY was father of the following sons: DAVID, m. Susannah (N); SAMUEL, d. before 14 May 1752; JOHANAH, m. William Shirvan.

Second Generation

2. DAVID MURPHY, son of Nicholas (1) Murphy, m. Susannah (N) who later m. Thomas Herwood.

On 13 April 1752 David Murphy of Duck Creek Hundred and Susannah his wife for £39 sold to Wm. Shirvan of same place a tract of land, whereas Henry Pearmain did obtain a 600 a. patent called *Pearmains Choice* on w. branch of Duck Creek to Pearmains Branch and he did give 1/2 of all his land to his wife Wadder, and Wadder Pearmain his widdow and Wm. Reynolds, son of afsd. Wadder sold to Nicholas Murphy 60 a. of the land (Book H, fol. 18) part of the afsd. tract adj. Nicholas Murphy's land, and Nicholas did bequeath the same to his son ye afsd. David Murphy (Book F, N9 fol. 2) ... 60 a. {KEDELR O:137}

David Murphey d. by 19 Nov 1770 when Susannah Murphey, widow, was appointed admx. of his estate. {Reg. of Wills, L:85} Note: Arch. A87:85 shows that Susannah Murphey later married Thomas Herwood.

3. JOAHANAH MURPHEY, dau. of Nicholas (1) Murphey, m. William Shirvan.

On 15 Nov 1752 William Shirvan of Duck Creek Hundred, Kent Co., yeoman, and Johanah his wife, for £14 sold to John Joy of same place a tract of land called *Pearmains Choice* in Duck Creek Hundred on s. side of Duck Creek and Pearmain did by his will give to his wife Waddy 1/2 of his real estate and pursuant to the will she together with William Reynolds her son did sell to a certain Nicholas Murphey part of the tract called *Pearmains Choice* adj. Nicholas Murphey's land, 60 a., and he did will the 60 a. to his son David Murphey and he sold the same to the afsd. William Shirvan. {KEDELR O:162}

Unplaced

(N) MURPHY m. Jean Boogs, dau. of William Boogs.

William Boogs d. leaving a Will dated 25 Nov 1771, proved 21 Dec 1771. Heirs: daus. Elizabeth Kearsey, Jean Murphy, Esther Boogs; sons John, Joseph and David. Execs., dau. Esther. Wits., James Caldwell, John Meekins, Ann Darling. {Arch. A4:184. Reg. of Wills, L:105}

On 25 May 1739 was made a deposition. Whereas some evill disposed persons have reported that I William Phillips have said that the Reverand Arthur Usshuer keeps a whore in his house named ANN MURPHY and that I saw her on Monday the 21st this instant May early in the morning undressed and in her bed and that he had but just risen from her, these are to certifie that the report is altogether false and groundless and that I never saw any immodest familiarity between them. {KEDELR M:pg 24}

CHARLES MURFEE m. Catherine (N).

On 15 Sep 1685 Charles Murfee and Catherine his wife assigned unto William Durvall of Kent Co. a tract of land. {KEDELR}

The Kent Co. Rent Roll, 1681-1688 shows Charles Murphy, owing rent on the tract *Gravesend*, 600 a. {Bendler:4}

DANIEL MURPHY m. Hannah Jacobs 22 Nov 1766. {Lewes and Coolspring Presbyerian Church}

ESTHER MURPHEY d. by 24 May 1774 when Thomas Murphey was appointed admin. {Reg. of Wills, L:154}

Petition of James Justice ca. 1737 that about five years ago Mary Boardman dec'd. on her death bed requested petitioner's wife take her child named REBECCA MURPHY into her care and tuition until she came of age. That petitioner has since her mother's decease had her child in care. He requests he and wife continue to care for her. {KEORCF Murphy, Rebecca - ca. 1737}

THOMAS MURPHY m. Jane (N).

On 19 Nov 1761 Thomas Murphy of Murtherkill Hundred, Kent Co., yeoman, and Jane his wife, for £280 sold to Timothy Mckeever now of same place yeoman ... a parcel of land and plantation whereon the said Timothy Mckeever now dwells in the forist of Murtherkill Hundred adj. the lands of Evan Lewis, *Howels Lott* ... 105 a., 154 perches, also one other small lott adj. the afsd. premisses surveyed for said Thomas Murphy by virtue of a warrant 12 March 1761 ... 4 a., 84 7/10 perches. {KEDELR Q:72}

THOMAS MURPHEW (Murphey) m. Rachel King, dau. of Richard King.

On 10 Feb 1731 Thomas Murphey of Kent Co., yeoman, and Rachell his wife, dau. and heiress to Richard King, late of Kent Co., dec'd., for £30 sold to Richard Dawson of same co. a tract of land (whereas Thomas Murphey in right of his wife Rachell became seized in a tract of land) on the s.w. branch of Duck Creek bounded by the Wild Branch ... 50 a. {KEDELR K:125}

On 11 Feb 1735 Thomas Murphew of Kent Co., yeoman, for £25 sold to John Hawkins of same place a tract of land (whereas Richard Dawson, the younger son of Richard Dawson the elder, both now dec'd., did become seized of 75 a. of land as one half of 150 a. of land left to him by the will of his father, and Richard Dawson the younger in his life time had the half part of the land divided out from the the other half and 10 Feb 1731 sold the same to Thomas Murphew. On 11 Feb 1735 Rachel Murphew wife of Thomas Murphew doth consent to the a deed of bargain and sale and every cause thereof doth hereby asign over all her right, title, interest, claim and demand to 75 a. of land to John Hawkins. {KEDELR L:125, 126}

THOMAS MURPHEY m. Sarah, widow of John Butcher. Butcher, John. Yeoman. Admin. of, to Sarah Butcher, widow. Dec. 29, 1760. Reg. of Wills, Liber K, folio 248. Note:Arch. vol. A7, page 8 shows Sarah, the widow, later married Thomas Murphey.

THOMAS MURPHEY m. Margaret Hendrickam, widow of Moses Henrickam.

Moses Hendricham [Hendrickam] d. leaving a will dated 11 May 1748, proved 21 May 1748. Heirs: wife Marget; sons John, Moses; dau. Mary; sister Keitren. Extx., wife Marget. Wits., Nicholas Lockerman, William Rees, John Ross. {Arch. A23:131-132. Reg. of Wills, 1:222-223} Note: Arch. A23:182 shows Margaret later married Thomas Murphey.

On 15 Nov 1752 Thomas Murphey of Kent Co., black smith, and Margret his wife, for £140 sold to Samuel Barnit of same place, taylor, a tract of land called *Blacksheirs Range* in the forrist of Dover Hundred on s. side of Dover River ... 100 a. {KEDELR O:160}

THOMAS MURPHY m. Margaret Moran.

Daniel McDavett, yeoman of Duck Creek, d. leaving a will dated 27 Feb 1759, proved 29 Aug 1759. Heirs: dau. Jane; Margaret Moran; Christopher Wan. Execs., Jacob Allee, Sr., and James McMullan, merchant. Trustee, motherin-law Jane Keith. Wits., Peter McGlew, John Mason, Patrick Moran. {Arch. A32:158-160, 162. Reg. of Wills, K:212} Note: Arch. A32:159-160 show Jane (Jean] later married Thomas Alston; Margaret Moran later married Thomas Murphy.

THOMAS MURPHEY d. by 30 Sep 1771 when Margrett Murphey, widow, was appointed admx. of his estate. {Arch. A37:104. Reg. of Wills, L:100}

WILLIAM MURPHEY m. Sarah (N).

William Murphey, yeoman, d. by 29 Aug 1760 when Sarah Murphey, widow, was appointed admx. of his estate. {Reg. of Wills, K:237-238} The admin. of the estate was later assigned to Thomas Harwood on 13 Oct 1760. {Reg. of Wills, K:242}

Sarah Murphy of Little Creek Hundred d. leaving a will dated 7 Oct 1760, proved 11 Oct 1760. Heirs: daus. Sarah and Rebecca; son Benjamin. Exec., bro. Paradee Courtney. Wits., Sarah Paradee, Mary Stewart, Daniel Smith. {Arch. A37:103. Reg. of Wills, K:241-242} Note: Will mentions husband William Murphy, dec'd.

William and Sarah were parents of the following children: SARAH; REBECCA; BENJAMIN.

WILLIAM MURPHEY m. Rebecca Denny, dau. of Philip Denny.

On 24 Feb 1773 in a petition of William Murphey he stated that Philip Denney was seized in his demesne died intestate leving sundry children among whom his said lands did descend and petitioner m. Rebecca Denny who was a dau. of said Philip Denny, dec'd., who has lately died also leaving issue one child named Nicholas Murphey who is the only heir of said Rebecca Denny and son of petitioner. {KEORCF Murphey, Nicholas - 1773}

THE NEEDHAM FAMILY

The first portion of this lineage is drawn from *The Welcome Claimants Proved, Disproved and Doubtful* by George E. McCracken, PhD., F.A.S.G., F.A.A.R., hereafter cited as Welcome Claimants.

1. EDMUND NEEDHAM.

Second Generation

2. EZEKIEL NEEDHAM, son of Edmund (1) Needham, was father of the following children {Welcome Claimants}[41]: SARAH, b. 27 May 1674; EZEKIEL, b. Dec 1676, d. Dec 1676; EZEKIEL, b. 15 Nov 1677; DANIEL, b. 15 March 1679/80; RALPH, b. 26 Aug 1682; EDMUND.[42]

On 10 Feb 1696/7 Ezekiell Needham of Kent Co. PA for love good will and affection gave to his well beloved son Ezekiell Needham a tract of land on s. side of Dover River being part of a 350 a. tract of land which he purchased of Thomas and Henry Bedwell of afsd. co., being part of a 1100 a. tract of land which said Thomas, Henry and Robert Bedwell and Adam Fisher took up and pattented called *The Long Reatch* beginning at the corner of Edmund Needham's land, 100 a. {KEDELR}

On 10 May 1697 Ezekiell Needham of Kent Co. PA for love and good will and affection gave to Edmund Needham, son of said Ezekiell Needham, a tract of land being part of a tract of land taken up by Thomas Bedwell, Henry Bedwell, Robert Bedwell and Adam Fisher, 100 a. {KEDELR}

On 10 Aug 1697 Ezekiell Needham of Kent Co. PA, for love good will and affection gave to his well beloved son Daniell Needham a tract of land on s. side of Dover River ... at the corner of his son Ezekiell Needham's land, part of a tract of land called *The Longwatch*, 100 a. {KEDELR}

Ca. 1697 Ezekiell Needham acknowledged a deed for 100 a. to his son Ezekiel Needham and a deed for 50 a. to Timothy Thorold. {Kent Ct.:103}

On 7 Aug 1731 Ralph Needham of Kent Co. yeoman for £20 sold to Mark Bardon of same place yeoman ... a tract of land whereas Ezekeil Needham, Junr., by sundry good conveyances became possessed of the 100 a.

---

41 Refers to an old Needham Bible that came down in the Cowgill family but has disappeared, printed in 1728 and purchased by the Cowgill family in 1829.

42 Shown below received a gift of land from his father, but not shown in the Needham Bible as quoted in Welcome Claimants Proved. {Welcome Claimants: 124}

called *Hammer Smith* and sold same to Ezekeil Needham, Senr., and he dyed possessed of the land and it descended to Daniel Needham his son and heir and he quitt claimed it unto Ralph Needham his brother, party to these presents. {KEDELR K:95}

Ezekiel was father of the following children: EZEKIEL; EDMUND; DANIELL; RALPH.

3. EDMUND NEEDHAM, son of Ezekiel (2) Needham, m. 24 Nov 1692, Anna Price, widow of John Price and dau. of Thomas Hewthat. Edmund d. by 10 Aug 1725.

On 22 Nov 1692 Edmund Needham and Anna Price both of Kent Co. have intentions of marriage and publish same. Arthur Meston, Clerk. {KEDELR}

On 24 Nov 1692 is announced the marriage of Edmond Needham and Anna Price who hath in solemn manner taken each other in holy estate of marriage. Wit: John Walker justice, Edmond Needham, Anna Needham, Thomas Heathard, Ezekell Needham, Henry Bedwell, Robert Edmond, John Robbison, Anna Heathard, Ellinor Needham, Ellinor Robbison, Sarah Bedwell, Prisilla Edmonds, Mellisent Bedwell, Robert Bedwell, William Nicolls, Adam Fisher, Stephen Simons, Thomas Skidmore.

Edmd. Needham is shown on the 1693 Tax Assessment List of Kent Co. {Bendler:24}

Thomas Hewthat mentions his dau. Ann Needham in his will written 29 Nov 1695, proved 24 Dec 1695. Heirs: daus. Priscilla Edmunds [Edmonds], Ann Needham, Elliner Robisson, Mellesent Bedwell; grandchildren not named; son Ralph Hewthat; son-in-law Robert Edmunds. Execs., son-in-law Robert Edmunds, Alexander Grans, schoolmaster. Wits., Henry Bedwell, Isaac Baker. {Arch. A23:196. Reg. of Wills, A:20}

On 10 Sep 1700 Thomas Price of Sussex Co., PA, planter, the only brother of John Price, late of Kent Co. PA, dec'd., whereas Thomas Heathard and Anna his wife, late of Kent Co., dec'd., by their deed bearing date 20 Feb 1687 for and in consideration of a marriage then had and solemnized betweene the said Thomas Heatherd and Anna his wife, dec'd., ... give unto their then son in law the said John Price, dec'd., his heirs all that tract of land of the said Thomas Heatherd, dec'd., which he then lived upon called *Ousbey*, beginning at the corner of John Robeson's land ... 200 a. ... Anna, widdow and relict of said John Price, dec'd., is since m. Edmund Needham of Kent Co. and none of the issue of the said John Price, dec'd., being at this day left alive but all of them are also since, dec'd., ... in consideration of the love good will and affection which he beareth unto the said Edmund Needham and Anna his wife as alsoe for £5 ... Thomas Price quitt claimes afsd. tract of land. {KEDELR}

On 2 Nov 1700 Edmond Needham and Anna his wife both of Kent Co., PA, for £63 sold to John Robeson of same co. ... a tract of land called *Cumberland* on upperside of Murder Creek, being taken out of a tract of land formerly belonging to Thomas Heatherd called *Ousbey* beginning at corner of John Robeson's land ... 200 a. {KEDELR F:14}

Shown in the Kent Co. Quit Rents, 1701-713, is the entry, Ezekiel Needham now Edmd. Needham, 300 (acres) purchased of Tho: Bedwell he to clear all rents. {Bendler:35}

On 14 Nov 1710 John Hall of Murtherkill Hundred Kent Co. yeoman for £50 sold to John Redman of same place bricklayer, a tract of land in

Murtherkill Hundred ... 105 a. and hath been purchased severally by Thomas Heathers, Edmond Needham and Anna his wife, Richard Shurley and Ezekiel Needham, dec'd., but now in the tenure of John Hall. {KEDELR E:278}

On 20 May 1713 Elenor Robertson wife of John Robertson of Kent Co., dau. and coheir of Thomas Hewthate of same co., yeoman, dec'd., whereas said Thomas Hewthate in his lifetime was seized of a tract of land, part of a greater tract on Mutherkill Creek called *Ousby* and by his will did give and bequeath his land to his son Ralph Hewthat and failing him said Ralph's heirs the said land to be equally divided among his four daus, Prisala Edmonds wife of Robert Edmonds, Anne Needum wife of Edmond Needum and the said Elenor Robertson wife of John Robertson and Mellecent Bedwell wife of Thomas Bedwell and whereas said Ralph Hewthat is since dec'd. without heirs of his body begotten the said lands were by the will vested in the said Prisalla, Anne, Elenor and Mellecent. {KEDELR E:89}

At the meeting of 16th da., 1st mo., 1713 no one was present to report the marriage of Moses Whiteacre and Ann Needham. {DCMM}

On 10 Aug 1725 Daniel Needham of Kent Co. gent for £80 sold to Wateman (Waitman) Sipple, Junr., of the same place, yeoman, a tract of land on n. side of Murther Creek in Murtherkill Hundred, 300 a., being part of a 1600 a. tract conveyed by Thomas Heathert unto Edmond Needham, dec'd., brother in the whole blood to the afsd. Daniel Needham and is now in the occupation of Wateman Sipple beginning at a corner of John Price's land ... 1/4 a. of land including that part thereof where the said Edmond Needham, dec'd., the brother, is buried and is always excepted out of the said 300 a. and is wholly reserved as a burying place. {KEDELR H:134}

4. DANIEL NEEDHAM, b. 15 March 1679/80, son of Ezekiel (2) Needham, m. Elizabeth, widow of John Nickolson.

On 1 Dec 1709 Daniell Needham of Kent Co., yeoman, and Elizabeth his wife relict and executrix of the will of John Nickolson late of same co., dec'd., for £50 sold to Joshua Clayton of same co., yeoman, a tract of land on Little Creek called *Northamtom* ... to corner of George Morgan's land ... 100 a. ... whereas John Nickollson by his will bequeathed to afsd. Elizabeth his then wife afsd. tract of land. {KEDELR D:75}

5. RALPH NEEDHAM, son of Ezekiel (2) Needham, m. 1720 Phebe Bunting.

On 18th da., 5th mo., 1720 the orderly marriage of Ralph Needham and Phebe Bunting was reported. {DCMM}

On 12 Feb 1746 Ralph Needham of Little Creek Hundred, yeoman, and Phebe his wife for £10 sold to Daniel Needham of Dover Hundred same co., yeoman ... a piece of marsh in Little Creek Hundred being part of an island of marsh surrounded by the water of the main s.w. branch of Duck Creek which was surveyed for the said Ralph Needham in pursuance of a warrant bearing date 27 Aug 1742 ... 100 a. {KEDELR N:119}

On 15 May 1747 Ralph Needham of Little Creek Hundred, Kent Co., yeoman, and Phebe his wife for 20 shillings sold to Nicholas Loockerman ... a small tract of marsh in an island by the s.w. branch of Duck Creek in Little Creek Hundred bounded by Daniel Needham's marsh ... 72 1/2 a., being part of an island called *Needham's Island* surveyed unto Ralph Needham in pursuance of a warrant bearing date 27 Aug 1742. {KEDELR N:150}

On 15 May 1747 Ralph Needham of Little Creek Hundred Kent Co., yeoman, and Phebe his wife for £2 sold to John Cowgill of same place yeoman ... a small tract of marsh in an island which is formed by the water of the main s.w. branch of Duck Creek in Little Creek Hundred beginning at Ralph Needham's bridge, to corner of Nicholas Lookerman's marsh ... 23 1/2 a. being part of *Needham's Island* surveyed unto Ralph Needham in pursuance of a warrant bearing date 27 Aug 1742. {KEDELR N:174}

Ralph Needham d. by 7 March 1752 when Phebee Needham, widow, was appointed admx. of his estate. {Arch. A37:156-157. Reg. of Wills, K:55}

On 28 Aug 1753 a commission was appointed to make division and distribution of lands and tenements of Ralph Needham, dec'd. [in Little Creek Neck and Hundred], between the widow and surviving children and legal representatives of said Ralph Needham, to wit, Phebe the afsd. widow and relict of said Ralph Needham, Benjamin Needham eldest son of said Ralph; Chaslinea, wife of William Maxwell; Rachel, wife of Thomas Brown; Sarah Needham; Lydia Needham and Ezekiel Needham, the youngest son. [The boundaries are described and a plat is shown.] {KEORCF Needham, Ralph - 1758-69}

On 14 Nov 1764 Thomas Parry of Kent Co. yeoman and Sarah his wife lately Sarah Needham one of the daus. and heirs of Ralph Needham late of same co., yeoman, dec'd., sold to William Killen of same co., atty at law, part of a tract of land, whereas the afsd. Ralph Needham in his lifetime was seized in a tract of land called *Mount Pleasant* in Little Creek Neck and Hundred and being so seized died intestate leaving issue, the afsd. Sarah Parry and several other sons and daus, and after the death of Ralph Needham by virtue of an order of an Orphans Court held 28 Aug 1753, the said tract of land was divided among the said children and widow, the division allotted and laid off to the said Sarah Parry, 62 a. {KEDELR Q:282}

On 25 Oct 1766 Thomas Brown of Chester Co. PA, weaver, and Rachel his wife, one of the daus. of Ralph Needham late of Kent Co., yeoman, dec'd., for £140, sold to Thomas Perry of Kent Co., a tract of land, whereas the said Ralph Needham in his lifetime became seized in a tract of land called *Mount Pleasant* in Little Creek Neck and Hundred and being so seized died intestate leaving issue, the said Rachel and 5 other sons and daus., by virtue of an order of the justices of the Orphans Court on 28 Aug 1753 the tract was divided among the sons and daus. of Ralph Neeham and Phebee his widow ... beginning at land late of Joshua Clayton now, dec'd. ... 62 a. {KEDELR R:110}

On 15 Jun 1767 Thomas Perry of Kent Co. and Sarah his wife, Joseph Price of said co., yeoman, and Lydia his wife and Benjamin Needham and Ezekiel Needham of said co., yeomen, which said Sarah Perry, Lydia Price, Benjamin Needham and Ezekiel Needham were sons and daus. of Ralph Needham of Kent Co. yeoman, dec'd., for £145 sold to Thomas Irons of same co. ... part of a tract of land, whereas the said Ralph Needham in his life time was seized in a 548 a. tract of land called *Mount Pleasant* in Little Creek Hundred adj. the lands late of Timothy Hanson and Joshua Clayton, dec'd., land of the said Thomas Irons and land called *Chippingnorton* and being so seized died intestate whereby the tract of land descended to the afsd. sons and daus. ... 62 a. {KEDELR R:201}

Phebee Needham d. by 14 Feb 1769 when son Ezekiel Needham was appointed admin. of her estate. {Reg. of Wills, L:53}

On 1 March 1769 appeared Benjamin Needham, Ezekiel Needham and

Thomas Parry, three of the heirs and legal representatives of Phebe Needham, dec'd., and by their petition prayed the court would appoint a commission to divide certain lands which were alloted to her as her thirds of her husband. {KEORCF Needham, Phebe - 1769}

Ralph was father of the following children {DCMM}: DANIEL, b. 19th(?) da., 6th mo., 1722; JOSHUA, b. 12th da., 11th mo., 1724/5; BENJAMIN, b. 6th da., 3rd mo., 1731; SARAH, b. 8th da., 5th mo., 1733, m. Thomas Perry; LYDIA, b. 8th da., 5th mo., 1733, m. Joseph Price; EZEKIEL; RACHEL, b. 14th da., 6th mo., 1727, m. Thomas Brown; CHASLINEA, m. William Maxwell.

Third Generation

6. DANIEL NEEDHAM, son of Ralph (5) Needham, recorded his cattle mark on 11 Jan 1726. {Kent Ct.:87}

Daniel Needham is mentioned in the will of Matthew Manlove who d. leaving a will dated 16 April 1743, proved 6 May 1743. Heirs: wife Mary; son George; daus. Mary, Elizabeth, Susanna, Sarah; bro. Jonathan. Extx., wife. Wits., John Brinckle, John Clark, Isaac King. {Arch. A32:44-46. Reg. of Wills, I:53} Page 44 mentions Daniel Needham and wife Mary Manlove; page 45 mentions father Matthew Manlove, dec'd; page 46 shows that Mary Manlove was wife of Phillip Reasin; mentions Benjamin Reasin, son of Phillip.

Daniel Needham, yeoman, d. by 28 Dec 1756 when his estate was administered by Susannah Needham, widow. {Arch. A37:142. Reg. of Wills, K:154}

7. EZEKIEL NEEDHAM, son of Ralph (5) Needham.

On 23rd da., 6th mo., 1770 a complaint was made against Ezekiel Needham, son of Ralph Needham, for accomplishing his marriage by assistance of a Priest (minister of another denomination) with a woman not of the Society. {DCMM}

8. SARAH NEEDHAM, dau. of Ralph (5) Needham of Little Creek, dec'd., m. 8th da., 3rd mo., 1764, Thomas Parry of Little Creek Hundred. {DCMM} Thomas Parry and his wife Sarah were parents of the following children: MARGARET, b. 12th da., 12th mo., 1764, d. 11th da., 8th mo., 1766; PHEBE, b. 27th da., 12th mo., 1766; NEEDHAM, b. 24th da., 9th mo., 1768; SARAH, b. 1770, d. 25th da., 10th mo., 1771; ---(dau.), b. 9th mo., 1772; THOMAS, b. 9th(?) da., 7th mo., 1775. Sarah, wife of Thomas Parry, d. 11th da., 10th mo., 1778. {DCMM}

On 22nd da., 12 mo., 1755 a certificate was prepared for Sarah Needham to recommend her to Nottingham Monthly Meeting. {DCMM}

On 28 Nov 1764 William Killen of Kent Co. atty at law for £100 sold to Thomas Parry of the same co., yeoman, ... a tract of land in Little Creek Neck and Hundred near the land of Thomas Irons ... 52 a., part of a larger tract called *Mount Pleasant* whereof Ralph Needham late of said co. yeoman, dec'd., died seized in and in the division was allotted to Sarah Needham his dau., now wife of Thomas Parry, also all his share of a parcel of marsh near Greens Creek in Little Creek Neck and Hundred ... {KEDELR R:2}

9. RACHEL NEEDHAM, dau. of Ralph (5) Needham of KE Co., m. Thomas Brown, son of Thomas Brown of East Nottingham of Chester Co., PA, dec'd.,

on 21st da., 12th mo., 1748/9 at Little Creek Meeting House. {Duck Creek Monthly Meeting}

Rachel was taken ill on 19th da., 4th mo., 1780 and d. 5th mo. following, about 7 a.m.; buried at East Nottingham on 13th da., 5th mo., 1780. {Nottingham Monthly Meeting}

10. BENJAMIN NEEDHAM, son of Ralph (5) Needham, b. 6th da., 3rd mo., 1731, m. c1769.

On 25th da., 2nd mo., 1769, Benjamin Needham acknowledged his outgoing in marriage. {DCMM}

Unplaced

On 10th da., 9th mo., 1753, a complaint was made against JESTINIA NEEDHAM, now Maxfield, for marrying out of the Unity of Friends and that she had had carnal knowledge of him before marriage. {DCMM}

On 14th da., 10th mo., 1754 Jestinia Maxwell brought a paper condemning her disorderly actions. {DCMM}

THE NEWELL FAMILY

1. JOHN NEWELL, m. Elizabeth (N). John bought land in Kent Co., DE, from Nicholas Bartlett.

On 16 Feb 1684 John Newell of Kent Co., PA, and Elizabeth his wife in consideration of 8400 pounds of tobacco sold to Henery Beckwith of Littell Choptanke in the Co. of Dorsett MD [DO Co.], planter, a plantation and parcell of land called *Gainsbrough* on w. side of Jones Creek containing 445 a. {KEDELR}

On 17 Feb 1684 John Newell of Kent Co., PA, planter and Elizabeth his wife, sold to Richard Mitchell of the same co. in consideration of 5300 pounds of tobacco ... a parcell of land called *The Reserve* on s.w. side of Dover River ... containing 400 a. {KEDELR}

On 10 Sep 1692 John Newell of Dover River in Kent Co., planter, do make and ordaine my well beloved wife Elizabeth Newell to be my true and lawfull atty ... to receive my debts and to pay what debts I owe out of my estate and also to make over and ackn 100 a. of land to James Maxwell which he bought of me and also to sue if they refuse to pay me as well as to abide judgment. {KEDELR}

Second Generation

2. JOHN NEWELL, son of John (1) Newell, m. Mary (N).

On 20 April 1730 John Bartlett of TA Co., MD, son and heir of Nicholas Bartlett, late of Kent Co., dec'd. for £60 sold to John Newell the younger of Kent Co., yeoman, a tract of land in Murderkill Hundred, beginning at the corner of Peter Groundick's ... (973 a. granted by warrant unto Nicholas Bartlett, dec'd., and surveyed on 18 Jan 1680 which he conveyed unto John Newell, dec'd. father of the afsd. John Newell 100 a. and to John Richardson dec'd. 300 a. ... John Bartlett the son since the decease of Nicholas Bartlett hath sold two other parcells to wit 100 a. to William Marchant and 100 a. more to

Thomas Skidmore) ... remaining part of the afsd. tract called *Bartletts Lott* ... 373 a. (excepting such land of Edward Williams lately sold him by the said John Bartlett as part of another tract). {KEDELR K:31}

In his will dated 27 March 1709, proved 31 March 1708, Henry Pennington mentioned among his heirs, Elizabeth Newell, dau. of John and Mary Newell. Admin. was John Newell. {Arch. A39:217. Reg. of Wills, B:60}

John Newell d. leaving a will dated 16 Jan 1739/40, proved 4 Feb 1739. Heirs: sons William, John, Thomas; dau. Elizabeth; grandson James Clayton; granddau. Ruth Betts; wife Mary. Extx., wife Mary. Wits., James Clayton, John Hall, Rebecca Welsh. {Arch. A37:190. Reg. of Wills, 1:14}

John was father of the following children: WILLIAM; JOHN; THOMAS; ELIZABETH.

Third Generation

3. WILLIAM NEWELL, son of John (2) Newell, m. Sarah who later m. Thomas Coe.

William Newell d. leaving a will dated 20 Feb 1748/9, proved 4 March 1748. Heirs: wife Sarah; daus. Sarah, Louisa, Mary, Elizabeth and Rachel; bro. Jno. Newell. Execs., wife and bro. Jno. Wits., Zachariah Goforth, Sylvester Tompson, James Clayton. {Arch. A37:199-201. Reg. of Wills, 1:258-259} Note: Arch. A37:200, shows Sarah, the widow, later married Thomas Coe; will mentions bro. Thomas, dec'd.

On 28 May 1751 whereas trustees of the General Loan Office in a Court of Common Pleas recovered a debt of £60.54.3 damages against William Newell late of Murtherkill Hundred, Kent Co., yeoman, dec'd. By virtue of a writ issued 28 Feb, Thomas Parke, high sheriff of Kent Co., seized a tract of land in the possession of John Newell, exec., and Thomas Coe and Sarah his wife, extx. of the will of William Newell in Murtherkill Hundred and sold the same for £70.17.6 to John Brown of same co., part of a larger tract called *Bartlets Lott* which William Newell dyed posest of and where Thomas Coe now dwells adj. to the dwelling plantation of John Newel 100 a., being the same land William Newell mortgaged including the dwelling house. {KEDELR O:89}

In a petition of John Newell, one of the execs of Wm. Newell, dec'd., it was stated that Wm. Newell made his last will and constituted execs., the petitioner and Sarah his wife, now the wife of Thos. Coe. Sd. Sarah took the goods and chattells of the testator into her hands and hath not passed an accoumpt of her administration or discharged the debts of the sd. testator and the petitioner believes that the estate will be embezzled and wasted by the sd. Thos. Coe. On 1 April 1755 John Newell petitioned to be appointed guardian to Sarah and Lovice Newell, children of Wm. Newell, dec'd. Whereas the petitioner's brother did by his last will leave to his two youngest daus., viz., Sarah and Lovice, the plantation whereon he lived and land belonging after his wife's decease and she is now dead but the plantation with 100 a. of land being mortgaged was sold with and the overplus of the land doth belong to the children afsd. and petitioner prayed that a guardian be appointed. {KEORCF Newell, William 1750-63}

William was father of the following daus: MARY, ELIZABETH; RACHEL; SARAH; LOUISA [the latter two being the youngest].

4. JOHN NEWELL, son of John (2) Newell, m. a dau. of Benjamin and Mary

Warren.

On 12 Feb 1754 John Newell of Kent Co., yeoman, for £15 sold to Daniel Robisson of same place a parcell of land being part of a larger tract called *Bartletts Lott* in Murderkill Hundred and being part of that land which John Newell late of this co., dec'd. father to the afsd. John Newell, bought of a certain Roger Burges and John Newell in his will bequeathed the same unto his son the afsd. John Newell ... 10 1/4 a. {KEDELR O:213}

John Newell d. leaving a will dated 14 Nov 1759, proved 20 Nov 1759. Heirs: sons Henry and William; daus. Tabitha Russell, Lydia, Hannah, Meriam Newell. Exec., Andrew Caldwell. Wits., Silvester Tomson, William Sipple, Durdin Wilson. {Arch. A37:191. Reg. of Wills, K:216} Note: Will mentions Mary Warren, grandmother.

Benjamin Warren of Murtherkill Hundred d. by 3 July 1762, proved 21 Sep 1762. Heirs: wife Mary; son Benjamin; grandsons Benjamin and John Warren; granddaus. Miriam and Lydia Newell. Execs. son Benjamin and wife Mary. Wits., Daniel Robisson, John Dunning, Mary Feagins. {Arch. A53:127. Reg. of Wills, K:290-291}

On 30 Aug 1764 Andrew Caldwell was admin. of the estate of John Newell. {Arch. A38:54} Note: Shown is that John Newell was guardian to Ruth Betts, wife of John McSparran, and Rachel Newell, wife of Henry Sapp; also mentions Henry and William Newell.

On 25 Nov 1766 William Newell of Kent Co., taylor, for all that parcel to the w. of the division now made release unto Henry Newell of same place, ship carpenter, the land to the e. of the division line, whereas John Newell of same co., father to the afsd. William Newell and Henry Newell, did in his life time make his will bearing date 14 Nov 1759 and did bequeath unto his 2 sons all his lands to be equally divided, whereas William Newell and Henry Newell have mutually agreed on the division of the lands ... beginning on n. side of Service Branch to *Bartletts Lott* to an ancient bounder called Peter Groundicke's white oak ... 154 1/2 a. Henry Newell made a similar release on the same day. {KEDELR R:129, 130}

John was father of the following children: HENRY; WILLIAM; TABITHA, m. (N) Russell; LYDIA; HANNAH; MERIAM.

5. THOMAS NEWEL, son of John (2) Newell, d. by 18 Nov 1744 when bros. William and John Newel were appointed admins. {Reg. of Wills, I:105} Fourth Generation

6. JOSEPH NEWELL, son of William (3) d. in 1745. John Bowers was appointed admin. of his estate on 21 Nov 1745. {Arch. A37:192. Reg. of Wills, I:116}

7. HENRY NEWELL, probable son of John (4) Newell, m. Margaret Wilson, dau. of George and Patience Wilson of TA Co., MD.

James Edmunds d. leaving a will dated 13 Feb 1770, proved 28 March 1770. Heirs: son John; cousin Henry Newell. Exec., Phillip Barratt. Wits., Wait-man Sipple, Jr.; George Wilson, John Mileway. {Arch. A16:31-38. Reg. of Wills, L:74}

Henry and Margaret were parents of the following children {DCMM}: PATIENCE, b. 23rd da., 3rd mo., 1764, m. Joseph George; MARY, b. 6th da., 2nd mo. 1766; ANN, b. 17th da., 3rd mo., 1768; SARAH, b. 11th da., 2nd mo., 1771; MARGARET, b. 10th da., 4th mo., 1775; TABITHA, b. 27th da., 11th mo., 1777, m. Ezekiel Hunn; LYDIA, b. 13th da., 5th mo., 1780.

On 25 Nov 1766 Henry Newell of Kent Co., ship carpenter, for all that part of land to the e. of the division now made, released unto William Newell of same place, taylor, the land to the w. of the division line beginning at Service Branch to *Bartletts Lott* to Heathers Road to Kings Road near the head of Skidmores Branch ... 140 1/2 a. {KEDELR R:130}

Margaret, wife of Henry Newell, d. 7th da., 2nd mo., 1789, age 44 years, 3 months, bur. Motherkiln Meeting. {DCMM}

8. WILLIAM NEWELL, probable son of John (4) Newell, d. by 12 Feb 1734, m. Mary (N) who later m. John Bowers.

William Newell d. leaving a will dated 9 Jan 1728/9, proved 3 Feb 1728. Heirs: sons Samuel, Joseph; wife Mary. Extx., wife. Wits., John Newell, Benjamin Barger, Joseph Barger. {Arch. A37:198. Reg. of Wills, G:19}

On 12 Feb 1734 Waitman Sipple, Junr, yeoman, for £25 (paid by John Bowers and Mary now his wife, extx. of the will of William Newell) sold to Joseph Newell, youngest son of William Newell, late of same co., yeoman, dec'd., and Mary his late wife ... whereas William Newell in his will devised to Mary his extx. to buy youngest son Joseph Newell, out of the personal estate, 100 a. of land which shall be made over to him at the age of 10 years ... a tract of land in the tenure of John Bowers being part of the land whereon Waitman Sipple now dwelleth which is part of the ancient tract called *Ousby* in Murderkill Hundred originally taken up by Thomas Hethard adj land which formerly belonged to Roger Shurly but now belongs to the heirs of the afsd. William Newell, dec'd. ... 138 a. {KEDELR L:11}

On 12 Aug 1747 whereas Joseph Newell, son of William Newell, late of Kent Co., dec'd., became seized in a tract of land in Murtherkill Hundred beginning by the road that passeth down the neck from the plantation late of Joseph Booth, dec'd., to the afsd. John Bowers dwelling plantation adj. land which formerly did belong to Roger Shurly but now belongs to the heirs of Thomas Skidmore dec'd. ... 138 a. part of an ancient tract called *Ousby*, conveyed by Wateman Sipple, Junr, on 12 Feb 1734 to the afsd. Joseph Newell (Book L, fol. 11), and Joseph Newell in 1745 dyed intestate and Letters of Administration was granted to the afsd. John Bowers of Kent Co., yeoman, on 29 May 1746, John Bowers having overpaid the estate £12.6.1 and still sundry demands against the estate, the Court impowered him to sell the lands belonging to the afsd. Joseph Newell, dec'd., to discharge the several debts ... on 13 Aug 1746 at a publick sale John Bowers for £37.10 sold the afsd. land to Edmund Kearny of same place, merchant. {KEDELR N:158}

William was father of JOSEPH who d. in 1745 intestate and SAMUEL.

Fifth Generation

9. PATIENCE NEWELL, dau. of Henry (7) and Margaret Newell, b. 23rd da., 3rd mo., 1764, m. Joseph George. The lived in Motherkiln area. They were parents of the following children {DCMM}: RACHEL, b. 28th da., 3rd mo., 1782; MARGARET, b. 27th da., 9th mo., 1785; JOHN, b. 20th da., 11th mo., 1787; MARY, b. 20th da., 4th mo., 1790; NEWELL, b. 26th da., 12th mo., 1792, d. 1855, a lunatic at Kent Co. Alms House.

10. TABITHA NEWELL, dau. of Henry (7) and Margaret Newell, b. 27th da.,

11th mo., 1777, m. Ezekiel Hunn (b. 1st da., 3rd mo. 1774). {DCMM}

11. SAMUEL NEWEL, probable son of William (8) Newell, m. Sarah (N).

On 7 Sep 1759 Samuel Newel and Sarah his wife of Kent Co. for £35 sold to John Edwards of DO Co., MD, a tract of land in the forest of Morderkill Hundred, surveyed 3 Oct 1758 for Samuel Newel by virtue of a warrant bearing date 19 Sep 1758 ... 104 a. {KEDELR P:160}

Unplaced

PETER NEWELL m. Mary (N).

On 10 Feb 1735 Peter Newell of Kent Co., taylor, and Mary Newell for £25 sold to Joseph Tumbelston of same place, cordwainder a tract of land called *Herrings Choice* in Mispillion Hundred on s. side of Black Swamp Branch ... 110 a. {KEDELR L:116}

THOMAS NEWELL m. Rachel (N).

On 7 Sep 1759 Thomas Newell and Rachel his wife of Kent Co., for £35 sold to John Edwards of DO Co., MD, a tract of land in the forrest of Murderkill Hundred, surveyed for Thomas Newell 30 Sep 1757 pursuant to a warrant bearing date 19 Sep 1757 ... 140 a. {KEDELR P:165}

THE NOCK FAMILY

1. THOMAS NOCK[43], yeoman, m. Sarah, mentioned as sister of Daniel Eyre in will below. Sarah later m. Jabez Jenkins.

Daniel Eyre of Sussex Co. d. leaving a will dated 14 Sep `1720, proved 24 Oct 1720. Heirs: wife Elizabeth Eyre; sisters Sarah Nock (wife of Thomas Nock of Kent Co.), Mary Mifflin (wife of Edward Mifflin of Northampton Co., VA) and Margaret Booth (wife of Joseph Booth, Jr. of Kent Co.). {Arch. A71:54. Reg. of Wills, A:138-139} Note: Arch. A71:54 mentions his dec'd. mother Anne Eyre.

On 15 Feb 1721/2 Thomas Knox (Nock) of Motherkill Hundred, Kent Co., farmer, for love, goodwill and affection give to Cherity Brooks of same place ... one cow & one calve. {KEDELR G:66}

Thomas Nock, d. 30th da., 8th mo., 1724. {DCMM} He left a will dated 26 Oct 1724, proved 4 Jan 1724. Heirs: wife Sarah; sons Ezekiell, Daniel & Thomas; daus. Patience, Ann, Sarah. Extx., wife. Trustees, Joseph Booth, Sr., Daniel Needham, Jabez Jenkins. Wits., William Rodeney, Jabez Jenkins, George Medcalfe, Benjamin Shurrner. {Arch. A38:34. Reg. of Wills, D:68}

Thomas and Sarah Nock were parents of the following children {DCMM}: ANN, b. 26th da., 11th mo., 1706; SARAH, b. 1708; EZEKIEL, b. 1710/11; DANIEL, b. 2nd mo., 9th mo., 1712/13; PATIENCE, b. 8th mo., 8th

---

[43] Thomas may be the same Thomas mentioned in the will of William Nock of Accomack Co., VA, who d. leaving a will dated 4 Sep 1724, proved 8 Feb 1726. {Accomack Co. Wills, Deeds 1715-1729:119}

da., 1715; ...ANNAH, b. 14th da., 1st mo., 1717/18; THOMAS.

On 21st da., 12th mo., 1725 the orderly marriage of Jabez Jenkins and Sarah Nock was reported. Friends were appointed to enquire into the settlement of her children's estate, left to them by their father. {DCMM}

Jabez Jenkins d. by 12 Feb 1732 when Sarah Jenkins was appointed admx. of his estate. {Reg. of Wills, H:101}

Sarah Jenkins, widow, d. leaving a will dated 13 Jan 1745/6, proved 3 Feb 1745. Mentioned were sons Ezekiel Nox, Daniel Nox, Thomas Nox, Jabez Jenkins; granddaus. Rachel and Sarah (daus. of James Willson), Mary Willson (dau. of George), Anne Willson (dau. of George). Execs. Ezekiel and Daniel Nox. Appraisers, John Holliday, James Gorrell. Wits., Peter Galloway, Samuel Robinson, James Gorrell. {Arch. A26:240. Reg. of Wills, I:120-121} Note: Will mentions second husband Jabez Jenkins, dec'd.

Second Generation

2. EZEKIEL NOCK, b. 1710/11, son of Thomas (1) and Sarah Nock, m. 1st 21st da., 11th mo., 1741, Elizabeth Hales at the Duck Creek Meeting House. {DCMM}

On 11 Aug 1749 Ezekeil Nock of Kent Co., yeoman, and Elizabeth his wife for £100 sold to Jabez Jenkins of same place, yeoman, a part of a tract of land in Murderkill Hundred called *Gainsborough*, formerly the property of a certain John Correy, late of same co. and conveyed by him to the afsd Ezekeil Nock (Lib. M, pg 84) ... on w. side of Newells Branch adj. Samuel Johns, on e. side of Tidbury Branch ... 150 a. {KEDELR O:9}

On 20th da., 8th mo., 1753 Ezekiel Nock requested a certificate in order for marriage with a Friend of Accomack Co., VA, at which place a monthly meeting was allowed to be held for that purpose. {DCMM}

Ezekiel Nock, of KE Co. on Dillaware m. 2nd Sarah Maxfeild of MD, 27 Sep 1753, at Daniel Mifflin's dwelling house in Accomack, VA, near *Lawnseys Goot* in VA. {TATH} Sarah was the widow of Joseph Maxfield of Worcester Co., MD. Sarah d. 8th da., 10th mo., 1773. Ezekiel d. 8th da., 11th mo, 1773. {DCMM}

On 27th da., 4th mo., 1765, Sarah Nock, by a Friend, requested a certificate on behalf of her son Stephen Maxfield who is bound an apprentice in Philadelphia. {DCMM}

Ezekiel left a will dated 28 Oct 1773, proved 30 Nov 1773. Heirs: sons Thomas, Joseph, Daniel; daus. Ann Griffin, Mary Nock; grandchildren Jabez, Daniel & Sarah Griffin, John & Thomas Brown. Exec., son Thomas. Wits., Thomas Nock, James Nock, Joseph Jenkins. {Arch. A38:22-24 & 27. Reg. of Wills, L:145}

Thomas Nock submitted a petition to the Orphan's Court on 1 Dec 1775, as guardian to Daniel Nock, minor, under age of 14, son of Ezekiel Nock, late of Murtherkill Hundred. He stated that Ezekiel Nock d. testate leaving a plantation to his son which plantation was now occupied by Elizabeth Perkins, tenant. {KEORCF Nock, Daniel 1775-76}

Ezekiel and Elizabeth were parents of the following children {DCMM}: SARAH, b. 25th da., 5th mo., 1743; ANN, b. 6th da., 11th mo., 1745; THOMAS, b. 29th da., 3rd mo., 1748.

Ezekiel and Sarah were parents of the following children {DCMM}: JOSEPH, b. 15th da., 5th mo., 1757; MARY, b. 31st da., 3rd mo., 1759;

EZEKIEL, b. 26th da., 3rd mo., 1762, d. 15th da., 11th mo., 1762; DANIEL, b. 29th da., 9th mo., 1766.

3. DANIEL NOCK of Duck Creek, b. 2nd mo., 9th mo., 1712/13, son of Thomas (1) and Sarah Nock, m. 28th da., 5th mo., 1736, Barthia Hales at the house of William Farson at Duck Creek. Following Daniel's death Barthia m. Isaac Hazell.

On 16th da., 6th mo., 1736 the orderly marriage of Daniel Nock and Barthia Hales was reported. {DCMM}

On 11 Aug 1740 Daniel Nock of Kent Co., yeoman, for £50 sold to Thomas Nock of same co., a tract of land called *New Lynn* on s. side of St. Jones Creek alias Dover River beginning at Tidbury Branch ... 445 a. (patent dated 6 Aug 1690 granted unto Ezekeil Needham and by his deed bearing date 10 Sep 1690 conveyed it unto William Clark) ... Daniel Nock doth acquit all his right and claim to the land, it being left him by his father decd. Wit: William Farson, Ezekiel Nock. {KEDELR M:84}

Daniel d. leaving a will dated 6 Dec 1749, proved 14 Feb 1749. Heirs: wife Barthia; sons Thomas, Daniel; dau. Ann; other child or children unnamed. Extx., wife Barthia. Trustees, bro. Ezekiel Nock, Thomas Nock & Henry Farson. Wits., William Farson, Richard Johns, John Woodall. {Arch. A38:18-19. Reg. of Wills, K:15-16} Note: Arch. A38:19 shows Elizabeth Pearson as dau. of William and Mary Pearson.

On 9 Feb 1768 Isaac Hazell, yeoman of Duck Creek Hundred, Kent Co, & Barthia his wife and Thomas Knock (Nock), late merriner of same place, and Nancy (signed deed as Ann) his wife for £370 the major part paid by John Spruance to discharge a judgment obtained against the said Thomas Knock by Bryan Bruin of Fredrick Co., VA, and the remaining part paid to Isaac Hazell sold to John Spruance, farmer of same place, a tract of land called *The Refuge*, except such part of it as the Bristol Company Hemp Manner has taken in. On 7 July 1740 at Philadelphia there was granted a warrant to survey the said tract to Daniel Knock, former husband of the said Barthia, now wife of the said Isaac Hazell, and father to the said Thomas Knock and the said Daniel Knock did by his will give the land to Thomas Knock his son reserving to his wife the third part thereof during her natural life, bounded by William Farson and Henry Farson ... 165 a. Wit: Danl. Smith, a Quaker, Charles Stewart. {KEDELR R:240}

Joseph Hales of Duck Creek d. leaving a will dated 27 June 1754, proved 21 Nov 1754. Heirs: nephew Joseph Nock, son of sister Barthia; cousin Thomas Hill; sisters Martha Clark, Barthia Nock, Rachel Liston; son-in-law Richard Holliday; Joseph Jenkins, son of Jabez; friend William Hammans; Robert Holliday, Hannah Jenkins, Susanna Hammans, Richard Holliday, Mary Holliday, Joseph Holliday, children of late wife. Execs., son-in-law Rob. Holliday, Thomas Hammans. Wits., William Farson, Roger Pugh, Jane Farson.
{Arch. A21:76-77. Reg. of Wills, K:98-99}

On 19th da., 3rd mo., 1755, there was a complaint against Bathia Hazle, former wife of Daniel Nock, dec'd., for her going out in marriage with one not of the Society. {DCMM}

Daniel and Barthia were parents of the following children {DCMM}: THOMAS, b. 4th da., 9th mo., 1737, m. Nancy (N); DANIEL, b. 10th da., 7th mo., 1739; EZEKIEL, b. 25th da., 7th mo., 1741; ANN, b. 19th da., 1st mo., 1744, d. 11th da., 2nd mo., 1752; MARY, b. 18th da., 1st mo., 1746, d. 1748;

SARAH, b. 18th da., 1st mo., 1747, d. 22nd da., 3rd mo., 1749; JOSEPH, b. 15th da., 6th mo., 1750.

Isaac Hazell of Duck Creek d. leaving a will dated 10 Feb 1768, proved 22 March 1768. Heirs: wife Barthia; nephew George Hill; George Hazell; Joseph Nock; Mary Nock; Isaac Curry; Jonathan Hazell; Moses Shelly; Thomas Nock, Jr.; Thomas Nock, son of Thomas Nock, Jr. Extx., wife Barthia. Wits., Molleston Correy, Andrew Jamison, Mary Farsons, Jr. {Arch. A23:88-91. Reg. of Wills, L:43}

Barthia Hazel of Duck Creek Hundred, widow, d. leaving a will dated 29 Dec 1784, proved 13 Aug 1787. Heirs: sons Joseph Nock; grandson Thomas Nock, son of son Thomas Nock; granddaus. Mary and Barthia Nock, daus. of son Thomas Nock. Exec. son Joseph Nock. Wits., John Brown, William Farson, Mary Smith. {Arch. A23:74. Reg. of Wills, M:148-149}

4. THOMAS NOCK, son of Thomas (1) and Sarah Nock, on 22nd da., 7th mo., 1746 produced a paper condemning his outgoing in marriage. {DCMM}

Thomas was father of the following children: THOMAS; MARY; BARTHIA. {See his mother's will above.}

5. ANN NOCK, b. 26th da., 11th mo., 1706, dau. of Thomas (1) and Sarah Nock, m. William Wilson.

On 17th da., 2nd mo., 1727 William Wilson, son of James Willson of Third Haven Montly Meeting and Ann Nock, dau. of Thomas Nock, late of Kent Co. on DE, dec'd., announced their intentions of marriage. On 17th da., 5th mo., 1727 the orderly marriage of William Wilson, with his parents' approval, and Ann Nock was reported. {DCMM}

Third Generation

6. ANN NOCK, b. 6th da., 11th mo., 1745, dau. of Ezekiel (2) and Elizabeth Nock, m. William Griffin, Junr.

On 24th da., 10th mo., 1767, representatives from the Monthly Meeting treated with Ann Nock, now the wife of William Griffin, Junr., for marrying a man not of the Society. {DCMM}

William and Ann were parents of the following children: JABEZ; DANIEL; SARAH.

7. SARAH NOCK, b, 1708, dau. of Ezekiel (2) and Elizabeth Nock, b. 25th da., 5th mo., 1743, m. John Brown. They were parents of the following children: JOHN, b. 22nd da., 3rd mo., 1765; THOMAS, b. 18th da., 7th mo., 1767.

John d. 17th da., 2nd mo., 1769. Sarah Brown, widow, was appointed admx. of his estate on 30 March 1769. {Reg. of Wills, L:57} Note: Arch. A6:53 shows Sarah Brown later m. John Morris. Sarah d. 6th da., 1st mo., 1773. {DCMM}

8. THOMAS NOCK, son of Ezekiel (2) and Elizabeth, b. 29th da., 3rd mo., 1748, m. Mary Caulk.

On 28th da., 11th mo., 1772, Duck Creek Preparative Meeting complained against Thomas Nock of Duck Creek Hundred for neglecting religious meetings, unnecessary frequenting of taverns, unprofitable company and using strong drink at times to excess. {DCMM}

Thomas Nock, Junr., of Kent Co. upon Delaware, and Mary Caulk of Cecil Co., with consent of parents, m. 13th da., 5th mo., 1773 at Sassafras Meeting House. Mary, b. 14th da., 12th mo., 1753, dau. of Oliver and Phebe Caulk. {CEMM}

On 28th da., 8th mo., 1773, Mary Nock, wife of Thomas Nock, produced a certificate from Cecil Monthly Meeting. {DCMM}

Thomas and Mary were parents of the following children {DCMM}: PHEBE, b. 1st da., 9th mo., 1775; EZEKIEL, b. 11th da., 4th mo., 1778; THOMAS, b. 18th da., 3rd mo., 1780; OLIVER, b. 1st da., 5th mo., 1783; MARY, b. 7th da., 3rd mo., 1790; DANIEL, b. 18th da., 11th mo., 1793.

Mary, wife of Thomas, d. 20th da., 8th mo., 1795, age 42 years, bur. Motherkiln Meeting. Thomas Nock d. 5th da., 10th mo., 1799, age 51 years, bur. Motherkiln Meeting. {DCMM}

9. MARY NOCK, dau. of Ezekiel (2) and Sarah Nock.

On 25th da., 2nd mo., 1775, there was a certificate drawn for Mary Nock, dau. of Ezekiel Nock, dec'd., to Philadelphia Monthly Meeting. {DCMM}

10. JOSEPH NOCK, son of Daniel (3) and Barthia Nock, b. 15th da., 6th mo., 1750, m. Sarah Smith (b. 11th da., 5th mo, 1752), dau. of Daniel and Jane Smith. Sarah d. 17th da., 10th mo., 1790. {DCMM}

On 26th da., 1st mo., 1771, Duck Creek Preparative Meeting complained against Joseph Nock and his wife Sarah, members of the Society, for accomplishing their marriage by the assistance of a priest. {DCMM}

Unplaced

On --- da., 8th mo., 1754 SARAH NOCK produced a certificate from Cecil Monthly Meeting, MD. {DCMM}

On 28th da., 3rd mo., 1761 there was a complaint against THOMAS NOCK, Junr., for accomplishing his marriage by a Priest. {DCMM}

THE ROBERT OFFLEY FAMILY

1. ROBERT OFFLEY[44], m. Margaret (N)

Robert Offley was nephew to Robert Hollinsworth. On 25 Jan 1724 Robert Hollinsworth and his wife Dorothy conv. to John Collins and Robert Offley in considerations of love and affection to their nephews and further payment of £100 - 396 a., a tract called *Castle Miles* and another called *Offley's Fortune.* {QALR IKB:302}

Robert Offley was witness to the will of Benjamin Benham, QA Co., written 10 July 1729. {MWB 19:839}

Robert Offley of QA Co. d. leaving a will dated 31 May 1755, proved 28 June 1764. Mentioned were wife Margaret and dau. Sarah Edward (or

---

[44] There was a Robert Offley who was transported into the province of Maryland by 1680. {MPL WC2:183}

Toward) to whom was left cattle at decease of wife, to be divided among children I have had by sd. wife, Margaret Offley. Extx. wife Margaret. In the probate of the will is mentioned Vincent (Vinson) Offley, eldest son and heir to testator Robert Offley. {MWB 32:238}

Robert was father of VINCENT; SARAH.

Second Generation

2. VINSON OFFLEY, eldest son of Robert Offley, m. Anne (N).

On 26 Feb 1768 Vinson Offley [and his wife Anne], oldest son of Robert Offley, dec'd., conv. to John Brown 62 a., part of *The Levell* and part of *Castle Miles.* {QALR RTH:173}

Vinson and Benton Offley were witnesses to the will of Richard Gould, QA Co., written 2 Jan 1766. {MWB 34:57}

THE CALEB OFFLEY FAMILY

1. CALEB OFFLEY, m. 1st Mary Mackie and m. 2nd Elizabeth Collins, m. 3rd Elizabeth England.

On 18th da., 2nd mo., 1709, Caleb Offley m. Mary Mackie, she producing a certificate from Friends at Cork, Ireland. {DCMM}

On 16th da., 5th mo., 1711, Caleb Offley was directed to speak to his brother Hasakiah to give an account about the Boston Collection. {DCMM}

Mary Offley, wife of Caleb Offley, d. 5th da., 9th mo., 1713. {DCMM} On 18th da., 2nd mo., 1716 CALEB OFFLEY to take a wife at Bristol in Bucks Co. {Duck Creek Monthly Meeting}

On 6th da., 5th mo., 1715, it was reported Caleb Offley of Duck Creek and Elizabeth Collins had married. {Falls Monthly Meeting, PA}

Elizabeth Offley, second wife to Caleb Offley d. 21st da., 11th mo., 1719.

On 10th da., 7th mo., 1722 the marriage of Caleb Offley and Elisabeth England at the house of said Elizabeth in the Province of Maryland, was reported. {DCMM}

Caleb Offley of Duck Creek, New Castle Co., yeoman, and Mary of same place but late of Ireland, m. 2nd mo., 17--, at Duck Creek. {DCMM}

Caleb Offley, yeoman, New Castle Co., d. leaving a will dated 12th da., 8th mo., 1727, proved 9 March 1727. Mentioned were wife Elizabeth Offley; eldest son Michael Offley; son Caleb Offley; son Daniel Offley; son David; sister's sons Hazadiah Shaw. Extx. wife Elizabeth. {New Castle Co. Wills Misc. I:373}

Caleb was father of the following children: MICHAEL, b. 18th da., 9th mo., 1718 {DCMM}; CALEB, b. 8th da., 4th mo., 1723 {DCMM}; DANIEL, b. 24th da., 5th mo., 1725; DAVID.

Second Generation

2. MICHAEL OFFLEY of Duck Creek in New Castle Co. upon Delaware, b. 18th da., 9th mo., 1718, son of Caleb (1) Offley.

On 20th da., 5th mo., 1741 Michael Offley and Elizabeth, dau. of John Hales, announced intentions of marriage. {DCMM}

Michael Offley and Phebe Corse of Kent Co., Maryland, m. with consent of parents, 8/4/1743 at Cecil Meeting House. {CEMM}

Michael Offley of New Castle Co. d. leaving a will dated 16 May 1767, proved 28 May 1767. Mentioned were wife; only son Michael; five daus. Elizabeth, Mary, Anne, Liddy and Phoebe. Extx. wife Phoebe and son. {New Castle Co. Wills Misc. I:381}

On 27th da., 1st mo., 1770 Phebe Offley now the wife of Nathan Newlin offered a paper of acknowledgment for her outgoing in marriage. {DCMM}

Michael was father of the following children: MICHAEL; ELIZABETH; MARY; ANNE; LIDDY; PHOEBE.

3. DAVID OFFLEY of Duck Creek Hundred, son of Caleb (1) Offley, m. Mercy (N) who later m. Buckingham.

On 25th da., 1st mo., 1751 David Offley by his brother Michael, requested a certificate to Philadelphia Monthly Meeting. {DCMM}

On 20th da., 8th mo., 1753 David Offley produced a certificate from Philadelphia Monthly Meeting. {DCMM}

On 18th da., 3rd mo., 1754, there was a complaint against David Offley who was found guilty of taking a certificate from Duck Monthly Meeting to Philadelphia Monthly Meeting in order for marriage with a young woman there and appeared with her and gave the certificate to Friends there and a little after another young woman was delivered of a bastard child by him begotten which he owned and married her in her bed by a Priest. {DCMM}

On 1 May -- David Offley of the Town of Salisbury in Duck Creek Hundred Kent Co., blacksmith, and Mercy (Mary) his wife for £8 sold to William Carpenter of same place yeoman ... a lott of ground in ye afsd. town beginning at Mary Carpenter's lott on High Street ... 1/4 a. Ackn 15 May 1754. {KEDELR O:233}

David d. leaving a will made 19 July 1755, proved 2 Aug 1755. Heir: wife unnamed. Wits., Charles Green, Mary Hammans. {Arch. A38:107-108. Reg. of Wills, K:119} Note: Arch. A38:108 shows Mercy, the widow, later married Howell Buckingham.

On 11 May 1769 the petition of Samuel Griffin most humbly sheweth that whereas a certain Enoch David obtained two judgments and executions in Feb Term 1757 against a certain Howell Buckinham and Mercy his wife late Mercy Offley, adminr. of David Offley, dec'd., that Casar Rodney, then sheriff of Kent co. did take in execution, expose to sale at publick vendue, a certain brick house and lott in Duck Creek Hundred, deemed the property of the afsd. David Offley dec'd., for £71 he being the highest bidder, but hath not as yet conveyed the premises and is since out of office. Samuel Griffin therefore prayed for an order of the Court commanding the present sheriff William Rhodes to execute a lawful deed. This was granted. {KEDELR Q:151}

3. CALEB OFFLEY, son of Caleb (1) Offley, b. 9th da., 4th mo., 1723.

On 16th da., 10th mo., 1751 there was a complaint against Caleb Offley for marrying out of the Unity of Friends. {DCMM}

Third Generation

4. MICHAEL OFFLEY, son of Michael (2) Offley, m. Elizabeth Wallis.

Michael Offley of New Castle on Delaware, son of Michael Offley and Pheby his wife, late of the same place, dec'd., and Elizabeth Wallis of Kent Co.,

MD, dau. of Samuel Wallis, and Saray Wallis his wife, m. at Cecil Meeting House, with consent of parents, 16/5/1781. {CEMM}

On 24th da., 11th mo., 1781 a certificate was presented to Duck Creek Monthly Meeting by Elizabeth Offley, wife of Michael, from Cecil Monthly Meeting. {DCMM}

Sarah, dau. of Michael and Elizabeth Offley, b. 12th da., 3rd mo., 1782, d. 6th(?) mo., 1784. {DCMM}

5. LYDIA (Liddy) OFFLEY, probable dau. of Michael (2) Offley, m. (N) McDaniels.

On 26th da., 8th mo., 1775, Lydia McDaniels, formerly Offley, charged with marrying a persons not of the Society. {DCMM}

6. ELIZABETH OFFLEY, dau. of Michael (2) Offley.

On 17th da., 6th mo., 1730, the marriage of Abraham Widdus and Elizabeth Offley was reported. {DCMM}

7. ANN OFFLEY, dau. of Michael (2) Offley, m. 31st da., 7th mo., 1771, Solomon Dawson, son of Benjamin Dawson of Kent Co., on Delaware, at Duck Creek. {DCMM}

Unplaced

(N) OFFLEY m. Margaret Cook.

On 23 Sep 1761 Margaret Offley of Duck Creek Hundred, Kent Co., widow, for £70 released unto John Cook of same place, yeoman, all her right unto a tract of land, whereas the said Margaret being collaterally an heiress to an undivided right in a tract of land now in the tenor and actual possession of the said John Cook in the afsd. hundred being the real estate of John Cook, late of said co., yeoman, dec'd., which lineally descended to his son Michael Cook who devised the same to his two sons John Cook and Michael Cook, and whereas the said Michael dyd intestate and seizd thereof by a deed from James Steel and Martha his wife unto the afsd. John Cook, yeoman, dec'd., whereby the said John Cook and Margaret Offley being the only brother and sister succeeding and surviving collatteral heirs of the said Michael Cook, Junr, dec'd. ... on w. branch of Duck Creek adj. land late of Nathaniel Lamplugh on Gravelly Run ... 350 a. {KEDELR Q:79}

JOHN OFFLEY was witness to the will of Thomas Joanes, TA Co., written 10 Sep 1680. {MWB 2:133}

JOHN OFFLEY of QA Co. m. Dorothey (N).

John d. leaving a will dated 16 March 1708/9, proved 20 April 1709. Mentioned were John Stead, Mary Stead, Susanna Walford to whom was bequeathed personalty to John Collins 200 a. of *Offley's Delight* at head of Chester River. Also mentioned was James Devige to whom was left 200 a. on Anderson's Branch. Wife Dorothey, extx. received residue of estate. {MWB 12:28, part 2}

The will of Thomas Collins of KE Co., MD, written 23 April 1698, mentions

Mother MABLE OFFLEY to be maintained from estate during life; the will was witnessed by Edward Offley among others. {MWB 6:118}

MARY OFFLEY m. Hans Johnson 14 Sep 1756. {QALU}

THE OLIVER FAMILY

1. RUBIN OLIVER m. Esther (N) who later m. George Lychum.

On 14 Sep 1765 Rubin Oliver of Kent Co., taylor, and Esther his wife, for £70 sold to David Peterkin of same place, merchant, a tract of land, in Mispillion Hundred, 200 a., part of a 2000 a. tract of land called *Fairfield* (Book F, fol. 28) ... 74 a. {KEDELR R:66}

On 25th da, 11th mo, 1769 Levi and Reuben Oliver requested for themselves, wives and children, to come under the care and notice of Friends. {DCMM}

Reuben Oliver d. by 10 June 1774 when Esther Oliver, widow, was appointed admx. of his estate. {Reg. of Wills, L:154} Note: Arch. A38:130 shows that Esther Oliver married George Lychum. Administration was assigned to Edward Fisher and John Furchase on 29 May 1776. {Arch. A38:129. Reg. of Wills, L:180}

On 22nd da, 4th mo, 1775, a testimony was drawn up a testimony against Esther Lathem, late widow of Reuben Oliver, for going out in her marriage after being precautioned. {DCMM}

Reuben and Esther were parents of the following children {DCMM}: SAMUEL, b. 15th da, 9th mo, 1757; GALLAUDETT, b. 5th da, 10th mo, 1759, d. 3rd da, 4th mo, 1846; ELISHA, b. 13th da, 9th mo, 1762; MARY, b. 2nd da, 3rd(?) mo, 1765; DEBORAH, b. 15th da, 11th mo, 1767; THOMAS, b. 23rd da, 5th mo, 1770.

2. LEVI OLIVER m. Jane (N). They resided near Milford.

They were parents of the following children {DCMM}: BENJAMIN, b. 16th da, 9th mo, 1762; MARY, b. 10th da, 1st mo, 1766; ANN, b. 13th da, 4th mo, 1768; RACHEL, b. 6th da, 5th mo, 1770, d. 27th da, 11th mo, 1770; AARON, b. 21st (or 27th) da, 2nd mo, 1772, d. 24th da, 1st da, 1796; JOSEPH, b. 6th da, 6th mo, 1774, d. 14th da, 1st mo, 1782; JAMES (or Jane), b. 18th da, 8th mo, 1776; LEVI, b. 8th da, 9th mo, 1778, d. 24th da, 1st mo, 1797; REUBEN, b. 22nd da, 2nd mo, 1781.

Levi, son of Levi, d. 24th da, 1st mo, 1797, age 68 years, bur. Milford Meeting. {DCMM}

Levi d. leaving a will dated 12 July 1797, proved 20 Nov 1797. Heirs: wife Jenny Oliver; sons Benjamin and Reuben Oliver; daus. Ann Morgan (wife of Parker Morgan), Mary Bowman (wife of Nathaniel Bowman), Je[an]nett Reed (wife of Elijah Reed); grandson Aaron Oliver (son of Benjamin). Extx., wife Jenny Oliver. Wits., Daniel Rogers, Alexander Draper, Hessy Wattson. {Sussex Co. Wills Arch. A91:153. Reg. of Wills, E:139-140}

Second Generation

3. GALLAUDIT OLIVER, son of Reuben (1) and Esther Oliver, b. 5th da, 10th mo, 1759, d. 3rd da, 4th mo, 1846, m. Eleanor (N). They were parents of the

following children {DCMM}: MARY, b. 26th da, 9th mo, 1789, d. 1862; CATHARINE, b. 27th da, 10th mo, 1791, m. William Redden and Samuel Anthony; JOSEPH, b. 8th da, 8th mo, 1794, m. Margaret Ray of Philadelphia.

4. SAMUEL, son of Reuben (1) and Esther Oliver, b. 15th da, 9th mo, 1757.

On 27th da, 4th mo, 1776, a complaint was made against Samuel Oliver for bearing arms in military service and enlisting himself as a soldier in one of their companies. {DCMM}

5. BENJAMIN OLIVER, son of Levi (2) and Jean Oliver, BENJAMIN, b. 16th da, 9th mo, 1762.

On 24th da, 6th mo, 1786, a complaint was made against Benjamin Oliver for outging in marriage with a person not of the Society. {DCMM}

Unplaced

On 2 May 1764 George Oliver m. Widow Montgomery. {LCPC}

THE PALMATARY FAMILY

Also see *Robert Palmatary of Duck Creek Delaware and his descendants* (1991) by Marjorie W. Nelson, 2315 S. E. Second St., Boynton Beach, FL 33435.

1. ROBERT PALMATARY m. 1st Ellinor (N). The following dates of birth are found in the Kent County Land Records {KEDELR}:

3 July 1676. Birth. Robert Palmatary, Junr., son of Robert Palmatary and Ellinor his wife was born in Kent Co. PA.

15 Nov 1679. Birth. Ellinor Palmatary dau. of Robert Palmatary and Ellinor his wife was born.

9 Nov 1681. Birth. John Palmatary son of Robert Palmatary and Ellinor his wife was born.

31 July 1684. Birth. Susanah Palmatary dau. of Robert Palmatary and Ellinor his wife was born.

Robert Palmatary m. 2nd Joanna (N) and d. 1692.

Rob. Palmontary is shown on the Kent Co. Rent Roll, 1681-1688, owning the tract *Parington*, 400 a. {Bendler:5} He is also listed in the 1693 Tax Assessment List of Kent Co. {Bendler:20}

On 2 April 1692 John Hilliard of Duck Creek Kent Co., PA, planter, quit claim Joanna Palmatary relict of Robert Palmatary, dec'd., in same co. from all bargains contracts suits and judgments. {KEDELR}

Robert d. 20 --- 1692. Heirs: wife, Joanna; sons, Robert and John; daus. Eleanor and Susanna. Wits., Jeffry Thomson, John Bradshaw. {Arch. A38:205. Reg. of Wills, A:3}

Robert was father of the following children: ROBERT; JOHN; ELEANOR; SUSANNA.

Second Generation

2. ROBERT PALMATARY, son of Robert (1) Palmatary, b. 3 July 1676, m. Elizabeth (N).

On 13 Aug 1765 Robert Palmatary of Kent Co. for £47.10 quit claim unto John Palmatary 1/3 part of a tract of land (which was given to us by our dec'd., father Robert Palmatary referring to his will) whereon the said John Palmatary now dwells binding on John Hawkins's land, 42 a. {KEDELR R:46}

Robert d. leaving a will dated 9 Nov 1748, proved 23 Nov 1748. Heirs: wife Elizabeth; sons John, Robert, Allen; daus. Grace, Elizabeth, Susannah Tompson and husband John Tompson. Exec., friend James Morris. Wits., Phebe Morris, William Hirons, John Hawkins. {Arch. A38:206-207. Reg. of Wills, I:247}

Robert was father of the following children: JOHN; ROBERT; ALLEN; GRACE; ELIZABETH; SUSANNAH, m. John Tompson.

3. JOHN PALMATARY, probable son of Robert (2) Palmatary, m. 1st Sarah Severson, dau. of John Severson and m. 2nd Margarett (N).

John Severson of Duck Creek Hundred d. leaving a will dated 2 April 1761, proved 24 Aug 1763. Heirs: wife Sarah; sons Simon and James; daus. Sarah Palmatary, Mary, Ann and Rachel Severson. Extx., wife Sarah. Wits., James Morris, William David, Elizabeth David. {Arch. A45:145-146. Reg. of Wills, K:314-315}

John Palmatree d. before 24 Oct 1772 when his estate was administered by Margarett Palmatree and James Severson. {Reg. of Wills, L:120}

<u>Unplaced</u>

ROBERT PALMETERRA, son of Clary Hall.

Clary Hall of Duck Creek d. leaving a will dated 4 Oct 1726, proved 22 Nov 1726. Heirs: sons Jonas and John Greenwood; daus. Mary and Elizabeth Greenwood. Exec., son Robert Palmeterra. Wits., James Morris, Thomas Taylor, Susannah Taylor. {Arch. A21:84. Reg. of Wills, F:17}

THE PARADEE FAMILY

1. STEPHEN PARADUE was awarded land for service to Lord Baltimore in Maryland 1665. {MPL 8:4}

On 29 Oct 1697 Stephen Paradee and Margarett Loober both of Kent Co., PA, had published their intention of marriage, William Rodeney, Clerk. {KEDELR} On 4 Nov 1697 the marriage of Stephen Paradee and Margaret Loeber both of Kent Co. PA was duly solomnized by Thomas Bedwell, Justice of the peace. {KEDELR} Margaret was the dau. of Peter Lowber.

Peter Loper mentioned Margaret Paradee when he d. leaving a will dated 2 April 1698, proved 2 May 1698. Heirs: wife Gartre; son Michael; daus. Mary Nichols (widow of William), Margaret Paradee, Gartre Loper, Agnes Smith. Extx. wife Gartre. Wits., Thomas Bedwell, William Nichols, Daniel Hudson. {Arch. A31:136. Reg. of Wills, B:27}

On 1 May 1711 Stephen Parradee of Kent Co., yeoman, and Margret his wife, for £20 sold to John Maron of same co., a tract of land lying in a fork of Little Creek being part of a tract of land purchased by Stephen Parradee of Richard Levick, 100 a. {KEDELR E:20} On 6 May 1721 Stephen and Margaret Parradee for £12 sold to Timothy Hirons (Irons) of same co. yeoman, a tract of land in Dover Hundred being part of a tract of land called *Edingtons Tract*, adj.

land called *Burtons Tract*, 26 a. {KEDELR G:16}

Stephen d. 11 --- 1727, proved 2 Jan 1727. Heirs: sons Stephen, Jr., John, Benjamin; daus. Susannah, Agnes and Elizabeth Paradee and Sarah Fitzgarrel; wife Margaret. Extx., wife Margaret. Wits., Thomas Harbutt, John Sturgis, Abraham Morris. {Arch. A38:241-242. Reg. of Wills, G:1}

Stephen was father of the following children: STEPHEN; JOHN; BENJAMIN; SUSANNAH; AGNES; ELIZABETH; SARAH, m. (N) Fitzgarrel.

Second Generation

2. STEPHEN PARADEE, son of Stephen (1) Paradee, m. Lydia (N).

On 24 Nov 1759 Stephen Paradee, Esqr., and Lydia his wife of Kent Co., for £100 sold to Daniel Lewis, farmer, and Margaret his wife of same co., a tract of land and plantation in Dover Hundred in actual possession of Daniel Lewis and Margaret his wife beginning at Pipe Elm Branch and land late of George Robinson now belonging to Aron Hart, the whole formerly belonging to William Winsmore called *Great Pipe Elm*, adj. and John Paradee's land, 176 a., also a small piece of meadow ground part of the tract of land called *Shoulder of Mutton* near Bucks Bridge to land called *Paradees Venture*, 5 a. {KEDELR P:164}

Stephen d. leaving a will dated 29 Nov 1759, proved 18 Dec 1759. Heirs: wife Lydia; dau. Mary; son Stephen; grandsons Daniel and Stephen Lewis; granddaus. Ruhamy, Hannah and Mary Lewis. Execs., wife Lydia and son-in-law Daniel Lewis. Appraisers, James Clayton and Charles Marim. Wits., Charles Inglis, Richard Wells, James Sykes. {Arch. A38:243-244 and vol. A39:1-2; Reg. of Wills, K:217-218} Note: Arch. A39:2 shows Jonathan Caldwell and wife Peggy, late Peggy Lewis, adms., d.b.n.

Daniel Lewis of Dover Hundred d. leaving a will dated 22 June 1761, proved 22 July 1761. Heirs: wife Peggy; sons Daniel and Stephen; dau. Elizabeth. Execs., wife Peggy and son Stephen. Wits., Caesar Rodney, Charles Marim, Wilson Buck [master]. {Arch. A30:59-62. Reg. of Wills, K:265} Note: Arch. A30:61 shows Daniel Lewis a relative of Stephen Paradee; also mentions Geo. Gordon and wife Mary, dau. of John Parradee; page 59 shows Margaret, the widow, later married Jonathan Caldwell.

Stephen was father of the following children: MARY; STEPHEN.

3. JOHN PARADEE, probable son of Stephen (1) Paradee, d. leaving a will date 24 Oct 1748, proved 29 Oct 1748. Heirs: sons John and David; daus. Mary and Elizabeth. Execs., bro. Stephen Paradee and Joshua Nickerson. Wits., Peter Pursel, William Manson, Dad. [David] Rees. {Arch. A38:236-238. Reg. of Wills, 1:235} Note: Arch. A30:60 shows dau. Mary m. George Gordon.

John was father of the following children: JOHN; DAVID; MARY, m. George Gordon; ELIZABETH.

Third Generation

4. STEPHEN PARADEE, probable son of Stephen (2) Paradee, m. Mary Marim, widow of John Marim. {See *Colonial Families of Delaware*, v. 2}

On 1 Jan 1760 David Finney of New Castle Co. for performing and fulfilling the Articles of Agreement on his part and for £200 paid by Stephen Paradee in his lifetime and £100 paid by Daniel Lewis sold to Daniel Lewis of Kent Co., yeoman, in trust for the use of Mary Paradee, a tract of land, by virtue of a deed pole made 11 Oct 1701 (Book C, fol. 267, 268) between Mary Naylor, widow and extx. of the will of John King of Memenson, Philadelphia Co., mariner, and Robert French of Philadelphia, merchant, the said Robert French became seized in a tract of land n.e. side of Dover River called *Troy*, 300 a., and Robert French by his will bearing date 23 Jan 1712 did devise to his dau. Elizabeth French the afsd. tract of land called *Troy* and died, and Elizabeth French m. a certain John Finney of New Castle Co. and is since, dec'd., leaving issue the afsd. David Finney her eldest son and heir and the said David Finney by Articles of Agreement 2 Jun 1759 between him and Stephen Paradee of Kent Co. esqr, David Finney for £300 would within 1 year sufficiently convey unto Stephen Paradee that tract of land called *Troy* in Dover Hundred, and Stephen Paradee would pay unto David Finney £200 and £100 the residue of £300 on executing the said conveyance, and Stephen Paradee died since having first made his will bearing date 29 Nov 1759 and did devise the said tract of land unto his dau. Mary when she shall attain the age of 18 years or is married, resurveyed 11 May 1739 by Thomas Noxon late deputy surveyor of Kent Co. adj. land called *Aberdeen* to land called *Lisburn*, 300 a. {KEDELR P:194}

5. JOHN PARRADEE, probable son of John (3) Parradee, m. Hannah Luff, dau. of Nathaniel Luff.

On 15 Feb 1758 John Parradee of Kent Co. farmer, and Hannah his wife for £60 sold to Casar Rodney of same co., a tract of land in the lower part of Dover Hundred near the dwelling plantation of said Casar Rodeney, part of a larger tract called *Great Pipe Elm* which was conveyd to John Parradee by Stephen Fitzjarrell on 13 Feb 1754, 50 a. {KEDELR P:52}

On 6 Aug 1758 John Paradee and Hannah his wife both of Dover Hundred, Kent Co., yeoman, for £55 sold to Daniel Lewis of same place, weaver, a tract of land in Joneses Hundred, part of a large tract called the *Shoulder of Mutton* on e. side of Pipe Elm Branch adj. land called *Great Pipe Elm* and land called *Paradees Venture* and now in the possession of the said Daniel Lewis on s.e. side of John Paradee's bridge to line between Daniel Lewis and John Paradee's land they now live on, 8 a. Wit: Stepn. Paradee, William Webley. {KEDELR P:85}

Hannah was mentioned as dau. in the will of Nathaniel Luff, Sr., Gentleman, written 3 Feb 1760, proved 27 Feb 1760. Heirs: wife Deborah; sons Caleb, Nathaniel, John; daus. Hannah Paradee, Deborth Pleasanton. Execs., sons Caleb and Nathaniel. Wits., Samuel Merydith, Sarah Maston, Thomas Clark. {Arch. A31:229-238. Reg. of Wills, K:225} Note: Arch. A31:235 shows John Paradee as husband of Hannah; David Pleasanton as husband of Deborah; Deborah later married Stephen Lewis. Page 236 shows Deborah, the widow, later married Jonathan Manlove. Page 238 shows Philip Reason [Rasin] only son of Sarah had heirs, Jemiah Ford, Robert Meeks and Joseph Rasin.

On 17 Jun 1762 Caleb Luff of Kent Co., farmer, Nathaniel Luff of same place, farmer, and John Paradee of same place, farmer, and Hannah his wife, for £201 sold to David Pleasanton of same place, farmer, a tract of land, whereas Mary Robisson afterwards called Mary Skidmore formerly Mary Luff late of this co., dec'd., was in her lifetime seized in a tract of land and died leaving no issue born of her body, by reason the estate of the said Mary Robisson descended to and became vested in the afsd. Caleb Luff, Nathaniel Luff and Hannah Paradee and Deborah wife of the said David Pleasanton, and to Philip Reason only son and heir of Sarah Reason formerly called Sarah Luff which said

Caleb, Nathaniel, Hannah, Deborah and Sarah were the brothers and sisters of the afsd. Mary Robisson, a tract of land in Murtherkill Hundred, 220 a. {KEDELR Q:104}

On 14 Feb 1764 John Paradee of Kent Co., farmer, for £240 sold to Benjamin Brown of Jones Neck same co., bricklayer, a parcel of land, part of a larger tract called *Aberdeen*, formerly surveyed for Thomas Clifford (R:5) ... 150 a. which land and premisses was lately conveyed by a certain Manlove Tarrant unto the afsd. John Paradee party hereto. {KEDELR R:9}

Fourth Generation

6. STEPHEN PARRADEE, probable son of Stephen (4) Parradee.

On 6 Feb 1739, whereas by a bargain of sale bearing date 20 Nov 1723 Charles Hillyard Esqr then sherriff of Kent Co. by virtue of certain powers of authority did for £40 sell unto John McDowell, a tract which was formerly a parcell of the estate of Stephen Parradee, dec'd., father of Stephen Parradee by whom it was sold unto Thomas Willson father of the afsd. Thomas Willson, but by some means the deed for the same is not to be found but is utterly lost ... Stephen Parradee of Kent Co, is very far from desiring to take any advantage to himself from the loss of the said deed of Stephen Parradee his father, to whom he is heir at law, and willing and desirous to preclude himself from any right, benefitt or claim to the said tract of land and for the consideration of 5 shillings, quit claims the 100 a. of land. {KEDELR N:17}

THE PARK/PARKE FAMILY

1. THOMAS PARK, mariner, m. Sarah, dau. of John Machan.

On 20 Dec 1715 Thomas Parke late of Murtherkill Hundred, Kent Co., marriner, and Sarah his wife for £75 sold to Nathaniel Hall of same place marriner ... a tract of land lying in Murtherkill Hundred on s. side of Jones Creek called *Shoemakers Hall* ... near Isaac's branch ... by Walker's branch ... patent for 400 a. bearing date 26 March 1684. {KEDELR E:55}

On 16 March 1729 Thomas Parke and Sarah his wife of Kent Co. for £300 sold to Andrew Magill and Mary his wife of same place, a tract of land being part of a tract called *Berrys Range* on n. side of Dover River ... 95 a. and also another tract of land adj. ... 80 a. {KEDELR I:260}

On 8 Oct 1730 Thomas Parke of Kent Co., yeoman, and Sarah his wife for good will and natural affection gave to their well beloved son John Parke ... two cows and their increase, one marked with a swallow fork in each ear and an over bitt in the right, one other black cow marked with a swallow fork in the right ear and an over bitt and a swallow fork in the left. {KEDELR K:51}

On 1 Aug 1717 John Machan of Kent Co. PA, planter, for naturall love and affection gave to dau. Sarah the wife of Thomas Park, marriner, a tract of land with a plantation called *Berrys Range* near the head of Jones Creek bounded by land purchased by James Maxwell of William Berry ... 95 a. and also part of a tract of land adj. being part of *Berry's Range* above the plantation where the said John Machan did live ... 80 a. {KEDELR I:7}

Sarah's father, John Machan, yeoman, d. leaving a will dated 10/24 June 1727, proved 23 April 1728. Heirs: grandsons Thomas and Theodorus Park, and John, son of Thomas and Sarah Park; granddaus. Charity and Cecilia

Park; dau. Sarah Park and dau. wife of Patrick Downs. Exec. grandson John Parks. Wits., Robert Potts, William Rodney, Susannah Tarrant, Thomas Tarrant. {Arch. A33:55-56. Reg. of Wills, G:12-13}

On 20 May 1728 Alice Machan of Kent Co., widow and relict of John Machan, late of same co., dec'd., for natural love and affection and good will gave to her grand children to wit., John Parke, Thomas Parke, Theodorus Parke, Hugh Parke and Cecelia Parke all being the sons and daus. of Thomas Parke and my dau. Sarah his wife ... all my right and dower in ye houses, buildings, lands and tenants which my husband John Machan afsd. dyed possessed of and also my 1/3 part of the estate which my said husband John Machan also dyed possessed of. {KEDELR I:131}

Sarah Parke d. leaving a will dated 19 Sep 1738, proved 19 Oct 1738. Heirs: sons Thomas, Theadore, Hugh; Ann, dau. of Thomas Tarrant; Rev. Arthur Ussher. Exec. friend Thomas Tarrant. Wits., Arthur Ussher, Mary Tuthill, Charles Tuthill. {Arch. A39:19-21. Reg. of Wills. I:4} Note: Arch. A39:20-21 show this account later administered, d.b.n., by Robert Willcocks and Rev. Arthur Ussher.

Thomas was father of the following children: THOMAS; THEODORUS; HUGH; JOHN; CHARITY; CECILIA.

Second Generation

2. THOMAS PARKE, son of Thomas (1) Parke, b. 1721, m. Ann (N).[45]

On 27 May 1747 Thomas Parke of Kent Co., hatter, and Ann his wife for £40 sold to Thomas Green of same co., yeoman, a lott of land in the Town of Dover being part of a parcel of land sold by Daniel Robinson to James Gorrel beginning where Kings Street and Water Street intersects to the said Parke's line, to Thomas Alford's lott which he purchased of the said Parke ... 1 a. {KEDELR N:154}

On 28 May 1747 Thomas Parke of Kent Co., hatter, and Ann his wife for £40 sold to Thomas Alford of same co., yeoman, a lott of land in the Town of Dover being part of a parcel of land sold by Daniel (Robisson) to James Gorril beginning where King Street and Water Street intersects Richard Richardson's land ... 1 a. {KEDELR N:144}

On 15 Feb 1755 Thomas Parke of the Town of Dover Kent Co. and Ann his wife for £60 sold to John Boggs of same place, house carpenter, a tract of land in the Town of Dover which Thomas Parke purchased of Wateman Sipple (Book N, fol. 55) beginning at King Street ... 30 1/8 sq perches. {KEDELR O:281}

On 13 Feb 1756 Robert Maxwell, exec. of James Maxwell, dec'd., of Kent Co. for £50.10 sold to Hugh Parke of same place, hatter, he being the highest bidder, a house and a lott in the Town of Dover and 100 a. of uncultivated land near the Bear Swamp conveyed by a certain Thomas Parke and

---

45 Perhaps her last name was Lecky. The will of Andrew Leckey, inn holder, was written 6 March 1744, proved 14 March 1744 in which he mentions son-in-law Thomas Parke as exec. Also mentioned were wife Esther; daus. Jane, Mary, Isabella; son Isaac. Execs., wife Esther and son-in-law Thomas Parke. Wits., Thomas Green, Timothy Cummins, Thomas Metcalf. {Arch. A29:222. Reg. of Wills, I:111-112}

Ann his wife to a certain Thos. Alford on 8 May 1747 (Book N, fol. 144) and after by him to the testator 10 Feb 1752 (Book O, fol. 130) beginning at King Street, ... 1 a. Robert Maxwell shall still have the right to a certain rent said to be due from Theodore Parke, dec'd., for which an action is now depending against said Theodore Parke's admin. {KEDELR O:329}

On 26 Nov 1762 Thos. Parke, aged 41 years, being solemnly sworn deposeth and saith that some time in the year 1750 he was high sherriff of Kent Co. and on 28 Dec 1750 he paid Jno. Green the sum of £84 being for an execution brought by Mr. Green against Phillip Fields. {KEDELR R:17}

Thomas Parke d. by 4 Nov 1766 when his estate was admin. by Ann Parke. {Arch. A39:27-29. Reg. of Wills, L: 21 and 48}

Ann Parke d. by 12 Nov 1768 when her estate was admin. by Cecilia Parke, next of kin. After the death of Ann, the estate of Thomas Parke was administered by Cecilia Parke, next of kin, d.b.n. on 12 Nov 1768. {Arch. A39:6-7 and 27-29. Reg. of Wills, L:48 and 21} Note: Arch. A39:6 and 27 shows that Cecillia Parke later m. Bertles Shee.

In a petition of 25 Feb 1767 Cecilia Parke stated that Thomas Parke of the town of Dover died intestate leaving a widow and 2 children: John and Cecilia Parke (petitioner) now 21 years of age. In a petition of Bertles Shee and Cecila his wife on 15 Nov 1769 it was sated that Thomass Parke died seized of several lots in the town of Dover and also in Murtherkill Hundred. Cecilia is now aged 21 years and upwards. {KEORCF Parke, Thomas 1767-78}

Thomas was father of the following children: CECILIA, m. Bertles Shee; JOHN.

3. THEODORE PARKE, tailor, son of Thomas (1) Parke, m. Frances Booth, dau. of Joseph Booth, and had a son Theodore who d. intestate and without issue.

Frances Park, dau. of Joseph Booth, dec'd., d. by 7 Aug 1753 when her estate was admin. by Theodore Park, husband, d.b.n. {Reg. of Wills, K:68}

On 16 April 1761 Thomas Parke of Kent Co. and Hugh Parke of same co., hatter, for £165 sold to Daniel Robisson of same co., a tract of land, whereas Joseph Booth, late of same co., gent., dec'd., was in his life time seized in 707 a. on s. side of St. Jones Creek or Dover River, part of a larger tract called *Whitwells Delight* and being so seizd d. intestate leaving issue, to wit, John Booth, his eldest son and 2 daus., Anna Booth and Frances Booth, and John Booth by his petition to the justices of the Orphans Court, 5 sufficient freeholders were appointed to make a division of the afsd. land on 15 March 1748 and did allot unto Frances Booth, 225 a., by the return of said division 25 Aug 1749, and whereas Frances Booth afterwards m. Theodore Parke who together did on 6 May 1751 convey the afsd. 225 a. unto the afsd. Thomas Parke, and Thomas Parke together with Anne his wife on 30 May 1751 did reconvey to the said Theodore Parke, gent., the afsd. land, and Theodore Parke sold to John Bowers 60 a. of the said tract but before disposition of the residue died intestate leaving issue only Theodore Parke his son which said Theodore Parke the younger died intestate also and without issue by means whereof the residue now is vested in the said Thomas Parke and Hugh Parke as uncles of the said Theodore Parke the younger and brothers of the said Theodore Parke the elder ... 225 a. Witnessed by Ceseia Parke, Vincent Loockerman. {KEDELR Q:49}

Theodore was father of an only child, THEODORE who d. intestate and without issue.

Theodore Parke, infant [*under the age of 21*], d. by 17 Aug 1759 when his estate was administered by Hugh Parke, hatter. {Reg. of Wills, K:210-211}

On 29 May 1767 Cecilia Parke stated that Theodore Parke, dec'd., intestate, of Dover, having issue only one child, Theodore Parke, who soon after died in his minority whereas rights to his land went to Thomas Parke and Hugh Parke, brothers and only surviving heirs of Theodore, dec'd. Said Thomas Parker d. intestate leaving 2 children, Cecilia Parke (petitioner) and John Parke. {KEORCF Parke, Theodore 1767}

Theodore Parke [apparently, son of Theodore (3) Parke], d. by 27 May 1767 when his estate was administered by Thomas Parke. {Arch. A39:25-26} Thomas Parke, admin. of the estate of Theodore Park, dec'd., of Motherkill Hundred, submitted a petition on 22 Feb 1757. {KEORCF Parke, Theodore 1757}

4. HUGH PARKE of Dover, son of Thomas (1) Parke, m. Elizabeth Edingfield. Following Hugh's death she m. John Carson.

Hugh d. leaving a will dated 15 July 1769, proved 22 July 1769. Heirs: wife Elizabeth; son Thomas. Extx. wife Elizabeth. Wits., William Rodney, Crawford Rees. {Arch. A39:8-11. Reg. of Wills, L:62} Note: Arch. A39:9 shows that Elizabeth Parke married John Carson.

Elizabeth's father John Edingfield of St. Jones Hundred, d. leaving a will dated 22 Oct 1771 [no date of probate]. Heirs: dau. Elizabeth Parke; grandsons Thomas Parke (son of Hugh and Elizabeth Parke) and John Clayton (son of James Clayton). Extx. dau. Elizabeth Parke. {Arch. A16:16. Reg. of Wills,
L:100-103}

Hugh was father of THOMAS.

Third Generation

5. JOHN PARKE, son of Thomas (2) Parke, d. by 16 July 1770 when his estate was administered by Bertles Shee and wife Cecilia. {Arch. A39:15-17}

6. CECILIA PARKE, dau. of Thomas (2) Parke, m. Bertles Shee.

7. THOMAS PARKE, probable son of Hugh (4) Parke, m. Jane (N). They were parents of the following children: ANN, b. 18th da., 5th mo., 1778; THOMAS, b. 13th da., 6th mo., 1780; SUSANNA HUDSON, b. 13th da., 8th mo., 1782; SAMUEL EMLEN, b. 2nd da., 3rd mo., 1787; HUDSON EMLEN, b. 4th da., 1st mo., 1789, d. 4th da., 8th mo., 1789. {DCMM}

Jane Parke produced a certificate from Philadelphia Monthly Meeting dated 30th da., 11th mo., 1787. {DCMM}

Unplaced

EDWARD PARK m. Alice or Alse (N) who later m. Wm. Ridgeway.

Edward Park, late of Kent Co., became seized in a tract of land on n.w. branch of Murder Creek ... 100 a. ... called *Nichols His Purchase* and being so seized d. inteste; his widow Alice after being married with William Ridgeway, in order to sattisfie unpaid debts did sell the afsd. land unto a certain William Clark on 6 Aug 1690. {KEDELR L:261}

Edward Park d. by 20 Dec 1683 when his estate was administered by

Alse Park. {Penna. Hist. Soc. Papers, AM 2013:9}

THE PARVIS FAMILY

1. ROBERT PARVIS m. Sirelly (N).

Robert d. leaving a will dated 8 Jan 1684, proved 10 July 1685. Heirs: sons, Robert and Jadwin; child unnamed; children of sisters Juda and Catterine Parvis; wife, Sirelly. Extx. wife. Trustees: William Santhers, Richard Mitchell, William Burry, Samuel Burrberry. Wits., Richard Ratliff, Samuel Mott, Benony Biship. {Penna. Hist. Soc. Papers, vol. AM. 2013:40-41} Note: Mentioned was Robert Parvis the uncle of William and Robert Parvis father of William as eldest son of the testator. Robert Parvis the uncle of William is since deceased.

On 10 July 1685 John Jadwin, relative, was appointed admin. of the estate of Robert Parvis. {Penna. Hist. Soc. Papers, AM. 2013:44. Arch. A39:100}

Robert was father of the following children: ROBERT; JADWIN.

Second Generation

2. ROBERT PARVIS, son of Robert (1) Parvis, m. Martha (N) who later m. John Castle.was father of the following daus.: DINAH, m. Thomas Pratt and had a son George; SARAH, m. William Downham and had a dau. Mary who m. James Willcocks; SUSANNAH, m. William Chance and had Aron and Francis.

On 20 April 1708 Robert Parviss, surviving son and heir of Robert Parviss, late of Kent Co, New Castle Co. and Sussex Co., dec'd., for £25 sold to John Wilson of TA Co., MD ... a tract of land called *Gilford,* on n. side of Murther Creek in fork of Bishops Branch ... 600 a. by virtue of a warrant from Kent Co. Court bearing date 17 Oct 1682 layed out for said Robert Parviss, dec'd. {E:332}

3. WILLIAM PARVISS, b. c1706, son of Robert (1) Parvis.

On 26 Aug 1724 William Parviss, son of Robert Parviss, late of QA Co., MD, dec'd., aged near 18 years hath put himself an apprentice and by these presents doth voluntarily and of his own, and with the free consent of his father in law John Castle and his mother Martha, wife of the said John, unto Christopher Penrose of Kent Co. cooper, with him after the manner of an apprentice to dwell, serve for and during the term of three years and a half ... at the end of three years and a half Christopher Penrose shall give him one thorough suit of good cloathes and shall also use his utmost endeavours to learn his said apprentice to read and write English well and arithmetic and the Golden Rule, teach, inform and instruct his said apprentice in all the arts and misteries of the coopers trade both sett and croos work to which occupation he the said Christopher Penrose now followeth. Wit: Benjamin Shurmer, John Russell, John Castle, Martha Castle. {KEDELR H:89}

William Parvis d. by 14 July 1739 when his estate was administered by Betty Parvis. {Reg. Of Wills, H:156}

Unplaced

RICHARD PARVIS was transported to the province of Maryland by 1669. {MPL 12:322}

RICHARD PARVIS, yeoman, d. by 14 Dec 1725 when his estate was administered by Hugh Perry. {Reg. of Wills, F:9}

THE PLEASANTON FAMILY

1. JOHN PLEASANTON, yeoman of Dover Hundred, m. Mary Campbell. Mary m. 1st Thomas Brinckle, m. 2nd (N) Campbell, m. 3rd John Pleasanton, and m. 4th Nimrod Maxwell.

George Lester of Dover Hundred d. leaving a will dated 6 April 1748, proved 14 May 1748. Heirs: sisters Mary Ware, Anna Roads; bros.-in-law Jonathan Pleasanton, David Pleasanton; nephew Johnny Ware. Exec., bro.-in-law William Ware. Wits., Benjamin Chew, Grace Morgan, Anna Morgan. {Arch. A30:17. Reg. of Wills, I:221}

On 10 Jan 1749 John Plesanton and Mary Campbel, both of Kent Co., have published their intention of maryage according to law at my house, these are therefore to certifie John Pleasanton and Mary Campbel did take each other to be lawful husband and wife before me one of the majesties justice of ye peace and a sufficient number of persons mett together for ye purpose being wittnesses present. Thos. Wilson, Ebenz. Manlove, Wm. Hirons, Charles Empson, Cesar Rodeney, John Allen, Charles Hemmey, Elizabeth Wilson, Elizabeth Rodeney, Jno. Hunn, David Plesenton, Mary Hememey, Sarah Manlove. {KEDELR O:60}

On 5 Dec 1753 John Pleasanton and Mary his wife for divers good causes and considerations hereunto moving give unto our well beloved son David Pleasanton one negro woman named Doll with one negro boy named Thomas and one negro boy named Frank ... in the penal sum of £70. {KEDELR O:245}

He d. leaving a will dated 8 Dec 1753, proved 15 Dec 1753. Heirs: wife Mary; sons John, Charles, George and David; granddau. Elizabeth Field; grandson Jonathan Pleasanton. Exec., son David. Wits., Ebenezer Manlove, William Shurmer, Abraham Barber. {Arch. A40:108-110. Reg. of Wills, K:88} Note: Will mentions wife's dau. Easter; Arch. vol. A40, page 109 shows Mary Maxwell and Thos. Brinckle as parents of Hester Brinckle, dec'd.

On 4 March 1755 a petition was submitted by Nimrod Maxwell and wife submitted an account for keeping one of dec'd. John Pleasanton's children named Charles and two negroes. To keeping the child £10.0.0. To keeping the two negroes £12.0.0. To buriing the child £3.0.0. On 1 April 1755 David Plesinton showed that he being left exec. of his father's will and by virtue of which he was left overseeer of his brother George Plesintine, begged that the court make Nimord Maxwell who married the widdow, give security for the afsd. George Plesinton's estate. On 29 Aug 1759 David Pleasanton stated that George Pleasanton, son of John Pleasanton, dec'd., at the time of the death of said John, was left a minor and under the guardianship of Mary Pleasanton, mother of said George. The afsd. Mary Pleasanton is since dec'd. and the said George still being a minor. The petitioner requests a guardian be appointed until the said George shall arrive to the age of 14 years. David Pleasantine was appointed quardian. {KEORCF Pleasanton, John - 1755-62}

There are two versions of a will for Hester Brinckle (Esther]. The first will shows it written on 13 Sep 1754, proved 10 Oct 1756. Heirs: sister Mary

Campbell; mother Mary Pleasenton. Extx., mother Mary Pleasenton. Wits., Stephen Paradee, Nimrod Maxwell, Anna Maxwell. {Arch. A5:167-169. Reg. of Wills, K:136} Note: Will mentions father Thomas Brinckle, dec'd.; Arch. A5:169 shows Mary Maxwell, nee Pleasanton, as extx. In the second will is shown Esther [Hester] Brinckle, dau. of Thomas, dec'd. Made 17 Sep 1754, proved 10 Oct 1754. Heirs: sister Mary Campbell; mother Mary Plesonton. Extx. mother. Wits., Stephen Paradee, Nimrod Maxwell, Annah Maxwell. {Arch. A5:167-168. Reg. of Wills, G: appendix 5} Note: The first unwitnessed will is recorded in Arch. A5:168 and Reg. of Wills, K:136}

John was father of the following children: JONATHAN; JOHN; CHARLES; GEORGE; DAVID.

Second Generation

2. JONATHAN PLEASASNTON, yeoman of Dover Hundred, son of John (1) Pleasanton, m. Mary Crawford, dau. of Thomas Crawford.

On 13 Feb 1744 Jonathan Pleasenton and Mary his wife of Kent Co. released unto Daniel Stevens and Letitia his wife of same co. ... 294 a., part of a tract of land called *The Cave* in the forrest of Murtherkill (granted by patent 20 Sep 1715 unto John French of Town and Co. of New Castle 588 a.) ... John French did on 10 Sep 1717 sell the said land and premisses unto John Brinkloe late of Kent Co., dec'd., who by his will did give the same to Mary Crawford and Letitia Crawford, daus of Thomas Crawford, which Mary is now the wife of afsd. Jonathan Pleasenton and Letitia is now the wife of Daniel Stevens, both parties agree to divide the land. {KEDELR N:57}

In a petition of Caesar Rodeney on 18 Dec 1753 he stated that whereas Jonathan Pleasanton late of this county, dec'd., did at the time of his death request of his father John Pleasanton to take care of his son Jonathan Pleasanton, then an infant and the said John Pleasanton being since dead, and the afsd. orphan having some considerable estate and nobody to take care of the same your petitioner prays your worship to appoint some carefull person as a guardian to the afsd. orphan Jonathan Pleasanton. Ceser Rodeney was appointed guardian. {KEORCF Pleasanton, Jonathan - 1753}

Jonathan d. leaving a will dated 8 Oct 1748, proved 1 Nov 1748. Heirs: son Jonathan; dau. Elizabeth; bros. John and David; Elizabeth Rodeney, Jr. Execs., John Pleasonton, Sr., father and John Pleasonton, Jr., bro. Wits., Richard Wells, Caesar Rodeney, William Clark. {Arch. A40:123, 127-128. Reg. of Wills, 1:236}

Jonathan was father of the following children: JONATHAN m. 29 July 1767, Ruhamah Lewis (b. ca. 22 Nov 1749); ELIZABETH.

3. JOHN PLEASANTON, probable son of John (1) Pleasanton, m. Sarah (N) who m. 2nd Elijah Anderson, and m. 3rd (N) Thomas.

John Pleasonton d. by 26 May 1770 when Sarah Pleasonton, widow, was appointed admx. of his estate. {Arch. A40:105-107. Reg. of Wills, L:79} Note: Arch. A40:105 show heirs, John, David, Elizabeth, Letitia and Rachel; page 106 shows that Elizabeth Pleasonton m. Daniel Thomas.

On 1 Sep 1770 John Pleasonton, a minor above the age of 14 years, son of John Pleasanton, late of sd. co., dec'd., prays to appoint David Pleasonton his uncle to be his guardian. On the same day David Pleasontine petitioned that he be appointed guardian to Elizabeth Pleasonton, a minor under the age of 14 years, dau. of John Pleasonton, late of sd. co., dec'd. On 27 Aug 1773, a petition was submitted by Sarah Anderson, widow of Elijah Anderson, dec'd., and late widow of John Pleasonton also dec'd., showing that the said John Pleasonton was seized in his demesne as of fee of and in a certain plantation in Murtherkill Hundred in Kent Co. and d. intestate leaving a widow, the petitioner, and sundry children - and that the petitioner is intituled to a third part of said plantation but she has never had the same laid off to her. On 25 Aug 1773 came John Pleasonton, eldest son and representative of John Pleasonton, dec'd., requesting the land be valued. On 24 Feb 1773 he stated that his father d. intestate leaving five children, to wit, John, Elizabeth, Latitia, David and Rachel. The petitioner was 21 years of age and upwards. On 27 May 1790, upon the application of Sarah Thomas, admin. of John Pleasonton, dec'd., for the sale of Letitia, David, and Rachel Pleasonton, dec'd., their undivided part of their father the said John Pleasonton, dec'd. real estate for the payment of their debts - in the whole containing about 189 a. {KEORCF Pleasanton, John - 1770-91}

John was father of the following children: JOHN; DAVID; ELIZABETH, m. Daniel Thomas; LETITIA; RACHEL.

4. DAVID PLEASANTON of Dover Hundred, son of John (1) Pleasanton, m. 1st Priscilla Hunn, dau. of Caleb Hunn and m. 2nd Deborah Luff, dau. of Nathaniel Luff. Deborah later m. Stephen Lewis.

Nathaniel Luff, Sr., Gentleman, d. leaving a will dated 3 Feb 1760, proved 27 Feb 1760. Heirs: wife Deborah; sons Caleb, Nathaniel, John; daus. Hannah Paradee, Deborth Pleasanton. Execs., sons Caleb and Nathaniel. Wits., Samuel Merydith, Sarah Maston, Thomas Clark. {Arch. A31:229-238. Reg. of Wills, K:225} Note: Arch. A31:235 shows John Paradee as husband of Hannah; David Pleasanton as husband of Deborah; Deborah later married Stephen Lewis. Page 236 shows Deborah, the widow, later married Jonathan Manlove. Page 238 shows Philip Reason [Rasin] only son of Sarah had heirs, Jemiah Ford, Robert Meeks and Joseph Rasin.

Caleb Hunn died intestate seized of a tract and leaving issue 3 daus, to wit Mary, the afsd. Hannah Levick and Ruth - and Priscilla who afterwards intermarried with David Pleasontine of Kent Co., yeoman, and is since dec'd. without issue living at the time of her death, by means of which said deaths of the said Caleb Hunn and Priscilla Pleasontine intestate the 98 a., 80 sq perches descended to the afsd. Mary, Hannah Levick, Ruth now w/o a certain John Rodeney, children and heirs of the said Caleb Hunn. Wit: Will Killen, William Ross. Hannah Levick ackn the within deed of her own free consent. Ackn 26 May 1762. {KEDELR Q:104}

David d. leaving a will dated 28 March 1774, proved 5 April 1774. Heirs: wife Deborah; dau. Sarah; sons Nathaniel, John, David, Caleb. Execs., wife Deborah and William Rodney. Commissioners, Caleb Luff, John Williams, James Sykes, Esq., William Rodney, Samuel Hanson. Wits., James Stevens, Jonathan Pleasanton, Benjamin Nixon. {Arch. A40:94-99. Reg. of Wills, L:152} Note: Arch. A40:96 shows that Deborah Pleasanton married Stephen Lewis.

David was father of the following children: SARAH; NATHANIEL; JOHN; DAVID; CALEB.

THE QUILLING/QUILLIN FAMILY

1. THOMAS QUILLING m. Barbara (N).

Thomas Quilling d. by 13 Feb 1741 when Barbary Quilling, widow, was appointed admx. of his estate. {Reg. of Wills, I:59} Note: Arch. A42:6 shows sons Teague, Alexander, Joseph; daus. Sarah, Lydia, Elizabeth Quilling; Benjamin, son of Thomas Quilling, Jr., dec'd.

On 25 Nov 1745 William Sidden of Dover Hundred, Kent Co. for divers, good causes and considerations him thereunto moving and also for 5 shillings released to Barbara Quillin of Murderkill Hundred same co., widow, a piece of land in Dover Hundred, being the w. part of that piece which was late conveyd to the said William Sidden by Thomas Green, high sheriff of same co. ... 75 a. called *Partners Lott*. {KEDELR N:103}

On 18 Sep 1762 John Miller of Kent co. yeoman for 330 pounds sold to John Barnett of same co. a parcel of land called *Maidstone* on s. side of Mill Branch or Main or Middle Branch of Dover River below the plantation whereon one Alexander Quilling lately dwelt ... 50 a., part of a larger tract called *Bushy Plain* which was sold to the John Miller by one Alexander Quilling, son and one of the heirs of Thomas Quilling, late of Kent Co, yeoman, dec'd. by deed poll bearing date 14 Nov 1749 and by one David Hannah and Elizabeth his wife, Henry Miller and Lydia his wife, John Quilling and Sarah his wife, Joseph Quilling and Elizabeth his wife and Benjamin Quilling heirs also and representatves of the said Thomas Quilling dec'd. by indenture bearing date 16 Sep instant. {KEDELR Q:120}

Thomas Quilling was father of the following children: THOMAS, d. by 13 Feb 1741; TEAGUE; ALEXANDER; SARAH, m. John Quilling; ELIZABETH, m. David Hannah; LYDIA, m. Henry Miller; JOSEPH, m. Elizabeth (N).

Second Generation

2. THOMAS QUILLING, probable son of Thomas (1) Quilling, d. by 13 Feb 1741, had a son BENJAMIN, mentioned in the will of Thomas's father.

3. ALEXANDER QUILLIN, probable son of Thomas (1) Quilling m. Mary (N).

On 14 Nov 1749 Alexander Quilling of Murtherkill Hundred, Kent Co., planter, and Mary his wife, for £14.11.6 sold to John Miller, Junr, of same place a parcel of land in the forrest of Murtherkill Hundred whereon I now dwell it being the lower n.e. part of the tract of land *Bushie*, beginning at a branch of Dover River ... 50 a. including ye plantation. {KEDELR O:29}

On 9 March 1761 Alexander Quilling and Mary his wife, John Quilling and Sarah his wife, David Hannah and Elizabeth his wife, and Henry Miller and Lydia his wife all of Kent co. for 5 shillings sold unto Joseph Quilling of of same co. a tract of land in the forrest of Dover Hundred called *Partners Choice* or *Lott* beginning at land conveyed to a certain William Sidden by Thomas Green the then high sheriff of Kent co. ... 75 a. {KEDELR Q:23}

4. SARAH QUILLING, dau. of Thomas (1) Quilling, m. John Quilling.

On 16 Sep 1762 David Hannah of Kent Co., yeoman, and Elizabeth his wife, Henry Miller of said co., husbandman, and Lydia his wife, John Quilling of said co., yeoman, and Sarah his wife, Joseph Quilling of said co., yeoman, and Elizabeth his wife and Benjamin Quilling of said co., yeoman, for £7 released unto John Miller of Kent Co., yeoman, all their shares in a tract of land, whereas Thomas Quilling late of Kent Co., carpenter, dec'd., was in his lifetime seized in 50 a. of land part of a larger tract called *Bushy Plain* on s. side of Main or Middle Branch of Dover River in the forest of Murtherkill Hundred and being so seized died intestate leaving issue one Alexander Quilling, the afsd. Elizabeth Hannah, Lydia Miller, Sarah Quilling wife of said John Quilling, Joseph Quilling and one Thomas Quilling now dec'd. father of the afsd. Benjamin Quilling, and whereas Alexander Quilling by his deed poll bearing date 14 Nov 1749 did convey to the said John Miller the 50 a. including the plantation whereon I now dwell (Book O, fol 28). (Q:pg 122)

John Quilling, chairmaker of Little Creek Hundred, d. by 26 Jan 1778 when Sarah Quilling and James Cummins were appointed admins. of the estate. {Arch. A42:3. Reg. of Wills, L:125}

5. JOSEPH QUILLING, probable son of Thomas (1) Quilling, m. Elizabeth (N).

Unplaced

(N) QUILLING m. Susannah, dau. of Dorathy Miller.

Dorathy Miller d. leaving a will dated 1761, proved 7 Dec 1762. Heirs: dau. Susannah Quilling; granddau. Mary Quilling; sons Henry, Peter, Adam, Chillen, John and Conrad Miller. Execs. sons Adam and Chillen Miller. Wits., John Wood, Joseph Quilling. {Arch. A35:74. Reg. of Wills, K:299. Note: Will mentions Clement Quilling.

(N) QUILLING, possibly Alexander (3) Quilling, m. Mary Jones, dau. of Barbara Jones.

Barbara Jones d. leaving a will dated 21 Nov 1768, proved 7 Dec 1763. Heirs: sons George Howard, John Benet, John Gould Howard; dau. Mary Quilling; son-in-law Benjamin Jones. Exec., son-in-law Benjamin Jones. Wits., Benjamin Jones, Jr., John Robearts, Susanah Steelman. {Arch. A27:133. Reg. of Wills, K:321-322}

THE RAWLINGS FAMILY

1. ANTHONY RAWLINS immigrated by 1645 to Maryland with wife Joan. Anthony was deceased c1652. {MPL ABH 15, 2:458, 479} John Rawlings of Stafford Freehold, Calvert Co., son of Anthony, living in 1664. {MPL 7:475, 8:90}

Second Generation

2. JOHN RAWLINGS, possibly son of Anthony (1) Rawlins, had a son Anthony.

John Rawlings, late of Kent Co., DE, yeoman, procured a warrant for a land patent bearing date 15 March 1680, surveyed on 9 May 1681, called *Camebridge* on n. side of Murderkill Creek which was since sold by Anthony Rawlings, son and heir of John Rawlings, unto Andrew Caldwell Senr., 100 a. {KEDELR N:11}

John Rawlings d. by 21/22 Sep 1681 when his estate was administered by John Richardson. {Reg. of Wills, Liber A:1}

On 23 Nov 1745 Anthony Rawlins (Rawlings) of Kent Co., yeoman, for £150 sold to Joseph Rawlins of same place, yeoman, a tract of land, part of a larger tract called *Rallings Lott*, surveyed and laid out on 10 May 1681 by Ephraim Harmon then surveyor by virtue of a warrant from St. Jones Court for John Rawlings, father to the afsd. Anthony Rawlins, to whom the tract of land did descend, in Mispillion Hundred on n. side of the s.w. prong of Murderkill Creek adj. Pemberton Brown's land ... 358 a. {KEDELR N:92}

3. ANTHONY RAWLINGS, son of John (2) Rawlings, m. Catherine (N).

On 11 May 1736 Anthony Rawlings and Catherine (Katherin) his wife for £15 released unto John Peirson, part of a tract of land called *Longford* near a branch of Murtherkill Creek beginning at a line of Manlove's land, 100 a. Witnessed by Joseph Rawlings, William Pegg. {KEDELR L:156}

On 9 Nov 1748 Anthony Rawlings of Kent Co., yeoman, for £27 sold to Peter Adams of same place, yeoman, a tract of land on n. side of Browns Branch in the upper part of Mispillion Hundred, being part of a larger tract beginning at William Eagle's land ... 112 a. Anthony Rawlings appointed his son Joseph Rawlings as atty to ackn this deed in open court. {KEDELR N:244}

Anthony Rawlings, trader, d. by 23 June 1762 when his estate was administered by Sarah Rawlings and Reynear Williams. {Reg. of Wills, K:286} Note: Arch. A42:134 shows this acct. was later admin. by Sarah Adams and Reynear Williams.

Anthony was father of JOSEPH.

Unplaced

JOHN RAWLINGS, yeoman, d. by 5 April 1735 when his estate was administered by Anthony Rawlings. {Reg. of Wills, H:93}

THE RODNEY FAMILY

For earlier ancestry see *The Welcome Claimants* ... See also *Somerset Sampler*.

First Generation

1. WILLIAM RODENEY[46], the immigrant, son of William and Rachel Rodeney and brother of Rachel and Elizabeth, was baptized 14 March 1660 at Christ Church, Bristol. William m. 1st 25th da., 11th mo., 1688 {Phila Monthly Meeting} Mary Hollyman of Philadelphia, dau. of Thomas and Sarah Hollyman, and m.

[46] An article in *The American Genealogist*, April 1989, pp. 97-111, Daniel Rodney Letter and Pedigree, Vol. 4, No. 1:1, shows that William Rodney was a grandson of William Rodney who m. Alice Caesar. William Rodney was the nephew of Capt. John Rodney of Philadelphia who d. leaving a Will dated 15 Sep 1694, proved 12 Dec 1694. He mentioned his wife Anne, minor son Caesar, dau. Penelopy Roach and nephew William Rodney of Jones Co. (Kent Co.) {Calendar of New Jersey Wills, V. 1:392; Philadelphia Wills A:279}.

2nd Sarah Jones. Sarah later m. George Nowell.

On 20 Feb 1693 William Rodeney and Sarah Jones both of Kent Co. having intentions of marriage duely published, certifie that said marriage was solomnized by George Martin, justice, at the house of Daniell Jones, Senr., father to Sarah Jones in presence of her father and mother. Witnessed by Daniell Jones Senr, John Brinckloe, John Betts, Daniell Jones, Junr.

Daniel Jones became seized in 791 a. called *Denbigh* and being so seized did by his will bearing date 21 Aug 1694 devise unto his dau. Sarah the afsd. tract of land at the head of St. Jones Creek with remainder to his son Daniel Jones. Sarah Jones afterwards intermarried with one William Rodney of Kent Co. Esqr now dec'd., by whom she had issue Daniel Rodney and Casar Rodney the elder, and afterward died leaving the afsd. Daniel Rodney her eldest son whereby an estate tail in the said tract became vested in the said Daniel Rodney and was thereof seized in fee tail general, and being so seized died without issue in the lifetime of the said Casar Rodney the elder his brother, whereby the tract vested in the said Casar Rodney, Casar Rodney afterwards died leaving issue Casar Rodney the younger of Kent Co. Esqr his eldest son who became seized of the land, whereas the said Casar Rodney the younger being so seized by indenture made between the said Casar Rodney, Richard Wells and Benjamin Chew did sell unto the said Richard Wells the afsd. tract of land in a good and perfect common recovery bearing date 1 April 1752 (Book O, fol. 145) ... on Walkers Branch adj. land formerly of John Walker now called *Dover Town* land ... 100 a. {KEDELR R:51}

Daniel Jones, Jones Creek, d. leaving a will dated 21 Aug 1694, proved 21 March 1694/5. Heirs: wife, Mary; son Daniel; dau. Sarah; son-in-law William Rodney. Execs., wife Mary and son Daniel. Wits., John Clayton, Joseph Osburne, Arthur Meston. {Arch. A27:150-151. Reg. of Wills, A:11}

On 14 Sep 1698 William Rodeney and Sarah his wife for love and naturall affection and 5 shillings sold to William Brinckloe and Elizabeth his wife, a tract of land being part of a tract of land called *Denbigh*, on w. side of Dover River, 394 a. {KEDELR}

Simon Hirons, Sr., d. leaving a will dated 12 Oct 1706, proved 16 Dec 1706. Heirs: sons Francis, Simon, Robert, William, and John; wife Pereess; dau. Margaret; Sarah Rodney, dau. of Capt. Wm. and Sarah Rodney; Anna Bedwell, dau. of Thomas and Milicent Bedwell; Samuel Berry, son-in-law; John Portess, son of John and Deborah Portess; Silvanus Portess, son of John and Deborah Portess. Extx. wife Percess. Wits., James Moore, Timothy Hanson, Joshua Clayton, Stephen Paradee. {Arch. A24:97. Reg. of Wills, B:56}

William Rodney d. 8 Sep 1708 and was buried on the Old Byfield Plantation in Jones' Neck. He left a will dated 1 May 1708, proved 4 Oct 1708. Heirs: sons William, Thomas, John, Anthony, George and Caesar; dau. Sarah; mother Rachel; sisters Rachel, Elizabeth; wife Sarah; orphans of Richard Willson. Extx. wife Sarah. Wits., Elizabeth Annand, William Annand. {Arch. A44:96-98. Reg. of Wills, B:63-64}

William Rodeney ye elder by severall purchases especially one from Frances Gibbons for 695 a. and James Maxfield for 50 a., both on s. side of Dover River on n. side of Mill Creek, together with 100 a. granted to him by the Commissioners of Property, and said parcels of land being resurveyed and found to be 840 a. called *Dover Farm*, Rodeney in his will bearing date 1 May 1708 did give to his two sons William and Thomas Rodeney all that afsd. tract of land. {KEDELR N:34}

On 1 Aug 1716 William Rodney of Kent Co., yeoman, for £28 sold to Isaiah Whitehead, carpenter, a tract of land called *Dover Farms*, on s. side of Dover River ... 800 a. made up of several parcels of land following ... 400 a. granted by pattent to Huber Frances, 200 a. granted by an order from the court at St. Jones 21 March 1684 to John Burton ... whereas Edmond Gibbson, dec'd., did in his life time purchase of Huberd Frances 400 a. and of John Burton 200 a. and devised the same by his will to his brother Frances Gibbson ... was resurveyed and found to have 695 a. and afterwards was conveyed by Frances Gibbson to William Rodeney, dec'd., father of afsd. William Rodeney and 50 a. more purchased by William Rodney of James Maxwell and 100 a. granted by virtue of a warrant and layed out to William Rodeney and all parcels resurveyed in one tract were found to contain 800 a. William Rodeney did make out his will 1 May 1708 and did bequeath unto his eldest sons William Rodeney and Thomas Rodeney all that tract of land called *Dover Farms*, s. side of Dover River, 840 a., to be equally divided between them ... when son William shall attain the age of 21. {KEDELR E:193}

On 11 March 1717 Daniel Rodeney and William Rodeney of Kent Co., yeomen, were bound and indebted unto George Nowell of same place gentleman in the sum of £660 due unto George Rodeney, Caleb Rodeney and Sarah Rodeney legatees of William Rodeney late of Kent Co., dec'd., gentlemen, £330, being their full dividends which had come to the possession of George Nowell and Sarah his wife, executors of the will of William Rodeney, dec'd. {KEDELR F:135}

Sarah Nowell, wife of George Nowell d. leaving a will dated 25 Dec 1729, proved 11 Feb 1729. Heir and exec.: son Daniel Rodney. Exec. son Daniel Rodney. Wits., John Wilson, Sr., James White. {Arch. A38:60. Reg. of Wills, H:2}

William and Mary were parents of the following children: WILLIAM, b. at Lewes 27 Oct 1689, d. 1731/2; RACHEL, b. Nov 1690, d. 1691; THOMAS, b. at Lewes 1692, d. Philadelphia 1709. Mary, wife of William d. Dec 1692. William m. 2nd on 20 Feb 1693, Sarah, dau. of Daniel Jones. Sarah later m. George Nowell. {Daniel Rodney Letter}

On 10 July 1696 a cattle mark was recorded for Daniell Rodney which had formerly belonged to Daniell Jones, his grandfather. {Kent Ct.:87}

On 12 Nov 1728 William Rodeney, eldest son of William Rodeney, late of Kent Co., dec'd., and Daniel Rodeney brother of the whole blood of John Rodeney, dec'd., another of the sons of the, dec'd., William Rodeney and a devisee named in his will send greeting ... know ye that the said William Rodeney the son of Daniel Rodeney for 5 shillings quitt claims unto Daniel Needham of Kent Co. gent in a tract of land called *Tiverton*. {KEDELR I:148}

William and Sarah were parents of the following children: DANIEL, b. 13 Feb 1694/5 in Kent Co., d. 19 Dec 1744, buried in Dover; JOHN, b. April 1696, d. Jan 1708; ANTHONY, b. March 1698, d. May 1720; GEORGE, b. Feb 1701/2, d. April 1721; SARAH, b. Aug 1704, d. April 1727; CESAR, b. 12 Oct 1707, d. May 1745. All the sons and daughters, except William the eldest and Cesar the youngest, d. without issue. {Daniel Rodney Letter and Rodney-Wilson Bible}

Second Generation

2. WILLIAM RODENEY, son of William (1) and Mary Rodeney, m. Ruth, dau.

of John Curtis whose widow later m. (N) Gilbert. Ruth later m. Mark Manlove.

On 9 May 1717. Whereas there was a certain sum of money in hand paid by Robert Bedwell in his life time to William Rodeney, dec'd., for a tract of land ... William Rodeney son and heir of William Rodeney late of Kent Co., dec'd., released to Robert and James Bedwell sons and coheirs of Robert Bedwell late of same co., dec'd., all his rights to tract of land called *Wedmore* ... 354 a. {KEDELR F:39}

Prissila Gilbert, widow, d. leaving a will dated 22 Jan 1719/20, proved 10 May 1721. Heirs: daus. Sarah Bowman, Prissila Walton and Ruth Rodney; son John Bowers; grandsons Nathaniel Hunn and Nathaniel Luff; granddau. Penelop Rodney, dau. of William and Ruth Rodney; Thomas Bowman, son of Nathaniel Bowman. Execs.. son John Bowers and son-in-law Nathaniel Bowman. Wits., Jonathan Manlove, Hannah Manlove. {Arch. A19:28. Reg. of Wills, D:44}

On 9 May 1717 William Rodeney, son of William Rodeney, late of Kent Co., dec'd., sold to Robert and James Bedwell, sons and coheirs of Robert Bedwell, late of Kent Co., dec'd., a tract of land called *Wedmore* wherewith the said William Rodeney, dec'd., did in his life time sell unto [page torn] by deed dated 14 Feb 1717 but not fully executed ... therefore son William Rodeney conveys unto Robert and James Bedwell the afsd. tract of land ... 254 a. {KEDELR E:289}

On 1 Nov 1721 William Rodeney of Kent Co. yeoman and Ruth his wife ... whereas a tract of land called *Dover Farms*, on s. side of Dover River ... by the line of William Darval's land ... by Mill Creek ... 840 a. being made up of several parcels of land: 400 a. granted by patent from Sir Edmond Andrews to Hubert Francis, 210 a. granted by Court of St. Jones and laid out 21 March 1684 to John Burton and whereas Edmond Gibbons, dec'd., did in his lifetime purchase of Hubert Francis the 400 a. and of the John Burton the 200 a. and devised the same by his will to his brother Francis Gibbons and resurveyed and found to contain 695 a. and afterwards conveyed by said Francis Gibbons to William Rodeney, dec'd., father of the afsd. William Rodeney and 50 a. more purchased by William Rodeney of James Maxwell and 100 a. granted by a warrant and being resurveyed together was found to contain 840 a. as afsd. and by confirmation by pattent bearing date 17 Oct 1701 by William Penn Esqr Governor of PA confirmed unto William Rodeney, and said William Rodeney did afterwards in his life time by deed 25 March 1699 sell unto Adam Fisher of same co. 92 a. part of afsd. 840 a. and also 1 May 1708 did make his will ... I bequeath unto my two eldest sons William and Thomas Rodeney all that tract of land called *Dover Farms* containing at this time 748 a. to be divided between them ... when my son William shall attain the age of 21. Thomas Rodeney dyeing without issue and before William Rodeney the brother came of age the same William Rodeney is heir to the whole 748 a. ... William Rodeney (after his attaining the age of 21) did sell to Isaiah Whitehead 50 a. and to Agnes Downham executrix of the will of Thomas Downham, dec'd., 57 a. ... this indenture William Rodeney for £350 sold to Waitman Sipple of same place, yeoman, remaining part of 748 a. {KEDELR G:39}

On 10 May 1725 William Rodeney and Ruth his wife of Kent Co. for £8 sold to Jehu Curtis of same place, Esqr., a tract of land which is not mentioned in the will of John Curtis late of same co., dec'd., father to the said Ruth ... in Mispilion Hundred called *Swamp Baron* 160 a. also two other parcells of land in Dorchester Co., MD, one called *Indian Quarter* and the other *Rochester*, 100 a. each. {KEDELR H:199}

On 4 May 1726 William Rodeney of Kent Co. and Ruth his wife for £25 sold to Niel Cook of Casil [Cecil] Co. MD, yeoman, a parcell of land in Murtherkill Hundred beginning at the corner of John Thompson's land ... 100 a. {KEDELR I:75}

On 10 May 1727 William Rodeney of Kent Co. PA esqr and Ruth his wife for £65 sold to John Craig of Cecill Co., MD, farmer and Moses Craig of the same place, farmer, two tracts of land (resurveyed 3 May 1727 for the said William Rodeney), part of the one tract begins at a corner of the land of Edward Williams ... to tract of land formerly laid out for Edward Cook ... 100 a. ... being one half of 200 a. laid out unto William Rodeney by virtue of a warrant granted to him 21 Jun 1716 ... also a tract of land beginning at the western line of land called *The Plains*, to corner line of Arthur Brooks ... 200 a. warrant granted at Philadelphia 21 Jun 1716 unto Edward Cook and by him assigned to the said William Rodeney by warrant remaining in the hands of Richard Smith deputy surveyor of Kent Co. ... in whole 300 a. {KEDELR I:87}

On 1 May 1731 John Rudolphus Bundelyn of Kent Co. yeoman for £20 sold to William Rodeney, Junr., and Penelope Rodeney both son and dau. to William Rodeney of same co., a tract of land whereon John Merry now dwells being part of a greater tract of land called *Rudolphus Range* on Murther Creek, 400 a. {KEDELR K:123}

William Rodeney d. 26 June 1732. His estate was administered 19 Oct 1732 by Ruth Rodeney. {Reg. of Wills, H:32 and 46}

On 27 Aug 1754 John Housman, Esqr., of the Town of Dover, Kent Co., sold to James Scott of same co., a tract of land, whereas Ruth Manlove widow and relict of Mark Manlove, dec'd., but was formerly the widow of William Rodeney of same co., dec'd., who was with Solomon Cale who is also, dec'd., one of the executors of the will of John Cale, dec'd., on 27 Dec 1730 at an Orphans Court before Charles Hilliard, John Hall, John Housman and William Manlove Esqr, William Rodeney and Solomon Cale obtained an order to sell the land of John Cale, dec'd., 50 a., being part of a larger tract called *Holly Neck* in Murderkil Hundred with the messuages thereon adj. the land then of Richard Jackson and John Jackson and *Caroon Mannor*, sold at vendue unto John Housman Esqr he being the highest bidder for £15 and now in his possession, William Rodeney and Solomon Cale died soon after and no deed to him made ... Ruth Manlove, admx., released unto John Housman the afsd. tract of land and for £45 paid by James Scott released her rights in the afsd. tract of land unto James Scott ... beginning at John Jackson's land to Beaver Dam Branch to William and John Jackson's land in the line of *Caroon Mannor* ... 102 a. {KEDELR O:237}

William was father of the following children: PENELOPE, b. 1712, m. James Gorrel, 1733 {Daniel Rodney Letter}; THOMAS, b. and d. Sep 1716; WILLIAM, b. March 1719, d. Jan 1735/6 at the house of Thomas Say, Philadelphia; MARY, b. 25 Jan 1721, d. 20 Aug 1724; JOHN, b. 7 Sep 1725, d. 23 Nov 1792 at his house in Lewes, buried St. Peters Church yard.

3. CESAR RODNEY, son of William (1) and Sarah Rodeney, b. 12 Oct 1707, m. 13 Oct 1727, Elizabeth Crawford (b. 8 June 1709), dau. of Rev. Thomas Crawford. {Welcome Claimants} They were parents of the following children:

CESAR, b. 7 Oct 1728 near midnight; ELIZABETH, b. 16 Oct 1730 on Friday about noon, d. 1765 without issue; GEORGE, b. 2 March 1731/2 minutes after 7 a.m., d. 1750 without issue; SARAH, b. 23 Oct 1733/4 on Monday about 2 a.m., d. 11 July 1734 about 2 p.m. without issue; MARY, b. 30 Oct 1735 Thursday about 3 p.m., d. 1782 leaving 3 children by Gordon?; WILLIAM, b. 19 July 1738 on Monday about 10 p.m, d. 9 or 10 Sep 1787 at Dover,[47] had 2 daus. whose issue became extinct; DANIEL, b. 22 July 1741 about 4 p.m., d. 1764, leaving 1 dau.; THOMAS, b. 4 June 1744 on Monday about 10 a.m., d. 2 Jan 1811, m. Elizabeth Fisher, dau. of Jabez Maud Fisher by whom he had issue, Cesar Augustus and Lavinia Rodney. {Rodney-Wilson Bible; Daniel Rodney Letter}

On 12 Nov 1728 Cesar Rodeney of Kent Co., gent., and Elizabeth his wife for £240 sold to Daniel Needham of same place a tract of land (pattent bearing date 9 Oct 1701 confirmed unto one William Morton and William Rodeney father of the said Cesar all his rights to 1300 a. of land called *London* [Patent Book A, vol 2, page 104] ... whereas by an indenture dated 11 Sep -William Morton and William Rodeney did divide the land, the tract called *Tiverton* did fall to William Rodeney, the other part called *St. Andrews* and did fall to William Morton, the great tract formerly purchased by them of John Stephens (Stevens), dec'd., and William Stephens of Dorchester Co. MD, planters, William Rodeney made his will about the year 1708 and did devise unto his son John Rodeney all parcells of land ... 300 a., it being the same Humphery Barret then divert and part of the land called *Tiverton* part also of the land called *London* to be only for the use of John Rodeney ... William Rodeney in the same will, that if any of his children should dye under age or without issue then the lands should decend from the eldest to the next in age to him, from his son William to Thomas, from him to John, from him to Anthony, from him to George, from him to his dau. Sarah, from her to his son Cesar and from him to William or in case of his, dec'd., to the next of them, always excluding his son Daniel by reason of his lands otherways falling to him far beyond any of his brothers, unless he should happen to survive all the rest, and they the said Thomas Rodeney, John Rodeney, Anthony Rodeney, George Rodeney and Sarah Rodeney also departed this life each of them under age or without issue and land is vested in the said Cesar, pursuant to the mind of the testator, who also is come of age and hath issue by his wife Elizabeth) ... n. side of Little Creek on the s. side of John Clayton's land ... to lands of Richard Richardson and Jabez Jenkins ... 300 a. ... will defend against the heirs of John Stephens the father, John Stephens the son and Williams Stephens, and against heirs of William Rodeney the father and against William Morton and his heirs. Witnessed by Wm. Rodeney, Daniel Rodeney, Jos. Booth Junr. Ackn 13 Nov 1728. {KEDELR I:146}

On 10 Feb 1731 Thomas Crawford of Kent Co. gent, Casar Rodeney of same place, gent., and Elizabeth his wife for £234.3 sold to John Curtis of Newcastle Co., gent., two tracts of land on Dover Hundred, one called *Brinkloes Range*, 258 a. and the other called *Popler Ridge*, 260 a. excepting 103 a. formerly conveyed by John Brinkloe to Arthur Meston and 40 a. lately conveyed by Thomas Crawford to his dau. Latetia Crawford. John Curtis to pay £234.3 at

---

47 His remains were interred at his late dwelling in St. Jones's Neck. {Rodney-Wilson Bible}

or before 1 Feb 1736 at the house of John Curtis in Newcastle Co. to Thomas Crawford, Casar Rodeney and Elizabeth his wife. {KEDELR K:134}

On 15 Aug 1733 Casar Rodeney of Kent Co. and Elizabeth, his wife for £188 sold to Peter Galloway of MD, gent., a tract of land near Little Creek beginning at the corner of Samuel Berry's land and also a corner of William Morton's land lately bought of John and William Stevens of Dorchester Co., MD, 200 a., called *Rodeneys Farm*, free of incumberances except one deed of mortgage between Casar Rodeney and Mark Manlove and John Hall of the same co., gent., trustees of the Loan Office, for £50.10 lent to Casar Rodeney and not yet redeemed. {KEDELR K:166}

On 18 Nov 1740 whereas Jehu Curtis at a Court of Common Pleas held at Dover the second Tuesday in Nov did recover a debt of £230.3 with interest and £3.10.6 damages against Cesar Rodeney and Elisabeth his wife, David Rees and Walter Dickenson and Catherine his wife, admins. of Thomas Crawford late of same co., dec'd., and by a writ dated 17 Nov Daniel Robisson, sheriff, seized in execution two tracts of land called *Brinckloes Range* and *Poplar Ridge* (excepting 103 a. formerly conveyed by John Brinckloe to Arthur Meston and 40 a. lately conveyed by Thomas Crawford to his dau. Letitia Crawford) which by an indenture bearing date 10 Feb 1731 were mortgaged by Thomas Crawford and Casar Rodeney and Elisabeth his wife unto Jehu Curtise afsd. ... sheriff sold the land at publick vendue to John Pleasentine for £300, he being the highest bidder. Whereas Daniel Robisson was suspended in his Office of Sheriff before he had duly conveyed the said land and Samuel Robisson, Esqr., being duely elected and in the Office of Sheriff conveyed the afsd. two tracts of land to John Pleasentine in Dover Hundred the one called *Brinckloes Range* adj. land late of Richard Basnet, 250 a. and the other tract called *Popler Ridge*, adj. land called *Popler Neck*. {KEDELR M:90}

Caesar Rodeney d. by 8 June 1745 when his estate was administered by Elizabeth Rodeney, widow. {Reg. of Wills, 1:111}

Following Caesar's death in 1745, Elizabeth m. Thomas Wilson. She d. Nov 1763. {Rodney-Wilson Bible}

Caesar was father of the following children {Welcome Claimants}: CAESAR, b. 7 Oct 1728, d. 20 Jan 1784 unm.; ELIZABETH, b. 16 Sep 1730, d. 1765; GEORGE, b. 2 March 1731/2, d. 1750; SARAH, b. March 1733/4, d. 1734; MARY, b. 30 Oct 1735, d. 1782, m. and had a dau. Elizabeth Gordon; WILLIAM, b. 19 July 1738, d. 10 Sep 1787, m. 19 March 1762 Lydia Paradee, dau. of John and Lydia (Edingfield) Paradee; DANIEL, b. 22 July 1741, d. 1764; probably m. Meriam, admx. of his estate on 18 Jan 1764; THOMAS, b. 4 June 1744, d. at Rodney, Jefferson Co., MS, 2 Jan 1811, m. 8 April 1771, Elizabeth Fisher, dau. of Jabez Maude Fisher.

4. ANTHONY RODENEY, son of William (1) Rodeney, d. by 7 May 1720 when his estate was administered by Daniel Rodeney. {Reg. of Wills, D:19}

5. DANIEL RODNEY, son of William (1) Rodney, b. 13 Feb 1694/5, d. 19 Dec 1744, m. Margaret, widow of George Nowell.

Daniel d. by 25 Jan 1744 when his estate was administered by wife Margaret Rodney. {Arch. A44:92. Reg. of Wills, 1:96} Note: Arch. A44:92 mentions John Bell, Jr., and his father's legacy.

On 11 Feb 1763 Margaret Rodeney of Kent Co., widow, formerly the wife of George Nowell late of said co. yeoman, dec'd., sold to Caleb Luff of same co., a tract of land, by patent bearing date 14 Aug 1678 did grant and confirm unto John Briggs and Mary Philips a 450 a. tract of land and 50 a. of marsh called *Kingston Upon Hull*, on n. side of St. Jones Creek adj. Robert Jones and land belonging to Town Point and by virtue of sundry conveyances duly made the said George Nowell in his life time became seized in the afsd. tract and being so seized did convey to divers persons 160 a. in sundry parcels and by his will bearing date 2 March 1730 did give unto the said Margaret Rodeney then Margaret Nowell his wife all the residue of the afsd. tract ... for the consideration that said Caleb Luff by his bond bearing even date with these presents hath bound himself unto the said Margaret Rodeney in the sum of £800 conditioned on the payment of £30 of like money yearly and every year unto the said Margaret Rodeney during the term of her natural life and also for 5 shillings in hand paid, conveys the residue of the afsd. tract unto Caleb Luff ... in Dover Hundred, 290 a. {KEDELR Q:148}

Third Generation

5. PENELOPE RODENEY, dau. of William (2) Rodeney, and sister of John Rodeney, b. 1712, m. 7 May 1733 James Gorrell. {Welcome Claimants}[48]
On 10 Aug 1749 James Gorrell of Kent Co. for 10 shillings and natural love and effection and other good causes and considerations quit claim unto his brother-in-law John Rodeney of Sussex Co. his full and peaceable possession in a tract of land on w. side of Murther Creek being half part of a 400 a. tract called *Rodulphus's Range* which was conveyed to one William Rodeney, Junr., and Penelope Rodeney the late wife of James Gorrell and sister to said John Rodeney (Book K, pg 123) ... 200 a. {KEDELR O:13}

6. WILLIAM RODNEY, son of William (2) and Ruth Rodney, b. March 1719, d. Jan 1735/6 at the house of Thomas Say, Philadelphia.

7. JOHN RODNEY, son of William (2) and Ruth Rodney, b. 7 Sep 1725, d. 23 Nov 1792 at his house in Lewes, buried St. Peters Church yard. John m. 1st 4 Oct 1748, Sarah, dau. of Samuel Paynter of Lewes. They had one son WILLIAM, b. 11 Feb 1749/50, and d. 22 Feb 1749. Sarah d. 17 June 1751.

John m. 2nd Ruth Hunn, dau. of Caleb and Ruth Hunn. They were parents of the following children: WILLIAM, b. Nov 1754, d. Jan 1756; MARY, b. 14 Feb 1756, d. 27 April 1791, m. Isaac Turner and left 2 daus.; PENELOPE, b. 9 Feb 1758, m. Phillips Kollock and left 2 sons and 4 daus.; JOHN, b. 22 Oct 1760, d. 10 Jan 1761; HANNAH, b. 5 June 1762, d. 18 May 1787; DANIEL, b. 10 Sep 1764; CALEB, b. 29 April 1767; RUTH, b. 9 Jan 1770, d. Aug following; JOHN, b. 11 March 1771; WILLIAM, b. 15 Sep 1773, d. 24 April 1774; THOMAS, b. 24 June 1775; GEORGE, b. March 1777, d. 30 June following.

Ruth, widow of John Rodney, d. in her 71st year and was also buried at St. Peters Church yard. {Daniel Rodney Letter; "an old record eaten by moths and yellow with age," copied by Rev. C.H.B. Turner}

---

48 Except that Welcome Claimants show James Garid vice Gorrell

On 20 Aug 1763 Nathaniel Hunn of Kent Co. yeoman, Mary Sipple of said co. widow, John Levick of said co. yeoman and Hannah his wife, John Rodney of Sussex Co., atty at law, and Ruth his wife sold to Benjamin Warren of Kent Co., yeoman, a tract of land. Whereas Anna Whitaker late of Kent Co. widow, dec'd., was in her lifetime seized in a 60 a. tract of land n. side of Murtherkill Creek in Murtherkill Hundred, part of a larger tract called *Ousby* bounded by said Benjamin Warren's land and land late of Waitman Sipple Junr, and Anna Whitaker being so seized made her will on 13 Aug 1741 and did devise the 60 a. unto her great grandson Caleb Sipple for life only, and whereas the said Ann soon after died leaving the afsd. Nathaniel Hunn and Mary Sipple her grandchildren and the afsd. Hannah Levick, Ruth Rodney and one Mary Williams now, dec'd., late wife of John Williams of Kent Co. yeoman her great grandchildren which Hannah Levick, Ruth Rodney and the said Mary Williams are the issue of one Caleb Hunn now, dec'd., who was brother of the said Nathaniel Hunn and Mary Sipple, and also one of the grandsons of Anna Whitaker but died in her lifetime, and whereas the said Caleb Sipple who was the eldest son of the said Mary Sipple, since the death of Anna Whitaker his great grandmother, is, dec'd., whereby his estate and the 60 a. descended to and is vested in Nathaniel Hunn, Mary Sipple, John Levick and Hannah his wife in right of the said Hannah and John Rodney and Ruth his wife in right of the said Ruth ... 60 a. {KEDELR Q:165}

8. DANIEL RODNEY, son of Caesar (3) and Elizabeth Rodney, b. 22 July 1741 about 4 p.m., d. 1764, m. Meriam (N). They were parents of a dau. {Daniel Rodney Letter}

Daniel's estate was administered 18 Jan 1764 by Meriam Rodney, widow. {Arch. A44:93. Reg. of Wills, K:334}

9. WILLIAM RODNEY, son of Caesar (3) and Elizabeth Rodney, b. 19 July 1738, d. 10 Sep 1787, m. 19 March 1762 Lydia Paradee, dau. of John and Lydia (Edingfield) Paradee.

On 4 Feb 1768 William Rodney of Dover Hundred Kent Co., gent., and Lydia his wife for £254 sold to Charles Marim of same place, a tract of swamp and plantation in Dover Hundred which premisses was conveyed by James Stevens to the said William Rodney by a deed poll bearing date 3 Dec 1766 (Book R, fol. 141) which is the undivided 1/3 part of the real estate of John Marim late of said co., dec'd., which was left by will to Ruhamah, dau. of said John Marim, being part of 2 tracts of land called *Little Pipe Elm* and *Edington* in the hundred afsd. {KEDELR R:241}

10. DANIEL RODNEY, son of John (7) and Ruth Rodney, b. 10 Sep 1764, d. 2 Sep 1846, m. 5 March 1788, Sarah Fisher, dau. of Henry and Margaret Fisher. They were parents of the following children: JOHN, b. 10 March 1789, d. same month; MARGARET, b. Aug 1790, d. 20 Oct following; MARY, b. 26 Nov 1791; HANNAH, b. 21 Feb 1794; JOHN, b. 20 Aug 1796; SUSAN, b. March 1799, d. 12 March 1799; HENRY, b. 13 July 1800; GEORGE, b. 2 April 1803; WILLIAM, b. 8 Oct 1805; SUSANNAH HUNN, b. 7 Oct 1808; NICHOLAS RIDGELY, b. 22 Dec 1810. {Daniel Rodney Letter. For more details on this family see this article.}

11. CALEB RODNEY, son of John (7) and Ruth Rodney, b. 29 April 1767, d. 29 April 1840, merchant of Lewes, speaker of Delaware Senate and acting governor of DE. {Welcome Claimants}

12. PENELOPE RODNEY, b. 9 Feb 1758, dau. of John (7) and Ruth Rodney, m. Phillips Kollock and was mother of the following children: JACOB; JOHN; MYRA; HESTER; HANNAH. {Welcome Claimants}

Unplaced

(N) RODENEY m. (N) Richardson and had sons THOMAS and WILLIAM RODNEY, grandchildren of John Richardson.

John Richardson, Little Creek, d. 12 Oct 1703, proved 3 Jan 1703. Heirs: wife Mary; grandsons John Richardson, Daniel Brady; Benjamin Brady; Richard Levick; John Levick; Thomas Rodney; William Rodney; children of George and Jude Roes. Extx., wife Mary. Wits., William Morton, Jesper Harwood, Mary Slaughter. {Arch. A43:164. Reg. of Wills, B:50}

Hezekiah, son of LYDIA RODNEY, adopted by grandmother, Indian River, bapt. 27 Nov 1774. {LCPC}

WILLIAM RODNEY

William, adopted son of Wm. and Mary Rodney b. 26 Jan 1768, bapt. 27 March 1768. {LCPC} John, grandson of WILLIAM RODNEY, bapt. 12 June 1768. {LCPC}

WILLIAM RODNEY of Indian River m. Sarah (N). They were parents of the following children {LCPC}: WILLIAM, bapt. 4 June 1769; JOHN, bapt. 29 Sep 1771; REBECCA, bapt. 13 June 1774.

WILLIAM RODNEY, planter, Worcester Co., MD,

On 17 Sep 1770 William Rodney, elder, below Indian River was buried. {LCPC}

William d. leaving a will dated 3 Dec 1767, proved 19 Oct 1770. Heirs: wife Mary Rodney; son William Rodney; daus. Lydia Rodney, Leah Simpler, Susannah Marvill, Comfort Marvill and Mary Magdaline Jones; son-in-law Thomas Prettyman. Extx. wife Mary Rodney. Wits., Wm. Kollock, Simon Kollock, Joshua Morris. {Arch. A97:28. [Not recorded in Sussex Co., DE}

THE SIPPLE FAMILY

Ref. A: Vernon L. Skinner, Jr., furnished much of the information on the early years of the Sipple family.

1. GARRET SIPPLE m. Mary Calvert, dau. of Christopher Calvert (b. c1600, d. c1681).

On 27 May 1667 Garrett Supple, as a servant of Mrs. Ann Toft, was brought to court and his age was judged as 17 years. He was to serve until reaching the age of 24 years. Garrett Suple came to Virginia aboard the ship *Dove*. On 19 May 1674 Garrett Supple petitioned to be released from his bond for good behaviour. Proclamation was made three times with no objections, so he was discharged from the bond and paid court charges. On 26 Jan 1674 Garret Supple had clandestinely m. Mary Colvert, servant to Mrs. Florence Parker. The court ordered that Supple pay Mrs. Parker 1500 lbs. of tobacco or serve one whole year; Mary was to return to the service of her mistress. On 16 Feb 1674 Garret Supple petitioned to appeal. On 17 March 1674 Garrot Supple refused obedience to the high sheriff and committed a misdemeanor in open court; at the sheriff's petition, it was ordered that Supple immediately receive 39 lashes upon his bare back well laid on and that he remain in the sheriff's custody till posting bond for his good behavior and keeping of the peace. {ACVACR}

On 19 March 1674 in a deed, Garret Supple and his wife Mary sold to Thomas Fookes 200 a., part of 800 a. granted to Christopher Calvert and assigned to Charles and Mary Calvert; it was on a neck of land by Onancoke Creek bordered by John Jenkinds. Supple had since m. Mary Calvert. Signed 17 March 1674/5 by Garret Suppill and Mary Suppill. Witnesses were John Stratton and Charles Holden. {ACVACR}

On 17 April 1675 John Savage sued Garret Suple, upon whose petition a nonsuit was ordered. On 17 July 1675, William Whittington impleaded Garret Supple to court but failed to file his petition; a nonsuit with court costs as granted to Supple. On 18 Sep 1675 the court found no cause of action in the suit of John Savage against Garret Supple for assault and battery; the suit was dismissed. On 17 Jan 1677 Garret Sepell assigned a power of attorney to Walter Tayler to acknowledge a judgment of 1037 lbs. of tobacco due to John West. On 20 Feb 1677 John Cole sued Garret Supple for 359 lbs. of tobacco, but Suplee failed to appear. On 16 April 1678 Garrt. Supple was sworn in as member of a jury. On 19 May 1681 Garret Supple claimed that he owned Richd. Marriner 600 lsb. of tobacco and that Joseph Browne owed Supple 800 lbs. of tobacco. Browne promised to pay Supple 200 lbs. of tobacco; it appeared to the court by the depositions of Jno. Bagwell and Xophr. Colvert that Marriner accepted the conditions, so it was ordered that Marriner pay the 200 lbs. of tobacco and court costs. On 14 July 1681, Garret Supple was ordered to be taken into sheriff's custody till he found security for his good behavior and payment of court charges; he had committed a misdemeanor. On 16 Aug 1681 Garret Supple, who had been bound for his good behavior, petitioned the court to be discharged. Proclamation was made and not objection appeared, so he was discharged. On 18 Feb 1681 Garret Supple was a member of a jury. On 16 May 1682 Garret Supple sued James Ewell and his wife for assault and battery. The court considered "that it was a cross action and it appearing by sufficient evidence that it was only a brabbling and vexatious business occasioned by drink and so fit to be cast out of court." {ACVACR}

Garret Supple/Sipple appeared as a tithable in Accomac Co., VA for 1676-1695. {ACVATithables}

On 3 Feb 1695 George Baynum sold to Garrett Sipple the tract called *Lock* in now Worcester Co. which Garrett and his wife Mary sold to James Duer. {Dryden Worcester Land:370}

Garret d. before 14 Nov 1724 and had a son Waiteman.

On 14 Nov 1724 Waiteman Sipple of Kent Co., yeoman, son and heir of Garret Sipple, late of same place, dec'd., for £50 sold to Francis Alexander of same place a tract of land called *Limerick*[?] except 1/4 a. reserved for a burying ground formerly purchased by the afsd. Garret Sipple of a certain John Townsend to whom it came from Benomi Bishop, s. side of the n.w. fork of Murder Creek bounded by Samuel Mott's land ... by Indian Field Branch ... 100 a. {KEDELR H:70}

Garret was father of the following children: WAITMAN; probably JOHN; probably CHRISTOPHER; probably ELLSE, who m. John Trippett.

Second Generation

2. WAITMAN SIPPLE, Senr., son of Garret (1), b. c1673, probably in Accomac Co., VA, m. Lydia (N). In 1730 Waitman Sipple of Kent Co., DE, and his wife Lydia, sold a tract in Murderkill Hundred to George Wilson, 100 a. {KEDELR K:34} Waitman Sipple and his wife Lydia on 22 Dec released unto George Hart a tract, part of a larger tract called *Pipe Elm*, 100 a. {KEDELR P:98}

On 22 Dec 1742 Waitman Sipple of Kent Co. and Liddea his wife for £60 sold to George Hart of same place, a tract of land being part of a tract called *Pipe Elm* now in the possession and occupation of Robert Maxwell in Dover Hundred on Pipe Elm branch ... 100 a. {KEDELR M:196}

On 23 May 1754 Waitman Sipple of Kent Co., gent., for natural love and affection and 5 shillings give to my son in law Andrew Caldwell of same place, a parcell of land and marsh in the forest of Murderkiln Hundred on w. side of Tapahanah Marsh to Waitman Sipple's line or land called *Long Chase* to fork in Little Marsh to Thomas Noxon's land to land whereon William Morris formerly did dwell ... 200 a. {KEDELR O:230}

On 12 Feb 1755 Wataman Sipple, Senr., of Kent Co. for natural love and affection and 5 shillings gave to his son-in-law Isaiah Wharton of same place, part of a tract of land on n.w. side of Tappahannah Marsh beginning at Mathias Stealman's land to land surveyed for the London Company to line of Charles Hylyard ... 153 a. {KEDELR O:274}

On 12 Feb 1755 Wataman Sipple, Senr., of Kent Co., yeoman, for naturall love and afection and 5 shillings give to his son-in-law Charles Hylyard of same place yeoman, part of a tract of land on the n.w. side of Tapahannah Marsh called *Tappahannah* beginning at land formerly given by said Wataman Sipple to his son in law Andrew Caldwell to line of the *Long Chase* to land surveyed for the London Company to Isaiah Wharten's land ... 270 a. {KEDELR O:273}

On 13 Feb 1756 Wataman Sipple, Senr., of Kent Co. for naturall love and afection and 5 shillings gave to his son-in-law Charles Hylyard of same place, part of two tracts of land in Murtherkill Hundred, one called *Carroon Manner* and the other *Dover Farms*, beginning near the line of Alexander Draper's heirs to St. Jones Creek to Pidgeon Branch Gutt ... 130 a. {KEDELR O:322}

Waitman Sipple was very aged in 1767 as noted in the following deed. On 24 Feb 1767 Waitman Sipple, Senr., of Murtherkill Hundred Kent Co., gent., for £84 sold to William Roberts of the forrest in same place, a tract of land and plantation, marsh and cripple, on s. of the middle of Tappahannah Marsh, part of *Tappahannah Tract*. The said Waitman Sipple, as he is very aged and not capable of coming to court, doth hereby appoint his well beloved son Garret Sipple to be his atty to ackn this indenture in open court. {KEDELR R:186}

Waitman Sipple, Sr., d. 7th inst., aged 99 years, wanting 5 days in Kent

Co. on Delaware. {Pennsyvania Gazette; The Sipple Family, Delaware Historical Society}

Waitman left a will dated 10 Jan 1772, proved 30 May 1772. Heirs: wife Lidia; son Garret; daus. Susanna Killen (wife of Henry Killen), Mary Caldwell (wife of Andrew Caldwell); granddau. Elizabeth Griffin, dau. of Susanna by her late husband Owen Griffin; grandson John Hilliard, son of Charles Hilliard and dau. Ruth, dec'd; Waitman Booth; son-in-law Henry Killen. Exec., son Garret. Wits., Benjamin Chew, Edward Tilghman, Jr., Joseph Alford, Elisha Morriss, Edward Cole, James Taggert. {Arch. A46:177. Reg. of Wills, L:115}

Waitman was father of the following children: GARRET; WAITMAN; MARY, m. 1st John Booth and m. 2nd Andrew Caldwell; SUSANNA, m. 1st Owen Griffin and had a dau. Elizabeth and m. 2nd Henry Killen; RUTH, m. Charles Hilliard and had a son John.

3. JOHN SIPPLE, probable son of Garret (1) Sipple, m. 1st Susannah, dau. of Stephen Simmons and m. 2nd Prudence (N).

On 14 Feb 1723 John Sipple of Kent Co. planter and Susanna his wife for £85 sold to Cornelious Swillavan of same place planter ... a tract of land formerly belonging to Thomas Williams of same co. called *Liverpool* on the n. side of Mother Creek on the n. side of Services Branch since in the tenure of John Courtney who sold the same to Stephen Simmons of same place, dec'd., father to the said Susanna, who by his will bequeathed the land and plantation unto his dau. Susanna ... 100 a. {KEDELR H:62}

On 17 Nov 1727 John Sipple and Susanah his wife of Kent Co., yeoman, for £130 sold to John Bowers of same co., yeoman, a parcell of land late in the tenour of a certain Cornelius Sullyvan but now in the possession of the said John Sipple being part of a tract of land called *New Seven Haven* which Cornelius Sullyvan by his deed bearing date 14 Feb 1723 conveyed unto John Sipple ... 220 a. {KEDELR I:109}

On 14 May 1729 John Sipple of Kent Co. and Susannah his wife, for £32 sold to David Leech of Sommersett Co., MD, but now of Kent Co., a tract of land (whereas a certain Griffith Hughs and Anne his wife did grant and convey unto the said John Siple and Susanna his wife a tract of land dated 1711) in the fork of Murderkill Creek ... intersects with Richard Wells land ... 50 a. ... the quit rents excepted being due and growing due of the fee thereof excepted and also about 1/4 a. at the head of a small branch excepted and also a passage way down to the said branch excepted ... {KEDELR I:187}

John Trippet d. leaving a will dated 17 Feb 1738, proved 7 March 1738. Heirs: sons John, Waitman and Gove; dau. Prinelopey; cousin Sarah Trippet; wife Ellse. Execs., wife and brother John Sipple. Wits., Mark Smith, Christopher Sipple. {Arch. A51:79, Reg. of Wills H:149}

On 13 Feb 1747 John Sipple, Senr., of Kent Co. yeoman, for naturall love and affection and the better maintenance of him, gave unto his son John Sipple, Junr., of same co. yeoman, part of a tract of land formerly called *Rights Lott* but since surveyed by Thomas Noxon and returned by him under the name of *Much Ado* in Murtherkill Hundred ... 117 a. {KEDELR N:192}

On 13 Feb 1747 John Sipple, Senr., of Kent Co., yeoman, for natural love and affection and for the better maintenance of him, gave to his son William Sipple of same co., yeoman, part of a tract of land formerly called *Rights Lott* but since surveyd and returned under the name of *Much Ado*, in Murderkill Hundred on s. side of Hudsons branch adj. with the line of Wm.

Mackado, near the line of John Virgin's land ... 103 a. {KEDELR N:192}

On 12 Aug 1748 John Siple and William Sipple, his son, both of the forrest of Mutherkil Hundred, yeoman, for £85 sold to John Virdin of same place, part of a tract of land (whereas there was formerly a tract of land in possession of the afsd. John Siple called *Wrights Lott* alias *Much a Do* and John Siple did give unto his son Wm. Siple afsd. a part of the tract) and whereas since the execution of the deed the said tract of land has been better confirmed to the said John Siple by the name of *Wrights Lot*, on s. side of Hudsons Branch ... 103 a. {KEDELR N:233}

John d. leaving a will dated 30 Oct 1752, proved 16 Dec 1752. Heirs: wife Prudence; sons Martinus, Nathaniel, Uriah, John, William; daus. Rachel, Sarah, Joanna; Sarah Millally. Execs., wife Prudence, sons William and John. Wits., Mark Smith, John Clother, James Berry. {Arch. A46: 141-142. Reg. of Wills, K:92}

On 13 Feb 1761 William Moris, the son in law of John Sipple, dec'd., humbly sheweth that your petitioner have purchased a tract of land of the late sheriff Thomas Parke in the forrist of Motherkiln Hundred part of a larger tract called *Oxford* which formerly belonged to William Hirons, 92 a., and have paid the sum of £25 which said land sold for at publick vendue but it was not conveyed. Therefore your petitioner humbly prays your worships to impower William Rhodes, Esqr., the present sheriff of this co. to execute a deed. {KEDELR Q:25}

On 28 May 1766 John Sipple of Kent Co., yeoman, for £174.6.10 1/2 penny sold to Henry Peterson May of same place yeoman, a tract of land, surveyed pursuant to a warrant bearing date 27 Feb 1739 for John Sipple late of said co., dec'd., father of the afsd. John Sipple, in the forrest of Murtherkill Hundred called *Wrights Lott*. John Sipple, dec'd., became seized in the land and did release unto his son John Sipple part of the afsd. tract ... 99 a., 100 perches, the burying ground in the orchard including the grave and ground 40 ft sq and the fence thereon excepted. KEDELR R:167}

On 13 Aug 1754 Prudence Sipple, Wm. Sipple and John Sipple, executors of the will of John Sipple, dec'd., for £90 sold to Joseph Campbell of same place, yeoman, a tract of land (whereas John Sipple, dec'd., did by his will bearing date 16 Dec 1752 impower his executors to sell a parcel of land conditionally devised to his son Uriah which conditions his said son Uriah not performing, the afsd. executors became vested with the right to dispose of the said land) called *Mary and Ann* in Murtherkill Hundred ... 175 a. {KEDELR O:244}

On 16 Sep 1757 was a petition to the Orphan's Court of Kent Co. of Prudence Sipple, Wm. Sipple and John Sipple, execs. of John Sipple. In the same case file is recorded that testator John Sipple lately dec'd. together with Alice Manlove by the name of Alice Trippet was appointed execs. of John Trippet lately before dec'd. and although the sd. John Sipple proved the will together with the sd. Alice of sd. John Trippett yet the afsd. John Sipple did not intermiddle with any of the estate of afsd. nor took administration of any of the goods and chattels. {KEOJRCF Sipple, John - 1757-59}

John was father of the following children: MARTINUS; NATHANIEL; URIAH; JOHN; WILLIAM; RACHEL; SARAH; JOANNA.

4. CHRISTOPHER SIPPLE, probable son of Garret (1) Sipple, m. Mary (N)

who later m. Ezekiel Cowgill.

On 10 May 1744 Christopher Sipple of Kent Co. PA yeoman for divers, good causes and considerations me hereunto moving have given unto Zachary Goforth, who marryed my dau. Sarah Sipple, of same co., yeoman, a tract of land on which he the said Zachary now dwells being near Jonecake Landing in Murther Kill Hundred, 100 a., beginning at Murther Kill Creek to line of Ebenr Hathorne's land, part of a larger tract called *Saint Collom.* Wit: Mark Smith Junr, William Radet. Ackn 10 May 1744. {KEDELR N:35}

Christopher d. leaving a will dated 7 Dec 1751, proved 24 Feb 1752. Heirs: wife unnamed; sons Christopher, Raymond, Silva; daus. Mary, Elizabeth, Alice and Priscilla Sipple and Sarah Goforth and Mary Ann Jenkins; granddau. Mary Jenkins. Execs., wife, bro. John Sipple and friend Mark Manlove. Wits., John Emerson, William Gray, Unity Emerson. {Arch. A46:110-115. Reg. of Wills, K:52} Note: Arch. A46:115 shows Mary, the widow, later married Ezekiel Cowgill.

On 15 Aug 1753 Mary Cowgill and Mark Manlove of Kent Co., surviving executors of Christopher Sipple, dec'd., for £100 released unto Thomas Christophers of same place, a tract of land (whereas Christopher Sipple, dec'd., did in his life time bargain with said Christophers to let him have a tract of land called *Sipples Choice* in Murderkill Hundred and whereas by Sipple's will bearing date 7 Dec 1751 he impowered his executors, to wit the afsd. Mark Manlove, Mary Cowgill then Mary Sipple and John Sipple since, dec'd., to comply with his part of the said covenants upon said Christophers complying with his.) {KEDELR O:199}

Christopher was father of the following children: CHRISTOPHER; RAYMOND; SILVA; MARY; ELIZABETH; ALICE; PRISCILLA; SARAH, m. Zachary Goforth; MARY ANN, m. (N) Jenkins and had a dau. Mary.

Third Generation

5. WAITMAN SIPPLE, Junr., son of Waitman (2) Sipple, m. Mary, dau. of Nathaniel Hunn in 1724.

The orderly marriage of Waitman Sipple and Mary Hunn was reported on 19th da., 8th mo., 1724.

On 10 March 1728 Caleb Hunn and Nathaniel Hunn of Kent Co., yeoman, sons of Nathaniel Hunn, late of same place, dec'd., Waitman Sipple, Junr. of same place, yeoman, and Mary his wife, dau. of the afsd. Nathaniel, dec'd., sold to John Killinsworth of Mispelion Hundred, yeoman, a tract of land in Mispelion Neck. Nathaniel Hunn in his lifetime did sell but not actually convey the 100 a. unto John Bowers of same co., cooper, bearing date 21 May 1716 and did bind himself to convey the same but hapened to dye intestate before he could perform the conveyance. {KEDELR I:181}

Anna Whitaker (Whitacre] d. leaving a will dated 30 Aug 1741, proved 1 Oct 1741. Heirs: grandson Caleb Hunn's four children Mary, Hannah, Ruth, Pricilla Hunn; grandsons Nathaniel Hunn, Waitman Sipple, Jr.; great-grandson Caleb Sipple. Exec. grandson Waitman Sipple, Jr. Wits., George Morgan, Benjamin Warren, James Dickson. {Arch. A54:75. Reg. of Wills, 1:54-55}

On 11 Aug 1749 Waitman Sipple, Junr., and Mary his wife for £30 sold unto John Hunn of same co. all our rights in two tracts of land which Nathaniel Hunn of Kent Co. late, dec'd., in his life time did purchase from Isaac Hill of same co. on the n. side of St. Jones Creek, 170 a., called *Town Point* and also one other parcel of 65 a., adj. the afsd. tract and purchased from George Newell, and Nathaniel Hunn d. intestate and his dau. Mary Hunn since m. with Waitman Sipple, Junr., of same co. {KEDELR O:10}

On 12 Nov 1755 Waitman Sipple, Junr., of Kent Co. yeoman for natural love and affection and the better maintainance, livelihood and preferment of him, give to my son Waitman Sipple the younger of same place, a parcell of land in Murderkill, part of a larger tract taken up by Thomas Hethers called *Ousbey* beginning at Phillips Barret's land lately conveyed to him by the afsd. Waitman Sipple, Junr., ... 109 a. {KEDELR O:333}

Waitman d. leaving a will dated 27 Jan 1762, proved 11 Feb 1762. Heirs: wife Mary; sons Waitman, Jonathan and Elijah; daus. Anna Furbee and Meriam Barrett; children of son Caleb. Execs., sons Waitman and Jonathan. Wits., Daniel Robisson, Silvester Tomson, Henry Whitacur. {Arch. A46:174-176. Reg. of Wills, K:276}

On 26 May 1762 Mary Sipple, widow, relict and late wife of Waitman Sipple, Junr., late of Kent Co., yeoman, dec'd., and dau. and one of the heirs of Nathaniel Hunn late of said co. yeoman, dec'd., for £20 sold to Nathaniel Hunn of same co. yeoman, a tract of land, whereas the said Nathaniel Hunn, dec'd., was in his lifetime seizd of a 303 a. tract of land called *Peters Neck* on the s. side of Bawcombriggs Creek in Mispillion Neck and being so seized died intestate leaving issue living at the time of his death, to wit Caleb Hunn since, dec'd., the said Nathaniel Hunn and Mary Sipple parties hereto, and John Hunn also since, dec'd., and whereas after the death of Nathaniel Hunn the father on 28 July 1744 the justices of the Orphans Court did on the humble petition of the afsd. John Hunn make an order thereby appointing 5 discreet freeholders of said co. to go on the lands whereof the said Nathaniel Hunn, dec'd., died seizd and make a division thereof among his children, and in pursuance of the order of the said court the 5 freeholders with the assistance of a skilfull surveyor did make a division of the said tract and thereby did lay off and allott unto the said Mary Sipple ... 49 a., 40 sq perches. {KEDELR Q:88}

Mary Sipple was granddau. of Ann Whitaker and sister of Nathaniel Hunn and Caleb Hunn. Mary had an eldest son Caleb Sipple as shown in the following deed. On 20 Aug 1763 Nathaniel Hunn of Kent Co. yeoman, Mary Sipple of said co. widow, John Levick of said co., yeoman, and Hannah his wife, John Rodney of Sussex Co., atty at law, and Ruth his wife, sold to Benjamin Warren of Kent Co. yeoman, a tract of land, whereas Anna Whitaker late of Kent Co., widow, dec'd., was in her lifetime seized in a 60 a. tract of land n. side of Murtherkill Creek in Murtherkill Hundred part of a larger tract called *Ousby* bounded by said Benjamin Warren's land and land late of Waitman Sipple Junr, and Anna Whitaker being so seized made her will on 13 Aug 1741 and did devise the 60 a. unto her great grandson Caleb Sipple for life only, and whereas the said Ann soon after died leaving the afsd. Nathaniel Hunn and Mary Sipple her grandchildren and the afsd. Hannah Levick, Ruth Rodney and one Mary Williams now, dec'd., late wife of John Williams of Kent Co. yeoman her great grandchildren which Hannah Levick, Ruth Rodney and the said Mary Williams are the issue of one Caleb Hunn now, dec'd., who was brother of the said Nathaniel Hunn and Mary Sipple, and also one of the grandsons of Anna Whitaker but died in her lifetime, and whereas the said Caleb Sipple who was the eldest son of the said Mary Sipple, since the death of Anna Whitaker his great grandmother, is, dec'd., whereby his estate and the 60 a. is ceased and descended to and is vested in Nathaniel Hunn, Mary Sipple, John Levick and Hannah his wife in right of the said Hannah and John Rodney and Ruth his wife in right of the said Ruth ... 60 a. {KEDELR Q:165}

Waitman was father of the following children: WAITMAN; JONATHAN; ELIJAH; ANNA, m. (N) Furbee; MERIAM, m. (N) Barrett; CALEB.

6. GARRET SIPPLE, son of Waitman (2) Sipple, residing Motherkiln, m. Elizabeth Berry, dau. of James and Sarah Berry of Maryland. They were parents of the following children: SARAH, b. 13th da., 4th mo., 1764; THOMAS, b. 1st da., 12th mo., 1765; WAITMAN (d. 8th da., 2nd? mo., 1769) and JAMES, b. 29th da., 11th mo., 1768; LYDIA and WAITMAN (d. 19th da., 5th mo., 1778), b. 14th da., 9th mo., 1771; ELIZABETH, 12th da., 5th mo., 1776; JOHN, b. 1st da., 7th mo., 1779, d. 12th mo., 1787. {DCMM}

Elizabeth, wife of Garrett of Motherkiln Hundred, d. 25th da., 8th mo., 1788; buried at Motherkiln Meeting. {DCMM}

Fourth Generation

12. MERIAM SIPPLE, dau. of Waitman (5) Sipple, m. Phillip Barrett.

On 13 Aug 1755 Waitman Sipple, Junr., of Kent Co. yeoman for love goodwill and effection give to Phillip Barret of same place farmer and Miriam his wife dau. of the afsd. Waitman Sipple, a tract of land in Murtherkill Hundred part of a larger tract called *Ousby*, part of a parcel of land which said Sipple lately purchased of heirs of Richard Richardson ... 94 1/2 a. {KEDELR O:306}

13. CALEB SIPPLE, son of Waitman (5) Sipple, m. Sarah (N) who later m. David Lewis.

On 24 Aug 1763 David Lewis of Kent Co., yeoman, and Sarah his wife, late the wife of Caleb Sipple late of said co. yeoman, dec'd., and adminr of Caleb Sipple, dec'd., sold to Benjamin Warren of same co., yeoman, a tract of land, part of a larger tract called *Ousby*, on n. side of Murtherkill Creek in Murtherkill Hundred beginning at land late of Benjamin Warren Senr, to land late of Waitman Sipple, Junr., ... 142 1/2 a., also that other parcel on s. side of Service Branch in the hundred afsd. beginning ... 84 a. {KEDELR Q:170}

Caleb d. by 10 Feb 1762 when his estate was administered by his widow, Sarah. {Reg. of Wills, K:275} Note:-Arch. A46:87-89 shows Sarah, the widow, later m. David Lewis; also mentions children Nancy, John, Caleb, Mary, Thomas, Elizabeth and Garret.

On 27 Feb 1765 Joseph Brinckle and John Brinckle (Brinckley) of Kent Co. for 5 shillings released unto John Sipple, Caleb Sipple, Garret Sipple and Thomas Sipple of same co., yeomen, Nancy Sipple, Mary Sipple and Elizabeth Sipple of same co., spinsters, the children and heirs of Caleb Sipple late of same co., yeoman, dec'd., ... a tract of land, 220 a. on n. side of the Murther Creek beginning below Kings Road from Dover to the draw bridge ... to Johnneycake Bridge. {KEDELR R:20}

John Sipple, minor above age of 14 years, and Caleb, minor above age of 14 years, sons of Caleb, were appointed guardian, Phillip Barrett, Jan 1768. {KE Co. Orphans Court B:31}

Caleb was father of the following children: NANCY; JOHN, b. c1750; CALEB, b. c1750; MARY; THOMAS; ELIZABETH; GARRET.

www.ingramcontent.com/pod-product-compliance
Lightning Source LLC
Chambersburg PA
CBHW050503270326
41927CB00009B/1886

* 9 7 8 1 5 8 5 4 9 0 1 9 6 *

7. MARTINUS SIPPLE, son of John (3) Sipple, m. Anna (N) who had a son John Cole.

On 10 May 1759 Prudence Sipple of Kent Co. for £12 released unto Martinus Sipple of same place, all her third part and dowery of my husband John Sipple's land left her by his will. {KEDELR P:125}

On 15 Nov 1759 Martinus Sipple of Murtherkill Hundred Kent Co., yeoman, and Anna (Anne) his wife for £26 sold to Henry Peterson of same place, storekeeper, a tract of land, whereas Prudence Sipple the relict and widow of John Sipple of same place, dec'd., hath by a deed of release on 10 May 1759 (Book P, fol. 125) conveyd unto the afsd. Martinus all her thirds of her husband John Sipple his land as left her by her husbands will, and whereas Martinus Sipple by his prayer and petition to the Orphans Court obtained an order dated 11 Sep 1759 appointing John Caton Esqr, William Rhodes, Henry Peterson, George Pratt and Preston Berry gent to meet with a survyeor and lay off the said thirds as right of dower by said will, completed the said division on 8 Oct 1759 ... beginning at the Kings Manner near Michael Furbee his land ... 53 a. {KEDELR P:228}

On 25 Nov 1761 Marteenas Sipple (Martinus) and Anna his wife both of Kent Co. for natural love, good will and affection and also divers other good causes and considerations give to John Cole son of Anna Sipple now wife of Marteenas Sipple, a tract of land in the forest of Murderkill Hundred adj. John Cloather's land where said Cloather dwelleth and also adj. Michal Furbey part of 100 a. surveyed for the said Martennas Sipple by virtue of a warrant ... 36 a. including the dwelling house where the afsd. Marteenas Sipple and Anna his wife dwelleth under the restriction that they doth reserve to themselves the afsd. 36 a. during their natural lives. {KEDELR Q:74}

8. JOHN SIPPLE, son of John (3) Sipple, m. Ann, sister of Mary Howard.

On 12 May 1749 Mary Midleton of Kent Co. spinster for £12 released unto Jno. Sipple, Junr., of same co., yeoman, a tract of land (whereas on 27 Feb 1739 the afsd. Mary called Mary Howard together with her sister Ann now wife of John Sipple, Junr., obtained a warrant for taking up a tract of land in Murderkill Hund) near the Black Swamp adj. Simon Irons land, to Armwell Howard's land, called the *Flying Jibb* ... 155 a. Mary Midleton and Ann wife of of Jno. Siple, Junr., have since held as joynt tenants. {KEDELR N:284}

On 11 Aug 1749 John Sipple, Junr., and Ann his wife of Kent Co. yeoman for £50 sold to his father John Sipple, Senr., of same co., a tract of land surveyed for Mary and Ann Howard. {KEDERL O:9}

9. WILLIAM SIPPLE, probable son of John (3) Sipple, m. Elizabeth (N). On 20 March 1754 Wm. Sipple and Eliza his wife both of Kent Co. for £100 sold to Nimrod Maxwell of same place, yeoman, a tract of land, 100 a. {KEDELR O:224}

10. CHRISTOPHER SIPPLE, son of Christopher (4) Sipple, m. Ann (N). Christopher d. by 8 Jan 1771 when his estate was administered by his widow Ann. {Arch. A46:116. Reg. of Wills, L:89}

11. RAYMOND SIPPLE, son of Christopher (4) Sipple.

On 12 Aug 1755 Raymon Sipple of Kent Co. for finding the said

Raymond Sipple during his naturall life in sufficient meat, drink, washing aparall, and lodging and likewise for 5 shillings sold to Zachery Goforth of same place, yeoman, a negroe man named Cezar now in the possession of Ezekiell Cowgill which the said Raymond holds by the bequeath of his father Christopher Sipple, dec'd., and likewise all his right in a remainder or not yet received of his, dec'd., fathers personall estate also the rents and services growing due in the lands left him by his dec'd., father. {KEDELR O:291}

Fifth Generation

14. CALEB SIPPLE Jr., son of Caleb (12) Sipple, d. by 29 Oct 1770 when his estate was administered by Jonathan Sipple, next of kin. {Reg. of Wills, L:84}

15. THOMAS SIPPLE, son of Caleb (12) Sipple, b. 8 Sep 1760, m. 25 Jan 1785 Jemima, dau. of Jonathan and Elizabeth Molleston. She d. 19 Jan 1796, leaving a son Caleb, b. 22 May 1791. {Runk:358}

Unplaced

(N) SIPPLE, dau. of John Sipple and sister of William Sipple, m. William Swift.

William Swift of QA Co., MD, d. leaving a will dated 3 Sep 1742, proved 25 Feb 1742. Heirs: wife Mary; sons John and Richard; bros. Thomas Swift and William Eubank; daus. Elizabeth and Neomy Swift. Execs., father-inlaw John Sipple and bro.-in-law William Sipple. Wits., James Horsley, Thomas Swift, Emanuel Swift. {Arch. A49:137-138. Reg. of Wills, K:17-18}

ELIZABETH SIPPEL m. Richard Holiday.

On 27th da. 9th mo., 1760, it was reported that the marriage of Richard Holiday and Elizabeth Sippel had been accomplished with the consent of parents and parties concerned. {DCMM}

LYDIA SIPPEL m. Benjamin Warren, Jr.

On 20th da., 2nd mo., 1751 it was reported that the marriage of Benjamin Warren, Junr. and Lydia Sippel, Junr., had been accomplished with consent of parents and relations. {DCMM}

PRISCILLA SIPPLE, dau. of Weightman Sipple, m. Samuel Hanson, son of Timothy Hanson of Little Creek, 22nd da., 12th mo., 1741. at the public meeting house at Little Creek Meeting House. {DCMM}

THE WALKER FAMILY

1. JOHN WALKER d. leaving a will dated 2 Nov 1707, proved 13 Nov 1707. Heirs: dau. Mary; sons John and Daniel; Elizabeth Coal. Execs., John, Daniel and Mary Walker. Guardians, Mark Manlove, Nathaniel Hunn and Edmond Needham. Wits., Abraham Skidmore, Zachariah Goeforth, John Robisson. {Arch. A52:185. Reg. of Wills, B:59}

On 8 July 1735 Zachariah Goeforth, aged 70 years or thereabout, being sworn saith that about 22 years agoe a certain John Walker and Daniel Walker since dec'd., requested of him to be one of the chain carriers in running out a tract of land whereon said John and Daniel then did live being on the Mutherkill Creek in Mispillion Hundred in order to the dividing the same between them, said John and Daniel and their sister Mary, according to their fathers will and this deponant saith that the butts and bounds relating to the whole running out of said tract of land being 900 a. {KEDELR L:213}

On 12 May 1743 Daniel Brown and Elizabeth his wife and Mary Manlove being daus and coheirs of Luke Manlove and Mary his wife for £30 sold to Charles Dickinson, yeoman, of same co. ... a tract of land part of a 100 a. tract called *Woodfort* in Mispillion Hundred which tract of land John Walker, dec'd., by his will did bequeath to his dau. Mary Walker who m. Luke Manlove beginning at the line of John Killingsworth, dec'd., on s.e. side of Beaverdam Branch ... 67 2/3 a. which is our part of the said tract. {KEDELR N:181}

On 14 Aug 1745 Charles Dickerson of Kent Co. and Grace his wife and George Pratt and Mary his wife for £200 sold to George Manlove, 100 a., part of a larger tract of land formerly laid out for John Walker on s. side of Murtherkill Creek formerly given by John Walker to his dau. Mary Walker beginning on e. side of Beverdam Branch to line of John Walker's land. {KEDELR N:69}

John was father of the following children: MARY[49], m. Luke Manlove; DANIEL; JOHN.

Second Generation

2. DANIEL WALKER, son of John (1) Walker, d. before 8 July 1735, had a dau. Jemimah who m. James McClemons.

On 25 Feb 1754 John Walker of Kent Co. for £17 sold to Henry Molleston of same place a tract of land (whereas John Walker, late of same co., dec'd., was seized of a parcel of land in Mispillion Hundred and did by his will bequeath part of the same unto his son Daniel Walker and he dec'd. leaving only one dau. Jemimah Walker and she m. James McClemons and he with his wife did convey part of the same parcel of land unto afsd. John Walker). {KEDELR O:236}

3. JOHN WALKER, possible son of John (1) Walker, had sons THOMAS and RICHARD.

On 6 Feb 1716 Thomas Walker of Kent Co., yeoman, for £21 sold to Elisha Snow of same place ... a tract of land on s. side of s.w. branch of Duck Creek being part of a 100 a. tract formerly laid for Thomas Willson called *Denby Town* and since conveyed by deed to Evin Jones ... 1702 Rachel Hoskings, extx. of Henry Hoskings and since conveyed from the said Evin Jones to John Walker by deed dated 10 Oct 1703 and said John Walker, dec'd., seized in actual possession of same did make his will and did give his dwelling plantation and land to be equally divided between his two sons Richard and Thomas Walker which division was made 4 Feb 1716 ... the eastern part of said land being the part of said Thomas ... 53 a. {KEDELR E:263}

On 11 Nov 1718 Richard Walker of Little Creek Hundred, Kent Co., yeoman, son of John Walker, dec'd., for £25 sold to James Whitehart of same place, yeoman ... (whereas John Walker in his lifetime was seized of a tract of

---

49 See The Manlove Family for her descendants.

land on s. side of s.w. branch of Duck Creek being part of a larger tract called *Denby Town* and in his will bequeathed to his two sons Thomas Walker and Richard Walker all his said tract or 100 a. together with plantation to be equally divided between them ...) the afsd. tract of land called *Walker's Landing* ... 50 a. {KEDELR F:48}

On 10 Dec 1725 Richard Walker and Mary his wife of Kent Co., yeoman, for £16 sold to Arther Alstone of same place ... a tract of land on s. side of s.w. branch of Duck Creek on n.w. side of Ellenworth Branch ... 170 a. {KEDELR I:30}

Third Generation

4. JEMIMA WALKER, only child of Daniel (3) Walker, m. James Clemmons (McClemmons).

On 6 Jun 1737 Jemima Walker of Kent Co., spinster, for £55 sold to Luke Manlove, Junr., part of a tract of land (whereas John Walker, late of same co., dec'd., did by his will bearing date 2 Nov 1707 bequeath unto his son Daniel Walker, father to the said Jemima, 400 a. of land and the said Daniel Walker afterwards did dye intestate and left no other child but her by which means she became possessed of the said land) ... the lower part of said 400 a. on s. side of Murtherkill marshes at corner of John Walker's land ... 200 a. KEDELR L:212}

On 4 Dec 1742 James Clemins (Clemmons) and Jemima, his wife, of Kent Co. for £50 sold to John Walker of same place, yeoman, a tract of land (whereas a certain Daniel Walker, late of same co., dec'd., was possessed by a tract of land in Mispillin Hundred on s. side of Murder Creek and did leave one dau. Jemima and she m. afsd. James Clemins). 200 a. was first sold unto Luke Manlove Junr., late dec'd., by Jemima before she m. James. {KEDELR M:207}

Fourth Generation

5. RICHARD WALKER, probable son of John (4), m. Mary, dau. of Edward Fitzgarrall and granddau. of Thomas Bolstock.

On 9 Aug 1721 Richard Walker of Little Creek Hundred, Kent Co., yeoman, and Mary his wife for £40 sold to Thomas Ellitt of same place, a tract of land patent at Philadelphia, granted unto Arthur Alston, late of Little Creek Hundred, dec'd., bounded on the n. by s.w. branch of Duck Creek, 800 a. Arthur Alston did convey 400 a. unto Thomas Bolstock then of same co. Thomas Bolstock dying intestate the 400 a. descended into the possession of Mary Fitzgarrall (Fitzjarrell) grandau. and only surviving heir to the said Thomas Bolstock ... Mary Fitzgarrall, dau. to Edward Fitzgarrall and Ann his wife (which said Ann was dau. of the said Thomas Bolstock) is now become lawfully married to Richard Walker afsd. ... 230 a. that part of the afsd. 400 a. tract whereon said Thomas Bolstock did in his lifetime dwell. {KEDELR G:31}

On 18 Jan 1725 Richard Walker of Little Creek Hundred, Kent Co., yeoman, and Mary his wife for £8 sold to Elizabeth Cockrall of same place spinstris ... a tract of land (patent granted unto Arthur Alstone, now dec'd.) 800 a. in Little Creek Hundred, bounded to the n. to s.w. branch of Duck Creek and to the n.w. with Allstones Branch. Arthur Alstone in his life time did sell unto Thomas Bolstock 400 a. and Thomas Bolstock dyed intestate, the land descended to Mary Fitzgerald, granddau. and only surviving heir to Thomas Bolstock, she being the dau. of Edward Fitzgerald and Anne his wife who was dau. to the said Thomas and the said Mary Fitzgerald being now the wife of

Richard Walker, partie to these presents) beginning at the s.w. corner of a part of the afsd. land late sold by the said Richard and Mary his wife to Thomas Ellit now in his possession, 50 a. {KEDELR I:28}

Richard Walker d. by 5 April 1727 when Mary Walker, widow, was appointed admx. of his estate. {Reg. of Wills, F:25}

THE JOHN WALKER FAMILY

1. JOHN WALKER m. Ann (N).

John d. leaving a will dated 9 Dec 1771, proved 1 July 1772. Heirs: wife Ann; sons William and John; daus. Ailse Frazier, Elizabeth Walker; grandson John King; granddau. Mary King. Execs., wife Ann and son John. Wits., Samuel Meridith, Henry Molliston, Sarah Molliston. {Arch. A52:187. Reg. of Wills, L:116}

John was father of the following children: WILLIAM; JOHN; AILSE, m. John Frazier; ELIZABETH; (N), m. (N) King and had children John King and Mary King.

Second Generation

2. AILSE WALKER, dau. of John (1) Walker, m. John Frazier.

John Fraizer of Little Creek Hundred d. leaving a will dated 1782, proved 13 March 1782. Heirs: wife Alice; sons John, William, James, George; daus. Mary Hanson, Rebeccah and Elizabeth. Execs., wife Alice and son John. Guardian, son William. Wits., James McManus, James Smith, Samuel Maxfield. {Arch. A18:96. Reg. of Wills, L:256-257}

Unplaced

JOHN WALKER m. Mary (N).

On 10 Feb 1687 John Walker of Kent Co., PA, and Mary his wife for 300 a. of land sold to Richard Williams of same co., 100 a. being part of a tract of land on s. side of Murther Creek. {KEDELR}

On 14 Feb 1693/4 John Walker of Kent Co., PA, and Mary his wife for £80 silver, sold to Peter Bisaillon of afsd. co. ... 400 a. being lower part of a tract containing 600 a. called *Williams Choice* on n. side of Murther Creek. {KEDELR}

JOHN WALKER m. Margret (N).

John Walker d. leaving a will dated 27 Oct 1708, proved 17 Dec 1708. Heirs: wife Margret; Elizabeth Willson, dau. of Richard Willson and dau.in-law of Vincent Emerson; Vincent Emerson; servant, Easther Hillyard; William Annand. Execs., Easther Hillyard, Vincent Emerson. Wits., Abraham Taylor, Weakman Sippen, Elizabeth Sippen. {Arch. A52:186. Reg. of Wills, B:69}

JOHN WALKER, son of Richard Walker.

Land was conveyed by James Steel to Richard Walker on 5 Nov 1718, and since conveyed by John Walker, son of the afsd. Richard Walker to George Swallow on 12 May 1747 (Book N, fol. 130). Ackn 12 Feb 1752. {KEDELR O:125}

JOHN WALKER d. by 30 Dec 1747 when John Walker was appointed admin. of his estate. {Reg. of Wills, I:190-191}

JOHN WALKER m. Mary, dau. of Mary Little.

Mary Little d. leaving a will dated 6 Jan 1748, proved 14 Jan 1748. Heirs: daus. Susannah Edmonds, Sarah Morgan, Mary Walker; grandson Addam Fisher; granddaus. Mary Fisher, Eliner Booth, dau. of Sarah Fisher; children of John and Mary Walker; Molliston Fisher; Robert and Susannah Edmonds. Execs., friends John Walker and John Fisher. Wits., William Newell, John Waller, William Silliven. {Arch. A30:196-197. Reg. of Wills, I:261}

JOHN WALKER m. Alice (N) by whom he had sons JOHN and WILLIAM and dau. ALICE.

William Green d. leaving a will (nunc.) made on 26 Jan 1736, proved 28 Jan 1736. Heir: Alice Rhoades, mother of Wm. Walker. Wits., William Fisher, William Walker. {Arch. A20:124. Reg. of Wills, I:55}

Alice Rhodes, widow, d. leaving a will dated 3 March 1745, proved 7 Jan 1746. Heirs: sons John Walker, William Walker. sons of first husband John Walker, dec'd.; dau. Alice Rhodes and son William Rhodes, children of dec'd husband John Rhodes; dau. Elizabeth Boyer. Exec., son William Walker. Wits., Joseph Dowding, Elizabeth Dowding, George Walton. {Arch. A43:131. Reg. of Wills, I:131-132}

On 13 May 1747 William Walker of Kent Co., yeoman, released unto John Walker of same co. his brother, a tract of land (whereas John Walker, late of this co. dec'd. father to the afsd. John and William did by his will give his two sons a tract of land of 400 a. to be equally divided between them and whereas Alce Roads of same co., dec'd., by her will did give unto her son the afsd. William Walker a percel of land provided he would give unto the afsd. John Walker his brother all his rights that he hath unto the land gave to them by their father John Walker) ... 400 a. {KEDELR N:148}

RICHARD WALKER d. by 17 Dec 1684 when Anna Walker, widow, was appointed admx. of his estate. {Penna. Hist. Soc. Papers, AM. 2013:35}

On 20 Jun 1687 John Price of Sussex Co., PA, and Anne Walker of Kent Co., having intentions of taking each other in mariage ... Wm. Berry, clerk.

On 25 July 1687 John Price and Anna Walker m. at the house of Thomas Heathers. Wit: Naomy Berry, Ellinor Roboson, Margret Nicholas, Katherin Price, Ana Heathord, Moloson Heathord, Isabella Price, Mary Walker, Mary Williamson, Henry Skidmore, Patrick Grady, Robert Nicholas, Henry Smith, Samuell Pollard, Stephen Simons, Wm. Berry, Comlock Curtice, Thomas Price, Thomas Walford, James Syckes, Daniell Jones, Thomas Price, Thomas Groves, Cortem Nicholas, Richard Renolds.

ROBERT WALKER, son of Jean Walker, m. Mary (N) had sons John and Robert; SAMUEL WALKER. Robert Walker d. by 6 Jan 1749/50.

Jean Walker d. leaving a will dated 6 Jan 1749/50, proved 17 Oct 1750. Heirs: grandsons John and Robert Walker; children of son Robert Walker; children of son Samuel Walker; Mary, widow of Robert Walker. Execs., friend James White and Joseph Mason. Wits., William Manlove, Thomas Ellet, Joseph

Lain. {Arch. A52:181-184. Reg. of Wills, K:24} Note: Arch. A52:182 mentions heirs, Ann, Jane, and Robert Walker; also shows that this account was later administered, D. B. N. by Charles Mason.

Robert Walker d. by 15 April 1749 when Mary Walker, widow, was appointed admx. of his estate. {Reg. of Wills, I:254}

SAMUEL WALKER, son of Jean Walker, m. Mary (N).

Samuel d. by 24 July 1749 when Mary Walker, widow, was appointed admx. of his estate. {Arch. A52:198. Reg. of Wills, 1:257-258 and K:2}

WILLIAM WALKER m. Agnes Lowber.

Michael Lowber d. leaving a will dated 2 Jan 1744, proved 7 April 1746. Heirs: daus. Unity (wife of John Emerson), Susannah Lewis; sons Michael, Peter, Matthew, Isaac; daus. Garty Muncy, Margarett Manlove, Agnes Walker; wife Rachel; grandchildren of dau. Grace Brown; grandsons Michael (son of Peter Lowber), John and Michael Reynalds, Michael Emerson (son of Unity and John Emerson), granddau. Susannah Reynalds. Exec'rs, wife Rachel and son Peter. Wits., Isabella Brooks, Arthur Brooks, Mary Brooks, now Mary Jackson. {Arch. A31:172-174. Reg. of Wills, I:122-123}

William Walker d. by 23 Feb 1769 when Agnes Walker, widow, was appointed admx. of his estate. {Arch. A52:201. Reg. of Wills, L:54}

WILLIAM WALKER d. by 9 Feb 1764 when William Walker of New Castle Co. was appointed admin. of the estate. {Arch. A52:200. Reg. of Wills, K:338}

WILLIAM WALKER m. Jemimah (N).

On 13 May 1762 William Walker of New Castle Co., cordwainer, and Jemimah his wife for £36 sold to James Sykes of Kent Co. a lott of ground part of a tract called *Town Land* in the Town of Dover bounded by North Street and King Street ... 36 sq. ft. Wit: William Walker, Junr, Roger McBride. {KEDELR Q:87}

WILLIAM WALKER m. Mary Craige by whom he had a dau. Isabella.

Isabella Craige, widow, d. leaving a will dated 11 Feb 1754, proved 21 March 1754. Heirs: daus. Jane Craige and Mary Walker; granddau. Isabella Walker. Execs., dau. Jane Craige and son-in-law William Walker. Wits., Samuel Harris, John Caten, John Chambers. {Arch. All:156. Reg. of Wills, K:91}

THE WALLACE FAMILY

1. BENJAMIN WALLACE d. leaving a will dated 19 Oct 1754, proved 21 Nov 1755. Heirs: sons Matthew, Solomon, William, Benjamin, Ruben, Josiah, Joshua; daus. Deborah Williams, Hannah Caldwell. Exec. son Joshua. Wits., Richard Lockwood, Mary Horn, William Wallace. {Arch. A52:210-211. Reg. of Wills, K:122}

On 12 Feb 1761 Reuben Wallace and Josiah Wallace, both of Kent Co., yeoman, for £150 sold to Hillarey Herbert (Harbert) of same co., ship right, a tract of land in Murtherkill Hundred part of two tracts one couled *Pilton*, the other *Long Reach*, and left to the afsd. Rubin Wallace and Josiah Wallace by their father's will on Isaacs Branch adj. Benjamin Wallace's lane ... 160 a. {KEDELR Q:29}

Benjamin was father of the following children: MATTHEW; SOLOMON; WILLIAM; BENJAMIN; RUBEN; JOSIAH; JOSHUA; DEBORAH, m. (N) Williams; HANNAH, m. (N) Caldwell.

Second Generation

2. MATTHEW WALLACE, son of Benjamin (1) Wallace, m. Agnis (N).

Mathew Wallace d. leaving a will dated 21 Aug 1762, proved 25 Sep 1762. Heirs: wife Agnes; sons Thomas, David; daus. Barbary Rash, Barsheba and Jenet Wallace; granddau. Agnes Rash. Extx. wife Agnes. Wits., James Hussey, Elizabeth Wallace, Deborah Williams. {Arch. A53:5. Reg. of Wills, K:291-292}

Agnis Wallace of Murtherkill Hundred, widow of Matthew, d. leaving a will dated 16 April 1770, proved 14 May 1770. Heirs: dau. Jennet Wallace; sons Thomas and David; son-in-law James Lukons; grandchildren Agnis, John and Mirim Rash, children of dau. Barbre. Exec., son Thomas. Wits., James Caldwell, Stephen Lewis, Mary Lee. {Arch. A52:168. Reg. of Wills, L:79}

Mathew and Agnis were parents of the following children: JENNET; THOMAS; DAVID; BARBARY, m. (N) Rash; BARSHEBA, m. 11 April 1764 Reedy Salmonds {LCPC}.

3. REUBEN WALLACE, son of Benjamin (1) Wallace, d. leaving a will dated 11 Dec 1771, proved 9 March 1772. Heirs: William, Joshua and Margret (children of Solomon and Margret Wallace); friend William Rhodes, Esq.; bro. Solomon Wallace. Exec., bro. Solomon Wallace. Wits., James Tilton, William Collins, John Rhodes. {Arch. A58:7. Reg. of Wills, L:110}

4.SOLOMON WALLACE, son of Benjamin (1) Wallace, was exec. of the will of his bro. Reuben Wallace. Solomon m. Margaret (N).

On 16 Dec 1754 Solomon Walace and Margrett his wife of Kent Co. for £60 sold to John Vickory of same place, yeoman, part of a tract of land ... 100 a. {KEDELR O:271}

On 9 March 1761 Solomon Wallace and Margaret his wife of Kent Co., yeoman, for £450 sold to John Purden of same place, yeoman, two tracts of land, *Shewforth* in Murtherkill Hundred ... 150 a. and *Trippetts Lott* or *Long Day* adj. *Shewforth* ... 116 a. {KEDELR Q:pg 37}

Solomon was father of the following children: WILLIAM; JOSHUA; MARGRET.

5. WILLIAM WALLACE, Sr., probable son of Benjamin (1) Wallace, m. Catherine (N).

John Kelly, farmer of Murderkill Hundred, d. leaving a will dated 14 March 1764, proved 24 April 1764. Heirs: son Enock; son-in-law Samuel Goodwin; dau.in-law Elizabeth Goodwin. Exec. friend William Wallace, Sr. Trustee, Charles Ridgly. Wits., Mark Harper, Daniel Coudret, Joshua Wallace. {Arch. A28:99, 106-108. Reg. of Wills, K:342} Note: Arch. A28:106 shows William Wallace, dec'd., and Catherine, his wife, admins.

William d. by 17 Dec 1767 when Catherine Wallace, widow, was appointed admx. of his estate. {Arch. A52:220-222. Reg. Of Wills, L:38} Note: Arch.

A6:108 shows that William Wallace was guardian of John Ryan and this acct. was later administered by widow Catharine Wallace.

In a petition of 30 Aug 1771 Elizabeth Wallace stated that she was the dau. of WilliamWallace, dec'd., and she requested that a valuation of the land be done. In an undated petition Elisabeth stated that William Wallace died intestate and was seized of land in Murtherkill Hundred and left the following issue: Mary the elder; Isball (Isabella); Elizabeth (petitioner) who is 21 years or older; Elinor; Robert, eldest son; William; Catharine; Thomas; John; Joseph. In a subsequent petition son William submitted a similar petition mentioning that the widow was Catharine Wallace. {KEORCF Wallace, William 1771-91}

William was father of the following children: MARY; ISABELLA; ELIZABETH; ELINOR; ROBERT; WILLIAM; CATHARINE; THOMAS; JOHN; JOSEPH.

6. BENJAMIN WALLACE, son of Benjamin (1) Wallace, m. Rachel (N).

Benjamin d. by 8 Jan 1772 when Rachel Wallace, widow, was appointed admx. of his estate. {Arch. A52:212-213. Reg. of Wills, L:105} Note: Arch. A52:212 mentions a son Benjamin Wallace.

Benjamin was father of BENJAMIN.

Unplaced

DAVID WALLACE m. Barbara (N).

David d. leaving a will dated 19 April 1751, proved 31 Aug 1751. Heirs: wife Barbara; sons Matthew, Solomon, William, Benjamin, Reuben, Joshua, Josiah; daus. Deborah Williams, Hannah Caldwell, Rhoda; granddau. Sarah Wallace. Execs., wife and son Reuben. Wits., Joseph Howell, George Meoller, John Brinkle. {Arch. A52:223-224. Reg. of Wills, K:40-41} Note: Arch. A52:224, shows James Caldwell as the husband of Hannah Caldwell.

David was father of the following children: MATTHEW; SOLOMON; WILLIAM; BENJAMIN; REUBEN; JOSHUA; JOSIAH; DEBORAH, m. (N) William; HANNAH, m. (N) Caldwell; RHODA.

DAVID WALLACE was father of the following sons: SOLOMON; JOSHUA, d. young; JOSIAH; RUBIN.

On 3 March 1767 Solomon Wallace of Murtherkill Hundred, Kent Co., gent., for 5 shillings and to fulfill the design of his fathers will confirmed unto Hillery Herbert of same place, shipwright, a tract of land now in the possession of William Streep, whereas the afsd. Solomon Wallace hath heretofore been seized of a larger tract of land called *Long Reach* in the forrest of Murtherkill Hundred on n. side of Isaacs Branch formerly conveyed to the said Solomon Wallace by a certain Robert Maxwell and being so seized conveyed a part thereof to a certain Nathan Williams and whereas David Wallace father to the said Solomon Wallace in his life time became seized in a part of the whole tract and being so seized died having first made his will and devised a part thereof to his son Joshua but in case of the death of the said Joshua without legal issue that then the land should decend to 2 other sons, viz Josiah and Rubin Wallace, and whereas the said Joshua Wallace died in his minority thereby the said Josiah and Rubin Wallace became intilted to the land and conveyed the same to the afsd. Hillery Herbert, whereas it may be hereafter alledged that deficiency may be found in the conveyances in the deeds from Nathan Williams to John Barns Esqr and by Barns to Harbert or from the said Josiah and Rubin Wallace to the said Harbert and the said Solomon Wallace being desirous like an honest man to do every act of justice in his power to confirm a title to the said Hillery Harbert ... 150 a. and also part of the said tract which was conveyed by the said Josiah and Rubin Wallace to the said Hillery Harbert adj. the lands of Benjamin Wallace and the said Rubin Wallace ... 154 a., 156 perches. {KEDELR R:180}

JOSHUA WALLACE, yeoman, d. by 28 Aug 1756 when Reuben Wallace was appointed admin. of his estate. {Arch. A53:1. Reg. of Wills, K:142}

JOSIAH WALLACE d. leaving a will dated 22 April 1763, proved 12 May 1763. Heirs: housekeeper Easther Knott; bro. Benjamin; cousin Josiah Wallace, son of Benjamin; Nancy Knott, dau. of Easther Knott. Execs., Easther Knott and bro. Benjamin Wallace. Wits., Jabez Jenkins, James Gordon. {Arch. A52:240-244. Reg. of Wills, K:311}

RICHARD WALLACE m. Mary Brown, dau. of Joshua Brown.

On 8 Feb 1763 James Brown, William Brown, John Brown, James Anderson and his wife Elizabeth, Richard Wallace Junr and Mary his wife, James Berry and Sarah his wife for £40.16.6 release unto Benjamin Brown all of Kent Co., part of a 468 a. tract of land surveyed for Joshua Brown 21 March 1746 by virtue of a warrant bearing date 30 July 1737 and Joshua Brown dying intestate the land fell unto all his children ... 156 a. {KEDELR Q:133}

THOMAS WALLACE m Elizabeth Woodle.

Joseph Woodle, Duck Creek, d. by 13 March 1750 when Mary Woodle, widow, was appointed admx. of his estate. {Arch. A56:106-108. Reg. of Wills, K:34-35} Note: Arch. A56:106 shows that Mary Woodle, widow, later married Matthew Hutchisson; also page 108 mentions heirs, Joseph Woodle and Elizabeth Woodle, wife of Thomas Wallace.

THOMAS WALLACE, yeoman, d. by 21 March 1761 when Ruth Wallace, widow, was appointed admx. of his estate. {Reg. of Wills, K:259-260}

WILLIAM WALLACE m. Margaret Ross, widow of John Ross.

John Ross d. by 24 May 1764 when John Parker and wife Elizabeth, late Elizabeth Ross were appointed admins. of his estate. {Arch. A44:137-138, 140141} Note: Arch. A44:140 shows that Margaret Ross later married William Wallace; page 141 mentions dau. Margaret Ross and son William Ross.

WILLIAM WALLACE m. Unity (N).

On 13 May 1752 Wm. Wallace of Murthur Creek Hundred, Kent Co., yeoman, and Unity his wife for £33 sold to Daniel Smith of Mispillen Hundred, same co., yeoman, a tract of land in the forrest of Mispillen Hundred ... 232 a.
{KEDELR O:148}

THE LUKE WATSON FAMILY

According to *First Settlers of Piscatawsay and Woodbridge*, Luke Watson was son of John Watson of Connecticut, who d. before 1638 and had a dau. Anna Watson by a former wife; his then wife, Elizabeth was called mother in law (step-mother) to Anna Watson in 1639. William Cramer of Elizabethtown, NJ, sold out on 1 Sep 1677 to John Tow, weaver, and soon after removed with Luke Watson to Whore-Kill, Lewes, DE. Cramer d. in 1695. {*First Settlers of Ye Plantations of Piscataway and Woodbridge, Olde East New Jersey*, by Orra Eugene Monnette, hereafter cited as Monnette:721}

According to *Biographical And Genealogical History of the State of Delaware ...* published by J. M. Runk and Co. (hereafter cited as Runk), Luke Watson, son of John Watson and wife Elizabeth, dau. of William Frost of Fairfield, CT, was b. 1630-40, d. Oct 1705. His mother after the death of his father, m. 2nd John Gray in 1644 and moved to Jamaica, Long Island, NY. Luke m. 1st Sarah (N) by whom he had Luke Watson, Jr., d. 1708, constable 1687, member of PA assembly. Luke moved to Lewes c1677.

A great deal of additional information has been supplied on the Watson family by Vernon L. Skinner, Jr. {A}

1. LUKE WATSON on 7 Oct 1678 petitioned for land at the Whorekill. {NY Col. Mss., v. 21, p. 10}. Associated with him in Whorekill and similarly a removal from New York to Delaware was Hon. Peter Alrichs. Luke Watson. Luke was a representative from Delaware to Governor's Council of PA, 1683-88; member of Provincial Council, PA, 1685; Delaware Assembly from Sussex Co., 1682, 83, 87, 94, 97, 98. He was called Captain, 1684-1705; High Sheriff, 1705. {*First Settlers of Ye Plantations of Piscataway and Woodbridge, Olde East New Jersey*, by Orra Eugene Monnette:722}

Luke Watson m. 1st Sarah (N), and m. 2nd Margery (Margaret), dau. of Capt. Henry Smith and m. 3rd Sarah Paynter, widow of John Paynter.[50] Sarah was mother of the following children: MARY Watson; and John, Richard, and Thomas Paynter.

A tract of land, warrant bearing date 21 Jan 1681, was surveyed and laid out 1500 a. for Luke Watson of Sussex Co., Esqr., in Mispillion Hundred called *Hunting Quarter*, and Luke Watson by his will bearing date 6 Sep 1705 did bequeath all the residue of his estate unto my well beloved wife Sarah and my dau. MARY to be equally divided between them, and the afsd. Sarah Watson died intestate leaving issue John Paynter, Richard Paynter and Thomas Paynter, afsd. Thomas Paynter died leaving Mary who intermarried with Peter Hoffman and Lydia, his lawful issue to whom his share of the half of 1500 a.

---

[50] Sarah Paynter, widow, administered the estate of Richard Paynter of Sussex Co.; she was appointed admx. on 4 March 1694. {Penna. Hist. Soc. Papers, AM. 2013:166} Monnette gives evidence that Luke Watson m. 1st Sarah Whitehead and had at least four sons, Luke, John, Samuel and Isaac. Monnette states that Richard Paynter was one of the original 80 associates of Elizabethtown in 1665, together with Luke Watson, John Gray and Barnabas Wines, all four of whom were interrelated by both blood and marriage.

did equally descend ... beginning on Mispillon Creek ... 112 a. {KEDELR O:136}

Luke and Sarah Wattson were witnesses at the marriage of Henry Malestyn of Lewis and Margarettt Hart, widow of Cedar Creek. on 17th da., 1st mo., 1686. {Sussex County Court Records}

At court, 4-6 Oct 1687 William Evitt, servant of Thomas Price, Senr., and Sarah Watson were presented for having carnal copulation together. Evitt later admitted that he had told the same to William Mosely but that it was untrue. At court 6-8 March, his master acquainted the court that he had severely whipt him for lying and slandering the young woman [Sarah Watson]. {Sussex County Court Records}

An order was produced by Justices of Sussex Co. for fees due them from the estate of John Bellamy, dec'd., according to accounts delivered which Capt. Luke Watson and his son Luke, admins. of said Bellamy refused to pay. The court also demanded fees against Luke Watson, Junr. for fees due in the preceding tryalls of his wife Mary and John Jones his servant. {Sussex County Court Records}

Luke Wattson, Sr., Esq., Lewes, d. leaving a will dated 6 Sep 1705, proved 6 Nov 1705. Heirs: wife Sarah Wattson; sons Luke, John, Samuel and Isaac Wattson; daus. Mary Wattson (by former wife Margery, dau. of Capt. Henry Smith), and Elizabeth Morris, wife of Antoney Morris, Sr. of Philadelphia). Extx. wife Sarah Wattson. Wits., Phillip Russell, Sarah Russell, Dorothy Givens, Anna Corbett, Roger Corbett. Overseers: son-in-law Richard Paynter, Justice Phillip Russell. {Arch. A106:27. Reg. of Wills, A:52-54}

Sarah Watson, late widow and extx. of Capt. Luke Watson, dec'd., and former widow and admx. of Richard Paynter, Senr., taylor, dec'd., (intestate) was summoned to the court of 7 May 1706 at the complaint of her son Richard Paynter, surety for his mother's administration of his father's estate. Reference was made to his eldest brother John Paynter and brother Thomas Paynter. Payments had not been received. {Sussex County Court Records}

On 8 April 1718 Adam Lewis of Philadelphia and Mary his wife, dau. of Luke Watson, late of Lewis Town, Sussex Co., dec'd., conveyed land to Berkly Cood. Whereas Luke Watson by his will bearing date 6 Sep 1705 did devise to his then wife Sarah and his dau. Mary Watson all the rest of his estate and he died seized of a tract of land n. side of Main branch of Mispilion, 1500 a. of which said land by virtue of the devise afsd. does of right belong to the said Mary Lewis. By this indenture Adam Lewis and Mary his wife for £20 sold to Berkly Cood and Mary his wife halfe part of the afsd. tract. {KEDELR H:174}

On 24 May 1748 a commission entered on a tract called *Hunting Quarter* and divided the same among the heirs of Sarah Watson. For the heirs and representatives of John Painter her eldest son his two shares ... for the heirs of Richard Painter her second son 225 a. ... for the heirs of Thomas Painter her third son, for his the said Thomas's dau. Lidia now the wife of Adam Fisher 112 a. and 1/2 and for his other dau. Mary now wife of Peter Hopman 112 a. 1/2. {KEORCF Watson, Sarah - 1748}

On 29 Oct 1748 Dogood Paynter and Luke Sheilds, both of Sussex Co., and Adam Fisher and Lidia his wife sold to Robert Killen of Kent Co., two tracts of land, warrant dated 21 Jan 1681 surveyd and laid out for Luke Watson of Sussex Co., Esqr, in Mispillon Hundred 1500 a. called *Hunting Quarter*, and Luke Watson by his will bearing date 6 Sep 1705 (in the Registers Office at the Town of Lewes Sussex Co) did devise all the residue of my estate both real and personal unto my well beloved wife Sarah and my dau. Mary to be equally divided between them, and Sarah Watson died intestate leaving issue John Paynter, Richard Paynter and Thomas Paynter, and partition was made between the afsd. heirs of Sarah Watson, dec'd., and the representatives of the assignees of the afsd. Mary, and whereas Richard Paynter by his will bearing date 21 Nov 1722 (in the Registers Office afsd) did devise unto my wife Margaret and my son Dogood all the residue of my estate, and Thomas Paynter died leaving the afsd. Lidia who afterwards intermaried with Adam Fisher and Mary his lawfull issue to whom his share of the afsd. 1500 a. of land did equally desend, the 1500 a. called *Hunting Quarter* was divided and part thereof was allotted to the afsd. Dogood Paynter and Luke Shields heirs under the will of Richard Paynter, dec'd., second son of Sarah Watson, dec'd., ... beginning at corner of the share allotted to the heirs of John Paynter, dec'd., to corner of the share allotted to Lydia the wife of Adam Fisher ... 225 a. and also 1/2 of the share of the afsd. Thomas Paynter, dec'd., was allotted to Lydia one of the daus. of the afsd. Thomas beginning n. side of Mispellen Creek to share allotted to the heirs of John Paynter, dec'd., to share allotted to the afsd. Mary the other dau. of Thomas Paynter ... 112 1/2 a. {KEDELR N:248}

Luke was father of the following children (by his 1st wife Sarah): LUKE; JOHN; SAMUEL; ISAAC; ELIZABETH, m. Antoney Morris, Sr. of Philadelphia. Luke was father of (by his 2nd wife Margery) MARY, b. 28th da., 12th mo., 1685 at Prime Hooke, Sussex Co.[51], m. Adam Lewis of Philadelphia.

Sarah, widow of Luke Watson, was mother of the following children: John, m. Mary (N) and had a son John Paynter; Richard Payner (2nd son of Sarah), m. Margaret (N) and had a son Doggod; Thomas Paynter had daus., Lydia who m. Adam Fisher and Mary who m. Peter Hoffman.

Second Generation

2. LUKE WATSON, Junr., son of Luke (1) Watson, m. Mary (N).

Mary Watson was presented at court of 4 Sep 1694 for receiving butter from John Jones who had stolen it from William Crafford.

Luke Watson, Junr. in behalf of Mary his wife and his servant John Jones, entered into recognizance of £100 guaranteeing the appearance of Mary his wife and John Jones his servant at the next court of Quarter Sessions. {Sussex County Court Records}

At court of 5 Sep 1694 Luke Watson, Junr., produced in open court sundry papers brought from England relating to the vindication of his wife Mary from a former slander which then had dependance in open court about having a child before her arrival into these parts of America and desired that the same might be read and put upon recorde. The report was given by Thomas Bawdewin, Esq., Mayor of Shrewsbury, that a falce reporte had been raised of Mary Lemme, late of the City of Chester in the County of Chester, England. He stated that certain statements were false and that Mary Lemme was a lodger and a scholar for 3 years, Aug 1681 to Aug 1684, lodged at the house of Lucy Minors of Shrewsbury, seamstriss - a virtuous and good woman.

---

51 *Some Records of Sussex County, Delaware* by C. H. B. Turner (1909), p. 137.

Elizabeth Lem of Westchester, widow, on 8 June 1687, deposed that her dau. Marie Lem with her mother's consent on 6 Sep 1686 did put her self a free passenger on board the Morning Starr whereof Thomas Hayes was Commander for Pennsylvania in America. And that siad Marie never had childe, nor was with childe. {Sussex County Court Records} During the same period Sarah Price of Leverpoole, widow, deposed that she was Aunt to Marie Lem and that Mary had behaved herselfe modestlie, civilly and virtuously. {Sussex County Court Records}

Watsons Marsh near Prime Hook Creek was purchased by Luke Watson from his father Luke Watson on 6 Feb 1704. Luke Watson the younger 4 Feb 1706 gave the land to his bro. John Watson. Sarah Watson relinguished her dower rights on 7 May 1724. John Watson conveyed land to John Smith. {F6:113}

Luke Watson d. leaving a will dated 10 Oct 1707, proved 26 April 1708. Heirs: wife unnamed; bros. Isaac and Samuel Watson; granddau. Mary Lillington. Extx., wife unnamed. Wits., Hannah Crosswell, Richard Davis, Samuel Watson. Trustee: bro. Samuel Watson. {Arch. A106:28. Reg. of Wills, A:440441} Reg. of Wills, A:440 mentions heirs of son Luke.

On 28 Oct 1747 William Till of Philadelphia, gent., and Mary his wife, grandau. and heiress at law of Luke Watson, Junr., late of Sussex Co., dec'd., for £100 quit claim unto Mathew Hillford of Sussex Co., yeoman, a tract of land (warrant granted by Court of Kent bearing date 15 Aug 1682 laid out for Luke Watson, Junr., called *Heyfeild* n. side of Mispilion Creek 600 a. surveyed 5 Feb 1685) William Till and Mary his wife by their deed poll bearing date 12 May 1735 for £50 paid by Robert Killen did convey unto Robert Killen 300 a. of land and by their deed poll the same date for £50 conveyed unto Matthew Hilford the other 300 a., Robert Killen by his deed bearing date 12 Aug in the present year for £50 conveyed unto Mathew Hilford his 300 a. ... and it has lately been discovered that the tract of land called *Heyfeild* doth not lye within the bounds and limits discribed in the said deeds ... for rectifying the mistake afsd. and for conveying the said Mathew Hilford the land called *Heyfield* beginning at the land late of Luke Watson, Senr., called *Hunting Quarter*, to the low grounds at the head of Mispillion Creek ... 600 a. {KEDELR N:189}

On 10 May 1735 William Till of Sussex Co. and Mary his wife ... whereas there is a tract of land warrant granted by Kent Co. Court bearing date 15 Aug 1682 laid out for Luke Wattson, Junr., called *Hayfeild* n. side of Mispillion Creek 500 a. [sic] surveyed 5 Feb 1685 ... Luke Wattson is since, dec'd., and William Till haveing intermaried with the afsd. Mary, grandau. and heir at law to the afsd. Luke Wattson, Junr., ... for £50 sold to Mathew Hillford of Kent Co. half part of the afsd. tract of land now divided between the said Mathew Hillford and a certain Robert Killing who has purchased the other part of said tract ... 300 a. {KEDELR L:64}

On 15 March 1742 William Till of Philadelphia and Mary his wife for £100 sold to Andrew White of Kent Co. gent ... a tract of land (whereas a certain Luke Watson by his will did devise to his then wife Sarah and his dau. Mary Wattson all the residue of his real and personal estate ... he was seized in a tract of land n. side of Mispillian Creek beginning at the corner of William Clerk's (Clark) land ... 1500 a. one half belonging to the said Mary Watson who afterwards intermarried with a certain Adam Lewis, and they conveyed the 1/2 part to Birkly Codd and Mary his wife, and Mary Codd surviving Berkly Codd her husband, by her will ordered the said William Till to sell the land ... 1/2 of 1200 a. {KEDELR N:1}

Luke was father of LUKE and ELIZABETH who m. George Lillington[52] and had a dau. Mary who m. William Till.

3. JOHN WATSON, son of Luke (1) Watson, m. Sarah (N).

Sarah was dau. of James Cannon who d. 1711 in DO Co., MD. {MDPrerogative Court Wills 17:319 and Prerogative Court Inventory and Accts. 33B:111 and 35B:31}

John d. leaving a will dated 3 Jan 1729, proved 27 Feb 1729. Heirs: wife Sarah Wattson; sons James, Luke and Hezekiah Wattson; daus. Mary Wattson and Elizabeth Townsend (wife of Stephen). Extx. wife Sarah Wattson. Wits., Chris. Philipson, Elizabeth Cirwithin, Jas. White. {Arch. A106:18. Reg. of Wills, A:237-239}

According to a Sussex Co. deed, John Wattson of Sussex Co. by his will dated 3 Jan 1729 devised as follows, "I bequeath unto my three sons, James, Hezekiah and Luke Wattson ... all my plantation ... containing 300 a. in Prime Hook neck on the n. side of the road that goes up the Neck to the Kings Road ..." and whereas said James Wattson d. intestate and without issue, and the land vested in afsd Hezekiah and Luke Wattson, and said Luke's moiety of said lands were sold by sheriff for the discharge of his debts and the other moiety descended unto Thomas Wattson by the death of his father, the above named Hezekiah Wattson as next of kin and heir at law, which said Thomas d. intestate and without issue whereby the said moeity descended to the heirs of Elizabeth, wife of Stephen Townsend, dec'd., (one of the daus. of afsd. John Wattson the testator), namely ½ thereof to Stephen Townsend, Abigail the wife of Aaron Oliver, Coston Townsend since dec'd. leaving issue three children to wit, Littleton Townsend, Elizabeth wife of William Walton, and Stephen Townsend, Betty Spencer since dec'd. leaving issue (Samuel, Ebenezer, Sarah and Betty Spencer and Mary Mitcalf), Littleton, Noah and Jehu Townsend and the other half thereof to the heirs and representatives of Mary late wife of Coston Townsend the Elder, dec'd., one of the daus. of afsd John Wattson, the testator, namely Isaac Townsend, John Townsend and James Townsend. And whereas the above named Littleton Townsend purchased the undivided rights of the above name Jehu Townsend, Littleton Townsend, Jr., Isaac Townsend and John Townsend which rights with the said Littleton Townsend's own undivided right to the quantity of 75 a. for 105. {SUDELR N:400}

He was father of the following children: JAMES d.s.p.; LUKE; HEZEKIAH; MARY, m. Coston Townsend, Sr.; ELIZABETH, m. Stephen Townsend.

4. SAMUEL WATTSON, Cedar Creek Hundred, son of Luke (1) Wattson, m. the oldest dau. of Thomas Davis.

Thomas Davis d. leaving a will dated 13 Jan 1698, proved Feb 1697/8. The probate shows J. Hill resigned the administration to Samuel Watson, husband of decedent's eldest dau. {Sussex Wills Arch. A68:131. Reg. of Wills, A:26-27. Sussex Co. Court 1680-1699}

---

52 According to Runk:264

Samuel d. leaving a will dated 21 Dec 1724, proved 27 Jan 1724/25. Heirs: wife unnamed; sons John, Luke and Samuel Wattson; daus. Mary, Susanna, Elizabeth and Sarah Wattson. Execs, unnamed wife and son Luke Wattson. Wits., William Till, Thomas Davis, Andrew Haverlo. {Sussex Co. Probate - Arch. A106:41. Reg. of Willls, A:179-181}[53]

Samuel was father of the following children: JOHN; LUKE; SAMUEL; MARY; SUSANNA; ELIZABETH; SARAH.

5. ISAAC WATSON of Sussex Co., b. c1665, son of Luke (1) Watson, d. 1728 intestate. He m. Elizabeth (Purnell) Nutter, widow of John Nutter (d. 1702) and dau. of Thomas Purnell of Somerset Co., MD.{SUORCT 2:15, Admin. Accts}

The Sussex Co. Quite Rent, 1702-1713 included payment due from Isaac Watson on 1000 a. conveyed by Wm. Clark, admin. of Hen: Bowman's estate for paying his debts by deed dated 1697 to John Nutter whose widow I. Wats. married. {Bendler:57}

Thomas Purnell, SO Co., MD, d. leaving a will dated 5 March 1693, proved 31 May 1694. Mentioned was dau. Eliza: Nutter. {MWB 2:319}

On 4 Feb 1719 Isaac conveyed 200 a. to Samuel Watson, land in Prime Hook which Isaac obtained from his father Luke Watson by deed of gift on 6 Dec 1697, part of 600 a. called *Fairfield.* {SUDELR F6:114}

Elizabeth, widow of Isaac Watson, d. 1738. {SUORCT 2:110}

Isaac and Elisabeth were parents of the following children: ISAAC; THOMAS; BETHUEL, b. 1710; ELIZABETH,[54] m. William Burton. {A}

6. ELIZABETH WATSON, b. 1673, d. 2 Feb 1767, m. 30 Aug 1700, Antoney Morris, Sr. of Philadelphia.[55]

7. JOHN PAYNTER, son of Sarah Paynter, m. Mary (N). They were parents of JOHN.

On 22 March 1736 Mary Paynter of Philadelphia, widow. for 5 shillings and affection give to my son John Paynter ... my one full equal part of a tract of land (whereas Luke Wattson late of Port Lewis Sussex Co., dec'd., by virtue of some good conveyances became in his life time seized in a tract of land n. side of the main branch of Muspelion 1500 a. and by his will dated 6 Sep 1705 did devise 1/2 unto Sarah his wife and she afterwards died intestate seized of the half part of the lands and it descended unto John Paynter her son and heir and he intermarrying with the said Mary made his will and devised the same unto her) ... beginning at corner of the land of William Clark. {KEDELR M:81}

---

[53] See admin. accounts in the orphans court records of 1729 which refers to five children. {SUORCT 1:8}

[54] Mentioned in the will of Henry Pennington dated 30 Dec 1713. {Sussex Co. wills Arch. A81:8. Reg. of Wills, A:77-79}

[55] According to Monnette, Elizabeth m. 1st Thomas Coddington and as his widow m. 1700 Anthony Morris 2d of Burlington, NJ and Phila., citing Abridg. Compend. Vol. I, p. 985, Vol. II, p. 408, and Vol. III, p. 759. Other data from Runk:265

Third Generation

8. ELIZABETH WATSON, dau. of Luke (2) and Mary Watson, m. George Lillington and had a dau. Mary who m. William Till.

Elizabeth Lillingston, widow, d. leaving a will dated 1 Dec 1705, proved 8 Dec 1705. Heirs: dau. Mary Lillingston; mother Mary Watson; father Luke Watson. Exec. father Luke Watson. Wits., John Hill, John Watson, Saml. Watson. {Sussex Co. Wills. Arch. A84:76. Reg. of Wills, A:439-440}

9. HEZEKIAH WATSON, son of John (3) Watson, m. Affiance Carpenter, dau. of James and Affiance Carpenter. Affiance, widow of Hezekiah Watson m. 2nd Thomas Humphreys. {SUORCT 3:12}

Affiance Carpenter, widow of James Carpenter, d. leaving a will dated 20 Nov 1739, proved 8 Jan 1740. Heirs: sons William, James, Laben, Benjamin and Nepthali; daus. Elizabeth Carpenter and Affiance Wattson; granddau. Betty Davis; grandson Piles Carpenter, son of William. {Sussex Co. Wills. Arch. A63:214. Reg. of Wills, A:320-321} Note: Arch. A63:214 mentiones father William Piles.

Hezekiah was father of SARAH, m. Joshua Ready; THOMAS, b. c1745 {SUORCT 3:12}, "weak of understanding" {SUORCT 4:14}.

On 6 May 1761 Joshua Ready (Reedy) of Sussex Co. and Sarah his wife, dau. of Hezekiah Watson, late of same co., yeoman, dec'd., for £20 quit claim unto Thomas Watson, brother to the afsd. Sarah, all their right to 1/2 part of a tract of land in Primehook Neck in Cedar Creek Hundred on w. side of Brook Branch, formerly belonging unto the afsd. Sarah's father which land was by the will of his father John Watson, late of same co., dec'd., bequeathed unto the afsd. Hezekiah Watson, dec'd. {SUDELR I:316}

10. LUKE WATSON, son of John (3) Watson.

On 5 Nov 1760 Luke Watson of Sussex Co., yeoman, in compliance with his fathers bond and for £36 paid by John Smith, late of same co., yeoman, dec'd. (grandfather of Henry Smith) unto John Watson, late of same co., yeoman, dec'd. (father of said Luke Watson) sold to said Henry Smith of same co., yeoman, a parcel of marsh in Primehook Neck near *Long Pond* adj. Samuel Watson and Primehook Creek, 100 a. {SUDELR I:317}

11. MARY WATSON, dau. of John (3) Watson, m. Coston Townsend, Sr. They were parents of the following children: ISAAC; JOHN; JAMES. {A}

12. ELISABETH WATSON, dau. of John (3) Watson, m. Stephen Townsend. They were parents of the following children: STEPHEN; ABIGAIL, m. Aaron Oliver; COSTON; BETTY, m. (N) Spencer; LITTLETON; NOAH; JEHU. {A}

Elisabeth Townsend, widow, d. leaving a will dated 21 Sep 1745, proved 2 Nov 1745. Heirs: sons Steven, Costin, Solomon and Charles Townsend; daus. Elisabeth Deputy and Abigail Clendaniel; grandsons William Townsend (son of Steven), Costin and Charles Townsend; granddaus. Betty, Sarah and Mary Deputy, Sarah Townsend (dau. of Steven), Betty Townsend (dau. of Solomon), Elisabeth Townsend (dau. of Steven); Mary Clendaniel. Exec. loving son. Wits., Thos. David, Thomas Lay, Rebecca Lay. {Sussex Co. Wills Arch. A102:51. Reg. of Wills, A:490-491}

13. LUKE WATSON, son of Samuel (4) Watson, d. intestate 1751. {SUORCT 2:89}. He m. (N) (N) and was father of the following children: ELISABETH, m. Joseph Collings; ESTHER, m. John Killingsworth; SAMUEL, b. c1745 {SUORCT 3:168}; JOHN {SUORCT 3:168}; 5 OTHER CHILDREN. {A}

14.SAMUEL WATSON, son of Samuel (4) Watson, d. c1746. {SUORCT 2:31} Samuel m. Elizabet Hickman and had 5 children. {The admin. acct. of Rebecca Hickman refers to Elizabeth, admx. of Samuel Watson who is exec. of the estate of Rebecca Hickman and refers to legacies to Elizabeth Watson. SUORCT 2:6}

15. ISAAC WATSON, son of Isaac (5) Watson, m. 1st Ann (N) and m. 2nd Mary (N).

On 20 April 1730 William Till of Sussex Co., merchant, and Mary his wife for £40 sold to Isaac Watson of same co., yeoman, and Ann his wife, a tract of land on s. side of Cedar Creek, 300 a. pattented to Luke Watson, Junr., 6 May 1695. Wit: [blank]. Ackn 21 April 1730. {SUDELR I:425}

In 1734 Larrance (age 17) and Benjamin Vill (age 7), sons of Larrance Vill of Sussex Co. were bound out to Isaac Watson and wife Ann. {SUORCT 1:72, 73}

16. THOMAS WATSON, son of Isaac (5) Watson, m. 1st Elizabeth Manlove and m. 2nd Margaret (N). Thomas and Elizabeth were parents of the following children: MARY, m. Luke Watson; ANN, m. Draper May; THOMAS, d.s.p. 1770; PURNELL, d. 1785, m. Mary (N) who m. 2nd Isaac Beauchamp; ISAAC, 1788.

Thomas d. by 18 April 1755 when Margaret Watson, widow was appointed admx. of his estate. {Reg. of Wills, K:111-112}

17. BETHUEL WATSON, son of Isaac (5) Watson, b. 1710, d. 1794, m. Elizabeth Smith, dau. of David Smith, Esq. They were parents of the following children: JESSE; BETHUEL; HESTER; MARY; NAOMI; DAVID, d. 1794; ELIZABETH.

Bethuel Wattson, Sr., farmer, Cedar Creek Hundred, d. leaving a will dated 21 June 1794, proved 12 Sep 1797. Heirs: sons Jesse and Bethuel Wattson; Naomi Herrington; grandchildren Esther, Elizabeth, Jesse, John and Bethuel Wattson (children of dec'd., son David Wattson), Luke, Nehemiah, John, Wattson, Mary, Betty and Zipporah Walton (children of dec'd. dau. Elizabeth Walton). Exec. son Bethuel Wattson. Wits., George Cooke, Sarah Cooke, Luke Rickards. {Sussex Co. Wills. Arch. A105:190-191. Reg. of Wills, E:132-134}

Fourth Generation

18. MARY LILLINGTON, dau. of Elizabeth (8) and George Lillington, m. William Till.

On 20 April 1761 Mary and William Till, Esq., along with dau. in law Gertrude, were appointed guardians of grandson William Till. {SUORCT 4:11}

19. PURNELL WATSON, son of Thomas (16) Watson, m. Mary (N) who m. 2nd Isaac Beauchamp. Purnell and Mary were parents of the following children: THOMAS; SARAH; WILLIAM; MARY; ANN. {A}

20. ISAAC WATSON, son of Thomas (16), m. Susanna Halbert (or Albert). {SUORCT A:125, 126, 322, 326, 327, 404}

THE WILLIAM WATSON FAMILY

1. WILLIAM WATSON m. Rebecka (N) who later m. William Smith.

William d. leaving a will dated 1 Feb 1746, proved 6 March 1746. Heirs: sons William, Benony, Francis, Solomon; daus. Maryann, Rebacka, Elizabeth; wife Rebacka. Extx., wife Rebacka. Wits., Thomas Parke, Timothy Griffen. Samuel Bostick. {Arch. A53: 187-188. Reg. of Wills: I:138} Note:-Arch. vol. A53, page 188 shows Rebecca later married William Smith.

William was father of the following children: WILLIAM; BENONY; FRANCIS; SOLOMON; MARYANN, m. John Kent; REBACKA; ELIZABETH.

2. WILLIAM WATSON, probable son of William (1) Watson, m. Mary, dau. of John Craige.

On 1 March 1758 William Watson of Kent Co., yeoman, and Mary his wife and Rebecca Smith of same co., widow, for £100 sold to William Ford of same co., yeoman, a tract of land, whereas William Watson late of said co. yeoman, dec'd., by virtue of a deed from a certain John Long to the said Watson, dec'd., (Lib M, fol. 33) became in his lifetime and was at the time of his death seizd in part of a larger tract of land called *The School House Tract* in Murtherkill Hundred adj. William Rodeney's land ... 100 a. and William Watson being so seizd by his will did devise the same to his son William Watson party to these presents and the afsd. Rebecca his widow who by virtue of her marriage with the decedant was intitled to her dower in the premisses. {KEDELR P:56}

On 13 Aug 1765 William Watson of Kent Co. yeoman and Mary his wife for £155 sold to Alexander Hutson of same co. clerk ... a parcell of land s. side of Murther Creek in Mispillion Hundred adj. land late of George Morgan, dec'd., and land of John Arnell ... 147 a. part of a larger tract called *Seaton* and that part of the tract conveyed by a certain Benjamin Nixon to the said William Watson on 29 Aug 1759 ... subject to the principal money and interest due on a mortgage to the trustees of the General Loan Office and also subject to a judgment and execution for a certain sum of money at the suit of the afsd. Benjamin Nixon against the said William Watson. {KEDELR R:50}

On 14 Feb 1764 William Watson of Kent Co. yeoman and Mary his wife for £57.10 sold to William Whitacre of same place yeoman ... a tract of land, whereas Benjamin Noxon of Newcastle co. gent on 29 Aug 1759 did release unto the afsd. William Watson a tract of land s.e. side of the main branch of Murtherkill Creek in Mispillion Hundred 177 a. part of the tract called *Seaton* (Book P, fol. 137) adj. land lately belonging to George Morgan, dec'd., and land of Daniel Brown ... 50 1/3 a. (Q:pg 227)

John Craige, d. leaving a will dated 14 April 1766, proved 12 Nov 1766. Heirs: wife Agnes; son Thomas; daus. Mary (wife of William Watson), Prudence (wife of Andrew Neal), Ezabel, Ann, Margret and Elizabeth Craige. Extx., wife Agnes. Wits., John Arnett, Edward Gibbs, John Newman. {Arch. All:167-169. Reg. of Wills, L:18}

3. BENONY WATSON, son of William (1) m. Elizabeth (N).

On 25 March 1757 Benony Watson and Elizabeth his wife for £100 sold to Vincent Loockerman and William Smith both of Kent Co. ... a tract of land whereon William Watson father of the said Benony lately dwelt in the forrest of Little Creek Hundred adj. land intended to be laid out for Benjamin Shurmer, 200 a. {KEDELR P:25}

On 6 Dec 1757 Vincent Loockerman and William Smyth both of Kent Co. for £200 sold to Howell Buckinham of same co. yeoman ... a tract of land purchased of Benoni Watson and Elizabeth his wife 25 March 1757 (Lib P, fol. 25) whereon William Watson father to the afsd. Benoni lately dwelt in the forrest of Little Creek Hundred adj. land intended to be laid out for Benjamin Shurmer, 200 a. {KEDELR P:46}

4. FRANCIS WATSON, son of William (1) Watson.

On 13 Aug 1747 William Clark of Kent Co., yeoman, for £50 which was paid by William Watson in his life time sold to Francis Watson of same co. an infant under the age of 21 years son and divisee of William Watson of same co. lately, dec'd., ... whereas the said William Watson did in his life time purchase a tract of land being on a drain of Tapahana in the forrest of Murtherkill Hundred surveyed and laid our for the afsd. William Clark by virtue of a warrant bearing date at Philadelphia 28 June 1740 by George Stevenson surveyor n. side of the road from Tapahannah to the *Forest Landing* to Samuel Robinson's and Joshua Meredith's lands ... 200 a. {KEDELR N:165}

On 24 Feb 1767 John Chicken of Dover Hundred Kent Co., house carpenter, and Matthew Crosire of Duck Creek Hundred. same co.. yeoman for £130 sold to Edward Moore late of Queen Annes co. MD yeoman ... part of a tract of land in the forrest of Murtherkill Hundred, whereas a certain William Clark obtained a warrant bearing date 28 Jun 1740 by virtue of which a survey was made by George Stevenson then surveyor, and William Clark after said survey did contract with a certain William Watson for the conveyance of said tract and received the consideration for the same but the William Watson dying before the conveyance was made and having by his will left the said tract to the minor Francis Watson by deed poll dated 13 Aug 1747 (Book N, fol. 165), and Francis Watson did afterward convey the tract to the afsd. John Chicken on 10 March 1760 (Book P, fol. 224) ... beginning n. side of the road from Toppahannah to the *Forrest Landing* ... 217 a. {KEDELR R:180}

5. MARYANN WATSON, dau. of William (1) Watson, m. before 17 Oct 1765, John Kent.

John Kent and Mary Ann his wife and Rebecca Watson, daus. of William Watson of Little Creek Hundred. Land by warrant 17 June 1746 to William Watson. {Deed R:73, 17 Oct 1765}

Unplaced

ISAAC WATTSON, possibly son of Isaac (14), d. leaving a will dated 27 Jan 1773, proved 24 March 1773. Heirs: wife Mary Wattson; sons Joseph and Isaac Wattson; dau. Elizabeth Draper; grandson Isaac Riley; granddau. Mary Riley. Execs. wife Mary Wattson, son Isaac Wattson. Wits., Elijah Truitt, Alice

Wattson, Reynear Williams. {Sussex Co. Probate, Arch. A106:5-6. Reg. of Willis B: 476-478} Arch. A106:6 shows John Draper as the husband of Elizabeth Draper. JOHN WATSON, turner, d. leaving a will dated 11 Dec 1733, proved 173-. Heirs: sister Margit Watson; cousin Tabitha Watson. Extx. Tabitha Watson. Wits., Samuel Barratt, Jonathan Griffin, Lear Gaskins. {Arch. A53: 179. Reg. of Wills, H:48}

JOHN WATSON d. 1740. Admin. is Thomas Grove. {SUORCT 1:127}

LUKE WATSON has the following children bound out in 1728 to John Jones: JOHN, age 3; EPHRAIM, age 7; MARY, age 5. {SUORCT 1:4}

PETER WATSON m. Ann, widow of John Francis.

John Francis d. by 4 June 1740 when his estate was administered by Ann Francis. {Reg. of Wills, I:32} Note: Arch. A18:77 shows a later admin. by Peter Watson and wife Ann, widow of John Francis.

WILLIAM WATSON d. prior to 1773, m. Mary Halbert. He was father of the following children: LUKE; WILLIAM; SARAH; SUSANNAH; HALBERT. {SUORCT A:125, 126, 322, 326, 327, 404}

THE WEBB FAMILY

1. ISAAC WEBB m. in Richmond Co., VA {DE Recall I:3}, Mary Bedwell, dau. of Robert Bedwell, who m. 2nd James Clayton and m. 3rd Michael O'Donahoe.

On 4 Sept 1688 Thomas Bedwell of Kent co. gives a gift of one light gray maire filly about one year and a half olde unto his nephew Robert Webb, his sister Marie's son with her increase to him the said Robert Webb ... except first horse coult of said maire shall be James Clayton's his said sisters present husband and in case Robert Webb shall hapen to die before he comes of age then one half of ye increase to go to my said sister his mother and James Clayton her husband ... other half of increase to return to me ... {KEDELR}

On 8 Feb 1695 Thomas Bedwell, son and admin. of the estate of Robert Bedwell, gave to his sister Mary Clayton, late widow of Isack Webb, oldest dau. to sd. Robert Bedwell, and now wife to James Clayton, a tract called *Claytons Lott* on s.w. side of Dover River. ... 175 a. {KEDELR}

On 20 Dec 1715 Thomas Parke, late of Murtherkill Hundred, Kent Co., marriner, and Sarah his wife, for £75 sold to Nathaniel Hall of same place, marriner, a tract of land lying in Murtherkill Hundred on s. side of Jones Creek called *Shoemakers Hall* near Isaac's Branch by Walker's Branch, patent for 400 a. bearing date 26 March 1684, granted to Isaac Webb, dec'd., who dyed intestate whereas Mary Webb relict of said Isaac Webb dec'd. did sell 200 a. from said 400 a. to Wm. Lawrence and Michel Walter ... whereas Robert Webb son and heir of afsd. Isaac Webb dec'd. did sell to Thomas Parker 200 a. (afsd 200 a. only by Mary Webb relict of Isaac Webb dec'd. and mother of Robert Webb sold excepted) and also 2 a. at ye end of ye mill down of Thomas Park also excepted. {KEDELR E:55}

On 14 Feb 1737 John Raynalls and Catherine his wife of Kent Co. for £40 (and £20 for second tract) sold to Phillip Lewes a tract of land (warrant from the Whorekill Court laid out unto Isaac Webb of Kent Co., dec'd., surveyed 21 Jan 1679/80 called *Shoemakers Hall* on s. side of St. Jones Creek, 404 a., afterwards Robert Webb, son and heir of Isaac Webb, became possessed of the afsd. land and premises and did by his deed bearing date 10 May 1712 convey unto Thomas Park marriner. {KEDELR L:270}

Isack Webb d. by 15 March 1687 when Mary Webb, widow, as appointed admx. of his estate. {Penna. Hist. Soc. Papers, AM. 2013:77}

Isaac was father of ROBERT.

Second Generation

2. ROBERT WEBB, son of Isaac (1) Webb, m. Sarah (N).

On 10 May 1712 Robert Webb, son and heir of Isaac Webb, late of Murtherkill Hundred, Kent Co., yeoman, dec'd., for £50 sold to Thomas Parke of same place, mariner, a tract of land in Murtherkill Hundred on s. side of Jones Creek called *Shoemakers Hall* beginning at the mouth of Isaacs Branch on Walkers Branch, 400 a., patent bearing date 26 March 1684, granted to William Webb dec'd. who died intestate and whereas Mary the mother of said Robert Webb by deed did grant him 200 a. and William Larrance and Michel Willson by same deed ... and 200 a. belonging to his mother. {KEDELR E:85}

Robert d. leaving a will dated 8 Jan 1708, proved 8 Oct 1722. Heir: wife Sarah. Extx., wife Sarah. Wits., Elizabeth Goodin, Daniel Goodin, Will Annand. {Arch. A53:211. Reg. of Wills, D:59}

Robert was father of JOHN.

3. JOHN WEBB, son of Robert (1) Webb, m. Ann (N)[56] who later m. James Howell.

On 11 May 1738 John Webb, eldest son of Robert Webb, late of Mutherkill Hundred, Kent Co., yeoman, for £12 sold to George Morgan now of the same place, a tract of land in Mutherkill Hundred adj. to the s.w. side of land called *Dundee* being a tract of land laid out to the said Robert Webb by virtue of a warrant from the commissioners of property in Philadelphia and is the same whereon Robert at the time of his decease did dwell and one other tract of land adj. to the e. side of a tract called *Dundee* and to the s. side of Isaacs Branch whereon the said Robert Webb did also dwell formerly and did purchase from Thomas Bedwell dec'd. ... and right, title and interest whatsoever in any lands within Kent Co. {KEDELR L:273}

John Webb d. leaving a will dated 29 Oct 1760, proved 1 Dec 1760. Heirs: wife Ann; daus. Elizabeth and Sarah; sons Caleb and Daniel. Execs., wife Ann and John Caton, Esq. Wits., Stephen Lewis, James Howell, Thomas Cain. {Arch. A53:203-205. Reg. of Wills, L:195, 204-205} Note: Arch. vol. A53, page 205 shows that Ann Webb married James Howell.

John was father of the following children: ELIZABETH; SARAH; CALEB; DANIEL.

---

[56] This may be Ann Webb, dau. of Edward Mills, mentioned in the will of Edward Mills, written in 1751 and proved 14 Oct 1751. {DE Recall cites Sussex Wills B:4}

Unplaced

ANN WEBB, spinster of Sussex Co., dau. of Richard Webb, dec'd., and Edward Lay of same co., having consent of relations concerned, m. 20th da., 4th mo., 1730 at the meeting house at Cold Spring. {DCMM}

The marriage of MARY WEBB and Abraham Potter was announced orderly accomplished on 17th da., 2nd mo., 1732. {DCMM}

On 24th da., 4th mo., 1773, it was reported that MARY WEBB, now wife of Henry Martingdale, had gone out in marriage with one not a member of the Society. {DCMM}

THOMAS WEBB m. Frances (N).

In 1767 Thomas Webb of Kent Co., innkeeper, and Frances his wife for £275 sold to Jonathan Hunn of same co. a tract of land in the forrest of Murtherkill Hundred ... 125 a. heretofore conveyed by John Vining of same co. to the said Thomas Webb on 16 Sep 1759 also all that other tract in Murtherkill Hundred ... 75 a. heretofore conveyed by the afsd. John Vining and one James Caldwell to the said Thomas Webb on 16 Nov year last afsd. which parcels are part of a 900 a. tract called *Dundee*. {KEDELR R:173}

THE WHITEHART FAMILY

1. RICHARD WHITEHART[57] m. Elizabeth (N).

On 9 Jan 1691 William Johnson and Richard Whitehart and Elizabeth (his wife?) all of Kent Co., PA, for £34 sold to Thomas Sharp of same place ... a tract of land called *Little Towerhill* on s. side of Duck Creek ... 300 a. {KEDELR}

Richard Whitehart of Duck Creek d. leaving a will dated 11 Oct 1701, proved 7 Nov 1701. Heirs: wife Elizabeth; children unnamed. Extx., wife Elizabeth. Wits., Henry Hoskins, Sarah Kelly, Mary Tobias. {Arch. A54:186. Reg. of Wills, B:44}

On 10 May 1718 Samuel Freeman of Little Creek Hundred, Kent Co., planter, and Elizabeth his wife, dau. of Richard Whitehart, dec'd., and James Saterfield of same co., planter, and Mary his wife, dau. of said Whitehart ... whereas Richard Whitehart late of Kent Co., dec'd., ... in his lifetime was seized of a tract of land on s. side of s.w. branch of Duck Creek being part of a tract called *Denby Town* ... 150 a. ... by his will dated 11 Oct 1701 did give his worldly goods to be equally divided amongst his children ... Samuel Freeman and Elizabeth his wife and James Saterfield and Mary his wife for £10 sold to Richard Whitehard of Little Creek Hundred, Kent Co., planter, ... their part, right and title in afsd. tract of land. {KEDELR F:8}

On 11 Aug 1719 whereas Richard Whitehart in his lifetime became seized of a parcell of land on s. side of s.w. branch of Duck Creek by a deed of sale to him 10 June 1701 and sometime before his death did give and bequeath

---

57 A Richard Whitehart was transported into Maryland by 1671. {MPL 16:507}

said land to be equally divided amongst his children as by his will dated 11 Oct 1701 ... whereas some of his children did sell their share unto their brother Richard Whitehart ... Richard Whitehart, Samuel Whitehart and James Whitehart all of Little Creek Hundred Kent co. yeomen, sons of Richard Whitehart, dec'd., for £10 sold to Arthur Alston, yeoman, ... afsd. tract of land beginning at the corner of John Walker, dec'd., ... to land where said Richard Whitehart now dwelleth ... 40 a. {KEDELR F:125}

Elizabeth Whitehart d. leaving a will dated 18 March 1730, proved 18 March 1730. Heirs: sons John Horsted, Benjamin Whitehart, and James White-hart; dau. Mary Whitehart. Execs. Richard Whitehart and Arthur Allstone. Trustees, Thomas Allstone, Richard Whitehart, Arthur Allstone. Wits., Hannah Harwood, Rachel Hillyard. {Arch. A54:181. Reg. of Wills, H:13 and 66}

Richard was father of the following children: RICHARD, eldest son; BENJAMIN; JAMES; SAMUEL; ELIZABETH, m. Samuel Freeman; MARY, m. James Satterfield; JOHN.

Second Generation

2. RICHARD WHITEHART, eldest son of Richard (1) Whitehart, m. Grace (N).

On 28 March 1725 whereas a tract of land patent given at Philadelphia unto Thomas Wilson called *Denby Town* in Little Creek Hundred bounded on the n. and n.e. with the s.w. branch of Duck Creek and to the s. and to the e. with Wilsons Branch, and Thomas Wilson by deed of gift did give unto his son Thomas Wilson Junr a parcell of the said land being the lower part, and Thomas Wilson Junr by deed did sell to Richard Whitehart 150 a., and the said Richard in his will gave the land to his eldest son Richard Whitehart and he did convey to his youngest brother and sister 60 a. of the land as a gratuity to them for releasing all their right of the said 150 a. ... this indenture Richard Whitehart the son, of Little Creek Hundred, Kent Co., yeoman, and Grace his wife, for £37.12.6 sold to James Tybout late of Duck Creek Hundred same co. merchant, the remaining 90 a. ... to land late in the possession of Arthur Alston ... to a corner binding with land formerly conveyed by the said Whitehart to Samuel Freeman now dec'd.. Wit: George Martin, Hugh Durborow Junr. Ackn continued by adjournment till 31 March 1725. {KEDELR H:132}

Richard Whitehart d. by 2 Feb 1732 when Grace Whitehart was appointed admx. {Reg. of Wills, H:100}

3. JAMES WHITEHART, probable son of Richard (1) Whitehart.

On 14 Feb 1723 James Whitehart of Kent Co., yeoman, for £20 sold to Samuel Whitehart of same place, yeoman, a tract of land (whereas John Walker in his life time was seized of a tract of land on s. side of s.w. branch of Duck Creek being part of a larger tract called *Derbytown* and in his will did bequeath to his two sons Thomas Walker and James Walker all his said tract or 100 a. of land together with the plantation to be equally divided between them and afterward Richard Walker, son to the afsd. John Walker did by a deed of sale convey the same to James Whitehart) near Walkers Landing ... to corner of Samuel Freeman's land ... to a piece of land now in the possession of ELISHA SNOW ... 50 a. {KEDELR H:71}

4. SAMUEL WHITEHART, son of Richard (1) Whitehart, m. Sarah (N).

On 14 Aug 1728 Samuel Whitehart of Little Creek Hundred, Kent Co., yeoman, and Sarah Whitehart for £5 sold to George Martin of Duck Creek Hundred, same co., yeoman, a tract of land ... 5 a. {KEDELR I:175}

On 10 Feb 1729/30 Samuel Whitehart of Little Creek Hundred, Kent Co., yeoman, and Sarah his wife for £60 sold to John Hillyard, son of Charles Hillyard of Duck Creek Hundred, same co., a tract of land Samuel Whitehart did formerly purchase from William Ellis whereon Whitehart late did dwell in Little Creek Hundred ... on s. side of s.w. branch of Duck Creek near Chestnutt Landing being the uppermost corner of a tract of land called *Denby Town* ... 100 a. part of the said tract called *Denby Town* and another tract of land Samuel did also purchase of James Steel adj. to the w. side of the afsd. land ... to other lands of Samuel Whitehart to a corner of Richard Walker's land ... to land late of James Jackson ... 80 a. being part of a tract of land called *Ferry Brigg* ... in the whole 180 a. {KEDELR K:pg 10}

Samuel Whithart, planter, Little Creek Hundred, d. leaving a will dated 9 May 1748, proved 24 May 1748. Heirs: wife Sarah; son Powell. Extx., wife Sarah. Wits., James Whithart, Edward Norman, Elizabeth Morgan. {Arch. A54: 188. Reg. of Wills, I:224}

Sarah Whithart [Whitehart] of Little Creek Hundred, widow, d. leaving a will dated 11 Oct 1762, proved 11 Nov 1762. Heirs: grandsons Samuel, John, Allen, Solomon and Powell Whitehart; granddaus. Sarah and Mary Whitehart. Extx., dau. Grace Whitehart. Wits., Elizabeth Cremine, Silvester Luck, Thomas Alberry. {Arch. A54:189. Reg. of Wills, K:300-301} Note: Will mentions sons Solomon and Samuel, dec'd.

Samuel was father of the following children: GRACE; SOLOMON; SAMUEL.

5. JOHN WHITHART, son of Richard (1) Whitehart, d. leaving a will 1708, proved 18 Jan 1708/9. Heirs: bros. Richard, Samuel, James; sisters, Elizabeth, Mary; friend, Elizabeth Smith. Exec. Richard Whithart. Wits., Philemon Emerson, Thomas Ohorrill. {Arch. A54:185. Reg. of Wills, B:72}

Third Generation

6. SAMUEL WHITHART of Little Creek, son of Samuel (4) Whithart, d. leaving a will dated 27 Feb 1739/40, proved 8 April 1740. Heirs: sons James, Samuel, Solomon; dau. Sarah Snow; wife Sarah. Execs., wife and son Samuel. Wits., William Flintham, Joseph Freeman. {Arch. A54:187. Reg. of Wills, I:20.4}

7. SOLOMON WHITEHART, son of Samuel (4) Whitehart, m. Grace (N).

On 11 Feb 1752 Thomas Hawkins and Dorothy his wife, Joseph Thompson (Thomson) and Mary his wife, Solomon Whitehart and Grace his wife all of Kent co. for £60 sold to James Snow of Duck Creek Hundred, same co., farmer ... all their rights in two tracts of land, 100 a., part of a 200 a. tract called *Christiana* conveyd by exec. of Matthew Morgan, dec'd., unto James Wornell and since conveyd by Mary Wornell then widow of James Wornell unto Allen Hawkins of same co., dec'd., and 6 a. Allen Hawkins purchased from afsd. John Snow, dec'd. {KEDELR O:144}

Solomon Whitehart, yeoman, d. by 14 June 1762 when Grace Whitehart was appointed admx. {Arch. A54:191. Reg. of Wills, K:285-286}

Unplaced

JAMES WHITEHART d. by 20 March 1730 when Richard Whitehart and Arthur Allstone were appointed admins. {Arch. A54:182. Reg. of Wills, H:14}

JAMES WHITHART, weaver, d. by 18 May 1748, proved 24 May 1748. Heirs: friend Nancy Winterton; Arthur Duncan. Extx., Nancy Winterton. Wits., William Sherwin, Matthew Taylor, Edward Norman. {Arch. A54:184. Reg. of Wills, I:223-224}3.

POWELL WHITEHART, grandson of Nicholas and Mary Powell.

Nicholas Powell of Little Creek d. by 9 April 1762, proved 24 May 1762. Heirs: wife Mary; grandson Powell Whitehart; children of Thomas Jones; children of John Clark; Esther, dau. of William Siddin. Execs. wife Mary and grandson Powell Whitehart. Wits., John Torbert, Daniel Newnam, William Corse. {Arch. A41:43-44. Reg. of Wills, K:284} Note: Arch. A41:44 shows Mary, the widow, later married William Wilson.

On 27 Aug 1766 William Willson and Mary his wife of Little Creek Hundred, Kent Co., for £3 sold to Joseph David of same place ... all our right and part of that land which was bequeathed on the afsd. Mary by Nicholas Powell her former husband and to Powell Whitehart his grandson in Little Creek Hundred adj. on n. side of afsd. Joseph David's land part of which is now in the possession of Powell Whitehart. {KEDELR R:135}

SAMUEL WHITEHART and Sarah Whitehart.

On 10 Aug 1741 Sarah and Samuel Whitehart of Little Creek, Kent Co., for a certain sum of money to them paid sold to John Parsons of same place ... a tract of land in Little Creek being part of a larger tract called *Rester* to a corner near Francis Keith's plantation along Miderton's e. line ... 50 a. {KDELR M:119}

WILLIAM WHITEHART d. by 5 Feb 1707 when Richard Whitehart was appointed admin. {Reg. of Wills, B:60}

INDEX to volume 1 of Colonial Families of Delaware

-D-

-G-

-H-

-I-

-J-

-K-

-L-

-M-

-Q-

-R-

-U-